Forschungen zum Alten Testament
2. Reihe

Edited by

Corinna Körting (Hamburg) · Konrad Schmid (Zürich)
Mark S. Smith (Princeton) · Andrew Teeter (Harvard)

139

Inscribe It in a Book

Scribal Practice, Cultural Memory, and the Making
of the Hebrew Scriptures

Edited by

Johannes Unsok Ro and Benjamin D. Giffone

Mohr Siebeck

Johannes Unsok Ro, born 1971; 1998 MA in Theological Studies; 2002 Dr. theol. in Old Testament; 2007 MDiv; currently Professor of Biblical Studies and Director of the Institute for the Study of Christianity and Culture at International Christian University, Japan.
orcid.org/0000-0003-1835-3093

Benjamin D. Giffone, born 1984; 2009 MS in Biblical Studies; 2012 MTh, 2014 PhD in Old Testament; since 2014 Research Associate, Universiteit van Stellenbosch; currently Associate Professor of Biblical Studies at LCC International University, Klaipėda, Lithuania.
orcid.org/0000-0003-0907-6514

ISBN 978-3-16-161524-5 / eISBN 978-3-16-161525-2
DOI 10.1628/978-3-16-161525-2

ISSN 1611-4914 / eISSN 2568-8367 (Forschungen zum Alten Testament, 2. Reihe)

The Deutsche Nationalbibliothek lists this publication in the Deutsche Nationalbibliographie; detailed bibliographic data are available at *http://dnb.dnb.de*.

© 2022 Mohr Siebeck Tübingen, Germany. www.mohrsiebeck.com

This book may not be reproduced, in whole or in part, in any form (beyond that permitted by copyright law) without the publisher's written permission. This applies particularly to reproductions, translations and storage and processing in electronic systems.

The book was typeset by Martin Fischer in Tübingen using Minion typeface, printed on non-aging paper by Laupp & Göbel in Gomaringen, and bound by Buchbinderei Nädele in Nehren.

Printed in Germany.

Preface

This volume's journey to publication began with one researcher's initiative to study themes related to scribalism and scribal practice. Johannes Unsok Ro of International Christian University launched a collaborative project on these themes, generating reciprocal and critical communication among scholars across several continents. Contributions were solicited from scholars representing diverse cultural locations and backgrounds, drawing balance of early, mid-career, and senior scholars, with particular emphasis on the voices of East Asian scholars, which have historically been less represented in international biblical scholarship. All contributors have published monographs, and/or have forthcoming monographs, in their respective areas. The project developed more ambitiously and fruitfully than initially planned, so he sought the assistance of one of the contributors, Benjamin Giffone of LCC International University, to be co-editor of this volume.

After the papers were submitted to the editors, they were each read by two reviewers, including other contributors with complementary expertise. When necessary, outside reviewers were sought for papers with particularly specialized foci. The feedback from this process was communicated to each author, who then had the task of revising her/his contribution in light of the critical engagements of the peer reviewers.

As editors and contributors, we want to thank the following persons who were not contributors but who served as reviewers of one or more of the essays: Michael G. Cox, Daniel E. Fleming, Dominik Markl, Yigal Levin, Raymond F. Person, and Jon P. Radwan. Their critical engagements have significantly improved the quality of this book.

We also thank the series editors of FAT II, Konrad Schmid, Mark S. Smith, Hermann Spieckermann, and Andrew Teeter, for accepting our volume in this series. It was a great pleasure to work with the publishing team of Mohr Siebeck, in particular Elena Müller. We also thank Rebecca Armstrong for her assistance in preparing the manuscript for publication. The preparation of the manuscript was supported by a grant from LCC International University. The preparation of the indexes was supported by the Japan Society for the Promotion of Science (JSPS) through a KAKENHI research grant (22K00080).

December 2022   Johannes Unsok Ro
                                           and Benjamin Giffone

Table of Contents

Preface V
List of Abbreviations IX

Johannes Unsok Ro and Benjamin D. Giffone
Introduction 1

Part I
Comparative Studies

Daniel Bodi
A New Proposal for the Origin of the Term for 'Letter': Sumerian inim.gar, i₅-gar-ra; Akkadian *egirtu*; Aramaic *'iggĕrâ*, *'iggartâ*, Hebrew *'iggeret* 15

William R. Stewart
The Death of the Prophet? A Comparative Study of Prophetic Signs in the Royal Archives of Mari, Syria (ARM 26/1.206) and the Hebrew Bible (Jeremiah 19:1–13) 35

JiSeong James Kwon
Scribal Intertexts in the Book of Job: Foreign Counterparts of Job 67

Sungwoo Park and Johannes Unsok Ro
Collective Identity through Scribalism: Interpreting Plato's Menexenus and the Book of Chronicles 99

Part II
Writing about Writing in the Hebrew Bible

Benjamin Kilchör
"Then Moses Wrote This Torah" (Deut 31:9): The Relationship of Oral and Written Torah in Deuteronomy 125

Lisbeth S. Fried and Edward J. Mills III
Ezra the Scribe 139

Johanna Erzberger
Israel's Salvation and the Survival of Baruch the Scribe 155

Peter Altmann
Tracing Divine Law: Written Divine Law in Chronicles 165

Part III

Case Studies

Jin H. Han
Did the Deuteronomist Detest Dreams? 193

Benjamin D. Giffone
Regathering Too Many Stones? Scribal Constraints, Community Memory, and the 'Problem' of Elijah's Sacrifice for Deuteronomism in Kings 213

Woo Min Lee
The "Remnant" in the Deuteronomistic Cultural Memory:
A Case Study on 2 Kings 19:30–31 235

Roger S. Nam
Nehemiah 5:1–13 as Innerbiblical Interpretation of Pentateuchal Slavery Laws 255

Kristin Weingart
Chronography in the Book of Kings: An Inquiry into an Israelite Manifestation of an Ancient Near Eastern Genre 273

Benjamin Ziemer
Radical Versus Conservative? How Scribes Conventionally Used Books While Writing Books 301

List of Contributors 329

Index of Biblial and Ancient Sources 331
Index of Modern Authors 335
Index of Subjects 338

List of Abbreviations

ÄAT	Ägypten und Altes Testament
AB	Anchor Bible
ABZ	*Assyrisch-babylonische Zeichenliste*
AC	*Acta Classica*
AdSem	Advances in Semiotics
AfO	*Archiv für Orientforschung*
Ahw	*Akkadisches Handwörterbuch*
AIL	Ancient Israel and Its Literature
AMD	Ancient Magic and Divination
ANEM	Ancient Near East Monographs/Monografias sobre el Antiguo Cercano Oriente
ANET	*Ancient Near Eastern Texts Relating to the Old Testament*
ANETS	Ancient Near Eastern Texts and Studies
AOAT	Alter Orient und Altes Testament
AOS	American Oriental Series
AOTC	Abingdon Old Testament Commentaries
APSR	*American Political Science Review*
ARAM	*Journal for the ARAM Society for Syro-Mesopotamian Studies*
ARM	Archives Royales de Mari
AS	Assyriological Studies
ATANT	Abhandlungen zur Theologie des Alten und Neuen Testaments
AUMSR	Andrews University Monographs Studies in Religion
AYBRL	Anchor Yale Bible Reference Library
BA	La Bible d'Alexandrie
BASOR	*Bulletin of the American Schools of Oriental Research*
BBR	*Bulletin for Biblical Research*
BBRSup	Bulletin for Biblical Research, Supplements
BeOl	Berit Olam
BETL	Bibliotheca Ephemeridum Theologicarum Lovaniensium
Bib	*Biblica*
BibOr	Biblica et Orientalia
BibSem	The Biblical Seminar
BJS	Brown Judaic Studies
BJSUCSD	Biblical and Judaic Studies from the University of California, San Diego
BK	*Bibel und Kirche*
BN	*Biblische Notizen*
BO	Bibliotheca Orientalis
BSac	*Bibliotheca Sacra*
BuL	*Bibel und Liturgie*
BW	BibleWorld

BWANT	Beiträge zur Wissenschaft vom Alten und Neuen Testament
BZ	*Biblische Zeitschrift*
BZABR	Beihefte zur Zeitschrift für altorientalische und biblische Rechtsgeschichte
BZAW	Beihefte zur Zeitschrift für die alttestamentliche Wissenschaft
CAD	*The Assyrian Dictionary of the Oriental Institute of the University of Chicago*
CBQ	*Catholic Biblical Quarterly*
CBQMS	Catholic Biblical Quarterly Monograph Series
CCGG	*Cahiers du Centre Gustave-Glotz*
CHANE	Culture and History of the Ancient Near East
CMP	Cultural Memory in the Present
ConBOT	Coniectanea Biblica: Old Testament Series
COS	*The Context of Scripture*
CP	*Classical Philology*
CRPOGA	Université des sciences humaines de Strasbourg, Travaux du Centre de Recherche sur le Proche-Orient et la Grèce Antiques
CurBR	*Currents in Biblical Research*
DBAM	*The Dictionary of the Bible and Ancient Media*
DEC	*Driot et Cultures*
DJD	Discoveries in the Judaean Desert
DNWSI	*Dictionary of the North-West Semitic Inscriptions*
DO	Docet Omnia
DULAT	*A Dictionary of the Ugaritic Language in the Alphabetic Tradition*
EA	El-Amarna tablets
ÉAHA	Études d'archéologie et d'histoire ancienne
EdF	Erträge der Forschung
EI	*Encyclopædia Iranica*
EJL	Early Judaism and Its Literature
FAT	Forschungen zum Alten Testament
FAT II	Forschungen zum Alten Testament, 2. Reihe
FiHi	*Fides et Historia*
FIOTL	Formation and Interpretation of Old Testament Literature
FOTL	Forms of the Old Testament Literature
FRLANT	Forschungen zur Religion und Literatur des Alten und Neuen Testaments
GBibS	Gorgias Biblical Studies
GBS	Guides to Biblical Scholarship
GMTR	Guides to the Mesopotamian Textual Record
HAT	Handbuch zum Alten Testament
HCOT	Historical Commentary on the Old Testament
HdO	Handbuch der Orientalistik
HeBAI	*Hebrew Bible and Ancient Israel*
HSM	Harvard Semitic Monographs
HSS	Harvard Semitic Studies
HThKAT	Herders Theologischer Kommentar zum Alten Testament
HTR	*Harvard Theological Review*
HUCA	*Hebrew Union College Annual*

IBC	Interpretation: A Bible Commentary for Teaching and Preaching
IBHS	Bruce K. Waltke and Michael O'Connor, *An Introduction to Biblical Hebrew Syntax* (Winona Lake, IN: Eisenbrauns, 1990)
ICC	International Critical Commentary
ITL	International Theological Library
ITQ	*Irish Theological Quarterly*
IVPBD	*InterVarsity Press Bible Dictionary*
JAJ	*Journal of Ancient Judaism*
JAJSup	Journal of Ancient Judaism Supplement Series
JANESCU	*Journal of the Ancient Near Eastern Society of Columbia University*
JAOS	*Journal of the American Oriental Society*
JBL	*Journal of Biblical Literature*
JBTS	*Journal of Biblical and Theological Studies*
JBQ	*Jewish Bible Quarterly*
JCS	*Journal of Cuneiform Studies*
JDT	*Jahrbuch für deutsche Theologie*
JEA	*Journal of Egyptian Archaeology*
JEOL	*Jaarbericht van het Vooraziatisch-Egyptisch Gezelschap (Genootschap) Ex oriente lux*
JHebS	*Journal of Hebrew Scriptures*
JHS	*Journal of Hellenic Studies*
JNES	*Journal of Near Eastern Studies*
JORH	*Journal of Religion and Health*
JSJ	*Journal for the Study of Judaism in the Persian, Hellenistic, and Roman Periods*
JSJSup	Journal for the Study of Judaism in the Persian, Hellenistic, and Roman Periods Supplement Series
JSOT	*Journal for the Study of the Old Testament*
JSOTSup	Journal for the Study of the Old Testament Supplement Series
JTS	*Journal of Theological Studies*
Judaica	*Judaica: Beiträge zum Verständnis des jüdischen Schicksals in Vergangenheit und Gegenwart*
KAT	Kommentar zum Alten Testament
KEH	Kurzgefasstes exegetisches Handbuch
Ktèma	*Ktèma: Civilisations de l'Orient, de la Grece et de Rome antiques*
LAPO	Litteratures anciennes du Proche-Orient
LCL	Loeb Classical Library
LD	Lectio Divina
LHBOTS	The Library of Hebrew Bible/Old Testament Studies
LLC	*Language and Linguistics Compass*
MAOG	*Mitteilungen der Altorientalischen Gesellschaft*
MARI	*Mari: Annales de recherches interdisciplinaires*
MC	Mesopotamian Civilizations
MCAAS	Memoirs of the Connecticut Academy of Arts and Sciences
MDOG	*Mitteilungen der Deutschen Orient-Gesellschaft*
MSO	Mémoires de la Sociéte d'etudes Orientales "Ex Oriente Lux"
MSSMNIA	Monograph Series of the Sonia and Marco Nadler Institute of Archaeology

MUN	Mémoires de l'Université de Neuchâtel
NABUM	Mémoires de *Nouvelles assyriologiques breves et utilitaires*
NAPR	Northern Akkad Project Reports
NGC	New German Critique
NSKAT	Neuer Stuttgarter Kommentar, Altes Testament
OBC	Orientalia Biblica et Christiana
OBib	*Oxford Bibliographies Online*
OBO	Orbis Biblicus et Orientalis
OIS	Oriental Institute Seminars
OLA	Orientalia Lovaniensia Analecta
OLZ	*Orientalistische Literaturzeitung*
OPSNKF	Occasional Publications of the Samuel Noah Kramer Fund
Or	*Orientalia*
OrNS	*Orientalia Nova Series*
OS	Oudtestamentische Studiën/Old Testament Studies
OT	Oral Tradition
OTE	Old Testament Essays
OTL	Old Testament Library
PBA	Proceedings of the British Academy
PFES	Publications of the Finnish Exegetical Society
PFFAR	Publications of the Foundation for Finnish Assyriological Research
PHSC	Perspectives on Hebrew Scriptures and Its Contexts
PIPOCF	Publications de l'Institut du Proche-Orient ancient du College de France
PJTC	Perspectives on Jewish Texts and Contexts
PRSt	*Perspectives in Religious Studies*
PT	Political Theory
RA	*Revue d'assyriologie et d'archeologie orientale*
RAI	Rencontre assyriologique international
RB	*Revue biblique*
RBI	*Rivista Biblica Italiana*
RBS	Resources for Biblical Study
RGRW	Religions in the Graeco-Roman World
RHR	*Revue de l'histoire des religions*
RlA	*Reallexikon der Assyriologie*
RP	The Review of Politics
RSJB	*Recueils de la Societé Jean Bodin*
R&T	*Religion and Theology*
SAA	State Archives of Assyria
SAAS	State Archives of Assyria Studies
SAOC	Studies in Ancient Oriental Civilizations
SBLDS	Society of Biblical Literature Dissertation Series
SBLMS	Society of Biblical Literature Monograph Series
SBLSymS	Society of Biblical Literature Symposium Series
SBT	Studies in Biblical Theology
SBTS	Sources for Biblical and Theological Study
SCaE	Supplement to Cahiers evangile
SCS	Septuagint Commentary Series

SemeiaSt	Semeia Studies
SHCANE	Studies in the History and Culture of the Ancient Near East
SJOT	*Scandinavian Journal of the Old Testament*
SOTBT	Studies in Old Testament Biblical Theology
SOTSMS	Society for Old Testament Studies Monograph Series
SPCC	Sheffield Phoenix Critical Commentary
SR	*Studies in Religion*
SRSup	Studies in Religion Supplements
ST	Studienbücher Theologie
StBL	Studies in Biblical Literature
STDJ	Studies on the Texts of the Desert of Judah
Sy	*Syria*
TAD	Bezalel Porten and Ada Yardeni, *Textbook of Aramaic Documents from Ancient Egypt: 1–4* (Hebrew University, Department of the History of the Jewish People, Texts and Studies for Students; Jerusalem: Hebrew University Press, 1986–99)
TynB	*Tyndale Bulletin*
TCS	Texts from Cuneiform Sources
TDOT	*Theological Dictionary of the Old Testament*
ThPh	*Theologie und Philosophie*
TJ	*Trinity Journal*
TLJS	The Taubman Lectures in Jewish Studies
TOTC	Tyndale Old Testament Commentaries
TRE	*Theologische Realenzyklopädie*
TSAJ	Texte und Studien zum antiken Judentum
TZ	*Theologische Zeitschrift*
UB	Understanding the Bible Commentary Series
UCOP	University of Cambridge Oriental Publications
UF	*Ugarit-Forschungen*
VT	*Vetus Testamentum*
VTSup	Supplements to Vetus Testamentum
WAS	Wiener Alttestamentliche Studien
WAW	Writings from the Ancient World
WBC	Word Biblical Commentary
WMANT	Wissenschaftliche Monographien zum Alten und Neuen Testament
WUNT	Wissenschaftliche Untersuchungen zum Neuen Testament
ZA	*Zeitschrift für Assyriologie*
ZABR	*Zeitschrift für altorientalische und biblische Rechtsgeschichte*
ZAW	*Zeitschrift für die alttestamentliche Wissenschaft*
ZBK	*Zürcher Bibelkommentare*
ZDMG	*Zeitschrift der deutschen morgenländischen Gesellschaft*
ZTK	*Zeitschrift für Theologie und Kirche*
ZWT	*Zeitschrift für wissenschaftliche Theologie*

Introduction

Johannes Unsok Ro and Benjamin D. Giffone

In the field of biblical studies, the topic of "scribal culture" gained limited attention until the 1980s and 1990s. The interest in the subject has dramatically increased in publications since the 2000s.[1] It has become *de rigueur* within biblical scholarship to acknowledge that the texts of the Hebrew Bible were products of scribal communities operating within an oral culture. This is a welcome devel-

---

[1] The literature that discusses the cultural aspects of the life of scribes is extensive. Selected volumes since 1990 would be enough to give a general picture of current scholarship: Susan Niditch, *Oral World and Written Word* (Louisville: Westminster John Knox, 1996); Philip R. Davies and Thomas Römer, eds., *Writing the Bible: Scribes, Scribalism and Script* (London: Routledge, 2014); Raymond F. Person Jr. and Robert Rezetko, *Empirical Models Challenging Biblical Criticism*, AIL 25 (Atlanta: Society of Biblical Literature, 2016); Jonathan G. Kline, *Allusive Soundplay in the Hebrew Bible*, AIL 28 (Atlanta: Society of Biblical Literature, 2016); Hindy Najman and Konrad Schmid, eds., *Jeremiah's Scriptures: Production, Reception, Interaction, and Transformation*, JSJSup 173 (Leiden: Brill, 2016); Scott B. Noegel, "Wordplay" in Ancient Near Eastern Texts, ANEM 26 (Atlanta: Society of Biblical Literature, 2021); David M. Carr, *Writing on the Tablet of the Heart: Origins of Scripture and Literature* (New York: Oxford University Press, 2005); Brian Schmidt, ed., *Contextualizing Israel's Sacred Writings: Ancient Literacy, Orality, and Literary Production*, AIL 22 (Atlanta: Society of Biblical Literature, 2015); Seth L. Sanders, *From Adapa to Enoch: Scribal Culture and Religious Vision in Judea and Babylon*, TSAJ 167 (Tübingen: Mohr Siebeck, 2017); William M. Schniedewind, *The Finger of the Scribe: How Scribes Learned to Write the Bible* (New York: Oxford University Press, 2019); idem, *How the Bible Became a Book: The Textualization of Ancient Israel* (Cambridge: Cambridge University Press, 2004); Karel van der Toorn, *Scribal Culture and the Making of the Hebrew Bible* (Cambridge, MA: Harvard University Press, 2007); Jonathan S. Greer, John W. Hilber, and John H. Walton, eds., *Behind the Scenes of the Old Testament: Cultural, Social, and Historical Contexts* (Grand Rapids: Baker Academic, 2018); Ruth Ebach and Martin Leuenberger, eds., *Tradition(en) im Alten Israel: Konstruktion, Transmission und Transformation*, FAT 127 (Tübingen: Mohr Siebeck, 2019); Wolfgang Oswald, ed., *Textgestalt und Komposition: Exegetische Beiträge zu Tora und Vordere Propheten*, FAT 69 (Tübingen: Mohr Siebeck, 2010); David W. Jamieson-Drake, *Scribes and Schools in Monarchic Judah: A Socio-Archaeological Approach*, JSOTSup 109, (Sheffield: Almond Press, 1991); Piotr Bienkowski et al., eds., *Writing and Ancient Near Eastern Society: Papers in Honour of Alan R. Millard*, LHBOTS 429 (New York: T&T Clark, 2005); David M. Carr, *The Formation of the Hebrew Bible: A New Reconstruction* (New York: Oxford University Press, 2011); Sara J. Milstein, *Tracking the Master Scribe: Revision through Introduction in Biblical and Mesopotamian Literature* (New York: Oxford University Press, 2016); Juha Pakkala, *God's Word Omitted: Omissions in the Transmission of the Hebrew Bible*, FRLANT 251 (Göttingen: Vandenhoeck & Ruprecht, 2013); Hans Jürgen Tertel, *Text and Transmission: An Empirical Model for the Literary Development of Old Testament Narratives*, BZAW 221 (Berlin: de Gruyter, 1994); John Van Seters, *The Edited Bible: The Curious History of the "Editor" in Biblical Criticism* (Winona Lake, IN: Eisenbrauns, 2006); Sidnie White Craw-

opment, as it permits the calibration and testing of source-, redaction-, and text-critical models, and allows for more realistic inquiry into the diverse strands that comprise the biblical texts.[2]

A great deal of biblical literary-historical scholarship has tended to proceed with the implicit assumption that biblical literature evolved solely by the medium of writing. However, it is now clear that even within the literate circles of scribes, oral correspondence/performance may have become the standard, with written texts playing a secondary role – at least until the text itself was regarded as sacred and the scrolls themselves became objects of veneration.[3] Philip Davies and Thomas Römer ask a useful question at this point: "in a world very largely preliterate, and before the institution of public reading (and translation) in synagogue, how were the scriptures disseminated (if at all) beyond literate circles?"[4] According to Davies and Römer, orality stresses efficiency, which not only requires but promotes elaboration, variation, and modification within certain limits.[5] As if each new rewriting were indeed a new "performance," the written form is constantly elaborated and changed. At least until a stage when not only the work, but also its textual fixation, was canonized, the roles of copying and composition did

---

ford, *Rewriting Scripture in Second Temple Times* (Grand Rapids: Eerdmans, 2008); Molly M. Zahn, *Rethinking Rewritten Scripture: Composition and Exegesis in the 4QReworked Pentateuch Manuscripts*, STDJ 95 (Leiden: Brill 2011); Benjamin Ziemer, *Kritik des Wachstumsmodells: Die Grenzen alttestamentlicher Redaktionsgeschichte im Lichte empirischer Evidenz*, VTSup 182 (Leiden: Brill, 2020); Raymond F. Person Jr., *The Deuteronomic History and the Book of Chronicles: Scribal Works in an Oral World*, AIL 6 (Atlanta: Society of Biblical Literature, 2010); Anne Fitzpatrick-McKinley, *The Transformation of Torah: From Scribal Advice to Law*, JSOTSup 287 (Sheffield: Sheffield Academic, 1999); Michael LeFebvre, *Collections, Codes, and Torah: The Re-Characterization of Israel's Written Law*, LHBOTS 451 (New York: T&T Clark, 2006); Jonathan Vroom, *The Authority of Law in the Hebrew Bible and Early Judaism: Tracing the Origins of Legal Obligation from Ezra to Qumran*, JSJSup 187 (Leiden: Brill, 2018); Paul S. Evans, "Creating a New 'Great Divide': The Exoticization of Ancient Culture in Some Recent Applications of Orality Studies to the Bible," *JBL* 136.4 (2017): 749–64.

[2] Important examples include: Saul M. Olyan and Jacob L. Wright, *Supplementation and the Study of the Hebrew Bible*, BJS 361 (Providence, RI: Brown University Press, 2018); Reinhard Müller, Juha Pakkala, and Bas ter Haar Romeny, *Evidence of Editing: Growth and Change of Texts in the Hebrew Bible*, RBS 75 (Atlanta: Society of Biblical Literature, 2014); Joshua A. Berman, *Inconsistency in the Torah: Ancient Literary Convention and the Limits of Source Criticism* (New York: Oxford University Press, 2017); Hanne von Weissenberg, Juha Pakkala, and Marko Martilla, eds., *Changes in Scripture: Rewriting and Interpreting Authoritative Traditions in the Second Temple Period* (Berlin: de Gruyter, 2011); Jan Christian Gertz et al., eds., *The Formation of the Pentateuch: Bridging the Academic Cultures of Europe, Israel, and North America*, FAT 111 (Tübingen: Mohr Siebeck, 2016); Kristin Weingart, *Gezählte Geschichte: Systematik, Quellen und Entwicklung der synchronistischen Chronologie in den Königebüchern*, FAT 142 (Tübingen: Mohr Siebeck, 2020); Joshua Berman, "Empirical Models of Textual Growth: A Challenge for the Historical-Critical Tradition," *JHebS* 16/12 (2016):1–25, doi:10.5508/jhs.2016.v16.a12.

[3] Davies and Römer, *Writing the Bible*, 2.
[4] Davies and Römer, *Writing the Bible*, 2.
[5] Davies and Römer, *Writing the Bible*, 2.

not seem to be divided. The production of texts might well be assigned to mere copyists, whose social standing was likely lower than that of an author.[6]

Research into cultural aspects of life of a scribe is frequently combined with memory studies.[7] Recently, a body of study has arisen which includes memory in conversations about transmission of tradition and scribal practices. For example, the studies by Raymond Person and David Carr pay attention to the function of recollection in the history of scribal transmission regarding biblical texts, Qumran material and other ancient literature.[8] The essays in a collection edited by Ehud Ben Zvi and Christoph Levin also consider scribal memory as a noticeable element in transmission of tradition.[9] The term "scribal memory" applies narrowly to the awareness of the standard texts within the collective memory of scribes and, more generally, to the influence of that knowledge on the biblical texts and their manuscripts.[10] Scribal memory can affect how the individual scribe makes copies of biblical texts, creating manuscripts that may vary from others but are not alien because they represent the conscious or subconscious understanding by the scribe of other versions of the same text, of other texts, or even of a wider tradition.[11] Raymond Person has used the idea of scribal memory in a variety of studies that contradict the consensus paradigm regarding the interaction between Samuel-Kings and Chronicles. Person articulates that the parallel texts between Samuel-Kings and Chronicles are better interpreted not as indicating textual dependency or derivatives, but rather as two loyal reproductions of the larger heritage retained in the collective memory of the scribes.[12] In this way, the present biblical texts can be considered instantiations of individual scribes in specific time and place based on the larger repertoire of the collective memory. For example, this idea could also be insightful for clarifying literary relationship within some heterogeneous traditions of biblical manuscripts such as MT-Samuel, LXX-Samuel, and 4QSam^a. Person's hypothesis reminds of Ferdinand de Saussure's distinction between *langue* and *parole* which is a theoretical linguistic dichotomy. *Langue* means the abstract and

---

[6] Davies and Römer, *Writing the Bible*, 3.

[7] For bibliography and issues related to "memory" in the Hebrew Bible cf. Barat Ellman, "Memory and History in the Hebrew Bible," *OBib* (2017), doi: 10.1093/obo/9780199840731-0143.

[8] Raymond F. Person Jr., "The Ancient Israelite Scribe as Performer," *JBL* 117 (1998): 601–9; Carr, *Formation of the Hebrew Bible*.

[9] Ehud Ben Zvi and Christoph Levin, eds., *Remembering and Forgetting in Early Second Temple Judah*, FAT 85 (Tübingen: Mohr Siebeck, 2012).

[10] Raymond F. Person Jr., "Scribal Memory," *DBAM* 1:352.

[11] Person Jr., "Scribal Memory," 352.

[12] Raymond F. Person Jr., "Text Criticism as a Lens for Understanding the Transmission of Ancient Texts in Their Oral Environments," in *Contextualizing Israel's Sacred Writing: Ancient Literacy, Orality, and Literature Production*, ed. Brian Schmidt (Atlanta: Society of Biblical Literature, 2015), 197–215; idem, "The Role of Memory in the Tradition Represented by the Deuteronomic History and the Book of Chronicles," *OT* 26 (2011): 537–50; idem, *The Deuteronomic History and the Book of Chronicles*.

formal system of linguistic rules and conventions which exists independently before individual language user; *parole* indicates particular instances in utilizing and employing langue and it differs in each individual. If Person is correct, the current biblical text is a collection of *parole* based on scribal collective memory which functions as a *langue*.

Furthermore, for David Carr, ancient scribal elitism was the result of advanced curricula and schooling, and therefore there is a complex social stratification between the different forms of Judahite literacy. Carr does not dispute that reading and writing may have been skills used by many of the ancient Judahite population, but a group of learned elites should be investigated separately from the scribal craftsmen. Only these elites were able to learn and memorize the texts which formed and shaped the social discourse of the Judahite community.[13] Carr argues that Deuteronomy and the so-called Deuteronomistic History were at the heart of an emerging curriculum in ancient Israel, one that had a significant impact during the exile and subsequent periods.[14]

For the recognition of more nuanced social stratification, perhaps it is worth noting that literacy is not a simple skill, but an intricate combination of techniques applied to texts.[15] In addition to the technical rigors of literacy, there are distinct categories in skills. Ancient literacy can practically be separated into three completely different areas: (1) reading, (2) writing by a copyist or a craftsman; and (3) writing by a composer. These roles were usually not overlapping; the different tasks were possibly assigned to persons of different social classes. Members of the priestly class, in particular, seem to have been frequently divided based on social rankings and religious authorities. For example, a priestly class such as Levites and Hasidim were not considered as upper-class since they were priests who were ranked lower than the כהנים (Ezra 2:36; 3:2; 6:9; Neh 3:22; 5:12; 7:64; 12:41)[16] – thereby experiencing "status inconsistency."[17]

---

[13] Carr, *Writing on the Tablet of the Heart*, 111–73.

[14] Carr, *Writing on the Tablet of the Heart*, 142.

[15] Cf. Johannes Unsok Ro, *Poverty, Law, and Divine Justice in Persian and Hellenistic Judah* (Atlanta: Society of Biblical Literature, 2018), 21.

[16] Cf. Ro, *Poverty, Law, and Divine Justice*, 179–80.

[17] Cf. Ro, *Poverty, Law, and Divine Justice*, 180. The term "status inconsistency" refers to a social phenomenon that occurs when a person's resources vary due to different social class systems: According to Gerhard E. Lenski, it is human nature to strive for maximum gratification, even though it means harming others (*Power and Privilege: A Theory of Social Stratification* [New York: McGraw-Hill, 1966], 44). An individual with strong economic power but limited political power, for example, would think about himself or herself in terms of the economic class system's high-ranking status. An individual with a low occupational rank but a high level of education would act or think in the same way. Others who associate with him or her in society, on the other hand, have a vested interest in treating him or her in the opposite orientation, that is, in terms of his or her lowest rated ranking (Lenski, *Power and Privilege*, 86–88). Status inconsistency may be a factor in social dispute. People whose social statuses are inconsistent have a proclivity to resist the status quo (Lenski, *Power and Privilege*, 87). This definition provides a rational explanation to the significant issue of why some members of the

The above brief sketch indicates several prominent developments of recent research regarding cultural aspects of scribalism. In our view, this volume contributes to the ongoing conversation within biblical and cognate studies concerning the scribal processes that produced biblical texts. The terms used within the title reflect the nodes that we seek to connect:

A. "Scribal practice": In contrast to "scribal culture," which could be narrowly construed as the subculture inhabited by scribes themselves, the term *practice* focuses on the production and social function of written texts within an oral culture.
B. "Cultural memory": Along with similar terms such as "social memory," "community memory" and "collective memory," this signifies the body of unwritten knowledge, understandings, and beliefs of a largely non-literate society of which scribes were part.[18]
C. "Hebrew scriptures": Not merely several *biblia*, but *graphai*: diverse texts which come to be regarded collectively as holy writ.
D. "Making": Includes various stages of text production, from oral utterance up to the extant manuscript forms: oral transmission, writing, copying, revision, supplementation, etc.

The essays in this volume take up the following subjects:

A. Tools and processes of scribal education, and the production of texts by scribes
B. Scribal culture in ancient Israel/Judea compared with those of other ANE cultures
C. The interaction between scribal texts and cultural/collective/community memory within an oral culture such as ancient Israel/Judea
D. The overlap and/or intersections of the roles "prophet," "priest," and "scribe" in ancient Israel/Judea and beyond
E. Conceptions of writing and scribal process within biblical texts themselves

The essays in Part I employ comparative methodologies to the topic of the scribal origins of biblical texts. The first essay, Daniel Bodi's "New Proposal for

---

upper and middle classes in a society dedicate themselves to revolutionary sociopolitical causes. To put it another way, despite their elevated status within the educational and vocational class systems, lower-ranking priests such as Levites and Hasidim did not hold a high place within the political and economic class systems. The active and dedicated involvement of Levites and Hasidim in writing and composing the Theology of the Poor can be persuasively explained using this principle of status inconsistency (Ro, *Poverty, Law, and Divine Justice*, 7–10).

[18] See the very recent collection facilitated by one of the editors: Johannes Unsok Ro and Diana Edelman, eds., *Collective Memory and Collective Identity: Case Studies in Deuteronomy and the Deuteronomistic History*, BZAW 534 (Berlin: de Gruyter, 2021). Many current works in biblical studies build off the seminal work of Jan Assmann applying "social memory" studies in the ancient world: *Cultural Memory and Early Civilization: Writing, Remembrance, and Political Imagination* (Cambridge: Cambridge University Press, 2011).

the Origin of the Term 'Letter,'" analyzes the relationship between the Akkadian word *egirtu*, the Biblical Aramaic *'iggrâ* and the Biblical Hebrew *'iggeret*. Bodi evaluates scholarly suggestions as to the etymology of this term, and argues that the most useful comparison is the Old Babylonian *egirrû/igerrû* – with the sense of "placing a word" with someone about another person – in Mari texts. The chain of transmission connoted in the term *egirrû*, from god to scribe to king, has implications for the understanding of the Hebrew scriptures perceived as a "letter," a "word that has been placed" with human transmitters for other humans informing them about God.

William R. Stewart likewise appeals to Mari literature in evaluating recent scholarly claims that biblical accounts of preexilic prophets are predominantly (or exclusively) the product of the literary activity of postexilic scribes. In offering "A Comparative Study of Prophetic Sign-Reports in the Royal Archives of Mari, Syria (ARM 26/1.206) and the Hebrew Bible (Jeremiah 19:1–13)," Stewart responds to John Barton's influential suggestion that the postexilic scribes (mis) perceived preexilic prophecy as a "mantic" activity. Stewart identifies parallels between Jeremiah 19 and the Mari text, which is the earliest extant extrabiblical prophetic sign-report, and argues that the reported activities of Jeremiah are credible as a preexilic prophecy enacted and exegeted by a historical prophet.

In "Scribal Intertexts in the Book of Job: Foreign Counterparts of Job," JiSeong Kwon evaluates attempts to identify a particular source text for the book of Job. Many Egyptian, Sumerian, Ugaritic, and Edomic texts with the "righteous sufferer" theme and similar motifs have been proposed as background for Job, but no clear demonstration of direct dependence has been successfully achieved. Kwon proposes not a direct line of literary dependence, but rather a general awareness of non-Israelite "sufferer" texts among the Israelite literati, who then recreated and adapted the motifs to their own cultural memory and aims.

The final contribution to Part I ranges a bit farther afield than the more obvious comparisons to Mesopotamian, Syro-Palestinian and Egyptian scribal communities and corpora. In "Collective Identity through Scribalism: Interpreting Plato's *Menexenus* and the Book of Chronicles," Sungwoo Park and Johannes Unsok Ro compare the ways in which Plato and the Chronicler adapted earlier literary forms – in this case, leaders' speeches at moments of national transition. Park and Ro show that in the *Menexenus* Socrates coopts the form of Pericles's famous funeral speech, but in service of a new kind of Athenian collective identity – one that is less militaristic and more focused on national and personal virtue. By comparison, in the Chronicler's re-presented history of the Israelite monarchy the speeches of David at key junctures serve to (among other aims) re-formulate the All-Israel collective identity independent of a kingship, more focused on national virtue and loyalty to YHWH.

The essays in Part II approach the topic of scribal practice starting from Hebrew Bible texts that make reference to scribes and the act of writing itself. Each of these essays, in its own way, interacts with the notion of a "divine torah," a written text taking on divine authority and its presence/performance in some way representing the deity's presence in the community.

In the essay titled, "Then Moses Wrote This Torah," Benjamin Kilchör argues for three levels of communication within Deuteronomy: an initial oral audience of Moses's speech, written communication for the benefit of the priestly and scribal elites, and – significantly – the future generations of laity who would be addressed by the oral performance of the written text, for pedagogical purposes and in cultic contexts.

In their contribution, Lisbeth S. Fried and Edward J. Mills III examine the story of "Ezra the Scribe" as that character is presented in Ezra 7–10 and Nehemiah 8. Building on Fried's recent proposed reconstruction of an original letter from Artaxerxes to Ezra,[19] Fried and Mills here suggest that the distance between the reconstructed original and the received text can be explained by the evolution of meaning of the Aramaic term דת, and the corresponding role of Ezra as a ספר מהיר. Through comparison with Daniel 2, 6 and 7, Fried and Mills argue that as דת changes from royal *ad hoc* decree to written statute, the role of the "scribe" changes from personal agent of the king (as in the reconstructed letter) to the biblical author's understanding of Ezra: as judge and expositor of written divine "torah."

Similarly, Johanna Erzberger suggests that the evolution of the character "Baruch" reflects the textualization of prophetic authority. In "Israel's Salvation and the Survival of Baruch the Scribe," she compares the role of Baruch in the extant versions of Jeremiah and the book of Baruch, with particular focus on the structural significance of MT Jer 36 and 45 – corresponding to LXX Jer 43 and 51:31–35 – within the books of Jeremiah. She concludes that the book of Baruch may be read as furthering the textualization of prophetic authority, in closer affinity to the conception presented in MT Jeremiah, despite the closer structural continuity with LXX Jeremiah.

In "Tracing Divine Law: Written Divine Law in Chronicles," Peter Altmann analyzes references to "YHWH's torah" in Chronicles, over-against Samuel–Kings, in search of insight into the significance of written "divine law" in the late-Persian / Early Hellenistic period. Altmann observes that "YHWH's torah" is most prominent in Chronicles when good kings apply the cultic ordinances of the Pentateuch, whereas connections to other legal spheres are largely absent. The Chronicler's use of written "torah," then, points to the Pentateuchal texts' ongoing application to new cultic situations, rather than as positive, practical judicial law, with implications for our understanding of the Pentateuch's formation and promulgation in the Persian period.

---

[19] Lisbeth S. Fried, *Ezra: A Commentary*, SPCC (Sheffield: Sheffield Phoenix, 2015), 309–31.

The essays in Part III employ a variety of approaches to specific cases in the Hebrew Bible where the scribal process becomes evident, and can be illumined by careful study of mainly internal evidence. These studies reflect a range in the degree of confidence with which the developmental history of a specific text may be reconstructed. In each case one may see behind the text a community of scribes, working to negotiate the constraints of cultural memory while furthering their own aims and purposes.

The first three essays take up the interaction of law and narrative. In a study of Deuteronomy 13:1–5 and the Former Prophets, Jin Han alliteratively asks, "Did the Deuteronomist Detest Dreams?" Even though Deuteronomy 13 casts a shadow of doubt upon the practice of dream divination as leading to the worship of other gods, dream revelations are presented positively in several instances within the Deuteronomistic History. Han suggests that the Deuteronomists are balancing the strong, positive cultural memory of leaders experiencing revelation through dreams at key moments in Israel's story, with the desire to discourage their audience from adopting dream divination instead of relying on written "torah."

Benjamin Giffone likewise addresses another instance of apparent conflict between the written "torah" and a narrative text. In "Regathering Too Many Stones? Scribal Constraints, Community Memory, and the 'Problem' of Elijah's Sacrifice for Deuteronomism in Kings," Giffone examines the narrative elements of 1 Kings 18–19 that might have been considered problematic for a Deuteronomistic conception of cultic centralization. Giffone proposes that the editors' apparent lack of concern about Elijah's sacrifice can be explained by a desire to balance cultural memory and theological advocacy, and also by specific narrative elements that render the story at least *tolerable* from the standpoint of Persian-period, pro-Jerusalem editors.

In "Nehemiah 5:1–13 as Innerbiblical Interpretation of Pentateuchal Slavery Laws," Roger Nam reminds that conceptions of scribal practice must account for the intricacies of social systems, economic power, and political authority. Nam shows how the scribal appropriation (or application) of the slavery laws in the Nehemiah 5 narrative must be "translated" through the lens of differing economic settings.

Kristin Weingart proposes that the well-attested ancient scribal activity of "chronicle-writing" can provide insight into the scribal culture that produced the biblical texts. In "Chronography in the Book of Kings: An Inquiry into an Israelite Manifestation of an Ancient Near Eastern Genre," Weingart identifies the elements of a "Chronicle of the Kings of Israel," a continuously updated chronographic work going back to the Omrides, which served as an informational source for the book of Kings as Israel and Judah developed a scribal culture and substantial literature in the late 9th and early 8th centuries.

Woo Min Lee searches for an element of scribal preservation of cultural memory in the story of Hezekiah's prayer and YHWH's response, in "The 'Remnant' in the Deuteronomistic Cultural Memory: A Case Study on 2 Kings 19:30–31." Lee argues that the passage reflects the scribes' interweaving of historical and cultural memory and eschatological perspective as a part of Isaiah's message to Hezekiah during Sennacherib's attack against Jerusalem.

Benjamin Ziemer's bold essay, "Radical Versus Conservative? How Scribes Conventionally Used Books While Writing Books," is overarching in its scope and culturally self-aware in its approach. Ziemer takes issue with the axioms of the "growth model" of redaction criticism, in particular, the principles of addition and differentiation which would theoretically allow editorial layers to be identified. Having marshaled many examples from the biblical texts – including various recensions and versions – and Mesopotamian literature, Ziemer argues that we should rather think in terms of "master scribes" (following Milstein) who never reproduced the original in its entirety without omission, but instead were inclined to add, combine, omit, substitute, rearrange, and otherwise update in ways that cannot be clearly excavated without the *Vorlage(n)*.

As readers will easily recognize, the present volume explores a wide-ranging landscape of materials and incorporates a variety of research into one volume. Each of the fourteen essays advances its own fresh perspective and insights, while also providing a window into larger scholarly projects related to scribal practice, cultural memory, and the making of the Hebrew Scriptures. The editors sincerely hope that this volume succeeds in making significant contributions to the ongoing paradigm shift in Hebrew Bible studies.

Bibliography

Assmann, Jan. *Cultural Memory and Early Civilization: Writing, Remembrance, and Political Imagination*. Cambridge: Cambridge University Press, 2011.

Ben Zvi, Ehud, and Christoph Levin, eds. *Remembering and Forgetting in Early Second Temple Judah*. FAT 85. Tübingen: Mohr Siebeck, 2012.

Berman, Joshua. "Empirical Models of Textual Growth: A Challenge for the Historical-Critical Tradition." *JHebS* 16/12 (2016):1–25. doi:10.5508/jhs.2016.v16.a12.

Berman, Joshua. *Inconsistency in the Torah: Ancient Literary Convention and the Limits of Source Criticism*. New York: Oxford University Press, 2017.

Bienkowski, Piotr, et al., eds. *Writing and Ancient Near Eastern Society: Papers in Honour of Alan R. Millard*. LHBOTS 429. New York: T&T Clark, 2005.

Carr, David M. *The Formation of the Hebrew Bible: A New Reconstruction*. New York: Oxford University Press, 2011.

Carr, David M. *Writing on the Tablet of the Heart: Origins of Scripture and Literature*. New York: Oxford University Press, 2005.

Crawford, Sidnie White. *Rewriting Scripture in Second Temple Times*. Grand Rapids: Eerdmans, 2008.

Davies, Philip R., and Thomas Römer, eds. *Writing the Bible: Scribes, Scribalism and Script*. London: Routledge, 2014.

Ebach, Ruth, and Martin Leuenberger, eds. *Tradition(en) im Alten Israel: Konstruktion, Transmission und Transformation*. FAT 127. Tübingen: Mohr Siebeck, 2019.
Ellman, Barat. "Memory and History in the Hebrew Bible." *OBib* (2017). doi:10.1093/obo/9780199840731-0143.
Evans, Paul S. "Creating a New 'Great Divide': The Exoticization of Ancient Culture in Some Recent Applications of Orality Studies to the Bible." *JBL* 136.4 (2017): 749–64.
Fitzpatrick-McKinley, Anne. *The Transformation of Torah: From Scribal Advice to Law*. JSOTSup 287. Sheffield: Sheffield Academic, 1999.
Fried, Lisbeth S. *Ezra: A Commentary*. SPCC. Sheffield: Sheffield Phoenix, 2015.
Gertz, Jan Christian, et al., eds. *The Formation of the Pentateuch: Bridging the Academic Cultures of Europe, Israel, and North America*. FAT 111. Tübingen: Mohr Siebeck, 2016.
Greer, Jonathan S., John W. Hilber, and John H. Walton, eds. *Behind the Scenes of the Old Testament: Cultural, Social, and Historical Contexts*. Grand Rapids: Baker Academic, 2018.
Jamieson-Drake, David W. *Scribes and Schools in Monarchic Judah: A Socio-Archaeological Approach*. JSOTSup 109. Sheffield: Almond Press, 1991.
Kline, Jonathan G. *Allusive Soundplay in the Hebrew Bible*. AIL 28. Atlanta: Society of Biblical Literature, 2016.
LeFebvre, Michael. *Collections, Codes, and Torah: The Re-Characterization of Israel's Written Law*. LHBOTS 451. New York: T&T Clark, 2006.
Lenski, Gerhard E. *Power and Privilege: A Theory of Social Stratification*. New York: McGraw-Hill, 1966.
Milstein, Sara J. *Tracking the Master Scribe: Revision through Introduction in Biblical and Mesopotamian Literature*. New York: Oxford University Press, 2016.
Müller, Reinhard, Juha Pakkala, and Bas ter Haar Romeny. *Evidence of Editing: Growth and Change of Texts in the Hebrew Bible*. RBS 75. Atlanta: Society of Biblical Literature, 2014.
Najman, Hindy, and Konrad Schmid, eds. *Jeremiah's Scriptures: Production, Reception, Interaction, and Transformation*. JSJSup 173. Leiden: Brill, 2016.
Niditch, Susan. *Oral World and Written Word*. Louisville: Westminster John Knox, 1996.
Noegel, Scott B. *"Wordplay" in Ancient Near Eastern Texts*. ANEM 26. Atlanta: Society of Biblical Literature, 2021.
Olyan, Saul M., and Jacob L. Wright. *Supplementation and the Study of the Hebrew Bible*. BJS 361. Providence, RI: Brown University Press, 2018.
Oswald, Wolfgang, ed. *Textgestalt und Komposition: Exegetische Beiträge zu Tora und Vordere Propheten*. FAT 69. Tübingen: Mohr Siebeck, 2010.
Pakkala, Juha. *God's Word Omitted: Omissions in the Transmission of the Hebrew Bible*. FRLANT 251. Göttingen: Vandenhoeck & Ruprecht, 2013.
Person, Raymond F., Jr. "Text Criticism as a Lens for Understanding the Transmission of Ancient Texts in Their Oral Environments." Pages 197–215 in *Contextualizing Israel's Sacred Writing: Ancient Literacy, Orality, and Literature Production*. Edited by Brian Schmidt. Atlanta: Society of Biblical Literature, 2015.
Person, Raymond F., Jr. "The Ancient Israelite Scribe as Performer." *JBL* 117 (1998): 601–9.
Person, Raymond F., Jr. *The Deuteronomic History and the Book of Chronicles: Scribal Works in an Oral World*. AIL 6. Atlanta: Society of Biblical Literature, 2010.
Person, Raymond F., Jr. "The Role of Memory in the Tradition Represented by the Deuteronomic History and the Book of Chronicles." *OT* 26 (2011): 537–50.

Person, Raymond F., Jr., and Robert Rezetko. *Empirical Models Challenging Biblical Criticism*. AIL 25. Atlanta: Society of Biblical Literature, 2016.

Ro, Johannes Unsok. *Poverty, Law, and Divine Justice in Persian and Hellenistic Judah*. Atlanta: Society of Biblical Literature, 2018.

Ro, Johannes Unsok, and Diana Edelman, eds. *Collective Memory and Collective Identity: Case Studies in Deuteronomy and the Deuteronomistic History*. BZAW 534. Berlin: de Gruyter, 2021.

Sanders, Seth L. *From Adapa to Enoch: Scribal Culture and Religious Vision in Judea and Babylon*. TSAJ 167. Tübingen: Mohr Siebeck, 2017.

Schmidt, Brian, ed. *Contextualizing Israel's Sacred Writings: Ancient Literacy, Orality, and Literary Production*. AIL 22. Atlanta: Society of Biblical Literature, 2015.

Schniedewind, William M. *How the Bible Became a Book: The Textualization of Ancient Israel*. Cambridge: Cambridge University Press, 2004.

Schniedewind, William M. *The Finger of the Scribe: How Scribes Learned to Write the Bible*. New York: Oxford University Press, 2019.

Tertel, Hans Jürgen. *Text and Transmission: An Empirical Model for the Literary Development of Old Testament Narratives*. BZAW 221. Berlin: de Gruyter, 1994.

Toorn, Karel van der. *Scribal Culture and the Making of the Hebrew Bible*. Cambridge, MA: Harvard University Press, 2007.

Van Seters, John. *The Edited Bible: The Curious History of the "Editor" in Biblical Criticism*. Winona Lake, IN: Eisenbrauns, 2006.

Vroom, Jonathan. *The Authority of Law in the Hebrew Bible and Early Judaism: Tracing the Origins of Legal Obligation from Ezra to Qumran*. JSJSup 187. Leiden: Brill, 2018.

Weingart, Kristin. *Gezählte Geschichte: Systematik, Quellen und Entwicklung der synchronistischen Chronologie in den Königebüchern*. FAT 142. Tübingen: Mohr Siebeck, 2020.

Weissenberg, Hanne von, Juha Pakkala, and Marko Martilla, eds. *Changes in Scripture: Rewriting and Interpreting Authoritative Traditions in the Second Temple Period*. Berlin: de Gruyter, 2011.

Zahn, Molly M. *Rethinking Rewritten Scripture: Composition and Exegesis in the 4QReworked Pentateuch Manuscripts*. STDJ 95. Leiden: Brill 2011.

Ziemer, Benjamin. *Kritik des Wachstumsmodells: Die Grenzen alttestamentlicher Redaktionsgeschichte im Lichte empirischer Evidenz*. VTSup 182. Leiden: Brill, 2020.

Part I

Comparative Studies

A New Proposal for the Origin of the Term for 'Letter': Sumerian inim.gar, i₅-gar-ra; Akkadian *egirtu*; Aramaic *'iggĕrâ*, *'iggartâ*, Hebrew *'iggeret*

Daniel Bodi

1. Akkadian *egirtu* "Letter" Derived From *egēru* Meaning, "To Be Crossed, or Twisted"?

The latest study of the Akkadian word *egirtu* in a published Harvard Ph.D. dissertation by Paul Mankowski reiterates the argument offered by Kaufman more than forty years ago[1]:

Kaufman has proposed the only plausible etymology for *egirtu*. In a 1977 article he suggested that *egirtu* is the feminine verbal adjective of the Akkadian *egēru*, "to be crossed, twisted," arguing that from the Mesopotamian (cuneiform) point of view, the orientation of Aramaic writing appeared "crosswise," and the *egirtu* was simply the Akkadian name for an Aramaic document, later having itself become a loanword in Aramaic with the specific meaning "letter."[2]

Kaufman sought corroboration for this explanation in the ninth-century bilingual Assyrian Aramaic inscription from the Tell Fekheryeh statue, where the cuneiform text is written running parallel to the long axis, at ninety degrees to the Aramaic text. Thus, Kaufman and in his vein Mankowski derive *egirtu* from *egēru* "to be crossed, twisted," presumably reflecting how the Assyrians perceived the Aramaic alphabetic writing as "lying transversally across" in respect to the cuneiform Akkadian script. This explanation may appear as an ingenious illustration of the meaning of the Akkadian verb *egēru* "to be crossed, twisted" but seems contrived.

First, Landsberger had already pointed out that *egirtu* was falsely derived from the verb *egēru* "to be twisted." He thought that this connection was not self-evident and might be erroneous.[3] Second, the way Assyrians perceived Aramaic

---

[1] Stephen A. Kaufman, "An Assyro-Aramaic *egirtu ša šulmu*," in *Essays on the Ancient Near East in Memory of J.J. Finkelstein*, ed. Maria deJong Ellis, MCAAS 19 (Hamden, CT: Archon Books, 1977), 119–27 (124n44).

[2] Paul V. Mankowski, *Akkadian Loanwords in Biblical Hebrew*, HSS 47 (Winona Lake, IN: Eisenbrauns, 2000), 22–25 (25). The word is variously spelled *egirrû/igerrû/igirrû/egerrû*.

[3] Benno Landsberger, "Das 'gute Wort'," *MAOG* 4 (1928–29): 294–321 (316). "Von *egēru* = 'über Kreuz,' spez. 'kompliziert sein' … ist *egirtu* schwer abzuleiten."

script is expressed differently as (^lúA.BA) "the scribe of the alphabetic script" (see below). Third, the position of the Aramaic inscription written horizontally at 90 degrees in respect to the Assyrian inscription written vertically on the Tell Fekheryeh statue is unusual. It is therefore hazardous to generalize out of a single case with a peculiar bilingual Assyrian-Aramaic disposition of an inscription. Moreover, Oppenheim suggested that the connection between *egirrû* and *egirtu* is based on some "popular" etymology used by scribes but that the precise way they relate these two terms escapes us.[4]

In this context, the use of the Sumerogram ^LÚA.BA in Neo-Assyrian documents to designate the Aramaic scribe using the alphabetic script might be significant. The usual Akkadian term for scribe is *ṭupšarru* that transcribes the Sumerogram ^LÚDUB.SAR means "the man who writes a tablet." However, the Sumerogram ^LÚA.BA is remarkably different, where LÚ stands for "man" and is usually found as a determinative before the name of professions. The following logograms A.BA have been interpreted as an attempt to indicate a scribe who uses the Aramaic alphabet, i. e. *'aleph-beth* as if ^LÚA.BA stood for "the man of the alphabet," or, an "alphabet scribe."[5] The Assyrian court had scribes who wrote Akkadian on clay tablets and scribes who wrote Aramaic on *sipru* (writing material made out of parchment or papyrus). Zadok equates *tupšar armā'a*, written ^LÚA.BA ^KUR *armā'a*, with *sepīru* which would be a term of Aramaic or Northwest Semitic origin for "scribe" like Hebrew *sōpēr*.[6] In analyzing sources from the first millennium BCE, Laurie Pearce concludes that the majority of Aramaic scribes were individuals of West Semitic parentage who bore Assyrian names, who performed their scribal duties in regions known to be heavily Aramaized and in contexts in which the services of an individual literate in Aramaic would facilitate the transaction.[7] Tadmor considers ^LÚA.BA to be a "pseudo-logogram" designating a scribe who uses alphabetic writing which he renders with "ABC-man."[8] This logogram seems to have originated in thirteenth-century Ugarit where the syllabic cuneiform Akkadian and the thirty alphabetic cuneiform signs for writing Ugaritic were employed side by side. That the "pseudo-logogram" ^LÚA.BA is of Northwest Semitic origin is confirmed beyond any doubt by the

---

[4] A. Leo Oppenheim, "Sumerian: inim.gar, Akkadian: *egirrû* = Greek: *kledon*," *AfO* 17 (1954–55): 49–55.

[5] Stefan M. Maul, "La fin de la tradition cunéiforme et les 'Graeco-Babyloniaca'," *CCGG* 6 (1995): 3–17 (6).

[6] Ran Zadok, *Assyrians in Chaldean and Achaemenid Babylonia* (Malibu, CA: Undena, 1984), 12.

[7] Laurie Pearce, "*Sepīru* and ^LÚA.BA: Scribes of the Late First Millennium," in *Languages and Cultures in Contact: At the Crossroads of Civilizations in the Syro-Mesopotamian Realm*, ed. Karel Van Lerberghe and Gabriella Voet, OLA 96 (Leuven: Peeters, 1999), 355–68 (361).

[8] Hayim Tadmor, "The Aramaization of Assyria: Aspects of Western Impact," in *Mesopotamien und seine Nachbarn: Politische und kulturelle Wechselbeziehungen im Alten Vorderasien vom 4. bis 1. Jahrtausend v. Chr.*, 3 vols., RAI 25 (Berlin: Reimer, 1982), 2:449–70 (459).

lexical lists found at Ugarit where one finds the following equation: [dub].sar = [a].ba = úmbisag = *ṭup-šar-rum* (*PRU* 3,212.12´-14´, *AHw*, 1395b) and ab.[ba] = [d]ub.sar.[9] At Ugarit, the Sumerogram ᴸᵁ́A.BA stands for a scribe writing the alphabetic cuneiform script and does not designate a scribe writing Aramaic. In the first millennium BCE, however, ᴸᵁ́A.BA stands for the scribe writing the alphabetic Aramaic script.

2. The Akkadian *egirtu* Is Related to *egirrû* as Some Kind of "Utterance"

The traditional explanation of the term *egirtu* is to connect it with the masculine noun *egirrû*. The *Chicago Assyrian Dictionary* entry on *egirrû* offers three different meanings for this word: 1.) Reputation (as expressed in utterances of others), 2.) Mood (as evoked by or expressed in utterances), 3.) An oracular utterance of uncertain nature.[10]

However, Akkadian *egirtu* is a feminine verbal adjective or noun identified by the final (*t*) and meaning, 1.) a letter, 2a.) a tablet as a legal document 2b.) a tablet of a specific form.[11] All the examples cited come from Neo-Assyrian times.[12]

The discussion on the origin of the term *egirtu* has a long and contentious history. In his dictionary and an article, von Soden argued that the Akkadian term for a letter is an Aramaic loanword.[13] However, Zimmern had already pointed out that Aramaic *'iggĕrâ* is a loanword from Akkadian.[14] Moreover, Mankowski rejects this derivation referring to an article by Köbert who argued that an Aramaic derivation was unlikely on the ground that the West Semitic noun type *qittil, qittal* was largely limited to physical defects, concluding that regarding its meaning and structure the Aramaic word *'iggĕrâ* is unique and stands alone.[15] Moreover, Köbert reviewed the earlier German philological scholarship on this term and aligned himself with the Akkadian derivation of the Aramaic word, but tried to explain its unusual form by saying that it was first adopted by the Persians

---

[9] Jean Nougayrol, "'Vocalises' et 'Syllabes en liberté' à Ugarit," in *Studies in Honor of Benno Landsberger*, ed. Hans G. Güterbock and Thorkild Jacobsen, AS 16 (Chicago: Oriental Institute of the University of Chicago, 1965), 29–39 (37n78).

[10] *CAD E*, 43–45.

[11] Simo Parpola, "Assyrian Library Records," *JNES* 42 (1983): 1–29 (2, 18), translates *egirtu* with "one-column tablet."

[12] *CAD E*, 45–46.

[13] *AHw*, 190a; Wolfram von Soden, "Aramäische Wörter in neuassyrischen und neu- und spätbabylonischen Texten: Ein Vorbericht I," *OrNS* 35 (1966): 1–20 (8).

[14] Heinrich Zimmern, *Akkadische Fremdwörter als Beweis für babylonischen Kultureinfluß* (Leipzig: Hinrichs, 1915), 19.

[15] Raimund Köbert, "Gedanken zum semitischen Wort- und Satzbau. 1–7," *OrNS* 14 (1945): 273–83 (278–79); "Gedanklich und strukturell steht *iggerā* also allein" (279). Köbert's article offers a series of earlier views by nineteenth century philologists.

and from there into Aramaic. However, the intermediary role of the Persians is unnecessary.

The two most important articles on this topic are still the ones by Landsberger and by Oppenheim. While Landsberger collected the greatest number of texts in which the Akkadian term *egirrû* occurs, Oppenheim's article on Sumerian inim. gar, Akkadian *egirrû*, Greek *klēdōn*[16] offers a valuable history of research. Oppenheim's suggestion to relate Akkadian *egirrû* with the Greek *klēdōn,* however, has now been completely abandoned since *egirrû* does not mean a word of chance, "overheard and considered endowed with ominous meanings." Both Wilcke and Durand criticized his understanding of the term (see below). Since the nineteenth century, Assyriologists have surmised that *egirrû* was some kind of utterance but were unable to determine the exact nuance of this word. Oppenheim enumerates the various early attempts since the end of the nineteenth and the beginning of the twentieth century to translate the term *egirrû* showing the difficulties in determining its precise meaning: Ungnad,[17] "*Stimmung*" ("mood") followed by Thureau-Dangin "*belle humeur*"[18] (i.e. "good mood," which is one of the meanings listed in *CAD* under the entry *egirrû*); Albright: "thought;"[19] Landsberger:[20] "*Formel*" ("formula" i.e. utterance in the sense of a good or evil wish, directly influencing the person to whom it is addressed); von Soden,[21] "*Formel*" and "*Schicksalsformel*."

Misled by Oppenheim's definition of *egirrû* as a chance word endowed with ominous meanings, Cogan and Sperling compared it with the rabbinic use of the expression *bat qôl*, "daughter of the voice" as a chance utterance or word.[22]

---

[16] Oppenheim, "Sumerian: inim.gar, Akkadian: *egirrû* = Greek: *kledon*," 49–55; Landsberger, "Das 'gute Wort'," 294–321.

[17] Arthur Ungnad, "Review of *Assyriologische und archäologische Studien, Festschrift H.V. Hilprecht (1909),*" *ZDMG* 65 (1911): 109–30 (127).

[18] François Thureau-Dangin, "L'exaltation d'Ištar," *RA* 11 (1914): 141–58 (148–51 "Que mon fidèle messier, dont les livres sont inestimables, qui connaît mes secrets, que Ilabrat, mon insigne messager, soit ton commissionaire; (148 l. 23) que, devant toi, il mentienne en constante belle humeur les dieux et les déesses (*ina maḫ-ri-ka e-gir-e ili u* ᵈ*iš-ta-ri li-dam-me -iq sa-an-tak[-ka]*)."

[19] William F. Albright, "Some Cruces in the Langdon Epic," *JAOS* 39 (1919): 65–90 (76n19) KA-GAR = *egirrû*, and (77) *banû egirrûya* "my thoughts were bright." Heinrich Zimmern, "Zu den 'Keilschrifttexten aus Assur religiösen Inhalts,'" *ZA* 30 (1915/1916): 184–229, KA-GAR *egirrū* "Deutung" = "meaning."

[20] Landsberger, "Das 'gute Wort'," 315.

[21] Wolfram von Soden, "Die Unterweltvision eines assyrischen Kronprinzen," *ZA* 43 (1939): 1–31, l. 14 *egerrê* (INIM.GAR) *lum-ni* "die Formel des Bösen" (20); Idem, "Ein Zwiegespräch Hammurabis mit einer Frau," *ZA* 49 (1950): 151–94 (170, rev. IV:5; 190–91).

[22] Saul Lieberman, *Hellenism in Jewish Palestine* (New York: Jewish Theological Seminary of America, 1950), 194–99, quoted in Mordechai Cogan, "The Road to En-dor," in *Pomegranates and Golden Bells: Studies in Biblical, Jewish, and Near Eastern Ritual, Law, and Literature in Honor of Jacob Milgrom*, ed. D.P. Wright, D.N. Freedman, and A. Hurvitz (Winona Lake, IN: Eisenbrauns, 1995), 319–26 (323n22). Also David Sperling, "Akkadian *egerrû* and Hebrew *bt qwl*," *JANESCU* 4 (1972): 63–74.

The entry on *egirrû,* and *egirtu* in the *CAD*, volume E, dating from the year 1958, offers almost four pages of examples. However, not a single one comes from the Old Babylonian Mari texts, which is understandable since the Mari letters mentioning *egirrû* were published about fifteen years later.

It might be worthwhile quoting the summary which the *CAD* E, 45 offers on the three basic meanings of *egirrû*:

The meaning of *egirrû* seems to have developed in three main directions. First, it refers to utterances of approval and admiration or disapproval and contempt which, either as interjections, short curses, or blessings, follow a person in public and are considered a reflection and measure of his social acceptability (cf. German "Nachrede," and cf. mng. 1a). In a slightly different nuance, the word refers to the ways in which an interceding deity can make or undo the standing of a worshipper before an important deity, thus transferring to the religious sphere the typical relationship of a subject with an interceding courtier and with his king (cf. mng. 1b).

In another sphere of meaning, *egirrû* describes the mood of the individual as evoked by utterances of his fellow men in direct contact or as revealed by his own utterances, such as sighs, interjections, etc. (cf. mng. 2).

As a third aspect should be regarded oracular utterances of a somewhat undetermined kind which are either accidental in origin (comparable with Greek *klēdon*) or hallucinatory in nature (corresponding to dreams). In both instances, they are acoustic (cf. the use of the verbs *apālu, šemû, šūṣû* (ka ... è), etc.) and considered (as) released by the deity in reply to prayers or as warnings (cf. mng. 3).

3. Sumerian inim.gar "To Place a Word" and Akkadian *egirrû* "Utterance"

Let us first state what has been secured so far with a certain degree of certainty in the course of Assyriological research. That the Akkadian term *egirrû* comes from Sumerian inim/i₅.gar had been established by Landsberger some time ago. Sumerian and Akkadian bilingual lexical lists make the following equation:

inim.gar = *i-gi-r[u]-u* (Erim-ḫuš III:175)

in[im.gar] = *e-gir-ru-u* (Antagal VIII:263)

inim.gar = *e-gir-ru-u* (Igituh short version 74).[23]

The meaning of the Sumerian inim.gar from which the Akkadian *egirrû* is derived is literally "to place a word," hence "utterance." Translated into Akkadian, it would be something like *awātam šakānum*. This also explains why *egirrû* is

---

[23] *CAD E*, 43, and Oppenheim, "Sumerian: inim.gar, Akkadian: *egirrû* = Greek: *kledon*," 49n3; Rykele Borger and Friedrich Ellermaier, "nº 15 inim/i₅-gar *egirrû* 'Leumund,' = 'reputation,'" *ABZ*, 64.

frequently followed with the adjective *damiqu* "good." It literally means, "to place a good word" either with the king or with the deity, i.e. to put in a good word for someone. The term *egirrû* designates a word or a discourse concerning somebody else held by an intermediary. In the case of *egirrû* as a divine message, it is given in the absence of the king. The tablet with the written *egirrû* has to be brought and read to the king. In both cases, there is an absent person, which necessitates either oral or written transmission of the message.

In a late bilingual Sumerian-Akkadian text in the Louvre Museum (A.6458), line 1, and dating from the Seleucid period, the Sumerian term in[im].k[a] is rendered in Akkadian with *zikir pîšu* "the word of his mouth."

An azag-ga gal-bi in[im]-k[a]-na nu-mu-[um]-til-li(ti-il)-e-ne

ᵈ*A-nu el-lu zi-kir pi-i-šu la ga-ma-ru*

"Anu, the holy and great, whose word is without end."[24]

4. From Sumerian inim.gar, "To Place a Word" to Akkadian *egirtu*, "Letter"

My suggestion is that the original meaning of inim.gar, "to place a word," has influenced the understanding and development of *egirrû*-message and *egirtu* as "letter, message," in the sense of placing a word with someone about a third person. The following data tend to confirm such an understanding.

A. There is a text where *egirrû* occurs with the verb *šakānu*, "to place":

egirrû(inim.gar) *dumqi u mēšari šukun elīya* literally: "place a good and just word on my behalf" (King,[25] *Magic* nº 1,22; BMS 1:22), cf. the translation in *CAD* E, 44c "grant me a happy and optimistic mood."

B. In a bilingual Sumero-Akkadian prayer,[26] one finds a highly significant variant (CT 16 8:280/281):

igi.mu.ta inim.gar sig₅.ga ḫé.en.dug₄.ga:

ana panīya e-gir-ri (var.-*tum*) *damiqti liqabbi arkīya ubānu damiqti littariṣ*

"In front of me may good words be said (about me) and may I be pointed out

with approval behind my back" (cf. *CAD* E, 43d).

---

[24] Thureau-Dangin, "L'exaltation d'Ištar," 141–58, (cuneiform text, 144; transcription, 147; translation, 150) "Anu, le saint et grand, dont la parole est sans fin." The Akkadian line differs. It does not render Sumerian gal *rabû* "great."

[25] Leonard W. King, *Babylonian Magic and Sorcery: Being "the Prayers of the Lifting of the Hand"* (London: Luzac, 1896; repr., Hildesheim: Olms, 1978).

[26] *Cuneiform Texts from Babylonian Tablets in the British Museum* (London: Trustees of the British Museum, 1903), Part 16 (50 Plates).

The texts in CT vol. 16, come from Neo-Assyrian times. There are three duplicates of this text with one variant which instead of *egirrû* has *egirtum*. In his time, Landsberger voiced the opinion that this single example is not enough to prove the case that Sumerian inim.gar was rendered into Akkadian as *egirtu* "letter, message."

C. However, now another example can be adduced where Sumerian inim.gar was understood and pronounced as *egirtu*. The Standard Babylonian Omen series from the library of Aššurbanipal, known as *Šumma ālu ina mēlê šākin*, "If a city is set on a height," is a catalog of omens, part of which date from Old Babylonian times. This is important since it would bridge the chronological gap between Sumerian inim.gar, Standard Babylonian, and Neo-Assyrian *egirtu*:[27]

diš *bi-ir-ṣu ina* gúb-šú igi.[du₈ n]a bi inim.gar sig₅-*ta* uš.uš-šú

"If a light-flash is se[en] on someone's left, favorable rumors will persistently follow that [m]an" (*Šumma ālu*, Tablet 20, Omen 35; CT 38 28:35).

The feminine adjective *damiqta*(sig₅-*ta*)[28] following the Sumerograms inim.gar normally agrees with the feminine noun that precedes it, indicating that in this case, the scribe read inim.gar as *egirtu*. Such examples show that there is a close connection between the terms inim.gar, *egirrû* and *egirtu*, and that the Akkadian feminine noun *egirtu* is yet another way of rendering Sumerian inim.gar.

D. There is an additional feature in the omen series *Šumma ālu* that might be pertinent for our demonstration. In a couple of omens, the term inim.gar is closely associated with writing and placing a written message. The prayer request is submitted to the god in a written form, to which the god answers with an oracular message. Four types of letters are part of the so-called "divine correspondence" between gods and humans: 1) Letters addressed to the gods, 2) Letters addressed to humans by gods, 3) Reports of military campaigns addressed to gods, and 4) An incantatory letter addressed to a god by a person during a divination ritual.[29]

---

[27] Sally M. Freedman, *If a City is Set on a Height: The Akkadian Omen Series Šumma Alu ina Mēlê Šakin*, OPSNKF 17 (Philadelphia: University of Pennsylvania Press, 1998), 298–99. Although the *Šumma ālu* series were copied in Neo-Assyrian times, these omen texts had Old Babylonian precursors, cf. David B. Weisberg, "An Old Babylonian Forerunner to *šumma ālu*," *HUCA* 40–41 (1969–70): 87–104 (87); Friedrich Nötscher, "Die Omen-Serie: *šumma âlu ina mêlê šakin* (CT 38–40)," *Or* 39/42 (1929): 1–247 (41–48); Idem, *Or* 51/54 (1930): 1–243 (Fortsetzung); Idem, "Zur Omen-Serie šumma âlu," *OrNS* 3 (1943): 177–95.

[28] Borger and Ellermaier, "n° 454 sig₅ = *damāqu* 'gut'," *ABZ*, 174.

[29] Daniel Bodi, "Les différents genres de la correspondance divine," *Ktèma* 33 (2008): 245–58. Beate Pongratz-Leisten, *Herrschaftswissen in Mesopotamien: Formen der Kommunikation zwischen Gott und König im 2. und 1. Jahrtausend v. Chr.*, SAAS 10 (Helsinki: Neo-Assyrian Text Corpus Project, 1999), 202–9: "Échange de lettres avec les dieux' in der Mari Zeit"; 210–65: "Literarisierte Formen der Kommunikation: 'Gottesbriefe' und 'Königsberichte.'"

Tablet 11 of the *Šumma ālu* omen series describes a variety of activities performed by the king, especially cultic activities. Freedman renders Sumerian inim.gar with "oracle."

Omen 26´: diš bará *a-na* dingir.meš *i-kar-rab-ma* inim.gar.bi [...] a.ra.zu-*šú* [...]

"If the king is praying to the gods and his oracle [...] his prayer [...]"

As a parallel, Freedman adduces a similar omen with a man as a subject rather than a king found in (K.2238+CT 39 41):[30]

1. diš lú *a-na* dingir *i-kar-rab-ma* inim.gar *ar-ḫiš i-ta-nap-pal-šú* 2. *ar-ḫiš im-man-gar* dingir-*šu tes-lit-su iš-me*

"If a man is praying to god and an oracle answers him promptly, it will promptly be granted; his god has heard his prayer."

Tablet 11 omen 35´:

[diš bará *ina* ki.]za.za-*šú šá* ḫur-ra x [...] dingir a.ra.[zu ...]

"[If the king, when b]owing (in prayer), ... [...] a god [...] his prayer."

Here again, Freedman adduces a parallel from Tablet 95 (K.2238+CT 39 41) which contains a similar omen with a man as a subject rather than a king:

3. diš lú *ina* ki.za.za-*šu šu* ḫur-ra *la na-da-at-ma* [inim.gar *i-pu*]-*ul- šú* 4. dingir a.ra.zu-*šú* iš-[*me* ... *š*]a *iq-bu-ú im-gur-šú*

"If, when a man is bowing (in prayer), ...? and [an oracle ans]wers him, the god has heard his prayer [...] and granted him what he said."[31]

Freedman's comment may be quoted in full:[32]

The reading of *šá* ḫur-ra in omen 35' and *šu* ḫur.ra *la na-da-at-ma* on CT 39 41:3 is uncertain. Despite grammatical difficulties, it is tempting to relate these passages to the idiom *uṣurta nadû* 'to set down a drawing, to write something down,' which is frequently used in religious contexts, where drawing or inscription is made as part of a supplication ritual. ḫur.ra denotes the verb *eṣēru*, 'to draw' or 'write down,' and the form *nadāt* indicates a feminine subject – but the logogram for *uṣurtu*, 'drawing' is giš.ḫur.ra, not ḫur.ra. However, if one accepts an anomalous spelling ḫur.ra for *uṣurtu*, the protasis of these omens may seem something like 'If, when a king/man is bowing (in prayer), the (appropriate ritual) drawing has not (yet) been set down but an oracle (already) answers him.'

Despite the uncertainty in understanding the exact meaning of ḫur.ra, what is pertinent for our analysis is that the divine oracular answer (inim.gar, *egerrû*) is obtained after a written request had been submitted to the divinity in the

---

[30] Freedman, *If a City is Set on a Height*, 184–85 (184n26).
[31] inim.gar *i-pu-ul- šú* is restored on the basis of the similar context in Tablet 95:2.
[32] Freedman, *If a City is Set on a Height*, 185.

form of a letter to the god.[33] The term inim.gar is associated with the practice of writing letters to the gods or receiving letters that gods were supposed to write to individuals through the intermediary of the temple personnel. It would be part of the "divine correspondence" between gods and humans.

In Mesopotamia, the practice of writing a "letter to the god" has older Sumerian antecedents. Ungnad and Falkenstein named this genre "*Gottesbrief.*"[34] It includes letters to the deities. Hallo prefers to call this genre "letter-prayers."[35] Mari Old Babylonian letters attest to the existence of the genre in the Northwest Semitic domain: ARM 1 3:1 (Yasmaḫ-Addu writes to the god Nergal);[36] Zimrī-Līm writes a letter to the river god asking for protection.[37] In ARM 4 68:17–22, what was interpreted by Speiser as Išme-Dagan of Assur writing to his personal god Lamassu, has now been understood as him simply writing to his wife whose full name was Lamassī-Aššur meaning "Assur is my protective spirit."[38] In Assyria, Sargon II (721–705 BCE) writes a detailed report about his eighth campaign which is presented as a letter to the god Aššur.[39] In 2 Kgs 19:14 // Isa 37:14 Hezekiah receives a letter from Sennacherib (704–682 BCE), goes to the Jerusalem temple, and spreads it out before YHWH as he prays for deliverance from the Assyrian besieger.

Another detail about this genre might be pertinent to our analysis. The Mesopotamian literary tradition also knows another subgenre within this category which may be rendered in English as "divine letter" meaning a letter sent from a divinity to a king.[40] We have a "divine letter" sent by the god Ninurta to As-

---

[33] Jack M. Sasson, "The Posting of Letters with Divine Messages," in *Florilegium marianum II: Recueil d'études à la mémoire de Maurice Birot*, ed. Dominique Charpin and Jean-Marie Durand, NABUM 3 (Paris: Société pour l'Etude du Proche-Orient Ancien, 1994), 299–316 (300) defines *egerrûm* as belonging to native Mari vocabulary applied to a document with prophetic content.

[34] Arthur Ungnad, "Der Gottesbrief als Form assyrischer Kriegsberichterstattung," *OLZ* 21 (1918): cols. 72–75. Adam Falkenstein, "Ein sumerischer 'Gottesbrief'," *ZA* 44 (1938): 1–25.

[35] William W. Hallo, "Individual Prayer in Sumerian: The Continuity of a Tradition," *JAOS* 88 (1968): 71–89 (75–89); "II. The Neo-Sumerian Letter-Prayers" (bibliography).

[36] Jean-Marie Durand, *Documents épistolaires du palais de Mari III*, LAPO 18 (Paris: Cerf, 2000), 72–74.

[37] Georges Dossin, "Les archives épistolaires du palais de Mari," *Sy* 19 (1938): 105–26 (126).

[38] Jean-Marie Durand, *Documents épistolaires du palais de Mari II*, LAPO 17 (Paris: Cerf, 1998), 118–19. Idem, "Annexe III: Les femmes de l'époque assyrienne non comprises dans la liste du harem," *MARI* 4 (1985): 433–35, and in particular, Pierre Marello, "Documents pour l'histoire du royaume de la Haute-Mésopotamie IV: Lamassi-Aššur," *MARI* 7 (1993): 271–79, who pointed out that Lamassī-Aššur is the wife of Išme-Dagan.

[39] François Thureau-Dangin, *Une relation de la huitième campagne de Sargon* (Paris: Geuthner, 1912); and see comments by A. Leo Oppenheim, "The City of Assur in 714 B.C.," *JNES* 19 (1960): 133–47 (145n22).

[40] Ephraim A. Speiser, "The Idea of History in Ancient Mesopotamia," in *Oriental and Biblical Studies: Collected Writings of E.A. Speiser*, ed. Jacob J. Finkelstein and Moshe Greenberg (Philadelphia: University of Pennsylvania Press, 1967), 270–312 (297–305) "VI. Omens and Letters to the Gods" (bibliography).

surnasirpal II (?) (883–859 BCE) (K. 2764).[41] The colophon of this tablet names it *šipirti* ᵈ*Nin*[*urta*] "a letter from the god Ninurta." There is a letter sent by the god Aššur to Šamši-Adad V (823–811 BCE) giving him an itemized acknowledgment of the things he previously mentioned to his addressee.[42] The oracular answer received from the god was written down by the scribe and sent to the king as a "letter from the god" providing an answer to his request. It would be tempting to assume that the feminine noun *egirtu* might have been used to designate such a written oracular answer obtained from the god. To confirm this supposition, however, it would be necessary to find additional texts making this connection explicit.

5. The Term *egirrû/igerrû* in Old Babylonian Mari

The Old Babylonian documentation from Mari brings some new and important data on the meaning and use of the term *egirrû*. Furthermore, it brings additional precision or correction to the third meaning of *egirrû* as offered in *CAD*, E, quoted above.

As established by Durand who has offered the most thorough analysis so far of the fifty Mari letters with prophetic content, in Mari the term *egirrû* has a double meaning. On the one hand, it has a purely secular meaning being a technical term for the act of "placing a favorable word" with the king. On the other hand, it has a religious or specialized meaning that stands for prophecy or a message from the god. What is highly significant in the Mari examples is the fact that the transmission of the *igerrû*-message involves at least three persons, sometimes more: the god inspiring it, the person uttering it, the witness hearing it, the scribe writing it down, and the king receiving it. There is something of a chain of transmission. It is a message carried from the source to the king.

A. First, in Mari texts, one finds a purely secular or profane meaning of the term *egirrû* which is illustrated in the Mari letter ARM(T) 10 78. The Queen of Ašlakkā, Inib-šarri, writes a letter to Šunuḫra-ḫālû asking him to place before the king a good word on her behalf:

ARM(T) 10 78:9–10, *i-ge-er-re* igi lugal *du-um-me-eq*

"Make good my *egirrû* or place good words before the king on my behalf."[43]

---

[41] Jean Nougayrol, "Parallèles, duplicats, etc.," *RA* 36 (1939): 29–40 (33–34).

[42] KAH II, 142 = VAT 9628, transliterated and translated by Ernst F. Weidner, "Die Feldzüge Šamši-Adads V. gegen Babylonien," *AfO* 9 (1933–34): 89–104 (101–4) "Ein Gottesbrief über den fünften Feldzug Šamši-Adads V."

[43] Jean-Marie Durand, *Archives épistolaires de Mari I/1*, ARM 26/1 (Paris: Èditions Recherche sur les Civilisations, 1988), 385, "Les textes prophétiques."

Šunuḫra-ḫalû is a high official in the palace of the King Zimrī-Līm. One of his duties is to introduce people living outside the palace to his lord's attention. Šunuḫra-ḫalû is supposed to plead their cause. The secular usage of *egirrû* has immediately found its place in the religious context. This is exactly what humans expect protective spirits to do on their behalf in front of great deities. In the Epilogue of his Codex (CH xli 52), the King Ḥammurabi of Babylon implores the guardian and protecting deities *šēdum lamassum … igirrê ūmišam ina maḫar Marduk bēlī-ya Zarpānītum bēltī-ya lidammiqū* "May (the protective spirits) Šedum and Lamassum give me a good report daily before Marduk my lord and Zarpanitum my lady."[44] We could also translate "may the protective spirits daily place a good word on my behalf in front of Marduk and Zarpanitum."

B. Another example of the secular use of *egerrû* in Mari texts is found in the letter A.730. In this text, a Benjaminite sheikh complains of being slandered before the king while he is away fighting and defending a dangerous frontier region. He is appealing to Ḫabdu-Malik to uphold his cause before King Zimrī-Līm. He is asking for the slanderers to be silenced and for his standing before the king to be restored. This last request is formulated with the expression, "make good *egirrû* on my behalf" (before the king):

A.730, l. 23: *a-ki-il kar-ṣí-ia ù qa-bi la dam-qa-ti-iq ma-ḫa-ar a-bi-i[a] [l]i-qí-lu-ma i-ge-re-e du-um-mi-iq*

"Hold back the one who is slandering me and saying bad things before my father and make good *egirrû* on my behalf."[45]

In this text, the spelling *i-ge-re-e* is the Mari form for *egerrī-ya*.

C. The religious meaning of *egirrû*: the term occurs in a letter from Queen Šibtu to King Zimrī-Līm describing a solicited prophecy brought about by the drinking of some liquid. Persons called "signs" both male and female (Akkadian *ittum* pl. *ittātum*, corresponding to Hebrew *'ôt*), drink an undetermined beverage and then make verbal communication. The *igerrû* or prophetic message obtained through such a technique predicts Zimrī-Līm's complete victory.

ARMT 10 4: 1–13 = ARM 26/1 207 [A.996]:[46]
1. *a-na be-lí-ia qí-bí-ma*　　　　　　　To my lord speak:
2. *um-ma ⸢ši-ib-tu amat*(geme₂)*-ka-a-ma*　thus (says) Šibtu, your servant,
3. *aš-šum ṭe₄-em ge-er-ri-im*　　　　　concerning the project[47] of the campaign

---

[44] *CAD E*, 44a.
[45] Durand, *AÉM I/1*, 385 who relates *li-qí-lu* to *qullum* "to silence." The term *kullum* can mean "to contain, to hold back."
[46] Durand, *AÉM I/1*, 435.
[47] For a discussion of the term *ṭēmu*, see Wilfred G. Lambert, *Babylonian Wisdom Literature* (Oxford: Clarendon, 1960), 325; Wolfram von Soden, "Der Mensch bescheidet sich nicht: Überlegungen zu Schöpfungserzählungen in Babylonien und Israel," in *Symbolae Biblicae et Mesopotamicae F.M. Th. De Liagre Böhl dedicatae*, ed. M.A. Beek et al. (Leiden: Brill, 1973), 349–58

4. ša be-lí i-la-ku it-ta-tim	which my lord is undertaking, (to the) "signs"
5. zi-ka-ra-am ù sí-in-ni-iš-ti	male and female
6. aš*-qi* áš-ta-al-ma i-ge-er-ru-ú-um	I gave to drink and I inquired: The *igerrûm*-message (of the god)[48]
7. a-na be-lí-ia ma-di-iš da-mi-iq	for my lord is very good.
8. a-na iš-me-ᵈda-gan qa-tam-ma	For Išme-Dagan in the same way
9. zi-ka-ra-am ù s[í]-in-ni-iš-tam	male and female
10. áš-ta-al-ma i-ge-er-ru-šu	I inquired, his *igerrû*-message (of the god)
11. ú-ul da-mi-iq	is not good.
12. ù ṭe₄-em-šu ša-pa-al še-ep be-lí-ia	and his project is placed at my lord's feet.
13. ša-ki-in.	

Wilcke translates the lines 4–7 in a different way: "Wegen der Nachricht über den Feldzug, den mein Herr unternehmen will, befragte ich Mann und Weib nach Vorzeichen, während ich (sie mit Wein) bewirtete, und das *egerrûm*-Omen ist für meinen Herrn sehr gut …"[49] He explains it as a consultation of public opinion, "Volksbefragung (Meinungsforschung)."

Sasson offers yet another interpretation of these lines: "I have waited for the signs (*ittātum*) by consulting everyone (lit. male and female) concerning tidings (*ṭēmu*) from the campaign which my lord is undergoing (as follows): 'Is the (verbal) report (*igerrûm*) favorable to my lord?' Similarly, I consulted everyone (lit. male and female) (with regard) to Išme-Dagan (as follows): 'Is the (verbal) report (*igerrûm*) not favorable? Consequently, the report (*ṭēmu*) about him is (now) placed at my lord's feet".[50] Sasson subsequently modified his translation and rendered (*igerrûm*) with "portent."[51] The majority of Assyriologists render the term (*igerrûm*) with synonyms: "Omen" (Wilcke), "augury" (Dossin and

---

(353) "Planungsfähigkeit," or "ability to plan." Note the uses of *ṭēmu* in the Amarna letters, often to mean "message, order, report" (EA 17:48; 21:29).

[48] Georges Dossin and André Finet, *Correspondance féminine*, ARM 10 (Paris: Geuthner, 1978), 25, translate *igerrû* with "l'augure." This brings to mind the augur of ancient Rome, representing any of a body of officials, divination experts, who interpreted omens as being favorable or unfavorable in connection with an undertaking.

[49] Claus Wilcke, "*ittātim ašqi aštāl*: Medien in Mari?" *RA* 77 (1983): 93.

[50] Jack M. Sasson, "Reflections on an Unusual Practice Reported in ARM X:4," *Or* 43 (1974): 404–10 (405). Idem, "The Posting of Letters with Divine Messages," 308: "As we are not given any inkling on how the soothsayers were psychologically affected, it is difficult to ascertain the kind of potion they were administered. It is possible that she was emulating on earth an activity she herself reported a few months earlier in XXVI: 208, where someone (Qišti-Diritum?) had a vision of male and female deities taking solemn oaths to protect Mari just after they were made to imbibe clay from Mari's gates dissolved in water. If so, there is no reason to think the soothsayers of XXVI: 207 drunk."

[51] Jack M. Sasson, *From the Mari Archive: An Anthology of Old Babylonian Letters* (Winona Lake, IN: Eisenbrauns, 2015), 283, "For a report (*ṭēmu*) on the campaign that my lord wants to undertake. I gave everyone (lit. male and female) signs to drink. I queried (them), and the portent (*igerrûm*) concerning my lord is favorable. However, when I similarly queried everyone, the portent (*igerrûm*) concerning Išme-Dagan was not favorable. The report (*ṭēmu*) is now set under my lord's feet."

Finet), and "portent" (Sasson). In the context of this letter, the (*igerrûm*) stands for a message from the gods obtained through a divinatory consultation. A particular technique of oracular consultation has been employed. That human beings, male and female, could be called "signs" is paralleled by Hebrew prophets. In Ezek 12:6, YHWH says to Ezekiel: "I have made you a portent (*môpēt*) for the house of Israel." There are three Mari prophetic texts (ARM 10 4; 10 6; and 10 9)[52] illustrating a solicited or induced prophecy. In the first two cases, the prophet ingests a beverage that would bring on a revelation. According to Durand, the male and female persons serving as signs would ingest some liquid, either wine or more probably spring water as in ancient Greece (spring water having the more ominous character pouring forth from under the ground, springing forth from the realm of chthonic divinities).[53]

In letter ARM 10 4, the act of absorbing the liquid transforms the person drinking it into a "sign" (*ittum*) a portent or an omen. Just as in the case of Ezekiel, the Hebrew term "sign" (*môpēt*) and Akkadian *ittum* are used as metonyms. A similar idea is found in Isa 8:18, where both Hebrew words, *'ôt* and *môpēt* are used in parallelism: "I and the children YHWH has given me. We are signs (*lĕ'ōtôt*) and portents (*ûlĕmôpĕtîm*) in Israel from YHWH-*ṣĕbā'ôt* of armies." Similarly, Ezekiel could be called a *'ôt* "sign" while personifying the siege of Jerusalem (Ezek 4:3). In these contexts, Hebrew *'ôt* stands for an "omenological sign." Deuteronomy 13:2–6 states that the Hebrews perceived dream interpreters as providing *'ôt ôw môpēt* "a sign or portent."[54]

In light of these Mari texts, one should modify Oppenheim's and *CAD*'s comparison with *klēdōn* (etym. *kaleō* "to call") which means "a chance utterance of a person which is overheard by another, taken out of the context in which it occurred and considered by the latter (as) a revelation of divine intentions concerning his own plans."[55] In this context, *igerrû* is not a chance utterance. On the contrary, it is provoked and solicited through a particular oracular technique. Both Wilcke and Durand agree that the term cledonomancy is inappropriate here to describe the term *egerrû*. Sasson is right in suggesting that *egerrû* should

---

[52] Durand, *AÉM I/1*, 392.

[53] Jean-Marie Durand, "In Vino Veritas," *RA* 76 (1982): 43–50 (48).

[54] Scott B. Noegel, "'Sign, Sign, Everywhere a Sign': Script, Power, and Interpretation in the Ancient Near East," in *Divination and Interpretation of Signs in the Ancient World*, ed. Amar Annus, OIS 6 (Chicago: Oriental Institute of the University of Chicago, 2010), 143–62 (152–54). The Egyptians referred to the hieroglyphic script as *mdw nṯr* "the words of the gods" while the presumed inventor of writing, the ibis-headed god Thoth, is called *nb mdw nṯr* "Lord of the words of the gods (hieroglyphs)" (145). In Mesopotamia, a text states "God Šamaš … who inscribes oracles and sets the judgment (divinatory sentence *dīnu*) in the entrails of the sheep" (^dŠamaš… *ina libbi immeri ta-šaṭ-ṭar šīra ta-šá-kan di-nu*), Jean Bottéro, "Symptômes, signes, écriture en Mésopotamie ancienne," in *Divination et rationalité*, ed. Jean-Pierre Vernant et al. (Paris: Seuil, 1974), 70–197 (159). Some extispicy omens were interpreted on a similarity in shape between features of the exta and various cuneiform signs.

[55] Oppenheim, "Sumerian: inim.gar, Akkadian: *egirrû* = Greek: *kledon*," 52.

be translated as a "verbal report." An *egerrû* was produced by human beings and was received by hearing, which implies that it was spoken and written down as attested in the following Mari letter.

D. In another text from Mari, *egerrû* stands for the prophetic message or oracle delivered in the temple. Before launching a military campaign the King Zimrī-Līm asks his servant who "dwells in the city of the god" to forward to him any *egerrû*-message that might occur in the temple of the god of that city. The Mari letter A. 3719 is written by Zimrī-Līm's servant Šamaš-naṣir, a majordomo at the Terqa palace, where he reiterates the specific mission that the king had given him:

ARM 26/1 196 [A.3719]:1–10[56]

1. *a-na be-lí-ia*	To my lord
2. *qí-bí-ma*	say:
3. *um-ma* ᵈutu *na-ṣir*	thus ᵈŠamaš-naṣir
4. *warad*(ìr)-*ka-a-ma*	your servant.
5. *i-nu-ma be-lí a-na ge-ri-im*	When my lord toward a military campaign
6. *pa-né-[šu] iš-ku-nu ki-a-am ú-wa-e-ra-an-ni*	set his face, he instructed me
7. *um-m[a-mi] i-na a-al* AN-*lim wa-ša-ba-at*	thus: You dwell in the city of the god. (If)
8. *i-g[e-e]r-ru-ú-um ša i-na é* AN-*lim*	an *igerrû*-message in the temple of the god
9. *i-[ba-a]š-š[u]-ú ú te-še-mu-ú*	would occur and you would hear (it),
10. *a-[n]a ṣe-r[i-i]a šu-up-ra-am*	write to me (about it).

In this Mari letter, the term *igerrû* is synonymous with a prophetic oracle or prophecy. There is nothing fortuitous in it. The city in question is Terqa since this official was stationed there. There are several people involved in this transaction: The one uttering the prophetic message *igerrû* that is revealed by the god Dagan in the city of Terqa, located about 50 kilometers north of Mari. There is a witness who is probably a scribe posted in the temple to write it down. Moreover, a courier is carrying the tablet to the king so that he may have it read to him by the scribe in the palace. The prophetic message and the written tablet are closely connected. This connection might have facilitated the semantic shift from *egirrû* "message" to *egirtu* "letter."

6. The Word for "Letter" in Aramaic and Hebrew

Dion notices the dimorphism of the Aramaic term for the letter written both *'grh* and *'grt* in Imperial and Middle Aramaic.[57] Could one see in this dimorphism a reflection of Akkadian *egirrû* and *egirtu*?

---

[56] Durand, *AÉM I/1*, 422.
[57] Paul E. Dion, "Aramaic Words for 'Letter,'" *Semeia* 22 (1981): 77–88 (78–79).

In Biblical Aramaic the term for "letter" occurs in Ezra 4:8 אגרה n.f.; emphatic form אגרתא in Ezra 4:11; 5:6. In Hebrew, the following occurrences are attested: אגרת n.f (abs.) Neh 2:8; 6:5; אגרת (cstr.) Esth 9:29; f. pl.: אגרות Neh 2:9; 6:19; 2 Chr 30:1,6; with suffix: אגרתיהם Neh 6:17. *BDB*, 8 especially royal letter 2 Chr. 30:1, 6; Neh 2:7, 8, 9; but also others Neh 6:5, 17, 19; Esth 9:26, 29// ספרים vv 20, 30.

Esther 3:13 tells of "letters sent by couriers to all the king's provinces" (ספרים ביד הרצים אל כל מדינות המלך) which the Septuagint renders with διὰ βιβλιαφόρων ("scroll-carriers"), while 8:10 tells of letters sent "by mounted couriers, riding on fast steeds" (ספרים ביד הרצים בסוסים רכבי הרכש; LXX βιβλιαφόρων). In his book *Histories* 8.98, Herodotus describes the Persian royal couriers as the fastest on earth. Along the roads of the Persian Empire, there were way stations at a riding distance of one day. At each station, one could find horses and riders ready to receive the royal mail and to set out immediately bringing it to the next relay. Snow, rain, heat, or night did not prevent them from completing their journey in the fastest time possible. Herodotus compares the Persian mail to the Greek torch race that was held in honor of the god Hephaestus and states that the Persian word for this kind of post was ἀγγαρήιον (*Histories* 8.98). The Greek word designating the Persian royal courier would be ἄγγαρος, indicating a mounted rider requisitioned for the royal postal service.[58] According to Naveh,[59] the word came into Persian from Akkadian *egirtu*, the same way it came into Aramaic and Hebrew. When the word was adopted into Syriac, Jewish Aramaic, and Mishnaic Hebrew it was used mainly to designate "forced labor" for the king. Thus, the Babylonian Talmud *Baba Meṣiʿa* 6:3 reads: "If a man hired an ass and it went blind or it was seized for the king's service (*sngry'* סנגריא)," meaning a donkey requisitioned for the corvée work. The double (*gg*) in Aramaic *'iggĕrâ, 'iggartâ*, is probably a reflection of an assimilated *n* as confirmed from the related Mandaic term for "letter" *'ngr*.[60]

7. Conclusion

The Akkadian word *egirtu* that gave the Aramaic and Hebrew words for the "letter" would have developed from an original connection with the action of a person placing a word for another person, using an intermediary. The letter would mean etymologically, placing or sending a word through an intermediary

---

[58] A. Bailly, *Dictionnaire grec-français* (Paris: Hachette, 1950), 7: "courier perse, requis par corvée de relais en relais pour le service du roi."

[59] Joseph Naveh, "The Aramaic Ostraca from Tel Arad," in *Arad Inscriptions*, ed. Y. Aharoni (Jerusalem: The Israel Exploration Society, 1981), 176n67.

[60] Marco Mancini, "Etimologia e semantica del gr. ἄγγαρος," *Glotta* 73 (1995/1996): 210–22 (221).

such as the scribe and the courier on behalf of another person who would hear or read it. The meaning of *egirtu* as "letter, message," was facilitated by the original meaning of the term *egirrû*. The term for letter developed from Sumerian inim. gar "to place a word." It was rendered into Akkadian as *egirrû*, a masculine noun meaning "utterance, message." The Sumerian term inim.gar was occasionally rendered with the feminine form *egirtu* in Akkadian confirming the derivation of the term "letter, message" from Sumerian and not from *egēru* "to be twisted." Furthermore, the Sumerian inim.gar, Akkadian *egirrû* is associated with the practice of writing letters to the gods. The Old Babylonian Mari texts show that the term *egirrû* was used at an early period in the Northwest Semitic domain. This could have facilitated the adoption of the term into Aramaic where it means "letter." From there it has been adopted into Biblical Hebrew of the post-exilic period. One still has to explain, however, why an original Sumerian inim.gar was rendered both with a masculine and a feminine noun and what influenced this development? Moreover, the development proposed here together with the connection with the ancient Near Eastern practice of the so-called "divine correspondence" can have some bearing on the theological understanding of the Scripture as a word from God sent to humans, transmitted by the prophets and disciples for the readers or auditors and intended as a recommendation on behalf of the divine author. The term *'iggeret* "letter," is used for modern Hebrew translation of the Greek ἐπιστολή from which English "epistle" is derived.[61]

Bibliography

Albright, William F. "Some Cruces in the Langdon Epic." *JAOS* 39 (1919): 65–90.
Bailly, Anatole. *Dictionnaire grec-français*. Paris: Hachette, 1950.
Bodi, Daniel. "Les différents genres de la correspondance divine." *Ktèma* 33 (2008): 245–58.
Borger, Rykele, and Friedrich Ellermaier. *Assyrisch-babylonische Zeichenliste*. AOAT 33. Kevelaer: Butzon & Bercker; Neukichen-Vluyn: Neukirchener Verlag, 1978.
Bottéro, Jean. "Symptômes, signes, écriture en Mésopotamie ancienne." Pages 70–197 in *Divination et rationalité*. Edited by Jean-Pierre Vernant, et al. Paris: Seuil, 1974.
Cogan, Mordechai. "The Road to En-dor." Pages 319–26 in *Pomegranates and Golden Bells: Studies in Biblical, Jewish, and Near Eastern Ritual, Law, and Literature in Honor of J. Milgrom*. Edited by David P. Wright, David Noel Freedman, and Avigdor Hurvitz. Winona Lake, IN: Eisenbrauns, 1995.
Cuneiform Texts from Babylonian Tablets in the British Museum. London: Trustees of the British Museum, 1903.
Dion, Paul E. "Aramaic Words for 'Letter.'" *Semeia* 22 (1981): 77–88.
Dossin, Georges. "Les archives épistolaires du palais de Mari." *Sy* 19 (1938): 105–26.

---

[61] 2 Cor 7:8; 2 Thess 3:17; Franz Delitzsch used the term אגרת, in his translation of the NT "epistle." In 2 Tim 3:16, the Rabbi Saul of Tarsus writes a letter to his disciple Timothy saying that "All Scripture is God-breathed" (θεόπνευστος).

Dossin, Georges, and André Finet. *Correspondance féminine*. ARM 10. Paris: Geuthner, 1978.
Durand, Jean-Marie. "Annexe III: Les femmes de l'époque assyrienne non comprises dans la liste du harem." *MARI* 4 (1985): 433–35.
Durand, Jean-Marie. *Archives épistolaires de Mari I/1*. ARM 26/1. Paris: Editions Recherche sur les Civilisations, 1988.
Durand, Jean-Marie. *Documents épistolaires du palais de Mari II*. LAPO 17. Paris: Cerf, 1998.
Durand, Jean-Marie. *Documents épistolaires du palais de Mari III*. LAPO 18. Paris: Cerf, 2000.
Durand, Jean-Marie. "In Vino Veritas." *RA* 76 (1982): 43–50.
Falkenstein, Adam. "Ein sumerischer 'Gottesbrief.'" *ZA* 44 (1938): 1–25.
Freedman, Sally M. *If a City Is Set on a Height: The Akkadian Omen Series Šumma Alu ina Mēlê Šakin*. OPSNKF 17. Philadelphia: University of Pennsylvania Press, 1998.
Hallo, William W. "Individual Prayer in Sumerian: The Continuity of a Tradition." *JAOS* 88 (1968): 71–89.
Kaufman, Stephen A. "An Assyro-Aramaic *egirtu ša šulmu*." Pages 119–27 in *Essays on the Ancient Near East in Memory of J. J. Finkelstein*. Edited by Maria deJong Ellis. MCAAS 19. Hamden, CT: Archon Books, 1977.
King, Leonard W. *Babylonian Magic and Sorcery: Being "the Prayers of the Lifting of the Hand."* London: Luzac, 1896. Repr., Hildesheim: Olms, 1978.
Köbert, Raimund. "Gedanken zum semitischen Wort- und Satzbau. 1–7." *OrNS* 14 (1945): 273–83.
Lambert, Wilfred G. *Babylonian Wisdom Literature*. Oxford: Clarendon, 1960.
Landsberger, Benno. "Das 'gute Wort'." *MAOG* 4 (1928–29): 294–321.
Lieberman, Saul. *Hellenism in Jewish Palestine*. New York: Jewish Theological Seminary of America, 1950.
Mancini, Marco. "Etimologia e semantica del gr. ἄγγαρος." *Glotta* 73 (1995/1996): 210–22.
Mankowski, Paul V. *Akkadian Loanwords in Biblical Hebrew*. HSS 47. Winona Lake, IN: Eisenbrauns, 2000.
Marello, Pierre. "Documents pour l'histoire du royaume de la Haute-Mésopotamie IV: Lamassi-Aššur." *MARI* 7 (1993): 271–79.
Maul, Stefan. "La fin de la tradition cunéiforme et les 'Graeco-Babyloniaca'." *CCGG* 6 (1995): 3–17.
Naveh, Joseph. "The Aramaic Ostraca from Tel Arad." Pages 153–76 in *Arad Inscriptions*. Edited by Yohanan Aharoni. Jerusalem: The Israel Exploration Society, 1981.
Noegel, Scott B. "'Sign, Sign, Everywhere a Sign': Script, Power, and Interpretation in the Ancient Near East." Pages 143–62 in *Divination and Interpretation of Signs in the Ancient World*. Edited by Amar Annus. OIS 6. Chicago: Oriental Institute of the University of Chicago, 2010.
Nötscher, Friedrich. "Die Omen-Serie: *šumma âlu ina mêlê šakin* (CT 38–40)." *Or* 39/42 (1929): 1–247.
Nötscher, Friedrich. "Die Omen-Serie: *šumma âlu ina mêlê šakin* (CT 38–40)." *Or* 51/54 (1930): 1–243 (Fortsetzung).
Nötscher, Friedrich. "Zur Omen-Serie *šumma âlu*." *OrNS* 3 (1943): 177–95.
Nougayrol, Jean. "Parallèles, duplicats, etc." *RA* 36 (1939): 29–40.

Nougayrol, Jean. "'Vocalises' et 'Syllabes en liberté' à Ugarit." Pages 29–39 in *Studies in Honor of Benno Landsberger*. Edited by Hans G. Güterbock and Thorkild Jacobsen. AS 16. Chicago: Oriental Institute of the University of Chicago, 1965.

Oppenheim, A. Leo. "Sumerian: inim.gar, Akkadian: *egirrû* = Greek: *kledon*." *AfO* 17 (1954–55): 49–55.

Oppenheim, A. Leo. "The City of Assur in 714 B.C." *JNES* 19 (1960): 133–47.

Oppenheim, A. Leo, Erica Reiner, and Martha T. Roth, eds. *The Assyrian Dictionary of the Oriental Institute of the University of Chicago*. 26 vols. Chicago: Oriental Institute of the University of Chicago, 1956–2010.

Parpola, Simo. "Assyrian Library Records." *JNES* 42 (1983): 1–29.

Pearce, Laurie. "*Sepīru* and ᴸᵁ́A.BA: Scribes of the Late First Millennium." Pages 355–68 in *Languages and Cultures in Contact: At the Crossroads of Civilizations in the Syro-Mesopotamian Realm*. Edited by Karel Van Lerberghe and Gabriella Voet. OLA 96. Leuven: Peeters, 1999.

Pongratz-Leisten, Beate. *Herrschaftswissen in Mesopotamien: Formen der Kommunikation zwischen Gott und König im 2. und 1. Jahrtausend v. Chr.* SAAS 10. Helsinki: Neo-Assyrian Text Corpus Project, 1999.

Sasson, Jack M. *From the Mari Archive: An Anthology of Old Babylonian Letters*. Winona Lake, IN: Eisenbrauns, 2015.

Sasson, Jack M. "Reflections on an Unusual Practice Reported in ARM X:4." *Or* 43 (1974): 404–10.

Sasson, Jack M. "The Posting of Letters with Divine Messages." Pages 299–316 in *Florilegium marianum II: Recueil d'études à la mémoire de M. Birot*. Edited by Dominique Charpin and Jean-Marie Durand. NABUM 3. Paris: Société pour l'Etude du Proche-Orient Ancien, 1994.

Soden, Wolfram von. "Aramäische Wörter in neuassyrischen und neu- und spät-babylonischen Texten. Ein Vorbericht I." *Or* NS 35 (1966): 1–20.

Soden, Wolfram von. "Die Unterweltvision eines assyrischen Kronprinzen." *ZA* 43 (1939): 1–31.

Soden, Wolfram von. "Der Mensch bescheidet sich nicht: Überlegungen zu Schöpfungserzählungen in Babylonien und Israel." Pages 349–58 in *Symbolae Biblicae et Mesopotamicae F. M. Th. De Liagre Böhl dedicatae*. Edited by M. A. Beek, A. A. Kampman, C. Nijland, and J. Ryckmans. Leiden: Brill, 1973.

Soden, Wolfram von. "Ein Zwiegespräch Hammurabis mit einer Frau." *ZA* 49 (1950): 151–94.

Speiser, Ephraim A. "The Idea of History in Ancient Mesopotamia." Pages 270–312 in *Oriental and Biblical Studies: Collected Writings of E. A. Speiser*. Edited by Jacob J. Finkelstein and Moshe Greenberg. Philadelphia: University of Pennsylvania Press, 1967.

Sperling, David. "Akkadian *egerrû* and Hebrew *bt qwl*." *JANESCU* 4 (1972): 63–74.

Tadmor, Hayim. "The Aramaization of Assyria: Aspects of Western Impact." Pages 449–70 in vol. 2 of *Mesopotamien und seine Nachbarn: Politische und kulturelle Wechselbeziehungen im Alten Vorderasien vom 4. bis 1. Jahrtausend v. Chr.* RAI 25. Berlin: Reimer, 1982.

Thureau-Dangin, François. *Une relation de la huitième campagne de Sargon*. Paris: Geuthner, 1912.

Thureau-Dangin, François. "L'exaltation d'Ištar." *RA* 11 (1914): 141–58.

Ungnad, Arthur. "Review of Assyriologische und archäologische Studien, Festschrift H. V. Hilprecht (1909)." *ZDMG* 65 (1911): 109–30.

Ungnad, Arthur. "Der Gottesbrief als Form assyrischer Kriegsberichterstattung." *OLZ* 21 (1918): cols. 72–75.

Weidner, Ernst F. "Die Feldzüge Šamši-Adads V. gegen Babylonien." *AfO* 9 (1933–34): 89–104.

Weisberg, David B. "An Old Babylonian Forerunner to *šumma ālu*." *HUCA* 40–41 (1969–70): 87–104.

Wilcke, Claus. "*ittātim ašqi aštāl*: Medien in Mari?" *RA* 77 (1983): 93.

Zadok, Ran. *Assyrians in Chaldean and Achaemenid Babylonia*. Malibu, CA: Undena, 1984.

Zimmern, Heinrich. *Akkadische Fremdwörter als Beweis für babylonischen Kultureinfluß*. Leipzig: Hinrichs, 1915.

Zimmern, Heinrich. "Zu den 'Keilschrifttexten aus Assur religiösen Inhalts.'" *ZA* 30 (1915/1916): 184–229.

The Death of the Prophet?
A Comparative Study of Prophetic Signs in the
Royal Archives of Mari, Syria (ARM 26/1.206)
and the Hebrew Bible (Jeremiah 19:1–13)*

William R. Stewart

> We have not seen our signs [אתותינו];
> there is no longer a prophet [נביא],
> and there is no one with us who knows how long. (Psalm 74:9)[1]

1. The Death of the Prophet

With the appearance of the law came to an end the old freedom, not only in the sphere of worship, now restricted to Jerusalem, but in the sphere of the religious spirit as well. There was now in existence an authority as objective as could be; and this was the death of prophecy.[2]

Thus the German biblical scholar Julius Wellhausen (1844–1918) declared in his *Prolegomena zur Geschichte Israels* (1878, 2nd ed. 1883, ET 1885), "a work which has cast its shadow over all subsequent attempts to reconstruct the history of

---

* Earlier versions of this essay were read at Emmanuel College, University of Queensland, in July 2009, and in the Prophets Group at the International Meeting of the Society of Biblical Literature, University of Helsinki, in August 2018. I thank Dr Geoffrey Jenkins, Prof. hon. Jean-Georges Heintz (University of Strasbourg and École du Louvre), Prof. José Andrés Sánchez Abarrio (Instituto Bíblico y Oriental, Madrid), and the reviewer, for commenting on earlier versions. I am grateful to Alphacrucis University College, Hobart, for my appointment as Honorary Scholar in Theology during which I completed the final draft. I also thank Prof. em. Kari Syreeni (Åbo Akademi University) for his hospitality in Finland. My essay is dedicated to Melanee, Zoë, and Jordan Clare.

[1] I interpret אתותינו here as the revelatory "signs" or "omens" of a "prophet" (נביא) with Robert P. Gordon, "'We Do Not See Our Signs' (Psalm 74:9): Signs, Prophets, Oracles, and the Asaphite Psalter," in *New Perspectives on Old Testament Prophecy and History: Essays in Honour of Hans M. Barstad*, ed. Rannfrid I. Thelle, Terje Stordalen, and Mervyn E. J. Richardson, VTSup 168 (Leiden: Brill, 2015), 95–97; and J. J. M. Roberts, "Of Signs, Prophets, and Time Limits: A Note on Psalm 74:9," *CBQ* 39 (1977): 475–78.

[2] Julius Wellhausen, *Prolegomena to the History of Israel: With a Reprint of the Article Israel from the Encyclopaedia Britannica*, trans. J. Sutherland Black and A. Menzies (Atlanta: Scholars Press, 1994), 402 (my emphasis).

ancient Israel."³ Wellhausen's assertion of "the death of prophecy" presupposed his fundamental assumption that the Mosaic legal code was based upon the ethical teachings of the so-called "classical" prophets (mid-eighth century to the Babylonian exile, 587 BCE) who were the true founders of Israelite monotheism. Lurking beneath this assumption is Wellhausen's belief that the presumed legalization of religion represented a decline – from *pre*-exilic "Israel" to decadent *post*-exilic "Judaism."⁴ After the Babylonian exile (post-539 BCE), the law supplanted the prophets as *the* authority in Judean religion. Whereas true prophecy was an oral phenomenon, postexilic "prophecy" increasingly imitated the priestly law which was scripture-based.

In a 2006 essay, Joachim Schaper concurs with Wellhausen's view that the biblical book of Ezekiel represented "a turning point in Israelite religious history, and that new departure has to do with 'books.'"⁵ Schaper also invokes the French semiotician Roland Barthes (1915–80) who, in a (famously or notoriously) iconoclastic 1967 essay, pronounced "the death of the Author" as the authoritative past of his/her text.⁶ For Schaper, the increase in literacy and textualization in Judean society and religion from the late preexilic period onwards was the basis for "a *textualization* of prophecy",⁷ a consequence of which was "the 'death of the prophet' – the prophet, that is, as he was conceived in 'classic' pre-exilic Israelite prophetic literature."⁸

For my purposes here, Schaper's phrase "the death of the prophet" offers a convenient label for the scholarly view that texts in the Nevi'im/Prophets division of the Hebrew Bible canon ostensibly reporting the *historical* activity of *pre*-exilic prophets are predominantly, or even exclusively, the product of the *literary* activity of *post*-exilic scribes.⁹ Some scholars are emphatic in pronouncing

---

³ J. W. Rogerson, "Setting the Scene: A Brief Outline of Histories of Israel," in *Understanding the History of Ancient Israel*, ed. H. G. M. Williamson, PBA 143 (Oxford: Oxford University Press, 2007), 3.

⁴ See Rolf Rendtorff, "The Image of Postexilic Israel in German Bible Scholarship from Wellhausen to von Rad," in *Sha'arei Talmon: Studies in the Bible, Qumran, and the Ancient Near East Presented to Shemaryahu Talmon*, ed. Michael Fishbane and Emanuel Tov (Winona Lake, IN: Eisenbrauns, 1992), 166–68.

⁵ Joachim Schaper, "The Death of the Prophet: The Transition from the Spoken to the Written Word of God in the Book of Ezekiel," in *Prophets, Prophecy, and Prophetic Texts in Second Temple Judaism*, ed. Michael H. Floyd and Robert D. Haak, LHBOTS 427 (London: T&T Clark, 2006), 63–79 (quotation 65).

⁶ Roland Barthes, "The Death of the Author," in *Image-Music-Text*, ed. and trans. Stephen Heath (New York: Hill & Wang, 1977), 142–48.

⁷ Schaper, "Death," 79 (original emphasis).

⁸ Schaper, "Death," 67.

⁹ For essay collections illustrative of this "literary paradigm," see, e.g., Ehud Ben Zvi and Diana V. Edelman, eds., *The Production of Prophecy: Constructing Prophecy and Prophets in Yehud*, BW (London: Equinox, 2009); Ehud Ben Zvi and Michael H. Floyd, eds., *Writings and Speech in Israelite and Ancient Near Eastern Prophecy*, SBLSymS 10 (Atlanta: Society of Biblical Literature, 2000); Michael H. Floyd and Robert D. Haak, eds., *Prophets, Prophecy, and Prophetic*

what amounts to the "death" of the historical preexilic prophet, asserting that preexilic prophecy bore little or no resemblance to the phenomenon portrayed in the Nevi'im. Others allow that the Nevi'im may contain accurate information about preexilic "prophets," or at least of the phenomenon of "prophecy," but believe that we can know preexilic prophecy only via what we can reconstruct working backwards through the postexilic books of the Prophets. Although not an extreme sceptic, Martti Nissinen, for instance, can, nevertheless, assert that: "Biblical prophecy, for its part, is no longer a representative of the 'authentic' prophetic phenomenon, … which, however, is historically and literally rooted in ancient Hebrew Prophecy."[10]

This view has emerged in the context of a wider agenda in scholarly research summarized by Ben-Dov in 2008:

> This new agenda centers on the relation between the mantic arts, prophecy, and the scribal culture. Based on the commonly accepted view that the lion's share of the production of prophetic books was carried out by scribes rather than prophets, scholarly effort is increasingly focussed on the relationships among prophets, diviners, and scribes in order to ascertain the precise role each of these parties played in the "publishing" process of a prophetic book. In addition, more attention is being paid to the relevance of extrabiblical prophetic texts, the study of which has introduced new data to the weighty discourse on biblical prophetic literature. Finally, acknowledgment of early Judaism's textual orientation has augmented the consideration being given to the gradual textualization of prophecy.[11]

I aim to contribute to this now not-so-new agenda by means of a case study in the phenomenology of Israelite prophecy in the preexilic period with reference to the relation between the mantic arts and prophecy and extra-biblical sources of prophecy. As Ben-Dov observes, a feature of recent scholarly theorizing about the composition of the Nevi'im concerns the mantic arts or what has been termed "mantological" or "mantic exegesis" (from Greek μαντική)[12] or "divinatory hermeneutics" (from Latin *divinatio*).[13] According to Schorch's definition, "the art

---

Texts in Second Temple Judaism, LHBOTS 427 (London: T&T Clark, 2006); Lester L. Grabbe and Martti Nissinen, eds., *Constructs of Prophecy in the Former and Latter Prophets and Other Texts*, ANEM 4 (Atlanta: Society of Biblical Literature, 2011). For a survey of research on Israelite prophecy since the 1980s identifying two main paradigms: prophecy as a socio-historical or a literary phenomenon, see Brad E. Kelle, "The Phenomenon of Israelite Prophecy in Contemporary Scholarship," *CurBR* 12 (2014): 275–320 (with bibliography 308–20).

[10] Martti Nissinen, "What is Prophecy? An Ancient Near Eastern Perspective," in *Prophetic Divination: Essays in Ancient Near Eastern Prophecy*, BZAW 494 (Berlin: de Gruyter, 2019), 73.

[11] Jonathan Ben-Dov, "Writing as Oracle and as Law: New Contexts for the Book-Find of King Josiah," *JBL* 127 (2008): 223–24.

[12] See Michael Fishbane, *Biblical Interpretation in Ancient Israel* (Oxford: Clarendon, 1985), 443–524; Stefan Schorch, "Between Science and Magic: The Function and Roots of Paronomasia in the Prophetic Books of the Hebrew Bible," in *Puns and Pundits: Word Play in the Hebrew Bible and Ancient Near Eastern literature*, ed. Scott B. Noegel (Bethesda, MD: CDL, 2000), 212, 215–17.

[13] E. g., Scott B. Noegel, *Nocturnal Ciphers: The Allusive Language of Dreams in the Ancient Near East*, AOS 89 (New Haven: American Oriental Society, 2007), 24.

of interpreting signs considered to be a medium of revelation is mantic. One of the most common methods for this interpretation tries to reveal the meaning of the sign from its representation in speech. That means, not the sign itself, but its name is interpreted, mostly with the help of paronomasia."[14] A relationship between "prophets" and the manifestation of a divine "sign" (Hebrew אות, Greek σημεῖον) or "portent" (מופת, τέρας) (often paired) is axiomatic in the literature of ancient Israel and Judah (e. g., Deut 13:1–3; 34:10–12; 1 Kgs 13:1–3; Ps 74:9; Isa 20:2–4; Jer 44:24–30; Ezek 4:1–8).[15] Moreover, paronomastic (phonetic) puns[16] characteristic of Near Eastern mantic praxis constitute the exegetical key to several revelations (oracles, signs, dreams, and visions) attributed to prophets in the Nevi'im (Amos 8:2; Jer 1:11–12; 1:13–14; 19:1–13; cf. Dan 5:25–28).[17]

2. Perceptions of Ancient Prophecy

While I have borrowed Schaper's phrase "the death of the prophet," my primary interlocutor is the seminal monograph *Oracles of God* by John Barton (1986, repr. 2007), instructively subtitled *Perceptions of Ancient Prophecy in Israel after the Exile*.[18] Barton's study is important here for two reasons. Firstly, because it is a seminal contribution to this debate and, secondly, because the relationship between mantic exegesis, prophecy and the scribal culture is at the crux of his argument. In *Oracles of God* Barton argues that during the Second Temple period (ca. 539 BCE–70 CE) the Israelite/Judean scribes who composed the biblical prophetic books increasingly perceived of "prophecy" as a "mantic" activity and embraced mantic "modes" of reading what was for them *ancient* prophecy.[19] Prophecy of the ancient (i. e., preexilic) kind – moral rebuke and warning, according to Barton[20] – continued, although it was no longer described as such but rather (Barton supposes) in language drawn from the wisdom tradition (e. g.,

---

[14] Schorch, "Science," 215 with nn31–33.

[15] See Jeffrey Gibson's over sixty references to "signs" sought to validate a "prophet" or prophecy in the Hebrew Bible and dependent literature: "Jesus' Refusal to Produce a 'Sign' (Mark 8.11–13)," in *The Historical Jesus: A Sheffield Reader*, ed. Craig A. Evans and Stanley E. Porter, BibSem 33 (Sheffield: Sheffield Academic, 1995), 274n8.

[16] Schorch distinguishes between *paronomastic* (phonetic or sound-based) and *polysemous* (semantic or sense-based) puns ("Science," 207 with n9).

[17] Fishbane, *Biblical Interpretation*, 451–52; Schorch, "Science," 215–16.

[18] John Barton, *Oracles of God: Perceptions of Ancient Prophecy in Israel after the Exile* (London: Darton, Longman & Todd, 1986; Oxford: Oxford University Press 1988, repr., 2007). The importance of Barton's work is demonstrated in the contributions by eminent scholars to "Rereading *Oracles of God*: Twenty years after John Barton, *Oracles of God: Perceptions of Prophecy in Israel after the Exile*" (ed. Ehud Ben Zvi, *JHebS* 7/14 [2007]: 29–33, doi:10.5508/jhs.2007.v7.a14) written in response to the republication of *Oracles of God* in 2007.

[19] See Barton, *Oracles*, 96–140; and for Barton's "modes" of reading preexilic prophecy, see 141–265.

[20] See Barton, *Oracles*, 131.

The Death of the Prophet? 39

"wise," "teachers," "learned").[21] Consequently, "much that did pass as 'prophecy' in the post-exilic age corresponded not to prophecy as it had been in earlier times, but to prophecy as it was (falsely) imagined to have been."[22] The scribes, having thus misperceived preexilic prophecy, (mistakenly) interpreted prophetic texts in accordance with this misperception. Barton believes that their misperception generated exegetical adaptations, elaborations, and insertions which resulted in radically distorted representations of the preexilic prophets of whom we purportedly read in Nevi'im to such an extent that it is difficult to identify the "real" prophets behind these texts.

It is by no means my intention here to downplay the significance of Barton's *Oracles of God* which identifies and examines fundamental questions concerning the phenomenon of prophecy and the composition and interpretation of prophetic books. Rather, my intention is to explore one avenue of inquiry which Barton himself highlighted – the phenomenology of preexilic Israelite prophecy, and a possibility which he himself later conceded – namely, that there may in fact have been greater continuity between pre- and post-exilic prophecy than he allowed in *Oracles of God*.[23] I am, however, asserting what I consider to be an inherent methodological problem involving a critical assumption Barton makes in *Oracles of God* – he believes he knows what preexilic prophets were like and contrasts them with postexilic prophecy on the basis of that assumption, following Wellhausen, whose modern perception of ancient prophecy was right.[24] If Barton has misperceived the preexilic prophets, then the contrast he makes may be incorrect or at least overstated.

It is notable, even if only coincidental, that Barton, like Wellhausen before him,[25] omitted any consideration of ancient Near Eastern sources. This is presumably because of his methodological approach of beginning with the *known* (i.e., biblical prophetic books) and working backwards to the *unknown* (earlier stages of composition, including, perhaps, the oracles and signs of historical prophets).[26] Other relevant *known* texts exist, however, in ancient Near Eastern sources of prophecy. Barton cites many extrabiblical sources, but his index of primary sources does not include a single reference to a preexilic, extrabiblical prophetic text. In fairness, it must be noted that Barton's 1986 monograph predated the publication by Durand in 1988 of the extended corpus of prophecies from Mari in modern-day eastern Syria (ARM 26/1), with which I

---

[21] Barton, *Oracles*, 201.
[22] Barton, *Oracles*, 269.
[23] See Barton's retrospective remarks in "*Oracles of God* Revisited," in Ben Zvi, "Rereading," 32.
[24] Barton, *Oracles*, 266–73.
[25] See Peter Machinist, "The Road Not Taken: Wellhausen and Assyriology," in *Homeland and Exile: Biblical and Ancient Near Eastern Studies in Honour of Bustenay Oded*, ed. Gershon Galil, Mark Geller, and Alan Millard, VTSup 130 (Leiden: Brill, 2009), 469–531.
[26] See Barton, *Oracles*, 3–5.

am concerned here (see further below), and the full corpus of Neo-Assyrian prophecies from Nineveh (modern Kuyunjik) in northern Mesopotamia (SAA 9) by Parpola in 1997, followed in 1998 by the Neo-Assyrian references to prophecy by Nissinen (SAAS 7).[27] Nevertheless, many extrabiblical sources (including twenty-eight Mari prophecies) were available when Barton was writing *Oracles of God*. The corpus of letters reporting prophecies from the kingdom based upon the city of Mari (modern Tell Hariri) near the modern Syria-Iraq border now includes some fifty-two letters reporting prophetic content (WAW 41, nos. 1–50b) and seventeen administrative documents mentioning prophets (WAW 41, nos. 51–65b), all written in cuneiform script representing the Babylonian dialect of the Akkadian language.[28] Through the Mari corpus, as Dominique Charpin, a doyen of Mari studies, recently observed, we are able "to analyse the prophetic phenomenon, at 'first hand', so to speak, that is to say through primary documentation with a clear geopolitical and historical context."[29] I believe that the critical assumption underlying Barton's influential thesis should be reconsidered in the light of these sources.

3. Dramatic, Flamboyant, Symbolic Acts

In 1997 when Huffmon published English translations of new Mari prophetic texts published by Durand in 1988, he concluded:

Obviously there is a temporal and geographical gap between the Mari texts and early Israel, ... It is clearly not a matter of direct continuity. Nonetheless, the Mari activity does provide a phenomenological background for biblical prophecy, both in the cultic and non-cultic forms. Biblical prophecy can now be seen as part of an ancient and honourable history of such activity in Greater Syria and as an instance of the wider phenomenology of prophetic mediation for the divine realm. As the new Mari texts make clear, that ancient story includes bold, assertive actions by the prophets, as well as very dramatic, even flamboyant, symbolic acts ... To be sure, biblical religion differs from the religion of the Amorite provinces of Mesopotamia, and Mari prophecy differs from biblical prophecy. Phenomenologically, however, the parallel is clear, and that is the proper point of com-

---

[27] Jean-Marie Durand, *Archives épistolaires de Mari I/1*, ARM 26/1 (Paris: Éditions Recherche sur les Civilisations, 1988); Simo Parpola, *Assyrian Prophecies*, SAA 9 (Helsinki: Neo-Assyrian Text Corpus Project, 1997); Martti Nissinen, *References to Prophecy in Neo-Assyrian Sources*, SAAS 7 (Helsinki: Neo-Assyrian Text Corpus Project, 1998).

[28] Transcriptions and English translations of Mari prophecies quoted here are from Martti Nissinen, with contributions by C. L. Seow, Robert K. Ritner, and H. Craig Melchert, *Prophets and Prophecy in the Ancient Near East*, 2nd ed., WAW 41 (Atlanta: Society of Biblical Literature, 2019).

[29] Dominique Charpin, "Prophetism in the Near East according to the Mari Archives," in *Gods, Kings, and Merchants in Old Babylonian Mesopotamia*, PIPOCF 2 (Leuven: Peeters, 2015), 57–58.

parison. One cannot require identity in detail; that would mean virtually an equation of the religious world of the Mari prophets and that of biblical Israel.[30]

More recently, on the basis of over two decades of research into ancient Near Eastern prophecy, Nissinen concluded that there are sufficient points of comparison to justify applying the concept of "prophecy" across the cultures of Mesopotamia and the Levant and to study prophecy in the Hebrew Bible as a local variation of that phenomenon.[31] I am concerned here with the Mari evidence for prophecy by means of the "symbolic acts" or, in the ancient terminology, "signs," to which Huffmon refers. My contribution is a comparative study of biblical and extrabiblical prophetic signs which both feature "mantic exegesis" in the form of paronomastic puns. A sign attributed to the Hebrew prophet Jeremiah (Jer 19:1–13) in Jerusalem, in the southern Levantine kingdom of Judah, late-seventh to the early-sixth century BCE, is compared with an extrabiblical prophetic sign (ARM 26/1.206 = WAW 41, no. 16) recorded in the royal archives of Mari during the reign of King Zimri-Lim, ca. 1776–1761 BCE.[32]

In the biblical book of Jeremiah, the prophet receives a "word" from YHWH, the god of Israel: "Go and buy a potter's earthenware jug." Jeremiah gathers the "elders" and "senior priests" at the city gate of Jerusalem leading to the valley of ben-Hinnom which, he ominously declares, will become "the valley of slaughter." Having condemned the kings of Judah and the people of Jerusalem for "making offerings in it to other gods," filling the city with "the blood of the innocent," and burning "their children in the fire as burnt offerings to Baal," the prophet was instructed to break the jug and announce: "Thus says YHWH of hosts: So will I break this people and this city, as one breaks a potter's vessel, so that it can never be mended."[33]

The biblical narrative does not specifically designate Jeremiah's action a sign, but the overall pattern, circumstances and intention characteristic of the phenomenon of signs suggests that witnesses would have called it an אות ("sign") or מופת ("portent").[34] "Signs" terminology and formulae are used with reference to prophetic "signs" elsewhere in Jeremiah (אות in 32:20, 21; 44:29) and explicitly used to designate symbolic actions attributed to his contemporary Ezekiel (אות, Ezek 4:3; 14:8; מופת, 12:6, 11; 24:24, 27).

---

[30] Herbert B. Huffmon, "The Expansion of Prophecy in the Mari Archives: New Texts, New Readings, New Information," in *Prophecy and Prophets: The Diversity of Issues in Contemporary Scholarship*, ed. Yehoshua Gitay, SemeiaSt (Atlanta: Scholars Press, 1997), 17–18.

[31] See Martti Nissinen, "Biblical Prophecy from a Near Eastern Perspective: The Cases of Kingship and Divine Possession," in *Prophetic Divination*, 351–76.

[32] ARM 26/1.206 was first published in Durand, *AÉM I/1*, 434–35. For further bibliography, see Nissinen, *Prophets*, 39–40.

[33] Quotations here are from Jer 19:3, 6, 4–5, 11. Quotations from the Bible in English in this essay are from the New Revised Standard Version (NRSV). I have substituted YHWH, the Hebrew name for Israel's god, for "the Lord."

[34] See Gibson, "Jesus' Refusal," 274.

In the text on a tablet from the Mari archives, a prophet asks: "Verily, what shall I eat that belongs to Zimri-Lim? Give me one lamb and I shall eat it!" The "prophet," called a *muḫḫum* ("ecstatic") in Akkadian, or perhaps the city governor, then gathers the elders in front of the city gate and the prophet devours the lamb "raw" before warning the assembly of an impending calamity: "A devouring will take place!" The prophet then issues demands: "Give orders to the cities to return the taboo material. Whoever commits an act of violence shall be expelled from the city."[35] The *muḫḫum* probably spoke his "oracle" in the name of the god Dagan, the leading deity of the Mari pantheon.

This prophecy is referred to as the prophet's *têrtum* (lines 28, 32, 34; cf. ARM 26/1.197:5, 22; 200:6; 216:8), significantly using terminology characteristic of the divination of "signs" practiced by Babylonian "diviners."[36] A *bārûm* "seer" or "diviner" determined if an observed phenomenon (most often the *exta* – the liver, lungs, or heart of a lamb) was a "sign" or "omen" (*ittum*)[37] and the divine "instruction" or "oracle" (*têrtum*) it signified.[38] The use of *têrtum* here indicates that the action of eating the lamb was a divine "sign" which the Mari prophet interpreted in his "oracle." The term *ittum* is used at Mari with reference to prophecy and oneiromancy (dream divination) (ARM 26/1.207:4; 212:2'; 237.5; FM 14:iii 35). It is probably etymologically related to the Hebrew אות (*ʾôt*)[39] used in the Hebrew Bible for divinatory "signs" (e.g., 1 Sam 14:10; Ps 86:17; Jer 10:2) including "signs" attributed to prophets (Isa 8:18; 20:3–4; Ezek 4:1–3).[40] The prophet's action in ARM 26/1.206 is thus rightly referred to as a "sign" comparable to those in the Hebrew Bible.[41] In both texts being compared here, therefore,

---

[35] Quotations are from ARM 26/1.206:7–9, 10, 18, 19–22.

[36] Concerning the "divination" of the *bārûm* at Mari, see Durand, *AÉM I/1*, 3–373, with texts 1–190 (published in English translation by Wolfgang Heimpel, *Letters to the King of Mari: A New Translation, with Introduction, Notes, and Commentary*, MC 12 [Winona Lake, IN: Eisenbrauns, 2003], 174–248). On Babylonian divination, see Ulla Susanne Koch, *Mesopotamian Divination Texts: Conversing with the Gods: Sources from the First Millennium* BCE, GMTR 7 (Münster: Ugarit-Verlag, 2015), esp. 15–18, 291–94, concerning prophecy; and Stefan M. Maul, *The Art of Divination in the Ancient Near East: Reading the Signs of Heaven and Earth*, trans. Brian McNeil and Alexander Johannes Edmonds (Waco, TX: Baylor University Press, 2018). The major study by Jean Bottéro is still important although subsequent source material must be considered (especially for Mari prophecy) and some of his hypotheses are now contested (Jean Bottéro, "Symptômes, signes, écritures en Mesopotamie ancienne," in Jean-Pierre Vernant et al., *Divination et rationalité*, Recherches anthropologiques [Paris: du Seuil, 1974], 70–197).

[37] s.v. "*ittu* A," *CAD* I/J (meaning 2).

[38] Koch, *Divination Texts*, 27, 291; Maul, *Art*, 20 with n24.

[39] F. Stolz, "אות," *TLOT* 1:67.

[40] See Roberts, "Signs," 475–78.

[41] See, esp., Jean-Georges Heintz, "La 'fin' des prophètes bibliques? Nouvelles theories et documents sémetiques anciens," in *Oracles et Prophéties dans l'antiquités: Actes du colloque de Strasbourg 15–17 juin 1995*, ed. Jean-Georges Heintz, CRPOGA 15 (Paris: de Boccard, 1997), 203 with nn21–22; also Kelvin G. Friebel, *Jeremiah's and Ezekiel's Sign-Acts: Rhetorical Nonverbal Communication*, JSOTSup 283 (Sheffield: Sheffield Academic, 1999), 62–63; Lester L. Grabbe, *Priests, Prophets, Diviners, Sages: A Socio-Historical Study of Religious Specialists in Ancient Is-*

the prophet's actions may rightly be termed a "sign," but the phenomenological significance of this observation has not been fully explored.

4. A Prophet at the Gate

We owe our knowledge of the Mari prophetic sign to an official, probably named Yaqqim-Addu, governor of Saggaratum, a regional city of the Mari kingdom. Yaqqim-Addu (if this identification is correct) dutifully wrote a report and had it delivered to the intended recipient, King Zimri-Lim, which now constitutes the earliest extant evidence of a prophetic sign. Mari prophecies were often recorded on or soon after the day they were delivered (e.g., ARM 26/1.196:8–10; 199:54–55; 217:27–28; 26/2.414:29–42).[42] They may be considered "firsthand written records of prophecy,"[43] composed (with interpretation and application) by a royal official (not the prophet). When it comes to examining ancient Near Eastern prophecy, "We can get no closer to hearing an oracle from a prophet's mouth."[44] Durand concludes from the non-professional writing of ARM 26/1.206 that Yaqqim-Addu wrote the text himself which indicates the importance of the information being reported to the king.[45] The governor's report may be compared to biblical texts in which a prophet or his scribe is instructed to write a prophecy (Isa 8:1–4, 16–20;

---

rael (Valley Forge, PA: Trinity Press International, 1995), 90; André Lemaire, "Les textes prophétiques de Mari dans leurs relations avec l'ouest," in *Amurru 1: Mari, Ébla et les Hourrites – premiere partie: Actes du colloque international (Paris, mai 1993)*, ed. Jean-Marie Durand (Paris: Éditions Recherche sur les Civilisations, 1996), 433.

[42] See Antti Laato, *History and Ideology in the Old Testament Prophetic Literature: A Semiotic Approach to the Reconstruction of the Proclamation of the Historical Prophets*, ConBOT 41 (Stockholm: Almqvist & Wiksell, 1996), 163–64; Lemaire, "Les textes," 433; Alan Millard, "La prophétie et l'écriture: Israël, Aram, Assyrie," *RHR* 202 (1985): 125–44. Millard's conclusions should be weighed against those of Martti Nissinen ("Spoken, Written, Quoted, and Invented: Orality and Writtenness in Ancient Near Eastern Prophecy," in Ben Zvi and Floyd, *Writings*, 235–71), Simon B. Parker ("Official Attitudes toward Prophecy at Mari and in Israel," *VT* 43 [1993]: 57–60), and Jack M. Sasson ("Water beneath Straw: The Adventures of a Prophetic Phrase in the Mari Archives," in *Untying Knots: Biblical, Epigraphic, and Semitic Studies in Honor of Jonas C. Greenfield*, ed. Ziony Zevit, Seymour Gitlin, and Michael Sokoloff [Winona Lake, IN: Eisenbrauns, 1995], 599–608). Nevertheless, the obligation to report oracles to the king (FM 7.39:34–45; ARM 26/1.196:8–10; 233:40–43), which parallels the protocol for diviners (ARM 26/1.1), is significant evidence in favor of the general reliability of the reports (Laato, *History*, 163). Charpin believes the prophet's messages were faithfully transmitted in most cases ("Prophetism," 30–31).

[43] See Martti Nissinen, *Ancient Prophecy: Near Eastern, Biblical, and Greek Perspectives* (Oxford: Oxford University Press, 2017), 83–85 (quotation 83).

[44] Simon B. Parker, "The Ancient Near Eastern Literary Background to the Old Testament," in *General and Old Testament Articles, Genesis, Exodus, and Leviticus*, ed. Leander E. Keck, vol. 1 of *The New Interpreter's Bible* (Nashville: Abingdon, 1994), 237.

[45] Jean-Marie Durand, "'Un habit pour un oracle!' À propos d'une prophétie de Mari," in *Muhibbe Darga Armağanı*, ed. Taner Tarhan, Aksel Tibet, and Erkan Konyar (Istanbul: Sadberk Hanim Müzesi, 2008), 232 with n2.

30:8–11; Jer 29:24–32; 36:1–8; 51:59–64a; Hab 2:2–4). The sign reported in the Mari text and those narrated in the Hebrew Bible are especially important because they reveal something of how the prophecies actually took place, whereas oracles focus on content rather than the performance.[46] At Mari, we can also get no closer to seeing a "sign" performed at the city gate!

My question then is this: in the light of the Mari evidence, how credible is the narrative in Jeremiah 19:1–13 as an authentic *pre*-exilic "sign" prophecy enacted and exegeted by a historical prophet? My essay adopts a comparative approach in the contextual sense advocated by Hallo.[47] The term "contextual" recognizes the methodological importance of identifying both similarities and differences between the phenomena under comparison, as well as continuity and change. My purpose is such that I am primarily concerned with similarities. Differences been biblical and Mari prophecy have been identified (e.g., polytheism rather than monotheism, the importance of extispicy and the prominence of female prophets at Mari, and in Israel and Judah the production of prophetic books),[48] although it is difficult to ascertain the extent to which some apparent differences are genuine or merely a consequence of the occasional character of the extant sources. While the most significant difference in terms of this study is arguably the respective source materials – from Mari an autograph copy of a contemporaneous letter and from Judah a book known from manuscripts written centuries later – I believe (in view of the phenomenological observations of Huffmon and Nissinen cited in the previous section) it is reasonable to draw analogous comparisons.[49] While what has been called "parallelomania" has been rightly criticized,[50] so has "parallelophobia."[51]

I suggest that a way forward is found in beginning with the firmest available historical material and the criterion of coherence. If a reasonable degree of coherence between Jeremiah 19 and the reliable historical material from Mari

---

[46] Cf. Nissinen, *Ancient Prophecy*, 335.

[47] William W. Hallo, "Compare and Contrast: The Contextual Approach to Biblical Literature," in *The Bible in the Light of Cuneiform Literature: Scripture in Context III*, ed. William W. Hallo, Bruce William Jones, and Gerald L. Mattingly, ANETS 8 (Lewiston, NY: Mellen, 1990), 1–30.

[48] The most recent comparison is by Charpin ("Prophetism," 48–57) who notes similarities and differences but concludes that some alleged differences now "prove less significant than previously thought, or even nonexistent ..." (52). See also Jésus Asurmendi, "Les textes ... et la Bible," in Jésus Asurmendi, et al., *Prophéties et oracles 1: Dans les Proche-Orient ancien*, SCaE 88 (Paris: Cerf, 1994), 75–78; Lemaire, "Les textes," 437–38.

[49] Mark W. Chavalas, "Assyriology and Biblical Studies: A Century and a Half of Tension," in *Mesopotamia and the Bible: Comparative Explorations*, ed. Mark W. Chavalas and K. Lawson Younger Jr. (Grand Rapids: Baker Academic, 2002), 39. On "analogous" and "homologous" comparisons, see Jack M. Sasson, "About 'Mari and the Bible'," *RA* 92 (1998): 98–99.

[50] Samuel Sandmel, "Parallelomania," *JBL* 81 (1962): 1–13.

[51] Robert Ratner and Bruce Zuckerman, "'A Kid in Milk'? New Photographs of KTU 1.23, Line 14," *HUCA* 57 (1986): 52.

can be established, I will argue that it is therefore possible that the narrative in Jeremiah 19 may portray not just authentic historical *prophecy* but also an event in the life of the historical *prophet*. I believe that Twelftree's observation in relation to study of the historical Jesus is pertinent here: "if a class or category of sayings has been established as belonging to the bedrock of historical material then reported activities which cohere with this (while not automatically, without further discussion, thereby established as authentic) can at least be given the benefit of the doubt in relation to historicity."[52]

My comparison of ARM 26/1.206 and Jeremiah 19:1–13 MT (*BHS*) identifies the following parallel features in the signs from Syria and Judah.

4.1 A Prophet with a Message from a Deity (ARM 26/1.206:5–6 and Jer 19:1–3, 11, 14)

Both signs involve the activity of a figure identified with the phenomenon of "prophecy"[53] who communicates a message from a deity. Yaqqim-Addu's report in ARM 26/1.206 identifies the sign as the activity of a "prophet" and a deity:

ARM 26/1.206:5–6: A prophe[t of Dagan] [*muḫḫûm ša Dagan*] came to me [and spoke as foll]ows.

The prophet is designated a *muḫḫûm*-"ecstatic" (fem. *muḫḫūtum*) (from *maḫûm*, to "rave," "become frenzied") which with the *āpilum/āpiltum*-"spokesperson" was one of the two principal types of "prophet" active at Mari.[54] While ecstasy is apparently also experienced by some biblical prophetic figures (e.g., Num 11:24–30; 1 Sam 10:5–6; 1 Kgs 18:28–29), there are few details of that experience in either Mari or Israel/Judah.[55] Most translations, beginning with

---

[52] Concerning "historical method" and the "criterion of coherence," see Graham H. Twelftree, *Jesus the Exorcist: A Contribution to the Study of the Historical Jesus* (Peabody, MA: Hendrickson, 1993), 130–35 (quotation 135).

[53] Since the 1980s "prophecy" has increasingly been classified as a sub-type of a wider phenomenon of divine-human intermediation referred to by the generic term "divination." A "prophet" is defined as a non-technical diviner whose activity does not involve learning specialized techniques and, while they might interpret "signs," does not engage in the systematic observation and organization of phenomena as a technical diviner does, in extispicy and astrology, for example. According to this working definition, I believe both Jeremiah (a נביא in the MT; προφήτης in the LXX) and the Mari *muḫḫum* may be identified as "prophets" for the purpose of my comparison. See Martti Nissinen, "Prophecy and Omen Divination: Two Sides of the Same Coin," in *Prophetic Divination*, 75–85 (with additional references 75n3); and Jonathan Stökl, *Prophecy in the Ancient Near East: A Philological and Sociological Comparison*, CHANE 56 (Leiden: Brill, 2012), 7–11 (with references 8n35). On "prophecy" and other types of "divination" at Mari, see Charpin, "Prophetism," 38–45.

[54] On the *muḫḫûm/muḫḫūtum*, see Durand, *AÉM I/1*, 386–90. For Mari prophecy in general, see Durand, *AÉM I/1*, 377–412; Charpin, "Prophetism"; and Stökl, *Prophecy*, 29–100 (I do not share Stökl's view that the *muḫḫum*'s prophetic role was secondary [37, 57, 99–100, 229–32]; see Nissinen, *Ancient Prophecy*, 34 with n166; 37n181).

[55] See Nissinen, *Ancient Prophecy*, 171–200.

Durand's original, restore the probable association of the *muḫḫum*'s prophecy with the god Dagan (line 5; cf. ARM 26/1.215:15–17; 220:16–18; 221:9–12), known in the Bible as the Philistine god Dagon (Judg 16:23; 1 Sam 5:2–7; 1 Chr 10:10). It is not certain that the expression "Dagan/The god has sent me," used occasionally at Mari (ARM 26/1.210:11; 220:19; 221:13), is a formula indicating consciousness of a divine commission, as in biblical examples (e.g., Isa 6:8; Jer 1:7; Ezek 2:3–4).[56] Nevertheless, with few exceptions Mari letters specify the deity for whom the prophet speaks, most frequently Dagan, and often the delivery of their message is "in the temple of" the respective deity (e.g. ARM 26/1.195:5; 196:8; 202:7; 213:5).[57] It is notable that Dagan is associated with another prophetic sign in the Epic of Zimri-Lim (FM 14 = WAW 41, no. 64), where Zimri-Lim interprets an *āpilum*-"prophet" as an *ittum*-"sign" (iii 35) from Dagan signifying his victory (cf. the victory *ittum* from Dagan in the Code of Hammurabi of Babylon [iv 23–31]).[58]

Jeremiah's sign is also identified with a deity and prophetic activity:[59]

Jer 19:1–3, 11, 14: Thus says YHWH ... go out to the valley of the son of Hinnom ... and proclaim there the words that I shall tell you. You shall say: Hear the word of YHWH ... and shall say to them: Thus says YHWH of hosts ... When Jeremiah came from Topeth, where YHWH had sent him to prophesy [להנבא] ...

At the beginning of the book, YHWH informs Jeremiah: "I appointed you a prophet [נביא; LXX: προφήτης]" (1:5). נביא (fem. נביאה) is the term most frequently used in Jeremiah and in the Hebrew Bible to denote a prophetic figure. Recently, some scholars have concluded that preexilic "prophets" like Jeremiah were not called נביא.[60] While the reference to Jeremiah's appointment as a נביא in the call narrative (1:5) may be postexilic redaction, it is possible that the historical Jeremiah had the title נביא or, if not, later interpreters believed that he (like the eighth-century Isaiah) could justifiably be referred to as such because he fulfilled the socio-religious role of a prophet (cf. 1 Sam 9:9).[61]

---

[56] Stökl, *Prophecy*, 221–24.

[57] See Charpin, "Prophetism," 19–25.

[58] See Michaël Guichard, "L'apparition d'un prophète anonyme dans un poème épique paléo-babylonien," in *Comment devient-on prophète? Actes du colloque organisé par le Collège de France, Paris, les 4–5 avril 2011*, ed. Jean-Marie Durand, Thomas Römer, and Micaël Bürki, OBO 265 (Fribourg: Academic Press; Göttingen: Vandenhoeck & Ruprecht, 2014), 38–45.

[59] On prophecy in the Hebrew Bible, see Nissinen, *Ancient Prophecy*, 144–67; Stökl, *Prophecy*, 155–202.

[60] For a summary, see William L. Kelly, *How Prophecy Works: A Study of the Semantic Field of* נביא *and a Close Reading of Jeremiah 1:4–19, 23:9–40 and 27:1–28:17*, FRLANT 272 (Göttingen: Vandenhoeck & Ruprecht, 2020), 28–32.

[61] See Stökl, *Prophecy*, 178–86, 201.

4.2 A Crude, Violent Action (ARM 26/1.206:10–12 and Jer 19:10)

Both prophets performed a crude, violent action. The ARM 26/1.206 sign involved an action in which, as Gordon remarks, "the crudity of the action exceeds anything attributed to the Israelite prophets."[62]

ARM 26/1.206:10–12: [I gave] him a lamb and he devoured it raw [*balṭussuma*, lit. "alive"] [in fr]ont of the city gate.

Gordon may be right, although Malamat suggests a resemblance to the Israelite judge Samson who "tore apart" a young lion "barehanded as one might tear apart a kid" (Judg 14:6).[63] Nelson considers this sign "bizarre."[64] He compares it with biblical prophetic symbolic actions (e.g., 1 Kgs 22:11; Ezek 4–5, 12; Jer 19:10–13; 27–28) which he describes as "eccentric and abnormal," some even "irrational," although paradoxically he also deems them "stereotypical behaviour" for prophets.[65] To modern readers this action may well seem bizarre but the governor's report certainly does not suggest that he considered this an instance of "prophetic lunacy."[66]

Both the choice of a "lamb" (lines 9, 10) as the sign and the manner of its consumption are probably quite deliberate and significant. As noted above, in Babylonian divination a lamb was sacrificed to a deity to serve as a medium of divine communication.[67] Moreover, it was always the unusual behavior or physical abnormalities of the medium that were considered to be "warning signs."[68] In extispicy a *bārûm* examined the *exta* of the sacrifice for deformities (splits, cuts, lacerations or perforations) which he exegeted as physical "signs" of divine communications (literally) written in the *exta*.[69] The earliest extant

---

[62] Robert P. Gordon, "From Mari to Moses: Prophecy at Mari and in Ancient Israel," in *Of Prophet's Visions and the Wisdom of Sages: Essays in Honour of R. Norman Whybray on his Seventieth Birthday*, ed. Heather A. McKay and David J.A. Clines, JSOTSup 162 (Sheffield: JSOT Press, 1993), 69.

[63] Abraham Malamat, *Mari and the Bible*, SHCANE 12 (Leiden: Brill, 1998), 136.

[64] Richard D. Nelson, "Priestly Purity and Prophetic Lunacy: Hosea 1.2–3 and 9.7," in *The Priests in the Prophets: The Portrayal of Priests, Prophets, and Other Religious Specialists in the Latter Prophets*, ed. Lester L. Grabbe and Alice Ogden Bellis, JSOTSup 408 (London: T&T Clark, 2004), 121n10.

[65] Nelson, "Priestly Purity," 119–22; cf. Robert P. Gordon who presumes that it "was within the bounds of familiar or accepted behaviour in the Mari region" ("Where Have All the Prophets Gone? The Disappearing Israelite Prophet Against the Background of Ancient Near Eastern Prophecy," *BBR* 5 [1995]: 77).

[66] Nelson, "Priestly Purity."

[67] See Maul, *Art*, 17–19. For Mari, see Durand, *AÉM I/1*, 36–37.

[68] Maul, *Art*, 190. Abraham Winitzer identifies "the structural opposition between soundness and abnormality" as "the 'first paradigm' of divination" ("The Divine Presence and Interpretation in Early Mesopotamian Divination," in *Divination and Interpretation of Signs in the Ancient World*, ed. Amar Annus, OIS 6 [Chicago: Oriental Institute of the University of Chicago, 2010], 191).

[69] On the semiotics of diviners' exegesis of deformities as divine "signs," see Jean-Jacques

signs/omens (inscribed on clay models of deformed sheep livers from the Mari palace, ca. 1875 BCE[70]) refer to calamities believed to correlate with deformities in the liver: military success or failure or death in bizarre circumstances. Signs and their prognostications were subsequently systematized so that a person might take action to persuade the gods to release them from a signified calamity by performing a *namburbû* release-ritual.[71] As I will demonstrate below, the *muḫḫum*'s lamb-sign announces an impending calamity unless restitution is made to release the kingdom from the consequences of sacrilegious action.

Jeremiah's sign of the earthenware jug signified the destruction of a city and its inhabitants:

Jer 19:10: Then you shall break the jug …

While this prophetic action might be considered less crude or grotesque than the devouring of a raw lamb by the Mari *muḫḫûm*, I would contend that the "breaking" which it signified was at least equivalent to the "devouring" signified by the Mari sign. Sherwood has demonstrated that, "Traditionally prophetic criticism has drawn on the language of Romanticism, rhetoric, gentlemanliness (and cleanliness); it has focussed on eschatology, transcendence and the individual prophetic heart. But prophecy [in the Hebrew Bible] is also a crudely embodied discourse."[72] She cites a litany of crudely embodied images from biblical prophecies (e. g., Jer 8:1–2; 13:22; Mal 2:3; Zech 14:12).[73] Notably, as I will demonstrate below, some feature the verb אכל (e. g., Isa 49:26; Mic 3:1–3).

4.3 A Paronomastic Pun (Mantic Exegesis) (ARM 26/1.206:9–10, 12, 18 and Jer 19:1–2, 10–12)

Arguably the most significant parallel is that the meaning of both signs is revealed exegetically by means of a paronomastic pun. An exegetical "pun-text" creates a second semantic level which is independent of the surrounding "grammatical" text in the sense that it is not bound by the rules of syntax but only by phonetic or semantic links.[74] Paronomasia has been defined as "the relationship that obtains between two or more words that sound similar, differ in meaning, occur in close

---

Glassner, "La fabrique des presages en Mésopotamie: la sémiologie des devins," in *La raison des signes: Présages, rites, destin dans les sociétés de la Mediterranée ancienne*, ed. Stella Georgoudi, Renée Koch Piettre, and Francis Schmidt, RGRW 174 (Leiden: Brill, 2012), 29–53.

[70] Maggie Rutten, "Trente-deux modèles de fois en argile inscrits provenant de Tell-Hariri (Mari)," *RA* 35 (1938): 36–52.

[71] See Stefan M. Maul, "How the Babylonians Protected Themselves against Calamities Announced by Omens," in *Mesopotamian Magic: Textual, Historical, and Interpretative Perspectives*, ed. Tzvi Abusch and Karel van der Toorn, AMD 1 (Groningen: Styx, 1999), 123–29.

[72] Yvonne M. Sherwood, "Prophetic Scatology: Prophecy and the Art of Sensation," *Semeia* 82 (1998): 183.

[73] See Sherwood, "Prophetic Scatology," 192–97.

[74] See Schorch, "Science," 206–7, 211–12.

proximity, and have been deliberately juxtaposed in order to draw the reader's [or hearer's] attention."[75] In both prophecies being studied here the pun-text is based on root modification: *'-k-l* (Akkadian) and שׁבר, *š-b-r* (Hebrew) respectively. A "metaphoric re-use"[76] of the root is juxtaposed with a literal usage. The Mari prophet's pun is formed by juxtaposing *ukultum* (line 18), a nominal derivation of the Akkadian verb *akālum*, meaning to "eat" or (of gods, fire or other agents) to "devour,"[77] with previous uses of that verb (lines 9–10, 12):

ARM 26/1.206:5–18: A prophe[t of Dagan] came to me [and spoke as foll]ows:

[Sign] "V[erily, what] shall I eat [*akkal*] that belongs to Z[imri-Lim]? [Give me] one la[mb] and I shall eat it [*lūkul*]." [I gave] him a lamb and he devoured it [*īkulšu*] raw [in fr]ont of the city gate.

[Oracle] He [or I] assembled the elders in front of the gate of Saggaratum and he said: "A DEVOURING [*ukultum*] will take place!"[78]

The metaphorical use of the *'-k-l* root (capitalised above) indicates that the lamb the prophet "devoured" signifies a metaphorical divine "devouring" (line 18).

The *muḫḫûm*'s paronomastic pun identifies his sign with the language of "signs" which characterized Babylonian divination and shows that it makes sense within that context. Punning, including paronomasia, was used as an exegetical tool in sign/omen texts ranging from the Old Babylonian (2004–1595 BCE) through to the Hellenistic Seleucid period (312–140 BCE).[79] Noegel concludes that punning "served as one of the most pervasive hermeneutics throughout Mesopotamian history" and "in most cases, it is the very essence of the message."[80] The sign and its interpretation (oracle) were linked by association created by *semantic* (usually based upon analogy) or *phonetic* similarity (as in ARM 26/1.206).[81]

---

[75] Jonathan G. Kline, *Allusive Soundplay in the Hebrew Bible*, AIL 28 (Atlanta: Society of Biblical Literature, 2016), 8; see further 6–13, with references (8n19).

[76] Susan Niditch, *The Symbolic Vision in Biblical Tradition*, HSM 30 (Chico, CA: Scholars Press, 1983), 34.

[77] s.v. "*akālu*," *CAD* A/1 (meaning 5).

[78] My analysis of texts featuring puns is adapted from the "analogical analysis" methodology formulated by David P. Wright ("Analogy in Biblical and Hittite Ritual," in *Religionsgeschichtliche Beziehungen zwischen Kleinasien, Nordsyrien und dem Alten Testament: Internationales Symposion Hamburg 17.–21. März 1990*, ed. Bernd Janowski, Klaus Koch, and Gernot Wilhelm, OBO 129 [Freiburg: Universitätsverlag Freiburg; Göttingen: Vandenhoeck & Ruprecht, 1993], 473–506; idem, "Ritual Analogy in Psalm 109," *JBL* 113 [1994]: 385–404). In accordance with Wright's methodology the METAPHORICAL ELEMENTS are capitalized.

[79] For Old Babylonian examples, see Sheldon W. Greaves, "Ominous Homophony and Portentous Puns in Akkadian Omens," in Noegel, *Puns*, 110–12.

[80] Noegel, *Nocturnal Ciphers*, 24, 279; citing examples from omens and dreams (11–24).

[81] For examples, see Giovanni Manetti, *Theories of the Sign in Classical Antiquity*, trans. Christine Richardson, AdSem (Bloomington: Indiana University Press, 1993), 9–10. On wordplay, esp. paronomasia, as the mechanism of association, see also Nicla De Zorzi, "The Omen Series *Šumma izbu*: Internal Structure and Hermeneutic Strategies," *KASKAL* 8 (2011): 67–

Before turning to Jeremiah's pun, I note that while the reporting of prophecies at Mari was not necessarily verbatim,[82] it is possible, even probable, that the pun-text (*akkal*, *lūkul*, *īkulšu*, and *ukultum*) of the pun in ARM 26/1.206 includes *ipsissima verba* (authentic words) of the prophet, for two reasons. Firstly, the Mari governor was probably one of the witnesses to the sign he reports. Secondly, Mari prophecies were probably spoken as well as written in (East Semitic) Akkadian rather than in the (West Semitic) Amorite vernacular because the pun functions in Akkadian.[83]

Paronomastic puns are widely attested in the Hebrew Bible, including the Nevi'im.[84] The parallels between ARM 26/1.206 and puns in the visions in Amos 8 and Jeremiah 1 are obvious. YHWH shows Amos "a basket of summer fruit [קיץ, *qāyiṣ*]," saying, "The end [הקץ, *haqqēṣ*] has come upon my people Israel" (Amos 8:1–2). Jeremiah sees "a branch of an almond [שקד, *šāqēd*] tree." YHWH says: "for I am watching [שקד, *šôqēd*] over my word to perform it" (Jer 1:11–12). Likewise, a pun on the Hebrew verb הפך (to "overturn") correlates both the sign in a dream and its interpretation as the sign of an Israelite victory over Midian overheard by Gideon (Judg 7:13–15).[85] Jeremiah's sign in chapter 19 signifies a metaphorical divine "breaking" by means of a pun on the Hebrew verb שבר (to "break" or "smash") used both for an action Jeremiah is commanded to perform with the jug (v. 10) and what YHWH will do (v. 11):

Jer 19:1–2, 10–12: Thus said YHWH: Go and buy a potter's earthenware jug. Take with you some of the elders of the people and some of the senior priests, and go out to the valley of the son of Hinnom at the entry of the Potsherd Gate, and proclaim there the words that I tell you …

[Sign] Then you shall break [ושברת, *wěšābarĕtā*] the jug in the sight of those who go with you, and shall say to them:

71; Victor Avigdor Hurowitz, "Alliterative Allusions, Rebus Writing, and Paronomastic Punishment: Some Aspects of Word Play in Akkadian Literature," in Noegel, *Puns*, 78–83.

[82] Stökl concludes: "I do not think the prophecies as we have them are *verbatim*, but they are probably fairly close …" (*Prophecy*, 75).

[83] See Dominique Charpin, "Prophètes et rois dans le Proche-Orient amorrite," in *Prophètes et rois: Bible et Proche-Orient*, ed. André Lemaire, LD (Paris: Cerf, 2001), 32–33 with 33n1; Jack M. Sasson, "The Posting of Letters with Divine Messages," in *Florilegium marianum II: Recueil d'études à la mémoire de Maurice Birot*, ed. Dominique Charpin and Jean-Marie Durand, NABUM 3 (Paris: Société pour l'étude du Proche-Orient ancien, 1994), 300n5; contra Malamat, *Mari and the Bible*, 65.

[84] On punning in the Hebrew Bible and ancient Near Eastern literature, see Noegel, *Puns*; idem, *"Wordplay" in Ancient Near Eastern Texts*, ANEM 26 (Atlanta: Society of Biblical Literature, 2021). For the Nevi'im, see, esp., Gerald Morris, *Prophecy, Poetry and Hosea*, JSOTSup 219 (Sheffield: Sheffield Academic, 1996), 74–100. On the influence of "Babylonian" or "analogical" hermeneutics on the Hebrew Bible, see Daniel Bodi, *Israël et Juda: À l'ombre des Babyloniens et des Perses*, ÉAHA (Paris: de Boccard, 2010), 177–207.

[85] See the discussion by Jin H. Han, "Did the Deuteronomist Detest Dreams?" in this volume and his comparison with Babylonian divination by extispicy.

[Oracle] Thus says YHWH of hosts: So WILL I BREAK [אשבר, *'ešĕbōr*] this people and this city, as one breaks [ישבר, *yišĕbōr*] a potter's vessel, so that it can never be mended … Thus will I do to this place, says YHWH, and to its inhabitants, making this city like Topeth.

As in ARM 26/1.206, the verb שבר is metaphorically re-used: "So will I break [metaphorically] this people and this city, as one breaks [literally] a potter's vessel." Another prophecy in Jeremiah 13:1–11 features a pun juxtaposing a literal (v. 7) and metaphorical (v. 9) use of the verb שחת (to "ruin," "spoil"). The prophet was commanded to bury then dig up a loincloth which now "was ruined [נשחת, *nišĕḥat*]; it was good for nothing …" YHWH then declares through the prophet: "Just so I WILL RUIN [אשחית, *'ašĕḥît*] the pride of Judah and the great pride of Jerusalem" (Jer 13:7, 9).[86] As Wright's analysis shows, although a verbal pun is not fully expressed in the biblical narrative, Jeremiah's action in chapter 13 is similar to the action of the prophet Ahijah who "tore" his garment into twelve pieces saying that YHWH was "TEARING" the kingdom from King Solomon (1 Kgs 11:29–31),[87] and to Jeremiah commanding Seraiah to throw a scroll tied to a stone into the Euphrates river saying it will "SINK AND NOT RISE," signifying the destruction of Babylon (Jer 51:59–64a MT).[88]

4.4 Cognate Vocabulary and Metaphors (ARM 26/1.206:9–10, 12, 18 and Jer 19:9)

Both signs have in common the metaphorical use of the cognate verbs *akālum* in the Akkadian and אכל, *'ākal*, in the Hebrew – both with semantic domains related to the action "to eat" or "devour." In Akkadian *akālum* is often used metaphorically "in describing 'consumption' or 'destruction' by enemies, sword, fire and pestilence, etc.,"[89] as it is in ARM 26/1.206:9–10, 12, 18 (quoted in the previous subsection). The Hebrew אכל is used analogously to its Akkadian cognate,[90] as in Jeremiah 19:9 (quoted below). Likewise, in an אות-sign (cf. Ezek 4:3) in Ezekiel:

Ezek 5:10, 12: Surely, parents shall eat [יאכלו, *yōʾkĕlû*] their children in your midst, and children shall eat [יאכלו, *yōʾkĕlû*] their parents … One third of you shall die of pestilence or be consumed [יכלו, *yikĕlû*] by famine among you.

Another significant biblical example is an oracle attributed to the prophet Isaiah which shares a similar pun to the prophetic sign from Mari. The verb is not only the vehicle of a phonetic pun but is from the אכל root. Isaiah declares:

---

[86] See Wright, "Ritual Analogy," 389.
[87] See Wright, "Analogy," 485.
[88] See Wright, "Analogy," 484.
[89] Ottosson, "אכל," *TDOT* 1:236.
[90] See Ottosson, "אכל," *TDOT* 1:238–39.

Isa 1:19–20: If you are willing and obedient, you shall eat [תֹּאכֵלוּ, *tōʾkēlû*] the good of the land; if you refuse and rebel, YOU SHALL BE DEVOURED [תְּאֻכְּלוּ, *tĕʾukĕlû*] by the sword ...

4.5 Treaty/Covenant Curse Maledictions (ARM 26/1.206:18 and Jer 19:6–9)

It is also of significance that both puns signify maledictions typically invoked for violations of treaty/covenant relationships with a deity:[91] a "paronomastic punishment."[92] In the Mari report the word *ukultum* signifies a divine "devouring" involving "plague" or "pestilence" (cf. Exod 9:1–7 and 10:1–20):

ARM 26/1.206:18: "A devouring [*ukultum*] (plague) will take place!" (Nissinen and Roberts),[93] or "Pestilence [*ukultum*] is at hand" (Huffmon).[94]

The word *ukultum* may refer to an epidemic "plague" considered the "devouring" of a god (*ukulti*, ARM 26/1.259:5; cf. ARM 3.61:9–13).[95] Alternatively, *ukultum* may denote "pestilence" which was a standard curse (Deut 28:38; SAA 2.6:442–43, 599–600). During recurrent infestations at Mari locusts are often said to have "devoured" the grain (e.g., ARM 27.32:18; cf. Aramaic אכל in the eighth-century BCE Syrian treaty Sefire 1, A:27–30). Calamities such as plague and pestilence are often predicted in Babylonian omen texts, sometimes using the same metaphor and vocabulary (e.g., "If bitches barked in the city gate, there will be pestilence [*ukulti*] in the land," *Šumma ālu* 1.48).[96] While there is no Mari evidence of a divine-human treaty comparable to the Israelite covenants with YHWH, there are early examples of political treaties (LAPO 16.282 and 292).[97]

It is probable that Jeremiah's sign also enacts a covenant curse malediction.[98] The breaking of weapons and the royal scepter are traditional curses.[99] Furthermore, Jeremiah's breaking of the jug signifies that Judah and Jerusalem will be broken "so that it can never be mended" (v. 11). An incurable wound is also

---

[91] The relationship with treaty/covenant curses was first observed by Huffmon ("Expansion," 13).

[92] See Hurowitz, "Alliterative Allusions," 83–86.

[93] J. J. M. Roberts, "The Mari Prophetic Texts in Transliteration and Translation," in *The Bible and the Ancient Near East: Collected Essays* (Winona Lake, IN: Eisenbrauns, 2002), 231.

[94] Huffmon, "Expansion," 13.

[95] See Durand, *AÉM I/1*, 544–49.

[96] Text and translation from Jack Newton Lawson, *The Concept of Fate in Ancient Mesopotamia of the First Millennium: Toward an Understanding of* Šīmtu, OBC 7 (Wiesbaden: Harrassowitz, 1994), 85.

[97] See examples in Jack M. Sasson, *From the Mari Archives: An Anthology of Old Babylonian Letters* (Winona Lake, IN: Eisenbrauns, 2015), 100–103. On treaty and covenant relationships in the ancient Near East, see Dominique Charpin, *'Tu es de mon sang': Les alliances dans le Proche-Orient ancien*, DO 4 (Paris: Les Belles Lettres, 2019), doi:10.4000/books.lesbelleslettres.258.

[98] See Michael L. Brown, *Israel's Divine Healer*, SOTBT (Carlisle: Paternoster, 1995), 191–95.

[99] Delbert R. Hillers, *Treaty-Curses and the Old Testament Prophets*, BibOr 16 (Rome: Pontifical Biblical Institute, 1964), 60–61.

a traditional curse (cf. Deut 28:27, 35).[100] In verses 6–9 the prophet employs covenant curse language in an oracle interpreting his sign: dead bodies will be devoured by birds and wild animals (v. 7), astonished passers-by will hiss in horror (v. 8), and the people will resort to cannibalism (cf. Lev 26:29; Deut 28:53–57),[101] denoted by אכל (v. 9):[102]

Jer 19:9: And I will make them eat [והאכלתים, wĕha'ăkalētîm] the flesh of their sons and the flesh of their daughters, and all shall eat [יאכלו, yōʾkēlû] the flesh of their neighbors in the siege.

The cannibalism curse is found in a Neo-Assyrian treaty (SAA 2.6:547–50) and invoked by Ezekiel in the prophetic sign quoted above (Ezek 5:10, 12).

The language of "covenant curses" (Deut 29:20) is often used in the Hebrew Bible for the sanctions for covenant violation (esp. Lev 26:14–33; Deut 27:11–26; 28:15–68). The general content of these calamities is often summarised according to literary convention, such as Jeremiah's "war, famine, and pestilence" (Jer 28:8 MT; cf. 2 Sam 24:13; Jer 14:12; Ezek 5:12).[103] Prophecies of destruction by pestilence occur in Amos 7, Jeremiah 27–28, and Joel 1–2 (with אכל in 1:19–20). Several biblical prophetic אתות ומופתים enact covenant maledictions, such as the curse of nakedness in Isaiah 20:2–4 (also Jer 28:10–11; Ezek 4:3; 5:1–17; 12:6, 11).[104]

4.6 Condemnation of Sacrilegious Acts (ARM 26/1.206:19–22 and Jer 19:4–5, 13)

Both signs condemn sacrilegious acts in violation of cultic obligations to a deity. After performing and interpreting his sign, the Mari prophet issues two demands for restitution:

---

[100] Hillers, *Treaty-Curses*, 64–66.
[101] Hillers, *Treaty-Curses*, 62–63.
[102] The maledictions in this prose section are often considered inauthentic compositions of "Deuteronomistic" scribes using conventional formulae, albeit perhaps from an original oracle (see, e. g., Moshe Weinfeld, *Deuteronomy and the Deuteronomic School* [Oxford: Clarendon, 1972; repr., Winona Lake, IN: Eisenbrauns, 1992], 138–46). However, Deuteronomistic theology and phraseology is a problematic criterion for determining the origin of a text or its relationship to a historical prophet like Jeremiah (cf. the methodological criticisms of Laato [*History*, 15–17, 138–45] contra Weinfeld). The idiom of the Deuteronomists may well have been Jeremiah's idiom (see Mark Leuchter, "Jeremiah: Structure, Themes, and Contested Issues," in *The Oxford Handbook of the Prophets*, ed. Carolyn J. Sharp [Oxford: Oxford University Press, 2016], 182–86). The "Deuteronomistic" sense of the prose oracles may have originated with Jeremiah even if they were redacted according to Deuteronomistic literary conventions (Mark Leuchter, "The Pen of Scribes: Writing, Textuality, and the Book of Jeremiah," in *The Book of Jeremiah: Composition, Reception, and Interpretation*, ed. Jack R. Lundbom, Craig A. Evans, and Bradford A. Anderson, VTSup 178, FIOTL 8 [Leiden: Brill, 2018], 17n48).
[103] Hillers, *Treaty-Curses*, 43.
[104] See Weinfeld, *Deuteronomy*, 135–38.

ARM 26/1.206:19–22: Give orders to the cities to return the taboo material [*asakkam*]. Whoever commits an act of violence [*rīsam*] shall be expelled from the city.

The first call for restitution in ARM 26/1.206 relates to the return of the "*asakkum*," "something set apart (for god, or king, a taboo)."[105] In another Mari prophecy the *asakkam* is the property of the god Adad (ARM 26/1.194:13–17) suggesting that ARM 26/1.206 refers to the removal of items sacred to the cult of Dagan. Several other Mari prophecies criticize the king for failing to honor his cultic responsibilities to a deity (e. g., ARM 26/1.198:3'–5'; 215:15–21; 220:13–23; 221:7–18).[106] The most striking feature of the prophet's demand in ARM 26/1.206 is the expression *asakkam akālum*, "eating the taboo," which refers to the violation of consecrated property (e. g., ARM 5.72).[107] Anyone who violated the *asakkum* had to be punished. Malamat argues that this parallels the biblical חרם ("ban," "consecrated" object or person).[108] Violation of חרם was an offense against YHWH which could be punished by death (Josh 7:2–26). Malamat even suggests that חרם is equivalent to an "*asakkum* of Yahwe."[109] I concur with Guichard's conclusion that because the entire community is not threatened with destruction (cf. Num. 21:2–3; Deuteronomy 7:1–5; 20:16–18; Josh 6:17–21; 1 Sam 15:3; denoted by the verb אכל in Deut 7:16) this is not an exact parallel, although he draws attention to Dagan's demands in ARM 26/1.206.[110] What the association in ARM 26/1.206 of *asakkum* and *akālum* with a prophetic sign signifying a divine "devouring" does demonstrate is that Mari gods could respond to violations of their sacred property with the weapons of plague or pestilence, thereby invoking sanctions typical of treaty curses, centuries before the existence of Israel.

The second demand is uncertain because the translation of *rīsam* suggested by Durand is based upon the only other occurrence of this word which is Late Babylonian.[111] If Durand's translation is correct, Dagan demands the expulsion of whoever committed an "act of violence" (*rīsam*, line 21). Several Mari prophecies invoke royal responsibility to enact social justice (FM 7.38:7'–11'; FM 7.39:53–54; also ARM 26/1.232:22–25).[112] In another, Zimri-Lim is called to de-

---

[105] s. v. "*asakku* B," *CAD* A/2. For the Mari evidence, see Abraham Malamat, *Mari and the Early Israelite Experience* (Oxford: Oxford University Press, 1989), 70–79.

[106] See Robert P. Gordon, "Prophecy in the Mari and Nineveh Archives," in *"Thus Speaks Ishtar of Arbela": Prophecy in Israel, Assyria, and Egypt in the Neo-Assyrian Period*, ed. Robert P. Gordon and Hans M. Barstad (Winona Lake, IN: Eisenbrauns, 2013), 47; and Charpin, "Prophetism," 22–23.

[107] See s. v. "*akālu*," *CAD* A/1 (meaning 7 a).

[108] See Malamat, *Mari and the Early Israelite Experience*, 70–79. On חרם, see N. Lohfink, "חרם," *TDOT* 5:180–99; Philip D. Stern, *The Biblical HEREM: A Window on Israel's Religious Experience*, BJS 211 (Atlanta: Scholars Press, 1991).

[109] Malamat, *Mari and the Early Israelite Experience*, 72.

[110] Michaël Guichard, "Les aspects religieux de la guerre à Mari," *RA* 93 (1999): 41–43, 47–48.

[111] Durand, *AÉM I/1*, 434. Heimpel leaves this word untranslated (*Letters*, 256).

[112] See Gordon, "Prophecy," 48–49.

clare an edict of *andurārum* ("remission [of debts]," "manumission [of slaves]") (ARM 26/1.194:32–43; cf. Isa 61:1; Jer 34:8–22).[113] Prophetic criticism of the king at Mari does not extend to the kingdom or society as a whole, as it often does in biblical prophecy.[114] However, in two texts (ARM 1.3; FM 7.38) a god claims the right to revoke the rule of kings for sacrilegious acts in a similar manner to biblical incidents involving prophets (1 Sam 15:28; 1 Kgs 11:11).[115] Bodi argues that these texts represent Northwest Semitic precursors to the theological principle of divine retribution attributed to biblical "Deuteronomistic" historiography.[116]

Mari prophecies invoking cultic and social justice responsibilities are strikingly similar to biblical prophecies concerning משפט ("justice") and צדקה ("righteousness"), especially in Jeremiah (e.g., Isa 1:17; 5:7; Jer 4:2; 7:5–7; 21:12; 22:3–5; Amos 5:24; Mic 6:8).[117] In Jeremiah's sign of the jug YHWH condemns sacrilegious actions (idolatrous offerings and child sacrifice) but there is no demand for restitution, only condemnation:

Jer 19:4–5, 13: Because the people have forsaken me, and have profaned this place by making offerings in it to other gods … and because they have filled this place with the blood of the innocent, and gone on building the high places of Baal to burn their children in the fire as burnt offerings to Baal … the houses of Jerusalem and the houses of the kings of Judah shall be defiled …

Interestingly, Jeremiah 34:8–22 contains a proclamation of "liberty" (דרור, *dĕrôr*, cf. Neo-Assyrian Akkadian *durāru*) for slaves by King Zedekiah of Judah.[118] When the Judahites renege, YHWH's condemnation through the prophet is based upon covenant violation to be punished by "a release to the sword, to pestilence, and to famine" (vv. 17–20).

4.7 Witnesses at the Gate (ARM 26/1.206: 11, 13–16, 33 and Jer 19:1–2)

Both signs were performed before witnesses ("elders" and "priests") at the city gate. Yaqqim-Addu's report indicates that the Mari prophecy was addressed to the king but delivered at the city gate of a regional city (lines 11, 14):

---

[113] See Dominique Charpin, "L'*andurârum* à Mari," *MARI* 6 (1990): 253–70; and Moshe Weinfeld, *Social Justice in Ancient Israel and in the Ancient Near East* (Jerusalem: Magnes; Minneapolis: Fortress, 1995), 75–96 (Mari 86–88).

[114] Martti Nissinen, "Das kritische Potential in der altorientalischen Prophetie," in *Prophetic Divination*, 191.

[115] See Malamat, *Mari and the Bible*, 157–62.

[116] Daniel Bodi, "The Retribution Principle in the Amorite View of History: Yasmaḫ-Addu's Letter to Nergal (ARM I 3) and Adad's Message to Zimrī-Līm (A. 1968)," *ARAM* 26.1/2 (2014): 285–300 (Mari 286–94).

[117] See Lemaire, "Les textes," 432–33; Weinfeld, *Social Justice*, 7–8, 87–88.

[118] See Bodi, *Israël*, 231–45; Weinfeld, *Social Justice*, 152–68.

ARM 26/1.206:11, 13–16, 32–34: he devoured it [the lamb] raw [in fr]ont of the city gate. He [or I] assembled the elders in front of the gate of Saggaratum ... He did not utter his oracle in private [*ina simmištim*], but he delivered his oracle in the assembly of the elders.

Both the location and the use of witnesses imply that the prophet's intention was to identify his sign as a legal action. Across the ancient Near East the city gate was a "legally significant site."[119] The city elders were responsible for the administration of justice at the gate.[120] Mari prophecies are often delivered in a temple (ARM 26/1.195:5; 196:12; 199:53; 214:5), but also at other public places such as the gate of a city or palace (ARM 26/1.208:7; ARM 26/2.371:9, 18).[121] The governor's letter emphasizes both the public location and audience of this prophecy. It would surely have been preferable from a political perspective for such an affair to have been kept "private" or "secret" (*simmištim*, line 32).[122] However, the oracle had already been delivered publicly to the elders. Yaqqim-Addu's concluding remark, therefore, attests to the authenticity of at least the sense of the prophecy's content as it was recorded.[123]

Similarly, Jeremiah's sign was performed before the "elders" and "senior priests" at a city gate:

Jer 19:1–2: Take with you some of the elders of the people and some of the senior priests and go out to the valley of the son of Hinnom at the entry of the Potsherd Gate, and proclaim there the words I tell you.

In the cities of Israel and Judah gates were the place for a jury of elders to judge legal disputes (e. g., Deut 21:18–21; Ruth 4:1–11; Prov 31:23; Amos 5:10; Isa 29:21). The context of prophecy was often a temple (Amos 7:10–17; Jer 19:14; 36:5–10) but prophets, like other citizens, often stood at the gate to initiate legal action (e. g., Jer 7:1–2; 19:1). Notably the venue of the trial is sometimes transferred to the divine "assembly." Two Mari letters may attest to prophetic involvement in the divine assembly (ARM 26/1.196 and 208).[124] An "assembly" or "council" of YHWH analogous to the human gate court is widely attested in the Bible (e. g., Gen 1:26–27; Job 15:8; Pss 82:1; 89:5–7). Like Babylonian diviners,[125] biblical prophets sometimes witness the divine council (1 Kgs 22:19–23; Jer 23:18–22; cf.

---

[119] Victor H. Matthews, "Entrance Ways and Threshing Floors: Legally Significant Sites in the Ancient Near East," *FiHi* 19 (1987): 25–40.

[120] For a recent study of the social and theological significance of city gates, see Natalie N. May, "Gates and their Functions in Mesopotamia and Ancient Israel," in *The Fabric of Cities: Aspects of Urbanism, Urban Topography and Society in Mesopotamia, Greece and Rome*, ed. Natalie N. May and Ulrike Steinert, CHANE 68 (Leiden: Brill, 2014), 77–121, esp. 95–100 on the gate as a place for judicial activities.

[121] Lemaire, "Les textes," 433.

[122] Durand, "Habit," 234–35.

[123] See Durand, *AÉM I/1*, 381.

[124] Martti Nissinen, "Prophets and the Divine Council," in *Prophetic Divination*, 465–68; but cf. Stökl, *Prophecy*, 224–26.

[125] See Maul, *Art*, 25–33.

Isa 6:1–8; Amos 3:7),[126] and could be sent to announce the verdict of the divine court.[127] The biblical ריב or covenant "lawsuit" (e.g., Isa 1:2–20; Jer 2:4–13; Mic 6:1–8)[128] may represent the litigation of the council of YHWH mediated by prophets against kings who violated Israel's covenant with YHWH.

In sum, my comparison of the prophetic signs in ARM 26/1.206 and Jeremiah 19 has identified phenomenological parallels which, when considered together, are substantive evidence of common patterns of prophetic activity despite the geographical distance between Mari and Judah and the temporal distance between the prophets of YHWH and Dagan.

5. Prophets from Ancient Times

Is Jeremiah 19:1–13 therefore credible as a *pre*-exilic prophetic sign enacted and exegeted by a historical prophet? Is the prophet dead? While it is important to be cautious in making generalizations from one case, I hope this comparison has demonstrated that, while we cannot require identity in every detail (rightly, Huffmon above), there is a significant degree of coherence between the activities attributed to Jeremiah in chapter 19 and reliable comparative historical material from Mari. We know that in a context which was not just preexilic but pre-Israel, prophetic signs were performed. But we can, I believe, also go further. It *is* possible that Jeremiah 19 reflects an actual event in the life of the historical (preexilic) Jeremiah ben-Hilkiah which can, at least initially, be given the benefit of the doubt in relation to historicity.[129]

Even though the canonical form of the Nevi'im was produced by scribes, this does not *necessarily* imply anything about the historical veracity of the content. Verisimilitude does not prove history, but in my judgment Brettler overstates the case when he asserts that "Verisimilitude proves absolutely nothing – authors of

---

[126] See Robert P. Gordon, "Standing in the Council: When Prophets Encounter God," in *The God of Israel*, ed. Robert P. Gordon, UCOP 64 (Cambridge: Cambridge University Press), 190–204; and for Mari, Malamat, *Mari and the Bible*, 134–39.

[127] See Victor H. Matthews and Don C. Benjamin, *Social World of Ancient Israel, 1250–587 BCE* (Peabody, MA: Hendrickson, 1993), 217–26; E. Theodore Mullen Jr., *The Divine Council in Canaanite and Early Hebrew Literature*, HSM 24 (Chico, CA: Scholars Press, 1980), 209–26.

[128] On the ריב, see Julien Harvey, *Le plaidoyer prophétique contre Israël après la rupture de l'alliance: Étude d'une formule littéraire de l'Ancien Testament*, Studia 22 (Bruges: de Brouwer; Montreal: Bellarmin, 1967).

[129] The question of the "historical Jeremiah" or "preexilic Jeremiah" remains a contested issue. For a recent summary, see Leuchter, "Jeremiah," esp. 180–87. Recent volumes devoted to Jeremiah studies with contributions representing the spectrum of views of the prophet – from historical person to literary character – include Hans M. Barstad and Reinhard G. Kratz, eds., *Prophecy in the Book of Jeremiah*, BZAW 388 (Berlin: de Gruyter, 2009); Lundbom, Evans, and Anderson, *Jeremiah*; and Hindy Najman and Konrad Schmid, eds., *Jeremiah's Scriptures: Production, Reception, Interaction, and Transformation*, JSJSup 173 (Leiden: Brill, 2016).

historical fiction, and even of other types of fiction, often aim at verisimilitude, and make up probable names and dates for the characters they create."[130] To my mind, he does not explain how ancient authors would have been able to "construct" verisimilitude in texts purporting to narrate events taking places centuries earlier; at best they could produce something archaistic rather than something genuinely archaic,[131] and his modern historical fiction analogy is anachronistic. Of course, this does not mean we can simplistically

assume that prophetic literature preserves that which prophets wrote or spoke ...

this notion presents an overly simple answer to a complex question: what is the relation of a prophet to the literature associated with him or her? The prophet as the author of literature is only one among several answers. An amaneunsis, a circle of disciples, a later redactor – any of these could serve as author of prophetic literature.[132]

Yet neither does it mean that we must exclude the possibility that Jeremiah, who, according to the biblical evidence, was a priest (Jer 1:1) "immersed in a scribal/textual culture" (e.g., Jer 32:6–15; 36:4–8, 32; 45:1; 51:59–64a) including Pentateuchal traditions and especially Deuteronomistic thought, may have had a role in the textualization of his own prophecies (Jer 30:2; 36:2; 51:60).[133]

This is not to suggest we ignore the textualization process or scribal updating of tradition (*Fortschreibung*) and inner-biblical exegesis (*Schriftauslegung*), although methodologies for reconstructing textual development need to be supported by empirical evidence.[134] Rather, I question the oversimplification (in my view) of asserting a fundamental phenomenological transformation "from prophet to exegete."[135] Certainly, prophecy was a dynamic not a static phenomenon – there was both continuity and change throughout its long history across the ancient Semitic world. It is possible to suppose, however, that the differences which Barton and those who share his hypothesis (under the shadow of Well-

---

[130] Marc Zvi Brettler, "Method in the Application of Biblical Source Material to Historical Writing (with Particular Reference to the Ninth Century BCE)," in Williamson, *Understanding*, 316.

[131] James K. Mead, "The Biblical Prophets in Historiography," in *Ancient Israel's History: An Introduction to Issues and Sources*, ed. Bill T. Arnold and Richard S. Hess (Grand Rapids: Baker Academic, 2014), 284.

[132] David L. Petersen, "Rethinking the Nature of Prophetic Literature," in Gitay, *Prophecy*, 31.

[133] On Jeremiah and scribal practice, see Leuchter, "Jeremiah," 178, 181–82 (quotation 181); and idem, "Pen," 10–13. On Jeremiah and Pentateuchal traditions, see Dalit Rom-Shiloni, "The Forest and the Trees: The Place of Pentateuchal Materials in Prophecy as of the Late Seventh/Early Sixth Centuries BCE," in *Congress Volume Stellenbosch 2016*, ed. Louis C. Jonker, Gideon R. Kotzé, and Christl M. Maier (Leiden: Brill, 2017), 56–92.

[134] See, e.g., the criticism of the literary "growth model" (*Wachstumsmodell*) by Benjamin Ziemer, "Radical Versus Conservative? How Scribes Conventionally Used Books While Writing Books," in this volume.

[135] Joachim Schaper uses this phrase taken from William M. Schniedewind's monograph *The Word of God in Transition: From Prophet to Exegete in the Second Temple Period* (JSOTSup 197 [Sheffield: Sheffield Academic, 1995]) in Schaper, "Death," 79.

hausen?) of a sharp discontinuity between pre- and post-exilic prophecy have perceived to be differences of *kind* are only differences of *degree*. Even in the postexilic era so-called *Schriftprophetie*, the inspired interpretation of texts, was, as Thomas observes, "but one trajectory of prophetic activity as it continues into the Second Temple period."[136] Conversely, ARM 26/1.206 demonstrates that even *very* ancient Semitic prophets could act as mantic exegetes. The presence of mantic exegesis is not ipso facto evidence of the absence of reliable historical material. The difference in the postexilic era was not the use of mantic exegesis per se but, as Tigay has demonstrated, the increasing application of techniques used to decipher actual ominous phenomena to the exegesis of their "written counterpart" in scriptural texts.[137] I believe the significance of Barton's work (notwithstanding his misperception of ancient prophecy) lies in his elucidation of the increasing tendency to exegete scriptures as signs in the late Second Temple period, as Davies emphasized in his response to the republication of *Oracles of God*.[138]

In the Hebrew Bible, the prophet Jeremiah says: "The prophets who preceded you and me from ancient times prophesied war, famine, and pestilence against many countries and great kingdoms" (Jer 28:8). While it is beyond the scope of this essay, in my judgment biblical texts narrating prophetic signs other than Jeremiah 19 may contain a core of authentic historical material.[139] Although in most instances we are probably restricted to the *ipsissimus sensus* (authentic sense) of the prophecy, my comparison suggests that in the case of some pun-texts it is even possible that *ipsissima verba* (authentic words) may have been preserved. Perhaps we may yet conclude (with apologies to Mark Twain) that reports of the death of the (historical) prophet are an exaggeration?

Bibliography

Asurmendi, Jésus. "Les textes … et la Bible." Pages 75–78 in Jésus Asurmendi, et al., *Prophéties et oracles 1: Dans les Proche-Orient ancien*. SCaE 88. Paris: Cerf, 1994.

Barstad, Hans M., and Reinhard G. Kratz, eds. *Prophecy in the Book of Jeremiah*. BZAW 388. Berlin: de Gruyter, 2009.

---

[136] Samuel I. Thomas, *The "Mysteries" of Qumran: Mystery, Secrecy, and Esotericism in the Dead Sea Scrolls*, EJL 25 (Atlanta: Society of Biblical Literature, 2009), 193.

[137] Jeffrey H. Tigay, "An Early Technique of Aggadic Exegesis," in *History, Historiography and Interpretation: Studies in Biblical and Cuneiform Literatures*, ed. H. Tadmor and M. Weinfeld (Leiden: Brill; Jerusalem: Magnes, 1983), 172–76 (quotation 172).

[138] Philip R. Davies, "Beginning at the End," in Ben Zvi, "Rereading," 10.

[139] I cite as one example Matthijs de Jong's study in which he concludes that Isaiah 20:1–5 "probably is an early report that reflects a symbolic act performed by the prophet … The prophet Isaiah may well have actually performed such an act around 712–711 BCE, in order to warn the Judeans against trusting Egypt for assistance against Assyria" (*Isaiah among the Ancient Near Eastern Prophets: A Comparative Study of the Earliest Stages of the Isaiah Tradition and the Neo-Assyrian Prophecies*, VTSup 117 [Leiden: Brill, 2007], 153).

Barthes, Roland. "The Death of the Author." Pages 142–48 in *Image-Music-Text*. Edited and translated by Stephen Heath. New York: Hill & Wang, 1977.

Barton, John. *Oracles of God: Perceptions of Ancient Prophecy in Israel after the Exile*. London: Darton, Longman & Todd, 1986. Oxford: Oxford University Press 1988.

Barton, John. "*Oracles of God* Revisited." Pages 29–33 in Ben Zvi, "Rereading."

Ben-Dov, Jonathan. "Writing as Oracle and as Law: New Contexts for the Book-Find of King Josiah." *JBL* 127 (2008): 223–39.

Ben Zvi, Ehud, ed. "Rereading *Oracles of God*: Twenty Years after John Barton, *Oracles of God: Perceptions of Prophecy in Israel after the Exile*." *JHebS* 7/14 (2007). doi:10.5508/jhs2007.v7.a14.

Ben Zvi, Ehud, and Diana V. Edelman, eds. *The Production of Prophecy: Constructing Prophecy and Prophets in Yehud*. BW. London: Equinox, 2009.

Ben Zvi, Ehud, and Michael H. Floyd, eds. *Writings and Speech in Israelite and Ancient Near Eastern Prophecy*. SBLSymS 10. Atlanta: Society of Biblical Literature, 2000.

Bodi, Daniel. *Israël et Juda: À l'ombre des Babyloniens et des Perses*. ÉAHA 2. Paris: de Boccard, 2010.

Bodi, Daniel. "The Retribution Principle in the Amorite View of History: Yasmaḫ-Addu's Letter to Nergal (ARM I 3) and Adad's Message to Zimrī-Līm (A. 1968)." *ARAM* 26.1/2 (2014): 285–300.

Bottéro, Jean. "Symptômes, signes, écritures en Mesopotamie ancienne." Pages 70–197 in Jean-Pierre Vernant, et al., *Divination et rationalité*. Recherches anthropologiques. Paris: du Seuil, 1974.

Botterweck, G. Johannes, Helmer Ringgren, and Heinz-Josef Fabry, eds. *Theological Dictionary of the Old Testament*. Translated by John T. Willis, et al. 17 vols. Grand Rapids: Eerdmans, 1974–2021.

Brettler, Marc Zvi. "Method in the Application of Biblical Source Material to Historical Writing (with Particular Reference to the Ninth Century BCE)." Pages 305–36 in Williamson, *Understanding*.

Brown, Michael L. *Israel's Divine Healer*. SOTBT. Carlisle: Paternoster, 1995.

Charpin, Dominique. "L'*andurârum* à Mari." *MARI* 6 (1990): 253–70.

Charpin, Dominique. "Prophètes et rois dans le Proche-Orient amorrite." Pages 21–53 in *Prophètes et rois: Bible et Proche-Orient*. Edited by André Lemaire. LD. Paris: Cerf, 2001.

Charpin, Dominique. "Prophetism in the Near East according to the Mari Archives." Pages 11–58 in *Gods, Kings, and Merchants in Old Babylonian Mesopotamia*. PIPOCF 2. Leuven: Peeters, 2015.

Charpin, Dominique. *'Tu es de mon sang': Les alliances dans le Proche-Orient ancien*. DO 4. Paris: Les Belles Lettres, 2019. doi:10.4000/books.lesbelleslettres.258.

Chavalas, Mark W. "Assyriology and Biblical Studies: A Century and a Half of Tension." Pages 21–67 in *Mesopotamia and the Bible: Comparative Explorations*. Edited by Mark W. Chavalas and K. Lawson Younger Jr. Grand Rapids: Baker Academic, 2002.

Davies, Philip R. "Beginning at the End." Pages 6–11 in Ben Zvi, "Rereading."

De Zorzi, Nicla. "The Omen Series *Šumma izbu*: Internal Structure and Hermeneutic Strategies." *KASKAL* 8 (2011): 43–75.

Durand, Jean-Marie. *Archives épistolaires de Mari I/1*. ARM 26/1. Paris: Éditions Recherche sur les Civilisations, 1988.

Durand, Jean-Marie. "'Un habit pour un oracle!' À propos d'une prophétie de Mari." Pages 231–35 in *Muhibbe Darga Armağanı*. Edited by Taner Tarhan, Aksel Tibet, and Erkan Konyar. Istanbul: Sadberk Hanim Müzesi, 2008.

Fishbane, Michael. *Biblical Interpretation in Ancient Israel.* Oxford: Clarendon, 1985.
Floyd, Michael H., and Robert D. Haak, eds. *Prophets, Prophecy, and Prophetic Texts in Second Temple Judaism.* LHBOTS 427. London: T&T Clark, 2006.
Friebel, Kelvin G. *Jeremiah's and Ezekiel's Sign-Acts: Rhetorical Nonverbal Communication.* JSOTSup 283. Sheffield: Sheffield Academic, 1999.
Gibson, Jeffrey. "Jesus' Refusal to Produce a 'Sign' (Mark 8.11–13)." Pages 271–99 in *The Historical Jesus: A Sheffield Reader.* Edited by Craig A. Evans and Stanley E. Porter. BibSem 33. Sheffield: Sheffield Academic, 1995.
Gitay, Yehoshua, ed. *Prophecy and Prophets: The Diversity of Issues in Contemporary Scholarship.* SemeiaSt. Atlanta: Scholars Press, 1997.
Glassner, Jean-Jacques. "La fabrique des presages en Mésopotamie: la sémiologie des devins." Pages 29–53 in *La raison des signes: Présages, rites, destin dans les sociétés de la Méditerranée ancienne.* Edited by Stella Georgoudi, Renée Koch Piettre, and Francis Schmidt. RGRW 174. Leiden: Brill, 2012.
Gordon, Robert P. "From Mari to Moses: Prophecy at Mari and in Ancient Israel." Pages 63–79 in *Of Prophet's Visions and the Wisdom of Sages: Essays in Honour of R. Norman Whybray on His Seventieth Birthday.* Edited by Heather A. McKay and David J.A. Clines. JSOTSup 162. Sheffield: JSOT Press, 1993.
Gordon, Robert P. "Prophecy in the Mari and Nineveh Archives." Pages 37–57 in *"Thus Speaks Ishtar of Arbela": Prophecy in Israel, Assyria, and Egypt in the Neo-Assyrian Period.* Edited by Robert P. Gordon and Hans M. Barstad. Winona Lake, IN: Eisenbrauns, 2013.
Gordon, Robert P. "Standing in the Council: When Prophets Encounter God." Pages 190–204 in *The God of Israel.* Edited by Robert P. Gordon. UCOP 64. Cambridge: Cambridge University Press, 2007.
Gordon, Robert P. "'We Do Not See Our Signs' (Psalm 74:9): Signs, Prophets, Oracles, and the Asaphite Psalter." Pages 90–103 in *New Perspectives on Old Testament Prophecy and History: Essays in Honour of Hans M. Barstad.* Edited by Rannfrid I. Thelle, Terje Stordalen, and Mervyn E. J. Richardson. VTSup 168. Leiden: Brill, 2015.
Gordon, Robert P. "Where Have All the Prophets Gone? The Disappearing Israelite Prophet against the Background of Ancient Near Eastern Prophecy." *BBR* 5 (1995): 67–86.
Grabbe, Lester L. *Priests, Prophets, Diviners, Sages: A Socio-Historical Study of Religious Specialists in Ancient Israel.* Valley Forge, PA: Trinity Press International, 1995.
Grabbe, Lester L., and Martti Nissinen, eds. *Constructs of Prophecy in the Former and Latter Prophets and Other Texts.* ANEM 4. Atlanta: Society of Biblical Literature, 2011.
Greaves, Sheldon W. "Ominous Homophony and Portentous Puns in Akkadian Omens." Pages 103–13 in Noegel, *Puns.*
Guichard, Michaël. "L'apparition d'un prophète anonyme dans un poème épique paléo-babylonien." Pages 35–49 in *Comment devient-on prophète? Actes du colloque organisé par le Collège de France, Paris, les 4–5 avril 2011.* Edited by Jean-Marie Durand, Thomas Römer, and Micaël Bürki. OBO 265. Fribourg: Academic Press; Göttingen: Vandenhoeck & Ruprecht, 2014.
Guichard, Michaël. "Les aspects religieux de la guerre à Mari." *RA* 93 (1999): 27–48.
Hallo, William W. "Compare and Contrast: The Contextual Approach to Biblical Literature." Pages 1–30 in *The Bible in the Light of Cuneiform Literature: Scripture in Context III.* Edited by William W. Hallo, Bruce William Jones, and Gerald L. Mattingly. ANETS 8. Lewiston, NY: Mellen, 1990.
Han, Jin H. "Did the Deuteronomist Detest Dreams?" Within this volume.

Harvey, Julien. *Le plaidoyer prophétique contre Israël après la rupture de l'alliance: Étude d'une formule littéraire de l'Ancien Testament.* Studia 22. Bruges: de Brouwer; Montreal: Bellarmin, 1967.

Heimpel, Wolfgang. *Letters to the King of Mari: A New Translation, with Introduction, Notes, and Commentary.* MC 12. Winona Lake, IN: Eisenbrauns, 2003.

Heintz, Jean-Georges. "La 'fin' des prophètes bibliques? Nouvelles theories et documents sémetiques anciens." Pages 195–214 in *Oracles et Prophéties dans l'antiquités: Actes du colloque de Strasbourg 15–17 juin 1995.* Edited by Jean-Georges Heintz. CRPOGA 15. Paris: de Boccard, 1997.

Hillers, Delbert R. *Treaty-Curses and the Old Testament Prophets.* BibOr 16. Rome: Pontifical Biblical Institute, 1964.

Huffmon, Herbert B. "The Expansion of Prophecy in the Mari Archives: New Texts, New Readings, New Information." Pages 7–22 in Gitay, *Prophecy*.

Hurowitz, Victor Avigdor. "Alliterative Allusions, Rebus Writing, and Paronomastic Punishment: Some Aspects of Word Play in Akkadian Literature." Pages 63–87 in Noegel, *Puns*.

Jenni, Ernst, and Claus Westermann, eds. *Theological Lexicon of the Old Testament.* Translated by Mark Biddle. 3 vols. Peabody, MA: Hendrickson, 1997.

Jong, Matthijs de. *Isaiah among the Ancient Near Eastern Prophets: A Comparative Study of the Earliest Stages of the Isaiah Tradition and the Neo-Assyrian Prophecies.* VTSup 117. Leiden: Brill, 2007.

Kelle, Brad E. "The Phenomenon of Israelite Prophecy in Contemporary Scholarship." *CurBR* 12 (2014): 275–320.

Kelly, William L. *How Prophecy Works: A Study of the Semantic Field of* נבאי *and a Close Reading of Jeremiah 1:4–19, 23:9–40 and 27:1–28:17.* FRLANT 272. Göttingen: Vandenhoeck & Ruprecht, 2020.

Kline, Jonathan G. *Allusive Soundplay in the Hebrew Bible.* AIL 28. Atlanta: Society of Biblical Literature, 2016.

Koch, Ulla Susanne. *Mesopotamian Divination Texts: Conversing with the Gods: Sources from the First Millennium* BCE. GMTR 7. Münster: Ugarit-Verlag, 2015.

Laato, Antti. *History and Ideology in the Old Testament Prophetic Literature: A Semiotic Approach to the Reconstruction of the Proclamation of the Historical Prophets.* ConBOT 41. Stockholm: Almqvist & Wiksell, 1996.

Lawson, Jack Newton. *The Concept of Fate in Ancient Mesopotamia of the First Millennium: Toward an Understanding of* Šīmtu. OBC 7. Wiesbaden: Harrassowitz, 1994.

Lemaire, André. "Les textes prophétiques de Mari dans leurs relations avec l'ouest." Pages 427–38 in *Amurru 1: Mari, Ébla et les Hourrites – premiere partie*: *Actes du colloque international (Paris, mai 1993).* Edited by Jean-Marie Durand. Paris: Éditions Recherche sur les Civilisations, 1996.

Leuchter, Mark. "Jeremiah: Structure, Themes, and Contested Issues." Pages 171–89 in *The Oxford Handbook of the Prophets.* Edited by Carolyn J. Sharp. Oxford: Oxford University Press, 2016.

Leuchter, Mark. "The Pen of Scribes: Writing, Textuality, and the Book of Jeremiah." Pages 3–25 in Lundbom, Evans, and Anderson, *Jeremiah*.

Lundbom, Jack R., Craig A. Evans, and Bradford A. Anderson, eds. *The Book of Jeremiah: Composition, Reception, and Interpretation.* VTSup 178. FIOTL 8. Leiden: Brill, 2018.

Machinist, Peter. "The Road Not Taken: Wellhausen and Assyriology." Pages 469–531 in *Homeland and Exile: Biblical and Ancient Near Eastern Studies in Honour of Bustenay*

Oded. Edited by Gershon Galil, Mark Geller, and Alan Millard. VTSup 130. Leiden: Brill, 2009.

Malamat, Abraham. *Mari and the Bible.* SHCANE 12. Leiden: Brill, 1998.

Malamat, Abraham. *Mari and the Early Israelite Experience.* Oxford: Oxford University Press, 1989.

Manetti, Giovanni. *Theories of the Sign in Classical Antiquity.* Translated by Christine Richardson. AdSem. Bloomington: Indiana University Press, 1993.

Matthews, Victor H. "Entrance Ways and Threshing Floors: Legally Significant Sites in the Ancient Near East." *FiHi* 19 (1987): 25–40.

Matthews, Victor H., and Don C. Benjamin. *Social World of Ancient Israel, 1250–587 BCE.* Peabody, MA: Hendrickson, 1993.

Maul, Stefan M. *The Art of Divination in the Ancient Near East: Reading the Signs of Heaven and Earth.* Translated by Brian McNeil and Alexander Johannes Edmonds. Waco, TX: Baylor University Press, 2018.

Maul, Stefan M. "How the Babylonians Protected Themselves against Calamities Announced by Omens." Pages 123–29 in *Mesopotamian Magic: Textual, Historical, and Interpretative Perspectives.* Edited by Tzvi Abusch and Karel van der Toorn. AMD 1. Groningen: Styx, 1999.

May, Natalie N. "Gates and their Functions in Mesopotamia and Ancient Israel." Pages 77–121 in *The Fabric of Cities: Aspects of Urbanism, Urban Topography and Society in Mesopotamia, Greece and Rome.* Edited by Natalie N. May and Ulrike Steinert. CHANE 68. Leiden: Brill, 2014.

Mead, James K. "The Biblical Prophets in Historiography." Pages 263–85 in *Ancient Israel's History: An Introduction to Issues and Sources.* Edited by Bill T. Arnold and Richard S. Hess. Grand Rapids: Baker Academic, 2014.

Millard, Alan. "La prophétie et l'écriture: Israël, Aram, Assyrie." *RHR* 202 (1985): 125–44.

Morris, Gerald. *Prophecy, Poetry and Hosea.* JSOTSup 21. Sheffield: Sheffield Academic, 1996.

Mullen, E. Theodore, Jr. *The Divine Council in Canaanite and Early Hebrew Literature.* HSM 24. Chico, CA: Scholars Press, 1980.

Najman, Hindy, and Konrad Schmid, eds. *Jeremiah's Scriptures: Production, Reception, Interaction, and Transformation.* JSJSup 173. Leiden: Brill, 2016.

Nelson, Richard D. "Priestly Purity and Prophetic Lunacy: Hosea 1.2–3 and 9.7." Pages 115–33 in *The Priests in the Prophets: The Portrayal of Priests, Prophets and Other Religious Specialists in the Latter Prophets.* Edited by Lester L. Grabbe and Alice Ogden Bellis. JSOTSup 408. London: T&T Clark, 2004.

Niditch, Susan. *The Symbolic Vision in Biblical Tradition.* HSM 30. Chico, CA: Scholars Press, 1983.

Nissinen, Martti. *Ancient Prophecy: Near Eastern, Biblical, and Greek Perspectives.* Oxford: Oxford University Press, 2017.

Nissinen, Martti. "Biblical Prophecy from a Near Eastern Perspective: The Cases of Kingship and Divine Possession." Pages 351–76 in Nissinen, *Prophetic Divination.*

Nissinen, Martti. "Das kritische Potential in der altorientalischen Prophetie." Pages 163–94 in Nissinen, *Prophetic Divination.*

Nissinen, Martti. "Prophecy and Omen Divination: Two Sides of the Same Coin." Pages 75–85 in Nissinen, *Prophetic Divination.*

Nissinen, Martti. *Prophetic Divination: Essays in Ancient Near Eastern Prophecy.* BZAW 494. Berlin: de Gruyter, 2019.

Nissinen, Martti. "Prophets and the Divine Council." Pages 461–77 in Nissinen, *Prophetic Divination.*

Nissinen, Martti. *References to Prophecy in Neo-Assyrian Sources.* SAAS 7. Helsinki: Neo-Assyrian Text Corpus Project, 1998.

Nissinen, Martti. "Spoken, Written, Quoted, and Invented: Orality and Writtenness in Ancient Near Eastern Prophecy." Pages 235–71 in Ben Zvi and Floyd, *Writings.*

Nissinen, Martti. "What is Prophecy? An Ancient Near Eastern Perspective." Pages 53–73 in Nissinen, *Prophetic Divination.*

Nissinen, Martti, with contributions by C. L. Seow, Robert K. Ritner, and H. Craig Melchert. *Prophets and Prophecy in the Ancient Near East.* 2nd ed. WAW 41. Atlanta: Society of Biblical Literature, 2019.

Noegel, Scott B. *Nocturnal Ciphers: The Allusive Language of Dreams in the Ancient Near East.* AOS 89. New Haven: American Oriental Society, 2007.

Noegel, Scott B. *"Wordplay" in Ancient Near Eastern Texts.* ANEM 26. Atlanta: Society of Biblical Literature, 2021.

Noegel, Scott B., ed. *Puns and Pundits: Word Play in the Hebrew Bible and Ancient Near Eastern Literature.* Bethesda, MD: CDL, 2000.

Oppenheim, A. Leo, Erica Reiner, and Martha T. Roth, eds. *The Assyrian Dictionary of the Oriental Institute of the University of Chicago.* 26 vols. Chicago: Oriental Institute of the University of Chicago, 1956–2010.

Parker, Simon B. "Official Attitudes toward Prophecy at Mari and in Israel." *VT* 43 (1993): 50–68.

Parker, Simon B. "The Ancient Near Eastern Literary Background to the Old Testament." Pages 228–43 in *General and Old Testament Articles, Genesis, Exodus, and Leviticus.* Edited by Leander E. Keck. Vol. 1 of *The New Interpreter's Bible.* Nashville: Abingdon, 1994.

Parpola, Simo. *Assyrian Prophecies.* SAA 9. Helsinki: Neo-Assyrian Text Corpus Project, 1997.

Petersen, David L. "Rethinking the Nature of Prophetic Literature." Pages 23–40 in Gitay, *Prophecy.*

Ratner, Robert, and Bruce Zuckerman. "'A Kid in Milk'? New Photographs of KTU 1.23, Line 14." *HUCA* 57 (1986): 15–60.

Rendtorff, Rolf. "The Image of Postexilic Israel in German Bible Scholarship from Wellhausen to von Rad." Pages 165–73 in *Shaʿarei Talmon: Studies in the Bible, Qumran, and the Ancient Near East Presented to Shemaryahu Talmon.* Edited by Michael Fishbane and Emanuel Tov. Winona Lake, IN: Eisenbrauns, 1992.

Roberts, J. J. M. "Of Signs, Prophets, and Time Limits: A Note on Psalm 74:9." *CBQ* 39 (1977): 474–81.

Roberts, J. J. M. "The Mari Prophetic Texts in Transliteration and Translation." Pages 157–253 in *The Bible and the Ancient Near East: Collected Essays.* Winona Lake, IN: Eisenbrauns, 2002.

Rogerson, J. W. "Setting the Scene: A Brief Outline of Histories of Israel." Pages 3–14 in Williamson, *Understanding.*

Rom-Shiloni, Dalit. "The Forest and the Trees: The Place of Pentateuchal Materials in Prophecy as of the Late Seventh/Early Sixth Centuries BCE." Pages 56–92 in *Congress Volume Stellenbosch 2016.* Edited by Louis C. Jonker, Gideon R. Kotzé, and Christl M. Maier. Leiden: Brill, 2017.

Rutten, Maggie. "Trente-deux modèles de fois en argile inscrits provenant de Tell-Hariri (Mari)." *RA* 35 (1938): 36–52.
Sandmel, Samuel. "Parallelomania." *JBL* 81 (1962): 1–13.
Sasson, Jack M. "About 'Mari and the Bible'." *RA* 92 (1998): 97–123.
Sasson, Jack M. *From the Mari Archives: An Anthology of Old Babylonian Letters.* Winona Lake, IN: Eisenbrauns, 2015.
Sasson, Jack M. "The Posting of Letters with Divine Messages." Pages 299–316 in *Florilegium marianum II: Recueil d'études à la mémoire de Maurice Birot.* Edited by Dominique Charpin and Jean-Marie Durand. NABUM 3. Paris: Société pour l'étude du Proche-Orient ancien, 1994.
Sasson, Jack M. "Water beneath Straw: The Adventures of a Prophetic Phrase in the Mari Archives." Pages 599–608 in *Untying Knots: Biblical, Epigraphic, and Semitic Studies in Honor of Jonas C. Greenfield.* Edited by Ziony Zevit, Seymour Gitlin, and Michael Sokoloff. Winona Lake, IN: Eisenbrauns, 1995.
Schaper, Joachim. "The Death of the Prophet: The Transition from the Spoken to the Written Word of God in the Book of Ezekiel." Pages 63–79 in Floyd and Haak, *Prophets.*
Schniedewind, William M. *The Word of God in Transition: From Prophet to Exegete in the Second Temple Period.* JSOTSup 197. Sheffield: Sheffield Academic, 1995.
Schorch, Stefan. "Between Science and Magic: The Function and Roots of Paronomasia in the Prophetic Books of the Hebrew Bible." Pages 205–22 in Noegel, *Puns.*
Sherwood, Yvonne M. "Prophetic Scatology: Prophecy and the Art of Sensation." *Semeia* 82 (1998): 183–224.
Stern, Philip D. *The Biblical HEREM: A Window on Israel's Religious Experience.* BJS 211. Atlanta: Scholars Press, 1991.
Stökl, Jonathan. *Prophecy in the Ancient Near East: A Philological and Sociological Comparison.* CHANE 56. Leiden: Brill, 2012.
Thomas, Samuel I. *The "Mysteries" of Qumran: Mystery, Secrecy, and Esotericism in the Dead Sea Scrolls.* EJL 25. Atlanta: Society of Biblical Literature, 2009.
Tigay, Jeffrey H. "An Early Technique of Aggadic Exegesis." Pages 169–90 in *History, Historiography and Interpretation: Studies in Biblical and Cuneiform Literatures.* Edited by H. Tadmor and M. Weinfeld. Leiden: Brill; Jerusalem: Magnes, 1983.
Twelftree, Graham H. *Jesus the Exorcist: A Contribution to the Study of the Historical Jesus.* Peabody, MA: Hendrickson, 1993.
Weinfeld, Moshe. *Deuteronomy and the Deuteronomic School.* Oxford: Clarendon, 1972. Repr., Winona Lake, IN: Eisenbrauns, 1992.
Weinfeld, Moshe. *Social Justice in Ancient Israel and in Ancient Near East.* Jerusalem: Magnes; Minneapolis: Fortress, 1995.
Wellhausen, Julius. *Prolegomena to the History of Israel: With a Reprint of the Article Israel from the Encyclopaedia Britannica.* Translated by J. Sutherland Black and A. Menzies. Atlanta: Scholars Press, 1994.
Williamson, H. G. M., ed. *Understanding the History of Ancient Israel.* PBA 143. Oxford: Oxford University Press, 2007.
Winitzer, Abraham. "The Divine Presence and Interpretation in Early Mesopotamian Divination." Pages 177–97 in *Divination and Interpretation of Signs in the Ancient World.* Edited by Amar Annus. OIS 6. Chicago: Oriental Institute of the University of Chicago, 2010.
Wright, David P. "Analogy in Biblical and Hittite Ritual." Pages 473–506 in *Religionsgeschichteliche Beziehungen zwischen Kleinasien, Nordsyrien und dem Alten Testament:*

Internationales Symposion Hamburg 17.–21. März 1990. Edited by Bernd Janowski, Klaus Koch, and Gernot Wilhelm. OBO 129. Freiburg: Universitätsverlag Freiburg; Göttingen: Vandenhoeck & Ruprecht, 1993.

Wright, David P. "Ritual Analogy in Psalm 109." *JBL* 113 (1994): 385–404.

Ziemer, Benjamin. "Radical Versus Conservative? How Scribes Conventionally Used Books While Writing Books." Within this volume.

Scribal Intertexts in the Book of Job: Foreign Counterparts of Job

JiSeong James Kwon

1. Introduction

The intellectual background of the book of Job has been investigated through a variety of methodologies by Assyriologists and Egyptologists who have suggested similarities to non-Israelite sources and their literary traditions.[1] This is because the book of Job, which consists of a prose-tale and a dialogue, is substantially divergent from the instruction and admonition genre found in Proverbs and from the Hellenistic sceptical theme and biographical genre of Ecclesiastes. Furthermore, the author of Job does not engage any events of Israel's narratives, but begins its story in a foreign land, Uz. Literary elements such as the motif of the innocent sufferer, the framing narrative, the form of dialogue, and the theme of theodicy have been compared to Egyptian, Sumerian-Babylonian, and Ugaritic texts.[2] Many scholars have insisted that the origins of the book of Job should be located outside the literary tradition represented by the Hebrew Bible. However, although ancient Near Eastern counterparts have been suggested as source texts of the book of Job and provide helpful insights into its compositional process, my claim is that it is hardly possible to designate a literary tradition that inspired the formation of Job, and to locate the place of its composition. Thus, the question in this article is as follows: does the study of non-Israelite texts tell anything of the historical origin of the Book of Job? If the hypotheses proposed by scholars cannot reveal anything definite about Job's origin, how should one understand resemblances of Job with other non-Israelite sources? Instead, it should be understood that its scribes – educated literati[3] – were aware of a variety of non-Israelite texts, and recreated the well-known story of the sufferer in their scribal milieu.

---

[1] Robert Gordis, *The Book of God and Man: A Study of Job* (Chicago: University of Chicago Press, 1978), 53–64.

[2] Earlier research, see Morris Jastrow, *The Book of Job: Its Origin, Growth and Interpretation: Together with a New Translation Based on a Revised Text* (Philadelphia: J.B. Lippincott Company, 1920), 46–49; Norman H. Snaith, *The Book of Job: Its Origin and Purpose*, SBT 11 (London: SCM, 1968), 19–33; JiSeong James Kwon, *Scribal Culture and Intertextuality: Literary and Historical Relationships between Job and Deutero-Isaiah*, FAT II 85 (Tübingen: Mohr Siebeck, 2016), 152–64.

[3] "Scribes" should not be misunderstood as a sort of an independent professional group such as a prophetic group, a priestly group, or a sage group, but the term "scribe" should be seen as

This study attempts to trace foreign counterparts – Egyptian, Mesopotamian (Sumerian-Babylonian), Ugaritic, Edomic texts – that have strongly been claimed to be the origin of the book of Job. I maintain that Job's intellectual discourse is best understood by placing the book in the scribal milieu[4] that contains diversity in genres and forms, rather than the direct literary adoption of foreign literature. After examining many theories concerning the origin of Job, I will present how we might understand the intertexts and multivocality of Job in ancient Near Eastern contexts, and describe how scribal ideas evolve.

2. Egyptian Origin

The possible Egyptian origin of the book of Job has not received much scholarly attention. Not much notice has been paid to Egyptian texts about an innocent sufferer, although some studies reference the Egyptian influence on Yahweh's speech of Job 38–41.[5]

2.1 Middle Egyptian Literature

Firstly, there are some noteworthy Middle Egyptian materials whose literary structure and highly cultural theme, such as theodicy,[6] are close to those of Job.[7]

---

the social circle of the Israelite or Jewish literate elite, so that scribes may compose any types of literary genres including prophetic, history, wisdom, and eschatological texts. I discussed this issue elsewhere in detail; see Kwon, *Scribal Culture*, 122–23, in which I argue that "a scribe" as an author in the Hebrew Bible "refers to all the skillful literate who could read and write texts, whether they were educated in the temple, at school, or in the home and whether later on they had jobs in public institutions, private businesses, or were unemployed. All the biblical writings could be composed and conducted by these scribes, the literati." I "understand the term סֹפֵר as the 'literate person', who regarded themselves as members of a class, including but not confined to vocational specialists who were in the temple/royal service."

[4] The extent of the scribal discourse and intertexts that I am arguing here is not limited only to written or oral texts but includes floating texts around cultural memory and knowledge.

[5] Paul Humbert, *Recherches Sur les Sources égyptiennes de la littérature Sapientiale d'Israël*, MUN 7 (Neuchâtel: Secrétde l'Univ, 1929), 75–106; Snaith, *Job*, 19–20. Georg Fohrer, *Das Buch Hiob*, KAT 16 (Gütersloh: Mohn, 1963), 46; Marvin H. Pope, *Job*, AB 15 (New York: Doubleday, 1965), LI–LIII; Edouard Dhorme, *A Commentary on the Book of Job*, trans. Harold Knight (London: Nelson, 1967), clxxi; Gordis, *Man*, 212; Ludger Schwienhorst-Schönberger, "Das Buch Ijob," in *Stuttgarter Altes Testament: Einheitsübersetzung mit Kommentar und Lexikon*, ed. Erich Zenger (Stuttgart: Katholisches Bibelwerk, 2004), 335–47; John Gray, *The Book of Job*, ed. David J.A. Clines (Sheffield: Sheffield Phoenix, 2010), 7, 55.

[6] Richard B. Parkinson, *Poetry and Culture in Middle Kingdom Egypt: A Dark Side to Perfection* (Oakville: Equinox, 2010), 129–30.

[7] Kwon, *Scribal Culture*, 159–63.

2.1.1 Dialogue of a Man and His Ba (Soul)

The first composition is "The Man Who Was Tired of Life" or "The Dialogue of a Man and His Ba (Soul)" (abbr., *A Man and His Ba*; Papyrus Berlin 3024)[8] from the 12th Dynasty which presents the dialogical debate between a tired suffering man and his *ba*.[9] Three symmetrical speeches between a man and his *ba*, including four poems in the fourth speech of the man, are similar to the dialogical poetry of Job in three cycles. Both dialogues present two opposing disputations on the value of life and the prospect of death.[10]

When this man is thoroughly isolated from his society (86–129) and his "death" stands before him (130–42), he wishes to be released from his earthly life. The sceptical view of life, the distrust in the community, and the longing for death are like elements found in Job's speeches (Job 3; 19:13–20). His *ba*, however, dissuades him from reaching into Sheol but threatens to abandon him if he persists in his sceptical view on life (147–54).

> … and cling to life by the means you describe! Yet love me here, having put aside West, and also still desire to reach the West, your body making landfall! I shall alight when you are weary; so shall we make harbour together! (150–53)

The tired man's positive view on death contrasts with the negative view of his *ba*, but as Parkinson observes, "the conflict is suspended not through the argument but performative 'perfect speech' before an audience."[11]

2.1.2 The Tale of the Eloquent Peasant

The second composition is "The Tale of the Eloquent Peasant" (abbr., *Eloquent Peasant*; Papyrus Berlin 3023, 3025, 10499; Papyrus Butler 527; British Museum 10274), probably dated to the 12th or 13th Dynasty,[12] although its setting would be in the 10th Dynasty.[13] This work is framed by narratives about the peasant Khunanup, and in its core contains nine petitions in terms of the personal com-

---

[8] For the English translation, see Richard B. Parkinson, *The Tale of Sinuhe and Other Ancient Egyptian Poems: 1940–1640 BC* (Oxford: Clarendon, 1997), 151–65. Also, see R. O. Faulkner, "The Man Who Was Tired of Life," *JEA* 42 (1956): 21–40; Miriam Lichtheim, ed., *The Old and Middle Kingdoms*, vol. 1 of *Ancient Egyptian Literature* (Berkeley: University of California Press, 1973), 163–69; "The Dispute between a Man and His Ba," trans. Nili Shupak (*COS* 3.146:321–26).

[9] James P. Allen, *The Debate between a Man and His Soul: A Masterpiece of Ancient Egyptian Literature*, CHANE 44 (Leiden: Brill, 2010), comments that *ba* symbolises "an entity immanent in the individual during life and then surviving in non-physical form after death or a mode of existence associated with the afterlife" is unclear (*Debate*, 6).

[10] "A Man and His *Ba*," *COS* 3.146:321 supposes that the narrative part was lost in Berlin 3024.

[11] Parkinson, *Poetry and Culture*, 226.

[12] I use the English translation from Parkinson, *Sinuhe*, 54–88. See also "The Eloquent Peasant," trans. Nili Shupak (*COS* 1.43:98–104); Lichtheim, *Kingdoms*, 169–84.

[13] Richard B. Parkinson, *Voices from Ancient Egypt: An Anthology of Middle Kingdom Writings* (London: British Museum, 1991), 64.

plaint of the peasant – just as the book of Job consists of the combination of a tale and a poetic dialogue.[14] Peasant's persistent appeals for social justice are unanswered and rejected by Rensi the High steward, son of Meru:

And this peasant said. 'You beat me, you steal my belongings? And then you'll rob my mouth of complaint? O Lord of Silence, may You give me back my belongings, so I shan't cry out to Your fearsomeness!' (BI 59–62)

Just as the dialogue of Job adopts many of the forms of psalms, the peasant offers a eulogy for his Maat.[15] Although his god Maat does not engage in the violent oppression, the peasant identifies the official as the divine representative and accuses the deity of crooked justice:

Your surroundings are awry, you who should be right!" (BI 293)

The delayed decision by Rensi and the king Nebkaure for Nemtinakht the oppressor, and the injustice of the innocent sufferer at a personal and a social level, aggravates the peasant's agony. Finally, the affliction of the peasant is apparently resolved by the order of the king, but the issue of theodicy is not seriously dealt with at the end of the narrative. In many ways, the themes and the structure of Job are similar to those of *Eloquent Peasant*. Firstly, both Job and *Eloquent Peasant* indicate a dichotomy between the objective reality and the subjective rhetoric of sufferers.[16] Secondly, in discourses of theodicy, both innocent persons continue to experience the absence of God (in Job) or "a creator of Truth" (in *Eloquent Peasant*) in series of poems, though they call to their deities for justice. Thirdly, instead of resolving the peasant's and Job's pleas, both *Eloquent Peasant* and Job are swiftly converted into the simple ending of narrative.

2.1.3 The Dialogue of Ipuur and the Lord of All

Job seems to be related to two Egyptian texts (*Ipuur*, *Neferti*) which may have the same historical setting and are frequently classified as prophecy, although they are unlikely to be prophetic texts equated to the category of biblical prophecy. The third intertext with Job[17] is the composition of "The Dialogue of Ipuur and

---

[14] Richard B. Parkinson, "Literary Form and the Tale of the Eloquent Peasant," *JEA* 78.1 (2017): 164 mentions that as "with the book of Job, the juxtaposition of the two modes of narrative and discourse in the Tale has been taken as evidence that the extant text was a redaction of at least two sources".

[15] Parkinson, *Poetry and Culture*, 169.

[16] Parkinson, *Sinuhe*, 55 maintains that in the Tale "there is a continuous dichotomy between the actual audience's awareness of the situation (shared with the fictional audience of the High Steward) and the peasant's awareness" and "between the rhetoric of his appeals and the simplicity of the narrative".

[17] Annette Schellenberg, "Hiob und Ipuwer: Zum Vergleich des alttestamentlichen Hiobbuchs mit ägyptischen Texten im Allgemeinen und den Admonitions im Besonderen," in *Das Buch Hiob und seine Interpretationen: Beiträge zum Hiob-Symposium auf dem Monte Verità vom 14.–19. August 2005*, ATANT 88 (Zürich: TVZ, 2007), 79 points out that (1) "sowohl im Hiob-

the Lord of All" (abbr., *Ipuur*) which is dated to the early 13th Dynasty, but whose fragment (Leiden 344) is dated to the 19th Dynasty.[18] The sage Ipuur in front of the royal court witnesses the state of national chaos and social subversion, just as his ancestors foretold. He complains of the turmoil of all the social classes, and laments the catastrophe of the suffering city (1.10–6.14). While observing the savage nature of humans – "O, but the river is blood, and they still drink from it; they push people aside, and still thirst for water" (2.10) – the sage doubts the efficacy of religious offerings (5.7–9).[19] However, different from the book of Job, Ipuur emphasises the observance of cultic actions in the temple (10.12–11.10).[20] After the two parts of structural "injunctions" – "Destroy …" and "Remember …" – Ipuur's complaint (12.1–13.9) concentrates on the innocent suffering due to the absence of divine intervention, and this leads him to reject the justice of the Sun-god (e.g., 11.11):

Look, why did He seek to shape (mankind), when the meek are not set apart from the savage so that He might have brought coolness upon the heat? (12.1)

No good can be found on the road – only conflict has come forth, and the driver-off of wrong is now its creator. There is no Pilot in their hour of duty – where is He today? So can He be sleeping? Look, no sign of His power can be seen. (12.5–6)

The aggressive accusation against the Sun-god, whose power is inactive and even generates evil (12.11–12; 13.1–2), is similar to Job's protest against his deity, who never appears in court and yet oppresses Job (Job 19:21; 23:8–9). After the series of poems, when Ipuur as a representative of Egyptians or humans asks the reasons of the national desolation, the interlocutor – who is probably "Lord of All," the creator God (Lord) – dialogues with Ipuur regarding of human suffering (14.10–17.1). One may discern similarities to Yahweh's speech, following human discourse, appearing in the form of a storm-god (Job 38–41). The Lord answers Ipuur that the responsibility for human disaster is attributed to inherited sinfulness of humans (14.14–15.1), but Ipuur contradicts the self-defence of the Lord, mentioning that the Lord turns away from the abandoned and innocent child (15.13–16.1; 16.1–5).[21] The final reply of the Lord reaffirms that human suffering as punishment is not caused by gods, but by human rebellion (16.10–17.1). Since the final ending of *Ipuur* is lost and the scribe left the space for approximately forty

---

buch als auch in den Admonitions wird die Welt als ein Chaos beschrieben und hier wie dort wird dieser Zustand in aller Schärfe Gott bzw. Dem Allherrn albst zur Last gelegt" and (2) "bei allen enttäuschten Erwartungen und einem Krisen-Bewusstsein scheint an dieser Theologie in den Admonitions auch nicht gerüttelt zu werdern".

[18] For the English translation, see Parkinson, *Sinuhe*, 166–99; Parkinson, *Voices*, 60; "The Admonitions of an Egyptian Sage: The Admonitions of Ipuwer," trans. Nili Shupak (*COS* 1.42:93–98); Lichtheim, *Kingdoms*, 149–63.

[19] Parkinson, *Poetry and Culture*, 206.
[20] Parkinson, *Poetry and Culture*, 207.
[21] Parkinson, *Poetry and Culture*, 212.

verses,[22] it is uncertain whether it ends with another dialogue speech of two disputants, or with an epilogue. It seems unlikely that the sage finally won over the aggressive denunciation of the Lord. In contrast, Yahweh in Job by no means answers Job's questions concerning innocent suffering, and Job does not directly rebut Yahweh's argument but renounces his persistent request of justice before the divine power (Job 42:2–6).

2.1.4 The Words of Neferti

The fourth composition is "The Words of Neferti" (abbr., *Neferti*) whose compositional setting is dated to the 12th Dynasty.[23] It describes the social chaos which gave rise to the expectation of the coming king Ameny (Amenemhet) in the Middle Kingdom. "The Dual King Sneferu" in the 4th Dynasty commands his courtiers to bring a wise man who is perfect in his behaviour, to provide entertainment. They summon Neferti, the great lector-priest and scribe, who is a wise man and can foretell future events. In reaction to Sneferu's request, Neferti tells the King to select either the past or future events. The King prefers to hear the future and then begins to write down what the sage foretells. Neferti's speeches (P 20–71), although Lichtheim and Shupak designate them as prophecy, should not be identified as such,[24] since his words represent past, present, and future events. He commands his heart to mourn in the face of the national disaster (P 20). Neferti then offers a dialogue with his heart ("Stir my heart", P 20), determining not to tell the King. Neferti as a sage predicts that "there will be no officials in the affairs of the land" (P 23), witnesses the political (P 20–24) and natural calamity in his time (P 25–29), and laments the overturn of social justice (P 54–56).

Distinct from the poetic dialogue of Job, Neferti specifies the historical background: the triumphant king upcoming from southern Egypt, King Amenemhet I in the 12th Dynasty (P 58–60), takes the double crowns that symbolise the two powers of "Upper and Lower Egypt respectively";[25] this is utilised as political propaganda in the Middle Kingdom. However, *Neferti* is broadly related to Job's ethos, in that it intertwines the social and political disorder with the gloomy future, without apparent explanation of the cause of the national disaster.

---

[22] Parkinson, *Sinuhe*, 169, 199 (n122).
[23] For English translation, see Parkinson, *Sinuhe*, 131–43; Lichtheim, *Kingdoms*, 139–45; Parkinson, *Voices*, 34–36; "The Prophecies of Neferti," trans. Nili Shupak (*COS* 1.45:106–10).
[24] Kwon, *Scribal Culture*, 172 mentions that "the Word of Neferti" "is neither a real prophetic form nor is it related to historical events known to us".
[25] Parkinson, *Sinuhe*, 142n25.

2.2 New and Later Kingdom

2.2.1 The Instruction of Ankhsheshonq

There are two more relevant cases in late Egyptian demotic literature. Firstly, "The Instruction of Ankhsheshonq" (abbr., *Ankhsheshonq*; BM 10508) was probably composed in the Ptolemaic period (323–30 BCE).[26] Its structure, similar to the Egyptian instruction genre, consists of a fictitious story followed by commands and proverbs of Ankhsheshonq, a priest of Re. When the priest visits his friend Harsiese the chief physician, he hears about the secret plot to assassinate the king. Though Ankhsheshonq did not align himself with the plan of Harsiese, Wahibre-makhy discloses the conspiracy to Pharaoh; after Harsiese and others actively involved were caught conspiring to rise in revolt, Ankhsheshonq is sent to prison. Then Ankhsheshonq composes his words for his son "on the sherds of jars," and the rest of the document consists of his self-reflective instructions. The basic theme in the proverbs of *Ankhsheshonq* is retaliation and punishment by the universal principle of cause-and-effect, even presenting "the Golden Rule" (12.6; 15.23) shared in the pool of international proverbs.[27] In the use of maxims, however, instructions of *Ankhsheshonq* frequently reflects the circumstance of the undeserved suffering of the priest:[28]

There is imprisonment for giving life.
There is release for killing.
There is he who saves and does not profit.
All are in the hand of the fate and the god. (26.5–8)

These instructions also tell that what will happen in human affairs under the capriciousness of the divinity – an arbitrariness quite like the unpredictability of the deity of Job:

Every hand is stretched out to the god (but) he accepts (only) the hand of his beloved. (23.14)

The plans of the god are one thing, the thoughts of [men] are another. (26.14)

---

[26] Janet H. Johnson, *Thus Wrote Onchsheshonqy: An Introductory Grammar of Demotic*, SAOC 45 (Chicago: Oriental Institute of the University of Chicago, 1991), 1. For the English translation, see Miriam Lichtheim, ed., *The Late Period*, vol. 3 of *Ancient Egyptian Literature* (Berkeley: University of California Press, 1980), 159–84; idem, *Late Egyptian Wisdom Literature in the International Context: A Study of Demotic Instructions*, OBO 52 (Freiburg: Universitätsverlag, 1983), 66–92.

[27] Lichtheim, *Late EWL*, 31–35. Also, they share common proverbs; e.g., in Ankhsh 17.12–13 and Job 14:19, though the implication is different. In Job, the force of water portrays the arbitrary power on the innocent, while in Ankhsheshonq there is no such basic meaning (Lichtheim, *Late EWL*, 36).

[28] Lichtheim, *Late EWL*, 40.

2.2.2 The Instruction of Papyrus Insinger

The second work of demotic literature in the late Ptolemaic period is "The Instruction of Papyrus Insinger" (abbr., *Insinger*)[29] that has been preserved at the Rijksmuseum in Leiden; the composition is earlier than 1st–2nd century AD. *Insinger* lacks the narrative before the instructions, instead consisting of organized, self-contained maxims and grouped sentences. The text is concerned with the character and morality of the wise and the fool (3.2–8), a concern shared with the morality of Hellenistic philosophy.[30] The work furthermore deals with the contingency of human sufferings in the divine order (20.13–17)[31] and with the paradox of the fate that humans cannot control (19.18–20).[32] Notions of human powerlessness in the act-consequence principle and of human fate and determinism that are presented in *Insinger* are common Hellenistic themes in Qoheleth and Sirach, though it is hard to prove that Ben Sira directly used *Insinger*.[33] According to Thomas Schneider, a notable example of the literary connection between Job and *Insinger* is Yahweh's first speech in Job 38, comparable to *Insinger* 24.[34]

3. Mesopotamian Origin

Mesopotamian (Sumerian-Babylonian) texts concerning suffering, theodicy, and pessimism are proposed as sources of the book of Job.[35]

3.1 Sumerian Man and His God

The Sumerian literary text "Sumerian Man and His God" is the earliest text exhibiting the motif of the undeserved sufferer that is frequently compared to

---

[29] For the translation, see Lichtheim, *Late Period*, 184–217; idem, *Late EWL*, 197–234.
[30] Lichtheim, *Late EWL*, 118–22.
[31] Lichtheim, *Late EWL*, 128–38.
[32] Lichtheim, *Late EWL*, 141–43 points out concepts of "fate" in Insinger in five ways: "reversals of fortune come from God"; "Paradoxes"; "God's creation is a union of opposites"; "man's freedom confronts the opposites"; "opposites reside in man's heart".
[33] Jack T. Sanders, *Ben Sira and Demotic Wisdom*, SBLMS 28 (Chico, CA: Scholars Press, 1983) supposes that Demotic wisdom texts like Insinger were the source of Ben Sira, but Goff argues that those similarities belong to the common Hellenistic features and each composition was written in its native wisdom tradition. See Matthew J. Goff, "Hellenistic Instruction in Palestine and Egypt: Ben Sira and Papyrus Insinger," *JSJ* 36.2 (2005): 147–72.
[34] Thomas Schneider, "Hiob 38 und Die Demotische Weisheit (Papyrus Insinger 24)," *TZ* 47.2 (1991): 108–24.
[35] Morris Jastrow, "A Babylonian Parallel to the Story of Job," *JBL* 25.2 (1906): 135–91; Fohrer, *Das Buch Hiob*, 43–46; Moshe Weinfeld, "Job and Its Mesopotamian Parallels: A Typological Analysis," in *Text and Context: Old Testament and Semitic Studies for F. C. Fensham*, ed. Walter T. Claassen, JSOTSup 48 (Sheffield: JSOT Press, 1988), 217–26; Gerald L. Mattingly, "The Pious Sufferer: Mesopotamia's Traditional Theodicy and Job's Counselors," in *Bible in the Light of Cuneiform Literature*, ed. William W. Hallo (Lewiston, NY: Mellen, 1990), 305–48.

the book of Job.[36] According to Samuel Kramer, all five fragments excavated at Nippur could be probably dated to 1700 BCE, and the original composition was written in the Third Dynasty of the city of Ur (Ur III Period), which is known as the era of the Sumerian renaissance.[37] According to Jacob Klein, *Sumerian Man and His God* contains a mixture of literary forms such as instruction, narration, penitential psalm, and a monologue by the sufferer.[38] The entire structure confirms the instruction in the Prologue (1–9), that humans should praise their gods and should appease the heart of their deities:

Let his lament soothe the heart of his god,
(For) a human being without a god would not obtain food. (8–9).

The wise and righteous man, similar to the figure of Job, suffers from sudden diseases by a demon entering his body, and laments his painful situation and the social exclusion from his community. He feels betrayed by friends and family members whom he once trusted (28–55), and he desires to encounter his deity (56–58, 96–100). Lastly, his unceasing prayer and worship (27–28, 118–19) are answered by his god and his sickened body is restored, as the demon is driven out. Though this text is a type of monologue, not a dialogue like the book of Job, biblical Job and *Man and His God* introduce the lament of the undeserved sufferer toward a deity. Differences are apparent, as well. As mentioned by Kramer, *Sumerian Man and His God* confirms the basic teaching that sufferings result from human misbehaviours and sins, and that prayer to the deity and the confession of sins effect relief and deliverance. By contrast, the voice of Job tells us that the faithful life and prayer does not always result in a positive reaction from the deity. While biblical Job does not end up with praise to his deity, *Sumerian Man and His God* finishes the story with an act of praise (127).

3.2 The Dialogue between a Man and His God

The first work of Babylonian literature compared to the book of Job is "The Dialogue between a Man and His God" or "Babylonian Man and His God" (abbr., *A Man and His God*; AO 4462, Louvre) which is probably dated to the late Old Babylonian period (late 17th century BCE).[39] This seventy-line dialogue is often

---

[36] Samuel N. Kramer, "'Man and His God': A Sumerian Variation on 'Job' Motif," in *Wisdom in Israel and in the Ancient Near East: Presented to Professor Harold Henry Rowley*, ed. Martin Noth and David W. Thomas, VTSup 3 (Leiden: Brill, 1955), 170–82; "Man and His God: A Sumerian Variation of the 'Job' Motif," trans. Samuel N. Kramer (*ANET*, 589–91); "Man and His God," trans. Jacob Klein (*COS* 1.179:573–75).
[37] Kramer, "'Job' Motif," in *Wisdom*, 170.
[38] Jacob Klein, "Man and His God: A Wisdom Poem or a Cultic Lament?" in *Approaches to Sumerian Literature: Studies in Honor of Stip (H.L.J. Vanstiphout)*, ed. Piotr Michalowski and Niek Veldhuis (Leiden: Brill, 2006), 123–43.
[39] Jean Nougayrol, "Une Version Ancienne Du 'Juste Souffrant,'" *RB* 59 (1952): 239–50; Wolfram von Soden, "Das Fragen nach der Gerichtigkeit Gottes im alten Orient," *MDOG* 96

called "the Poem of the Just Sufferer" – but the sufferer, unlike Job, does not claim to be innocent before his deity, and confesses his sins. The narrative explains the agony of the sufferer praying in lament (1–11),[40] and in the monologue (12–36) against increasing distress he confesses his hidden sins against others and his deity. Lastly, the rescue, healing, and restoration of his deity come upon him (37–47), and his health is quickly restored (esp. 46–47).[41] In the epilogue (48–67), his deity delivers a message of hope and comfort – "your path is straight and compassion is bestowed on you" (55). The creator establishes a relationship with the sufferer, promising protection and offering eternal life (58–61) and advice concerning social justice (esp. 63). The appendix ends with the petition to the deity for the sufferer (68–69). According to Klein, *A Man and His God* and *Sumerian Man and His God* have in common "the cultic genre" of "the Penitential Psalm."[42] John Gray mentions that the epilogues of *A Man and His God* and the book of Job (esp. Job 42:7–8) indicate the happy ending and divine assurance, though the Old Babylonian text lacks the motif of the innocent sufferer.[43]

3.3 Ludlul bēl nēmeqi ("I will Praise the Lord of Wisdom")

The most noteworthy possible intertext with Job is *Ludlul bēl nēmeqi* ("I Will Praise the Lord of Wisdom" – shortened to *Ludlul*, also known as "The Babylonian Job", or "The Poem of the Righteous Sufferer"). The text was composed in the Cassite Dynasty of the Babylonian Empire (1600–1155 BCE).[44] The poem of *Ludlul* consists of four tablets and presumed 480 lines in total (120 lines in each tablet; the beginning and end of Tablet I is missing).[45] It describes the pious man who experieced many misfortunes and physical disease, and whose health was finally restored by his deity. Given that the protagonist Šubši-mešrê-Šakkan (III 43–44), to whom Marduk brought prosperity, begins to praise the lord of wisdom, *Ludlul* could be considered a religious text to honour Marduk. But *Ludlul*

(1965): 41–59. I use the English translation from Wilfred G. Lambert, "A Further Attempt at the Babylonian 'Man and His God,'" in *Language, Literature, and History: Philological and Historical Studies Presented to Erica Reiner*, ed. Francesca Rochberg-Halton, AOS 67 (New Haven: American Oriental Society, 1987), 187–202. Also see "Dialogue between a Man and His God," trans. Benjamin R. Foster (*COS* 1.151:485); Foster, *Before the Muses*, 78–80.

[40] Nougayrol, "Une Version Ancienne Du 'Juste Souffrant'" assumably supposes that its introduction, just as the prologue of Job has, would have had the description explaining the blissful life of the sufferer.

[41] Klein, "Man and His God," 134–36.

[42] Klein, "Man and His God," 133.

[43] John Gray, "Book of Job in the Context of Near Eastern Literature," *ZAW* 82 (1970): 259–60.

[44] Lambert, *BWL*, 21–62; Foster, *Before the Muses*, 306–23; "The Poem of the Righteous Sufferer," (*COS* 1.153:486–92); Amar Annus and Alan C. Lenzi, *Ludlul Bēl Nēmeqi: The Standard Babylonian Poem of the Righteous Sufferer*, PFFAR (Helsinki: Neo-Assyrian Text Corpus Project, 2010). Here I use the translation of Annus and Lenzi.

[45] Lambert, *BWL*, 21.

also portrays the loss and restoration of a pious sufferer. Due to many of its features, interpreters have regarded *Ludlul* as a main source text of Job.[46]

In Tablet I, Šubši-mešrê-Šakkan praises the erratic nature of Marduk (I 1–10) and the omnipotence and omniscience of the deity are foremost among other gods (I 29–36).

Without his consent, who could assuage his striking?
Apart from his intention, who could stay his hand? (I 35–36)

Here a parallel is found to Job's confession that nothing can affect God's purpose for human lives (Job 23:13): nobody can escape Marduk's decision. The sufferer then laments the punishment on himself, feels rejection and terror due to the absence of the divinity (I 41–49), and experiences the isolation, abandonment, and marginalization from his family, peers, and community (I 50–90). The sufferer observes that, since the principle of retribution is not being applied, the one who speaks calumny against him receives divine help (I 93–99, esp. 95); all property and social honour were taken away from the sufferer (I 99–104). Tablet I concludes with sorrow but also hope (I 105–20). The marginalisation of the Babylonian sufferer from his community parallels Job's experience of being mistreated by friends and community (Job 6:14–23; 19:13–22; 30:1–15).

Tablet II concentrates on his increasing misfortune and physical suffering a year later. Although he pleaded his case to his deities, his deities are not concerned with his prayers, and no diviners, dream interpreters, or exorcists could tell the cause of his suffering (II 4–9). Because the sufferer does not know the intention of the gods, he continues to experience seemingly undeserved misfortune. Although he has performed all his religious pleas and duties, and even as a teacher instructed his people in religious rites and morality (II 10–32), he is baffled by the gods' ill-treatment. In a bitter complaint, the sufferer says:

That which is wretched to one's heart may be good to one's god.
Who can learn the plan of the gods in the heavens?
Who understands the counsel of the deep?
Where did humanity learn the divine decree of the gods? (II 35–38)

Just as the sceptical speech is found in rhetorical questions of the unpredictable nature of gods and human ignorance, it is discovered in Job 28 where wisdom cannot in any way be found by human faculties. Human fragility and uncertain existence are irresistible, in that circumstances influence human be-

---

[46] Snaith, *Job*, 21–27 argues that the author of Job directly owes his theme and structure to the Babylonian Job (esp. Job 3; 29–31; 38–39), although the book of Job is essentially Hebrew wisdom literature. Gray, "Book of Job," 262–64; Weinfeld, "Job and Its Mesopotamian Parallels," 219–22; Michael Cheney, *Dust, Wind and Agony: Character, Speech and Genre in Job* (Stockholm: Almqvist & Wiksell, 1994), 36; Hans-Peter Müller, *Das Hiobproblem: seine Stellung und Entstehung im Alten Orient und im Alten Testament*, EdF 84 (Darmstadt: Wissenschaftliche Buchgesellschaft, 1995), 49–51.

haviour which will end in death (II 39–47). The Babylonian sufferer cannot find the meaning in his misfortune (II 48–49) and in the rest of Tablet II laments the pain in his many body parts: "skull", "neck", "chest", "breast", "back", "innards", "limbs", "belly", "skins", "eyes", "ears", "loins", "throat", "bones", and "tissues" (II 50–107). The author of Job likewise employs a variety of metaphors to describe the sickness of his body parts (e. g., Job 16:8–16; 17:6–7; 19:20; 30:16–31).[47] The Babylonian sufferer heard no hopeful answer from exorcists and diviners since his deities are indifferent to his suffering (II 108–13). His weeping at being prepared for the grave deepens the frustration of his friends and families (II 114–20). The confession of the sufferer's pain in Tablet II is similar to the disputational soliloquy in Job 29–30,[48] although the Babylonian sufferer does not confidently claim his innocence.

Repeating the Babylonian sufferer's dire catastrophes (III 1–8), Tablet III and IV concentrate on his restoration by Marduk. In three dreams, he meets a figure of outstanding physique, an unspecified figure, and a young woman whom Marduk sent a release, cure, and deliverance (III 9–39). In another dream, Ur-Nintinugga an exorcist speaks that "Marduk sent m[e]" and "I brought this band[age] to Šubši-mešrê-Šakkan" (III 40–44). After his prayer is accepted by divine mercy, his liberation is pronounced and forgiveness is presumably given to him (III 45–60). While the list of his illness in III 69–75 reverses that of II 51–57,[49] the resurgence of his bodily pain in III 80–100 is described.

The sufferer in Tablet IV honours Marduk who ended his suffering and rescued him from all the disasters (IV 1–11), and explains how Marduk vindicated him by defeating his adversary (IV 12–21). After a renewal through ceremony (IV 28–35), he walks through the twelve gates in the Esagil temple in Babylon, and in each gate receives beneficences such as a guardian, well-being, prosperity, life, purification, etc (IV 36–50), concluding with cultic rituals of gratitude at the temple (IV 51–61). Just as the sufferer's community in Job 42:10–11 witnessed Job's restoration, all the Babylonian residents testify in doxology how the protagonist was saved by the power of Marduk (IV 69–90). Its ending invites readers who are in trouble to consider this lesson (IV 113–20).

---

[47] Alec Basson, "Just Skin and Bones: The Longing for Wholeness of the Body in the Book of Job," *VT* 58.3 (2008): 287–99; Scott C. Jones, "Corporeal Discourse in the Book of Job," *JBL* 132.4 (2013): 845–63; Yosefa Raz, "Reading Pain in the Book of Job," in *The Book of Job: Aesthetics, Ethics, Hermeneutics*, ed. Leora Batnitzky and Ilana Pardes, PJTC 1 (Berlin: de Gruyter, 2014), 77–97; Edward L. Greenstein, "Metaphors of Illness and Wellness in Job," in *"When the Morning Stars Sang": Essays in Honor of Choon Leong Seow on the Occasion of His Sixty-Fifth Birthday*, ed. Scott C. Jones and Christine R. Yoder, BZAW 500 (Berlin: de Gruyter, 2017), 39–50. For the malady of Job, see Katharine J. Dell, "What Was Job's Malady?" *JSOT* 41.1 (2016): 61–77; JiSeong James Kwon, "Psychosomatic Approach to Job's Body and Mind: Based on Somatic Symptom Disorder," *JORH* 59.4 (2020): 2032–44.

[48] Choon Leong Seow, *Job 1–21: Interpretation and Commentary* (Grand Rapids: Eerdmans, 2013), 52.

[49] Annus and Lenzi, *Ludlul Bēl Nēmeqi*, xxiii.

There are significant commonalities between the texts of *Ludlul* and Job. Firstly, the description of the sufferer's trouble in Job 3 and 31:15–34 is comparable to Tablet I/II, and Job's restoration by God in epilogue corresponds to the renewal in Tablet III/IV.[50] Secondly, hymnic forms in praise play an important role in each context: Eliphaz's speech in Job 5:18–20; and *Ludlul* II 34–35, 39–42.[51] Thirdly, the motif of salvation in Elihu's speech[52] – from שחת ("sword") and שלח ("pit") (Job 33:18) – resembles the Babylonian sufferer's conviction of Marduk's deliverance in Tablet IV 29–31.

3.4 The Babylonian Theodicy

The composition of *the Babylonian Theodicy* (abbr., *Theodicy*; "the Babylonian Ecclesiastes") is not earlier than the Cassite dynasty and its linguistic style makes us place its date approximately to 1,000 BCE.[53] The form of dialogue between the sufferer and the anonymous friend in *Theodicy*, whose acrostic poem consists of "twenty-seven stanzas in 11 lines each",[54] shares several themes and literary forms with the dialogue between Job and his three friends in Job 4–37; there are cases in which the book of Job has been compared with *Theodicy*.[55]

The theological wrestling of the sufferer, "Saggilkinamubbib, the incantation priest" who is "adorant of god and king,"[56] is even more closely similar to the suffering of Job than that in *Ludlul*. The literary structure in which a friend accuses the sufferer, and both present contrasting views of the relationship between human behaviours and prosperity, exhibits many affinities between the two texts. Just as Job curses the deliverance from mother's womb (Job 3:10) and laments his restless life, the Babylonian sufferer mourns the circumstance in which none can be his protector and even his parents forsook him (I). The doctrine of the friend in *Theodicy* concerning the retribution principle, comparable to the rigorous belief of Job's friends, is presented:

The poor man's son advanced, someone helped him get rich,
Who did favors for the sleek and wealthy?
He who looks to his god has a protector,
The humble man who reverses his goddess will garner wealth. (II 19–22)

---

[50] Snaith, *Job*, 26.
[51] Seow, *Job*, 53–54.
[52] Weinfeld, "Job and Its Mesopotamian Parallels," 218.
[53] Lambert, *BWL*, 63–91; "The Babylonian Theodicy," trans Benjamin R. Foster (*COS* 1.154:492–96); I refer to the translation by Foster, *Before the Muses*, 790–98.
[54] Lambert, *BWL*, 63.
[55] Snaith, *Job*, 20; Gray, "Book of Job," 256–58; Weinfeld, "Job and Its Mesopotamian Parallels," 222–25; Cheney, *Dust, Wind and Agony*, 34–35; Müller, *Das Hiobproblem*, 51–53; Linda J. Sheldon, "The Book of Job as Hebrew Theodicy: An Ancient Near Eastern Intertextual Conflict between Law and Cosmology" (PhD diss., University of California, Berkeley, 2002), 96–101.
[56] Lambert, *BWL*, 63.

The sufferer stresses his bodily pain alongside the loss of property (III 27–30), and grieves the uncertainty of future happiness in his life (III 30–31). The friend condemns the sufferer for neglecting cultic rituals such as "choicest offerings" (IV 37, 42) and recommends the reestablishment of "prayer" (IV 39). The sufferer replies that he did not refrain from offerings and prayers (V 54–55). Similarly, Job cries out his pleading is not answered (e. g., Job 9:16; 14:15; 19:7) in response to Eliphaz's challenge of prayer (5:8a). In both texts, the imagery of a lion is used to describe the fate of the wicked (VI 59–64; Eliphaz in Job 4:10–11).[57]

The friend employs the remoteness ("Netherland", "innermost heaven") of the divinity from the human world to rebuke the sufferer's protest of "divine design" (VI 58; also see VIII 79, 82):

You are a mere child, the purpose of the gods is remote as the netherworld. (VI 58)

You have cast off justice, you have scorned divine design. (VIII 79)

In Job, this theological idea is likewise found in the entire speech of Yahweh (esp. Job 38:2), as well as Zophar's speech (11:7–11; esp. v. 8), which emphasise the unknowability of divine power and the futility of human beings.

The Babylonian sufferer witnesses the incomprehensible reversal of divine justice in his society as well as in his individual life (VII 70–75; XXV 266–74). Such a speech contrasts with his friend's persistent indictment of his irreverent attitude, asking him to perform cultic rites (VIII 79; XX 219–20; XXII 240–42); this structural correspondence is observed in Job's dialogue (e. g., Job 21:7–33; 22:2–30). At some points, the complaint of the Babylonian sufferer that the hand of a deity is behind the suffering (XXIII 243–44) is the same as that of Job (Job 3:20–26; 10:1–22). Highlighting the transcendence of the divinity in comparison of human ignorance, the friend designates the freedom of divine activity in the world (e. g., the diversity of cow's offspring; XXIV 254–64). Yahweh's speeches in Job 38–39 describes God's freedom in creating the nature of animals (Job 38:39–39:30). The Babylonian sufferer criticises in detail the false witnesses of the unknown powerful class, and the harshness against the innocent and the pious. He alleges that, in supporting the injustice of the tyrant, they snatch provisions from the poor (XXV 265–75). While Job's friends in no way blame human sufferings on their deity, the friend in *Theodicy* responds to the sufferer's question by telling him that gods (Enlil and Ea) granted "lies and falsehood" to powerful men for injustice (XXVI 279–80). Finally, the dialogue between the sufferer and friend concludes with plea of 'not guilty' and a call to the gods to call for protection (XXVII 287–97); this corresponds to the declaration of innocence in Job 31. The theological answer of the friend that their gods caused the persecution of the protagonist does not seem to be accepted by the sufferer, who still seeks saving help from his deity.

---

[57] Sheldon, "Theodicy," 97. The image of a lion in Job 10:16 is sarcastically used in the voice of Job to regard Job himself as the innocent victim by God.

3.5 A Pessimistic Dialogue between Master and Servant

Lastly, "A Pessimistic Dialogue between Master and Servant" ("The Dialogue of Pessimism" or "The Obliging Slave"; abbr., *Pessimism*)[58] is worthy of mention for its sceptical ideas in comparison with the poetic dialogue of Job.[59] Distinct from the form of pessimistic philosophy, Ephraim Speiser maintained that *Pessimism* more appropriately belongs to the genre of satire, due to its humorous tone.[60] However, determining the dominant literary purpose is quite complex; Jean Bottéro maintained that its sceptical and pessimistic content in its performance could include both the humorous and serious purposes.[61] The reference to an "iron dagger" (L 52) has made interpreters suppose that *Pessimism* is dated to the Cassite period (1550–1155 BCE).[62] In ten dialogues, the master gives orders in pessimistic and fickle moods to his slave. His slave does not protest the master but informs him of the consequences that his master's action will bring. In an exceptional case, when in the seventh dialogue the master repeatedly states that he will not give a sacrifice to his god, the servant sarcastically replies that humans cannot instruct the deity (58–60). The deity who is worshipped by the master is compared to a dog which is subservient to humans. In the last dialogue, when the master questions what goodness is, the servant recommends suicide to his owner, and also asks him to kill the slave himself. The rhetorical questions in Prov 30:4 and Deut 30:12–13 would be much closer to the question in *Pessimism* regarding who is the tallest and the broadest one (83–84).[63]

4. Ugaritic Origin

Although mainly Egyptian and Mesopotamian origins of Job have been mentioned, the association between Ugaritic literature and the book of Job needs

---

[58] Lambert, *BWL*, 139–49; "A Pessimistic Dialogue between Master and Servant," trans. Robert H. Pfeiffer (*ANET*, 437–38); "Dialogue of Pessimism or the Obliging Slave," trans. Alasdair Livingstone (*COS* 1.155:495–96).

[59] Fohrer, *Das Buch Hiob*, 43.

[60] Ephraim A. Speiser, "The Case of the Obliging Servant," *JCS* 8 (1954): 105. Lambert, *BWL*, 140 proposes an alternative possibility (except for "a philosophical tractate" or "a joke"), that "the writer" "owed his outlook to his emotional state".

[61] Jean Bottéro, *Mesopotamia: Writing, Reasoning, and the Gods* (Chicago: University of Chicago Press, 1995), 260–61 suggests that the sceptical view of life in "Pessimism" is compared with the book of Ecclesiastes (e.g., 3:1–9). Also see Edward L. Greenstein, "Sages with a Sense of Humor: The Babylonian Dialogue between a Master and His Servant and the Book of Qohelet," in *Wisdom Literature in Mesopotamia and Israel*, ed. Richard J. Clifford, SBLSymS 36 (Atlanta: Society of Biblical Literature, 2007), 55–65.

[62] Lambert, *BWL*, 140.

[63] Abigail Pelham, "Job as Comedy, Revisited," *JSOT* 35.1 (2010): 89–112; James W. Whedbee, "The Comedy of Job," in *On Humour and the Comic in the Hebrew Bible*, ed. Yehuda T. Radday and Athalya Brenner-Idan, JSOTSup 92 (Sheffield: Almond Press, 1990), 217–49.

to be assessed as well. The weight given to Ugaritic language may be validated based on the assumption that the Ugaritic language is the earliest antecedent to classical Hebrew among Northwest Semitic languages.[64] As modern scholarship has discovered numerous linguistic similarities between Ugaritic literature and the book of Job,[65] attention has been focused on the sources of Job's prosetale and poetic part.[66] For instance, Charles Feinberg in a short article from 1946 argued that the poetic structure and literary techniques – parallelism, 3+3 meter, lines, rhythms, and sentence structure – in Ras Shamra texts are similar to those employed in the book of Job so that there is a definite literary contact between Hebrew and Ugaritic poetry.[67] Ugaritic influence on the book of Job has been investigated as even more original and direct than other foreign counterparts. Mitchell Dahood provides "the hapax- or dis-legomena parallel pairs in Job that recur in Ugaritic" but are absent from the Hebrew Bible, and concludes in agreement with Albright's view that the results "point to a 'Phoenician-influenced origin in Galilee or the Syrian diaspora during the seventh – or possibly – the early sixth century BCE'".[68] Johannes de Moor notices that the text of Job is not monotheistic and that the God of the book of Job is much closer to El of Canaanite religion with a similar motif of clay and pottery (Job 33:6) and in particular he considers the link between Job 19:25–27 and "the Ugaritic Baal myth".[69] Further, based on "Ugaritisms" in the book of Job, he boldly argued

---

[64] Aaron D. Rubin, "The Subgrouping of the Semitic Languages," *LLC* 2.1 (2008): 79–102; https://doi.org/10.1111/j.1749-818X.2007.00044.x.

[65] See Mitchell J. Dahood, "Some Northwest Semitic Words in Job," *Bib* 38 (1957): 306–20; idem, "Northwest Semitic Philology and Job," in *The Bible in Current Catholic Thought* (New York: Herder, 1962), 55–74. For other proponents of Ugariticism, see Anton C. M. Blommerde, *Northwest Semitic Grammar and Job*, BO 22 (Rome: Pontifical Biblical Institute, 1969); Anthony R. Ceresko, *Job 29–31 in the Light of Northwest Semitic: A Translation and Philological Commentary*, BO 36 (Rome: Pontifical Biblical Institute, 1980); Lester L. Grabbe, *Comparative Philology and the Text of Job: A Study in Methodology*, SBLDS 34 (Missoula, MT: Scholars, 1977). For an interesting debate regarding Ugaritic and Hebraic in Job, see Oswald Loretz, "Ugaritisch-Hebräisch in Job 3:3–26: Zum Disput Zwischen M. Dahood Und J. Barr," *UF* 8 (1976): 123–27.

[66] Charles L. Feinberg, "The Poetic Structure of the Book of Job and the Ugaritic Literature," *BSac* 103 (1946): 283–92; Peter C. Craigie, "Job and Ugaritic Studies," in *Studies in the Book of Job*, ed. Walter Emanuel Aufrecht, SRSup 16 (Waterloo, ON: Wilfrid Laurier University Press, 1985), 28–35; Daniel O'Connor, "The Keret Legend and the Prologue-Epilogue of Job," *ITQ* 55 (1989): 1–6; Lowell K. Handy, "The Authorization of Divine Power and the Guilt of God in the Book of Job: Useful Ugaritic Parallels," *JSOT* 60 (1993): 107–18; Johannes C. de Moor, "Ugarit and the Origin of Job," in *Ugarit and the Bible*, ed. George J. Brooke (Münster: Ugarit-Verlag, 1994), 225–57; Robert S. Fyall, *Now My Eyes Have Seen You: Images of Creation and Evil in the Book of Job* (Leicester: Inter-Varsity Press, 2002), 191–94.

[67] Feinberg, "Poetic," 292.

[68] Mitchell J. Dahood, "Some Rare Parallel Word Pairs in Job and in Ugaritic," in *The Word in the World: Essays in Honor of Frederick L. Moriarty, S.J.*, ed. Richard J. Clifford and George W. MacRae (Cambridge, MA: Weston College Press, 1973), 30.

[69] De Moor, "Ugarit," 239–41.

that the Canaanite city-ruler *Ayyabu* from *Ashtartu* who lived in the fourteenth century BCE was the biblical Job.[70]

The *Epic of Keret* (abbr., *Keret*)[71] discovered during the archaeological digs at Ras Shamra (1930–31) consists of three clay tablets each with six doubled-ruled columns on both sides.[72] Keret's writing was recorded by a scribe Elimelek during the reign of a Ugaritic king, Niqmadd in the fourteenth century BCE.[73] Both Keret and Pabil the king of Udum, as John Gibson maintains, could be historical figures and the theme of *Keret* might be ideological as exemplifying the ideal kingship in ancient Near East.[74] In contrast, Baruch Margalit argues that "the view of the *Keret* poem as a work of royal propaganda" endorsing the ideology of the kingdom of Ugarit founded by *Keret* "is hugely mistaken" and that "the poet actually ridicules it".[75]

The story of *Keret* begins with the devastation of the Keret's clan – "the house of the king did come to an end" (CTA 14 i.7–8) – in which seven wives of the king were suddenly deceased so that he failed to have the heir of his kingdom (i.9–25). When Keret, mourning in his chamber at night, falls asleep, his deity El appears in a dream, asking the cause of his wretchedness (i.26–51). Keret asks to have sons to succeed his kingdom, and El gives detailed instructions, where the devotee needs to offer sacrifices to El and Baal (i.52–ii.79) and to prepare to march his army to the city of Udum during seven days to take the daughter of Pabil, Huray (ii.85–iii.153). After Keret awakens, his army marches forth and on the seventh day camps near Udum. Keret finally accepts Pabil's surrender and takes Huray as his bride (iii.154 – CTA 15 i.8). Consequently, in the gods' assembly, El promises that Keret's wife will deliver eight sons (CTA 15 ii.1–28). However, Keret's promised blessing was still not accomplished after seven years. Then Asherah announces the demise of Keret (iii.20–25ff), and suddenly physical illness comes upon Keret (iv.14) and causes earthly disasters like drought (iii). After the temple ceremony, El intervenes in Keret's illness, expelling plagues, and finally the health of the hero is dramatically restored (vi.14). The story ends with the rebellion by one of Keret's younger sons, and with the scolding and curse of the king.[76]

---

[70] De Moor, "Ugarit," 246–57.
[71] Different vocalizations of k-r-t are transcribed as Keret, Kirta, Karrate, Kuriti, Karta. See n3 in "The Kirta Epic," trans. Dennis Pardee (*COS* 1.102:333).
[72] For the translation, see "Kirta Epic," *COS* 1.102:333–43. Also, refer to "The Legend of King Keret," trans. Harold L. Ginsberg (*ANET*, 142–49); John C. L. Gibson, *Canaanite Myths and Legends*, 2nd ed. (Edinburgh: T&T Clark, 1978), 19–23, 82–102; For a recent introduction, see Baruch Margalit, "The Legend of Keret," in *Handbook of Ugaritic Studies*, ed. Wilfred G. E. Watson, HdO 39 (Leiden: Brill, 1999), 203–4.
[73] See the end of KRT (C. Ginsberg, "The Legend of King Keret," 142).
[74] Gibson, *Canaanite*, 23.
[75] Margalit, "The Legend of Keret," 207–8.
[76] Margalit, "The Legend of Keret," 231 interprets this ending as "its tragi-comic equivalent".

Both Keret and Job encounter the lack of children and experience the loss of physical health and the recovery of what they have lost (although, in the case of Job, there is no mention of the healing of physical pain), and they are accused of oppressing the marginalized by friends (Job) and by his son (*Keret*). Daniel O'Connor provides striking parallels in the prose-tale that describes the sudden loss of the sufferer's household, his long illness, and the restoration of his health; (1) the loss of children (Job 42:13–14//Keret III.iii 5–12); (2) "the assembly of the gods" (Job 1–2) and protagonists described as servants (Keret I iii.49, 51); (3) "animal sacrifices" (Job 1:5//Keret I ii.8–18).[77] Contrary to the indifference to cult and sacrifice in Job, the ritual and ceremony to deities at the centre of the story of *Keret* play an important role in resolving personal and national sufferings.

5. Edomic Origin

The last suggestion about the origin of the book of Job is the widespread theory of Edomic wisdom.[78] This was earlier initiated by Robert Pfeiffer saying that Job has its origin in Edomite wisdom and that attributes of Job's deity as the cosmic Creator were influenced by Edomite wisdom.[79] According to Pfeiffer, the original author of Job was an Edomite who had the pessimistic philosophy about Edomite deities and humans and who was aware of Edomic wisdom literature, and afterwards, Jewish editors of Job added the pre-existent folktale to it.[80] For another example, John Day claims that since sages of Israel would be indebted to Edomite wisdom, the author of Job could set up the protagonist as an Edomite who is

---

[77] Those similarities "suggest the possibility that the author of the Job poem consciously drew on an ancient folk-tale of the Keret type in which the upright hero suffered the loss of family and property, but was eventually restored to his former happiness." See O'Connor, "The Keret Legend and the Prologue-Epilogue of Job," 2–3. Craigie, "Job and Ugaritic Studies," 34–35 argues that "the story of Job and the story of AQHAT" "were similar popular traditions," widely known throughout the Ancient Near East. Simon B. Parker, *The Pre-Biblical Narrative Tradition: Essays on the Ugaritic Poems Keret and Aqhat*, RBS 24 (Atlanta: Scholars Press, 1989), 146, 184, 195 also claims that the prologue of "Keret" is "reminiscent of the prose prologue of the book of Job".

[78] Robert H. Pfeiffer, "Edomitic Wisdom," *ZAW* 44 (1926): 13–25; Otto Eissfeldt, *The Old Testament* (New York: Harper & Row, 1965), 169–70; Bernardo Boschi, "Saggezza Di Edom: Mito o Realtà?" *RBI* 15 (1967): 358–68; John Day, "How Could Job Be an Edomite?" in *The Book of Job*, ed. Willen A. M. Beuken, BETL 114 (Leuven: Leuven University Press; Peeters, 1994), 392–99; Bradley L. Crowell, "A Reevaluation of the Edomite Wisdom Hypothesis," *ZAW* 120.3 (2008): 404–16; recently, Juan M. Tebes, "The 'Wisdom' of Edom," *BN* 143 (2009): 114 finds the evidence of the wisdom of Edom from Jer 47:9 and Obad 7b–8 and argues that "the magic facet of the indigenous metallurgy industry was part of this wisdom experience."

[79] Pfeiffer, "Edomitic Wisdom." Pfeiffer argues that Deutero-Isaiah combines the motif of the transcendent God in Job that was shaped by Edomitic wisdom with the monotheistic doctrine in the history of Israel. See Robert H. Pfeiffer, "The Dual Origin of Hebrew Monotheism," *JBL* 46 (1927): 193–206.

[80] He supposes that Job and Genesis 1–11 (S [Seir or South] -document) shared the Edomite mythic document and worldview. Pfeiffer, "Edomitic Wisdom."

the admirable model of piety, though Edom was not the opponent of Israel.[81] The Edomic wisdom hypothesis was also supported by Victor Sasson who, by presenting parallels between the ostracon dated to the second half of 17th century BCE and the Hebrew book of Job (esp. 27:10–17), argues that the ostracon was composed by a circle of Edomite scribes and its linguistic obscurity was not different from the ambiguity of Job.[82]

Then, how can we evaluate the Edomite wisdom hypothesis regarding the origin of Job? Unfortunately, we have no complete Edomite composition to assess their wisdom literature, as Sasson himself has already noted. Although there is a close similarity between Job and an allegedly Edomite wisdom text on the ostracon, this need not be evidence that the author of Job had ethnic origin from Edom or even that the setting of Job is Edomite wisdom school. For instance, Pfeiffer argues that Job and Genesis 1–11 (S [Seir or South] document) shared the Edomite mythic document and worldview.[83] However, such reasoning is not decisive. In contrast, Bradley Crowell, using socio-political analysis, reevaluates the "Edomite wisdom hypothesis", arguing that Job's literary background (not the social location) is Edom, but dismissing the claim that Edomite writers composed the discourse in terms of the innocent sufferer.[84] According to Crowell, Edom, having "such a small, decentralized polity", did not develop a scribal training and administration where their scholars who recognised a variety of Egyptian, Mesopotamian, and Judean literature could compose sophisticated texts like Job and Proverbs.[85]

6. Intertexts, Forms, Genres, and Ideas

In this survey, we have observed many scholars' assertions that the book of Job is directly inspired by a specific non-Israelite text or the influence of a particular literary tradition. Yet, those claims concerning the origin of Job in foreign counterparts remain unproven, since the origin cannot be identified with just one text. For instance, Job's wailing in Job 3 in which he curses his birth and prefers

---

[81] Day, "How Could Job Be an Edomite?"

[82] Victor Sasson, "An Edomite Joban Text: With a Biblical Joban Parallel," *ZAW* 117.4 (2005): 601 supposes that one text published in 1993 from inscriptions "unearthed at Horvat Uza (Hebrew: חורבת עוזה)" in the northeast of the Negeb (1982–88) provides the elusive transcription and translation of the ostracon by F.M. Cross. In conclusion, Sasson even assumes that "the author of Job could have been half-Israelite or half-Jewish, half-Edomite, a converted Edomite".

[83] Pfeiffer, "Edomitic Wisdom."

[84] Crowell, "Reevaluation," 409–16.

[85] Crowell, "Reevaluation," 406, 414. Bob Becking, "Does Wisdom Come from Edom? Remarks on an Ostracon from Horvat 'Uza," in *Weisheit und Schöpfung: Festschrift für James Alfred Loader zum 65. Geburtstag*, ed. Stefan Fischer and Marianne Grohmann, WAS 7 (Frankfurt am Main: Lang, 2010), 29–42 similarly is sceptical that the ostracon is Edomite and is classified as a wisdom text.

to die could be derived from specific Egyptian texts such as *Ipuur* and *A Man and His Ba*.[86] However, these references are not unique, since a striking parallel is found in biblical texts such as Jer 20:14–18.[87] It is accordingly reasonable to suppose that common expressions in Job 3 were prevalent among scribes. Also, it is not always necessary to contend narrowly that scribes referred to the literary tradition of a specific foreign civilization. Moshe Weinfeld, for example, argues that Mesopotamian parallels with the book of Job remind us of several psalms of thanksgiving in biblical literature, and that those similarities reflect common "liturgies of thanksgiving of the sufferer to his god".[88] Literary resemblances between the texts of Job/Psalms and the two Mesopotamian compositions, *Sumerian Man and His God* and *Ludlul*, are suggested as notable evidence of literary dependence.[89] Then Weinfeld claims that the Babylonian literary tradition produced "typological affinities" with the book of Job.[90] Similarly, John Gray claims that the book of Job adopted the literary tradition common to Mesopotamia and Israel (cf. Ps 73).[91] In a broad sense, it would be appropriate to say that Mesopotamian texts like *Ludlul* show significant resemblances with Job, but substantial resemblances with Egyptian texts make it too difficult for us to suppose that the author of Job directly utilised only the Babylonian literary tradition. For another instance, Konrad Schmid presumes that Job originated from Babylonian texts and that the book of Job thematically combines *Ludlul* (Job's plea and Yahweh's speech in Job 3; 29–31; 38–41) with *Theodicy* (in the dialogue with Job's friends).[92] However, the literary form of "dialogue" also appears in *A Man with His Ba* and *Ipuur*, and the lament of the sufferer is also found in *Eloquent Peasant* and *Neferti*.

It is more likely that the way of using genres and forms known to the author(s) of Job – narrative, hymns, laws, lament, disputation, parody, proverbs, prophecy, didactic, etc – is so amalgamated and diverse that determining a dominant genre and setting from the perspective of form criticism is not possible. For instance, even though Job might use hymns, its reinterpretation is not quite typical, but its author sarcastically reverses the intention for exalting the greatness of God

---

[86] See Fohrer, *Das Buch Hiob*, 116; Shupak notices the literary echo between the "Dialogue of a Man with His Soul", Ipuur and Job's texts (cf. 3:3 ff., 20–22; 10:18–19; 13:15; 14:13; 17:13–14). See Shupak, "The Dispute between a Man and His Ba," *COS* 3.146:321–26; Foster, "Dialogue between a Man and His God," *COS* 1.151:485.

[87] See David J.A. Clines, *Job 1–20*, WBC 17 (Dallas: Word, 1989), 83.

[88] Weinfeld, "Job and Its Mesopotamian Parallels," 217.

[89] Weinfeld, "Job and Its Mesopotamian Parallels," 218.

[90] Weinfeld, "Job and Its Mesopotamian Parallels," 222–25.

[91] See Gray, "Book of Job": "The anticipated relief suggests again the theme of his suffering, and here the language is reminiscent of Job and the Plaint of the Sufferer in the Psalms" (263); "The affinities of the Book of Job with the sophisticated sapiential tradition of Mesopotamia are not to be denied" (265).

[92] See Chapter 5 in Konrad Schmid, *Literaturgeschichte des Alten Testaments: eine Einführung* (Darmstadt: WissBuchges, 2008).

by heavily misusing the original context.[93] Additionally, it is notable to mention that laws and legal texts were shared in the dialogue of Job. Central to the entire language in Job's dialogue is the prominent form of trial or disputation which commonly emerges in ancient Near Eastern literature, Neo-Babylonian literature in particular. For instance, F. Rachel Magdalene examines resemblances between Neo-Babylonian litigation procedure and the book of Job, and she then proposes that suffering, divine action, and a lawsuit in the ancient context of theodicy are related to Job's legal disputation in disease, disability and disaster and that there is a "direct influence on that of Israel during the period when the author of Job created this work."[94] It is assumed by Magdalene that the author of Job intentionally used litigation documents of the Neo-Babylonian period to produce Job's text. If the argumentation of Magdalene and other scholars is acceptable, we could say that these scribal texts were broadly shaped by legal language in Babylonian texts; although it is unlikely that the author of Job refers to a specific text from cuneiform texts.

Indeed, those intertextual links make it nearly impossible for us to trace what precedes Job's texts. Although Job's form and theme might be explained by a direct dependence from foreign counterparts, a better explanation, as I suppose, is that the scribe of Job would be aware of shared ancient Near Eastern stories, texts, and related motifs and that he could utilise that cultural memory and knowledge for his personal or communal agenda.

6.1 Suffering

Foreign counterparts relating to the book of Job are generally bound up with the issue of human suffering and misery in the individual life and the world. In Job, suffering and injustice occupy a central theme, although the text of Job is unlikely to give the rational explanation of the innocent sufferer. Let us consider four different pieces of literature: *Ludlul*, *Eloquent Peasant*, *Keret*, and *Sumerian Man and His God*. These compositions are dealing with issues of individual tragedies (e.g., individuals, peasant, king); though there are national calamities in the case of *Ipuur*. In these texts, restoration of loss and reconciliation of the conflict at the end of the stories are given to sufferers; an exception is in *Pessimism*. Although

---

[93] Katharine J. Dell, *The Book of Job as Sceptical Literature*, BZAW 197 (Berlin: de Gruyter, 1991) provides a good example of the "misuse" in Job of psalmic texts.

[94] Magdalene alongside Dick, Gemser, Sheldon, and Westbrook argues that "the author of Job incorporated the worldview reflected in the Mesopotamian ritual incantations, hymns, prayers, and theodicies in shaping his book" (F. Rachel Magdalene, *On the Scales of Righteousness: Neo-Babylonian Trial Law and the Book of Job*, BJS 348 (Providence, RI: Brown Judaic Studies, 2007), 24, 28–29; idem, "The ANE Legal Origins of Impairment as Theological Disability and the Book of Job," *PRSt* 34 (2007): 23–59; Michael B. Dick, "Legal Metaphor in Job 31," *CBQ* 41 (1979): 37–50; Sheldon, "Theodicy"; Berend Gemser, "The Rib- or Controversy Pattern in Hebrew Mentality," in *Wisdom in Israel and in the Ancient Near East: Presented to Professor Harold Henry Rowley*, ed. Martin Noth and David W. Thomas, VTSup 3 (Leiden: Brill, 1955), 120–37.

the detailed literary descriptions are diverse and they do not all deal with the case of the purely innocent sufferer, all of them are engaged with the sufferer's motif which is the same as in the book of Job.

6.2 Prose-Tale

In its literary form, Job's intertexts, except for the psychological conflict in the main body, appear as an adaptation from the tradition of prose-tales similar to *Eloquent Peasant*, *Ankhsheshonq*, *A Man and His God*, *Ludlul*, *Theodicy*, and *Keret*. Just as texts such as *A Man and His Ba*, *Ludlul*, and *Theodicy* feature dialogical conflicting and polyphonic voices in terms of suffering and order, the arrangement of the prose-tale and the poetic dialogue in Job produces such a complicatedly intertwined discourse. Yet again, this does not mean that one can reconstruct the origin of Job's text. For this issue, Michael Cheney comments:

> The classification of a story as a frame tale does not constitute a claim for or against the 'authenticity' or 'originality' of the text or any of its portions. Nevertheless the fact that such complex structures have come from a variety of cultural backgrounds and are attested for several different periods in the history of the ANE counsels against equating literary tension and complexity with diversity of origin.[95]

6.3 Dialogue

Another literary genre shared by Job and non-Israelite sources, we say, is "dialogue", which usually consists of the debate or discussion between two speakers and which explores questions of human suffering. It is tempting to assert that the author of Job adopted the framework of the dialogue form to draw attention to individual suffering and social chaos in his time. While it was a prevailing genre shared in ancient Near East cultures, this cannot, however, be simply compared with the structure of the Platonic dialogue in Greek culture or with the modern dialogue genre.[96]

Except for the dialogue form, there is almost nothing which can link texts in Job to the Babylonian compositions *A Man and His God*, *Ludlul*, *Theodicy*, and *Pessimism*, or Egyptian texts *A Man and His Ba*, *Eloquent Peasant*, and *Ipuur*. Van der Toorn, for instance, proposes the literary "dialogue" as one of the prevalent genres, comparing three ancient texts, *A Man and His Ba*, *Theodicy*, and the Book of Job.[97] According to van der Toorn, the dialogue genre in each literature

---

[95] Cheney, *Dust, Wind and Agony*, 35–36.

[96] Denning-Bolle regards a literary dialogue in Akkadian literature as an established genre in the disputation and ritual setting. See Sara Denning-Bolle, *Wisdom in Akkadian Literature: Expression, Instruction, Dialogue*, MSO 28 (Leiden: Ex Oriente Lux, 1992), 85–133.

[97] In conclusion, he says that "on the strength of these formal and material resemblances, one is led to posit the existence of the literary dialogue as a distinct literary genre in the ancient Near East." See Karel van der Toorn, "The Ancient Near Eastern Literary Dialogue as a Vehicle of

is placed in various literary settings such as "legal metaphors", "judicial trials" or "wisdom disputation",[98] and, further, it combines the subject-matter of theodicy with other works of pessimistic literature which reflect the mood of an individual's chaos and distress in its own right. On the contrary, the structure of *Eloquent Peasant* seems to escape the dialogue genre and to adopt "tale" as a prominent genre, but in the main body, it seems to adopt the "internal dialogue" (or monologue) where the correspondent is silent.[99] The literature most similar to the book of Job, the Sumerian *Man and His God* likewise lacks the dialogue form but instead includes the long monologue expressed to his deity. The Ugaritic composition *Keret* has less dialogue than other compositions, but it also includes a dialogue between Keret and the supreme god El.

The dialogue was a literary tool used to reflect the many voices of ancient writers. Such a literary dialogue was very popular in Middle Kingdom Egyptian (1980–1630 BCE), in Babylonian – both in the Old Babylonian (2000–1595 BCE) and Cassite period – Sumerian, Ugarit, and Hebrew texts. For Middle Egyptian compositions, Parkinson says:

> The complaint-and-answer character of theodicy is particularly suited to the form of a dispute, and theodicy themes are most fully articulated in the discourse and dialogue genres, although the narratives often embody the issue of divine justice through anomic experiences, and the teachings assert Maat by guiding the audience through pragmatic problems of social behavior.[100]

Those non-Israelite texts wholly or partly revolve around the literary genre of dialogue, as they are applied into different contents and different styles, and forms. Indeed, it may be supposed that scribes were aware of a literary genre of dialogue common in other cultures.

6.4 Personal Religion and Piety

When the dimension of religiosity and the divine-human relationship in Job is portrayed in broader ideas in ancient Near Eastern cultures, it is probable to draw close parallels between attitudes to God in Job and attitudes to God that we find in several late texts from other foreign countries. For instance, by the time of the New Kingdom (18th–20th dynasties) in ancient Egypt, a new religiosity that is connected to notions of the personal piety and a single and powerful god emerged particularly from the Ramesside period (19th and 20th dynasties). Jan Assmann has argued that the "new solar theology" in the pre-Amarna period

---

Critical Reflection," in *Dispute Poems and Dialogues in the Ancient and Mediaeval Near East*, ed. Gerrit J. Reinink and Herman L. J. Vanstiphout (Louvain: Department Oriëntalistiek, 1991), 71.

[98] See van der Toorn, "Dialogue," 62–65.

[99] Parkinson points out that "Khakheperreseneb", "Sasobek", and "the Eloquent Peasant" fall into this pattern. See Parkinson, *Poetry and Culture*, 200.

[100] Parkinson, *Poetry and Culture*, 137–38.

was converted by the Amarna religion into a new theology in the Ramesside age that underscores "personal piety."[101] By the time of the Hellenistic and Greco-Roman period, literature in demotic Egyptian script which is full of sayings about the inability of humans to control individual lives is prevalent, such as the instruction of *Papyrus Insinger* (2nd century CE).[102] Although several Egyptian texts paralleled with Job (see §2.1) were composed in the Middle Egyptian Kingdom, Job's theology of the divine is much closer to the religious discourse of the transcendent super-god that started from the Ramesside Period.

The elevated idea of a personal god may also be observed approximately in the Late Bronze Age of Mesopotamia, in which a deity is concerned with personal affairs such as protection, forgiveness, punishment, and help.[103] Thorkild Jacobsen argues that when the aspect of cosmic and terrifying gods is changed into that of the loving and forgiving deities having a parental persona, this reality causes paradoxical problems with incomprehensible contradictions:

> Thus experience could not but drive its cruel wedge ever more deeply between the dispassionate, terrifying, cosmic aspect of the divine which governed the way things really are and really happen, and the personal, concerned, angry, forgiving, loving aspect in which I, the individual, matter so profoundly that love for me must sway the universe off its course to help and sustain me. This is the problem of the righteous sufferer. It forces itself upon righteous consciousness in Mesopotamia about the middle of the second millennium and is dealt with in two remarkable works, Ludlul bēl nēmeqi ... and the Babylonian Theodicy.[104]

Jacobsen, then, insists that such an insoluble contradiction about injustice in the view of the cosmic god(s) was partly resolved in Israelite religion as in the book of Job, where "the personal, egocentric view of the sufferer" "is rejected" and "the full stature of God as the majestic creator and ruler of the universe is reinstated".[105] Although at the time of Job's composition, its author attempts to advance the discourse on human pain, it is more accurate to say that the conflict between two different views on a god – between a personal god and a terrifying,

---

[101] Jan Assmann, *The Search for God in Ancient Egypt* (Ithaca, NY: Cornell University Press, 2001), 222; However, Assmann sometimes tends to put too much emphasis on so-called religious changes and reforms. John Baines and Elizabeth Frood bring interesting corrections, nuances to Assmann's views. See "Piety, Change and Display in the New Kingdom," in *Ramesside Studies in Honour of K.A. Kitchen*, ed. Mark Collier and Steven R. Snape (Bolton: Rutherford, 2011), 1–17.

[102] Lichtheim, *Late Period*, 184–217.

[103] Thorkild Jacobsen, *The Treasures of Darkness: A History of Mesopotamian Religion* (New Haven: Yale University Press, 1976), 147–55 (esp. 152) mentions that "the Mesopotamian genres in which the attitude of personal religion first appears are the 'Penitential Psalms' and the 'Letters to Gods'" and that "as an early example of the first of these one might cite the composition called 'A Man and His God'". The change to personal religion, according to Jacobsen, is linked with notions such as "fortunes", "success", the "responsibility" and "identifiability" of a deity, and the image of "parent" for individuals (155–60).

[104] Jacobsen, *Treasures of Darkness*, 161.

[105] Jacobsen, *Treasures of Darkness*, 163.

cosmic god – is dramatized in Job than to say that the eminence of God as a universal ruler is reinstated. If we look at late Babylonian literature such as the *Sayings of Ahiqar* written on an Aramaic papyrus which represents broad Mesopotamian ideas (written approximately 500 BCE, though being circulated before 6th century BCE),[106] one may find a high idea of the gods controlling the world alongside with the emphasis on the personal piety.

In this sense, although the book of Job shares crucial affinities with *Eloquent Peasant, A Man and His God*, and *Ludlul* from early ancient Near Eastern literature, it is also worth noting the obvious differences between Job and other foreign counterparts.[107] Certainly, Yahweh's speech (Job 38–41) highlights the sovereignty and freedom of divinity independent from human justice and its idea of the cosmic power conflicts with Job's request of justice in the poetic dialogue. The book of Job implies an intellectual debate beyond the discussion of theodicy of the previous generation, and consequently, those scribal ideas found in Job, in terms of theology, is even closer to those found in later texts (e.g., *Ahiqar*).

This is the point at which the ancient Israelite religion and early Judaism closely interact with religious thought in other foreign nations. For this issue, Rainer Albertz notices the emergence of "the personal theology" or "the theologizing of personal piety" in the book of Job which was developed in the post-exilic period for the upper-class.[108] Likewise, Susan Niditch discusses biblical passages related to "personal religion among Yahwists of the Neo-Babylonian and Persian period"[109] and concludes:

... late biblical texts such as the confessions of Jeremiah, the soliloquies of Job, and the social critiques of Qohelet, the characterizations of and interactions between characters in Ruth and Jonah portray individuals' emotions, disappointments, and doubts with greater attention to detail and urgency than do classical texts. ... religious ideas and expressions

---

[106] James M. Lindenberger, *The Aramaic Proverbs of Ahiqar* (Baltimore: Johns Hopkins University Press, 1983).

[107] It is more so in that those Egyptian and Mesopotamian texts do not have the notion of an innocent sufferer in a strict sense; human suffering there is mostly explained by the human ignorance of gods' will or the human corruption, and the misconduct against gods. See Daniel P. Bricker, "Innocent Suffering in Mesopotamia," *TB* 51 (2000): 193–214; idem, "Innocent Suffering in Egypt," *TB* 52 (2001): 83–100.

[108] Albertz maintains that the personal theology in Job corresponds to "theological or theologized wisdom" in Proverbs 1–9 that is classified as a late redactional stage. Rainer Albertz, *From the Exile to the Maccabees*, vol. 2 of *A History of Israelite Religion in the Old Testament period*, trans. John Bowden (Louisville: Westminster John Knox, 1994), 507–11; idem, "The Sage and Pious Wisdom in the Book of Job: The Friends' Perspective," in *Sage in Israel and the Ancient Near East*, ed. John G. Gammie and Leo G. Perdue (Winona Lake, IN: Eisenbrauns, 1990), 243–61; idem, "Personal Piety," in *Religious Diversity in Ancient Israel and Judah*, ed. Francesca Stavrakopoulou and John Barton (London: T&T Clark, 2010), 135–46.

[109] Susan Niditch, *The Responsive Self: Personal Religion in Biblical Literature of the Neo-Babylonian and Persian Periods* (New Haven: Yale University Press, 2015), 16.

are privatized and personalized, albeit always within the contours of traditional content, structures, and turns of phrase.[110]

Among biblical wisdom literature, the book of Ecclesiastes which highlights the impossibility of controlling human life and death together with a strong idea of God's free will (Eccl 7:13; 8:7–8) is another example of the personal theology.

7. Conclusion

The origin of the book of Job and its diverse sources have been investigated by many from the perspective of literary dependence and influence, which to some degree provide useful clues concerning its compositional process. However, when considering its intertextual links with foreign counterparts, it is hardly possible to reconstruct a single origin or to present the book as the odd combination of a few sources. What the diversity in genres/forms and the literary structure of Job tell us is that the author of Job as a Jewish scribe reflects the cultural memory of the discourse of innocent suffering, the cosmic power of a deity, and personal piety – and the scribe adopts the literary forms of prose-tale and dialogue to present those ideas. The diverse intertexts and genres present in Job compels one to dismiss the old assumption of the wisdom tradition, that consists of unified terms, styles, and themes, and the conception of a historical setting by which "sages" or "the wise men" composed wisdom materials. While the author of Proverbs is concerned with Jewish Law (e.g., Prov 3:1–10; 4:1–9) and Qoheleth undermines the worldview of the Torah (contrary to its editor in Eccl 12:13), the author of Job neither discusses any type of written laws nor at some points opposes the value of practising laws.[111] What form criticism has argued is that there were certain professionals (priests, Levites, Deuteronomists, sages, etc.) who involved in specific manufacture of a literary genre. However, as seen above, it is doubtful to think that one may delimit the literary features of Job as a subgenre of wisdom literature. Beyond such modern ideas about its compartmentalisation of form criticism, it would be reasonable to assume that any highly-educated literati could memorise, produce, and perform heterogeneous genres and works and that their collective memory was used for making many kinds of books.

---

[110] Niditch, *Self*, 134–35.
[111] JiSeong James Kwon, "Divergence of the Book of Job from Deuteronomic/Priestly Torah: Intertextual Reading between Job and Torah," *SJOT* 32.1 (2018): 49–71. The similar deduction may be observed in the article of the Peter Altmann in this volume telling that the recognition of Chronicles about the Torah is distinctive from that of the divine Torah in Deuteronomi(sti)c History, though they both employed the same materials; Altmann argues, "This no doubt fits well with Chronicles' focus on the temple and on cultic worship, but it is also surprising that little evidence of judicial application of the divine Torah appears."

Bibliography

Albertz, Rainer. *From the Exile to the Maccabees*. Vol 2. of *A History of Israelite Religion in the Old Testament Period*. Translated by John Bowden. Louisville: Westminster John Knox, 1994.

Albertz, Rainer. "Personal Piety." Pages 135–46 in *Religious Diversity in Ancient Israel and Judah*. Edited by Francesca Stavrakopoulou and John Barton. London: T&T Clark, 2010.

Albertz, Rainer. "The Sage and Pious Wisdom in the Book of Job: The Friends' Perspective." Pages 243–61 in *Sage in Israel and the Ancient Near East*. Edited by John G. Gammie and Leo G. Perdue. Winona Lake, IN: Eisenbrauns, 1990.

Allen, James P. *The Debate Between a Man and His Soul: A Masterpiece of Ancient Egyptian Literature*. CHANE 44. Leiden: Brill, 2010.

Annus, Amar, and Alan C. Lenzi. *Ludlul Bēl Nēmeqi: The Standard Babylonian Poem of the Righteous Sufferer*. PFFAR. Helsinki: Neo-Assyrian Text Corpus Project, 2010.

Assmann, Jan. *The Search for God in Ancient Egypt*. Ithaca, NY: Cornell University Press, 2001.

Baines, John, and Elizabeth Frood. "Piety, Change and Display in the New Kingdom." Pages 1–17 in *Ramesside Studies in Honour of K.A. Kitchen*. Edited by Mark Collier and Steven R. Snape. Bolton: Rutherford, 2011.

Basson, Alec. "Just Skin and Bones: The Longing for Wholeness of the Body in the Book of Job." *VT* 58.3 (2008): 287–99.

Becking, Bob. "Does Wisdom Come from Edom? Remarks on an Ostracon from Horvat 'Uza." Pages 29–42 in *Weisheit und Schöpfung: Festschrift für James Alfred Loader zum 65. Geburtstag*. Edited by Stefan Fischer and Marianne Grohmann. WAS 7. Frankfurt am Main: Peter Lang, 2010.

Blommerde, Anton C.M. *Northwest Semitic Grammar and Job*. BO 22. Rome: Pontifical Biblical Institute, 1969.

Boschi, Bernardo. "Saggezza Di Edom: Mito o Realtà?" *RBI* 15 (1967): 358–68.

Bottéro, Jean. *Mesopotamia: Writing, Reasoning, and the Gods*. Chicago: University of Chicago Press, 1995.

Bricker, Daniel P. "Innocent Suffering in Egypt." *TynB* 52 (2001): 83–100.

Bricker, Daniel P. "Innocent Suffering in Mesopotamia." *TynB* 51 (2000): 193–214.

Ceresko, Anthony R. *Job 29–31 in the Light of Northwest Semitic: A Translation and Philological Commentary*. BO 36. Rome: Pontifical Biblical Institute, 1980.

Cheney, Michael. *Dust, Wind and Agony: Character, Speech and Genre in Job*. Stockholm: Almqvist & Wiksell, 1994.

Clines, David J.A. *Job 1–20*. WBC 17. Dallas: Word, 1989.

Craigie, Peter C. "Job and Ugaritic Studies." Pages 28–35 in *Studies in the Book of Job*. Edited by Walter Emanuel Aufrecht. SRSup 16. Waterloo, ON: Wilfrid Laurier University Press, 1985.

Crowell, Bradley L. "A Reevaluation of the Edomite Wisdom Hypothesis." *ZAW* 120.3 (2008): 404–16.

Dahood, Mitchell Joseph. "Northwest Semitic Philology and Job." Pages 55–74 in *The Bible in Current Catholic Thought*. New York: Herder, 1962.

Dahood, Mitchell Joseph. "Some Northwest Semitic Words in Job." *Bib* 38 (1957): 306–20.

Dahood, Mitchell Joseph. "Some Rare Parallel Word Pairs in Job and in Ugaritic." Pages 19–34 in *The Word in the World*. Edited by Richard J. Clifford and George W. MacRae. Cambridge: Weston College, 1973.

Day, John. "How Could Job Be an Edomite?" Pages 392–99 in *The Book of Job*. Edited by Willen A. M. Beuken. BETL 114. Leuven: Leuven University Press; Peeters, 1994.

Dell, Katharine J. *The Book of Job as Sceptical Literature*. BZAW 197. Berlin: de Gruyter, 1991.

Dell, Katharine J. "What Was Job's Malady?" *JSOT* 41.1 (2016): 61–77.

Denning-Bolle, Sara. *Wisdom in Akkadian Literature: Expression, Instruction, Dialogue*. MSO 28. Leiden: Ex Oriente Lux, 1992.

Dhorme, Edouard. *A Commentary on the Book of Job*. Translated by Harold Knight. London: Nelson, 1967.

Dick, Michael B. "Legal Metaphor in Job 31." *CBQ* 41 (1979): 37–50.

Eissfeldt, Otto. *The Old Testament*. New York: Harper & Row, 1965.

Faulkner, R. O. "The Man Who Was Tired of Life." *JEA* 42 (1956): 21–40.

Feinberg, Charles L. "The Poetic Structure of the Book of Job and the Ugaritic Literature." *BSac* 103 (1946): 283–92.

Fohrer, Georg. *Das Buch Hiob*. KAT 16. Gütersloh: Mohn, 1963.

Foster, Benjamin R. *Before the Muses: An Anthology of Akkadian Literature*. Bethesda: CDL Press, 2005.

Fyall, Robert S. *Now My Eyes Have Seen You: Images of Creation and Evil in the Book of Job*. Leicester: Inter-Varsity Press, 2002.

Gemser, Berend. "The Rib- or Controversy Pattern in Hebrew Mentality." Pages 120–37 in *Wisdom in Israel and in the Ancient Near East: Presented to Professor Harold Henry Rowley*. Edited by Martin Noth and David W. Thomas. VTSup 3. Leiden: Brill, 1955.

Gibson, John C. L. *Canaanite Myths and Legends*. 2nd ed. Edinburgh: T&T Clark, 1978.

Goff, Matthew J. "Hellenistic Instruction in Palestine and Egypt: Ben Sira and Papyrus Insinger." *JSJ* 36.2 (2005): 147–72.

Gordis, Robert. *The Book of God and Man: A Study of Job*. Chicago: University of Chicago Press, 1978.

Grabbe, Lester L. *Comparative Philology and the Text of Job: A Study in Methodology*. SBLDS 34. Missoula, MT: Scholars Press, 1977.

Gray, John. "Book of Job in the Context of Near Eastern Literature." *ZAW* 82 (1970): 251–69.

Gray, John. *The Book of Job*. Edited by David J. A. Clines. Sheffield: Sheffield Phoenix, 2010.

Greenstein, Edward L. "Metaphors of Illness and Wellness in Job." Pages 39–50 in *"When the Morning Stars Sang": Essays in Honor of Choon Leong Seow on the Occasion of His Sixty-Fifth Birthday*. Edited by Scott C. Jones and Christine R. Yoder. BZAW 500. Berlin: de Gruyter, 2017.

Greenstein, Edward L. "Sages with a Sense of Humor: The Babylonian Dialogue between a Master and His Servant and the Book of Qohelet." Pages 55–65 in *Wisdom Literature in Mesopotamia and Israel*. Edited by Richard J. Clifford. SBLSymS 36. Atlanta: Society of Biblical Literature, 2007.

Hallo, William W., ed. *Archival Documents from the Biblical World*. Vol 3. of *The Context of Scripture*. Leiden: Brill, 2002.

Hallo, William W., ed. *Canonical Compositions from the Biblical World*. Vol 1. of *The Context of Scripture*. Leiden: Brill, 1997.

Handy, Lowell K. "The Authorization of Divine Power and the Guilt of God in the Book of Job: Useful Ugaritic Parallels." *JSOT* 60 (1993): 107–18.
Humbert, Paul. *Recherches sur les sources égyptiennes de la littérature sapientiale d'Israël*. MUN 7. Neuchâtel: Secrétde l'Univ, 1929.
Jacobsen, Thorkild. *The Treasures of Darkness: A History of Mesopotamian Religion*. New Haven: Yale University Press, 1976.
Jastrow, Morris. "A Babylonian Parallel to the Story of Job." *JBL* 25.2 (1906): 135–91.
Jastrow, Morris. *The Book of Job: Its Origin, Growth and Interpretation: Together with a New Translation Based on a Revised Text*. Philadelphia: J. B. Lippincott Company, 1920.
Johnson, Janet H. *Thus Wrote Onchsheshonqy: An Introductory Grammar of Demotic*. SAOC 45. Chicago: Oriental Institute of the University of Chicago, 1991.
Jones, Scott C. "Corporeal Discourse in the Book of Job." *JBL* 132.4 (2013): 845–63.
Jones, Scott C. "Man and His God: A Wisdom Poem or a Cultic Lament?" Pages 123–43 in *Approaches to Sumerian Literature: Studies in Honor of Stip (H. L. J. Vanstiphout)*. Edited by Piotr Michalowski and Niek Veldhuis. Leiden: Brill, 2006.
Kramer, Samuel N. "'Man and His God': A Sumerian Variation on 'Job' Motif." Pages 170–82 in *Wisdom in Israel and in the Ancient Near East: Presented to Professor Harold Henry Rowley*. Edited by Martin Noth and David W. Thomas. VTSup 3. Leiden: Brill, 1955.
Kwon, JiSeong J. "Psychosomatic Approach to Job's Body and Mind: Based on Somatic Symptom Disorder." *JORH* 59(4) (2020): 2032–44.
Kwon, JiSeong J. *Scribal Culture and Intertextuality: Literary and Historical Relationships between Job and Deutero-Isaiah*. FAT II 85. Tübingen: Mohr Siebeck, 2016.
Lambert, Wilfred G. "A Further Attempt at the Babylonian 'Man and His God.'" Pages 187–202 in *Language, Literature, and History: Philological and Historical Studies Presented to Erica Reiner*. Edited by Francesca Rochberg-Halton. AOS 67. New Haven: American Oriental Society, 1987.
Lambert, Wilfred G. *Babylonian Wisdom Literature*. Oxford: Clarendon, 1960.
Lichtheim, Miriam. *Ancient Egyptian Literature*. Vol. 1. Berkeley: University of California Press, 1973.
Lichtheim, Miriam. *Ancient Egyptian Literature*. Vol. 3. Berkeley: University of California Press, 1980.
Lichtheim, Miriam. *Late Egyptian Wisdom Literature in the International Context: A Study of Demotic Instructions*. OBO 52. Freiburg: Universitätsverlag, 1983.
Lindenberger, James M. *The Aramaic Proverbs of Ahiqar*. Baltimore: Johns Hopkins University Press, 1983.
Loretz, Oswald. "Ugaritisch-Hebräisch in Job 3:3–26: Zum Disput zwischen M. Dahood und J. Barr." *UF* 8 (1976): 123–27.
Magdalene, F. Rachel. *On the Scales of Righteousness: Neo-Babylonian Trial Law and the Book of Job*. BJS 348. Providence, RI: Brown Judaic Studies, 2007.
Magdalene, F. Rachel. "The ANE Legal Origins of Impairment as Theological Disability and the Book of Job." *PRSt* 34 (2007): 23–59.
Margalit, Baruch. "The Legend of Keret." Pages 203–33 in *Handbook of Ugaritic Studies*. Edited by Wilfred G. E. Watson. HdO 39. Leiden: Brill, 1999.
Mattingly, Gerald L. "The Pious Sufferer : Mesopotamia's Traditional Theodicy and Job's Counselors." Pages 305–48 in *Bible in the Light of Cuneiform Literature*. Edited by William W. Hallo. Lewiston, NY: Mellen, 1990.

Moor, Johannes C. de. "Ugarit and the Origin of Job." Pages 225–57 in *Ugarit and the Bible*. Edited by George J. Brooke. Münster: Ugarit-Verlag, 1994.

Müller, Hans-Peter. *Das Hiobproblem: seine Stellung und Entstehung im Alten Orient und im Alten Testament*. EdF 84. Darmstadt: Wissenschaftliche Buchgesellschaft, 1995.

Niditch, Susan. *The Responsive Self: Personal Religion in Biblical Literature of the Neo-Babylonian and Persian Periods*. New Haven: Yale University Press, 2015.

Nougayrol, Jean. "Une Version Ancienne Du 'Juste Souffrant.'" *RB* 59 (1952): 239–50.

O'Connor, Daniel. "The Keret Legend and the Prologue-Epilogue of Job." *ITQ* 55 (1989): 1–6.

Parker, Simon B. *The Pre-Biblical Narrative Tradition: Essays on the Ugaritic Poems Keret and Aqhat*. RBS 24. Atlanta: Scholars Press, 1989.

Parkinson, Richard B. "Literary Form and the Tale of the Eloquent Peasant." *JEA* 78.1 (2017): 163–78.

Parkinson, Richard B. *Poetry and Culture in Middle Kingdom Egypt: A Dark Side to Perfection*. Oakville: Equinox, 2010.

Parkinson, Richard B. *The Tale of Sinuhe and Other Ancient Egyptian Poems, 1940–1640 BC*. Oxford: Clarendon, 1997.

Parkinson, Richard B. *Voices from Ancient Egypt: An Anthology of Middle Kingdom Writings*. London: British Museum, 1991.

Pelham, Abigail. "Job as Comedy, Revisited." *JSOT* 35.1 (2010): 89–112.

Pfeiffer, Robert H. "Edomitic Wisdom." *ZAW* 44 (1926): 13–25.

Pfeiffer, Robert H. "The Dual Origin of Hebrew Monotheism." *JBL* 46 (1927): 193–206.

Pope, Marvin H. *Job*. AB 15. New York: Doubleday, 1965.

Pritchard, James B., ed. *Ancient Near Eastern Texts Relating to the Old Testament*. 3rd ed. Princeton: Princeton University Press, 1969.

Raz, Yosefa. "Reading Pain in the Book of Job." Pages 77–97 in *The Book of Job: Aesthetics, Ethics, Hermeneutics*. Edited by Leora Batnitzky and Ilana Pardes. PJTC 1. Berlin: de Gruyter, 2014.

Rubin, Aaron D. "The Subgrouping of the Semitic Languages." *LLC* 2.1 (2008): 79–102; https://doi.org/10.1111/j.1749-818X.2007.00044.x

Sanders, Jack T. *Ben Sira and Demotic Wisdom*. SBLMS 28. Chico, CA: Scholars Press, 1983.

Sasson, Victor. "An Edomite Joban Text: With a Biblical Joban Parallel." *ZAW* 117.4 (2005): 601–15.

Schellenberg, Annette. "Hiob und Ipuwer: Zum Vergleich des alttestamentlichen Hiobbuchs mit ägyptischen Texten im Allgemeinen und den Admonitions im Besonderen." Pages 55–79 in *Das Buch Hiob und seine Interpretationen: Beiträge zum Hiob-Symposium auf dem Monte Verità vom 14.–19. August 2005*. Edited by Thomas Krüger. ATANT 88. Zürich: TVZ, 2007.

Schmid, Konrad. *Literaturgeschichte des Alten Testaments: eine Einführung*. Darmstadt: WissBuchges, 2008.

Schneider, Thomas. "Hiob 38 und die Demotische Weisheit (Papyrus Insinger 24)." *TZ* 47.2 (1991): 108–24.

Schwienhorst-Schönberger, Ludger. "Das Buch Ijob." Pages 335–47 in *Stuttgarter Altes Testament: Einheitsübersetzung mit Kommentar und Lexikon*. Edited by Erich Zenger. Stuttgart: Katholisches Bibelwerk, 2004.

Seow, Choon-Leong. *Job 1–21: Interpretation and Commentary*. Grand Rapids: Eerdmans, 2013.

Sheldon, Linda J. "The Book of Job as Hebrew Theodicy: An Ancient Near Eastern Intertextual Conflict between Law and Cosmology." PhD diss., University of California, Berkeley, 2002.

Snaith, Norman H. *The Book of Job: Its Origin and Purpose*. SBT 11. London: SCM, 1968.

Soden, Wolfram von. "Das Fragen nach der Gerichtigkeit Gottes im Alten Orient." *MDOG* 96 (1965): 41–59.

Speiser, Ephraim A. "The Case of the Obliging Servant." *JCS* 8 (1954): 98–105.

Tebes, Juan M. "The 'Wisdom' of Edom." *BN* 143 (2009): 97–117.

Toorn, Karel van der. "The Ancient Near Eastern Literary Dialogue as a Vehicle of Critical Reflection." Pages 59–75 in *Dispute Poems and Dialogues in the Ancient and Mediaeval Near East*. Edited by Gerrit J. Reinink and Herman L. J. Vanstiphout. Louvain: Department Oriëntalistiek, 1991.

Weinfeld, Moshe. "Job and Its Mesopotamian Parallels: A Typological Analysis." Pages 217–26 in *Text and Context: Old Testament and Semitic Studies for F. C. Fensham*. Edited by Walter T. Claassen. JSOTSup 48. Sheffield: JSOT, 1988.

Whedbee, James W. "The Comedy of Job." Pages 217–49 in *On Humour and the Comic in the Hebrew Bible*. Edited by Yehuda T. Radday and Athalya Brenner-Idan. JSOTSup 92. Sheffield: Almond Press, 1990.

Collective Identity through Scribalism: Interpreting Plato's Menexenus and the Book of Chronicles*

Sungwoo Park and Johannes Unsok Ro

1. Introduction

Plato's *Menexenus* has often been treated as an enigmatic dialogue.[1] Above all, readers find in the dialogue an "un-Socratic" Socrates who shows assertive confidence in making a public speech. The Socrates in most other Platonic dialogues condemns rhetoric as the chief cause of moral and political corruption.[2] In the *Menexenus*, however, Socrates is depicted as the master of rhetoric, in contrast to his typical characterization. He delivers a funeral speech, which allegedly surpasses the most famous funeral speech by Pericles. What attracts more attention is that Socrates in this dialogue dares to employ some elements of mendacity the "philosophical" Socrates would never apply. For instance, he commits some historical distortions with his alleged premise that the funeral speech necessarily praises the fatherland. Socrates appears to be insensitive to historical inaccuracy, anachronism, and even forgery.

How is it possible that Socrates departs from his typical style of dialectics and turns to such a rhetorical means? How is it possible that Socrates, who is known as a "gadfly" for criticizing the drowsiness of his fellow citizens, now appears to hypnotize people with the distorted history of Athens? Scholars vary in the understanding of the question of whether or not Socrates was sincere in bragging about his rhetorical capability and presenting distorted history. Some argue that the *Menexenus,* unlike other Platonic dialogues, is not aimed at presenting a philosophical message. Instead, they find Socrates to be an ironic figure who apparently makes himself self-contradictory.[3] Despite the huge volume of scholarly

---

* The present article has benefited from a JSPS KAKENHI research grant (22K00080).
[1] For example, Friedländer says: "This is Plato's most confusing work and among his numerous portraits of Socrates, it is most paradoxical" (Paul Friedländer, *Plato II: The Dialogues*, trans. Hans Meyerhoff [London: Routledge & Kegan Paul, 1964], 216); Similarly, Kahn also states that "This little work is almost certainly the most enigmatic of all Plato's writings" (Charles Kahn, "Plato's Funeral Oration: The Motive of the Menexenus," *CP* 58.4 [1963]: 220–34).
[2] The *Gorgias* is the most prominent example to show Socrates' condescending attitude toward rhetoric. In the dialogue Socrates calls himself the true politician and says he could never make a persuasive speech in front of the Athenian jury (Plato, *Plato*. 166.521d–2a [Lamb, LCL]).
[3] For details see Bruce Rosenstock, "Socrates as Revenant: A Reading of the *Menexenus*," *Phoenix* 48.4 (1994): 331–47; Nicole Loraux, *The Invention of Athens: The Funeral Oration in the*

work on the enigmatic character of the *Menexenus*, the most fundamental question remains unanswered concerning Plato's motivation to write such an enigmatic dialogue.

This paper, separating Plato as a writer and Socrates as a character in the dialogue, attempts to answer the question of why Plato wrote such a problematic dialogue by placing Socrates in an unusual context. Above all, it is noteworthy that Plato mutely yet quite appealingly compares Socrates' speech with the famous funeral speech of Pericles documented in Thucydides' *History* (Thuc. II.35–46). The initial exchange between Socrates and Menexenus in the dialogue is concerning the political choice of the public speaker for the upcoming national funeral ceremony.[4] Socrates evokes Pericles by intimating that his speech is, in fact, an unspoken part of Pericles's speech, which actually Aspasia had written for him. Oddly enough, Socrates even informs that he learned how to make a speech from Aspasia, Pericles's mistress. It is reasonable to assume that Socrates' speech in the *Menexenus* is a rejoinder to Pericles's speech. Again, the question is what is Plato's intention in figuratively juxtaposing the two funeral speeches.

The paper argues that Plato here intends to present a new collective identity for Athenians, just as Pericles did earlier through delivering the famous funeral speech to the Athenian public during the War. Plato attempted to replace Pericles's version of Athenian collective identity with his own version in order to rebuild the ruined morality among Athenians in the wake of the Peloponnesian War. What is peculiar to Plato is that he did not deliver the funeral speech directly to the Athenian people, but wrote a dialogue that includes the speech in a dramatic setting. Plato's action of 'writing' is deliberately aimed at political intention to reshape the Athenian collective identity. This interpretation is based on the understanding that Plato's conscious action of 'writing' philosophical dialogues, so-called 'Platonic scribalism' is his political decision to depart from Socrates' insistence that philosophers should never write according to the nature of philosophy.

After examining 'Platonic scribalism,' the paper turns to David's speech in the book of Chronicles. In biblical scholarship, it has been widely recognized that a glaring contrast can be established between the Deuteronomistic David and the Chronistic David, particularly in the Succession Narrative in 1 Chr 22–29. For example, the author(s) of the book of Chronicles (hereafter "the Chronicler"[5])

Classical City, trans. Alan Sheridan (Boston: Harvard University Press, 1986); M. M. Henderson, "Plato's Menexenus and the Distortions of History," *AC* 18 (1975): 25–46; Sara Monoson, "Remembering Pericles: The Political and Theoretical Import of Plato's Menexenus," *PT* 26.4 (1998): 489–513; Stephen Salkever, "Socrates' Aspasian Oration: The Play of Philosophy and Politics in Plato's Menexenus," *APSR* 87.1 (1993): 133–43.

[4] For the beginning of the practice see Rosalind Thomas, *Oral Tradition and Written Record in Classical Athens* (Cambridge: Cambridge University Press, 1989), 207.

[5] In this paper, the term "the Chronicler" is employed to indicate the author or group of authors to whom biblical researchers have attributed the production of the book of Chronicles.

links 2 Sam 24 with the discovery of the temple location.[6] In sharp contrast to Deuteronomistic History, 1 Chr 28:3 describes David as a man of bloodshed, providing an interpretation of 2 Sam 7 on why David will not build the temple but Solomon will.[7] On the other hand, the Deuteronomistic David is ambitious and struggles to get to the top while the Chronistic David desires to endow wisdom and virtue to his nation.

Of course, unlike Plato, the Chronicler is not juxtaposing an older speech with a newer occasion (Pericles vs. Socrates), but he is re-writing the stories and re-formulating the speeches.[8] On the other hand, by doing so the Chronicler, just like Plato, revises and tweaks historical details related to David and Solomon for his own political purpose and ideological agenda by reshaping symbols of the temple, king, Torah and all-Israel for the new collective identity of the Judean community in the Persian or Hellenistic period.[9]

The Chronicler records some battles. However, he makes them a response to David's care for the cultus (1 Chr 18–20, following ch. 16) and to slights against the Israelite people (1 Chr 19:1–5). Foreign relations or expansion is more about trade and peace (2 Chr 8–9), and the nations recognizing Solomon's wisdom and YHWH's temple (2 Chr 2:11–18; ch. 9). David's military expansion was of little interest for the Chronicler because it would not have been a reality in his day. Emphasizing voluntary devotion and virtue as opposed to coercion, nationalism[10] and militarism, the Chronicler, like Plato, made efforts to redefine communal memory and transform the collective identity of his community.

For convenience sake, the singular form of the noun is used; however, it does not mean that the authors of this paper assume an individual author for the book of Chronicles. For the dating and the circumstance of the composition see among others Gary Knoppers, "Hierodules, Priests, or Janitors? The Levites in Chronicles and the History of the Israelite Priesthood," *JBL* 118 (1999): 49–72; Kai Peltonen, "A Jigsaw without a Model: The Date of Chronicles," in *Did Moses Speak Attic? Jewish Historiography and Scripture in the Hellenistic Period*, ed. Lester L. Grabbe, JSOTSup 317 (Sheffield: Sheffield Academic, 2001), 225–71; William M. Schniedewind, *How the Bible Became a Book: The Textualization of Ancient Israel* (Cambridge: Cambridge University Press, 2004), 20–22, 166, 184–87.

[6] For details see section 4, "The Chronicler's David in the Transition of the Kingdom" below.

[7] For details see section 4, "The Chronicler's David in the Transition of the Kingdom" below.

[8] For an interpretation of the interaction between the oral and written Torah in Deuteronomy, see the contribution by Benjamin Kilchör in this volume: "'Then Moses Wrote This Torah' (Deut 31:9): The Relationship of Oral and Written Torah in Deuteronomy."

[9] For a discussion of balance or negotiation regarding collective identity in Persian-era Yehud, see also the contribution by Benjamin D. Giffone in this volume, "Regathering Too Many Stones? Scribal Constraints, Community Memory, and the 'Problem' of Elijah's Sacrifice for Deuteronomism in Kings."

[10] Since the late 18th century, the term "nationalism" has been used to describe the revolutionary movement that established the French nation (Dominik Markl, "Does Deuteronomy Promote a Proto-Nationalist Agenda?" in *Political Theologies in the Hebrew Bible*, ed. Mark Brett and Rachelle Gilmore, JAJSup [Paderborn: Brill, forthcoming]). Thus, applying this term to the Deuteronomistic History or Chronicles could sound somewhat anachronistic. However, Hans Kohn regards the Hebrew Bible as one of the sources of modern nationalism whose essential

In the following sections, this paper tries to illustrate a cross-cultural analogy between the funeral oration of Socrates in the *Menexenus* on the one hand and speeches of David in the book of Chronicles on the other. Specifically, section 2 argues that although both the Platonic and Periclean collective identities encompass the value of liberty, they ultimately differ on what constitutes the "true" liberty: the former consists of the pan-Hellenistic orientation of liberty, while the latter embodies national and, later, the imperialistic feature of liberty. Section 3 shows that Plato's rhetorical scheme for the persuasion is to exhort the younger generation to be virtuous on the one hand and to encourage the older generation to have a reserved attitude toward life. Section 4 emphasizes the role of David's speeches in the book of the Chronicles in the context of the transition of the Kingdom. Finally, section 5 returns to the discussion about the way Plato considered the fundamental relationship between politics and philosophy. At issue is the question about how this "practical Plato," who actively engaged in forming the Athenian collective identity, can go with the other "theoretical Plato," who allegedly devoted himself wholeheartedly to philosophical life. Platonic scribalism, a conscious decision to "write" a philosophical dialogue on the most controversial political issue was a consequence of Platonic compromise between philosophical and political Plato. Our argument is that Plato as well as the Chronicler reformed collective memories and reshaped collective identities through their respective scribal media.

2. Problematizing Periclean Collective Identity

Before analyzing Plato's intention in "writing the funeral speech" in *Menexenus*, it is necessary to note first how the funeral speech in Athens played a significant role in formulating collective identity for the ordinary people. The funeral speech, ἐπιτάφιος λόγος, was generally presented at the national funeral for the war dead.[11] According to Loraux, the speeches consisted of not only the list of glorifying patriotic exploits but Athens' whole trajectory of history for the sake of justifying the regime. Thus, the public speech at the national funeral could be an effective means for revitalizing the city's prideful history. Hearing such praise, ordinary Athenians presumably took pride in their city and felt as if they belonged to such a great city.

---

features are the idea of the chosen people, the consciousness of national history and national Messianism (Hans Kohn, *The Idea of Nationalism: A Study on its Origins and Background* [New York: Macmillan, 1944], 36). According to Markl, "Nationalism is … a useful term to address a central issue among the political ideas expressed in the Pentateuch and, in particular, in the book of Deuteronomy" because Deuteronomy advocates a political agenda, the collective identity of an ethnically defined people to be established on the basis of a specified region, which has some parallels to the modern nation state (Markl, "Proto-Nationalist Agenda," 1–7).

[11] Loraux, *The Invention of Athens*, 28.

Therefore, the funeral speech reflected the collective identity of the Athenians, while also giving them a chance to re-formulate it. When delivered in the public space, it had an effect of creating the "imagined community" for Athenians to continue their collective identity.[12] In this respect, to deliver a funeral speech was an influential and important political activity. It is no surprise that Pericles, the most prominent politician at the time, delivered the famous funeral speech during the early period of the Peloponnesian War and was seriously concerned about the collective identity of his fellow citizens. Now, Plato in the *Menexenus* has Socrates give the same kind of public speech, while appearing to emulate Pericles. What else could be his motivation than to form a new collective identity? However, Plato does not seem straightforward in presenting his morally desirable version of collective identity, since he must know that the candid presentation of moral necessity does not lead to people's agreement. To shape a collective identity requires complicated consideration, in particular, for the multiple strata of social composition, rich and poor, old and young, intellectual and ignorant, etc. Thus, Plato, in order to succeed in forming a new collective identity, must have considered not only the contents of the collective identity but also the forms in which it is presented.

The *Menexenus* begins with a brief conversation between Socrates and Menexenus. Socrates comes across Menexenus, who has just come from the council meeting where people discuss who would be the public speaker of the national funeral. Socrates teases the young Menexenus by asking whether he believes that he has completed education and finished philosophy enough to rule over others, since he now attended the council meeting, one of the major political institutions of Athens. Menexenus retorts that he would like to listen to Socrates' opinion. In reply, Socrates first brings up the nature of funeral speeches. He argues that people are dazzled by those speeches – the speeches are full of praise for the fatherland, its ancestors, and contemporaries. Socrates mocks those who deliver such speeches by intimating that they merely praise people in front of them. Having heard Socrates' mockery, Menexenus provokes Socrates into showing how he can make the "easy" speech. Surprisingly enough, Socrates does not mind presenting his own funeral speech. So begins Socrates' funeral speech.

Beforehand, it should be noted that Socrates explicitly juxtaposes his speech with Pericles's. When he begins his speech, Socrates enunciates the name of Pericles twice as well as the name of Aspasia, who according to Socrates, has

---

[12] Ibid. The expression "imagined community" derives from Benedict Anderson. According to Anderson, the legally formed community is ideally envisioned as a collection of individuals who share features of common identity based on ethnic, linguistic, cultural, or religious factors. He articulates that the interaction between book printing, capitalism, Protestantism, and the emergence of vernacular languages produced a new type of imagined community, which in its fundamental morphology prepared the ground for the modern nation (Benedict Anderson, *Imagined Communities: Reflections on the Origin and Spread of Nationalism* [London: Version, 1983], 37–46).

taught Pericles. Therefore, it is a prerequisite to briefly examine the features of Pericles's funeral speech. Like other funeral speeches, Pericles's speech aims at both praising the warriors and consoling the bereaved. What is peculiar to his speech is that the praise is focused on the Athenian empire and its democratic regime, rather than the individual exploits. In addition, Pericles, unlike other funeral speakers, does not spend much time either identifying Athens' origins or honoring older Athenian generations. Instead, briefly commenting on the ancestors, Pericles honors his contemporary generation for both "augmenting" the empire and "equipping the city in every way to be the most self-sufficient in both war and peace" (Thuc.II.36.3). It is the imperial generation that Pericles would refer to throughout his speech. He shortly mentions Athens's institutions and national mores which have made Athenian imperialism possible (Thuc.II.37.1–41.1). Finally, he praises the character of imperialism itself (Thuc.II.41.2–43.6). According to him, the Athenian empire bears testimony to the very virtue of the Athenians (Thuc.II.41.2).

Pericles continues praising the empire even when he has to console the bereaved. He exhorts the individual Athenian to sacrifice himself out of the love of Athens, precisely in her imperial splendor (Thuc.II.43.1). In this context, Pericles elevates courage and braveness to the status of the most praiseworthy virtue and urges his fellow citizens to emulate the courage of those who died gloriously at the battle (Thuc.II.41.1–6). By sacrificing themselves out of the love of their fatherland, Pericles promises, the citizens will find their true happiness. He speaks to the Athenians to "judge happiness to be freedom, and freedom to be courage." So, he argues that one should be courageous to lead a happy life. Moreover, Pericles emphasizes that it is in this virtue that they should not cower in terror when wars broke out (Thuc.II.43.4). He ends up his praise by mentioning the greatness of the empire. Athens becomes greater and nobler as it provides a condition for each citizen to lead the noblest and best life.

In comparison with Pericles's, Socrates' speech seems to respect more about Athens' older traditions rather than the cause of the contemporary empire. Socrates begins providing an extraordinary account of the origin of Athens. Based on the myth of autochthony,[13] he claims that the Athenians grew from their mother earth (237b–238b) and thus stresses the debt of gratitude and reverence the Athenians owe not only to their mother earth and their ancestors but even to the gods (238b). Then, Socrates speaks about the Athenian regime, featuring it as the "nurturer" and "educator" responsible for the Athenians' goodness: he

---

[13] The myth of autochthony is well described in Plato's *Republic* (415a–c). For Plato's use of autochthony, see Nicole Loraux, *The Children of Athena: Athenian Ideas about Citizenship and the Division between the Sexes*, trans. Caroline Levine. rev. ed. (Princeton: Princeton University Press, 1994); Arlene Saxonhouse, "Nature and Convention in Thucydides' History," *Polity* 10 (1978): 252–73.

narrates a long history of "kings" and then depicts democracy as a kind of aristocracy (238b–239a).

While describing the extended history, Socrates emphasizes that the Athenians who have been nurtured and educated in such a regime value freedom and equality. According to Socrates, the Athenians have cherished freedom constantly along with tradition: to preserve freedom, they have fought against Barbarians, even against Greeks.

To substantiate this claim, Socrates turns to the history of old wars that Athenians had experienced (239a–246a). This part differs the most from Pericles's account of Athenian history. While Pericles describes the brilliant undertakings that have achieved the ascending status of the Athenian empire, Socrates emphasizes how Athenians fought for freedom. First, Socrates gives the highest honors to the old heroes of the Persian Wars, notably, those who won the first victory over the Persians at Marathon [490 BCE] (240b–241a). Socrates stresses that they were not aggressors; instead, they fought for the safety and freedom of the Greeks (239a, 240e). Socrates declares that the brave at Marathon are "fathers not only of our bodies but also of our spirit of *freedom*, ours and that of everyone on this continent" (240e). He asserts that the attitude shown at the Marathon War has become a paragon for the following generations of Athens (240e). While giving the "top prize" to the heroes of the Marathon War, Socrates mentions the sea battles at Salamis and Artemisium [480 BCE] as a second-rank model to show the Athenian character at war. Finally, Socrates talks about the exploits at Plataea [479 BCE]. In these descriptions of the wars, Socrates constantly characterizes the entire history of Athens as one of defending safety and freedom.

As mentioned earlier, Socrates' historiography raises several doubts. Above all, Socrates never acknowledges the expansionist aspects of the Athenian foreign policy in the fifth century. He mentions only how Athenians "drove the Barbarians off the sea" (241d); however, he does not say a word about Athenians' aggressive actions against the other Greeks. Socrates commits historical distortions by omitting this significant part of Athenian history, the expansion of the Athenian empire.

More substantially, Socrates alludes to sea battles at the Eurymedon (466 BCE, cf. Thuc.I.100) and Cyprus (478 BCE, cf. Thuc.I.94–95) and to the Egyptian expedition (circa 460–455 BCE, cf. Thuc.I.104, 109, 110), all of which allegedly endeavored to root out the conspiracies of Barbarians and the Persian King to encroach the land of Greeks (241e). However, one can hardly deny that a series of foreign policies Athens took during this period were aimed at making Athens an empire.[14]

The most revealing case of historical distortion occurs in Socrates' analysis of the cause of the Peloponnesian War. He simply regards the period of Pentacon-

---

[14] John V. A. Fine, *The Ancient Greeks: A Critical History* (Boston: Belknap, 1983), 354–55.

taetia, the history of the fifty years after the Persian War, as peaceful. And he explains that it was "when the other Greeks' emulation of Athens' success turned into envy" that the War broke out (242a). However, in fact, the Greeks during that period lined up against each other in alliance with either Athens or Sparta. The cause of the outbreak of the Peloponnesian war is not as simple as Socrates explains. By pointing out envy as the main cause of the war, Socrates leaves out, at the very least, the fact that not the envy but the animosity of the Greeks against Athens, notably, their fear of Athenian expansion, played the decisive role in causing the War. Socrates here ignores the famous cause of the War explained by Thucydides: "The truest cause, even if the one least apparent in speech, I believe, to be that the Athenians by becoming great and instilling fear in the Lacedaimonians compelled them to make war" (Thuc.I.23.6). Moreover, emphasizing other Greeks' changed minds "from emulation to envy," Socrates, indeed, keeps silent about the most significant change of minds among Athenians themselves: an ambition to build an Athenian empire.

Largely disregarding historical accuracy, Socrates constantly asserts that all these elements of Athenian history point to the Athenians' veneration of freedom not only for themselves but also for other Greeks. He says that Athenians fought against Spartans on behalf of Boeotian freedom at the battle of Tanagra (457 BCE, 242a); Socrates takes it as an example of "helping Greeks against Greeks on behalf of freedom" (242b). Thucydides, however, reports that the Athenian engagement in Tanagra was mainly for conquest rather than liberation (Thuc.I.108).[15]

For Socrates, the Peloponnesian War is further evidence that the Athenians love freedom and hate unnecessary fighting, particularly among the Greeks. Socrates points out that the Athenians had seized the Spartan leaders at Sphacteria (425 BCE, Thuc.IV.1–39), but later sent them back in order to maintain the peace (421 BCE, 242c–d). Socrates' description of the Sicilian expedition also differs from the general understanding of this event, such as that of Thucydides. Thucydides describes the expedition as fueled by the "love" of imperial longings (Thuc. VI.24). In contrast, Socrates insists that it was undertaken for the freedom of the Leontinians (242e–243a).

Why does Socrates dare to commit such a myriad of historical distortions?[16] We would find the clue in the sheer fact that Socrates does not intend to leave a recorded history but makes a funeral speech as a way of participating in the political activity of formulating the Athenian collective identity. In particular, Socrates undertakes to form a new collective identity for Athenians, who would cherish freedom not only for themselves but also for other Greeks – the free-

---

[15] Fine, *Ancient Greeks*, 354–55.

[16] For the discussions of the historical distortions and lies Socrates commits, see Kahn, "Plato's Funeral Oration," 224–25; Henderson, "Plato's Menexenus," 38–46.

dom of universal value. This characterization is far from the existing one Pericles formed by his lavish praise of Athenian imperialism. Socrates' silence about Athenian imperialism and his extraordinarily biased historiography are meant not to justify imperialism but to mitigate its aggressiveness by offering a new collective identity that leans toward the universal value, the freedom of the entire Greek civilization.

When forming an identity, people do not write about past events exactly as they had happened – not about what people did, but about what they should have done, along with the idea that mistaken past deeds are responsible for the present deplorable situation. In this perspective, the funeral speech is a significant political space for the Athenians not to check historical accuracy but to recall the collective memory from the wishful thinking. Thus, it is necessary to understand Socrates' biased historiography, bearing in mind his motivation to make public speech.

As we noted above, Socrates describes the entire history of Athens as the history of promoting their own freedom and that of the other Greeks. In this respect, even the defeat in the Peloponnesian War and a series of civil wars following it are not necessarily taken as tragic events to Athens. They are meaningful in cultivating Athenians' spirit of freedom. Even when Socrates refers to the civil war of Athens (404 BCE), he recalls the Amnesty Law in order to emphasize that Athenians showed forgiveness and love of freedom (243e). Finally, he downplays the hatred and jealousy among the Greeks during the Corinthian War (244b). Socrates here ascribes all the negative sides of history merely to misfortunes that happened towards the end of the Peloponnesian War.

Socrates' speech never forgets to embellish Athenian role in defending freedom for themselves as well as the other Greeks, while recollecting history from the remote to the recent time. If we keep in mind that Socrates makes the funeral speech with the motivation to build a new collective identity, we can conclude that the new identity should be based on the love for universal liberty. Plato implies that the advent of the Athenian empire corrupted previously existing Athenian values. For him, the seed of this corruption is implanted in Pericles's adamant pride in empire, although the Periclean empire is not the most wretched example of empire. So, Plato has a good reason to rewrite the history of Athens both to cure the corrupted status of Athenian minds and to revitalize the older collective identity which must be distinguished from the current imperialistic collective identity Pericles heavily influenced.

To achieve this goal, Plato let Socrates discard historical accuracy. Perhaps Plato would have a good justification: Socrates' speech in this dialogue is in the form of the funeral speech, which is supposedly allowed to be tendentious history to some extent. His distorted history is further justified by the fact that the speech does not come directly from Socrates but from Aspasia, Pericles's mistress. Paradoxically, Socrates, through these historical distortions, criticizes implicitly what the Athenians did in the past and simultaneously envisions what direction they should take in the future concerning their collective identity. For example, the Athenians must have been aware that their expedition to Sicily was not as justified as is portrayed in Socrates' distorted description. Having heard Socrates' historical distortion, they must have felt guilty about their unspoken motivation: through the expedition they did not attempt to liberate Leontinians but to fulfill their ambition. Socrates' distorted history may help Athenians recognize past wrongdoings, and then suggest what should be envisioned for the future – thereby forming a desirable collective identity of Athens.

However, it is a tricky undertaking to formulate a reliable collective identity which citizens of an empire should opt for. Plato here does not seem to renounce the empire altogether. Plato agrees that the empire as such is not objectionable, as far as it guarantees the freedom of the city from external threats. However, Plato warns, an excessive desire for empire, the pursuit of excessive domination, or imperialistic ambition, seriously undermine the spirit of freedom from within. Concerning the danger posed by excessive expansion, Plato agrees with Thucydides. What is peculiar to Plato is that he tackles the issue of how to avoid falling into an excessively imperialistic – and thus, self-undermining – empire. Plato seeks a stable combination of empire and freedom. Plato finds the solution in formulating the new collective identity that matches such a liberal empire.

3. New Collective Identity through the Separate Messages to the Old and the Young

After having given the historical accounts of Athenians' wartime exploits, Socrates leaves special messages to the children and the parents of the soldier dead (246c–249c). To leave the messages to "those who remain" for the sake of consolation is a typical format of the funeral speech. It is remarkable that Pericles underrated the importance of consoling the bereft families while focusing more on the task of encomium of the Athenian empire. In particular, his "brief piece of advice to the widows" is infamous because he even encouraged the mourning mothers to send even more of their sons to the battlefields. Pericles's point was that they could achieve virtue and the highest good only by participating in the aggrandizement of the empire.

Then, what is the feature of Socrates' messages by comparison? It is notable that Socrates broadens the subject of his speech in the consolatory messages. He does not constrain his speech to talking about the war exploits or historical achievements, but he extends the subject to such a grave question of the end of life or worthy way of life. Socrates exhorts the children of the warriors to behave courageously on the fields of battle. Yet, more emphatically, he encourages them to live virtuously. Similarly, in the message given to the parents, Socrates asks them to reflect their entire lives on moderation, independence, and finally, self-sufficiency.[17] Although both messages appeal to virtue, the nuanced differences between the two messages serve Plato's motivation to enact the new collective identity more practically.

First, the message to the children does not come directly from Socrates himself. Here Socrates perports to represent the voice of the fathers who sacrificed themselves at war. In actuality, Socrates is two degrees removed from this voice of the fathers: first, Socrates' whole speech originates in the voice of Aspasia; and second, Socrates represents the voice of the dead fathers. Regardless, emphasizing the virtue of courage, the voice of the fathers reiterates that they died nobly at war. It warns that "life is not worth living for the one who brings shame upon his own, and that such a man will find no friend among either human beings or gods, neither on the earth nor under it once he died" (246d). However, the voice does not confine the subject to the virtue of courage at war. Instead, it quickly broadens the range of virtue by encouraging the offspring to consider how they should conduct in their pursuits in life.[18] Thus, the voice continues to urge the children: "Even if you should practice something else, practice it with virtue, knowing that without this *all possessions and pursuits* are shameful and base" (246e–247a). Unlike Pericles, Socrates is definitely dealing with the question of the good life, not merely the question of the good soldier.

However, it is remarkable that the way Socrates treats the issue of the good life is different from how he used to do so. Socrates' message to the bereft families differs subtly from what we may expect from the philosopher, Socrates. He exhorts the children to lead the life of moral virtue. In other words, unlike a "philosophical" Socrates, Socrates here appeals at best to the virtue that is generally agreed among ordinary citizens. He says not a word about philosophy. His exhortation may be taken as a practical advice to the bereaved children. Perhaps the apparent gap between the "philosophical" Socrates and the Socrates who is here interested in the practical implementation of moral virtues, requires Plato to depict that Socrates speak with the voice of the children's fathers, two steps away from Socrates' own voice.

The voice of the fathers exhorts their now-orphaned children to be virtuous in every sphere of life. This voice emphasizes the entirety of virtue. Yet, if the children have to choose one virtue, it should be justice rather than courage. The voice declares that even all knowledge when "severed from justice and the rest of virtue reveals itself as villainy, not wisdom" (246e–247a). Thus, the voice commands the children to "try to be zealous about justice – first and last, in all

---

[17] Scholars agree that Socrates seems to return to his own posture in these messages because they find the most serious and solemn moment in these messages. See Susan D. Collins and Devin Stauffer, "The Challenge of Plato's Menexenus," *RP* 61.1 (1999): 85–115; Salkever, "Socrates' Aspasian Oration."

[18] For a biblical analogy see 1 Chr 28:8; 29:18.

things and in every way." Moreover, with respect to the virtuous life, the voice of the fathers does not merely hold themselves as a model but challenges their offspring to surpass their accomplishments (247a). Finally, the voice of the fathers mentions afterlife: "if you live by what we have said, you will come to us as friends to friends when your own fate carries you off. But if you are neglectful and live basely, no one will welcome you favorably" (247c).

Considering the voice of the fathers as a guideline given to children, we can conclude that the way of life Socrates endorses is sharply contrasted with the way of life Pericles praised in his funeral speech. Pericles praised the ambitious political life, especially as a citizen of an empire. To lead the way of life Socrates encourages, one does not necessarily deny living as a citizen of an empire. While Socrates constantly emphasizes moral virtues in the entire sphere of life, he still appreciates the good an empire may offer, such as security, wealth, and freedom. In other words, the way of life Socrates here supports is still a political life that can be properly applied in the Athenian empire, however distinctive it is from the more ambitious and imperial Periclean political life. After all, the message given to the children is not about living a philosophical life but living a political life, although its version is subtly yet meaningfully different from Pericles's.

Why then does Socrates adopt the unexpected posture of giving up philosophical life and endorsing a specific political life? Socrates wants to direct Athenians' attention to a subtle connection between foreign policies and the moral ground of domestic politics. For Socrates, it is not forbidden to be a citizen of an empire, as far as the empire guarantees security and freedom. The problem is that the empire is inclined to expand its power such that it brings moral corruption to its citizens. As Collins and Stauffer point out correctly, "since there is no absolute line between the principles that guide the conduct of foreign affairs and those that apply in the domestic sphere, the conduct of foreign affairs naturally has an impact on a city's domestic life."[19]

People under the Periclean empire may understand that their empire is unrestricted by justice or any law that might limit its actions. People may overlook the unjust behaviors of their own empire by claiming that certain wrongdoings abroad are inevitable to maintain the empire. However, this self-understanding would result in overlooking morally unbridled actions within the empire.[20]

Socrates' assumption that moral corruption suffuses from foreign policies to domestic politics may explain why Socrates takes pains to bury the aggressive and expansionist nature of Athenian imperialism, as is often criticized as a historical distortion. Socrates invokes the spirit of the Marathon fighters, since they observed justice abroad and, at the same time, practiced virtue at home. In sum,

---

[19] Collins and Stauffer, "The Challenge," 12–13.
[20] For a discussion of the impact of foreign policy on domestic affairs, see Saxonhouse, "Nature and Convention," 252–73.

Socrates objects to the imperialism celebrated by Pericles, since Periclean imperialism ultimately threatens the moral virtue of citizens, undermines its fragile character, and even leads to loss of it altogether. Nevertheless, Socrates still does not deny the benefits of living in the "less ambitious" or moderate empire, such as security and freedom.[21] Now, the question is how Athenian people can become citizens of such a moderate or so-called Socratic empire, instead of being citizens of the imperialistic Periclean empire.

In our view, the message given to the older generation gives some hints to this question. Socrates speaks to the parents who lost their sons at war. Socrates now takes the voice of the sons. Strangely, the voice refers to the famous Delphic proverb "Nothing too much" and offers an extraordinary interpretation of it. Basically, the proverb is in line with the voice of the fathers, which touts moderation to their sons. Now the voice of the sons interprets the Delphic saying specifically as an injunction not to allow oneself to become overly dependent upon other human beings: it insists that he who "depends on himself for everything, or nearly everything" is the one who is "best prepared to live", because his independence from other human beings protects his own fortunes from being "compelled to wander" with the changing fortunes of others (247e–248a). According to the voice of the sons, only those who achieve both self-sufficiency and independence are moderate, courageous, and prudent; they can follow the proverb's teaching of self-sufficiency and independence even when facing birth and death.

In this message to the parents, Socrates apparently renounces Periclean political life, a characteristic of the expansionist imperialism; it instead shows the superiority of moderation over ambition and of self-sufficiency over patriotic zealotry. Moreover, the exhortation urging to become as independent as possible is quite apart from the earlier advice for the children to constantly pursue the virtue that fits in the greatness of the empire. Here the voice of the sons downplays the necessity of emulation for the virtue, as claimed earlier to meet their parents honorably in the afterlife. Instead, it asserts to the parents that all the virtue including moderation, courage, and prudence, finds common ground in achieving self-sufficiency. As Salkever points out, this message has signficant philosophical overtones.[22] In fact, the message is reminiscent of Socrates' famous dictum that virtue is knowledge, the dictum that is ultimately geared toward the priority of philosophical life.

However, it should also be noted that the "nothing-too-much" attitude toward life, no matter how much it is related to the philosophical life, is not exactly the same as the philosophical life; the philosophical life is meant to devote entirely

---

[21] The possibility of doing philosophy is another benefit coming from this moderate empire, although this claim is controversial and beyond the subject of the paper.

[22] Salkever, "Socrates' Aspasian Oration," 140–41.

to the pursuit of wisdom regardless of political affairs. The way of life Socrates encourages the parents to choose is close to the philosophical life only in the sense that it keeps some distance from the excessive passion towards the earthly goods, whatever they are.

Then, what does Plato aim to achieve by suggesting such a subtle but ambivalent way of life to the parents who must be despondent at losing their sons? He does not intend merely to console them; here again, Plato tries to formulate the collective identity of the Athenians. Our interpretation is that Plato considers a certain collaboration between the younger and the older generations. Thus, he lets Socrates address them separately: the former are exhorted to be actively virtuous in every sphere of life, whereas the latter are exhorted to be reserved and remote from the passionate attitude towards life. In doing so, Plato contrives a social reform so that the younger generation would devote their lives to build a moderate empire – the empire organized by the principle of universal freedom and detached from the Periclean expansionist imperialism – while the older generation would choose a temperate and semi-philosophical life.

If Plato does not reject the Athenian empire entirely yet approves it only in the moderate and liberal form, why does not he adhere to the concept of liberal empire that looks like a Periclean format of combining liberty and empire where citizens may devote themselves to the cause of freedom and, at the same time, take pride in the empire? Why does Plato instead make a difficult choice of presenting a worldly version of philosophical life? We believe it is because Plato thinks that the liberal empire can easily degenerate into the expansionist and eventually heinous imperialism. Plato's point must be that, no matter how attractive the liberal empire appears to be to the Athenians in its earlier stage, the empire should be ultimately swayed by citizens' excessive ambitions only to be degenerated.

Encouraging the older generation to live temperate and semi-philosophical lives, Plato wishes to contrive a social reformation in which all the citizens keep the empire untainted. Plato arranges an inter-generational cooperation by leading each generation to different values so that the younger and the older generations play their parts toward the goal of achieving balance in a moderate and durable empire.

However, we would point out that to give the older generation a message is not sufficient for them to choose such a semi-philosophical life. The genuine philosophers, however small the group is, need to exist in the empire in order to give tangible examples to the ordinary people; otherwise, the older generation could not find a model to follow. In order to achieve the goal of maintaining the moderate and liberal empire Plato envisions, philosophers and their way of life are necessary. From this perspective, philosophers, however irrelevant and thus useless they look in dealing with the affairs of the empire, play an important role in moderating imperial citizens and keeping the empire in a balanced position.

4. The Chronicler's David in the Transition of the Kingdom

The book of Chronicles within the Hebrew Bible provides a useful comparison with Plato's attempted revisionism. Of particular interest is the way in which the Chronicler rewrites and expands the presentation of the transfer of the kingdom from David to Solomon that is found within the books of Samuel and Kings (2 Sam 22 to 1 Kgs 2; 1 Chr 21–29). Like Plato's Socrates in the *Menexenus*, the Chronicler appears to have been slightly distorting – or, at the very least, fleshing out – the received history, in the interest of molding a morally stable collective identity.

It is generally[23] accepted within scholarship that the Chronicler draws from the so-called Deuteronomistic History (DtrH), mostly the books of Samuel and Kings, in re-presenting the history of the monarchic period of Israel. For the purposes of this comparison, it is not necessary to enter into the extensive debates regarding the dating of the various elements and the final forms of the DtrH and Chronicles; it is sufficient to note that for DtrH, proposed dates of finalization range from the Babylonian period to the early Persian period (roughly the sixth century BCE), whereas Chronicles would have been written considerably later, late in the Persian period or in the Hellenistic period (the fourth century BCE or even later).[24] For this reason, scholars also debate the degree of influence of Persian versus Hellenistic thought and historiographical approaches in Chronicles.[25]

Though there are similarities between ideas and approach in the Chronicler's re-presentation of David's legacy and Plato's presentation of Socrates, it is important first to note significant differences. First, both Socrates's and Pericles's orations are preserved (by Plato and Thucydides) in texts that were produced within a generation of the purported events (in the fifth century BCE); both Samuel–Kings and Chronicles are presenting events several centuries after they

---

[23] Though this point is not universally accepted – see, e.g., the important work of Raymond F. Person Jr., and A. Graeme Auld – the comparison to Chronicles would still be relevant even if the Deuteronomistic History and Chronicles were "contemporary competing historiographies," as Person contends; A. Graeme Auld, *Kings Without Privilege: David and Moses in the Story of the Bible's Kings* (Edinburgh: T&T Clark, 1994); Raymond F. Person Jr., *The Deuteronomic History and the Book of Chronicles: Scribal Works in an Oral World*, AIL 6 (Atlanta: Society of Biblical Literature, 2010).

[24] See the recent summary of discussions in Benjamin D. Giffone, *'Sit at My Right Hand': The Chronicler's Portrait of the Tribe of Benjamin in the Social Context of Yehud*, LHBOTS 628 (London: T&T Clark, 2016), 51–54.

[25] Gary N. Knoppers, *1 Chronicles 1–9*, AB (New York: Doubleday, 2004), 105; Kenneth G. Hoglund, "The Chronicler as Historian: A Comparativist Perspective," in *The Chronicler as Historian*, ed. M. Patrick Graham, Kenneth G. Hoglund, and Steven L. McKenzie, JSOTSup 238 (Sheffield: Sheffield Academic, 1997), 19–29; Diana Edelman and Lynette Mitchell, "Chronicles and Local Greek Histories," in *What Was Authoritative for Chronicles?* ed. Ehud Ben Zvi and Diana Edelman (Winona Lake, IN: Eisenbrauns, 2011), 229–52.

allegedly occurred. Furthermore, Pericles's and Socrates's orations were in fact distinct events, whereas the DtrH and Chronicles give competing accounts of the same event/process: David's handover of the kingdom to Solomon.

However, both Pericles and Socrates (in the speeches as presented) recount a common history of Athens; the later presentation is apparently presented as a competing account of history and its ongoing significance for Athenians. Moreover, Plato's Socrates claims to have received some of his material from a common "muse" with Pericles (Pericles's mistress). Even though David's speeches at the end of his life are not a "funeral oration," the Chronicler presents David's final words as a way of re-formulating the All-Israelite collective identity, independent of a kingship. Socrates represents the voice of the dead fathers; David is a dying father, who addresses his son, his people, and – unlike in Samuel and Kings – all who come after them.

The texts in view for this comparison are the collection of materials at the end of the book of Samuel that relate to the end of David's reign (2 Sam 22–24); the first two chapters of the book of Kings (1 Kgs 1–2); and the Chronicler's much-expanded account of the transition of power (1 Chr 21–29). The Chronicler has certainly revised details but has also given coherence of presentation to a historical moment that receives rather sparce and narrow treatment in the Deuteronomistic account.[26]

The Dtr's version (1 Kgs 1–2) is much more immediate, militarized, and concerned with the transfer of power. This court story, sometimes known as the "Succession Narrative,"[27] expands the account of David's rule from 2 Samuel 9–20. The dramaturgy is intense and the story recounts the progress of the conflict (1 Kgs 1:1–53), which was worsened by David's physical deterioration. David is weak and dying (1:1–4), and has not made public his intention to put Solomon on the throne after him, thereby leaving an opening for his other son to seize control (1:5–10). David's final words to Solomon consist of a personal, not a national, exhortation to virtue – but also instructions to settle David's personal vendettas (1 Kgs 2:1–10). David is not described as making any plans or material provision for the building of a permanent temple. His fidelity to YHWH is signaled not mainly by actions, but by two songs celebrating YHWH's past deeds: a psalm of deliverance (2 Sam 22:1–51//Ps 18), and his last words (2 Sam 23:1–7).

The Chronicler, seeking to recast David as an establisher of the cult, provider of stability, tradent of law, and example of virtue, clearly considers the Deuteronomistic account wholly unsatisfactory. In his account, the transfer is deliberate, detailed, and public (1 Chr 21–29). The Chronicler presents Solomon as

---

[26] Of course, it is debatable whether the text of 1 Chr 21–29 was composed by the Chronicler himself or by a later editor. For the detailed discussion related to the composition of 1 Chr 21–29 see Gary N. Knoppers, *1 Chronicles 10–29* (AB; New York: Doubleday, 2004), 788–98.

[27] For the recent status of research related to "Succession Narrative," see Andrew Knapp, "The Succession Narrative in Twenty-first-century Research" *CurBR* 19.3 (2021): 211–34.

both the Temple builder and the future king (1 Chr 22:10; 28:4–5). Throughout the narrative, Solomon's status as chosen successor is stressed. Solomon is appointed by David in preference to the other officials in David's reign (1 Chr 23:6–27:34). Solomon's mission is to build the Temple, and he should do so as king. The entire story unfolds overtly as David's preparations to hand on his kingdom to Solomon. The Chronicler has substituted Dtr's succession narrative, which is filled with murder and conspiracy, with his own succession story, which is much more harmonious. The words and deeds of the Chronicler's David acknowledge continuity with the past, but also open a new chapter characterized not by war, taxation and forced labor,[28] but by peace, wisdom, and cultic fidelity. As a reward, David dies "at a ripe old age, full of days, riches and honor" (1 Chr 29:28). The Chronicler's David is deeply interested in permanently ensuring the ongoing right-standing of the people before YHWH through the Jerusalem cultus. The Chronicler expands the story of David's humble repentance in the matter of the census (2 Sam 24) to make the episode the discovery of the divinely-ordained site for the future temple (1 Chr 21:1–22:1).[29] Rather than being funded through taxation, the temple construction and maintenance are funded by the voluntary contributions of the king (1 Chr 28:11–29:5), and of the people following his example (1 Chr 29:6–9).

In his funeral oration, Pericles celebrates the Athenian empire and expansionism; in the *Menexenus*, Socrates emphasizes the significance of national strength through virtue rather than through empire. In Chronicles, David is forbidden to build the temple because he "was a man of war and has shed much blood" (1 Chr 28:3); rather, his son Solomon ("peace"; 22:9) will build the temple in which YHWH will dwell. This is consistent with the characterization of David within the book of Samuel, but the causal connection is unique to Chronicles. Prior to the transition of kingship, the Chronicler attributes David's martial success to his care for the cults (1 Chr 18–20, following ch. 16), and a just response to the aggression against Israel (1 Chr 19:1–5). Subsequent foreign relations and expansion of Israelite influence are interested in trade and peace (2 Chr 8–9),

---

[28] "… The Chronicler, writing in the 4th century BCE, chooses to emphasize David's soliciting only voluntary contributions to the temple building fund (1 Chr 29:1–9), and Solomon only exacting forced labor from foreigners, not Israelites (2 Chr 2:17–18, contra 1 Kgs 5:13–14)." Jonathan Warner and Benjamin D. Giffone, "Economic Thought in the Hebrew Scriptures: Context and Reception," in *Economic Thought before Economics*, ed. Tomáš Evan (Prague: Czech Technical University Publishing, forthcoming).

[29] Yairah Amit, "Araunah's Threshing Floor: A Lesson in Shaping Historical Memory," in *What Was Authoritative for Chronicles?* ed. Ehud Ben Zvi and Diana Edelman (Winona Lake, IN: Eisenbrauns, 2011), 133–44; Louis C. Jonker, "Of Jebus, Jerusalem and Benjamin: The Chronicler's *Sondergut* in 1 Chronicles 21 against the Background of the Late Persian Era in Yehud," in *Chronicling the Chronicler: The Book of Chronicles and Early Second Temple Historiography*, ed. Tyler F. Williams and Paul S. Evans (Winona Lake, IN: Eisenbrauns, 2013), 81–102.

and the nations recognizing Solomon's wisdom and YHWH's temple (2 Chr 2:11–18; 2 Chr 9).

As we have seen, Socrates appeals to the myth of autochthony, Athenians' origin from mother earth, to shape their corporate identity and sense of responsibility. The Chronicler likewise begins his book with an account of the origins of nations, emphasizing the common humanity of Israel and its neighbors. Israel's uniqueness comes from the gift of YHWH's law (16:40; 22:12) and the land (1 Chr 22:13, 18).

Amasai's speech to David in 1 Chr 12:18 demonstrates that David and his dynasty were the recipients of divine grace and that "peace" was to be the sign of Davidic dynasty.[30] In 22:6–16, a speech attributed to David himself, the topic of "peace" is reiterated and further developed. This speech reveals the Chronicler's answer to the question of why the temple was not built by David, but by Solomon.[31] The delay of the temple building is regarded in 1 Kgs 5:3 as a consequence of historical circumstance rather than divine judgment or providence. In the speech of 1 Chr 22:6–16, a more comprehensive theological clarification is provided. In the Chronicler's view, David's reign did not know "rest" because the temple was not yet built.[32] The assertion that violence precludes a character from involvement in the construction of the temple (1 Chr 22:8) was a novel thought of the Chronicler, which is not present in the DtrH. The temple construction can be initiated and completed only by "a man of peace" (1 Chr 22:9), who is Solomon. Rather than attributing complete pacifism to the Chronicler (see the positive evaluation of David's military victories in the following section: 22:18), a more plausible interpretation would be that the Chronicler considers David as a second Moses, in particular as he receives and conveys the divine instructions for the construction of the temple and tabernacle, but ultimately was not able to complete the divine mission.[33]

It has often been claimed that the Chronicler portrays David as an idealized and flawless monarch.[34] However, as the stories in 1 Chronicles 13; 15 and 21 clearly indicate, this interpretation must be nuanced; King David is far from ideal in the eyes of the Chronicler.[35] Of course, there is a clear tendency in the books of Chronicles to emphasize David's glories and to overlook his flaws. For instance, the Chronicler excludes David's adultery with Bathsheba, his murder of Uriah, and the prophet Nathan's denunciation (1 Chr 20:1–3), and finishes the narrative

---

[30] Rex Mason, *Preaching the Tradition: Homily and Hermeneutics after the Exile based on the 'Addresses' in Chronicles, the Speeches in the Books of Ezra and Nehemiah and the Post-exilic Prophetic Books* (Cambridge: Cambridge University Press, 1990), 20.

[31] Sara Japhet, *The Ideology of the Book of Chronicles and Its Place in Biblical Thought*, trans. Anna Barbar (Frankfurt am Main: Lang, 1989), 396.

[32] Mason, *Preaching the Tradition*, 23.

[33] Mason, *Preaching the Tradition*, 25.

[34] Robert North, "Theology of the Chronicler," *JBL* 82 (1963): 376–78.

[35] Japhet, *Chronicles*, 473.

of David's battles by omitting a substantial chunk of the so-called "Court History of David" in 2 Sam 13–21. However, this tendency does not derive from the Chronicler's interest in David as a person, but from what might be called "theocracy".[36] David's emotional ties are of no concern to the Chronicler. Rather David is frequently represented as the founder of Jerusalem's most important cultic institutions, including the temple and Levitical as well as priestly functions (1 Chr 15:1–16:43; 17:1–15; 23:1–26:32; 28:1–29:9).

In 1 Chr 22:17–19 (David's address to the leadership of Israel), political and military leaders and their victories are portrayed as instrumental: the military victories give "rest" to Israel, thereby liberating them for their authentic mission which is the building of a theocratic community.[37] The divine providence which promoted David and his descendants to the throne is not for them as individuals, but for the theocratic community. In particular, it was revealed that Solomon has built the temple so that the Israelites would know that the true "rest" was present in their midst.[38] As the Davidic speeches demonstrate, the Chronicler's concerns are directed away from militaristic and nationalistic policies, and towards "theocratic" ones.[39]

The Chronicler draws a parallel between David and Moses, and between Solomon's temple and the tabernacle.[40] This illustrates that the key concern of the Chronicler is not so much the Davidic dynasty itself, but the temple, for whose sake the dynasty is inaugurated and in which it sought its fulfillment. For the Chronicler, the temple of Jerusalem is a symbol of the theocratic rule of YHWH based on the virtue of the Israelite community's voluntary obedience and contributions. The Chronicler aims not merely to more adequately bridge the gap between David and Solomon for the sake of David's reputation; rather, the transition itself sets forth for all time the purposes for which the kingship was established. These higher principles are applicable and universal (for Israel), regardless of whether there is actually a king around to implement them.

In the Davidic speeches we might hear a message from the Chronicler to his post-exilic audience. Indeed, the speech of 1 Chr 22:17–19 could well serve the purpose of connecting the call for concern of the temple with the post-exilic situation. It is a similar call which is repeated in the books of Haggai, Zechariah and

---

[36] Mason, *Preaching the Tradition*, 26.
[37] Mason, *Preaching the Tradition*, 26.
[38] Mason, *Preaching the Tradition*, 27.
[39] Mason, *Preaching the Tradition*, 27.
[40] Dominik Markl argues that the primary aim of the sanctuary texts in the final phases of Pentateuch is to establish continuity between the pre-exilic and the post-exilic cults in Jerusalem. This theological tendency is inherited and strengthened by the Chronicler (Dominik Markl, "The Wilderness Sanctuary as the Archetype of Continuity between the Pre- and the Postexilic Temples of Jerusalem," in *The Fall of Jerusalem and the Rise of the Torah*, ed. Peter Dubovský, Dominik Markl and Jean-Pierre Sonnet, FAT 107 [Tübingen: Mohr Siebeck, 2016], 228–45).

Malachi. In the environment of the Persian empire, the people are to follow the realization of divine promises of rest and prosperity given to David, but not in hopes of a political and military restoration of the Davidic dynasty.[41]

There are several instances in which expressions of God's care for the Davidic dynasty in the DtrH are deleted by the Chronicler. Rather, it is emphasized that Solomon would be protected for the sake of his divinely-assigned mission. This reveals a limitation in the interpretation of "messianism" in Chronicles on the sole basis of divine care for the Davidic line. In the Chronicler's focus on the election of David and the Davidic line, the aim of this election is the construction of the temple. In the Chronicler's view, the post-exilic theocracy is a valid successor to the pre-exilic monarchy.

We have seen several points of comparison between David's speeches in the book of Chronicles and Socrates' speech in *Menexenus*. The Chronicler shifts the nationalism and militarism of the DtrH into voluntary devotion, virtue and the theocratic rule of YHWH, just as Plato attempts to replace the imperialism of Pericles's oration with an emphasis on virtue, Athenian origins, philosophy, and pan-Hellenism. While there does not seem to have been an "Israelite empire" or much of an imperial impulse by the time the received Hebrew texts are being compiled, Yehudian scribes are also attempting to unify disparate groups through new and revised accounts of Israel's founding traditions, and principles of virtue and covenant faithfulness that will enable them to survive the Babylonian, Persian and Hellenistic empires.[42]

5. Collective Identity and Scribalism at the Crossroads of Philosophy and Theology

Thucydides commented that Pericles's absence resulted in a radical decline of the Athenian empire (Thuc.II.65). Thucydides warned the excessive ambition of people that led them to make the imprudent and reckless decisions on the imperial policies. Thus, Thucydides bolstered a Periclean empire and its ensuing collective identity among Athenians as a solution to prevent the empire from being swayed by excessively ambitious people. However, Thucydides could not have imagined how easily the Periclean empire, indispensably meeting the insatiable desires of the people, would slide into an excessively power-loving and thus aggressive empire.

This paper argues that Plato attempted to overhaul the tragic situation by presenting an alternative collective identity: Athenian citizens in a liberal and

---

[41] Mason, *Preaching the Tradition*, 27.

[42] For analyses of the appearances of YHWH's Torah in the books of Chronicles during the late Persian/early Hellenistic period, see the contribution by Peter Altmann in this volume, "Tracing Divine Law: Written Divine Law in Chronicles."

temperate empire. For Plato, the people mistakenly accepted the Periclean collective identity as if it were the only desirable option. The Periclean option was precarious, though appearing at first to be reliable. Plato therefore needed to raise the standard of politics by replacing the Periclean collective identity with a new one. Along this line, Plato had Socrates speak up once in the *Gorgias* that he is the only "true politician" who matches the enhanced standard of politics, while denouncing all the respectable politicians including Pericles (521d). The true standard Socrates sets up in the *Gorgias* is whether or not the politician makes people better. Socrates' claim of being a "true politician" in the *Gorgias* is definite and assertive. Yet, in that dialogue, Plato did not show how possibly Socrates could take a role as the true politician. It is in the *Menexenus* that Plato showed how Socrates, "the true politician," could perform true politics in practice.

Thus, in the *Menexenus*, Plato rejected the Periclean empire and collective identity, reformulating in its place a new collective identity with an image of a rather moderate and liberal empire. Replacing an old collective identity with a new one requires running the risk of historical distortions. Plato allowed himself to make historical distortions because he understood that making collective identity was to be brought about not by philosophical accuracy but by political deliberation.

However, Plato also understood that stability in the collective identity requires philosophy or philosophical attitude at least. According to our interpretation, the Periclean collective identity first appears to be moderate and liberal and yet quickly falls into a pit of excessive and aggressive imperialism. Plato's solution was to instill people with the philosopher-like reserved attitude towards life – a task both political and philosophical. It must be politically effective in making collective identity, but also philosophical because the only solution to the corruptive inclination of collective identity is found in philosophy. Plato undertook the task not by speaking but by "writing philosophically" on the most controversial political issues. Platonic scribalism was Plato's conscious decision for presenting philosophically affirmative and politically effective collective identity.

Platonic scribalism in the *Menexenus* is an attempt to compromise the seemingly irreconcilable confrontation between philosophy and politics. Platonic scribalism exemplifies how to hit the balance between theory and practice or how to compromise between a true politician and a practical rhetorician. Plato made Socrates a true rhetorician who was successfully engaged in reshaping the new collective identity.

In doing so, Plato hoped to avoid the usual antipathy toward philosophers. Plato implied that philosophers might play the role of making a stable collective identity, beneficial for the city. In this role, the philosophers need not play "gadflies" that should awaken ordinary people only at the risk of endangering their lives. They are thus able to remain philosophers as such, people who love the truth. Socrates in the *Menexenus*, the dialogue in which Plato involves his ideas most directly in real politics, still defends the priority of philosophical life no less than Socrates did in the *Apology*.

The speeches of David in the books of Chronicles are a useful cross-cultural comparison with the speech of Socrates in the Menexenus. Like Plato, the Chronicler attempted to redefine the collective identities of his community by stressing voluntary devotion and virtue, in place of coercion, nationalism and militarism.

The early types of biblical speech seem to chronologically precede the funeral oration of Athens; however, Athenian recitations of its own history spread rapidly in the sixth to fourth centuries BCE. Of course, we cannot suppose a direct influence between the two literary artefacts. However, perhaps these corresponding forms of mnemonic speeches reflect analogous social settings and demonstrate how two roughly contemporary ancient groups developed and sometimes shifted collective memories and collective identities via scribal media.[43]

Bibliography

Altmann, Peter. "Tracing Divine Law: Written Divine Law in Chronicles." Within this volume.
Amit, Yairah. "Araunah's Threshing Floor: A Lesson in Shaping Historical Memory." Pages 133–44 in *What Was Authoritative for Chronicles?* Edited by Ehud Ben Zvi and Diana Edelman. Winona Lake, IN: Eisenbrauns, 2011.
Auld, A. Graeme. *Kings without Privilege: David and Moses in the Story of the Bible's Kings.* Edinburgh: T&T Clark, 1994.
Buster, Aubrey. "Recited History and Social Memory in the Ancient Mediterranean." Pages 325–51 in *Collective Memory and Collective Identity: Case Studies in Deuteronomy and the Deuteronomistic History.* Edited by Johannes Unsok Ro and Diana Edelman. BZAW 534 Berlin: de Gruyter, 2021.
Collins, Susan D., and Devin Stauffer. "The Challenge of Plato's Menexenus." *RP* 61.1 (1999): 85–115.
Edelman, Diana, and Lynette Mitchell. "Chronicles and Local Greek Histories." Pages 229–52 in *What Was Authoritative for Chronicles?* Edited by Ehud Ben Zvi and Diana Edelman. Winona Lake, IN: Eisenbrauns, 2011.
Fine, John V. A. *The Ancient Greeks: A Critical History.* Boston: Belknap, 1983.
Friedländer, Paul. *Plato II: The Dialogues.* Translated by Hans Meyerhoff. London: Routledge & Kegan Paul, 1964.
Giffone, Benjamin D. "Regathering Too Many Stones? Scribal Constraints, Community Memory, and the 'Problem' of Elijah's Sacrifice for Deuteronomism in Kings." Within this volume.
Giffone, Benjamin D. *'Sit At My Right Hand': The Chronicler's Portrait of the Tribe of Benjamin in the Social Context of Yehud.* LHBOTS 628. London: T&T Clark, 2016.

---

[43] On this issue see also Aubrey Buster, "Recited History and Social Memory in the Ancient Mediterranean," in *Collective Memory and Collective Identity: Case Studies in Deuteronomy and the Deuteronomistic History*, ed. Johannes Unsok Ro and Diana Edelman, BZAW 534 (Berlin: de Gruyter, 2021), 325–51.

Henderson, M. M. "Plato's Menexenus and the Distortions of History." *AC* 18 (1975): 25–46.
Hoglund, Kenneth G. "The Chronicler as Historian: A Comparativist Perspective." Pages 19–29 in *The Chronicler as Historian*. Edited by M. Patrick Graham, Kenneth G. Hoglund, and Steven L. McKenzie. JSOTSup 238. Sheffield: Sheffield Academic, 1997.
Japhet, Sara. *The Ideology of the Book of Chronicles and Its Place in Biblical Thought*. Translated by Anna Barbar. Frankfurt am Main: Peter Lang, 1989.
Jonker, Louis C. "Of Jebus, Jerusalem and Benjamin: The Chronicler's *Sondergut* in 1 Chronicles 21 against the Background of the Late Persian Era in Yehud." Pages 81–102 in *Chronicling the Chronicler: The Book of Chronicles and Early Second Temple Historiography*. Edited by Tyler F. Williams and Paul S. Evans. Winona Lake, IN: Eisenbrauns, 2013.
Kahn, Charles. "Plato's Funeral Oration: The Motive of the Menexenus." *CP* 58.4 (1963): 220–34.
Kilchör, Benjamin. "'Then Moses Wrote This Torah' (Deut 31:9): The Relationship of Oral and Written Torah in Deuteronomy." Within this volume.
Knapp, Andrew, "The Succession Narrative in Twenty-first-century Research," *CurBR* 19.3 (2021): 211–34.
Knoppers, Gary N. *1 Chronicles 1–9*. AB. New York: Doubleday, 2004.
Knoppers, Gary N. *1 Chronicles 10–29*. AB. New York: Doubleday, 2004.
Knoppers, Gary N. "Hierodules, Priests, or Janitors? The Levites in Chronicles and the History of the Israelite Priesthood." *JBL* 118 (1999): 49–72.
Kohn, Hans. *The Idea of Nationalism: A Study on its Origins and Background*. New York: Macmillan, 1944.
Loraux, Nicole. *The Children of Athena: Athenian Ideas about Citizenship and the Division between the Sexes*. Translated by Caroline Levine. Rev. ed. Princeton: Princeton University Press, 1994.
Loraux, Nicole. *The Invention of Athens: The Funeral Oration in the Classical City*. Translated by Alan Sheridan. Boston: Harvard University Press, 1986.
Markl, Dominik. "The Wilderness Sanctuary as the Archetype of Continuity between the Pre- and the Postexilic Temples of Jerusalem." Pages 227–51 in *The Fall of Jerusalem and the Rise of the Torah*. Edited by Peter Dubovský, Dominik Markl and Jean-Pierre Sonnet. FAT 107. Tübingen: Mohr Siebeck, 2016.
Markl, Dominik. "Does Deuteronomy Promote a Proto-Nationalist Agenda?" In *Political Theologies in the Hebrew Bible*. Edited by Mark Brett and Rachelle Gilmore. JAJSup. Paderborn: Brill, forthcoming.
Mason, Rex. *Preaching the Tradition: Homily and Hermeneutics after the Exile based on the 'Addresses' in Chronicles, the Speeches in the Books of Ezra and Nehemiah and the Postexilic Prophetic Books*. Cambridge: Cambridge University Press, 1990.
Monoson, Sara. "Remembering Pericles: The Political and Theoretical Import of Plato's Menexenus." *PT* 26.4 (1998): 489–513.
North, Robert. "Theology of the Chronicler." *JBL* 82 (1963): 376–78.
Peltonen, Kai. "A Jigsaw without a Model: The Date of Chronicles." Pages 225–71 in *Did Moses Speak Attic? Jewish Historiography and Scripture in the Hellenistic Period*. Edited by Lester L. Grabbe. JSOTSup 317. Sheffield: Sheffield Academic, 2001.
Person, Raymond F., Jr. *The Deuteronomic History and the Book of Chronicles: Scribal Works in an Oral World*. AIL 6. Atlanta: Society of Biblical Literature, 2010.

Plato. *Lysis, Symposium, Gorgias.* Translated by W. R. M. Lamb. LCL. Boston: Harvard University Press, 1925.
Rosenstock, Bruce. "Socrates as Revenant: A Reading of the *Menexenus*." *Phoenix* 48.4 (1994): 331–47.
Salkever, Stephen. "Socrates' Aspasian Oration: The Play of Philosophy and Politics in Plato's Menexenus." *APSR* 87.1 (1993): 133–43.
Saxonhouse, Arlene. "Nature and Convention in Thucydides' History." *Polity* 10 (1978): 252–73.
Schniedewind, William M. *How the Bible Became a Book: The Textualization of Ancient Israel.* Cambridge: Cambridge University Press, 2004.
Thomas, Rosalind. *Oral Tradition and Written Record in Classical Athens.* Cambridge: Cambridge University Press, 1989.
Warner, Jonathan, and Benjamin D. Giffone. "Economic Thought in the Hebrew Scriptures: Context and Reception." In *Economic Thought before Economics.* Edited by Tomáš Evan. Prague: Czech Technical University Publishing, forthcoming.

Part II

Writing about Writing in the Hebrew Bible

"Then Moses Wrote This Torah" (Deut 31:9): The Relationship of Oral and Written Torah in Deuteronomy

Benjamin Kilchör

1. Introduction: Two Levels of Communication

Is Deuteronomy oral speech or written text? Obviously, it is both:

Almost all the book consists of reported speech, mostly in direct discourse and mostly of Moses, whereas only about fifty-six verses are reporting speech, the Deuteronomic narrator's, which form the context for Moses' utterances.[1]

Robert Polzin, in his ground-breaking study *Moses and the Deuteronomist*, applied Bakhtin's dialogic model[2] with its distinction between "reported speech" and "reporting speech" to Deuteronomy. Polzin distinguished between the Mosaic voice (reported speech) and the voice of the narrator (reporting speech), whereby the latter is identified with the Deuteronomistic (which Polzin called "Deuteronomic") narrator who presents himself as a "prophet like Moses."[3] According to Polzin, the "frame-breaks" of the narrator have the function to undermine the unique status of Moses:

The narrator's utterances are spoken in two ideological voices which interfere with one another: an overt, obvious voice that exalts Moses and plays down its own role, and a hidden voice that will soon exalt itself at the expense of Moses' uniqueness.[4]

Of course, the distinction of these two voices also includes a distinction of two different audiences: the audience of Moses, and the audience of the narrator.[5]

Jean-Pierre Sonnet picked up Polzin's observations but also modified them. Although the role of textualization is implied by the expression "reported speech," textualization plays no explicit role in Polzin's theory:

---

[1] Robert Polzin, "Reporting Speech in the Book of Deuteronomy: Toward a Compositional Analysis of the Deuteronomic History," in *Traditions in Transformation: Turning Points in Biblical Faith*, ed. Baruch Halpern and Jon D. Levenson (Winona Lake, IN: Eisenbrauns, 1981), 194.

[2] Mikhail Bakhtin, *Problems of Dostoevsky's Poetics* (Ann Arbor, MI: Ardis, 1973).

[3] Robert Polzin, *Moses and the Deuteronomist: Deuteronomy, Joshua, Judges*, vol. 1 of *A Literary Study of the Deuteronomy History* (New York: Seabury, 1980), 61. Cf. Polzin, "Reporting Speech," 200–211.

[4] Polzin, *Moses*, 34.

[5] Polzin, "Reporting Speech," 207.

In his opinion Deuteronomy's poetics consists in a dialectic of "speeches." Moses' communication, however, actually eventuates in the writing of the Torah "book." In other words, Deuteronomy includes the theme and aspect of *written* communication.[6]

Despite this and other critical remarks, Sonnet built on Polzin's basic observations. The interpolated comments of the narrator, according to Sonnet, reveal "a double act of communication":

> (1) from Moses to his addressees in the plains of Moab; (2) from the narrator to the readers. The starting point is that each group remains in its own sphere of communication (Moses never addresses the readers as such). The latter-day readers are in the position to receive information that is denied to Moses "historical" addressees.[7]

These two acts of communication are introduced in Sonnet's monograph on the first page:

> In this study I intend to describe Deuteronomy's way of combining the two levels of communication: Moses' address, in the represented world (to the sons of Israel in the plains of Moab), and the book's address to its reader.[8]

It becomes clear here that Moses' addressees are listeners to an oral Torah, while the book's addressees are readers of a written Torah. Indeed, Sonnet consistently refers to the addressees of the second level as "readers." In a later article he titles this as a process "From Oral to Written Communication":[9] while the oral communication remains on the level of the narrative, the written communication bridges the gap between Moses and a later audience. Moses himself "is apparently entirely on the side of orality."[10]

> This certainly raises questions about the effective transmission of the Torah from one bank of the Jordan to the other: what will assure the transmission and the reproduction of "all the words of this Torah" (Deut 27:3, 8) [...]? The enigma is solved in 31:9, when the narrator reports: "Moses wrote down this Torah" [...].[11]

If I understand Sonnet correctly, the oral communication belongs mainly to the past of Mosaic time, while the written communication reaches the readers of the coming generations.

Taking these observations as a starting point, and including some recent insights on scribal culture and the interaction of oral and written tradition processes, I will outline here a more nuanced interpretation of the interaction between oral and written Torah in Deuteronomy.

---

[6] Jean-Pierre Sonnet, *The Book within the Book: Writing in Deuteronomy* (Leiden: Brill, 1997), 2–3, emphasis original.

[7] Sonnet, *Book*, 239.

[8] Sonnet, *Book*, 1.

[9] Jean-Pierre Sonnet, "The Fifth Book of the Pentateuch: Deuteronomy in Its Narrative Dynamic," *JAJ* 3 (2012): 207.

[10] Sonnet, "Fifth Book," 209.

[11] Sonnet, "Fifth Book," 210.

2. The Interaction of Oral and Written Communication

While for Sonnet written communication seems to supersede and replace oral communication in Deuteronomy,[12] David Carr makes a strong case for a much closer interaction of oral and written communication in the ancient Near East:

> One starting point for this alternative picture is the fact that many ancient texts were not written in such a way that they could be read easily by someone who did not already know them well. [...] Though someone might have such a text before him or her in order to dictate to others or even perform the text, it would function more the way a musical score does for a musician who already knows the piece than like a book the reader has never encountered before.[13]

This fits well with the observation that "the picture presented by Deuteronomy is not one of Moses writing the 'book of the *torah*' first, and then reading it to the people."[14] Rather, when Moses writes the Torah down, it is already orally known

---

[12] Similarly already Julius Wellhausen, *Prolegomena zur Geschichte Israels,* 6th ed. (Berlin: Reimer, 1905), 408: "Die Einführung des Gesetzes, zunächst des Deuteronomiums, sodann des ganzen Pentateuchs, war in der Tat der entscheidende Schritt, wodurch die Schrift an die Stelle der Rede trat und das Volk des Wortes ein Volk des Buches wurde." Cf. also Karel van der Toorn, *Scribal Culture and the Making of the Hebrew Bible* (Cambridge, MA: Harvard University Press, 2007), 225: "The innovation of Deuteronomy lies not in the fact of its being written Torah, then, but in its claim to be a source of authority overruling the oral tradition."

[13] David M. Carr, *Writing on the Tablet of the Heart: Origins of Scripture and Literature* (New York: Oxford University Press, 2005), 4.

[14] Geert J. Venema, *Reading Scripture in the Old Testament: Deuteronomy 9–10; 31; 2 Kings 22–23; Jeremiah 36; Nehemiah 8*, OS 48 (Leiden: Brill, 2004), 41. The picture, however, is a bit more complicated since a written document is already mentioned in Deut 17:18; 29:19, 20, 26; 30:10. I concur with Eckart Otto, *Deuteronomium 1,1–4,43*, HThKAT (Freiburg: Herder, 2012), 205–6, that this tension cannot be resolved unless Deuteronomy is integrated into the narrative of the whole Pentateuch: "In gesamt-pentateuchisch-synchroner Lektüre löst sich die [...] Aporie in Bezug auf die *spr*-Belege in Dtn 29–30, da in pentateuchischer Perspektive die Sinaiperikope und damit Ex 24,3–8 und Moses Schreiben eines *spr* im Rahmen des Sinaibundesschlusses nicht nur als 'Wissensstoff', wie J.-P. Sonnet meint, sondern literarisch in der Leserichtung vorauszusetzen ist. [...] In Dtn 29,19.20.26 soll der Leser des Deuteronomiums wie bereits in Dtn 17,18 erkennen, dass er auf Moses Auslegung der am Sinai von Mose verschrifteten Bundesurkunde gewiesen ist. Die Frage, welcher Status der Auslegung im Verhältnis zur sinaitischen Bundesurkunde zukommen soll, wird mit der Verschriftung auch dieser Auslegung in Dtn 31,9.24 beantwortet. Sie erhält neben die Lade gelegt den Status einer Bundesurkunde des Moabbundes als Auslegung der Sinaitora. So soll einerseits die Identität von Sinai- und Moabtora unterstrichen werden, andererseits aber soll die Differenz zwischen der Moabtora als Auslegung und der Sinaitora als ausgelegter erkennbar bleiben." Cf. Eckart Otto, "Mose, der erste Schriftgelehrte: Deuteronomium 1,5 in der Fabel des Pentateuch," in *L'Ecrit et l'Esprit: Etudes d'histoire du texte et de théologie biblique en hommage a Adrian Schenker,* ed. Dieter Böhler, Innocent Himbaza and Philippe Hugo, OBO 214 (Fribourg: Academic Press; Göttingen: Vandenhoeck & Ruprecht, 2005); Benjamin Kilchör, *Mosetora und Jahwetora: Das Verhältnis von Deuteronomium 12–26 zu Exodus, Levitikus und Numeri*, BZABR 21 (Wiesbaden: Harrassowitz, 2015), 3–11.

to the audience.[15] Written communication then does not replace oral communication; rather, the writing down of the oral Torah serves its ongoing oral performance.[16] In the words of Geert Venema: "Moses writes down the words, in order that from now on the words he spoke may be spoken again in Israel."[17] This is what James Watts names "secondary orality based on written texts," referring to Exod 24:3–7, Deut 31:9–11, Josh 8:30–35, 2 Kings 22–23//2 Chronicles 34, and Nehemiah 8:

> This reminder that the interaction between oral and written compositions ran in both directions should warn interpreters against too sharp a distinction between the modes of presentation [...].[18]

Such an interaction between oral and written communication entails on the one hand that an oral knowledge of the text precedes its writing down, and on the other hand, that the writing down of the text does not stop its oral transmission. Both can be shown in Deuteronomy.

First, it is obvious that Moses performs his speech orally before he writes it down. This is indeed not just a narrative peculiarity in Deuteronomy but rather the natural sequence throughout the Old Testament (cf. Exod 24:3–7; Deut 31:1, 9–11; Jer 36:2; Ezek 43:10–11; Ezr 7:11;[19] probably also Isa 30:8). Jeremiah 36:2 especially, but possibly also Ezek 43:11, presuppose a certain time period between the first oral performance and the writing down and therefore a memorization process already on an oral stage.

Second, as Karin Finsterbusch has shown,[20] Deuteronomy constitutes Israel as a community of teaching and learning, whereby telling (e.g. Deut 4:10) and learning by heart (Deut 5:1; 6:6; 30:14) – oral transmission – play a crucial role. Of course, there are also elements of written transmission on a smaller level than Deut 31:9 (namely Deut 6:6–9; 11:18–21[21]); yet these are also integrated into a primarily oral memorization process.[22]

---

[15] Dominik Markl, *Gottes Volk im Deuteronomium*, BZABR 18 (Wiesbaden: Harrassowitz, 2012), 165, has convincingly argued that "this Torah" refers to Deut 5–28 at the least, possibly to Deut 5–30.

[16] Cf. Edgar W. Conrad, "Heard but not Seen: The Representation of 'Books' in the Old Testament," *JSOT* 54 (1992): 46–47.

[17] Venema, *Reading Scripture*, 42.

[18] James W. Watts, *Leviticus 1–10*, HCOT (Leuven: Peeters, 2013), 144.

[19] According to Fried and Mills in this volume, the formulation "copy of an order" in Ezra 7:11 "suggest[s] that this letter is a written copy of an original oral command."

[20] Karin Finsterbusch, *Weisung für Israel: Studien zu religiösem Lehren und Lernen im Deuteronomium und seinem Umfeld*, FAT 44 (Tübingen: Mohr Siebeck, 2005), 308–11.

[21] See Sonnet, *Book*, 51–58, 69–71.

[22] See also Jan Assmann, *Das kulturelle Gedächtnis: Schrift, Erinnerung und politische Identität in frühen Hochkulturen* (München: Beck, 1992), 219–21, who identifies eight different mnemonics in Deuteronomy.

These observations lead to the conclusion that it would be too narrowly considered to regard the Mosaic audience as the addressees of the Mosaic speech, and the later generations as the addressees of the written text. Rather, the written text becomes oral speech again when it is taught to the people. This introduces a third level of communication and raises the question anew: Who are the addressees of Deuteronomy?

3. Who are the Addressees of Deuteronomy?

According to Sonnet's comments on Deut 6:9, Moses' speech projects a covenantal world where "the people is capable of writing" (and reading).[23] With regard to Deut 31:9–11 he writes:

> In distinction from the tablets written by God and sealed off in the ark, the words of the Torah written by Moses are immediately destined for reading: "You will read this Torah," Moses says to all Israel (31:11). This solemn reading, every seven years, in front of the gathered population, will be nothing less than a new Horeb, eliciting the same effects.[24]

While it is true that the public reading of the Torah every seven years is a realization of the Horeb event, Sonnet's formulation that Moses speaks "to all Israel" in 31:11 is not precisely correct. Rather, according to 31:9, Moses addresses here only the priests and elders, to whom he hands over the written document. This indeed calls to mind the Sinai event in Exod 24:1, 9, 14, where the priests and elders have their place between Moses and the people. They are those who shall read the Torah while Israel shall listen to the spoken word: "You shall read/shout" (31:11) has its counterpart in, "they shall hear and learn" (31:12).

Therefore, three levels of communication and three groups of addressees can in fact be distinguished:

1. Moses' speech as oral communication and Israel on the plains of Moab as the addressees of this speech (primary orality).
2. The written document and the priests and elders as recipients of this document.
3. The periodical public reading of the written document and the coming generations as addressees of these public readings (secondary orality).

Leaving the first level aside for the moment, it is worthwhile to think about the distinction between the rhetorical function of Deuteronomy for the other two levels.

---

[23] Sonnet, *Book*, 56.
[24] Sonnet, "Fifth Book," 211.

3.1 The People as the Torah's Target Audience

It is not possible here to present a thorough analysis of signals within Deuteronomy by which one can draw conclusions about Deuteronomy's target audience. However, I briefly point to four texts which show that the laypeople are the target audience of the Mosaic speech.[25]

a. Deuteronomy 24:8. In this verse the target audience is explicitly distinguished from the Levitical priests who are the recipients of the written Torah in Deut 31:9:

Take care, in a case of leprous disease, to be very careful to do according to all that the Levitical priests shall direct you. As I commanded them, so you shall be careful to do. (ESV)

The addressee (2.P.Sg.) is informed what he has to do in case of leprous disease. More precisely, he is sent to the Levitical priests (3.P.Pl.) who will tell him what to do. The priests have already been instructed by the speaker of the oral speech (1.P.Sg.) who is Moses.[26] But they are not instructed *within* the oral speech of Moses. Rather, by the back reference "as I commanded them" the oral speech assumes an earlier instruction of the Levitical priests by Moses.[27] The layperson addressee of the current speech has not to know the content of this earlier instruction, he has just to know where to go in case of leprous disease. It is revealing to compare Deut 24:8 with Lev 13–14 where detailed instructions with regard to cases of leprous disease are given, to which Deut 24:8 refers.[28] While Deut 24:8 addresses the layperson directly in 2.P., according to Lev 13:2 and 14:2, a person

---

[25] See also Benjamin Kilchör, "The Reception of Priestly Laws in Deuteronomy and Deuteronomy's Target Audience," in *Exploring the Composition of the Pentateuch*, ed. L. S. Baker Jr. et al., BBRSup 27 (University Park, PA: Eisenbrauns, 2020).

[26] Thus also Jack R. Lundbom, *Deuteronomy: A Commentary* (Grand Rapids: Eerdmans, 2013), 685; cf. J. Gordon McConville, *Deuteronomy*, AOTC 5 (Downers Grove, IL: InterVarsity Press; Nottingham: Apollos, 2002), 361; Eckart Otto, *Deuteronomium 23,16–34,12*, HThKAT (Freiburg: Herder, 2017), 1837. That the "I" belongs to Moses and not to YHWH is supported by the reference to YHWH in 3.P.Sg. just in the following verse (24:9). As Eckart Otto notes with reference to Lev 10:10–11, the presupposed chain of revelation in Deut 24:8 goes from YHWH to Moses to the Levitical priests (Otto, *Deuteronomium 23,16–34,12*, 1837).

[27] In his contribution in this volume, Peter Altmann notes that in Chronicles the torah of YHWH is linked to the Zadokites, while the torah of Moses is relegated to the Levites. It might be worthwhile to think about the signals in the Pentateuch itself that trigger this hermeneutical distinction. On the one hand, the speaker of the laws in Exodus, Leviticus and Numbers is always YHWH, while the speaker of the laws in Deuteronomy is Moses; on the other hand, some of the laws in Exodus, Leviticus and Numbers are explicitly given to the priests, while others are designated for a larger audience. There is a certain tension on the storage of the torah in Deuteronomy: according to Deut 31:9, it is given to the Levitical priests and elders of Israel, while according to Deut 31:25, the Levites shall store the torah. As Altmann concludes, torah of YHWH in Chronicles refers to "pentateuchal cultic ordinances" which fits the observations here, that these cultic ordinances are presupposed in Deuteronomy as given to the priests.

[28] Cf. Moshe Weinfeld, *Deuteronomy 1–11*, AB 5 (New York: Doubleday, 1991), 30; Otto, *Deuteronomium 23,16–34,12*, 1837.

with leprous disease shall be brought (*hophal*) to Aaron and his sons. In both cases, the following verbs then have the priest as subject (13:3 and 14:3) and the instructions do not tell what the layperson has to do but rather what the priest has to do. In a synchronic reading of the Pentateuchal narrative we therefore find two different levels of addressees: While in Lev 13–14 the priests are instructed on their tasks in case of leprous disease, in the oral speech that includes Deut 24:8, the laypersons are simply informed that they have to go to the priests who have further instructions.

b. Deuteronomy 18:1–8. Another text within Deuteronomy's Mosaic speech where people and Levitical priests are distinguished is Deut 18:1–8. While Deut 16:18 and 17:15 addresses the people (2.P.Sg.) with regard to the appointment of judges, officials, and a king, the priests are presupposed as appointed previously in Deut 18:1–8 what is best explained by the Pentateuchal narrative, where the appointment of the priests takes place in Lev 8 and the appointment of the Levites in Num 3.[29] Therefore, the main issue in Deut 18:1–8 is not the appointment of the priests but their right of charges by the people (משפט הכהנים מאת העם Deut 18:3). The people are addressed in vv. 4–6 in 2.P.Sg., while the priests and Levites are only referred in 3.P. Again, it is revealing to compare Deut 18:1–8 with Num 18:8–24: In the latter text, Aaron as priestly representative is directly addressed by YHWH with regard to the charges received by the priests in the first part (Num 18:8–19), while he shall instruct the Levites regarding the charges they receive in the second part (Num 18:20–24). While it is relevant for the priests and the Levites in Num 18:8–24, who and where they shall eat their share, this is not relevant for the laypeople addressed in Deut 18:1–8. In other words: While Num 18:8–24 instructs the priests and Levites what they may eat from the sacrifices and charges, Deut 18:1–8 informs the laypeople about what they are obliged to give to the priests (Deut 18:3–4).

c. Deuteronomy 12. Of course, it is not possible to discuss this chapter here in its complexity. For the present question a few hints shall suffice. First, the people are addressed in 2.P.Pl. in the first half of the chapter (Deut 12:2–12) while they are addressed in 2.P.Sg. in the second half (Deut 12:1, 13–31). Second, there are no instructions which are specifically relevant for the cultic personnel, unlike Exod 20:24–26 (building of the altar; sacral clothing) and also unlike Lev 17:2–9 where both the priests and the people are addressed and both are instructed about their respective tasks in sacrificing.[30] Third, while Deut 12:15–18 addresses the consumption of meat by the people, the consumption of meat by the priests is not addressed in Deuteronomy at all (unlike Num 18). Fourth, among the sacrifices, Deut 12 mentions the עלה (6, 11, 13, 14, 27) and the זבח (6, 11, 27) but not

---

[29] On the distinction between priests and Levites in Deut 18:1–8 see Kilchör, *Mosetora*, 215–20.

[30] The same applies to Lev 3; cf. Watts, *Leviticus 1–10*, 271.

the חטאת and the אשם, possibly because "the flesh of these two sacrifices was to be consumed by priests only."[31] In sum, both the formulations and the contents of Deut 12 are directed at the laypeople, not the cultic personnel.

d. Deuteronomy 14:1–20. Deuteronomy's target audience can also be seen in a comparison between Lev 11:1–20 and Deut 14:1–20, according to Christophe Nihan "the most remarkable instance of legislation shared by Priestly and non-Priestly legal traditions within the Torah."[32] Without going into the details here, I agree with Reinhard Achenbach who interprets Deut 14:1–20 as a simplified food regulation for the common people while Lev 11 contains a more detailed version for priestly instructions.[33]

In sum, if "this Torah" in Deut 31:9 refers to Deut 5–30, as Jean-Pierre Sonnet and Dominic Markl have convincingly argued,[34] we do not find one single instruction for priests within the oral Torah, spoken by Moses to the Israelites (Deut 4:44). Not only in the narrative logic of Deuteronomy is the Mosaic speech addressed to the laypeople, but also the contents of the Mosaic speech obviously have the aim to teach laypeople. David Carr speaks of a "Deuteronomic utopia on education of *all*."[35] However, the "textual-torah" – the written text – is not given to all male Israelites but to a smaller elite. The written text therefore is not given to the group to which its content is addressed.

3.2 The Priests and Elders as Deuteronomy's Target Audience

While in Deut 5–30 the priests are never addressed, Deuteronomy contains two oral speeches where the priests (together with the elders of Israel) or the Levites, respectively, are addressed: Deut 31:10–13 and 31:26–29. Both of these two speeches are connected to the writing down of the oral Torah.

The only instructions for the priests and elders in Deuteronomy therefore have reference to the written Torah: they shall gather the Israelites (including men, women, children and sojourners) every seven years for a public reading of the

---

[31] J. Gordon McConville, *Law and Theology in Deuteronomy*, JSOTSup 33 (Sheffield: JSOT Press, 1984), 54.

[32] Christophe Nihan, "The Laws about Clean and Unclean Animals in Leviticus and Deuteronomy and Their Place in the Formation of the Pentateuch," in *The Pentateuch: International Perspectives on Current Research,* ed. Thomas B. Dozeman, Konrad Schmid and Baruch J. Schwartz, FAT 78 (Tübingen: Mohr Siebeck, 2011), 401.

[33] Reinhard Achenbach, "Zur Systematik der Speisegebote in Leviticus 11 und in Deuteronomium 14," *ZABR* 17 (2011): 173.

[34] Sonnet, *Book*, 248; Markl, *Gottes Volk*, 165.

[35] Carr, *Tablet*, 137. Cf. Seth L. Sanders, *The Invention of Hebrew* (Urbana, IL: University of Illinois Press, 2009), 170: "The Deuteronomistic covenant is not intended to constitute a state [...] but to imagine a people, constituted by their attention and response to a set of texts (both spoken and written); to the extent that the texts share a goal it is to elicit this attention and response: for addressees to imagine themselves as part of this people. The ideal reader it presupposes is not a member of an already constituted kingdom or polity, but a constituting member. This imagined people, mediated through Hebrew texts, constitutes Israel – the Bible's public."

written Torah (31:11–12) with the goal to transmit the Torah from generation to generation (31:13), and they shall store the written Torah in the sanctuary (31:26).

3.3 The Addressees of the Written and the Oral Torah

Taken these observations together, it becomes clear that "this Torah" in Deuteronomy addressees the common people. The priests and elders are addressed in two short speeches in Deut 31, both of which belong to Deuteronomy's framework outside the body of "this Torah" (e. g. Deut 5–30) or, in the words of Sonnet, outside "the book within the book."

To come back to the three suggested levels of communication: 1) the level of primary orality of the Mosaic speech in Deut 5–30 refers to the second generation of Israel after the Exodus; 2) this speech is written down and, accompanied by two short additional speeches, handed over to the responsibility of the priests as written text; 3) the contents of the written text, however, do not address those who administer the written Torah but the coming generations of the people.

This means that the addressees of the written Torah are not readers but listeners. Those who read the Torah are not addressed by the Torah; they just have the mandate to store and publicly read it. In addition, this means that the communication does not go from oral to written communication, but rather that the written texts serve an ongoing oral communication of the Torah. The written text therefore serves to bridge the gap of time. One of the main features of the oral performance of this text is the repetitive "today" throughout the book. As Dominik Markl and Georg Braulik have shown, the function of this "today" is that Deuteronomy's addressees hear their own "today" and appropriate the Mosaic speech for themselves.[36] Therefore, the "today" also has the function to distinguish between the audience of the primary orality and the audience of the secondary orality (most explicit in Deut 29:13–14).

Yet again, the concept of "a book within a book," whereby the smaller book (i.e. "this Torah," Deut 5–30) addresses the people while the framing of the larger book (i.e. Deuteronomy) also contains addresses to the priests and elders, points towards something like a double audience: While in the *written Torah* the people are always addressed directly and the priests and elders (and other officials) are only mentioned as far as it concerns the people, *Deuteronomy* as a whole instructs those who store the written texts, i.e. the priests and elders. Perhaps it could be boiled down as follows: "Deuteronomy" is something like the teaching materials for the teachers, while "this Torah" is the teaching content, tidied up for (secondary) oral performance in a way that by verbal recitation the target audience is immediately addressed as if they would be part of the original audience of Moses's (primary) oral performance.

---

[36] Cf. Markl, *Gottes Volk*, 70–79; Georg Braulik, "'Heute' im Buch Deuteronomium: Tora und Bundesschluss," *BuL* 90 (2017).

4. Conclusion: "What was once thought can never be unthought" (Friedrich Dürrenmatt, *The Physicists*)

According to David Carr, the education of all Israelites – not just a smaller elite – is a utopia.[37] While "utopia" could be understood as pure fiction in a time when only specialists had access to this sort of education, one still might ask: Even if the education of all Israelites is merely an ideal, what then is the function and the impact of such an ideal? Will such a thought only remain on the level of unrealistic fiction? What is the role, also the political and social role, of literature addressed to the people?[38]

The question is even more fundamental: If, as argued above ("The People as the Torah's Target Audience"), the Mosaic speech indeed is directed at the common people, what is then the rhetorical strategy behind the text if we do not assume that at least a subset of the target audience is reached by it?[39] Seth Sanders has made a case that the invention of Hebrew and Ugaritic as "the first attempts by people in the ancient Near East to write in their own, local spoken languages" entailed "new possibilities of participation, reflected in rituals written in Ugaritic (KTU 1.40) and Hebrew (Leviticus 16) that assumed the people as a central protagonist."[40] Of course, participation requires education. Consequently, Sanders assumes, based on the epigraphic evidence, a rather widespread access of the people to textual traditions: "What made the alphabet's new uses in the Iron Age Levant so important was the new set of assumptions behind them – assumptions about *participation*."[41]

Georg Fischer and Norbert Lohfink outlined with regard to Deut 6:7 a vivid picture of a meditative technique in Ancient Israel that might as a forerunner be in continuity with later monastic tradition (there, however, again limited to the clergy). According to them, this technique of reciting memorized texts would have been widespread at least in postexilic times.[42]

---

[37] Carr, *Tablet*, 137.

[38] Cf. the subtitle of Seth L. Sanders, "What Was the Alphabet For? The Rise of Written Vernaculars and the Making of Israelite National Literature," *Maarav* 11 (2004): 50: "The Political Role of a Literature Addressed to the Reader."

[39] Cf. Braulik, "Heute," 20: "Es gibt Phänomene im Deuteronomium, die zumindest auf der Ebene der Kompositionstechnik auch direkt auf den realen Leser zu zielen scheinen."

[40] Sanders, *Invention*, 75.

[41] Sanders, *Invention*, 169.

[42] Georg Fischer and Norbert Lohfink, "'Diese Worte sollst du summen:' Dtn 6,7 *wᵉdibbartā bām* – ein verlorener Schlüssel zur meditativen Kultur in Israel," *ThPh* 62 (1987): 71. The postexilic dating of this technique is established by them on the basis of dating assumptions of the respective biblical texts rather than on the basis of extrabiblical evidence, cf. Fischer and Lohfink, "Worte," n49. Seth Sanders, however, seems to have earlier times in mind when he speaks of "new possibilities in participation" with regard to the invention of Hebrew in the Iron Age (Sanders, *Invention*, 75).

A common insight of different studies is that cultic and ritual concerns might be of central importance for the spreading of textualization among the people. Seth Sanders, as previously quoted, speaks about "new possibilities of participation, reflected in rituals written in Ugaritic [...] and Hebrew [...]."[43] William Schniedewind points to the fact that already in the cuneiform tradition liturgical texts were the main types of advanced curriculum[44] and he interprets also some of the Kuntillet 'Ajrud inscriptions in this context.[45] He agrees with Seth Sanders's "rule of popularity," according to which "widely distributed material is more likely to be known,"[46] and concludes:

In the same way, it seems likely that some biblical texts that were repeated, widely cited, adapted, and interpreted inner-biblically or extra-biblically may have originally had a role in the advanced scribal curriculum of ancient Israel and Judah.[47]

The combination of people's participation in written texts with a liturgical and ritual context is in accord with the biblical text itself: according to Deut 31:10, the written Torah becomes oral Torah again in every year of release on occasion of the Feast of Booths by a public reading. Jean-Pierre Sonnet showed on the basis of the intertextual connections between Deut 5:22, 10:4, and 31:9 that the "solemn reading, every seven years, in front of the gathered population, will be nothing less than a new Horeb, eliciting the same effects."[48] According to Georg Braulik, in this event the time difference between Moses and the audience is liturgically suspended. Yet, as he emphasizes, it is not the book of Deuteronomy, but the Torah written down by Moses (according to him Deut 5–28) that is recited.[49] Deut 31:12 describes the task of the people in this event: They shall listen, learning by heart, fear YHWH, their God, and be careful to do according to all words of this Torah. This is, in Deuteronomy's conception, the precondition for religious education and participation in the families of Israel, where this Torah shall live in oral recitation (Deut 6:6–9).[50] The written Torah therefore is not the end of the oral Torah but rather the condition for a widespread life of the oral Torah among the people. Moreover, the addressees of the written Torah are not readers but listeners. To whatever extend one may reckon on the realization of this ideal: At least Deuteronomy plants the thought of an educational program for the common people and requests its realization. And, in the words

---

[43] Sanders, *Invention*, 75.
[44] William M. Schniedewind, *The Finger of the Scribe: How Scribes Learned to Write the Bible* (New York: Oxford University Press, 2019), 22.
[45] Schniedewind, *Finger*, 159.
[46] Seth L. Sanders, *From Adapa to Enoch: Scribal Culture and Religious Vision in Judea and Babylon*, TSAJ 167 (Tübingen: Mohr Siebeck, 2017), 233.
[47] Schniedewind, *Finger*, 169.
[48] Sonnet, "Fifth Book," 211.
[49] Braulik, "Heute," 20.
[50] Fischer and Lohfink, "Worte;" Finsterbusch, *Weisung*, 308–11.

of the physicist Möbius in Friedrich Dürrenmatt's drama *The Physicists* (1962): "What was once thought can never be unthought."

Bibliography

Achenbach, Reinhard. "Zur Systematik der Speisegebote in Leviticus 11 und in Deuteronomium 14." *ZABR* 17 (2011): 161–209.

Assmann, Jan. *Das kulturelle Gedächtnis: Schrift, Erinnerung und politische Identität in frühen Hochkulturen*. München: Beck, 1992.

Bakhtin, Mikhail. *Problems of Dostoevsky's Poetics*. Ann Arbor, MI: Ardis, 1973.

Braulik, Georg. "'Heute' im Buch Deuteronomium: Tora und Bundesschluss." *BuL* 90 (2017): 11–22.

Carr, David M. *Writing on the Tablet of the Heart: Origins of Scripture and Literature*. New York: Oxford University Press, 2005.

Conrad, Edgar W. "Heard but not Seen: The Representation of 'Books' in the Old Testament." *JSOT* 54 (1992): 45–59.

Finsterbusch, Karin. *Weisung für Israel: Studien zu religiösem Lehren und Lernen im Deuteronomium und seinem Umfeld*. FAT 44. Tübingen: Mohr Siebeck, 2005.

Fischer, Georg, and Norbert Lohfink. "'Diese Worte sollst du summen:' Dtn 6,7 $w^e dibbart\bar{a}$ $b\bar{a}m$ – ein verlorener Schlüssel zur meditativen Kultur in Israel." *ThPh* 62 (1987): 59–72.

Kilchör, Benjamin. *Mosetora und Jahwetora: Das Verhältnis von Deuteronomium 12–26 zu Exodus, Levitikus und Numeri*. BZABR 21. Wiesbaden: Harrassowitz, 2015.

Kilchör, Benjamin. "The Reception of Priestly Laws in Deuteronomy and Deuteronomy's Target Audience." Pages 213–25 in *Exploring the Composition of the Pentateuch*. Edited by L. S. Baker Jr., Kenneth Bergland, Felipe A. Masotti and A. Rahel Wells. BBRSup. University Park, PA: Eisenbrauns, 2020.

Lundbom, Jack R. *Deuteronomy: A Commentary*. Grand Rapids: Eerdmans, 2013.

Markl, Dominik. *Gottes Volk im Deuteronomium*. BZABR 18. Wiesbaden: Harrassowitz, 2012.

McConville, J. Gordon. *Law and Theology in Deuteronomy*. JSOTSup 33. Sheffield: JSOT Press, 1984.

McConville, J. Gordon. *Deuteronomy*. AOTC 5. Downers Grove, IL: InterVarsity Press; Nottingham: Apollos, 2002.

Nihan, Christophe. "The Laws about Clean and Unclean Animals in Leviticus and Deuteronomy and Their Place in the Formation of the Pentateuch." Pages 401–32 in *The Pentateuch: International Perspectives on Current Research*. Edited by Thomas B. Dozeman, Konrad Schmid and Baruch J. Schwartz. FAT 78. Tübingen: Mohr Siebeck, 2011.

Otto, Eckart. *Deuteronomium 1,1–4,43*. HThKAT. Freiburg: Herder, 2012.

Otto, Eckart. *Deuteronomium 23,16–34,12*. HThKAT. Freiburg: Herder, 2017.

Otto, Eckart. "Mose, der erste Schriftgelehrte: Deuteronomium 1,5 in der Fabel des Pentateuch." Pages 273–84 in *L'Ecrit et l'Esprit: Etudes d'histoire du texte et de théologie biblique en hommage a Adrian Schenker*. Edited by Dieter Böhler, Innocent Himbaza and Philippe Hugo. OBO 214. Fribourg: Academic Press; Göttingen: Vandenhoeck & Ruprecht, 2005.

Polzin, Robert. *Moses and the Deuteronomist: Deuteronomy, Joshua, Judges.* Vol. 1 of *A Literary Study of the Deuteronomy History.* New York: Seabury, 1980.

Polzin, Robert. "Reporting Speech in the Book of Deuteronomy: Toward a Compositional Analysis of the Deuteronomic History." Pages 192–211 in *Traditions in Transformation: Turning Points in Biblical Faith.* Edited by Baruch Halpern and Jon D. Levenson. Winona Lake, IN: Eisenbrauns, 1981.

Sanders, Seth L. *From Adapa to Enoch: Scribal Culture and Religious Vision in Judea and Babylon.* TSAJ 167. Tübingen: Mohr Siebeck, 2017.

Sanders, Seth L. *The Invention of Hebrew.* Urbana, IL: University of Illinois Press, 2009.

Sanders, Seth L. "What Was the Alphabet For? The Rise of Written Vernaculars and the Making of Israelite National Literature." *Maarav* 11 (2004): 25–56.

Schniedewind, William M. *The Finger of the Scribe: How Scribes Learned to Write the Bible.* New York: Oxford University Press, 2019.

Sonnet, Jean-Pierre. *The Book within the Book: Writing in Deuteronomy.* Leiden: Brill, 1997.

Sonnet, Jean-Pierre. "The Fifth Book of the Pentateuch: Deuteronomy in Its Narrative Dynamic." *JAJ* 3 (2012): 197–234.

Toorn, Karel van der. *Scribal Culture and the Making of the Hebrew Bible.* Cambridge, MA: Harvard University Press, 2007.

Venema, Geert J. *Reading Scripture in the Old Testament: Deuteronomy 9–10; 31; 2 Kings 22–23; Jeremiah 36; Nehemiah 8.* OS 48. Leiden: Brill, 2004.

Watts, James W. *Leviticus 1–10.* HCOT. Leuven: Peeters, 2013.

Weinfeld, Moshe. *Deuteronomy 1–11.* AB 5. New York: Doubleday, 1991.

Wellhausen, Julius. *Prolegomena zur Geschichte Israels.* 6th ed. Berlin: Reimer, 1905.

Ezra the Scribe

Lisbeth S. Fried and Edward J. Mills III

1. Introduction

It may be possible to use the story of Ezra to help us understand the growth of the image of the scribe as well as the growth and change in the image of the law over the long period in which the story was written. The story of Ezra is presented in Ezra 7–10 and in Nehemiah 8. These chapters primarily include narrative but also a letter putatively from Artaxerxes the king to this Ezra. The narrative introduction describes Ezra as "a ready or skilled scribe" ספר מהיר (Ezr. 7:6), and also as הכהן הספר ספר דברי מצות־יהוה וחקיו על־ישראל "the priest, the scribe, scribe of the words of the commandments of Yhwh and of his laws over Israel" (Ezr. 7:11). Our purpose here is to understand both the historical Ezra and the Ezra in the mind of the biblical author.

2. The Letter from King Artaxerxes

Understanding Ezra requires understanding the Aramaic letter from king Artaxerxes which appoints him to his role (Ezra 7:12–26).[1] Parts of the letter are likely authentic, but parts are not. The letter is as follows:

– *Verse 12:* "To Ezra, priest, scribe of the law of the God of Heaven. (May it be fulfilled!)" The form for the word "to" is ל-, a form characteristic of addressees in letters of the Hellenistic and Roman periods, not the Achaemenid.[2] Thus this verse has been at least rewritten in the Hellenistic period.

– *"priest"* The word used here is the Hebrew word for "priest," *kōhēn*, but written in Aramaic form: כהנא. It is not the actual Aramaic word for priest that the king would have known, *kamara'*, כמרא.[3] Rather than indicating that the Hebrew

---

[1] This section is based on portions of the coauthor's commentary on Ezra: Lisbeth S. Fried, *Ezra: A Commentary*, SPCC (Sheffield: Sheffield Phoenix, 2015). For translation details of the letter, see 309–31.

[2] Dirk Schwiderski, *Handbuch Des Nordwestsemitischen Briefformulars: Ein Beitrag Zur Echtheitsfrage der Aramäischen Briefe des Esrabuches*, BZAW 295. (Berlin: de Gruyter, 2000), 362.

[3] J. Hoftijzer and K. Jongeling, *Dictionary of the North-West Semitic Inscriptions* (Leiden: Brill, 1995); *TAD* D18.1; 18.2.

word had become a recognized official title in the Achaemenid chancellery,[4] the appearance of the Hebrew word suggests instead that this word has been added by the biblical writer and Ezra's identity as priest was not known to, or at least not relevant to, the king.

– *"scribe of the law"* The word used for "law" here is דתא, the Persian word *dātāʾ*. This term is discussed below.

– *"God of Heaven"* This is a term used by Judeans when talking to non-Judeans. It is not a word used by non-Judeans themselves, so it is not likely that this would have appeared in a letter from the Persian king.

– Verse 13: *"The people of Israel"* It is not likely that the Persian king would know the phrase "the people Israel" since the province was known as Yehud in the Persian period. It was likely added by the biblical author.

– *"and its priests and Levites who volunteers to go to Jerusalem with you, may go."* Again, the Hebrew rather than the Aramaic word for "priests" is used; nor would the Achaemenid king have had the concept of "Levites." Further, the word for "volunteer" is Hebrew, not Aramaic. This entire phrase is suspect.

– Verse 14: *"You are being sent"* This is the passive participle applied to Ezra, and the phrase is common to Persian-period letters. The same phrase appears in Dan 5:24 where the hand that writes "is being sent" by God himself. Parallels have been seen between the Aramaic term *šᵉliaḥ*, 'the one being sent', and the Mishnaic statement that the one being sent by a person is like that person (*m. Ber.* 5.5). The one being sent acts in the role of the sender, implying that Ezra here has royal authority.

– *"his seven counselors"* This notion of seven counselors or advisors has become a literary topos for Greek and other non-Persian writers. There is no mention of these in any authentic Persian document. The Great King operates alone.

– *"to act as the King's Ear"* That is, "to inspect" (*lᵉbaqqārāʾ*), to act as *mᵉbaqqēr*. This is likely authentic, as it was a common office in the Achaemenid Empire. This is the primary import of the letter: to appoint Ezra as *mᵉbaqqēr* "over Judah and Jerusalem." The infinitive *lᵉbaqqārāʾ* is translated in both 1 and 2 Esdras by the Greek infinitive ἐπισκέψασθαι. This is defined by Liddell and Scott (definition 5) as "one who 'watches over, as overseer, or guardian, specifically as the 'King's Eye'." Provincial governments were under the constant supervision of the 'eyes' or 'ears' of the king (Xenophon, *Cyr.* 8.2.10–12).[5] These royal agents were independent of the satraps and other local authorities and reported any seditious

---

[4] So Wilhelm Rudolph, *Esra und Nehemia Samt 3.Esra* (Tübingen: Mohr Siebeck, 1949), 73.

[5] Steven W. Hirsch, *The Friendship of the Barbarians: Xenophon and the Persian Empire* (London: Tufts University; University Press of New England, 1985), 131–34; Muhammad A. Dandamayev, "Courts and Courtiers: In the Median and Achaemenid Periods," *EI* 6:356–59, Fasc. 4.

speech directly to the king.[6] Reading and writing were not required for the job of *m^{e}baqqēr*. In fact, the *m^{e}baqqēr* would have had a secretary of his own to enable communication between himself and the king.

– *"by means of the* dāt *of your god"* This phrase is likely authentic. Ezra is told to carry out his role of *m^{e}baqqēr,* the king's "eye" or "ear", as well as his task of appointing judges "by means of the *dāt* of your god which is in your hand," בדת אלהך די בידך (7:14). The Persian term *dāt* is usually translated as 'law'. This is because of its Greek translation as νόμος (*nomos*), a term regularly translated into English as 'law'. *Nomos*, like *dāt,* however, actually refers to right behavior, custom, convention, the prevailing norms, principle, not to a written law code. *Nomos* did not come to refer to a written code of law until fifth century Athens,[7] but such a written unchanging concept of law was not part of the ancient Near East understanding of law at least until the Greek period.[8] According to Persian period inscriptions and to court cases, the *dāt* of the king always referred to his *ad hoc* orders and decrees, not to a written law code which did not exist.[9] Rather than a written code of law, *dāt* referred to right order and justice in the abstract, as well as each person being in his proper place. The *dāt* of the god, referred to in the letter, is, of course, the *dāt* or word of the king and inseparable from it; the word of the king was the word of the god and *vice versa*. Ezra, as the Eye and Ear of the king, was thus to ensure that each resident behaved as the king (and the god, i.e., Ahura Mazda) would want and to report back to the king if any acted otherwise. Both "the *dāt* of the king" and "the *dāt* of the god" would be the command of the king. "King" and "god" were viewed as synonymous.

---

[6] For further discussion see Fried, *Ezra*, 316–18.

[7] Kurt A. Raaflaub, "The Transformation of Athens in the Fifth Century," in *Democracy, Empire, and the Arts in Fifth-Century Athens*, ed. Deborah Boedeker and Kurt A. Raaflaub (Cambridge, MA: Harvard University Press, 1998), 15–41; see also the articles in Michael Gagarin and David Cohen, eds., *The Cambridge Companion to Ancient Greek Law* (Cambridge: Cambridge University Press, 2005).

[8] Wilhelm Spiegelberg, *Die sogenannte demotische Chronik des Pap. 215 der Bibliothéque Nationale de Paris* (Leipzig: Hinrichs, 1914); Charles Nims, "The Term *Hp* 'Law,' 'Right,' in Demotic," *JNES* 7 (1948): 243–60; Raymond Westbrook, "Cuneiform Law Codes and the Origins of Legislation," *ZA* 14 (1979): 201–22; Guillaume Cardasçia, "La Coutume dans les Droits Cunéiformes," *RSJB* (1990): 61–69; C. Janssen, "Samsu-Iluna and The Hungry Naditums," *NAPR* 5 (1991): 3–40; Nili Shupak, "A New Source for the Study of the Judiciary and Law of Ancient Egypt: The Case of the Eloquent Peasant," *JNES* 51 (1992): 1–18; Klaas R. Veenhof, "The Relation between Royal Decrees and 'Law Codes' of the Old Babylonian Period," *JEOL* 35/36 (1997): 49–83; Donald B. Redford, "The So-Called 'Codification' of Egyptian Law under Darius I," in *Persia and Torah: The Theory of Imperial Authorization of the Pentateuch*, ed. James W. Watts (Atlanta: Society of Biblical Literature, 2001), 135–59.

[9] Muhammad A. Dandamayev and Vladimir G. Lukonin, *The Culture and Social Institutions of Ancient Iran* (Cambridge: Cambridge University Press, 1989): 116–17; Sophie Démare-Lafont, "Datu Ša Šarri. La 'Loi Du Roi' dans la Babylonie Achéménide et Séleucide," *DEC* 52 (2006): https://doi.org/10.4000/droitcultures.544; Josef Wiesehöfer, "Law and Religion in Achaemenid Iran," in *Law and Religion in the Eastern Mediterranean: From Antiquity to Early Islam*, ed. Anselm C. Hagedorn and Reinhard G. Kratz (Oxford: Oxford University Press, 2013), 41–57.

– *"which is in your hand"* The *dāt* or word of your god "which is in your hand," furthermore, is not to be taken literally as implying a physical object like a written document. It simply means "which you know," "which you control," "which is yours." We read in Darius's Behistun inscription: "The lie made [these nine kings] rebellious, … afterwards Aḫuramazda put them into my hand; as was my desire, so I did unto them" (DB 4.36). We also have the following Akkadian example: "Try the case according to the judgment that is in your hands" (*dinam ša ina qatikunu ibaššu šuḫiza*; CAD Q 189). In other words, "Try the case according to your own judgment." Thus Ezra was to act as the Eye or Ear of the king and to appoint judges according to his own conception of what the King would want.

– Verse 15: *"and to carry the silver and gold which the king and his counselors have volunteered for the god of Israel whose dwelling is in Jerusalem"* The word "volunteered" is Hebrew (התנדבו), not Aramaic, and renders the verse suspect.

– Verse 16: *"and all the silver and gold that you will find in the whole province of Babylon"* This outlandish statement appears to be an addition of the biblical writer.

– *"along with the freewill offerings of the people and the priests, freely offered for the house of their god that is in Jerusalem"* Although the morpheme "their" in "their god" (אֱלָהֲהֹם) is the Persian-period spelling, and so was not updated in the Greek period, the word for "priests" is Hebrew not Aramaic (see comment on verse 12), rendering the entire phrase suspect.

– Verse 17: *"You shall quickly acquire"* The word for "quickly" is the Persian-period word (אספרנא), and was not updated to the Greek period equivalent.

– *"with this silver [and gold] bulls, rams, and their grain offerings, and their libation"* The morpheme "their" (וּמִנְחָתְהוֹן וְנִסְכֵּיהוֹן) has been updated to that of the Hellenistic period. This phrase has likely been added by the biblical writer.

– Verse 18: *"according to the will of your god."* The morpheme "your" has the Persian-period spelling (אֱלָהֲכֹם), but the word for "will" is not Aramaic, but Hebrew (רעות), rendering the phrase suspect.

– Verses 19–20: *"The vessels that are given to you for the service of the house of your god deliver safely before the god of Jerusalem. The rest of the requirements of the house of your god which falls upon you to give, give from the treasure-house of the king."* These verses appear to be authentic.

– Verse 21a: *"I, Artaxerxes the king, decree to all the treasurers who are in Beyond-the-River"* This seems authentic. This is the beginning of a second, embedded letter – common in Achaemenid epistolary. This second letter is addressed to the treasurers of all the provinces in the satrapy of Beyond-the-River, not just Yehud.

– *"that all that Ezra the priest"* This is again the Hebrew word for priest, and has been added by the biblical writer.

– *"and scribe of the dāt"* This possibly authentic phrase will be discussed below.

– *Verses 21b–22:* "*of the god of heaven will ask of you, you shall quickly do up to 100 talents of silver, 100 kors of wheat, 100 baths of wine, 100 baths of oil, and salt without counting.*" Another outlandish phrase, likely supplied by the biblical writer, writing in the Hellenistic period to offer the Achaemenid kings as a model for the Seleucid ones. These amounts are far too large to be real.

– *Verse 23:* "*All that is commanded by the god of heaven let it be done zealously for the house of the god of heaven lest Wrath come upon the realm of the king and upon his children.*" Since there is no limit to what the god of heaven would have demanded (by way of his priests), this is not likely part of an authentic letter.

– *Verse 24:* "*We inform all of you that*" The "we" is the royal we; the "you" is plural and is addressed to the treasures of the satrapy Beyond-the-River.

– "*[regarding] all the priests, Levites, singers, gatekeepers, temple servants, and cult officials of this house of God*" All of these terms, except "cult officials," are Hebrew terms specific to the temple in Jerusalem and would not have been known by the king. The term translated here as "cult official" (פלחי) was the normal Persian-period Aramaic word for one who serves a god, and could have been used by the king.

– "*neither tribute, poll tax, nor land tax is authorized to impose upon them.*" These taxes were common throughout the Achaemenid Empire, the terms are the normal Aramaic ones. The word for "them" (עֲלֵיהֹם) is the normal spelling used in the Achaemenid period. These sorts of exemptions were common, and the passage is likely authentic. Such favors to friends of the king as removing taxes for specific groups was common in the Achaemenid Empire.

– *Verse 25:* "*Now, you, Ezra*" This reverts back to the main letter.

– "*according to the wisdom of your god which is in your hand*" This line repeats verse 14 above, and takes the reader back to the main letter.

– "*appoint magistrates and judges who may become judges for all the people who are in Beyond-the-River*" Ezra's task was to appoint judges. These were to be royal judges (since he was an agent of the king), and they were to be appointed throughout the satrapy of Beyond-the-River, not just in Yehud. These judges would have all been Persian, except perhaps for an occasional Babylonian. Greek authors also report that the Persian kings sent Persians into the conquered areas to serve as judges.[10] Contemporary documents from both Egypt and Babylon reveal that the royal judges were ethnic Persians who took over the judicial system of the conquered areas. Even in Egypt, Egyptians, Judeans, Arameans all appeared before Persian judges. There were no Egyptian judges in Egypt, and there would not have been Judean judges in Yehud/Judah. The appointment of Persian judges throughout the empire was the primary way in which the empire enforced its decrees.[11]

---

[10] Dandamayev and Lukonin, *Culture*, 122.

[11] For further discussion see Lisbeth S. Fried, *The Priest and the Great King: Temple-Palace Relations in the Persian Empire*, BJSUCSD 10 (Winona Lake, IN: Eisenbrauns, 2004).

– *"who may become judges for all the people who are in Beyond-the-River"* Ezra is thus assigned to appoint judges for all the people in the satrapy Beyond-the-River, not just the Judeans in the satrapy, and not just the people who live in Yehud, but everyone in the entire satrapy. These judges he was to appoint would be Persian.

– *"to all who know the* dāt *of your god. Whoever does not know, you [plural, i.e., the judges and magistrates you appoint] will instruct."* This is part of the authentic letter. The term *dāt* is discussed further below.

– Verse 26: *"All who do not obey the* dāt *of your god and the* dāt *of the king, let judgment be quickly executed on him, either for death, or flogging, or fine, or imprisonment."* This is part of the authentic letter and concludes it. These punishments were all common in the Achaemenid empire.

2.1 The Authentic Letter from King Artaxerxes to Ezra

The letter purports to be a "copy of an order" (7:11) that a king Artaxerxes had given to this Ezra. Since the words 'copy' and 'order' are in Persian, a Persian original may be accepted. These terms suggest that this letter is a written copy of an original oral command. The letter itself is in Aramaic, the lingua franca of official letters of the Achaemenid Empire (cf. *TAD* and *ADAB*). Removing the problematic verses and phrases we have what may be the authentic letter from King Artaxerxes to Ezra:

Artaxerxes, King of Kings, to Ezra, and now [14.]you are being sent from before the king to act as the King's Ear (לְבַקָּרָא, *l^ebaqqārā*), over Yehud by means of the *dāt* of your god which is at your hand. [19.]The vessels that are given to you for the service of the house of your god deliver safely before the god of Jerusalem. [20.]The rest of the requirements of the house of your god which falls upon you to give, give from the treasure-house of the king [in Jerusalem].

[21] I, Artaxerxes the king, decree to all the treasurers who are in Beyond-the-River that regarding the cultic officials of this house of god, neither tribute, poll tax, nor land tax is authorized to impose upon them.

[25] Now, you, Ezra, according to the wisdom of god which is at your hand, appoint judges who may become judges for all the people who are in Beyond-the-River. [26] All who do not obey the law of god and the law of the king let judgment be quickly executed on him, either for death, or flogging, or fine, or imprisonment.

[From Artaxerxes, King of Kings, to Ezra, year seven of the king.]

3. The Law of God and the Law of the King

Marin Buss distinguishes two types of law: natural and positive. Natural law "expresses an intrinsic morality based on the presence of inner connections between participants in reality," whereas positive law "expresses a law-giver's free will, independent from others".[12] Natural law, or the law of God, is grounded in a socially constructed inner morality, based on perceived reality. Positive law, or the law of the king, can be changed on a whim. Natural law is permanent, on-going, and was the basis of Judges' decisions. In antiquity, judges decided their cases based on natural law. In Pharaonic Egypt, pharaoh was the source of positive law. In the Achaemenid Empire, the source of positive law was the king. The decrees of the king were on an *ad hoc* basis and did not comprise a law code. The Persian judges that Ezra appointed would have judged according to their own conscience and their own conceptions of right and wrong, except if the rare command of the king intervened.

3.1 Sōpēr of the Dāt of God

The historical Ezra thus had two roles: 1) to act as one of the King's 'Ears', i. e., as a spy for the king, and 2) to appoint Persian judges for the satrapy Beyond-the-River. Nevertheless, the biblical writer describes Ezra as *sōpēr* of the *dāt* of God (Ezra 7:6), as scribe of the law. So the question is why the author would have labeled him such, and what might he have meant by it. The statement that Ezra was a "scribe of the law" was likely due to the biblical writer's own contemporary understanding of the word *dāt*. A copy of the authentic letter of the king to Ezra was likely maintained in the temple's archives and the biblical writer evidently had access to it. He then based his own story of Ezra on it. When would that have been?

Ben Sira provides a date for the story of Ezra. Ben Sira knows the story of Zerubbabel and Jeshua who built the temple of Yhwh in Jerusalem which is told in Ezra 1–6 (Ben Sira 49. 11–12). He also knows the story of Nehemiah who built the wall around Jerusalem, told in Nehemiah 1–7.3 (Ben Sira 49.13). Nevertheless, he does not know the story of Ezra, told in Ezra 7–10 and in Nehemiah 8. This implies that the chapters regarding Ezra (Ezra 7–10, Nehemiah 8–10) were written after Ben Sira. Ben Sira, who extols both priest (BS 45:6–26; 50:1–21) and scribe of the Law of God (BS 39.1–11), would certainly have referred to Ezra's story had he known it, and if it had been written he would have known it.

The story of Ezra and of his reading the law (Neh. 8) must have been written after Ben Sira and so in the early second century BCE at the earliest, since scholars have concluded that Ben Sira wrote around 195 BCE.[13] These chapters in Ezra-Nehemiah regarding Ezra (Ezra 7–10, Neh. 8) were thus among the last chapters to be added to the book of Ezra-Nehemiah. Archaeological investigations also

---

[12] Martin J. Buss, "Legal Science and Legislation," in *Theory and Method in Biblical and Cuneiform Law: Revision, Interpolation and Development*, ed. Bernard Levinson (Sheffield: Sheffield Academic, 1994), 88–90.

[13] Otto Mulder, *Simon the High Priest in Sirach 50: An Exegetical Study of the Significance of Simon the High Priest as Climax to the Praise of the Fathers in Ben Sira's Concept of the History of Israel*, JSJSup 78 (Leiden: Brill, 2003), 13.

confirm that the towns listed in Nehemiah 11.25–36 could only have been described as belonging to Judah after the Maccabean wars, so this section too must have been composed after 160 BCE.[14] Thus while the authentic letter from Artaxerxes to Ezra would have been written at the beginning of the fourth century by Artaxerxes II, the entire story of Ezra, though based on that archival letter, seems to have been written in the Seleucid period, after Ben Sira.

4. Changing Meaning of *dāt*: Evidence from the Book of Daniel

What motivated the biblical author, writing in the Seleucid period, to use Artaxerxes' letter to create his story of Ezra? We propose it was the change in the meaning of the term *dāt*. This change is especially observable within the Aramaic portions of Daniel. Chapters 1–6 are dated by scholars to the late Persian period (fourth century BCE), and these chapters exhibit one meaning of the term.[15] In contrast, chapter 7, dated by these scholars to the time of the Seleucid king Antiochus IV, exhibits another. We examine the relevant verses one by one.

4.1 Daniel 2:9 – The words of Nebuchadnezzar to Daniel

די הן חלמא לא תהודענני חדה היא דתכון   If you do not tell me what the dream was, there will be only one *dāt* for you.

Here the word *dāt* simply means edict – the king's edict which results from his personal decision in an *ad hoc* situation. This verse and the next two are from the story of Nebuchadnezzar's dream of a giant statue. He has demanded that the sages and diviners not only interpret his dream, but that they tell him what the dream was.

4.2 Daniel 2:12–13 – The magicians could not tell the dream

כל קבל דנה מלכא בנס וקצף שגיא ואמר   Because [they could not tell him his dream] the
להובדה לכל חכימי בבל: king flew into a violent rage and commanded
ודתא נפקת וחכימיא מתקטלין ובעו דניאל   that all the wise men of Babylon be destroyed.
וחברוהי להתקטלה: The *dāt* went forth, and the wise men were about to be killed and [soldiers] sought Daniel and his comrades to kill them.

---

[14] Israel Finkelstein, *Hasmonean Realities behind Ezra, Nehemiah, and Chronicles* (Atlanta: Society of Biblical Literature, 2018); Deirdre N. Fulton, *Reconsidering Nehemiah's Judah*, FAT II 80 (Tübingen: Mohr Siebeck, 2015).

[15] Louis F. Hartman and Alexander A. Di Lella, *The Book of Daniel: A New Translation with Introduction and Commentary*, AB 23 (New York: Doubleday, 1978), 13; John E. Goldingay, *Daniel*, WBC 30 (Dallas: Word, 1989), 326; Carol A. Newsom and Brennan W. Breed, *Daniel, A Commentary*, OTL (Louisville: Westminster John Knox, 2014).

Here again *dāt* is an order or demand of the king. It is an *ad hoc* royal decree, not part of any permanent law code.

4.3 Daniel 2:15 – Daniel asks about the king's rage against the magicians

ענה ואמר לאריוך שליטא די מלכא על מה דתא מהחצפה מן קדם מלכא אדין מלתא הודע אריוך לדניאל:	He (Daniel) approached and asked Arioch, the royal official, "Why is the *dāt* of the king so harsh?" Arioch explained the thing to Daniel.

Again, the term refers here to an *ad hoc* decree of the king.

4.4 Daniel 6:6 – The officials of Darius's court try to entrap Daniel

אדין גבריא אלך אמרין די לא נהשכח לדניאל דנה כל עלא להן השכחנה עלוהי בדת אלהה:	Then these men said that we shall not find [fault] against this Daniel in the whole matter unless we find it against him in the *dāt* of his God. [ET 6:5]

That is, unless we find fault in the decrees or *dāt* of Daniel's god, we shall not find fault in Daniel, because Daniel follows the decrees of his god above all else.

Here, and in the following four passages in this chapter, Daniel's enemies are trying to remove Daniel and his influence from Darius's court. They convince Darius to sign an edict that for the next thirty days Darius alone may be worshipped, but no other god or human – under penalty of death in a lion's den. It is hoped this will force Daniel to disobey the king so that he may be killed.

4.5 Daniel 6:9 – The officials persuade the king to establish his rule in writing

כען מלכא תקים אסרא ותרשם כתבא די לא להשניה כדת מדי ופרס די לא תעדא:	Now, let the king establish a decree and sign a paper so that according to the *dāt* of the Medes and Persians it cannot be changed, it is a decree which cannot be revoked. [ET 6:8]

This verse implies that according to the customs and traditions of the Medes and the Persians, a decree of the king that is written down, unlike an oral statement, cannot be changed or revoked, but is permanent.

4.6 Daniel 6:13 – The officials inform the king that Daniel continues to worship only his god

באדין קריבו ואמרין קדם מלכא על אסר
מלכא הלא אסר רשמת די כל אנש די יבעה מן
כל אלה ואנש עד יומין תלתין להן מנך מלכא
יתרמא לגוב אריותא ענה מלכא ואמר יציבא
מלתא כדת מדי ופרס די לא תעדא:

Then they approached and said before the king concerning the prohibition, "O King, did you not decree and sign [it] that anyone who prays to anything, divine or human, besides you for thirty days, shall be thrown into a den of lions?" The king answered, "The word stands firm, according to the *dāt* of the Medes and Persians, which cannot be revoked." [ET 6:12]

Again, according to the traditions of the Medes and the Persians a written decree or statement cannot be revoked. Once written, it has the force of binding eternal law.

4.7 Daniel 6:16 – It is reiterated that a decree, written and signed, cannot be revoked

באדין גבריא אלך הרגשו על מלכא ואמרין
למלכא דע מלכא די דת למדי ופרס די כל
אסר וקים די מלכא יהקים לא להשניה:

Then the men came and approached the king and said to the king, "Know, O King, that it is the *dāt* of the Medes and the Persians that no order or decree that the king establishes [in writing] can be changed. [ET 6:15]

Again, we may translate *dāt* here as custom and tradition. It is asserted here that according to the custom of the Medes and Persians, a decree of the king once written may not be altered. For the first time, here in the book of Daniel the force of written law is signaled. Because it is a written decree, and because a written decree may not be altered or erased, the king puts it in force for a specified period of time only. This law is to be in effect for just thirty days.

4.8 Daniel 7:25 – The fourth beast

Daniel 7 records the King's dream of the four evil kingdoms each represented by a beast, followed by a fifth pure kingdom, represented by a human being. The first three evil kingdoms are the Babylonians, the Medes, and the Persians. The fourth kingdom, the Greeks, is the most heinous:

ומלין לצד עלאה ימלל ולקדישי עליונין יבלא
ויסבר להשניה זמנין ודת ויתיהבון בידה עד
עדן ועדנין ופלג עדן:

[The fourth king] shall speak words against the Most High, shall wear out the holy ones of the Most High, and shall attempt to change the times and the *dāt*; and they shall be given into his hand for a time, two times, and half a time.

Daniel 7 describes the depredations of Antiochus IV Epiphanes upon Judea and Jerusalem. By his attempt to "change the times" is meant an attempt to change the calendar used in the temple– to change the dates of the sacred holidays. The horror expressed at changing the *dāt* here suggests that the meaning of the word *dāt* had changed. It had now become a written code of law – as it was only a written decree which could not be changed.

5. Evolution in the Concept of Law

Thus, the book of Daniel allows us to track the evolution of the concept of law over time. The Aramaic word *dāt,* changed from a Persian-period concept of a simple *ad hoc* one-time decree to the later Hellenistic Period practice of an immutable written law. By the time of the Maccabees, as seen in Daniel 7, the meaning of *dāt* had evolved to a concept of a codified law. This change in meaning over time applies as well to the word *dāt* that appears in Ezra 7. If we posit that Ezra 7 contains a genuine letter from a king Artaxerxes, then we must conclude that the term *dāt* in that letter did not refer to a written permanent code of law, but to *ad hoc* royal decrees. When we realize, however, that the biblical writer wrote in the Hellenistic period and did not know that earlier meaning of the term we can understand the biblical writer's concept of Ezra.

5.1 Ezra as Sōpēr Māhîr

The biblical writer labels Ezra as *sôpēr* (scribe) and as *sôpēr māhîr*. As the meaning of *dāt* changed, so did the meaning of these titles. The phrase *sôpēr māhîr* is usually translated "skilled scribe." This description is elsewhere applied to Aḥiqar, an official in the court of Sennacherib, King of Assyria, and bearer of the king's seal. Heltzer and Avishur suggest translating the phrase *sôpēr māhîr* with the help of the Arabic.[16] Admittedly, the first meaning of the Arabic phrase is "skilled scribe", as the phrase is usually translated. The second meaning of *māher* in Arabic may be more appropriate, however. *Muher* means "stamp," and the person who seals by a stamp is a *māher*. The verb *mahara* means "he sealed by a stamp seal". Although the word is found in present-day Arabic, it seems to have been of Persian or of Aramaic origin. If Ezra were actually a *sôpēr māhîr* for king Artaxerxes, we could surmise, as Heltzer and Avishur do, that Ezra was an official in the court of Artaxerxes, and that he sealed his own edicts with the seal of the king.[17] The difficulty is that this phrase never appears in the authentic parts of the letter from the king detailing Ezra's task. It appears only in the biblical writer's introduction.

---

[16] Michael Heltzer and Y. Avishur, "The Term *Sofer Mahir* as Designating a Courtier in the Old Testament and the Ahiqar," *UF* 34 (2002): 217–21.

[17] Heltzer and Avishur, "The Term *Sofer Mahir*," 221.

5.2 The Torah as King

With the concept of *dāt* having changed by the Maccabean period from an *ad hoc* decree of the king to a permanent written law code, so did the understanding of Ezra's role and of Artaxerxes' letter to him authorizing it. The letter from Artaxerxes was reinterpreted by the biblical writer according to the new understanding of law and of written law codes. Ezra was no longer viewed as having been charged with the task of appointing judges who would judge according to their own sense of right and wrong and by the word of the king. Now he was viewed as tasked with appointing judges who were to judge according to a written law code. This code of law was not one legislated by a king, however, but rather it was now the immutable law of God, the torah of Moses. As we see, the biblical writer has labeled Ezra as ספר מהיר בתורת משה אשר־נתן יהוה אלהי ישראל, "a skilled scribe (*sôpēr māhîr*) in (or by means of, or according to) the torah of Moses which Yhwh, god of Israel gave [to Israel]" (Ezra 7:6). Thus, now Ezra writes decrees himself which he seals by torah. As Eskenazi puts it, Ezra's master is now the book of the torah.[18] The torah has become the king, the law-giver.[19]

5.3 Ezra as *sôpēr māhîr* of the Torah

In Nehemiah 8[20] Ezra is shown reading and teaching the torah to the people Israel. According to the text, Ezra stands on a wooden platform high above all the people (Neh. 8:4–5). We read the following (Neh. 8:5–6):

ויפתח עזרא הספר לעיני כל העם כי מעל כל העם היה וכפתחו עמדו כל העם: ויברך עזרא את יהוה האלהים הגדול ויענו כל העם אמן אמן במעל ידיהם ויקדו וישתחו ליהוה אפים ארצה:	And Ezra opened the book in the sight of all the people, for he was standing above all the people; and when he opened it, all the people stood up. Then Ezra blessed YHWH, the great God, and all the people answered, "Amen, Amen," lifting up their hands. Then they kneeled and bowed down to YHWH with their faces on the ground.

The text states that they kneeled touching their foreheads to the ground to Yhwh, but they are actually kneeling and bowing their heads before the torah

---

[18] Tamara Cohn Eskenazi, *In an Age of Prose: A Literary Approach to Ezra-Nehemiah* (Atlanta: Scholars Press, 1988), 136.

[19] Two other essays within this volume probe this "textualization" of divine authority, or – put differently – the divinization of written law. Johanna Erzberger, "Israel's Salvation and the Survival of Baruch the Scribe," finds that the figure of Baruch in the books of Jeremiah (LXX and MT) and the book of Baruch represents a development similar to what we suggest regarding the figure of Ezra the scribe in the developmental stages of Ezra–Nehemiah. Peter Altmann traces the phenomenon of "written divine law" in Chronicles during the late-Persian/early-Hellenistic period, and argues that the Chronicler's conception of divine law interpreted by judges tends toward cultic issues, rather than economic or other concerns; see "Tracing Divine Law: Written Divine Law in Chronicles."

[20] This section incorporates comments from Lisbeth S. Fried, *Nehemiah: A Commentary*, ed. David J. Clines, SPCC (Sheffield: Sheffield Phoenix, 2021).

scroll that Ezra is holding up. The torah scroll has thus come to represent the god. Some form of the phrase 'kneeled and bowed down' occurs fifteen times in the Bible. It is not always before a deity. Often it is before a king. Bathsheba kneels and bows twice before King David on behalf of her son Solomon (1 Kings 1.16, 31). Other times it is before a supernatural apparition, as when Bila'am kneels and bows before the Angel of Yhwh (Num. 23.31) and when Saul kneels and bows before Samuel's ghost (1 Sam. 28.14). Every other time that kneeling and bowing is mentioned however, it is to Yhwh that they kneel and bow down, with no physical representation of him at all (e. g., Gen. 24.28; Exod. 4.31; 2 Chron. 20.18). Only here does Yhwh have a representation before which the people kneel and bow. Here the people kneel and bow down before a *text*, before a piece of literature. At the time of writing, and in the mind of the author, the torah scroll had thus become an icon of the god Yhwh.[21] This attitude toward the torah is exhibited most clearly in 1 Macc. 3.48, when it had evidently become commonplace:

| καὶ ἐξεπέτασαν τὸ βιβλίον τοῦ νόμου περὶ ὧν ἐξηρεύνων τὰ ἔθνη τὰ ὁμοιώματα τῶν εἰδώλων αὐτῶν | And they opened the book of the torah to inquire into those matters about which the Gentiles consulted the likenesses of their gods. |

By the Maccabean period the torah had become the icon of the god, and Ezra, the scribe, the bearer of its seal.

Bibliography

Altmann, Peter. "Tracing Divine Law: Written Divine Law in Chronicles." Within this volume.
Buss, Martin J. "Legal Science and Legislation." Pages 88–90 in *Theory and Method in Biblical and Cuneiform Law: Revision, Interpolation and Development*. Edited by Bernard Levinson. Sheffield: Sheffield Academic, 1994.
Cardasçia, Guillaume. "La Coutume dans les Droits Cunéiformes." *RSJB* (1990): 61–69.
Dandamayev, Muhammad A. "Courts and Courtiers: In the Median and Achaemenid Periods." *EI* 6:356–59, Fasc. 4.

---

[21] Michael Fishbane, *Biblical Interpretation in Ancient Israel* (Oxford: Clarendon, 1985), 245; Susan Niditch, *Oral World and Written Word*, AIL (Louisville: Westminster John Knox, 1996), 106; Karel van der Toorn, "The Iconic Book Analogies between the Babylonian Cult of Images and the Veneration of the Torah," in *The Image and the Book: Iconic Cults, Aniconism, and the Rise of Book Religion in Israel and the Ancient Near East*, ed. Karel van der Toorn (Leuven: Peeters, 1997), 229–48; Jeffrey H. Tigay, "The Torah Scroll and God's Presence," in *Built by Wisdom, Established by Understanding: Essays on Biblical and Near Eastern Literature in Honor of Adele Berlin*, ed. Maxine L. Grossman (Bethesda, MD: University Press of Maryland, 2013), 323–40; Lisbeth S. Fried, "The Torah of God as God: The Exaltation of the Written Law Code in Ezra-Nehemiah," in *Divine Presence and Absence in Exilic and Post-Exilic Judaism: Studies of the Sofja Kovalevskaja Research Group on Early Jewish Monotheism, Vol. II*, ed. Nathan MacDonald and Izaak de Hulster, FAT II 61 (Tübingen: Mohr Siebeck, 2013), 283–300; Fried, *Ezra*, 300–302.

Dandamayev, Muhammad A., and Vladimir G. Lukonin. *The Culture and Social Institutions of Ancient Iran*. Cambridge: Cambridge University Press, 1989.

Démare-Lafont, Sophie. "Datu Ša Šarri. La 'Loi Du Roi' dans la Babylonie Achéménide et Séleucide = Datu Ša Šarri." *DEC* 52 (2006). https://doi.org/10.4000/droitcultures.544.

Erzberger, Johanna. "Israel's Salvation and the Survival of Baruch the Scribe." Within this volume.

Eskenazi, Tamara Cohn. *In an Age of Prose: A Literary Approach to Ezra-Nehemiah*. Atlanta: Scholars Press, 1988.

Finkelstein, Israel. *Hasmonean Realities behind Ezra, Nehemiah, and Chronicles*. Atlanta: Society of Biblical Literature, 2018.

Fishbane, Michael. *Biblical Interpretation in Ancient Israel*. Oxford: Clarendon, 1985.

Fried, Lisbeth S. *Ezra: A Commentary*. SPCC. Sheffield: Sheffield Phoenix, 2015.

Fried, Lisbeth S. *The Priest and the Great King: Temple-Palace Relations in the Persian Empire*. BJSUCSD 10. Winona Lake, IN: Eisenbrauns, 2004.

Fried, Lisbeth S. "The Torah of God as God: The Exaltation of the Written Law Code in Ezra-Nehemiah," Pages 283–300 in *Divine Presence and Absence in Exilic and Post-Exilic Judaism: Studies of the Sofja Kovalevskaja Research Group on Early Jewish Monotheism, Vol. II*. Edited by Nathan MacDonald and Izaak de Hulster. FAT II 61. Tübingen: Mohr Siebeck, 2013.

Fulton, Deirdre N. *Reconsidering Nehemiah's Judah*. FAT II 80. Tübingen: Mohr Siebeck, 2015.

Gagarin, Michael, and David Cohen, eds. *The Cambridge Companion to Ancient Greek Law*. Cambridge: Cambridge University Press, 2005.

Goldingay, John E. *Daniel*. WBC 30. Dallas: Word, 1989.

Hartman, Louis F., and Alexander A. Di Lella. *The Book of Daniel: A New Translation with Introduction and Commentary*. AB 23. New York: Doubleday, 1978.

Heltzer, Michael, and Y. Avishur. "The Term *Sofer Mahir* as Designating a Courtier in the Old Testament and the Ahiqar." *UF* 34 (2002): 217–21.

Hirsch, Steven W. *The Friendship of the Barbarians: Xenophon and the Persian Empire*. London: Tufts University; University Press of New England, 1985.

Hoftijzer, J., and K. Jongeling. *Dictionary of the North-West Semitic Inscriptions*. Leiden: Brill, 1995.

Janssen, C. "Samsu-Iluna and The Hungry Naditums." *NAPR* 5 (1991): 3–40.

Mulder, Otto. *Simon the High Priest in Sirach 50: An Exegetical Study of the Significance of Simon the High Priest as Climax to the Praise of the Fathers in Ben Sira's Concept of the History of Israel*. JSJSup 78 Leiden: Brill, 2003.

Newsom, Carol A., and Brennan W. Breed. *Daniel, A Commentary*. OTL. Louisville: Westminster John Knox, 2014.

Niditch, Susan. *Oral World and Written Word*. AIL. Louisville: Westminster John Knox, 1996.

Nims, Charles. "The Term *Hp* 'Law,' 'Right,' in Demotic." *JNES* 7 (1948): 243–60.

Raaflaub, Kurt A. "The Transformation of Athens in the Fifth Century." Pages 15–41 in *Democracy, Empire, and the Arts in Fifth-Century Athens*. Edited by Deborah Boedeker and Kurt A. Raaflaub. Cambridge, MA: Harvard University Press, 1998.

Redford, Donald B. "The So-Called 'Codification' of Egyptian Law under Darius I." Pages 135–59 in *Persia and Torah: The Theory of Imperial Authorization of the Pentateuch*. Edited by James W. Watts. Atlanta: Society of Biblical Literature, 2001.

Rudolph, Wilhelm. *Esra und Nehemia Samt 3.Esra*. Tübingen: Mohr Siebeck, 1949.

Schwiderski, Dirk. *Handbuch Des Nordwestsemitischen Briefformulars: Ein Beitrag Zur Echtheitsfrage der Aramäischen Briefe des Esrabuches.* BZAW 295. Berlin: de Gruyter, 2000.

Shupak, Nili. "A New Source for the Study of the Judiciary and Law of Ancient Egypt: The Case of the Eloquent Peasant." *JNES* 51 (1992): 1–18.

Spiegelberg, Wilhelm. *Die sogenannte demotische Chronik des Pap. 215 der Bibliothéque Nationale de Paris.* Leipzig: Hinrichs, 1914.

Tigay, Jeffrey H. "The Torah Scroll and God's Presence." Pages 323–40 in *Built by Wisdom, Established by Understanding: Essays on Biblical and Near Eastern Literature in Honor of Adele Berlin.* Edited by Maxine L. Grossman. Bethesda, MD: University Press of Maryland, 2013.

Toorn, Karel van der. "The Iconic Book Analogies between the Babylonian Cult of Images and the Veneration of the Torah." Pages 229–48 in *The Image and the Book: Iconic Cults, Aniconism, and the Rise of Book Religion in Israel and the Ancient Near East.* Edited by Karel van der Toorn. Leuven: Peeters, 1997.

Veenhof, Klaas R. "The Relation between Royal Decrees and 'Law Codes' of the Old Babylonian Period." *JEOL* 35/36 (1997): 49–83.

Westbrook, Raymond. "Cuneiform Law Codes and the Origins of Legislation." *ZA* 14 (1979): 201–22.

Wiesehöfer, Josef. "Law and Religion in Achaemenid Iran." Pages 41–57 in *Law and Religion in the Eastern Mediterranean: From Antiquity to Early Islam.* Edited by Anselm C. Hagedorn and Reinhard G. Kratz. Oxford: Oxford University Press, 2013.

Israel's Salvation and the Survival of Baruch the Scribe*

Johanna Erzberger

1. Introduction: The (Pre-)History of Baruch

Baruch, introduced as Jeremiah's scribe in Jer 32 and a seemingly secondary character in the larger book, plays an increasingly important role in a series of texts throughout the book. In Jer 36, Baruch writes a scroll under the dictation of Jeremiah, reads it in the temple, and rewrites it after it has been destroyed by Jehoiakim. There are, however, subtle differences inscribed into the image of Baruch in the different versions of the book preserved in the Septuagint and the Masoretic Text. According to the LXX (Jer 43:32), it is Baruch who takes the initiative to rewrite the scroll.[1] In Jer 43, Baruch is accused by the survivors of the events unfolding around Gedaliah's murder of having caused Jeremiah's opposition to the idea of taking refuge in Egypt. He then accompanies Jeremiah there. The announcement of Baruch's survival in Jer 45 closes both the biography of the prophet Jeremiah and the history of Judah's fall, ending with the disappearance in Egypt of Jeremiah and the seemingly last inhabitants of the land. In the Septuagint, this chapter closes the book, followed only by an appendix dealing with the fall of Jerusalem which is taken over from 2 Kgs 24–25. The book of Baruch reprises the Baruch tradition and casts Baruch as the reader or author of a(nother) book. This work has sometimes been read as a sequel to the book of Jeremiah, particularly the version of the LXX.

This article focuses on Baruch's final appearance in Jer 45 and his role in the opening chapter of the book of Baruch, which together indicate the scribe's function in the shifting contexts of the different versions of the book of Jeremiah and the book of Baruch. This article will demonstrate that the book of Baruch's own agenda serves to supplement the multiple perspectives already at play within the Jeremiah tradition. From this background, the book of Baruch can indeed be read as perpetuating the figure Baruch as the personification of textualization as it has been created by the book of Jeremiah.[2]

---

* The author acknowledges support as a Research Fellow of the University of Pretoria.
[1] According to the MT version of the book (36:32), it is Jeremiah.
[2] In this volume, Lisbeth S. Fried and Edward Mills III propose that the figure "Ezra the Scribe" as represented in the various hypothesized layers of Ezra 7 likewise represents shifting understandings of the divine authority as "textualized."

2. Jeremiah 45

2.1 A Close Reading

In both the LXX and MT versions of the book of Jeremiah, Jer 45 follows directly after the episode of Jeremiah and Baruch's enforced stay in Egypt (Jer 43–44). Against this textual context, Jer 45:1 introduces what follows as a word that Jeremiah has spoken to Baruch, when Baruch wrote "these words" at the dictation of Jeremiah in a book, in the fourth year of King Jehoiakim's reign. A prophetic messenger formula (45:2) introduces a divine speech that is said to be "about you, Baruch." In addressing Baruch directly, this divine speech then quotes a lamentation that is attributed to Baruch (v. 3). Apart from the introduction, "you [Baruch] said," this lamentation recalls the lamentations of Jeremiah appearing earlier in the book and, if taken on its own, does not explicitly identify Baruch as its speaker. Another divine speech follows, which now addresses Jeremiah and asks him to transfer the message to Baruch (v. 4aα), after which proceeds another prophetic messenger formula that gives a divine answer to the preceding lamentation. God announces disaster for all flesh, but promises the addressee his life "in every place to which you may go" (vv. 4b–5). The motif of God building and breaking down, planting and plucking reprises several parallels appearing earlier in the book.[3] The addressee's fate and seeking great things for himself – with the formulation בקש גדול, which is used elsewhere with regard to the people – is confronted with a global perspective of disaster (הנני מביא רעה על־כל־בשר).[4]

Excluding the brief mention of Baruch in v. 1 and in the supplement to the messenger formula in v. 2, both the lamentation and the divine answer could just as easily refer to Jeremiah. Verse 4aα, which underlines that Jeremiah addresses Baruch on God's order, creates a tension with regard to v. 3aα; both of these

---

[3] However, it differs from the earlier parallels in that it is part of an announcement of limited disaster rather than of salvation. This difference in meaning is underlined by the use of different tenses. Whereas in 45:4 *qatal* is used for the positive actions, the participle is instead used for the negative ones. In all of the parallels, the *yiqtol* is used throughout. While the parallels have typically been attributed to a Deuteronomistic redaction, the motif in Jer 45 has either been considered to be post-Deuteronomistic (Winfried Thiel, *Die deuteronomistische Redaktion von Jeremia 26–45*, WMANT 52 [Neukirchen-Vluyn: Neukirchener Verlag, 1981], 85) or – on the contrary – to have served as a model for the parallels (Axel Graupner, "Jeremia 45 als 'Schlusswort' des Jeremiabuches," in *Altes Testament und christliche Verkündigung*, ed. Manfred Oeming and Axel Graupner [Stuttgart: Kohlhammer, 1987], 290; Marion Ann Taylor, "Jeremiah 45: The Problem of Placement," *JSOT* 37 [1987]: 79–98 [92]; Hannelis Schulte, "Baruch und Ebedmelech: Persönliche Heilsorakel im Jeremiabuche," *BZ* 32.2 [1988]: 257–65 [261]) due to these differences in tense.

[4] This is usually considered to be Deuteronomistic due to the motif's global perspective (Schulte, "Baruch und Ebedmelech," 261). Thiel, who considers על־כל־בשר to instead refer to the Judeans in Judah and Egypt, more particularly identifies מביא רעה as Deuteronomistic (Thiel, *Die deuteronomistische Redaktion von Jeremia 26–45*, 86).

are subordinated to the messenger formula in v. 2 though they are addressing a different "you" (second pers. sg.). The subordination of the second messenger formula in v. 4aβ prevents it from being read on the same textual level as the first messenger formula in v. 2. The introduction in v. 1, the supplement to the messenger formula in v. 2, and the possibly secondary v. 4aβ,[5] attribute to Baruch a role that is elsewhere in the book attributed to Jeremiah.

2.2 Intra-textual Links and Shifting Perspectives Within the Book of Jeremiah

In the scholarly literature, the link between Jer 45 and 36 created by their common date "in the fourth year of King Jehoiakim's reign" and by both chapters' reference to Baruch writing these words in a book at Jeremiah's dictation[6] has been widely discussed. The fact that Jer 45 follows Jeremiah and Baruch's involuntary escape to Egypt rather than Jer 36 has led some scholars to argue that the date and the rendering את־הדברים האלה were secondarily added to this chapter.[7]

To complete the picture, the link between these two chapters and Jer 25:1, which also shares the same date, should equally be taken into consideration. The announcement of disaster for Judah in Jer 25:1–13(14), which is limited by the announcement of disaster for Babylon, closes out Jer 1–25. Exegetes who identify "all that is written in this book" in 25:13 with the first 25 chapters of the book of Jeremiah have further identified these chapters with the scroll written by Baruch in Jer 36. However, both the MT and the LXX version of 25:1–13(14) identify "that land" against which God has announced disaster according to "every-

---

[5] Duhm suggests either to delete v. 4aα or to change אמרת in v. 3 to אמר (Bernhard Duhm, *Das Buch Jeremia* [Tübingen: Mohr Siebeck, 1901], 335). See also Wilhelm Rudolph, *Jeremia*, HAT 1 (Tübingen: Mohr Siebeck, 1968), 264. Thiel considers v. 4aα to be part of the Deuteronomistic layer (Thiel, *Die deuteronomistische Redaktion von Jeremia 26–45*, 85; see also Graupner, "Jeremia 45 als 'Schlusswort' des Jeremiabuches," 288). Holladay does not consider v. 4aα to be secondary (William Lee Holladay, *Jeremiah 2: A Commentary on the Book of the Prophet Jeremiah Chapters 26–52*, Hermeneia [Minneapolis: Fortress, 1989], 309).

[6] ויכתב ברוך מפי ירמיהו את כל־דברי in Jer 45:1 echoes בכתבו את־הדברים האלה על־ספר מפי ירמיהו יהוה אשר־דבר אליו על־מגלת־ספר in Jer 36:4.

[7] Duhm, *Das Buch Jeremia*, 335; see also the presentation of Taylor, "Jeremiah 45," 79–80; Elena di Pede, "Jérusalem, Ebed-Melek et Baruch: Enquête narrative sur le déplacement chronologique de Jr 45," *RB* 111.1 (2004): 61–77 at 65–67. Thiel assumes that Jer 45 originally referred to Jer 43 with both the date and את־הדברים האלה in v. 1 constituting a secondary addition (Thiel, *Die deuteronomistische Redaktion von Jeremia 26–45*, 83–84, 85, 88). According to Graupner, את־הדברים האלה in Jer 45:1 originally referred to Jer 43 and was then predated under the influence of the later addition of the oracle to Seraiah (Jer 51:59–64), which refers to the oracle to Baruch but precedes the destruction of Jerusalem (Graupner, "Jeremia 45 als 'Schlusswort' des Jeremiabuches," 291). This impression is underlined by an observation of Duhm, that has hardly been repeated in scholarly debate. Though Jer 36 dates the writing of the scroll that announces disaster for Judah if the latter does not return to the fourth year of Jehoiakim's reign, its reading and its destruction would serve as a better reference point for Baruch's lamentation and is dated in the fifth year (Duhm, *Das Buch Jeremia*, 334; see also Thiel, *Die deuteronomistische Redaktion von Jeremia 26–45*, 87).

thing written in this book" with Judah's oppressor, Babylon.[8] They thus create a transition to what follows in each version. The LXX version of the book proceeds directly with the Oracles Against the Nations, with the final oracle being against Babylon. The MT version of the book instead continues with the oracle of the cup. While in both versions the oracle of the cup announces disaster for both the nations and for Judah, in the MT version of the book it also announces disaster for Babylon. Thus, the MT version of the book creates overt intertextual links between the oracle of the cup and the Oracles Against the Nations – through the use of an atbash for Babylon (25:26; 51:41) and in the order of the nations with Babylon appearing at the end of the list – so that the MT version of Jer 25 also points to the Oracles Against the Nations even though the two passages are separated by nearly 25 chapters.[9]

Notwithstanding the intertextual links, there is a shift in focus between Jer 25, Jer 36, and Jer 45. The emphasis of Jer 25 is squarely on Judah's disaster, which is limited by the announced calamity for Babylon.[10] While Jer 36 also focuses on the disaster for Jerusalem and Judah, this is put into a more global perspective with Jer 36:2 referring to the words that God has spoken "against/about Israel and Judah and all the nations" (אשר־דברתי אליך על־ישראל ועל־יהודה ועל־כל־הגוים). This more comprehensive outlook might have been established by the impression of the link to Jer 25 due to their common date. Finally, Jer 45 takes a fully global perspective and announces disaster for all flesh, though the MT reintroduces the perspective on the land (45:4, ואת־כל־הארץ היא).[11] Jer 45 further limits the announcement of salvation for Judah/Israel to an announcement of Baruch's mere survival.

The mere survival of Baruch the scribe proves the validity of Jeremiah's prophecy and secures its tradition. At the same time, it puts the preceding inter-texts into perspective. Judah's salvation is reduced to the survival of the messenger and the message. The book of Baruch echoes this tradition – this is most apparent when the book follows the LXX version of the book of Jeremiah that ends with Jer 45.

---

[8] In v. 14 the MT's "everything written in this book" (כל־הכתוב בספר הזה) is further identified with "what Jeremiah prophesied against all the nations" (אשר־נבא ירמיהו על־כל־הגוים).

[9] Beat Huwyler, *Jeremia und die Völker: Untersuchungen zu den Völkersprüchen in Jeremia 46–49* (Tübingen: Mohr Siebeck, 1997), 353.

[10] The role of the nations varies between the two versions. According to the LXX, Judah and the neighboring countries will be destroyed and Judah will serve among the nations until its enemy's fall. According to the MT, the nations will serve Babylon until its fall.

[11] In the MT, "I am going to break down what I have built, and pluck up what I have planted" refers to "this land," which occupies an awkward position within the phrase and is most likely a secondary addition. See William McKane, *A Critical and Exegetical Commentary on Jeremiah, Volume II: Jeremiah XXVI–LII* (Edinburgh: T&T Clark, 1996), 1096.

3. Baruch 1

3.1 Intertextual Links, Loose Ends, and Open Questions

The first verse of the first chapter of the book of Baruch identifies what follows as a book written by Baruch in the fifth year, on the seventh day of the month, when the Chaldeans took Jerusalem and set it on fire. It is not quite clear how the dating of this introduction and the conquest of Jerusalem relate to each other. In 2 Kgs 25:8 the destruction of Jerusalem is dated to "the fifth month, on the seventh day of the month" – in opposition to the "fifth month, the tenth day of the month" in Jer 52:12 quoting 2 Kgs 25:8. An understanding of the dating in Bar 1:2 as referring to the fifth anniversary of Jerusalem's destruction in the fifth month on the seventh day (following the dating in Kings) would have the additional benefit of offering an explanation for the somewhat cryptic dating wherein the name of the month is missing. It is also plausible that the name of the month might have fallen out by mistake due to the number five being mentioned twice.[12] The fifth month is also mentioned in Zech 7:3–5; 8:19 with regard to a fast in remembrance of the destruction of the temple, while the fifth year after the destruction of Jerusalem also has a parallel in the dating of Ezekiel's call to the fifth year after the exile of King Jehoiachin in Ezek 1:2. Within the Jeremiah tradition, the fifth year provides a reference point to the third deportation, which took place in Nebuchadnezzar's twenty-third year or five years after the second deportation, which occurred in Nebuchadnezzar's eighteenth year and is linked with the destruction of Jerusalem in the MT version of Jer 52:28–30 – these verses are missing in Jer[LXX]. Within Jer 52, the dating of the second deportation to Nebuchadnezzar's eighteenth year in v. 29 creates a tension with regard to Jer 52:12, where the destruction of Jerusalem and the following deportation is dated to Nebuchadnezzar's nineteenth year. According to an extra-biblical tradition reported by Josephus in *Ant.* 10.179, Egyptian Jews were deported to Babylon by Nebuchadnezzar in the course of a military campaign against Egypt five years after the destruction of Jerusalem.

Bar 1:2 mentions only the burning of the city, with no explicit reference to the burning of the temple, though it is possible that the latter might also be implied.[13] This silence in regard to the destruction of the temple has a parallel in the MT version of the book of Jeremiah at Jer 39:8. Jer 39 quotes from 2 Kgs 25//Jer 52, though more extensively in the MT version (39:1–10) than in the LXX version (39:1–3) of the text. Jer 39:8 appears only in the MT version, where it mentions

---

[12] Odil Hannes Steck, *Das apokryphe Baruchbuch: Studien zu Rezeption und Konzentration "kanonischer" Überlieferung*, FRLANT 160 (Göttingen: Vandenhoek & Ruprecht, 1993), 19. ובחדש החמישי has been lost.

[13] Sean A. Adams, *Baruch and the Epistle of Jeremiah: A Commentary Based on the Texts in Codex Vaticanus*, SCS (Leiden: Brill, 2014), 57.

the burning of Jerusalem, but skips over any explicit mention of the burning of the temple, which was part of its source.

Baruch is said to read this book in front of the exiled king, Jeconiah, and the assembly of the first *golah* at the river Sud. The list of addressees recalls the similar lists of Jer 36 and 2 Kgs 22, though the choice of vocabulary with regard to the functionaries (Bar: πρεσβύτεροι) does not follow the standard translation of the Hebrew term שרים used in Jer 36 and 2 Kgs 22 or that of the LXX of Jer 36 (ἄρχοντες). The list of those accompanying Jehoiachin to exile in Bar 1:9 recalls the political decision-makers of the book of Jeremiah, among whom are the ἄρχοντες, who in Jer 36 and 2 Kgs 22–23 are those close to the king and the addressees of one of three readings. Bar 1:4 has πρεσβύτεροι instead. The πρεσβύτεροι are mentioned among the listeners of the final reading in 2 Kgs 23:1–2, and as addressees of the letter which Jeremiah sends to the exiles in Jer 29:1, with the title of that episode closely resembling that of the book of Baruch. In Baruch, there is a clear break between the leaders of the people before and after the conquest of Jerusalem, as well as between the leaders in exile and those in the land. The latter are represented by the priests, who become merely the recipients of Baruch's words. The river Σουδ is otherwise unknown. As there is evidence for a river סור in the Jeremiah apocalypse from Qumran (4Q389 1.7),[14] it has been suggested that the reading of a river Σουδ is the result of a confusion between ר and ד in a Hebrew *Vorlage*.

Upon hearing Baruch's reading, the audience reacts with weeping, fasting, and prayers (v. 5). They collect donations (v. 6) and send a delegation to the priest Ioakim and the people who remain in Jerusalem (v. 7). An infinitive construction in vv. 8–9 gives the impression of a later addition, with this happening after either Baruch or Ioakim received the silver temple vessels that Sedekias had made as a replacement for those that had been brought to Babylon with Jeconiah in the course of the first deportation.[15] While both versions of the book of Jeremiah report the deportation of the temple vessels in the course of both the first (Jer 27, in retrospect) and second (Jer 52) deportation, in Jer 27:16–17 only the MT seems to envisage a return of the temple vessels. However, as the return is also stated elsewhere, cf. Ezra 1:7–11, the first chapter of the book of Baruch might not necessarily have built on the MT version of the book of Jeremiah at that point. In any case, it strengthens a motif that is central to MT Jeremiah but not the LXX version of the book. The reference to the δεσμῶται in the list of the deported

---

[14] Steck, *Das apokryphe Baruchbuch*, 23; Adams, *Baruch and the Epistle of Jeremiah*, 55.

[15] Due to the infinitive construction, the sentence seems overly long. Verse 10 would have connected to v. 7 without any difficulties. The reference to the month by name does not fit to the likely reference to the month by number in v. 1. The relation between both dates is unclear. If the month in v. 1 was the fifth and if the transmission of the temple vessels was concurrent with that of the delegation, the transfer would have taken place one year after the initial reading at the river.

seems to build on Jer 24:1 in the LXX version (which has τεχνίται καὶ δεσμῶται) rather than the version of the MT (which has החרש והמסגר). Both the return of the temple vessels that were produced by Sedekias and the presence of Baruch in Babylon argue for a setting some years after the destruction of Jerusalem.

The passage closes with a message from the *golah* addressing those who remain in Jerusalem, which asks for the latter's sacrifices, their prayers for Nebuchadnezzar in their favor, and for the forgiveness of sins.[16] Jer 41, which deals with the murder of a group of pilgrims, presupposes the possibility of sacrifices at the site of the destroyed temple. Ezra 3:1–6; 7:17; 8:35 explicitly mention burnt offerings at the site of the destroyed temple by the returnees, though it makes clear that an altar has to be first rebuilt, a tradition which was apparently not shared by the book of Baruch. The call for prayer for the foreign ruler is a widespread motif both within and outside of the bible (cf. Jer 29:7; 1 Macc 7:33; Philo, *Leg. ad Gaium*, 156–57; m. Avot 3.2). Ezra 6:10 more precisely asks for sacrifices and prayers for the foreign ruler and his sons, and Dan 1:12 calls for prayers for Nebuchadnezzar and his son Belshazzar. The addressees are further asked to read this book in the temple on the days of an unspecified feast and the appointed days.

3.2 A Sequel to the Book of Jeremiah ...

It has been discussed whether the book that is read by Baruch to the exiles and the book that is sent to Jerusalem to be read in the temple refer to the following prayer of repentance, to the following chapters including the prayer of repentance,[17] or – in a self-referential move – to the book of Baruch as a whole including the introduction. Based on the evidence of some Latin manuscripts in which the book of Baruch follows the book of Jeremiah without a break and the fact that both Latin and Greek church fathers quote the book of Baruch as the book of Jeremiah, Bogaert has proposed to read 1:1–14 as a subscription to the book of Jeremiah.[18]

There are several parallels in other biblical books that refer to the public reading of a text, which is almost always associated with the authorship of Moses (2 Kgs 22–23; Neh 9). Jer 36 is a prominent exception, and Jeremiah as the author of the scroll implies a moment of self-referentiality. There are several examples where the reading of a book authored by Moses or Jeremiah is answered by a prayer of repentance. In Neh 9, the reading of the Torah is followed by a prayer of repentance. In Dan 9:2, Daniel's (private) reading of the book of Jeremiah is also followed by a prayer of repentance. The parallel between Baruch and Daniel

---

[16] In fact, the first person plural might include the addressees in Jerusalem.
[17] Steck, *Das apokryphe Baruchbuch*, 5, 8.
[18] Pierre-Maurice Bogaert, "Les trois formes de Jérémie 52: (TM, LXX et VL)," in *Tradition of the Text*, ed. Gerard J. Norton and Dominique Barthélemy (Freiburg: Universitätsverlag, 1991), 9. See also Isabelle Assan-Dhôte and Jacqueline Moatti-Fine, *Baruch, Lamentations, Lettre de Jérémie*, BA (Paris: Cerf, 2008) 50; Adams, *Baruch and the Epistle of Jeremiah*, 50.

is further highlighted by the fact that the prayer of repentance in Bar 1:15–3:8 is an almost literal quote of the prayer of repentance in Dan 9. Notwithstanding the fact that there are no parallels for v. 1 functioning as a subscription,[19] the lack of clarity with regard to the question of whether the book mentioned in Bar 1 is represented or answered by the prayer of repentance allows for the possibility that the book Baruch reads to the exiles is indeed the book of Jeremiah rather than the book of Baruch.

3.3 … In Which of Its Versions?

If the book of Baruch is read as a subscription or sequel to the book of Jeremiah, then the question arises as to which version of the book of Jeremiah its authors had in mind. Neither the form nor the agenda of either version answer this question unequivocally.

The list of the deported in Bar 1:9 seems to build on Jer 24:1 according to the version of the LXX.[20] If the initial incomplete date, "the fifth year, on the seventh day of the month," refers to the anniversary of the destruction of Jerusalem, the closest parallel would be a version of the report of the fall of Jerusalem that is represented by neither version of the book of Jeremiah but rather by its parallel in 2 Kgs 24–25. The tradition of a third deportation five years after the second one is known from extra-biblical sources as well as from the MT version of Jeremiah.[21]

Neither can the specific agenda of the book of Baruch be used as an argument for the book's design as a sequel to the book of Jeremiah in one of its versions.[22] The continuation of the cult moves the book of Baruch closer to the MT version than to the LXX version of the book of Jeremiah. The silence of Bar 1:2 about the burning of the temple has a parallel in the quotation of 2 Kgs 25//Jer 52 in Jer 39:4–10, which does not include the explicit mention of the burning of the temple that was part of its source. Both the MT version of the book of Jeremiah and the book of Baruch show an interest in the return of the temple vessels that the LXX version of the book of Jeremiah does not display. The prayer for Nebuchadnezzar and his son has a parallel in Daniel, whose presentation of Nebuchadnezzar as having been temporarily granted supremacy by God has a closer parallel in the MT version of the book of Jeremiah than in the LXX version of the book.[23]

---

[19] Steck, *Das apokryphe Baruchbuch*, 15.

[20] See above.

[21] The underlying dating system creates tensions with regard to the dating of the destruction of the temple in Jer 52:12, suggesting different sources. These tensions are not smoothed out by the book of Baruch, which in v. 1 seems to refer to the dating system underlying Jer 52:12//2 Kgs 25:8 though referring to the tradition attested by 2 Kgs with regard to the day.

[22] The eventual misreading of a ר for a ד that might have resulted in the otherwise unknown river Σουδ would argue for a Hebrew original, though not necessarily for its being dependent on the Hebrew text of Jeremiah as represented by the MT version.

[23] Johanna Erzberger, "Nebuchadnezzar, Judah, and the Nations: Shifting Frames of Reference

However, there are also major differences between the agenda of the book of Baruch and that of the book of Jeremiah in both of its versions. In contradiction to what the book of Jeremiah seems to presuppose, the land is not empty and the cult is functioning even while the *golah* is still in exile. The high priest in Jerusalem acts as an executive organ of what the exiles, represented by the elders and inspired by the book that they read and sent to Jerusalem, demand.

4. The Aftermath: The Survival of Baruch the Scribe and the Jeremiah Tradition

Though the book of Baruch might be read as a sequel to any version of the book of Jeremiah, it also has its own agenda. The LXX version of the book of Jeremiah simplifies an argument for the book of Baruch as its sequel by presenting Jer 45 as a transitional text at its end. The manuscripts and the church fathers' testimonies suggest that the book of Baruch has, indeed, been read as a sequel to the LXX version of the book or of its Hebrew Vorlage. The MT version's ideology, however, comes closer to the ideology of the book of Baruch. Ultimately, the book of Baruch further develops tendencies that are present in either version of Jeremiah.

The replacement of the prophet by the scribe is a move that has already been prepared by the figure of Baruch in the book of Jeremiah. This move goes hand in hand with the shifting perspectives on the role and function of formative texts as they are presented by the texts themselves.[24]

The writing of the scroll in Jer 36 is implemented by divine order. In Jer 45, the presentation of Baruch as the living legitimizing proof of the Jeremiah tradition is part of a prophetic word, which quotes a divine word but is not itself legitimized by a divine word. The title of the book of Baruch differs from those of (other) prophetic books by the lack of a prophetic word transmission formula. Consequently, it lacks and does not claim an explicit divine legitimation. What legitimizes the book's content is a reference to an established tradition, not to a particular act of revelation.

If the book of Baruch is read as a continuation of the book of Jeremiah, it comments on it and further shifts its perspective as much as it continues it. But, then, this is not more than what the shifting perspectives within the book of Jeremiah have already done.

---

in Jer 25," in *Die Septuaginta: Geschichte, Wirkung, Relevanz*, ed. Siegfried Kreuzer et al., WUNT 405 (Tübingen: Mohr Siebeck, 2018), 685–700.

[24] See, by comparison, Peter Altmann's essay in this volume that traces the phenomenon of references to written divine law in Chronicles. Altmann argues that for the Chronicler written "torah" mainly pertained to cultic matters, rather than economic or social; see "Tracing Divine Law: Written Divine Law in Chronicles."

Bibliography

Adams, Sean A. *Baruch and the Epistle of Jeremiah: A Commentary Based on the Texts in Codex Vaticanus*. SCS. Leiden: Brill, 2014.

Altmann, Peter. "Tracing Divine Law: Written Divine Law in Chronicles." Within this volume.

Assan-Dhôte, Isabelle, and Jacqueline Moatti-Fine. *Baruch, Lamentations, Lettre de Jérémie*. BA. Paris: Cerf, 2008.

Bogaert, Pierre-Maurice. "Les trois formes de Jérémie 52: (TM, LXX et VL)." Pages 1–17 in *Tradition of the text*. Edited by Gerard J. Norton and Dominique Barthélemy. Freiburg: Universitätsverlag, 1991.

Duhm, Bernhard. *Das Buch Jeremia*. Tübingen: Mohr Siebeck, 1901.

Erzberger, Johanna. "Nebuchadnezzar, Judah, and the Nations: Shifting Frames of Reference in Jer 25." Pages 685–700 in *Die Septuaginta: Geschichte, Wirkung, Relevanz*. Edited by Siegfried Kreuzer, et al. WUNT 405. Tübingen: Mohr Siebeck, 2018.

Fried, Lisbeth S., and Edward J. Mills III. "Ezra the Scribe." Within this volume.

Graupner, Axel. "Jeremia 45 als 'Schlusswort' des Jeremiabuches." Pages 287–308 in *Altes Testament und christliche Verkündigung*. Edited by Manfred Oeming and Axel Graupner. Stuttgart: Kohlhammer, 1987.

Holladay, William Lee. *Jeremiah 2: A Commentary on the Book of the Prophet Jeremiah Chapters 26–52*. Hermeneia. Minneapolis: Fortress, 1989.

Huwyler, Beat. *Jeremia und die Völker: Untersuchungen zu den Völkersprüchen in Jeremia 46–49*. Tübingen: Mohr Siebeck, 1997.

McKane, William. *A Critical and Exegetical Commentary on Jeremiah, Volume II: Jeremiah XXVI–LII*. Edinburgh: T&T Clark, 1996.

Pede, Elena di. "Jérusalem, Ebed-Melek et Baruch: Enquête narrative sur le déplacement chronologique de Jr 45." *RB* 111.1 (2004): 61–77.

Rudolph, Wilhelm. *Jeremia*. HAT 1. Tübingen: Mohr Siebeck, 1968.

Schulte, Hannelis. "Baruch und Ebedmelech: Persönliche Heilsorakel im Jeremiabuche." *BZ* 32.2 (1988): 257–65.

Steck, Odil Hannes. *Das apokryphe Baruchbuch: Studien zu Rezeption und Konzentration "kanonischer" Überlieferung*. FRLANT 160. Göttingen: Vandenhoek & Ruprecht, 1993.

Taylor, Marion Ann. "Jeremiah 45: The Problem of Placement." *JSOT* 37 (1987): 79–98.

Thiel, Winfried. *Die deuteronomistische Redaktion von Jeremia 26–45*. WMANT 52. Neukirchen-Vluyn: Neukirchener Verlag, 1981.

Tracing Divine Law: Written Divine Law in Chronicles*

Peter Altmann

1. Introduction

The striking feature of divinely promulgated law separates Israel's Scriptures from all surrounding societies. Yet, what does it matter if the Torah is attributed to Yhwh? Little direct indication of its significance comes from the texts of the Pentateuch itself. It is also difficult to trace much importance of the connection of "law" with God in extra-biblical pre-Hellenistic texts or material culture.[1] Yet in the late literature of the Hebrew Bible, especially in Chronicles, the late Gary Knoppers and Paul Harvey Jr. note the increase of interconnections of *torah*, especially written *torah*, and its divine origin in comparison with the texts of Samuel–Kings.[2]

Similarly, this frequency of *torah* has attracted significant attention in recent scholarship, resulting in both an article and a monograph published in 2019: Shuai Jiang's "God's Law and Theocracy: The Use of 'YHWH's Torah' in Chronicles" and Lars Maskow's *Tora in der Chronik: Studien zur Rezeption des Pentateuchs in den Chronikbüchern*.[3] Within this well-trod path, however, it is surprising that key recent monographs on the development of notions of biblical

---

* This essay has been written as part of the European Research Council project "How God Became a Lawgiver: The Place of the Torah in Ancient Near Eastern Legal History." This project has received funding from the European Research Council (ERC) under the European Union's Horizon 2020 research and innovation programme grant agreement No 833222. I am grateful to my colleagues Anna Angelini, Dylan Johnson, Phillip Lasater, Lida Panov, and Konrad Schmid, as well as to Benjamin Giffone for their helpful feedback on earlier versions of this essay.

[1] The material culture becomes more intriguing with the rise of the Hasmonean Kingdom, while the only possibly related extra-biblical texts are the Yavneh Yam inscription, the amulets from Khirbet Beit Lei, and the so-called Passover Letter from Elephantine (TAD A4.1).

[2] Gary N. Knoppers and Paul B. Harvey Jr., "The Pentateuch in Ancient Mediterranean Context: The Publication of Local Lawcodes," in *The Pentateuch as Torah: New Models for Understanding Its Promulgation and Acceptance*, ed. Bernard M. Levinson and Gary N. Knoppers (Winona Lake, IN: Eisenbrauns, 2007), 134.

[3] Shuai Jiang, "God's Law and Theocracy: The Use of 'YHWH's Torah' in Chronicles," *ZAW* 131.3 (2019): 444–58; Lars Maskow, *Tora in der Chronik: Studien zur Rezeption des Pentateuchs in den Chronikbüchern*, FRLANT 274 (Göttingen: Vandenhoeck & Ruprecht, 2019). A sampling of earlier publications includes Félix García López and Heinz-Josef Fabry, "תּוֹרָה Tôrâ," *TDOT* 15:609–46; Thomas Willi, "Thora in den biblischen Chronikbüchern," *Judaica* 36 (1980): 102–5, 148–51; Jack N. Lightstone, "Torah Is Nomos – except When It Is Not: Prolegomena to the Study of the Law in Late Antique Judaism," *SR* 13 (1984): 29–37.

law/*torah* in early Judaism, such as those of LeFebvre, Fitzpatrick-McKinley, Collins, and Vroom, do not discuss Chronicles in much detail.[4]

Thus, following scholarship on Chronicles, my investigation turns to the appearance of the *torah* of Yhwh in Chronicles, especially as it relates to scripturalization. My specific contribution lies in the question of how this increased focus on written and divine *torah* relates to legal sphere in this period of early Judaism. For if, as Vroom postulates for the Persian period, the Pentateuch begins to function as written law at this time,[5] the question arises as to whether this conceptualization for *torah* makes a concrete appearance in Chronicles?[6] My discussion shows that Yhwh's *torah,* when specified, generally concerns cultic matters, as one might expect given the focus on the temple and cultic practice in Chronicles, indicating little interest in legal matters outside this realm.

2. Background of Written Torah

Overall, *torah* appears as written material around forty times in the Hebrew Bible. The first canonical appearance of a written (and divine) *torah* appears in Exod 24:12, with God's own writing of it.[7] The other appearances of a written *torah* in the Pentateuch are Deuteronomy's self-referential "this *torah,*" in Deut 17:18–19 and frequently in chs. 27–31. Joshua refers to a written *torah* of

---

[4] Michael LeFebvre, *Collections, Codes, and Torah: The Re-Characterization of Israel's Written Law*, LHBOTS 451 (New York: T&T Clark, 2006); John J. Collins, *The Invention of Judaism: Torah and Jewish Identity from Deuteronomy to Paul*, TLJS 7 (Oakland, CA: University of California Press, 2017); Anne Fitzpatrick-McKinley, *The Transformation of Torah: From Scribal Advice to Law*, JSOTSup 287 (Sheffield: Sheffield Academic, 1999); Jonathan Vroom, *The Authority of Law in the Hebrew Bible and Early Judaism: Tracing the Origins of Legal Obligation from Ezra to Qumran*, JSJSup 187 (Leiden: Brill, 2018). Fishbane proves something of an exception to this, but in spite of many mentions of Chronicles, very few of them concern the passages that refer directly to torah: Michael Fishbane, *Biblical Interpretation in Ancient Israel* (Oxford: Clarendon, 1985). The most considerable exception is Jackson. See, e.g., Bernard S. Jackson, "Law in the Ninth Century: Jehoshaphat's 'Judicial Reform,'" in *Understanding the History of Ancient Israel*, ed. Hugh G.M. Williamson (Oxford: Oxford University Press, 2007), 369–97; Bernard S. Jackson, *Studies in the Semiotics of Biblical Law*, JSOTSup 314 (Sheffield: Sheffield Academic, 2000), 120–21, 135, 170.

[5] Vroom, *The Authority of Law*, 198–99.

[6] I am not insinuating that Chronicles must be a pre-Hellenistic book. The most I am able to argue at this point is that my analysis shows that Chronicles presupposes very late pentateuchal textual traditions, such as those found in Num 28–29. Whether this indicates a late-Persian or early-Hellenistic date remains an open question.

[7] This text bears a special similarity to some texts in Chronicles (esp. 1 Chr 14:3 and 31:21), which, like Exod 24:12, concern the Torah and the commandment. For more discussion on this important phenomenon, see Reinhard Achenbach, "The Pentateuch, the Prophets, and the Torah in the Fifth and Fourth Centuries B.C.E.," in *Judah and the Judeans in the Fourth Century B.C.E.,* ed. Oded Lipschits, Gary N. Knoppers, and Rainer Albertz (Winona Lake, IN: Eisenbrauns, 2007), 253–85.

Moses in chs. 1; 8; and 23, as well as Joshua writing "these words in the scroll of the *torah* of God" (ויכתב יהושע את־הדברים האלה בספר תורת אלהים) in 24:26. A majority of references to a written *torah* in Kings appear in 2 Kgs 22–23.[8] While a generalization, these references are largely associated with the legal stipulations of Deuteronomy.[9]

In addition to the texts in the Primary History, a considerable number of references to a written divine *torah* appear in Chronicles. As noted by Jiang, mentions of *torah* in Chronicles generally seek to provide authority for a specific practice or event.[10] Building on his insight, the following textual analyses focus on appearances of the *torah* of Yhwh in texts of Chronicles for which this expression does not appear in Samuel–Kings in order to isolate the significance of this divine law in Chronicles.[11] This expression appears many times: in 1 Chr 16:40; 22:12; 2 Chr 6:16; 12:1; 17:9; 31:3, 4; 34:14; and 35:26. The importance of this evidence emerges from comparisons with Samuel–Kings, where there is only a single appearance of the *torah* of Yhwh: 2 Kgs 10:31: "But Jehu was not careful to follow the law of the Yhwh the God of Israel with all his heart."[12] By contrast, as mentioned above, the Torah of Moses appears a number of times in texts of the Primary History in Josh 8:31–32 (cf. 1:7–8); 1 Kgs 2:3; 2 Kgs 14:6; 23:25, and the law is linked to Moses in 2 Kgs 21:8.[13] A similar connection appears in Chronicles without Yhwh/God in 2 Chr 8:13; 24:6, 9; 30:16; 35:12, in texts adopted from

---

[8] More striking is their mention in 2 Kgs 14:6 and 2 Kgs 17:37, which warrant a separate discussion elsewhere. Westbrook notes the significance of 2 Kgs 14:6 // 2 Chr 25:4 because the king acts "in accordance to what is written in the book of the law of Moses," and then it continues by referring to Deut 24:16, the only place where something like this occurs in Kings: Raymond Westbrook, "The Character of Ancient Near Eastern Law," in *A History of Ancient Near Eastern Law*, ed. Raymond Westbrook, HdO 1 (Leiden: Brill, 2003), 1:20. A written *torah* also appears in 1 Kgs 2:3, which I discuss below.

[9] This connection goes back to de Wette, as noted by Mordechai Cogan and Hayim Tadmor, *2 Kings: A New Translation with Introduction and Commentary*, AB 11 (Garden City, NY: Doubleday, 1988), 294. One can point to the similar language in 2 Kgs 23:3 with Deut 6:5 and the destruction of the high places in 2 Kgs 23:8–15 with the focus on cult centralization in Deut 12, but especially the late vv. 2–3 ("high places"). However, there are some distinctions between the report of Josiah's actions and the prescriptions of Deuteronomy; for discussion see Peter Altmann, *Festive Meals in Ancient Israel: Deuteronomy's Identity Politics in Their Ancient Near Eastern Context*, BZAW 424 (Berlin: de Gruyter, 2011), 9–10. None of these connections need place these texts in the preexilic period, though I do ascribe to a historical core of Josiah's reform (see Altmann, *Festive Meals*).

[10] Jiang, "God's Law and Theocracy," 445.

[11] I am aware of the debate about the nature of Chronicles' sources, though I have not delved into this question for this discussion.

[12] Outside of Chronicles, it also appears in Ezra 7:10; Neh 9:3; Pss 1:2; 19:7; 119:1; Jer 8:8; Amos 2:4. The related expression "law of God" appears in Josh 24:26; Neh 8:8, 18; 10:28. I find it quite significant that most if not all of these texts are regularly dated quite late.

There are, of course, a number of related expressions. To name just a few, *torah* as an object of the Yhwh's commanding: Deut 33:8. Commandments/ordinances related to Yhwh are found in 1 Chr 28:7–8; 29:19; 2 Chr 7:17, 19; 17:4; 24:20; 29:25; 34:31.

[13] Also Ezra 3:2; 7:6; Neh 8:1; Dan 9:11, 13.

Kings. Finally, both Moses and Yhwh are linked to the *torah* rather seldom: in 2 Kgs 14:6 // 2 Chr 25:4; 2 Kgs 21:8 // 2 Chr 33:8; and in 2 Chr 34:14; 35:6, 12, which are part of the Josiah narratives.

As a result of this difference, the question arises as to why the emphasis on a divine *torah* increases in Chronicles, one quite often linked with scripturalization? Jiang makes an important observation in that they all occur – except for the one rejection of Yhwh's *torah* (2 Chr 12:1) – in relation to those kings that the Chronicler praises.[14] One may wonder whether this has anything to do with an increased *legal* conceptualization of *torah* in the texts.

3. First Chronicles 16:40: Yahweh's Torah as the Authority for New Applications of Torah

The first passage of interest is 1 Chr 16:40, the context of which parallels 2 Sam 6 (see 1 Chr 16:1–3 // 2 Sam 6:17–19a and 1 Chr 16:43 // 2 Sam 6:19b–20) but includes a long plus concerning David's installation of the temple musicians and a song of praise (1 Chr 16:4–36). This is followed by another insertion that addresses the establishment of temple personnel both before the Ark (in Jerusalem) and before the tabernacle (in Gibeon).

להעלות עלות ליהוה	to lift up burnt offerings to Yhwh
על־מזבח העלה	upon the altar of burnt offering
תמיד לבקר ולערב	daily in the morning and evening,
ולכל־הכתוב בתורת יהוה	namely according to everything written in the *torah of Yhwh*
אשר צוה על־ישראל	that he commanded Israel.[15] (1 Chr 16:40)

The Zadokite personnel (v. 39) were put in place in Gibeon, according to v. 40, to do "everything written in the *torah* of Yhwh that he commanded Israel." This text provides a clear reference to the divine cultic law that Chronicles claims was followed by David at Gibeon.

Naturally, neither Zadok nor Gibeon appear in the Pentateuch. Instead, two pentateuchal texts provide the background information for "everything written in the *torah* of Yhwh": Exod 29:38–42 and Num 28:3–8. Exodus 29:38–39 states that twice a day (morning and evening) a year-old lamb should be "done upon the altar" (תעשה על המזבח). In v. 42 it is then called an עלת תמיד "regular burnt offering," giving more detail on which kind of offering. Numbers 28:3–8 is more specific. In v. 3 it states:

---

[14] Jiang, "God's Law and Theocracy," 448. He argues, "If the basic materials of Chronicles could be dated to the late Persian period, this emphasis of the correlation between the law, God, and the Davidic kingship can be best explained by the theocratic position presented in Chronicles" (Jiang, "God's Law and Theocracy," 450).

[15] The OG, however, has: "for the *sons of* Israel *by the hand of Moses, the servant of God*" (ἐφ' υἱοῖς Ισραηλ ἐν χειρὶ Μωυσῆ τοῦ θεράποντος τοῦ θεοῦ), increasing the prominence of Moses.

ואמרת להם	And you say to them:
זה האשה	This is the food offering
אשר תקריבו ליהוה	that you shall bring to Yhwh:
כבשים בני־שנה תמימם שנים ליום	two wholesome year-old lambs per day,
עלה תמיד	a regular burnt offering:
את־הכבש אחד תעשה בבקר	the first lamb you shall do in the morning
ואת הכבש השני תעשה בין הערבים	and the second lamb you shall do at twilight.

(Num 28:3)

The comparison with 1 Chr 16:40 is quite close. The Chronicles text speaks of the offering at *evening* instead of *twilight,* and it uses a form of the verb עלה for performance of the offering in contrast to the עשה found in both pentateuchal texts. Furthermore, 1 Chr 16:40 specifies *which* altar,[16] while the pentateuchal texts concentrate on the nature of the offering, showing Chronicles' attempt to incorporate a wider range of pentateuchal texts. Nonetheless, both concern a twice-daily עלה-offering and the beginning and end of each day.

Several non-exclusive reasons come together for the use of a reference to the *torah* of Yhwh in this location. Two concern legitimation of David and Solomon. First, Maskow sees this text as presenting David as one who knows the cultic *torah* because he puts it into practice.[17] However, it is located in Gibeon, which, second, provides the reason for Solomon's great sacrifice there (from 1 Kgs 3).[18] Thus, what appears here is a very late literary application of pentateuchal cultic regulations,[19] which also accounts for the tabernacle. By placing it in Gibeon, this supports cultic practice there both by David in this chapter and in 2 Chr 1 by Solomon. Thus, it authorizes worship in this *new* location – Gibeon – and carried out by *previously unknown* personnel – the Zadokites. As such, in its attempt to accentuate David and Solomon, Chronicles depicts David following specific divine *torah* regulations as a way to show the kings' (David and Solomon's) obedience, thereby also raising the profile of the *torah* of Yhwh, which now includes the Priestly traditions of the tabernacle. As a result, the Chronicler can proudly present Solomon's offering in Gibeon as Torah conformant because it locates sacrifice around the centralizing cultic paraphernalia of the tabernacle and its altar.[20]

---

[16] Perhaps presupposing the late text of Exod 30:1–10: see Maskow, *Tora in der Chronik*, 80.

[17] Maskow, *Tora in der Chronik*, 236. It also legitimates him as one who can implement and change it: see Ehud Ben Zvi, "One Size Does Not Fit All: Observations on the Different Ways That Chronicles Dealt with the Authoritative Literature of Its Time," in *What Was Authoritative for Chronicles?* ed. Ehud Ben Zvi and Diana Vikander Edelman (Winona Lake, IN: Eisenbrauns, 2011), 30.

[18] Ralph W. Klein, *1 Chronicles: A Commentary*, Hermeneia (Minneapolis: Fortress, 2006), 369. The transformation of the two pentateuchal texts for its own purposes fits in well with the types of scribal uses of earlier texts on display in Benjamin Ziemer, "Radical Versus Conservative," in this volume.

[19] If it refers to Num 28.

[20] For a helpful discussion of the inclusion of P, and, as a result, its different notion of centralization, see Benjamin D. Giffone, "According to Which 'Law of Moses'? Cult Centralization

Finally, Jiang also notes that the *torah* of Yhwh links specifically to the Zadokites in Chronicles, while the Mosaic Torah is relegated to the Levites (2 Chr 23:18 and 30:16).[21] Thus, the use of the divine *torah* highlights the Zadokite's claims.

For my purposes, a version of the practice found in the Pentateuch appears prescriptive for cultic practice here in Chronicles, and Chronicles refers to the *textual* version of this divine *torah*: the pentateuchal stipulations are functionally prescriptive, though the Chronicles text can adjust details, especially through combinations of different regulations. What is most important is that the prescriptive nature of the pentateuchal text serves as an authoritative means to support David's action of directing this practice to take place *in Gibeon* and *by the Zadokites*. In other words, 1 Chr 16:39–40 applies pentateuchal ordinances to a new literary setting (with different personnel).

4. First Chronicles 22:12–13: Shifting Torah's Authority from Moses to Yhwh

In 1 Chr 22:12–13 David speaks to Solomon about the preparations for the Temple and calls for Yhwh's blessing upon his son in the construction process.

As many commentators have noted, this text bears many similarities to the commissioning of Joshua (Josh 1) and the *Vorlage* of 1 Kgs 2:2–3, such as the language on being courageous and not fearing.[22]

Most important here is the comparison with 1 Kgs 2:3:

ושמרת את־משמרת יהוה אלהיך	And keep the charge *of Yhwh your God*,
ללכת בדרכיו	Walking in his ways,
לשמר חקתיו מצותיו ומשפטיו ועדותיו	Keeping his ordinances, his commandments, his judgments, and his testimonies
ככתוב בתורת משה	*As is written in the torah of Moses*
למען תשכיל את כל־אשר תעשה ואת כל־אשר תפנה שם:	So that you may prosper [at] everything you do and everywhere you turn
	(1 Kgs 2:3)

---

in Samuel, Kings, and Chronicles," *VT* 67 (2017): 442. This is a radical bifurcation, one should note, of the centralizing practices found in P and H. For a masterful discussion of their notion of centralization for the Persian period and its contrast to Deuteronomy, see Julia Rhyder, *Centralizing the Cult: The Holiness Legislation in Leviticus 17–26*, FAT 134 (Tübingen: Mohr Siebeck, 2019), esp. 112–89.

[21] Jiang, "God's Law and Theocracy," 450.

[22] Among many others including Klein, *1 Chronicles*, 439. David's speech to the leaders of Israel in 1 Chr 28 covers similar territory, including the recapitulation of Yhwh's words to David intended for Solomon concerning the conditional promise in vv. 7–8, though it does not use the term *torah*: ... אם־יחזק לעשות מצותי ומשפטי כיום הזה ועתה לעיני כל־ישראל קהל־יהוה ובאזני אלהינו שמרו ודרשו כל־מצות יהוה אלהיכם ... However, in this chapter as well, the exhortation directly concerns David's plans for the temple's construction. See also 1 Chr 29:19.

אַךְ יִתֶּן־לְךָ יְהוָה שֵׂכֶל וּבִינָה	Indeed may *Yhwh* grant you skill and understand-
וִיצַוְּךָ עַל־יִשְׂרָאֵל	ing – and may he commission you over Israel[23] –
וְלִשְׁמוֹר אֶת־תּוֹרַת יְהוָה אֱלֹהֶיךָ:	namely to keep the *torah of Yhwh your God*.
אָז תַּצְלִיחַ	Then you will prosper,
אִם־תִּשְׁמוֹר לַעֲשׂוֹת אֶת־הַחֻקִּים וְאֶת־הַמִּשְׁפָּטִים	if you are careful to do the ordinances and judgments
אֲשֶׁר צִוָּה יְהוָה אֶת־מֹשֶׁה עַל־יִשְׂרָאֵל	that *Yhwh* commanded Moses concerning Israel.
חֲזַק וֶאֱמָץ אַל־תִּירָא וְאַל־תֵּחָת:	Be strong and courageous. Do not fear and do not be discouraged.
	(1 Chr 22:12–13)

All three passages (including Josh 1) also refer to a *torah*. Similar to the prior passage (1 Chr 16:40), however, the reference here is to Yhwh's *torah* instead of Moses' *torah* as found in both Josh 1 (התורה אשר צוך משה) and 1 Kgs 2.[24] Moses does, however, appear in the following verse (1 Chr 22:13) as the mediator of the ordinances and stipulations from Yhwh to Israel, just as they are "[Yhwh's] statutes, his commandments, his ordinances, and his testimonies" in 1 Kgs 2:3. Different in this case from 1 Chr 16, a *written torah* appears in the *Vorlage*, "as it is written in the law of Moses" (1 Kgs 2:3), but its ascription changes in Chronicles. One might imagine that this was taken for granted in Chronicles, but it is surprising and parallels a similar development in Ps 1, which also builds on Josh 1:7–8, though generalizing Joshua's experience into that of every Yhwh follower.[25] In any case, the shift of the Torah from Moses' Torah to Yhwh's Torah represents a subtle shift in the direct authority behind it. Furthermore, Chronicles re-orders the section so that "the *torah* of Yhwh your God" replaces "the charge of Yhwh your God." In bringing together the collage of texts, Chronicles lays extra weight on Yhwh's authority (3x), rendering Moses clearly secondary – as one receiving Yhwh's command. Again, one might speculate that the *contents* of the Torah have changed, now including a larger number of texts as posited above for 1 Chr 16, but little direct evidence from the text itself points in this direction. Instead, comparing the contexts of 1 Kgs 2 and 1 Chr 22 largely reveals one difference:

---

[23] I am reading ויצוך על ישראל here similarly to 2 Sam 7:11: ולמן־היום אשר צויתי שפטים על־עמי ישראל "And since the day when I commissioned judges over my people Israel."

[24] It has often been noted that the Chronicler models the passing of the torch from David to Solomon on the earlier transition from Moses to Joshua; see, e.g.., Raymond B. Dillard, "The Chronicler's Jehoshaphat," *TJ* 7 (1986): 17 and literature mentioned there. In contrast, the similar text of Ps 1:2 has בתורת יהוה followed in v. 3 with the motif of prospering (וכל אשר־יעשה יצליח). Maskow (Maskow, *Tora in der Chronik*, 87–91) makes much of the overlap with Josh 1:7–9, and indeed there is much that 1 Chr 22:12–13 picks up on here, but it is important to start with the *Vorlage* from Kings and see how this has been supplemented from Joshua.

[25] Kratz sees Ps 1:2 as dependent on 1 Chr 22: Reinhard Gregor Kratz, "Die Tora Davids: Psalm 1 und die doxologische Fünfteilung des Psalters: Odil Hannes Steck zum 60 Geburtstag," *ZTK* 93 (1996): 7.

1 Kgs 2 emphasizes David's charge for Solomon to repay the wrongs done to him (vv. 5–9), while 1 Chr 22, esp. vv. 8–9 and 18, notes that Solomon will be a man of rest (הוא איש מנוחה in v. 9), rendering him an appropriate ruler to build Yhwh's temple, while in 2 Sam 7, God brings rest for Israel during David's reign.[26] However, in 1 Kgs 2:2, David exhorts Solomon, "So be strong and be a man" (וחזקת והיית לאיש) in the face of David's impending death, which includes definitively violent overtones (cf. 1 Sam 4:9 for the same exhortation in plural form). Thus, Chronicles introduces a striking change when compared with 1 Kgs 2 in avoiding such a command to eliminate David's enemies. However, the passage does maintain a connection with Josh 1, with its fourfold encouragement to take courage and not be afraid (Josh 1:9 // 1 Chr 22:13, with a slight change from ערץ to ירא).

David's disqualification as one who "shed much blood and fought great battles" (1 Chr 22:8 raises questions because the battles David fought could even receive specific approval from Yhwh (e.g., 1 Chr 14:10, 13–16; 18:6, 13), though the summary nature of "Yhwh gave David victory wherever he went" may not represent *specific* approval, thus relegating explicit approval of fighting to defensive battles. This may indicate a closer connection to David's census of fighting men in 1 Chr 21, which leads to the death of 70,000.[27]

One might link the defensive nature of Israelite kingship to the change from Torah of Moses to the Torah of Yhwh. Perhaps, given the emphasis on peacefulness as a requirement for temple building in 1 Chr 22 versus the overtly militaristic and violent connections in Josh 1 and 1 Kgs 2, the change reflects a different *kind* of obedience. In particular, it may represent a different conception of the laws of kingship in Deut 17:14–20. In this reading, Chronicles emphasizes the *lack* of an offensive fighting force with David's standing army as an interpretation of Deut 17:16 (the increase of horses). Instead, the king focuses on learning and doing Yhwh's law (cf. 1 Chr 22:12–13 and Deut 17:18–19). Finally, perhaps one can even go so far as to link the prohibition on the king lifting himself up over his fellow Israelites in Deut 17:20 with the omission of Solomon eliminating David's enemies from 1 Kgs 2. These interpretive steps then entail also a transformation of the conception of Torah-conformant royal obedience for the fourfold encouragement found in both Josh 1 and 1 Chr 22.

---

[26] For discussion, see Klein, *1 Chronicles*, 435–38. The notion of rest connects back with Josh 1:13, and to Deut 12:9–11 for the chosen *location* for the sanctuary. Rest also appears for the *Ark* in 1 Chr 6:2.

[27] Cf. Klein, *1 Chronicles*, 437. He also points to further treatments of this issue. Another direction worth exploring is that it may also address the rejection of the accounts in 1 Kgs of Solomon carrying out David's final wishes of revenge. Note the discussion for the reasons of this more pacific orientation of Chronicles in Sungwoo Park and Johannes Unsok Ro, "Collective Identity through Scribalism: Interpreting Plato's *Menexenus* and the *Book of Chronicles*," in this volume. They suggest that this change represents an important turning point in the narrative.

The connection between royal obedience to Torah and rest, in Chronicles even in the face of foreign attack, receives support from other narratives in the book. It also appears in 2 Chr 20:30, when Yhwh ambushes Judah's enemies while Judah's army of singers praise their God. Significantly, these events take place under Jehoshaphat, for whom Yhwh's Torah plays a significant role (2 Chr 17:7–9).[28] The similar case of Asa in 2 Chr 14–15 strengthens this connection as well ("rest" in 14:6–7; 15:15; Torah obedience in 14:4; 15:3).

As a final note, the change from the Torah of Moses to the Torah of Yhwh in this text contrasts with the introduction of the Torah of *Moses* in two places in Chronicles: 2 Chr 23:18 and 30:16. Jiang notes that both of these cases address general cultic prescriptions and the Levites,[29] but there is more at play here. As Maskow notes, these two texts recur on the complex relationship between Moses and David in Chronicles. The first connects closely with Deuteronomy in its use of הכהנים הלוים (cf. Deut 17:9; 18:1), yet it mixes ordinances from the *Mosaic* Torah (Pentateuch) with those of David concerning singing-oriented service. David had "distributed" (חלק) these officials set over the sanctuary "to lift up the burnt offerings of Yhwh *according to what is written in the torah of Moses*" (להעלות עלות יהוה ככתוב בתורת משה), but it is done "in joy and in song by the authority of David" (בשמחה ובשיר על ידי דויד; cf. 1 Chr 15). Thus, the mentions of David and Moses together point to the specific associations with each authoritative figure.[30]

The use of the phrase in 30:16 is more difficult to explain, at least in terms of its differentiation from the Torah of Yhwh in the rest of the book. It concerns a revised Passover – taking place in the second month, though for different reasons than those given in Num 9. Furthermore, unclean people take part, which appears problematic both in this text (2 Chr 30:18–20) and Num 9:6–7. It may be the questionable nature of the execution of this event that leads to the evocation of Mosaic Torah:

ויעמדו על־עמדם	And they stood at their position
כמשפטם	According to their custom,
כתורת משה איש־האלהים	according to the *torah* of Moses, the man of God.
הכהנים זרקים את־הדם מיד הלוים	The priests [were] sprinkling the blood from the hands of the Levites. (2 Chr 30:16)

The phrase "according to the Torah of Moses, the man of God" is somewhat awkward in its context, appended to the phrase "according to their custom." Mas-

---

[28] See discussion below. It is quite significant that Jehoshaphat allows Yhwh to do the fighting in this instance, unlike his joint military action with Ahab in 2 Chr 18, which received divine reprimand in 2 Chr 19:2. Note a similar connection for Hezekiah in the appearance of the Torah of Yhwh in 2 Chr 31 and Yhwh defeating Judah's enemies and giving them rest in 32:22 (reading וינחם in place of וינהלם).

[29] Jiang, "God's Law and Theocracy," 450.

[30] Chronicles describes both as איש האלהים: David in 2 Chr 8:14, and Moses in 1 Chr 23:14 and here, in 2 Chr 23:18 (elsewhere only in Ps 90:1; Ezra 3:2; and Josh 14:6).

kow argues that the mention of the Mosaic Torah here refers to the initial installation of the Levites and priests akin to Num 3:6–8; 8:13. However, the "places" of the Levites had changed in the meantime: David, in 1 Chr 23:27–28 changed their roles from carrying the Tent of Meeting and its paraphernalia to assisting the Aaronide priests. This was now "their position" (מעמדם), showing again the confluence of Mosaic and Davidic rulings. Thus, one may conclude that Chronicles introduces a hierarchy between the Mosaic and Yahwistic Torahs, with the latter identified more closely with the divine will, while the former undergoes updating through David's ordinances.

5. Second Chronicles 6:16 and 12:1–5: The Identification between Yhwh and Yhwh's Torah

While these texts do not include an expressed mention of a written *torah*, so I am going a step outside my initial inquiry, they do provide an important change from their parallel texts. The distinctiveness of the text of 2 Chr 6:16 emerges as quite significant when contrasted with its parallel in 1 Kgs 8:25:

ועתה יהוה אלהי ישראל	And now, Yhwh, God of Israel
שמר לעבדך דוד אבי	Keep for your servant David, my father
את אשר דברת לו לאמר	What you promised him, saying
לא־יכרת לך איש מלפני	He will not cut off a man of yours from before me
ישב על־כסא ישראל	Sitting on the throne of Israel
רק אם־ישמרו בניך את־דרכם	If only your sons guard their way
ללכת לפני כאשר הלכת לפני:	To walk *before me* just as you walked before me.
	(1 Kgs 8:25)

ועתה יהוה אלהי ישראל	And now, Yhwh, God of Israel
שמר לעבדך דויד אבי	Keep for your servant David, my father
את אשר דברת לו לאמר	What you promised him, saying
לא־יכרת לך איש מלפני	He will not cut off a man of yours from before me
יושב על־כסא ישראל	Sitting on the throne of Israel
רק אם־ישמרו בניך את־דרכם	If only your sons guard their way
ללכת בתורתי כאשר הלכת לפני	To walk *in my torah* just as you walked before me.
	(2 Chr 6:16)

Many interpreters have noted that rather than "to walk before me" (ללכת לפני), Chronicles offers "to walk in my *torah*" (ללכת בתורתי).[31] However, Maskow argues that this represents the rise of a "theology of holy scripture," following Willi;[32] yet

---

[31] Note that LXX has ἐν τῷ ὀνόματί μου "in my name."

[32] Maskow, *Tora in der Chronik*, 237. The quotation is my translation from Thomas Willi, *Die Chronik als Auslegung: Untersuchungen zur literarischen Gestaltung der historischen Ueberlieferung Israels*, FRLANT 106 (Göttingen: Vandenhoeck & Ruprecht, 1972), 125. See also Marc Zvi Brettler, *The Creation of History in Ancient Israel* (London: Routledge, 2006), 24. As a result "Torah-piety" may be a better expression: see Ben Zvi, "One Size Does Not Fit All," 19–20.

it is surprising that the text itself provides no mention of writing. Neither does this change take place globally within Chronicles, for "before [Yhwh]" appears in 2 Chr 6:14 and its *Vorlage* in 1 Kgs 8:23,[33] which shows how closely linked the Chronicler understood Yhwh to be with his *torah*.

What does take place here is that Chronicles makes *torah* prescriptive: Solomon prays that his successors be treated according to their activity in relation to Yahweh's Torah. However, in this case *torah* could still signify a more general conception of justice or righteousness.[34] Solomon's prayer does go on to unfold Yhwh's role in this justice, which accords with that found throughout the ancient world in adjudicating justice in the case of sacred oaths in vv. 22–23.

In any case, the significance lies in the *torahization* of the divine will, though the meaning of this action remains broad, rather than recalling any specific pentateuchal legal stipulations. One might even imagine *torah* to refer to oral teaching, given the lack of written *torah* in 1 Chr 22:12–13 in contrast to its *Vorlage* (1 Kgs 2:3). In any case, the importance of this unspecified *torahization* lies rather in the importance of the royal *response* rather than the medium of its communication.

Such an identification of Yhwh and his Torah also appears in 2 Chr 12:1–5.[35] In expansions on 1 Kgs 14:25, the Chronicles version speaks of Rehoboam "abandoning the Torah of Yhwh" (v. 1: עזב את־תורת יהוה), and in v. 5 it explicates this phrase through the words of the prophet Shemaiah: "Thus says Yhwh: You abandoned me" (כה־אמר יהוה אתם עזבתם אתי), thereby making the same type of connection.[36] Furthermore, this text offers an adjudicatory connection in international diplomacy: In the intervening verses of vv. 2–4, it narrates Shishak's invasion "for/because they were unfaithful to Yhwh" (כי מעלו ביהוה, v. 2). The prophetic oracle in v. 5 cements this link: "so I also have abandoned you into the hand of Shishak" (ואף אני עזבתי אתכם ביד שישק). In other words, this text shows that unfaithfulness or abandoning Yhwh's Torah stands in for unfaithfulness or abandoning Yhwh himself, and that such action bears consequences.

The element of the prophetic declaration brings in an emphatic confirmation. The Chronicles commentary already noted the act-consequence connection

---

[33] Japhet takes this to mean that in this case "... the Chronicler simply replaces one Deuteronomistic idiom by another, giving the general and rather rare 'walk before the Lord' a more precise meaning, i.e. keeping God's commandments": Sara Japhet, *I & II Chronicles: A Commentary*, OTL (Louisville: Westminster John Knox, 1993), 592. What she misses is this idiom comes to mean something different in Chronicles, given that a written *torah*, named *torah of Yhwh*, takes on more definitive shape in Chronicles.

[34] Though, as Maskow notes, the LXX translates with ἐντολὰς: Maskow, *Tora in der Chronik*, 112n170. This translation likely indicates that the LXX has *concrete* commandments in mind, not simply an amorphous notion of "justice."

[35] By downplaying the importance of this text in order to argue for the significance of the connection between good kings and Yhwh's *torah*, Jiang's article overlooks these developments in his brief discussion of this passage: Jiang, "God's Law and Theocracy," 453–54.

[36] See also Japhet, *I & II Chronicles*, 676; Maskow, *Tora in der Chronik*, 112.

(*Tun-Ergehen Zusammenhang*) between king and deity in the interpretation of Shishak's invasion in v. 2, making Shemaiah's declaration in v. 5 of that interpretation unnecessary for the audience of the text. First, within the world of the text, v. 5 serves the purpose of informing Rehoboam and the leaders of Judah of the reason for their calamity. Second, within the literary context itself, this emphasis marks the loss of the Davidic-Solomonic golden age.[37] Finally, for the text's audience, this repetition serves especially to support the connection of the abandonment of Yhwh's Torah with abandoning Yhwh by means of Yhwh's own word through prophetic oracle. The decisive force of the divine law receives Egyptian military confirmation.

6. Second Chronicles 14–15: Torah-Centered Worship

The relationship between these chapters and 1 Kgs 15:9–24 includes some rearranging and additions. As an overview for Asa's reign as a whole, however, Chronicles inserts obedience to the Torah and the commandment in the overview of his reign in 2 Chr 14:3: ויאמר ליהודה לדרוש את יהוה אלהי אבותיהם ולעשות התורה והמצוה, "Then he [Asa] told Judah to seek Yhwh, the god of their ancestors, *and to do the Torah and the commandment.*" (cf. 1 Kgs 15:8–11). This reliance on Torah, similar to the case of Jehoshaphat, leads to Yhwh defeating Judah's enemy and leaving Judah the spoils, in this case in the insertion of the battle against Zerah the Ethiopian (2 Chr 14:9–15). In this way, Chronicles links the presence of Torah and acting accordingly as the central focus for maintaining peace, recalling the apology for the choice of Solomon to build the temple in 1 Chr 16; 28–29. In this case, some of the content of the Torah and the commandment take on strongly Deuteronomistic hues concerning improper cultic practice, as seen in a comparison between 2 Chr 14:2 and, e. g., Deut 7:4–5 (cf. 12:2), though this is less clear for 1 Chr 14:4.[38]

In another plus compared with its parallel in 1 Kgs 15, 2 Chr 15:1–15 contains the narration of the speech of the prophet Azariah to King Asa, which concerns the *torah*: וימים רבים לישראל ללא אלהי אמת וללא כהן מורה וללא תורה, "Now for a long time Israel [was] without true god, without teaching priest,[39] and without *torah.*" It goes on to recount the negative consequences of this state of affairs, though it then leads to their turning to Yhwh. As Japhet notes, unlike in Hos 3:4, where Israel was without king, sacrifice, and worship paraphernalia, 2 Chr 15:3 notes

---

[37] This turning point is also marked by the first use of מעל, "unfaithful" since the Saul narrative in 1 Chr 10:13.

[38] However, 2 Chr 14:4 may follow Lev 26:30, given the presence of במ(ו)ת and חמני(ם) in both texts, though the mere presence of two terms presents a relatively weak connection, cf. Maskow, *Tora in der Chronik*, 120.

[39] This phrase is missing from the LXX.

the dire situation of going without the true god,[40] a teaching priest, and, separate from the priest, a *torah*.[41] Thus, in comparison with Hosea, Chronicles understands appropriate worship to focus on instruction, highlighting its centrality for postexilic worship.[42]

7. Second Chronicles 17:7–9 and 19:5–11: Yahweh's Torah and Jehoshaphat's Judicial Reform

Witte comments, "Next to David, *Jehoshaphat ...* figures as an exemplary king, whose military and economic successes were grounded in his impeccable religious policy, *attention to the law*, and fidelity to Yhwh."[43] Yet was it really "attention to *the law*" that Chronicles records?

The recounting of Jehoshaphat's reign in 2 Chr 17 is part of the Chronicler's considerable additions to the material concerning this king's story. It recounts how Yhwh was *with* Jehoshaphat (v. 3: ויהי יהוה עם־יהושפט) because (or therefore)[44] Jehoshaphat followed his father's example and did not engage in improper worship (דרש לבעלים), but instead worshipped his ancestor's God and walked in his commandments. As a result, Jehoshaphat receives wealth and glory, and the king takes even more steps in eliminating improper worship (v. 6) from Judah.

As part of this action, vv. 7–9 report the king sending out his officials, Levites, and priests to teach (ללמד) throughout his realm. Specifically, (v. 9)

וילמדו ביהודה	And they taught in Judah,
ועמהם ספר תורת יהוה	And with them [was] *the scroll of the torah of Yhwh*.
ויסבו בכל־ערי יהודה	And they went around in all the cities of Judah
וילמדו בעם	And they taught the people.

The plurality of the teaching faculty – Levites, priests, and royal officials – shows the importance of this mission for the king (and Chronicler).[45] Japhet draws con-

---

[40] It is anarthrous, yet given the late date of the text, it should be interpreted in a monotheistic manner. Note the related but different formulation in Jer 10:10: ויהוה אלהים אמת.

[41] Japhet, *I & II Chronicles*, 719.

[42] Perhaps worthy of note here is the transition from cultic to book-oriented worship. See e.g., Konrad Schmid, "The Canon and the Cult: The Emergence of Book Religion in Ancient Israel and the Gradual Sublimation of the Temple Cult," *JBL* 131 (2012): 289–305. As Maskow notes, the teaching priest in this setting accords with a similar focus on the personnel in Jehoshaphat's reforms in 2 Chr 19: Maskow, *Tora in der Chronik*, 113.

[43] Markus Witte, "The Book of Chronicles," in *T&T Clark Handbook of the Old Testament: An Introduction to the Literature, Religion and History of the Old Testament*, ed. Jan Christian Gertz (London: T&T Clark, 2012), 686. Italics added.

[44] As argued by Kim Strübind, *Tradition als Interpretation in der Chronik: König Josaphat als Paradigma chronistischer Hermeneutik und Theologie*, BZAW 201 (Berlin: de Gruyter, 1991), 143.

[45] It also indicates the postexilic origins of this feature: see Strübind, *Tradition als Interpretation*, 138.

nections with Ezra's teaching of the *torah* to the people (Ezra 7:10, 25; also Neh 8:7).[46] However, 2 Chr 17:9 is quite surprising in that it does not say that they taught the *torah* or that they taught *from* the *torah*.[47] Instead, they had Yhwh's *torah with* them,[48] as Yhwh was *with* Jehoshaphat in v. 3.

As such, the *torah* serves as a reference, perhaps as an authority, yet not as the centerpiece or object of their message,[49] as that which they directly pass on to their audience. In this way it differs markedly from, e. g., Neh 8:8, where "they read *in* the book of the *torah* of God (ויקראו בספר בתורת האלהים).

This raises the question of why, since the Chronicler emphasizes the role of the *torah*, as I have shown above, did he not accord it a more central role in this section? A comparison of the actions that one does with *torah* may provide insight. The verses of 2 Chr 17:7–9 include a form of למד three times.[50] Unlike the majority of texts containing *torah*, and especially *torah of Yhwh/God* in the Hebrew Bible, the focus here is on *teaching* the *torah*, rather than on keeping or observing it. Elsewhere a form of learning or teaching *torah* only appears in Exod 24:12; Lev 10:11; Deut 4:1, 5, 14; 5:31; 6:1; 33:10. Arguments can be made for the lateness of all of these texts.[51] Furthermore, of them, only Exod 24:12 refers to something written:

ויאמר יהוה אל־משה	And Yhwh said to Moses,
עלה אלי ההרה והיה־שם	"Ascend the mountain to me and remain there,
ואתנה לך את־לחת האבן והתורה	and I will give to you the stone tablets and the *torah*
והמצוה	and the commandment
אשר כתבתי להורתם	that *I have written in order to teach them.*

---

[46] Japhet, *I & II Chronicles*, 592.

[47] Contra Frank Crüsemann, *The Torah: Theology and Social History of Old Testament Law*, trans. Allen W. Mahnke (Minneapolis: Fortress, 1996), 92.

[48] The closest parallel appears in Jer 8:8: איכה תאמרו חכמים אנחנו ותורת יהוה אתנו אכן הנה לשקר עשה עט שקר ספרים, "How can you say, 'We are wise, and the *torah* of Yahweh [is] with us.' Now truly the false stylus of the scribes makes [it] into falsehood." Note that the term for "with" (את) differs from 2 Chr 17:9.

[49] Contra Japhet, *I & II Chronicles*, 748.

[50] Jackson, *Semiotics of Biblical Law*, 121, 132–35. Jackson (ibid., 135) notes "But Jehoshaphat's didactic activity appears not to have been unique: Weinfeld has pointed to a parallel in the Sargon inscriptions from Assyria: 'to teach them (the natives of Assyria) the teaching of fearing God and king, I sent officers and overseers.'" See Moshe Weinfeld, "The Origin of the Apodictic Law: An Overlooked Source," *VT* 23 (1973), 70.

[51] On the Deuteronomy texts, see, e. g., Eckart Otto, *Deuteronomium 1–11*, HThKAT (Freiburg im Breisgau: Herder, 2012); idem, *Deuteronomium 12–34*, HThKAT (Freiburg im Breisgau: Herder, 2016). On Lev 10:11, see Christophe Nihan, *From Priestly Torah to Pentateuch: A Study in the Composition of the Book of Leviticus*, FAT II 25 (Tübingen: Mohr Siebeck, 2007), 590. On Exod 24:12, the narrative begun here continues to 1 Kgs 8:9; see Michael Konkel, "Exodus 32–24 and the Quest for an Enneateuch," in *Pentateuch, Hexateuch, or Enneateuch? Identifying Literary Works in Genesis through Kings*, ed. Thomas B. Dozeman, Thomas Römer, and Konrad Schmid, AIL 8 (Atlanta: Society of Biblical Literature, 2011), 177.

This text bears great significant for my discussion because it contains the *original* writing of the Torah by God, a phenomenon that rarely appears.[52] As such, this text directly links the *writing* of the law with its divine nature. Furthermore, this text grounds the original purpose for a written *torah* as teaching (להורתם).[53] Of course, there is an implied link to *doing* them, but no direct link exists to some type of judicial setting or use:[54] the conceptual context is instructional rather than legal.

In any case, no doubt such stone tablets would have proved impractical in the context of 2 Chr 17:7–9, hampering the kind of transportation of the Torah envisioned in by Jehoshaphat's officials. Replacement stone tablets elsewhere acquire a ritual significance when Moses places them inside the Ark. However, it is clear that the Chronicles text places little emphasis on the *contents* of the Torah in this setting.[55]

Turning to a related point of interpretation of Exod 24:12, it may be that the Torah and the commandment in Exod 24:12 differ from the stone tablets, depending on one's understanding of the *waws* before the two terms – are they phrasal or explicative?[56] Either way, the inclusion of the Torah and the commandment here serve to increase their level of authority.

Surprisingly, perhaps, *neither* of these two texts concern *adjudicating* by means of the Torah, as one might interpret Ezra 7:26 to indicate:

וכל די לא להוא עבד דתא די אלהך	And all that do not do the law of your god
ודתא די מלכא אספרנא	and the law of the king diligently,
דינה להוא מתעבד מנה	thus shall be done with him:
הן למות הן לשרשו	whether to death, whether to banishment,
הן לענש נכסין ולאסורין	whether to confiscation of goods, or to bondage.

This text, along with the earlier verse 7:10, imagine teaching "the law of your God" (Aram.: דתא די אלהך) *in order to make legal judgments on its basis*. Collins, for example, views this Ezra text as a key text in placing the rise of Torah's normativity in the mid to late Persian period, even though some references to it in Nehemiah differ from what the current Pentateuch prescribes.[57] Given the

---

[52] Also Exod 32:14; Deut 9:10; 10:4; and the hypothetical of Hos 8:12.

[53] Fitzpatrick-McKinley, *Transformation of Torah*, 101 considers this a monumental purpose for the laws, but they do not end up on a stela like those in 8:32–33. Nonetheless, writing on *stone* does constitute more permanence than writing on a scroll to be sure.

[54] There is mention concerning "whoever has a dispute" (מי בעל דברים) in v. 14, but they are to go to Aaron and Hur.

[55] Following von Rad, Strübind relates this with a general divine charge as a whole: Strübind, *Tradition als Interpretation*, 146.

[56] *IBHS*, § 39.2.1, 648–49. This presents a problem in the text, assuming that the *torah* and commandment are not typically understood to have been written by God. See, e.g., Brevard S. Childs, *The Book of Exodus: A Critical, Theological Commentary* (Louisville: Westminster, 1974), 499, 507. Childs takes ותורה ומצוה as a later addition.

[57] Collins, *Invention of Judaism*, 53–57.

180   *Peter Altmann*

placement of Chronicles in a similarly late or even later setting, it is striking that such a purpose remains absent from 2 Chr 17:9.[58]

Nonetheless, while the treatment of the mention of the Torah in 2 Chr 17 does not attribute it an official judiciary function, actual pentateuchal *texts* do appear in Jehoshaphat's instructions to the judges he establishes throughout his realm in 2 Chr 19:5–11. This section includes one mention of *torah*, but only as part of a list of possible disputed cases that could be referred to Jerusalem for adjudication:

ויאמר אל־השפטים	6 And he said to the judges:
ראו מה־אתם עשים	"Consider what you are doing,
כי לא לאדם תשפטו	for you judge not on behalf of human beings
כי ליהוה	but on Yhwh's behalf;
ועמכם בדבר משפט	and [he is] with you in matters of judgment.
ועתה יהי פחד־יהוה עליכם	7 Now, let the fear of Yhwh be upon you;
שמרו ועשו	take care what you do,
כי־אין עם־יהוה אלהינו עולה	for there is no injustice with Yhwh our God,
ומשא פנים ומקח־שחד:	or partiality, or taking of bribes." …
כה תעשון	9 "This is how you shall act:
ביראת יהוה	in the fear of Yhwh,
באמונה ובלבב שלם	in faithfulness, and with your whole heart;
וכל־ריב אשר־יבוא עליכם מאחיכם	10 whenever a case comes to you from your kindred
הישבים בעריהם	who live in their cities,
בין־דם לדם	*between one kind of homicide and another*,[59]
בין־תורה למצוה לחקים ולמשפטים	*between torah, commandment, statutes, and ordinances,*
והזהרתם אתם	then you shall caution them,
ולא יאשמו ליהוה	so that they may not incur guilt before Yhwh
והיה־קצף עליכם ועל־אחיכם	and wrath may not come on you and your kindred.
כה תעשון ולא תאשמו	Do so, and you will not incur guilt. (2 Chr 19:6–7, 9–10)

As Knoppers shows, links between chs. 17 and 19 establish continuity between the two texts: for example, Jehoshaphat goes throughout his realm as did the earlier officials (19:4–5; 17:1–2, 7),[60] though they represent different events.[61] In this case, the king assures the judges that Yhwh will be *with* them, recalling the divine presence with Jehoshaphat himself in 17:3. However, the role of *torah* is diminished from a catch-all term for the iconic divine/Mosaic support for teaching throughout the country to one of a number of kinds of stipulations that Jehoshaphat mentions in his charge to judges in Jerusalem.

Understanding the conception of *torah* here relies on the understood antecedent for "them" in the subsequent clause: והזהרתם אתם "then you shall caution them" (v. 10). If the antecedent is "your kindred that live in your cities,"

---

[58] See also Jackson, *Semiotics of Biblical Law*, 170.

[59] On this translation see *IBHS*, § 11.2.6c, 200, commenting on the same construction in Deut 17:8.

[60] Gary N. Knoppers, "Jehoshaphat's Judiciary and 'The Scroll of YHWH'S Torah,'" *JBL* 113.1 (1994): 66. His article also persuasively shows that 2 Chr 19 depends on Exod 18 and Deut 16.

[61] Knoppers, "Jehoshaphat's Judiciary," 67.

then this suggests that the central judges in Jerusalem provided advice to their judge colleagues spread throughout the realm.[62]

One difficulty arises with this reading: "between one homicide and another" is difficult to understand as part of the same series as "between *torah,* commandment, statutes, and ordinances." Yet if they are *two* related sequences that both envision advice from a more senior collegium, which the grammar allows, then they could fit together. If this is the case, then it appears that the text has in mind a variety of regulations (whether written or oral remains unclear) of which the various judges must decide what applies in specific situations. *This may represent some kind of reference to the application of legal statements in a positive law setting.*[63] The dispersed judges receive advice on *which torah,* commandment, etc. to apply to a given case.[64] This text may also intimate possible *"prima facie"* conflicts *between* various legal precepts, taken as contradictions in historical criticism, but dealt in other ways in early Judaism.[65] In this situation, they may be viewed as something like LeFebvre's "academic ideal."[66]

In general, in 2 Chr 19 various terms for pentateuchal legal precepts take on increased authority in the *training,* or at least *exhorting,* of judges, similar to Moses' role in Exod 18:20 and the Levitical priests and judge in Deut 17:10–11. However, the term does differ in 2 Chr 19:10, which concerns זהר, admonish rather than the clearly didactic ירה hiphil in Exod 18 and Deut 17. Perhaps a decisive distinction arises in 2 Chr 19:10 in the communication of the differences between various precepts *to the dispersed judges*, rather than to the people (Exod 18:20) or the litigants bringing the case (Deut 17:10–11).[67]

The text does directly link this development with the *divine* nature of these legal precepts. Their directives relate quite closely with the standing in as judges for Yhwh, "for you judge not on behalf of human beings but on Yhwh's behalf," כי לא לאדם תשפטו כי ליהוה (2 Chr 19:6),[68] which relates to avoiding guilt before

---

[62] This is the understanding promoted by Ralph W. Klein, *2 Chronicles: A Commentary*, Hermeneia (Minneapolis: Fortress, 2012), 276.

[63] A closely related option would be Westbrook's notion of laws as reference material to train judges: see Raymond Westbrook, "Biblical and Cuneiform Law Codes," *RB* 92 (1985): 254.

[64] Japhet, *I & II Chronicles*, 778, sees them as written, but this may overstate the case.

[65] The example of "cooking the Passover meat with fire" in 2 Chr 35:13 provides one such example.

[66] LeFebvre, *Collections, Codes, and Torah*, 97. However, it does seem that they are binding in the sense of Vroom's "practical authority": they seem more "commanded" than "persuasion," cf. Vroom, *The Authority of Law*, 21.

[67] So also Maskow, *Tora in der Chronik*, 165. He states, "Dabei wird in der Fortsetzung der Prätexte des Pentateuchs, insbesondere der dtr./dtn. Texte, ein Perspektivwechsel vollzogen. Anders als bspw. in Dtn 17,8 geht es hier nicht mehr um den in der 2.Ps.Sg. angesprochenen Rechtsuchenden, sondern um die Maßstäbe für die Richter selbst." He goes on to call it a "Sakralisierung der Rechtsprechung" (ibid., 166).

[68] Maskow calls this the "Schlüsselcredo" or Jehoshaphat's legal reform: *Tora in der Chronik*, 165.

Yhwh (v. 10). Furthermore, a number of the exhortations made by Jehoshaphat in this section recall pentateuchal verbiage. Deuteronomy 17:8–13 likewise offers the phrase בין־דם לדם, "between one type of bloodshed and another," though as part of a different list of cases.[69] Both sections also offer a two-tiered justice system (also found in Exod 18; Deut 1). Taking bribes (לקח + שחד) appears just after recognizing persons (though expressed differently) in Deut 16:19 (cf. the even more closely worded texts of Deut 10:17; Hos 3:4; Lev 19:14 as well).[70]

While hypothetical, given the limited evidence from the text, perhaps this text displays something of an *internal* narrative on the transformation from royal law into divine law as noted by Knoppers and Harvey,

> Chronicles is most unusual in its depiction of a king explicitly mandating the dissemination of Torah to effect this result [of justice]. Set against the background of ancient Near Eastern legal tradition, the Chronicler ingeniously presents a king promulgating not his own royal code but God's law. The result is something unprecedented in Israelite history: a monarch mandating education in Torah to his people.[71]

The impetus for the legal reform comes from the king, but Jehoshaphat keeps himself, and largely keeps his interests (but see "in matters of the king" in 19:11), out of the adjudicatory process. However, it should be noted that the "Torah" only serves as an iconic authority in 2 Chr 17, and it remains simply part of the reference material for the judges in ch. 19. Therefore, in 2 Chr 19, *justice,* more so than "the Torah," is connected with Yhwh (19:6–7, vs. v. 10), which relativizes the point made by Knoppers and Harvey.

8. Second Chronicles 31:3–4: Yhwh's Torah after Hezekiah's Passover

After the celebration of Passover-Unleavened Bread under Hezekiah, the people disperse and destroy the paraphernalia associated with other deities, quite in keeping with the Deuteronomistic style of the source verse of 2 Kgs 18:4. Upon everyone's return home, Hezekiah appoints cultic personnel. The verses mention the Torah of Yhwh, then describe, first, Hezekiah's provision for them and, second, his call for those living in Jerusalem to do the same. As a result, (most likely) the priests and Levites will be able to focus on the Torah of Yhwh.

---

[69] On the detailed connections with Deut 17:8–13, see esp. Sarah J. K. Pearce, *The Words of Moses*, TSAJ 152 (Tübingen: Mohr Siebeck, 2013).

[70] Also noted in Maskow, *Tora in der Chronik*, 167; Knoppers, "Jehoshaphat's Judiciary"; Louis C. Jonker, "Was the Chronicler More Deuteronomic than the Deuteronomist? Explorations into the Chronicler's Relationship with Deuteronomic Legal Traditions," *SJOT* 27 (2013): 195–96.

[71] Knoppers and Harvey Jr., "Pentateuch in Ancient Mediterranean Context," 134.

ומנת המלך מן־רכושו לעלות	Now the portion of the king from his possessions for
לעלות הבקר והערב	burnt offering: for the burnt offerings of the morning
והעלות לשבתות ולחדשים ולמעדים	and the evening, and for the burnt offering for Sabbaths, and for New Moons, and for appointed festivals
ככתוב בתורת יהוה	according to what is written in the Torah of Yhwh.
ויאמר לעם ליושבי ירושלם	And he told the people, to those living in Jerusalem,
לתת מנת הכהנים והלוים	to give the portion of the priests and the Levites
למען יחזקו בתורת יהוה	so that they could strengthen themselves in the Torah of Yhwh. (2 Chr 31:3–4)

These verses, along with vv. 2–19 as a whole, do not rely on a *Vorlage* from 2 Kgs 18. As Japhet notes, this is the first place in Chronicles (or Samuel–Kings) that deals extensively with the provisions for temple personnel.[72] The only pentateuchal text that includes the Sabbath burnt offering is Num 28–29, which suggests that Chronicles has this late textual tradition in mind.[73] Much like David's application of offering provisions from Numbers (and Exodus) to a new situation in the above-discussed text of 1 Chr 16:40, Hezekiah as well adapts the pentateuchal tradition to his own setting. However, because the Pentateuch provides no specific precept for the manner in which daily, Sabbath, and New Moon burnt offerings should be provided,[74] Chronicles/Hezekiah could not draw on any to support his specific action or command. Instead a similar combination appears in the cultic practice in Ezek 45:17,[75] with quite similar terminology: בחגים ובחדשים ובשבתות בכל־מועדי בית ישראל ("on the festivals and on the New Moons and on the Sabbaths – all the appointed times of the house of Israel"). Ezekiel has the "prince" provide not just for burnt offerings, but others as well, and a further difference is the twice-daily burnt offering from Num 28–29, rather than the daily burnt offering in Ezek 45:23, if one can apply this regulation outside of the festival period.

Therefore, this text calls on the general rhetorical power of a reference to "what is written in the *torah* of Yhwh," though only the carrying out of the rituals appears there,[76] likely attempting to gain support (on the narratival level) for a command thereby quite similar to "what is written," but in *Ezekiel* rather than in the Pentateuch. If this is the case, it radically broadens Chronicles' conception of Yahwistic Torah to include cultic ordinances found in the prophetic books.[77]

---

[72] Japhet, *I & II Chronicles*, 960. See the related issue in Neh 10:33–40; 13:10–13; Ezek 44:29–30; 45:17; Mal 3:8–10.

[73] Maskow, *Tora in der Chronik*, 224–25, following Shaver.

[74] One might be able to use the festival calendar texts to address offerings for the festivals.

[75] Klein, *2 Chronicles*, 445. Thanks to Benjamin Giffone for pointing me to this reference.

[76] Fishbane refers to this text only in passing (and incorrectly: "'as it is written in the Torah of Moses'"): Fishbane, *Biblical Interpretation*, 112n21.

[77] This is a contention that has been explored in more detail by Benjamin D. Giffone, "Atonement, Sacred Space and Ritual Time: The Chronicler as Reader of Priestly Pentateuchal

9. Second Chronicles 34:14–15 and 36:26–27: Josiah's Reign, His Passover, and Torah

Finally, as is well known, the Chronicler does not allow Josiah to wait until the scroll of the Torah is found in the eighteenth year of his reign to begin his reforms. Chronicles instead places the beginning of Josiah's reforms at the time when he reaches adulthood at age twenty (2 Chr 34:3).[78] This change results in deemphasizing the role of the scroll of the Torah in the reforms from the report in 2 Kgs 22.[79]

In the narrative of the discovery of the *torah* in the temple during Josiah's reign, 2 Chr 34:15 offers a statement lifted almost verbatim from 2 Kgs 22:8:

ויען חלקיהו ויאמר אל־שפן הסופר ספר התורה מצאתי בבית יהוה ויתן חלקיהו את־הספר אל־שפן	And Hilkiah *answered* Shaphan the scribe and said, "I have found the scroll of the *torah* in the house of Yhwh. And Hilkiah gave the scroll to Shaphan. (2 Chr 34:15)
ויאמר חלקיהו הכהן הגדול על־שפן הספר ספר התורה מצאתי בבית יהוה ויתן חלקיה את־הספר אל־שפן ויקראהו׃	And Hilkiah the high priest *said to* Shaphan the scribe, "I have found the scroll of the *torah* in the house of Yhwh." And Hilkiah gave the scroll to Shaphan, *and he read it*. (2 Kgs 22:8)

While this shared verse does not explicitly designate the divine origins of the Torah, though it does, of course, come from the temple, the previous verse in Chronicles, 2 Chr 34:14, offers a plus that makes its origin explicit: מצא חלקיהו הכהן את־ספר תורת־יהוה ביד־משה, "Hilkiah found the scroll of the *torah* of Yhwh by the hand of Moses." Commentators suggest that this addition takes place in order to show that the Chronicler has the entire Pentateuch in mind.[80] This interpretation does not explicitly follow from the immediate context itself. However, one could make this *inference* based on the nature of the report of the Passover celebration in 2 Chr 35:1–19 (cf. 2 Kgs 23:1–3), which includes attention to various parts of the pentateuchal discussions on Passover:

On the fourteenth day: v. 1 – Exod 12:1–6
Intermediary role of Levites: v. 3 – Num 3:6–9; 8:19[81]

Narrative," in *Chronicles and the Priestly Literature of the Hebrew Bible*, ed. Louis Jonker and Jaeyoung Jeon, BZAW 528 (Berlin: de Gruyter, 2021), 221–43.

[78] On the significance of this year, see Num 1:3; 26:2; 1 Chr 23:24, 27; 2 Chr 31:17, and Klein, *2 Chronicles*, 495.

[79] Klein, *2 Chronicles*, 492; Steven L. McKenzie, *I and II Chronicles*, AOTC (Nashville: Abingdon, 2004).

[80] Louis C. Jonker, *1 & 2 Chronicles*, UB (Grand Rapids: Baker Books, 2013), 290; McKenzie, *I and II Chronicles*.

[81] Japhet, *I & II Chronicles*, 1045–46.

Offering of cattle:	vv. 7, 9 – Deut 16:2, Num 28:19[82]
Priests splashed blood on the altar:	v. 11 – Lev 1:5, 11; 3:2, 8, 13[83]
Burnt offerings at Passover:	v. 12 – Num 28:19
Passover [offering] boiled over fire:	v. 13 – harmonizing Exod 12:8–9/Deut 16:7

The key point to emphasize here is that the regulations referred to in this text of Chronicles draw from a wide array of texts and sources in the Pentateuch – D and P, early and late. Thus, it shows that Chronicles was familiar with a broad diversity of texts and/or traditions for the depiction of Josiah's Passover.

There are, however, a number of discrepancies with the Pentateuch. Among other details is the remark "according to the word of Yhwh" in 35:6 for the Levites slaughtering the Passover lambs and consecrating themselves, which does not appear in the pentateuchal discussions.[84] Perhaps one can bring this together with the mention of the scroll of the Torah of Yhwh in 34:14 and combining it with the "boiling of the Passover [offering] on fire *according to the stipulation*" ויבשלו הפסח באש כמשפט.[85] These three plusses in comparison with the text of Kings, though not all concerning *Yhwh's torah,* still heighten the importance of actions according to the *Torah,* especially concerning the implementation of cultic law in a new setting, during the reign of Josiah.

Finally, as a subscript to Josiah's life, 2 Chr 35:26–27 notes that "the remainder of Josiah's deeds and his faithfulness according to what is written in the *torah* of Yhwh[86] … are written in the Scroll of the Kings of Israel and Judah." The phrase ככתוב בתורת יהוה also appears in 1 Chr 16:40 and 2 Chr 31:3, which as Maskow notes, connects David/Solomon, Hezekiah, and Josiah.[87] They become those who are adept at applying Yhwh's *torah* to new *cultic* situations. This insertion into the final epitaph on Josiah's life in 2 Kgs 23:28, however, goes beyond the golden ages of the United Monarchy and Hezekiah.[88] It appears as a subscript to Josiah's entire life. Nevertheless, his disobedience leads to his untimely death, bringing him back down to the realm of mortals.

---

[82] Following McKenzie, *I and II Chronicles*; contra the harmonizing view of Japhet, *I & II Chronicles*, 1050.

[83] Noted by Japhet, *I & II Chronicles*, 949. It accords with 2 Chr 29:34; 30:17.

[84] As noted by Klein, *2 Chronicles*, 520.

[85] Klein makes a brief connection with 34:14 as well: Klein, *2 Chronicles*, 529. This is a case of what Fishbane calls "synthetic exegesis" of the sub-type "synthesis by comparative supplementation": see Fishbane, *Biblical Interpretation*, 251.

[86] The LXX reads quite differently here, however: "And the matters of Josiah and his hope were written *in* the law of the Lord" (καὶ ἦσαν οἱ λόγοι Ιωσια καὶ ἡ ἐλπὶς αὐτοῦ γεγραμμένα ἐν νόμῳ κυρίου·).

[87] Maskow, *Tora in der Chronik*, 233.

[88] Japhet notes the difference from Hezekiah, but does not make anything of it: Japhet, *I & II Chronicles*, 1058.

10. Conclusion

These brief analyses of the appearances of Yhwh's Torah in the books of Chronicles, during the late-Persian / Early Hellenistic period, reveal several developments in comparison to the books of Samuel-Kings. And, returning to the overarching question of this essay, these developments offer insight into the significance of "divine law" in this time period, at least for the circles from which Chronicles develops and in which it is transmitted.

First, as frequently noted in previous scholarship, Yhwh becomes intricately identified with the divine Torah in texts such as 1 Chr 22:12–13; 2 Chr 6:16; and 12:1–5, a phenomenon that also appears in other early Second Temple texts, such as Ps 119.

Second, an important question is what this *torah* consists of? According to the evidence in Chronicles, Yhwh's Torah most frequently appears as a reference when good kings apply particular pentateuchal *cultic* ordinances in entirely new settings. Thus, the detailed conception of Yhwh's Torah in Chronicles, when one appears, addresses cultic stipulations, especially those that introduce the Zadokites, such as in 1 Chr 16:40. This text, which incorporates late Priestly, or Priestly-influenced texts such as Num 28, expands references beyond the material associated with Deuteronomy in, e.g., Josh 1, which serves as a source text for 1 Chr 22:12–13. Most striking, however, is the similarity, or even influence, of Ezek 45:17 in 2 Chr 31:3–4, which stretches Chronicles' authoritative divine Torah to include at least this prophetic conception of appropriate cultic worship.

In contrast, other legal spheres, such as economic provisions, torts, bodily harm, or family law – which are widely distributed throughout the contemporary epigraphic remains of the region (e.g., Elephantine, Babylonia, or even Egypt more broadly, if considering the Ptolemaic period) – make hardly any appearance whatsoever in connection with Yhwh's Torah in these texts. A small, hidden reference to *torah* as part of a list of types of regulations given to judges in the central judicial setting of Jerusalem appears in 2 Chr 19:10, but this is *as part of* various types of cases, suggesting that *torah* itself is a subset – exactly what kind remains unclear – of those issues this group of judges might face. However, the mentions of the divine Torah that extend beyond the cultic sphere to concern *teaching* throughout the countryside, though addressing a context concerned with proper worship that eliminated abhorrent practices (2 Chr 17:3, 6), with the support of the divine Torah. On the whole, Chronicles is far more concerned with gathering various types of cultic concerns into the Yahwistic Torah and using this material to address new cultic situations than with applying this divine Torah, broadly speaking, to the judicial realm. This no doubt fits well with Chronicles' focus on the temple and on cultic worship, but it is also surprising that little evidence of judicial application of the divine Torah appears. As a result, the depiction and conception of the divine Torah in Chronicles questions the extent and nature of the embrace of pentateuchal laws as practical judicial law – as positive law – during the Persian or perhaps the early Hellenistic period, an insight with wider ramifications for the nature of Torah as "law" in the early Second Temple Period and issues such as Persian authorization of Torah.

Bibliography

Achenbach, Reinhard. "The Pentateuch, the Prophets, and the Torah in the Fifth and Fourth Centuries B.C.E." Pages 253–85 in *Judah and the Judeans in the Fourth Century B.C.E.* Edited by Oded Lipschits, Gary N. Knoppers, and Rainer Albertz. Winona Lake, IN: Eisenbrauns, 2007.

Altmann, Peter. *Festive Meals in Ancient Israel: Deuteronomy's Identity Politics in Their Ancient Near Eastern Context.* BZAW 424. Berlin: de Gruyter, 2011.

Ben Zvi, Ehud. "One Size Does Not Fit All: Observations on the Different Ways That Chronicles Dealt with the Authoritative Literature of Its Time." Pages 13–35 in *What Was Authoritative for Chronicles?* Edited by Ehud Ben Zvi and Diana Vikander Edelman. Winona Lake, IN: Eisenbrauns, 2011.

Botterwick, G. Johannes, and Helmut Ringgren, eds. *Theological Dictionary of the Old Testament.* 15 vols. Grand Rapids: Eerdmans, 1974–2004.

Brettler, Marc Zvi. *The Creation of History in Ancient Israel.* London: Routledge, 2006.

Childs, Brevard S. *The Book of Exodus: A Critical, Theological Commentary.* Louisville: Westminster, 1974.

Cogan, Mordechai, and Hayim Tadmor. *2 Kings: A New Translation with Introduction and Commentary.* AB 11. Garden City, NY: Doubleday, 1988.

Collins, John J. *The Invention of Judaism: Torah and Jewish Identity from Deuteronomy to Paul.* TLJS 7. Oakland, CA: University of California Press, 2017.

Crüsemann, Frank. *The Torah: Theology and Social History of Old Testament Law.* Translated by Allen W. Mahnke. Minneapolis: Fortress, 1996.

Dillard, Raymond B. "The Chronicler's Jehoshaphat." *TJ* 7 (1986): 17–22.

Fishbane, Michael. *Biblical Interpretation in Ancient Israel.* Oxford: Clarendon, 1985.

Fitzpatrick-McKinley, Anne. *The Transformation of Torah: From Scribal Advice to Law.* JSOTSup 287. Sheffield: Sheffield Academic, 1999.

Giffone, Benjamin D. "According to Which 'Law of Moses'? Cult Centralization in Samuel, Kings, and Chronicles." *VT* 67 (2017): 432–47.

Giffone, Benjamin D. "Atonement, Sacred Space and Ritual Time: The Chronicler as Reader of Priestly Pentateuchal Narrative." Pages 221–43 in *Chronicles and the Priestly Literature of the Hebrew Bible.* Edited by Louis C. Jonker and Jaeyoung Jeon. BZAW 528. Berlin: de Gruyter, 2021.

Jackson, Bernard S. "Law in the Ninth Century: Jehoshaphat's 'Judicial Reform.'" Pages 369–97 in *Understanding the History of Ancient Israel.* Edited by Hugh G. M. Williamson. Oxford: Oxford University Press, 2007.

Jackson, Bernard S. *Studies in the Semiotics of Biblical Law.* JSOTSup 314. Sheffield: Sheffield Academic, 2000.

Japhet, Sara. *I & II Chronicles: A Commentary.* OTL. Louisville: Westminster John Knox, 1993.

Jiang, Shuai. "God's Law and Theocracy: The Use of 'YHWH's Torah' in Chronicles." *ZAW* 131.3 (2019): 444–58.
Jonker, Louis C. *1 & 2 Chronicles*. UB. Grand Rapids: Baker, 2013.
Jonker, Louis C. "Was the Chronicler More Deuteronomic than the Deuteronomist? Explorations into the Chronicler's Relationship with Deuteronomic Legal Traditions." *SJOT* 27 (2013): 185–97.
Klein, Ralph W. *1 Chronicles: A Commentary*. Hermeneia. Minneapolis: Fortress, 2006.
Klein, Ralph W. *2 Chronicles: A Commentary*. Hermeneia. Minneapolis: Fortress, 2012.
Knoppers, Gary N. "Jehoshaphat's Judiciary and 'The Scroll of YHWH'S Torah.'" *JBL* 113.1 (1994): 59–80.
Knoppers, Gary N., and Paul B. Harvey Jr. "The Pentateuch in Ancient Mediterranean Context: The Publication of Local Lawcodes." Pages 105–41 in *The Pentateuch as Torah: New Models for Understanding Its Promulgation and Acceptance*. Edited by Bernard M. Levinson and Gary N. Knoppers. Winona Lake, IN: Eisenbrauns, 2007.
Konkel, Michael. "Exodus 32–24 and the Quest for an Enneateuch." Pages 169–84 in *Pentateuch, Hexateuch, or Enneateuch? Identifying Literary Works in Genesis through Kings*. Edited by Thomas B. Dozeman, Thomas Römer, and Konrad Schmid. AIL 8. Atlanta: Society of Biblical Literature, 2011.
Kratz, Reinhard Gregor. "Die Tora Davids: Psalm 1 und die doxologische Fünfteilung des Psalters: Odil Hannes Steck zum 60 Geburtstag." *ZTK* 93 (1996): 1–34.
LeFebvre, Michael. *Collections, Codes, and Torah: The Re-Characterization of Israel's Written Law*. LHBOTS 451. New York: T&T Clark, 2006.
Lightstone, Jack N. "Torah Is Nomos – except When It Is Not: Prolegomena to the Study of the Law in Late Antique Judaism." *SR* 13 (1984): 29–37.
Maskow, Lars. *Tora in der Chronik: Studien zur Rezeption des Pentateuchs in den Chronikbüchern*. FRLANT 274. Göttingen: Vandenhoeck & Ruprecht, 2019.
McKenzie, Steven L. *I and II Chronicles*. AOTC. Nashville: Abingdon, 2004.
Nihan, Christophe. *From Priestly Torah to Pentateuch: A Study in the Composition of the Book of Leviticus*. FAT II 25. Tübingen: Mohr Siebeck, 2007.
Otto, Eckart. *Deuteronomium 1–11*. HThKAT. Freiburg im Breisgau: Herder, 2012.
Otto, Eckart. *Deuteronomium 12–34*. HThKAT. Freiburg im Breisgau: Herder, 2016.
Pearce, Sarah J. K. *The Words of Moses*. TSAJ 152. Tübingen: Mohr Siebeck, 2013.
Rhyder, Julia. *Centralizing the Cult: The Holiness Legislation in Leviticus 17–26*. FAT 134. Tübingen: Mohr Siebeck, 2019.
Schmid, Konrad. "The Canon and the Cult: The Emergence of Book Religion in Ancient Israel and the Gradual Sublimation of the Temple Cult." *JBL* 131 (2012): 289–305.
Strübind, Kim. *Tradition als Interpretation in der Chronik: König Josaphat als Paradigma chronistischer Hermeneutik und Theologie*. BZAW 201. Berlin: de Gruyter, 1991.
Vroom, Jonathan. *The Authority of Law in the Hebrew Bible and Early Judaism: Tracing the Origins of Legal Obligation from Ezra to Qumran*. JSJSup 187. Leiden: Brill, 2018.
Weinfeld, Moshe, "The Origin of the Apodictic Law: An Overlooked Source." *VT* 23 (1973): 63–75.
Westbrook, Raymond. "Biblical and Cuneiform Law Codes." *RB* 92 (1985): 247–64.
Westbrook, Raymond. "The Character of Ancient Near Eastern Law." Pages 1–90 in *A History of Ancient Near Eastern Law*. Edited by Raymond Westbrook. HdO 1. Leiden: Brill, 2003.

Willi, Thomas. *Die Chronik als Auslegung: Untersuchungen zur literarischen Gestaltung der historischen Ueberlieferung Israels.* FRLANT 106. Göttingen: Vandenhoeck & Ruprecht, 1972.

Willi, Thomas. "Thora in den biblischen Chronikbüchern." *Judaica* 36 (1980): 102–5, 148–51.

Witte, Markus. "The Book of Chronicles." Pages 683–94 in *T&T Clark Handbook of the Old Testament: An Introduction to the Literature, Religion and History of the Old Testament.* Edited by Jan Christian Gertz. London: T&T Clark, 2012.

Part III

Case Studies

Did the Deuteronomist Detest Dreams?

Jin H. Han

1. Introduction

The Deuteronomic warning in Deut 13:2–6 (ET 13:1–5) may generate a facile impression that the Deuteronomist seeks to ban oneiromancy outright.[1] The passage directs one to discard the oracle of a prophet or a dreamer who leads the people astray into worship of other gods, but the prohibition applies not to all diviners but to a specific subgroup who pushes forth a devious agenda. The Deuteronomistic corpus (traditionally known as the Former Prophets, the books from Deuteronomy to 2 Kings) includes a small number of references to a dream that suggest that apparently the Deuteronomistic Historian not only tolerates but also may even welcome dreams as a means of communication with the deity. Instead of adjudicating dreams that are notoriously uncontrollable, the matrix of the few dream reports that are committed to writing in the Deuteronomistic History displays a thoughtful reconfiguration guided not only by the immediate narrative context of the story but also by the overall Deuteronomistic Torah-based spirituality that values the practice of being in communion with God. Under the scribes' brush, the amorphous dreams find their integral place in the cultural memory of ancient Israel, while leaving their rough edges that the Deuteronomistic Historian preserves while maintaining the inchoate concern about oneiromancy.

2. What Does Deut 13 Really Say about Dreams?

In the larger literary context of 12:1–17:7, the rubrics are clear. The collection of the laws that govern cultic practices starts with the pronouncement of the designated place of worship in ch. 12, a location that shall be one of God's own choosing. The provision is repeated in the book of Deuteronomy with no clear

---

[1] In this article, the "Deuteronomic" refers to the law code or its adjutant legal tradition reflected in the core of the book of Deuteronomy, whereas the "Deuteronomistic," to the historiographic endeavor that has produced the corpus commonly known as the Deuteronomistic History guided by the Deuteronomic law.

explanation.[2] The laws that follow v. 29 stipulate that the people of God secure measures to keep themselves pure in God's sight.[3] The people who are privileged enough to live in the holy land must live a life worthy of God's presence in their midst and may not worship other gods.

The advisory about a misleading prophet or a dream interpreter in 13:2–6 (ET 13:1–5) is squarely in consonance with the overriding concern to preserve the unadulterated worship of Yahweh. The injunction on prophecy and dreams is preceded by 13:1, which mandates complete and non-deleterious obedience to God's commandment. This literary context suggests that the Deuteronomist seeks to warn against the prophet or the oneiromancer in light of the mandated observance of God's command (את כל הדבר אשר אנכי מצוה אתכם, v. 1a).

The casuistic commandment regarding the dream diviner in vv. 2–3 begins with the protasis with three parts, and each part builds upon the previous: (1) the appearance of a divinatory functionary who has an extramundane experience (v. 2); (2) the fulfillment of the predictive component of the diviner's divination (v. 3a); and (3) the possibility of the diviner's attempt to allure the people to worship other gods (v. 3b). The first item features "a sign (אות)" or "a wonder (מופת)." They do not need to trigger any immediate concern, however, for the sign simply promises a piece of extraordinary information, and the wonder may simply evince God's involvement in human affairs. How to adjudicate the second phenomenon is outlined elsewhere in Deut 18. Although the chapter limits its scope to the prophetic activities, it may well be broadly construed to include all functionaries of divination. The litmus test that ch. 18 provides to identify true prophecy is squarely based on the fulfillment or nonfulfillment of the prognostication postulated in the prophecy (vv. 21–22). The prophet whose words come true and is deemed to be a true prophet is not subjected to further scrutiny as to what the prophet does with the *true* prophecy.

By contrast, Deut 13 does not stop with the question of whether the words have come true or not. It offers an additional qualifying clause in v. 3b, for the fulfillment of the sign or the wonder in v. 3a signals the authenticity of the prophecy without establishing it. The scribal adjoining of the two halves of the verse presents a possibility in which ch. 13 intertextually engages ch. 18, voicing the main caveat that sounds an alarm for a disconcerting development in which the diviner attempts to lure the people away from the worship of Yahweh (13:3b). The nature of the interaction of the two elements of vv. 2–3a and v. 3b is complex. The scribe who has joined them may have intended them as complements.

---

[2] Rannfrid I. Thelle, *Approaches to the 'Chosen Place': Accessing a Biblical Concept*, LHBOTS 564 (London: T&T Clark, 2012), 1–3.

[3] Dale Patrick, "The Rhetoric of Collective Responsibility in Deuteronomic Law," in *Pomegranates and Golden Bells: Studies in Biblical, Jewish, and Near Eastern Ritual, Law, and Literature in Honor of Jacob Milgrom*, ed. David P. Wright, David Noel Freedman, and Avi Hurvitz (Winona Lake, IN: Eisenbrauns, 1995), 421–36.

In that case, the law can be construed as welcoming the rise of a prophet who can yield a sign or a wonder (which can be regarded as divine gifts as implied in the verb נתן "give" in v. 2b; cf. 18:18). Alternatively, the combination of the two parts may communicate a case of intersectional concern about the intermediary, whose numinous performance should not cause the hearer to let his guard down. Chapter 13 evinces no effort to adjudicate between the two possible scenarios, both of which presuppose previously known or imaginable cases (as insinuated in the conjunction כי that could be construed as conditional in. 13:2a). The Masoretic scribe inserts a stroke of clarification by placing the accent of ʾatnāḥ under לאמר in v. 3, suggesting that one should pause and pay a significant amount of attention to what follows in v. 3b – to watch out for the dangerous enticement that seeks to lead the people astray to the worship of other gods.

The preventive prohibition of listening to the diviner's misleading words in v. 4 (לא תשמע "you shall not listen") recalls the *Shema* passage in 6:4 (שמע ישראל "hear, O Israel"), which prescribes proper worship. The absolute nature of the injunction in 13:4a prefaced by the negative לא in v. 4a is followed by the exposition of the spirit of the law spelled out in v. 4b, whose כי clause characterizes the crisis as a test (מנסה) designed to ascertain or bolster fidelity to God. In the MT, the second half of v. 4 shifts to the second-person plural discourse, which critics take as a sign of later interpolation added "to counter potential resistance from readers who might otherwise respect such confirmatory prophetic signs."[4] While it is tempting to interpret this as a juxtaposition of the communal charge with an individual responsibility, the fluidity of the grammatical number cannot bear the burden of such theological finesse. The use of both the singular and the plural in addressing the audience may better be explained as a speech reflex that understands Israel as a collective of individuals charged with the responsibility of keeping the law.[5] At any rate, the scribe has preserved the element of dissonance in the text instead of smoothing out other ways to read and hear the sentence.

The Deuteronomistic basis of the passage frames the charge of faithfulness as a matter of love (אהב), a term which underscores the relationship of fidelity in ancient Near East (v. 4b).[6] The love command is further qualified with the Deuteronomistic standard ("with all your heart and with all your soul," 13:4b), again recalling the *Shema* passage (see 6:5).[7] The highly recommended response

---

[4] Richard D. Nelson, *Deuteronomy*, OTL (Louisville: Westminster John Knox, 2002), 166.

[5] For the debate on the alternation between the second person singular and plural pronouns in Deuteronomy, see Edward J. Woods, *Deuteronomy*, TOTC (Downers Grove, IL: InterVarsity Press, 2011), 34–36.

[6] Jason S. DeRouchie, *A Call to Covenant Love: Text Grammar and Literary Structure in Deuteronomy 5–11*, GBibS 30 (Piscataway, NJ: Gorgias, 2014), 227–49.

[7] The triple mode of devotion in 6:5 ("with all your heart, and with all your soul, and with all your might" is found only once more in 2 Kgs 23:25, suggesting that Josiah was the only one who fully lived out the call of Deut 6:4–5 completely. In 13:4 and elsewhere, the dual ("with all heart and with all soul") is used.

in 13:5 involves both correct conduct (תלכו "walk") and proper piety (תיראו "fear"), all of which manifest themselves in the observance of commandments (ואת מצותיו תשמרו), obedience of God's voice (ובקלו תשמעו), properly directed worship (ואתו תעבדו), and abiding allegiance to God (ובו תדבקון). The community is clearly warned, and the offender faces capital punishment (v. 6; compare with Exod 19:12; 21:12, 15; Lev 20:2, 9, 10, 11; 24:16–17 et al.). Under the pain of death, the law condemns the seditious speech (דבר סרה) that entices the people of God off course (להדיחך מן הדרך; LXX ἐξῶσαί σε ἐκ τῆς ὁδοῦ, Deut 13:6). Such evil needs to be thoroughly purged (ובערת, lit. "burned," v. 6b).

The directive against the subversive speeches of a deceitful diviner in vv. 2–6 is framed as a warning to the close relative and friends in the community in vv. 7–10, evoking a picture of the problematic prophets and dream interpreters as "outsiders ... who tempt households."[8] Their status as intrusive alien elements may not necessarily establish their provenance, but their obfuscating activities effectively render them strangers to the people of God. The Deuteronomist identifies their offense with the rampant disregard for the gracious act of God, who brought them out of the bondage of slavery, causing the harm to the identity of the redeemed people of God (v. 6a).

In the cultic advisory of ch. 13, the Deuteronomist highlights the inspiring power of divination, which, fallen in wrong hands, could facilitate the grave offence of leading the people to worship other gods (vv. 3, 7, 14), echoing the Deuteronomist's overriding concern (see also 7:4; 8:19; 11:16, 28).[9] There can be no lenience for the offense committed by these no-good troublemakers (בני בליעל, 13:14). One cannot afford dismissing their act as a trivial stunt. When their offence is permitted to grow and spread, the whole town will be subjected to the sweeping purge of חרם (v. 16). The Deuteronomic law displays no prejudice against dream divination itself, however, just as it is not against prophecy. The very addition of the qualifying clause in v. 2 suggests that not all dreams are to be categorically proscribed, for "the dream might be the channel of a genuine revelation ...; [although] it might readily become a source of self-deception."[10] The Deuteronomist is wary of the potential abuse of the awe of a numinous event and names the danger in no uncertain terms, while being no less mindful of the fact that a prophet and a dreamer may display awesome supernatural power, facilitating access to the numinous encounter with God.

Even as the Deuteronomic Code cracks down on perverting prophets and depraved dreams, the Deuteronomist may have found that a dream can be as

---

[8] Don C. Benjamin, *The Social World of Deuteronomy: A New Feminist Commentary* (Eugene, OR: Cascade, 2015), 105.

[9] Rob Barrett, *Disloyalty and Destruction: Religion and Politics in Deuteronomy and the Modern World*, LHBOTS 511 (New York: T&T Clark, 2009), 128.

[10] S. R. Driver, *A Critical and Exegetical Commentary on Deuteronomy*, ICC (New York: Scribner's Sons, 1895), 151.

helpful as it is dangerous. Instead of brushing the phenomenon of dreams aside, ch. 13 elevates, in effect, the dream divination to something that can be placed on par with prophecy. The Deuteronomist's tenuous, if not Janus-faced, posture toward dreams may be compared to Arthur Schopenhauer's parable of porcupines in *Parerga and Paralipomena*, vol. 2, § 396.[11]

On a cold winter's day a community of porcupines huddled very close together to protect themselves from freezing through their mutual warmth. However, they soon felt one another's quills, which then forced them apart. Now when the need for warmth brought them closer together again, that second drawback repeated itself so that they were tossed back and forth between both kinds of suffering until they discovered a moderate distance from one another, at which they could best endure the situation. – This is how the need for society, arising from the emptiness and monotony of our own inner selves, drives people together; but their numerous repulsive qualities and unbearable flaws push them apart once again. The middle distance they finally discover and at which a coexistence is possible is courtesy and good manners. In England, anyone who does not stay at this distance is told: 'Keep your distance!' – Of course by means of this the need for mutual warmth is only partially satisfied, but in exchange the prick of the quills is not felt. – Yet whoever has a lot of his own inner warmth prefers to stay away from society in order neither to cause trouble nor to receive it.

In a comparable manner, a dream can prick when it is presented from a wrong angle. Yet, it is a human tendency to be drawn to a dream – a powerfully attractive experience that can provide a slice of a realm that one cannot access in waking. Woefully, as the Deuteronomist discerns, it can be enlisted as a harmful tool to corrupt the people of God. One can still embrace the sublime dilemma of the dreamy events while keeping abuses at bay. One may find this kind of multi-pronged posture also reflected in the dream accounts in the Deuteronomistic History.

3. Dream Divination in the Deuteronomistic Corpus

The Deuteronomistic corpus includes a small number of remarkable references to a dream or a related event. They include Judg 7; 1 Sam 3; ch. 28; and 1 Kings 3. These instances neither display any type of apprehension toward oneiromancy, nor inspire suspicion that a dream would lead to apostasy or any comparably dangerous situation as Deut 13 warns. Yet they take on a direction that is not always anticipated by the dreamer or anyone who hears of the dream. For example, while the dream remains inherently private and cannot be falsified, the dream in Judg 7 leaps from a personal plane to evolve into a force that can shape

---

[11] Arthur Schopenhauer, *Parerga and Paralipomena: Volume 2: Short Philosophical Essays*, ed. and trans. Adrian Del Caro and Christopher Janaway (Cambridge: Cambridge University Press, 2017), 691–92.

the course of history. The instance in 1 Sam 3 begins without the explicit notice of a dream, only to leave behind what must have been an auditory message dream in the night. Saul's desperate inquiry at Endor takes place where he is deprived of a dream that could have granted him access to God's pleasure or displeasure. By contrast, Solomon's famous dream at Gibeon in 1 Kings 3 serves as a halcyon event that lays out a blueprint of a dream-world under his reign.

In these intermittent reports, one may find a dream featured not so much as a celebrated means of divination as a mere narrative prop. While this subtlety makes it difficult to assess whether or how a dream lends legitimacy to the spiritual experience, the very ambiguity also serves as a witness to the way the scribe was obliged to grapple with the dream divination deeply embedded in cultural memory. Crafting the account of a dream or a comparable experience that can point beyond the immediate context of the moment, the passages in the Deuteronomistic History display how the scribe has made it amply clear that a dream can have a profound impact upon all who come into contact with it.

3.1 Dream That Led to Victory (Judges 7)

The dream report in Judg 7 has its dramatic quality intensified at a critical time that threatens the very survival of the people of Israel, although the Midianite crisis that propels Gideon to the stage is only one of the series of crises that characterize the pre-monarchic period (chs. 3–16). Squarely following the programmatic statement of 2:11–19, which serves as "an interpretive framework which not only connects but also unifies" the main bulk of the book,[12] Gideon emerges as the military leader, traditionally known as "the judge (שפט)," called in the time of emergency to deliver the people of Israel (chs. 6–7). Subsequently, inspired by Gideon's saving act, the Israelites proffer him a dynasty, but he turns it down in the name of God's kingship (8:22–23). The narrator juxtaposes his theological clarity with a set of behaviors that clash with it, however. For example, he builds a large harem (v. 30) and names his son as Abimelech (lit. "my father is king," v. 31), leaving one to wonder whether he meant what he said. Gideon's confusing behavior only "shows that though [he] refused dynastic kingship he was not opposed to receiving extra payment or the trappings of kingship."[13] In addition, he molds a golden ephod, which Israelites worship to the Deuteronomistic Historian's horror (v. 27). The narrator offers a stringent criticism on the situation, naming it as religious harlotry (ויזנו) of the people and a snare (מוקש) for Gideon and his "house" (ולביתו, a surreptitious scribal ploy that foreshadows the ill-fated "dynasty" of Gideon in ch. 9).

In an already-multifaceted story, a dream is featured to advance the plot of the narrative in ch. 7. It is not Gideon's dream, however. It is an enemy soldier's,

---

[12] Frederick E. Greenspahn, "The Theology of the Framework of Judges," *VT* 36 (1986): 385.
[13] Tammi J. Schneider, *Judges*, BeOl (Collegeville, MN: Liturgical Press, 2000), 127.

which Gideon appropriates. The motif of a borrowed – if not stolen – dream produces a literary effect that suggests that a dream is commonplace and that one does not have to actively pursue it as a means of divination. Nonetheless, the dream plays a decisive role in Gideon's triumph over the Midianites by either showing or hewing the course of the event that is about to unfold.

The account of divination on the eve of a battle is well-known in antiquity.[14] For example, a king may resort to a means of divination, such as extispicy, to learn of the outcome of the war.[15] In addition to the ritualized practice, an oracle may be secured through the accidence of overhearing, as it takes place in Judg 7 (see vv. 13, 15). Susan Niditch locates Gideon's case in the traditional context of ancient divination:

> In this passage, the symbolic dream is combined with another sort of divinatory technique, the random overhearing of a statement by a passerby that can be understood as relevant to the listener's current situation. In Greek tradition, such a form of unintentional prophecy is called the *klēdōn* (see, e.g., *Odyssey* 18.117; 20.120). Gideon has a double divinatory experience, for he hears the dream report of a passerby and another's interpretation of it; what the interpreter says applies specifically and overtly to him. A rolling loaf of bread that upends a tent is interpreted to mean that Gideon will be victorious, rolling over his enemies. The tent clearly represents enemy troops and bivouac. The term for "bread" is identical to the root for another word "to make war," so perhaps in accordance with traditional dream interpretation, word association is assumed. Through the Near East, word association, like idea association, is a common divinatory technique.[16]

In Judg 7, the dream reporter uses the formula of "dreamed a dream" (v. 13), calling attention to the way the experience can be turned into an object (cf. Gen 37:5–10; 40:5–9; 41:11–15; 42:9; Dan 2:1). Now Gideon who overhears it can take it with him. According to the dreamer's fellow solider who serves as the initial clairvoyant interpreter, the dream signifies the triumph of the Israelites over the Midianites (Judg 7:14). Gideon takes the interpretation with him, too.

The images of the dream are highly suggestive with a scene of a roll of barley bread rolling into the enemy camp of the Midianites, causing it to collapse

---

[14] Jonathan Stökl, "Divination as Warfare: The Use of Divination across Borders," in *Divination, Politics, and Ancient Near Eastern Empires*, ed. Alan Lenzi and Jonathan Stökl, ANEM 7 (Atlanta: Society of Biblical Literature, 2014), 49–63.

[15] For example, a Babylonian text of K. 4061and K. 10344 (Obv. 1'–2') offers an illustrative example that states, "If a hole lies in the middle of the right surface of the finger (referring to a part of the sheep's liver): [... ... : The enemy] will besiege the town, he will t[ake (it_), / in battle: defeat of the army, [it will rai]in, a patient will rec[over"; Nils P. Heeßel, "The Calculation of the Stipulated Term in Extispicy," in *Divination and Interpretation of Signs in the Ancient World*, ed. Amar Annus, OIS 6 (Chicago: Oriental Institute of the University of Chicago, 2010), 170; Stefan M. Maul, *The Art of Divination in the Ancient Near East: Reading the Signs of Heaven and Earth*, trans. Brian McNeil and Alexander Johannes Edmonds (Waco, TX: Baylor University Press, 2018), 20.

[16] Susan Niditch, *Judges: A Commentary*, OTL (Louisville: Westminster John Knox, 2008), 97–98.

(vv. 13–14). The dream report in v. 13 bolsters the proposed interpretation by using the verb הפך "overturn." The word is repeated in different conjugations to correlate the action of the barley bread that tumbles on its own (see the reflexive form of *mithappēk*) and what it is expected to do to the camp of Midian (ויהפכהו "and it overturned it," v. 13). The two cases of the verb הפך "overturn" not only presents a graphic portrayal of the disaster but also simulates the crushing and collapsing of the Midianite camp with the sound effect of the consonants that the verb has with the guttural sound of *h* followed by the plosive sounds of *p* and *k*. Yet, it is the dreamer's comrade who seals the deal, casting away any possibility of ambiguity by equating the roll of bread with Gideon's role in breaking the opposing army. When he returns to the camp of Israel with the dream and its interpretation, Gideon raises a battle cry (קומו "Arise!") instead of simply repeating what he heard (v. 15). The ensuring battle (vv. 15–25) enlists "the tactics of shouting and trumpet blasting, reminiscent of the battle of Jericho in Joshua 6, and the use of torches and jar smashing are suggestive of ritual action and miracle accounts."[17] The battle ends in Gideon's triumph over the Midianites in a manner that may recall the words of Octavius Caesar in William Shakespeare's *Anthony and Cleopatra*: "The breaking of so great a thing should make / A greater crack" (V.i. 14–15).

Apart from the victory that is won, Gideon's approach to a certain man's dream may sound impulsive and even outright dangerous. No general would devise a sweeping military plan based on a report of a dream that he overheard, let alone a dream that he himself may have dreamed. There is no reflection on this in the passage at least within the confined context of the story of the battle against the Midianites. Both prediction and execution are given a religious tint, for they involve not just military maneuvers but more importantly a greater power than any of those human efforts. The tacit acknowledgment that revelation does come through a dream is a telltale, albeit unobtrusive, sign of the Deuteronomist's willingness to allow space for dream divination in the construction of the Deuteronomistic theology.

3.2 Auditory Dream Theophany (1 Sam 3)

The account of 1 Sam 3 does not introduce the event as a dream, but the *mise en scène* has enough clues to warrant a close look at the passage as a case of dream theophany.[18] The formative force of the revelation is even more pronounced in this episode than in any other examples of dream reports of antiquity. The scene

---

[17] Niditch, *Judges*, 98.
[18] Robert Gnuse, "A Reconsideration of the Form-Critical Structure of I Samuel 3: An Ancient Near Eastern Dream Theophany," *ZAW* 94.3 (1982): 379–90; see also id., *The Dream Theophany of Samuel: Its Structure in Relation to Ancient Near Eastern Dreams and Its Theological Significance* (Lanham, MD: University Press of America, 1984).

includes God taking divine stand (ויתיצב, v. 10a; cf. Exod 34:5) to issue a directive that will shape the course of history. Samuel's acknowledgement in 1 Sam 3:10 completes the scene of commission, in which the king enlists the royal servant's service.

The nocturnal event takes place at a time when divine communication has become rare (יקר), implying that revelation has become precious and much desired due to its paucity.[19] In the midst of poverty of numinous manifestations, Eli and Samuel lie down to sleep (שׁכב, v. 2b and v. 3a; cf. Gen 28:11; Deut 24:12 et al). Yahweh's voice wakes up Samuel, who mistakenly assumes Eli is asking for him (1 Sam 3:4–5). Eli denies calling Samuel and instructs the child to resume his sleep (שׁוב שׁכב "return to sleep," v. 5a); so Samuel sleeps (וישׁכב, v. 5b). The subsequent event does not include a visual expression but does suggest a case of an auditory dream.[20]

The message delivered in what must have been a dream is a communication from God, as Eli discerns (vv. 8–9). While the material content of divine message delineates the demise of Eli's house, the scribal design makes the most of it to mark the transition into a new era. The auditory dream of Samuel propels him into the stage of the Deuteronomistic History as the prophet of the Lord (vv. 19–20). To confirm this, Yahweh appears again to Samuel at the sanctuary site of Shiloh, where Eli has exercised his role as the leader of Israel (v. 21).

3.3 Down to Despair (1 Sam 28)

In 1 Sam 28:3–25, Israel mourns over the death of Samuel, who is there no more to interface between God and the people. Saul's ban of various forms of mediated revelation is in effect (v. 3b). Saul's purge of mediums (אבות; LXX ἐγγαστριμύθους, "belly-talkers" or "ventriloquists")[21] and wizards (ידענים; LXX γνώστας, "knowers" or "experts"), which would be in line with the Deuteronomist's commitment to religious purity (see Deut 18:10–11), receives no adulation from the scribe who offers no explanation for Saul's measure, and Saul's decline is narrated against the backdrop of his estrangement from Samuel. Saul, who banned divination earlier, now feels the deprivation from the measure he adopted to restrict access to the otherworldly realms. Eventually, Saul's story reaches a point where there is no dream. There is only despair.

---

[19] The second half of the verse reports a comparable situation with the unavailability of the version (אין חזון נפרץ). G. R. Driver posits another root of פרץ "command" and translates "there was no vision ordained" (v. 1b; "Studies in the Vocabulary of the Old Testament III," *JTS* 32 [1931]: 365); the LXX also supports Driver's proposal: οὐκ ἦν ὅρασις διαστέλλουσα ("there was no commanding vision").

[20] Gnuse, "A Reconsideration"; id., *The Dream Theophany of Samuel*.

[21] The Greek term refers to the ancient practice of the diviner, who uses ventriloquy and speaks as if a deity speaks through them.

Even before Samuel died, Saul had already been alienated from the prophet who once anointed him as the king of Israel (10:1–8). The spiritual destitution that sets in after Samuel is gone (28:6) recalls the time before Samuel begins his ministry (3:1). Perhaps, the comparison of the two chapters (chs 3 and 28) may suggest that the situation has gotten worse. In the early days, the word of Yahweh was "rare (יקר)," and there was no vision that bursts forth (אין חזון נפרץ, 3:1). Now in ch. 28, Saul's inquiry to Yahweh goes unanswered in any of the known means including dreams, Urim, and prophets (גם בחלמות גם באורים גם בנביאם, v. 6), depicting a complete severance of divine communication. Saul experiences a blockage of revelation all around him, for "three licit means of learning Yahweh's will have all failed Saul (v. 6); these licit means are balanced in this account by three terms associated with false divination and sorcery (vv. 7–8)."[22] Out of desperation, Saul is forced to turn to the illicit means and go to Endor, the place mentioned elsewhere only in Josh 17:11 and Ps 83:11, both of which "may suggest a locality where Israelite traditions are not strong."[23] There Saul finds a medium (בעלת אוב), who the narrative soon reveals is a necromancer (1 Sam 28:11–12a). The medium of Endor along with the wise woman from Tekoa (2 Sam 13:35–14:6) and others in Joel 3:1 (ET 2:28) "channel the dead, provide counsel to their monarchs and enter trances to access the divine plane."[24]

The story unfolds in a strange dream-like séance between Saul and Solomon. Saul asks her to do קסם ("practice divination," v. 8), having been denied any access to or revelation from God. When Saul speaks to Samuel, he protests that he cannot reach God either by prophets or by dreams (v. 15b), suggesting that he has finally been given a chance to be communication with God. Samuel discounts it as a futile exercise, a mere disturbance (הרגזתני, v. 15a; from the root רגז, possibly of an onomatopoeic origin), however, Saul can only mourn over the Philistine threat and his debilitated situation caused by the blocked communication with God, who no longer answers him by any agency or means (גם ביד הנביאם גם בחלמות, "by the hand of the prophets by dreams," v. 15b).

The encounter with Samuel's ghost brings no satisfaction to Saul. Saul has sought in vain the quasi-sense of immediacy with the divine. It is appealing to ask what this episode can reveal about the practice of necromancy in Israel; however, the Deuteronomistic Historian assigns no redeeming quality to the event at Endor.[25] The upshot of the story of 1 Sam 28 is that divine message will not be available to the king who sought it desperately.

---

[22] A. Graeme Auld, *I & II Samuel: A Commentary*, OTL (Louisville: Westminster John Knox, 2011), 327.
[23] Auld, *I & II Samuel*, 326.
[24] Benjamin, *The Social World of Deuteronomy*, 124.
[25] See the series of probing questions regarding the necromancer of Endor in Esther J. Hamori, *Women's Divination in Biblical Literature: Prophecy, Necromancy, and Other Arts of Knowledge*, AYBRL (New Haven: Yale University Press, 2015), 17.

The story of Endor is a sobering, if grotesque, picture of a world where there are no more dreams and where one is forced to resort to any desperate measure to peer into the world that is not available. The oblique inclusion of the uncanny story of the medium of Endor in the Deuteronomistic History sounds a silent alarm for those who may pursue the supernatural means of receiving revelation in such a highly unorthodox means of divination. The disjunctive nature of the story whose obscurity sets it apart from the rest of 1 and 2 Samuel may have come from the scribe's tactful framing of the story as an anomaly. Eventually, the end of Saul's reign bears out the sinister implication of this incident. Saul, who has lost touch with all who could give him counsel, is bound to fall. Nonetheless, the story paradoxically hints at a certain value of a dream, especially in times of spiritual destitution, without granting it a privileged status in the religious life of Israel. Instead of revising the séance through the medium of Endor, the Chronicler curtly condemns the visit in the summative statement of the reign of Saul as a king who was unfaithful and died in unfaithfulness (1 Chr 10:13).

3.4 Dream as the Channel of Wisdom (1 Kings 3)

In 1 Kings 3, the dream takes its ordinary revealing role. Introducing the inception of a new reign, the passage reports a dream that Solomon had. It promotes the kind of rule that Solomon is expected to administer, adumbrating "the particular contours of his reign"[26] and puts forth the promise embedded in the inauguration of the new reign.

The report of dream locates it in the high place of Gibeon, "which otherwise is not held in high esteem in biblical traditions" and may have had an etiological function based on "a living memory in [the storyteller's] time that provided an explanation for presence of the unliked Gibeonites in the temple of Jerusalem."[27] The scribe is clearly conscious of the problematic nature of Solomon's worship in a high place and meticulously excuses the king with a note of exigency: it was before the temple was built in Jerusalem (v. 2). After all, the story features none other than Solomon, who "loved Yahweh, walking in the statutes of David his father" (v. 3a).

The text presents the dream at Gibeon as an event in which Solomon receives something important from God. The reception of the grant is encoded in the passive Niphal form of the verb, נראה (LXX aorist passive ὤφθη). Both the Hebrew נראה and the Greek ὤφθη often serve as a prompt-word for theophany (e.g., Gen 48:3; Exod 16:10; Num 14:10 et al). The verbal form encodes the event as a

---

[26] Gary N. Knoppers, *The Reign of Solomon and the Rise of Jeroboam*, vol. 1 of *Two Nations under God: The Deuteronomistic History of Solomon and the Dual Monarchies*, HSM (Atlanta: Scholars Press, 1993), 81–82.

[27] Niels-Peter Lemche, "Solomon as Cultural Memory," in *Remembering Biblical Figures in the Late Persian and Early Hellenistic Periods: Social Memory and Imagination*, ed. Diana V. Edelman and Ehud Ben Zvi (Oxford: Oxford University Press, 2013), 174–75.

passive transaction, but English Bibles customarily render it with the active verb like "appear." In a dream that is ordinarily understood to be a case of incubation at Gibeon, God appears, and Solomon receives God's communication.[28]

The content of the dream presents an ideal reign of Solomon over the people of Israel. The wise king's political platform will be guided by the royal לב שמע, literally "a heart that listens" (v. 9), which is commonly understood as a metaphor for "wisdom."[29] Any historian would have held this ideal not just for Solomon but also all kings. The expectation of the wise rule by a king who listens (to the voice of any party that he should heed, including the voice of the people and the counsel of wisdom) is comparable to the ethos embedded in the famous medieval *Fürstenspiegel* ("mirror of the princes"), which encourages the rulers to seek the reign of peace and justice in their domain.[30] Solomon too is on track to become a good king *par excellence* (1 Kgs 3:12), although the superlative praise may be available to more than one including Hezekiah (2 Kgs 18:5) and Josiah (23:25).[31]

Solomon's dream at Gibeon places him in a favorable light, although the references to a dream remain in the framework of the story (vv. 5, 15). The dream is virtually devoid of any symbolic features that may be expected in an incubation (cf. Gen 28:12–16). In the parallel account of the event, the Chronicler stops short of calling it a dream, but the time stamp of "in that night" (בלילה) facilitates a tentative connection with a dream divination. The Chronicler's depiction of David and Solomon indicates that this later historian's desire to cast the Judean kings in the most favorable light possible may have crowded out a chance to mention an evaluation of the dream in 1 Kings 3. Given the paucity of dream reports in the books of Deuteronomy to 2 Kings that the Chronicler could have incorporated, it is not clear exactly what the Chronicler must have thought of dream divination. The differences one can find between the two accounts may even suggest a possibility that the Chronicler's account was not a revision of

---

[28] Shaul Bar, "Incubation and Traces of Incubation in the Biblical Narrative," *OTE* 28 (2015): 244.

[29] The Septuagint translators apparently recognized the metaphorically charged expression of a "listening heart" the king desires to be able to govern God's people in the MT and elaborates as καρδίαν ἀκούειν καὶ διακρίνειν τὸν λαόν σου ἐν δικαιοσύνῃ ("a heart to listen and judge [with discernment] your people in righteousness"). The Chronicler paraphrases Solomon's petition into mundane terms: "Give me now wisdom and knowledge to go out and come in before this people, for who can rule this great people of yours?" (2 Chr 1:10).

[30] Jin H. Han, "A Heart That Listens (1 Kings 3)," in *Handbook to Asian-American Biblical Hermeneutics*, ed. Uriah Kim and Seung Ai Yang (London: T&T Clark, 2019), 256–57; for ancient kings cited in *Fürstenspiel*, see Hans Hubert Anton, ed., *Fürstenspiegel des frühen und hohen Mittelalters* (Darmstadt: Wissenschaftliche Buchgesellschaft, 2006), 15.

[31] The apparent clash has been debated among scholars; for example, see A. Graeme Auld, *Kings without Privilege: David and Moses in the Story of the Bible's Kings* (Edinburgh: T&T Clark, 1994), 105.

1 Kings 3 but that of a shared source.[32] Alternatively, in the Chronicler's History, the scribe may have found the dream a superfluous distraction, when Solomon receives "a direct revelation" from the Lord (2 Chron 1:7; 7:12–22).[33] Instead, the Chronicler turns attention from the Deuteronomistic Historian's hint of apology to the large scale of worship at Gibeon, where God's tent of meeting that originates from the time of Moses was located (1:3; see also 1 Chron 16:39; 21:29). Even before Solomon did anything, David had already provided a tent for it in Jerusalem 2 Chron(1:4, which also recalls what David did in 1 Chron 17–29 in anticipation of Solomon's temple building). The sanctuary was complete with "the bronze altar that Bezalel son of Uri, son of Hur, had made" (1:5). Now that all components of proper worship already were in place, so that Solomon had only to ascend to the altar "and offered a thousand burnt offerings on it (v. 6). In the Chronicler's History, God's nocturnal visitation to Solomon (again with the passive forms of the Niphal נראה and the Greek ὤφθη, v. 7) presents Solomon's petition for wisdom yet another virtue of a good king (v. 10).

By contrast, the Deuteronomistic Historian's account of the event places the emphasis upon royal governance so strikingly encoded in the idea of לב שמע "a heart that listens" (1 Kings 3:9).[34] Solomon gains his fame as a wise king as intimated in 1 Kings 3. But the Deuteronomistic Historian emphasizes the king's religious failings (11:1–25), and Solomon's use of corvée (4:6; 5:13, 27; 28; 9:15, 21) suggests totalitarian grip, which the elders of Israel depict as "heavy yoke" (עלו הכבד; 12:4).

A kingdom on earth may seldom experience the rule of a king who has a heart that listens in pursuit of wisdom, but Solomon's dream at Gibeon reflects the aspiration of the people who would live under a king who listens. Solomon's dream at Gibeon provides the perspicacious moment of divine immediacy when what God desires is made known.[35]

4. Dream and Divine Immediacy

The few dream reports found in the corpus of Deuteronomy to 2 Kings demonstrate that the Deuteronomistic Historian, who alerts the people of Israel to its abuse in Deut 13, did not seek to root out the practice of dream and oneiromancy

---

[32] A. Graeme Auld suggests that both come from yet another source that they shared; see "Solomon at Gibeon: History Glimpsed," in *Samuel at Threshold: Selected Works of Graeme Auld*, SOTSMS (New York: Routledge, 2016), 107.

[33] Ralph W. Klein, *2 Chronicles: A Commentary*, ed. Paul D. Hanson, Hermeneia (Minneapolis: Fortress, 2012), 23.

[34] C.L. Seow, "The Syro-Palestinian Context of Solomon's Dream," *HTR* 77 (1984): 151.

[35] Micha H. Werner, "The Immediacy of Encounter and the Dangers of Dichotomy: Buber, Levinas, and Jonas on Responsibility," in *The Legacy of Hans Jonas: Judaism and the Phenomenon of Life*, ed. Hava Tirosh-Samuelson and Christian Wiese (Leiden: Brill, 2008), 203–30.

from the life of ancient Israel. Such a heavy-handed measure would not have been practical, for people dream, and no law can shield them from the experience. The recognizable, if not prominent, status of dreams in the Deuteronomistic History is certainly different from that of other means of divination of antiquity, which are virtually unmentioned in Deuteronomy to 2 Kings and only obscurely featured in the rest of the Hebrew Bible. For example, extispicy never gains popularity in Israel, and Jeremiah's prophecy regarding the law written on human hearts only offers a minuscule possibility that the prophet may have had such a method of divination in mind (ועל לבם אכתבנה, Jer 31:33).[36] Nor does rhabdomancy receive any more than a tangential reference when the prophet condemns those who "consult a piece of wood" expecting their divining rod to yield oracles (עמי בעצו ישאל ומקלו יגיד, Hos 4:12). In contrast to these other methods of divination, a dream takes a remarkable place as a means that facilitates communion with God in the Deuteronomistic History. Elsewhere in the Bible, the dream divination is not regarded as an anomaly, either (see Gen 20:3, 6; 28:12; 31;10; 37:5, 41; Dan 2; Joel 2:28).

The Deuteronomist is clearly aware of the power of dreams: a dream could predict the future and establish the numinous nature of the event (Deut 13). The danger comes from the possibility that dreams can be utilized to lure the people away from Yahweh and Torah. In negotiating with dreams and visionary experiences, however, the Deuteronomistic Historian has left much more than a cluster of useful metaphors, although critical scholarship has often failed to see beyond "mere poetic decoration" in the ancient text, which Samuel Taylor Coleridge, the Romanticist poet of the 19th century, famously deplored.[37] Dreams have a greater role than mere curious embellishments, helping advance the narrative without assuming a prominent place in the Deuteronomistic History.

The corpus of Deuteronomy to 2 Kings is too multifaceted to be summarized by a singular theological organizing principle, but there may be a way to explain the tacit acceptance that the dream divination receives in the Deuteronomistic History whose historiography is sustained by the unwavering commitment to Torah. Diviners who utilize dreams to entice the people to worship other gods will not be tolerated, for they violate Deuteronomistic commitment to the worship of one God as laid out. For the same reason, the worship of other gods is condemned, for it leads the people of God astray from communion with God.[38] By contrast, a dream will be given a niche in cultural memory and may, if obliquely, facilitate a limited form of access to divine immediacy.

---

[36] See also William R. Stewart's article in this volume.

[37] Christopher Rowland, Patricia Gibbons, and Vicente Dobroruka, "Visionary Experience in Ancient Judaism and Christianity," in *Paradise Now: Essays on Early Jewish and Christian Mysticism*, ed. April D. DeConick, SBLSymS 11 (Atlanta: Society of Biblical Literature, 2006), 41–42.

[38] H. N. Rösel, "Does a Comprehensive 'Leitmotif' Exist in the Deuteronomistic History?" in

5. Dream Divination and Cultural Memory

While the process of formation of the Deuteronomistic History that may have affected the manner in which the dreams are reported in the collection may require further investigation, the role that dreams must have played in the life of the people of Israel can find a meaningful tool in in the notion of cultural memory. As Jan Assmann, who has pioneered the studies of cultural memory along with Aleida Assmann, puts it,

> The concept of cultural memory comprises that body of reusable texts, images, and rituals specific to each society in each epoch, whose "cultivation" serves to stabilize and convey that society's self-image. Upon such collective knowledge, for the most part (but not exclusively) of the past, each group bases its awareness of unity and particularity.[39]

As an item in cultural memory, reflections on dreams in the Deuteronomistic History also provide a tangible, if subdued, clue to the way the people of Israel gained a sense of their identity as the people who worship God with fidelity.

In their self-understanding, as the small number of passages that report dreams in the Deuteronomistic History demonstrate, the people of Israel are not encouraged to adopt dream divination as a major mode of divine communication comparable to Torah, which the Deuteronomistic Historian advocates with utmost vigor. While the Torah and Yahweh-worship are presented as the mainstay of Israel's cultural memory, the corpus of the Deuteronomistic History has provided space for the cultural memory of the dreams of the past – the dreams that revealed the path of history that one was invited to imagine and experience. In the final analysis, the Deuteronomistic History embraces dreams, while drawing a clear line that indicates where the dream divination – or any other form of divination – will not be tolerated to transgress and lure the people away from Yahweh. The discrete passages in the Deuteronomistic History can still be analyzed as a witness or a reflection of a certain historical context, and the written form of the text should continue to receive attention with respect to its literary intricacies. At the same time, the dream reports will continue to yield insights into the way a dream can be embraced as a meaningful experience within the framework of the cultural and religious identity of the people of God.

The Deuteronomistic Historian's modulated attitude to dreams is guided by the identity of the people who are mandated to worship Yahweh alone. All other experiences are to be evaluated in light of this commitment to unadulterated worship. Jan Assmann observes that this dynamic force of cultural memory that combines faithfulness and tolerance is at work in the formation of the cultural

---

The Future of the Deuteronomistic History, ed. Thomas C. Römer, BETL 147 (Leuven: Leuven University Press, 2000), 203–5.

[39] Jan Assmann, "Collective Memory and Cultural Identity," *NGC* 65 (1995): 132.

identity of the Israelites as portrayed in the Bible, and particularly in the book of Deuteronomy.

The Israelites seem to have been the discoverers or inventors of this spiritual attachment, and it was made possible through their writings. Among the much discussed consequences of the written culture, the development of an extraterritorial or spiritual living space is probably the most significant. Deuteronomy is the text that focuses on and illuminates this process by developing mnemotechnics that help to keep all the decisive bonds alive in the collective memory, irrespective of the indispensable and thus, in this sense, natural framework.[40]

The clear and yet accommodating posture one finds in the direction on dreams in Deut 13 is reflected in Jeremiah, whose connections with the Deuteronomistic tradition have been vigorously debated among scholars. While it is hard to reconstruct the exact nature or chronology of Jeremiah's association with Josiah, Jeremiah's theology shows affinities with the Deuteronomistic platform of Josiah's reform, including the prophet's remembrance of Josiah as a king who did justice and righteousness (Jer 22:15; cf. 2 Chron 35:25). The compositional and redactional processes that have yielded the present form of the book of Jeremiah display no integrated effort to ban dreams. Jeremiah's posture to dreams is in consonance with the Deuteronomist's position of banning the dream and dreams that lure the people into the worship of other gods. Jeremiah also associates the dream diviners with false prophets in Jer 23:25–32; 27:9; 29:8–9. Considered in isolation, 23:28 seems to clearly privilege the oracular revelation over the dream divination, comparing the latter to straw, and the former to wheat. The thrust of the chapter, however, drives the polemic against the false prophets who promise hope and monger peace "when there is no peace" (6:14; 8:11; 28:9). In ch. 23, the scribal composition of the chapter makes it clear that Jeremiah's grievance is not with those who dream and practice dream divination but with those who falsely claim that their dreams came from Yahweh.[41]

Like other prophets, Jeremiah also receives visions (e.g., chs. 1, 24). It is not to dreams and other numinous experiences but to "lying dreams" (חלמות שקר, 23:32) that Jeremiah is opposed. The issue is "not the method in itself," and "dreams were not in themselves to be rejected as a way God could speak."[42] Jeremiah's seemingly lopsided polemic is best understood as a response to "the

---

[40] Jan Assmann, *Cultural Memory and Early Civilization: Writing, Remembrance, and Political Imagination* (Cambridge: Cambridge University Press, 2011), 192–93.

[41] One may compare this to Jeremiah's temple sermon in ch. 7. Jeremiah's declaration ("Do not trust in these deceptive words: 'This is the temple of the Lord, the temple of the Lord, the temple of the Lord'") is not an attack on the temple but on an attempt "to put one's security in such words" (William L. Holladay, *Jeremiah 1: A Commentary on the Book of the Prophet Jeremiah Chapters 1–25*, ed. Paul D. Hanson, Hermeneia (Philadelphia: Fortress, 1986, 242).

[42] Christopher J. H. Wright, *The Message of Jeremiah: Against Wind and Tide* (Downers Grove, IL: InterVarsity Press, 2014), 253.

popularity of dream revelations [that] evidently posed a greater threat."[43] Although this type of rhetorical slant is not unattested to in oral speeches, the scribe is obliged to depend on it without having oratorical cadence unavailable for a written text. When he denounces practitioners of divination in 27:9, the prophet includes dreamers, but his denunciation is not on the modes of divination but on the presumptuous utterance (see also Deut 18:20). In Jer 29:8–9, the prophet's warning is also not so much about the type of revelation as about the deceptive nature of the message the prophets and diviners advance to argue for an imminent return of those who were taken to Babylon in exile in 597 BCE. Jeremiah's concern is consonant with the Deuteronomist's warning in Deut 13, which is wary of what appears to be the work of a true prophet but lures the people's attention from its proper focus.

Unlike the endeavor of historical reconstruction, dreams can only be studied as imagined, for a question of falsifiability is foregone due to the nature of the experience. Nor is it to be categorized as creative literature whose only requirement is verisimilitude. Yet dreams can certainly be analyzed in terms of their effect on the communal identity. This is precisely the area where cultural memory can be invoked, for its "task … is to transmit a collective identity with all its norms and values,"[44] enabling the researcher to seek how it shapes the self-awareness of the identity of those to whom the content or pieces are bequeathed in remembrance. As artefacts of cultural memory, the dream reports can serve as what Pierre Nora calls *lieux de mémoire* (sites of memory), which carry cultural memory on, even after the historical course is either blurred or forgotten.[45] Such an exercise of cultural memory facilitates the construction of "'identity' on an individual and in particular on a collective level."[46]

6. Conclusion

Various scenarios regarding the provenance and progress of the collection of the books in the Deuteronomistic History have traversed through colorful trajectories and continue to produce many vehemently debated issues.[47] The

---

[43] Leslie C. Allen, *Jeremiah: A Commentary*, OTL (Louisville: Westminster John Knox, 2008), 271.

[44] Jan Assmann, "Introduction: What Is 'Cultural Memory'?" in *Religion and Cultural Memory: Ten Studies* (Stanford, CA: Stanford University Press, 2006), 6–7.

[45] See Pierre Nora, "Between Memory and History: *Les Lieux de Mémoire*," *Representations* 26 (1989): 7–9; he maintains that a *lieu de mémoire* can be a "purely material site, like an archive … with a symbolic aura" or "a purely functional site, like a classroom manual [or] a testament" (ibid., 18–20).

[46] Aleida Assmann, "Transformations between History and Memory," *SR* 75 (2008): 54–55.

[47] For evaluation of major proposals along with areas of suggested further research, see Thomas Römer and Albert de Pury, "Deuteronomistic Historiography (DH): History of

Deuteronomistic History as a defensible literary corpus, although its cohesion cannot be established with certainty, hints at the cultural dynamics that contribute to the construction of the identity of the people of Israel. It incorporates certain elements of religious practices like dream divination with a caveat that the purity of worship should be safeguarded. The latitude toward dreams preserved in cultural memory within the perimeters of the uncompromised worship of God highlights an important legacy of balancing what persists from the past religious experience of the people with the overarching commitment to Torah in the religious life of the people of Israel, who love God with all their heart, and with all their soul, and with all their might.

Bibliography

Allen, Leslie C. *Jeremiah: A Commentary*. OTL. Louisville: Westminster John Knox, 2008.
Anton, Hans Hubert, ed. *Fürstenspiegel des frühen und hohen Mittelalters*. Darmstadt: Wissenschaftliche Buchgesellschaft, 2006.
Assmann, Aleida. "Transformations between History and Memory." *SR* 75 (2008): 49–72.
Assmann, Jan. "Collective Memory and Cultural Identity." *NGC* 65 (1995): 125–33.
Assmann, Jan. *Cultural Memory and Early Civilization: Writing, Remembrance, and Political Imagination*. Cambridge: Cambridge University Press, 2011.
Assmann, Jan. "Introduction: What Is 'Cultural Memory'?" Pages 1–30 in *Religion and Cultural Memory: Ten Studies*. Stanford, CA: Stanford University Press, 2006.
Auld, A. Graeme. *I & II Samuel: A Commentary*. OTL. Louisville: Westminster John Knox, 2011.
Auld, A. Graeme. *Kings without Privilege: David and Moses in the Story of the Bible's Kings*. Edinburgh: T&T Clark, 1994.
Auld, A. Graeme. "Solomon at Gibeon: History Glimpsed." Pages 87–108 in *Samuel at Threshold: Selected Works of Graeme Auld*. SOTSMS. New York: Routledge, 2016.
Bar, Shaul. "Incubation and Traces of Incubation in the Biblical Narrative." *OTE* 28 (2015): 243–56.
Barrett, Rob. *Disloyalty and Destruction: Religion and Politics in Deuteronomy and the Modern World*. LHBOTS 511. New York: T&T Clark, 2009.
Benjamin, Don C. *The Social World of Deuteronomy: A New Feminist Commentary*. Eugene, OR: Cascade, 2015.
DeRouchie, Jason S. *A Call to Covenant Love: Text Grammar and Literary Structure in Deuteronomy 5–11*. GBibS 30. Piscataway, NJ: Gorgias, 2014.
Driver, G. R. "Studies in the Vocabulary of the Old Testament III." *JTS* 32 (1931): 361–66.
Driver, S. R. *A Critical and Exegetical Commentary on Deuteronomy*. ICC. New York: Scribner's Sons, 1895.
Gnuse, Robert. "A Reconsideration of the Form-Critical Structure in I Samuel 3: An Ancient Near Eastern Dream Theophany." *ZAW* 94.3 (1982): 379–90.

Research and Debated Issues," in *Israel Constructs Its History: Deuteronomistic Historiography in Recent Research*, ed. Albert de Pury, Thomas Römer, and Jean-Daniel Macchi, JSOTSup 306 (Sheffield: Sheffield Academic, 2000), 24–141.

Gnuse, Robert. *The Dream Theophany of Samuel: Its Structure in Relation to Ancient Near Eastern Dreams and Its Theological Significance*. Lanham, MD: University Press of America, 1984.

Greenspahn, Frederick E. "The Theology of the Framework of Judges." *VT* 36 (1986): 385–96.

Hamori, Esther J. *Women's Divination in Biblical Literature: Prophecy, Necromancy, and Other Arts of Knowledge*. AYBRL. New Haven: Yale University Press, 2015.

Han, Jin H. "A Heart That Listens (1 Kings 3)." Pages 252–60 in *Handbook to Asian-American Biblical Hermeneutics*. Edited by Uriah Kim and Seung Ai Yang. London: T&T Clark, 2019.

Heeßel, Nils P. "The Calculation of the Stipulated Term in Extispicy." Pages 163–76 in *Divination and Interpretation of Signs in the Ancient World*. Edited by Amar Annus. OIS 6. Chicago: Oriental Institute of the University of Chicago, 2010.

Holladay, William L. *Jeremiah 1: A Commentary on the Book of the Prophet Jeremiah Chapters 1–25*. Edited by Paul D. Hanson. Hermeneia. Philadelphia: Fortress, 1986.

Kamrada, Dolores G. "Urim and Thummim." Pages 267–89 in *Cultural Memory in Biblical Exegesis*. Edited by Pernille Carstens, Trine Bjørnung Hasselbach, and Niels Peter Lemche. PHSC 17. Piscataway, NJ: Gorgias, 2012.

Klein, Ralph W. *2 Chronicles: A Commentary*. Edited by Paul D. Hanson. Hermeneia. Minneapolis: Fortress, 2012.

Knoppers, Gary N. *The Reign of Solomon and the Rise of Jeroboam*. Vol. 1 of *Two Nations under God: The Deuteronomistic History of Solomon and the Dual Monarchies*. HSM. Atlanta: Scholars Press, 1993.

Lemche, Niels-Peter. "Solomon as Cultural Memory." Pages 158–81 in *Remembering Biblical Figures in the Late Persian and Early Hellenistic Periods: Social Memory and Imagination*. Edited by Diana V. Edelman and Ehud Ben Zvi. Oxford: Oxford University Press, 2013.

Maul, Stefan M. *The Art of Divination in the Ancient Near East: Reading the Signs of Heaven and Earth*. Translated by Brian McNeil and Alexander Johannes Edmonds. Waco, TX: Baylor University Press, 2018.

Nelson, Richard D. *Deuteronomy*. OTL. Louisville: Westminster John Knox, 2002.

Niditch, Susan. *Judges: A Commentary*. OTL. Louisville: Westminster John Knox, 2008.

Nora, Pierre. "Between Memory and History: *Les Lieux de Mémoire*." *Representations* 26 (1989): 7–24.

Patrick, Dale. "The Rhetoric of Collective Responsibility in Deuteronomic Law." Pages 421–36 in *Pomegranates and Golden Bells: Studies in Biblical, Jewish, and Near Eastern Ritual, Law, and Literature in Honor of Jacob Milgrom*. Edited by David P. Wright, David Noel Freedman, and Avi Hurvitz. Winona Lake, IN: Eisenbrauns, 1995.

Römer, Thomas, and Albert de Pury. "Deuteronomistic Historiography (DH): History of Research and Debated Issues." Pages 24–141 in *Israel Constructs Its History: Deuteronomistic Historiography in Recent Research*. Edited by Albert de Pury, Thomas Römer, and Jean-Daniel Macchi. JSOTSup 306. Sheffield: Sheffield Academic, 2000.

Rösel, H. N. "Does a Comprehensive 'Leitmotif' Exist in the Deuteronomistic History?" Pages 203–5 in *The Future of the Deuteronomistic History*. Edited by Thomas C. Römer. BETL 147. Leuven: Leuven University Press, 2000.

Rowland, Christopher, Patricia Gibbons and Vicente Dobroruka. "Visionary Experience in Ancient Judaism and Christianity." Pages 41–56 in *Paradise Now: Essays on Early*

Jewish and Christian Mysticism. Edited by April D. DeConick. SBLSymS 11. Atlanta: Society of Biblical Literature, 2006.
Schneider, Tammi J. *Judges*. BeOl. Collegeville, MN: Liturgical Press, 2000.
Schopenhauer, Arthur. *Parerga and Paralipomena: Volume 2: Short Philosophical Essays*. Edited and translated by Adrian Del Caro and Christopher Janaway. Cambridge: Cambridge University Press, 2017.
Seow, C. L. "The Syro-Palestinian Context of Solomon's Dream." *HTR* 77 (1984): 141–52.
Stewart, William R. "The Death of the Prophet? A Comparative Study of Prophetic Signs in the Royal Archives of Mari, Syria (ARM 26/1.206) and the Hebrew Bible (Jeremiah 19:1–13)." Within this volume.
Stökl, Jonathan. "Divination as Warfare: The Use of Divination across Borders." Pages 49–63 in *Divination, Politics, and Ancient Near Eastern Empires*. Edited by Alan Lenzi and Jonathan Stökl. ANEM 7. Atlanta: Society of Biblical Literature, 2014.
Thelle, Rannfrid I. *Approaches to the 'Chosen Place': Accessing a Biblical Concept*. LHBOTS 564. London: T&T Clark, 2012.
Werner, Micha H. "The Immediacy of Encounter and the Dangers of Dichotomy: Buber, Lavinia's, and Jonas on Responsibility." Pages 203–30 in *The Legacy of Hans Jonas: Judaism and the Phenomenon of Life*. Edited by Hava Tirosh-Samuelson and Christian Wiese. Leiden: Brill, 2008.
Woods, Edward J. *Deuteronomy*. TOTC. Downers Grove, IL: InterVarsity Press, 2011.
Wright, Christopher J. H. *The Message of Jeremiah: Against Wind and Tide*. Downers Grove, IL: InterVarsity Press, 2014.

Regathering Too Many Stones?
Scribal Constraints, Community Memory, and the 'Problem' of Elijah's Sacrifice for Deuteronomism in Kings*

Benjamin D. Giffone

1. Introduction

In this essay I attempt a modest contribution to the discussions surrounding scribal culture and the making of the Hebrew Bible. While much remains unknown about the specific circumstances of production and promulgation of biblical texts, our conjectures can become more refined as more becomes known generally about the Persian period and the production and use of texts in oral cultures.

Modern redaction criticism has sought to discern editorial seams in the texts and to identify possible sources through differences in style, vocabulary, theology/ideology, and other features. While these sorts of approaches have a great deal of heuristic value, at times a necessary next step goes overlooked: suggesting plausible reasons why – and means by which – a text was brought together into its extant form. Put more simply: we can often account for the pieces, but not always for the whole.

This study is an attempt to account for one piece, 1 Kings 17–19, in relation to the whole of the book of Kings. Previous studies have emphasized either these chapters' consistency with the rest of Kings (some pre-modern and contemporary interpreters of a traditional bent), or rather a divergent outlook in these chapters that belongs to a context earlier or later than much of the rest of the book of Kings (or a so-called Deuteronomistic History). In other words: some attempt to harmonize 1 Kings 17–19 with Kings; others regard it as either pre- or post-Deuteronomistic.

In a sense, my approach is an attempt at harmonization, but on different grounds than that of traditional interpreters. Rather, we must move beyond the questions of the order in which the pieces were created, to the question of a

---

* I am most grateful for a research grant from the Department of Higher Education and Training (South Africa) and travel support from LCC International University that allowed me to present this paper at the November 2018 meeting of the Institute for Biblical Research (Denver, CO). Gary Schnittjer, Michael Cox, and Kristin Weingart provided invaluable feedback on drafts of this paper at various stages, though I remain solely responsible for its shortcomings.

plausible context in which the recognizable pieces would have been combined into the present work we call "Kings" with its overall outlook that we might choose to call "Deuteronomistic" (or not). We presume that those who put forward a particular text such as Kings wanted to achieve *something* with this work, in a context of divergent beliefs and identities in Persian-era Yehud. In this view, terms such as "compromise," "consensus" or "consensus-building," "balancing," and "identity negotiation" might be used to describe the intention of authors, *authorizers*, or *storymakers*. Such storymakers were constrained by community memory and the desire to balance competing aims in their own circle.

One problematic aspect of 1 Kings 17–19 that has led to its assignment to various redactional stages is its apparent acceptance of multiple Yahwistic cultic centers, which would seem to be at odds with "Deuteronomistic" theology of centralization. I suggest that the prospect of incorporating 1 Kings 17–19 into the larger work entailed sufficient theological "rewards" greater than the "risks" – risks which were then creatively mitigated by the editors/redactors of Kings, yet within constraints of community memory.

My proposal has implications for our understanding of the development of a so-called "Deuteronomistic History" and the relationship of Northern Israelite traditions to the primarily Judah- and Levi-centered texts of the Hebrew Bible in their final forms. The final editorial hand exhibits a certain sophistication in balancing two notions: that Jerusalem is the special place where YHWH's name dwells, and that YHWH is the proper deity for Northern Israelites to worship. In adopting material from a Northern Israelite source, the storymakers assert that these ideas are complementary, not mutually exclusive – while cleverly excluding Mount Carmel as a legitimate place for YHWH worship in their own Babylonian- and Persian-era contexts.

2. The Deuteronomistic History and the "Trouble with Kings"

The compositional history of the book of Kings and its relation to a "Deuteronomistic History" or an "Enneateuch" are the subject of much debate.[1] Particularly relevant to the issue at hand is the question of whether the colorful Northern pro-

---

[1] Examples include: Thomas B. Dozeman, ed., *Pentateuch, Hexateuch, or Enneateuch: Identifying Literary Works in Genesis through Kings*, AIL 8 (Atlanta: Society of Biblical Literature, 2011); Reinhard Müller, Juha Pakkala, and Bas ter Haar Romeny, *Evidence of Editing: Growth and Change of Texts in the Hebrew Bible*, RBS 75 (Atlanta: Society of Biblical Literature, 2014); Thomas Römer, "The Case of the Book of Kings," in *Deuteronomy–Kings as Emerging Authoritative Books: A Conversation*, ed. Diana V. Edelman, ANEM 6 (Atlanta: Society of Biblical Literature, 2014), 187–201; Juha Pakkala, "Deuteronomy and 1–2 Kings in the Redaction of the Pentateuch and Former Prophets," in *Deuteronomy in the Pentateuch, the Hexateuch, and the Deuteronomistic History*, ed. Konrad Schmid and Raymond F. Person Jr., FAT II 56 (Tübingen: Mohr Siebeck, 2012), 133–62.

phet stories, including 1 Kings 17–19, are understood as pre- or post-Deuteronomistic incorporations into the book of Kings.

In the earliest decades of the broad acceptance of Noth's "Deuteronomistic History" thesis, it was more common to consider the Elijah–Elisha prophet cycles as having been incorporated by a Deuteronomistic editor.[2] That understanding has now come into question, as a number of scholars have designated such stories, including 1 Kings 17–19, as post-Deuteronomistic additions.[3]

These disputes are significant, though they are partly due to different understandings of the terms "editors" and "redactors," "Deuteronomists," and "Deuteronomism." I think it likely that the text that became 1 Kings 17–19 arose in a pre-Deuteronomistic situation – that is, a situation in which multiple Yahwistic cultic centers were widely accepted.

However, the problem that Elijah's sacrifice at Carmel presents in the received text is not very different whether 1 Kings 17–19 is understood as pre- or post-Deuteronomistic. While there are other possibilities, we can simply contrast the implications of the two options. In one scenario, a group of editors/redactors utilized Northern Israelite traditions when composing the book of Kings; those editors are what we might call "Deuteronomists." In the second scenario, a group of editors/redactors incorporated Northern prophet traditions into a previously-existing "Deuteronomistic History," which included material from what we call the book of Kings. Either way, the question of narrative and theological consistency that drives modern redactional study remains. Whether we call them "Deuteronomists" or not, how did the editors who put the final touches on the book of Kings justify Elijah's actions in 1 Kings 18? Given what we think we know of the scribal communities who "finalized" most of the texts of the Hebrew Bible, it seems quite likely that they would have affirmed Jerusalem centralization and some form of Levitical cultic oversight. What then, are the storymakers doing with 1 Kings 17–19 in the final form of the book? Do these texts indeed present a

---

[2] Jeremy M. Hutton, *The Transjordanian Palimpsest: The Overwritten Texts of Personal Exile and Transformation in the Deuteronomistic History*, BZAW 396 (Berlin: de Gruyter, 2009), 79; Antony F. Campbell, *Of Prophets and Kings*, CBQMS 17 (Washington, DC: Catholic Biblical Association of America, 1986); Nadav Na'aman, "Prophetic Stories as Sources for the Histories of Jehoshaphat and the Omrides," *Bib* 78 (1997): 153–73. See the helpful survey of opinions in Susanne Otto, "The Composition of the Elijah–Elisha Stories and the Deuteronomistic History," *JSOT* 27.4 (2003): 487–508.

[3] Otto, "The Composition of the Elijah–Elisha Stories"; Thomas C. Römer, *The So-Called Deuteronomistic History: A Sociological, Historical and Literary Introduction* (New York: T&T Clark, 2007), 103, 153–54; Steven L. McKenzie, *The Trouble with Kings: The Composition of the Book of Kings in the Deuteronomistic History*, VTSup 42 (Leiden: Brill, 1991), 81–87; Juha Pakkala, "Die Entwicklung der Gotteskonzeptionen in den deuteronomistischen Redaktionen von polytheistischen zu monotheistischen Vorstellungen," in *Die deuteronomistischen Geschichtswerke: Redaktions- und religionsgeschichtliche Perspektiven zur "Deuteronomismus"-Diskussion in Tora und Vorderen Propheten*, ed. Markus Witte et al., BZAW 365 (Berlin: de Gruyter, 2006), 243.

problem for Jerusalem centralization? What might be the other goals of including these narratives, and how are they balanced with one another?

3. The Problem: Approved Sacrifice Outside Jerusalem

Thus far we have only alluded to the problems with 1 Kings 17–19. A layperson might understandably protest that only a biblical scholar could find theological inconsistency in the chapters surrounding Elijah's sacrifice on Mount Carmel. A face-value reading of the narrative yields a straightforward significance and meaning: the sacrifice proves the existence of YHWH as the one true deity, overagainst Ba'al.

But the question is warranted by the literary context of this episode in the book of Kings. While there are various definitions of "Deuteronomism" and many opinions about the notion of a Deuteronomistic editorial hand in the Former Prophets (and at which stages of development), it is widely accepted that one of the hallmarks of these texts is an emphasis on centralizing cultic activity in "the place which YHWH will choose to set his name to dwell there" (Deut 12:11 ff.).[4] This turns out to be Jerusalem as the story unfolds; David "completes" the conquest of Canaan by capturing Jebus/Jerusalem and brings the ark of God there (2 Sam 5–6). I have argued elsewhere that the Deuteronomist and the Chronicler[5] have a nuanced disagreement over the proper centralized location for sacrifice during the time that the ark is in Jerusalem and the tabernacle/tent of meeting is elsewhere, until both are consolidated into the new temple (1 Kgs 8 // 2 Chr 5).[6] But after the Jerusalem temple is built, it is clear that Jerusalem is considered by the Deuteronomist (and by the Chronicler) to be the proper cultic center, even for Northern Israelites after YHWH orchestrates the division of the kingdom (1 Kgs 12:21–33).

The stories of the kings of Greater Israel, Northern Israel, and the Kingdom of Judah comprise the basic narrative of the book of Kings. The succession formula typically includes a moral assessment of the king's reign, stating whether he did what was "upright" or "evil" in YHWH's sight, and laying out his moral achievements and failures. One key criterion of assessment is whether the king tolerated or removed the "high places," which, in the view of the storymakers,

---

[4] Norbert F. Lohfink, "Was There a Deuteronomistic Movement?" in *Those Elusive Deuteronomists: The Phenomenon of Pan-Deuteronomism*, ed. Linda S. Schearing and Steven L. McKenzie, JSOTSup 268 (Sheffield: Sheffield Academic, 1999), 41.

[5] The occasional use in this paper of the singular – "the Deuteronomist," "the Chronicler," and "the storymaker" – is for simplicity's sake, not to imply a single authorial or editorial hand in either work. However, it will become apparent that I do presume some level of unified intentionality in the final editorial layer of the received texts.

[6] Benjamin D. Giffone, "According to Which 'Law of Moses'? Cult Centralization in Samuel, Kings and Chronicles," *VT* 67 (2017): 432–47.

were used for both YHWH worship and the worship of other deities.[7] Jeroboam is castigated for building an altar to YHWH (no other deity is mentioned in 1 Kgs 13) at Bethel, despite the well-documented pedigree of Bethel as a cultic site (Gen 12:8; 13:3–4; 28:18–19; 35; Jdg 20:18, 26; 1 Sam 7:16). Jerusalem is considered the only valid cultic location, because it is "the city which YHWH had chosen from all the tribes of Israel to put his name there" (1 Kgs 14:21).

So, why does the storymaker of 1 Kings 18 find it acceptable for Elijah to offer a burnt offering (עולה) at Mount Carmel? Furthermore, why was it permissible for Elijah, "a Tishbite of Gilead" (1 Kgs 17:1) – who was not an Aaronide priest or even a Levite – to officiate at the sacrifice? Elijah is clearly the officiating priest at the sacrifice at Carmel: building the altar, arranging the wood, slaughtering the ox (18:30–33). He has no assistant, emphasizing that he alone is left as prophet of YHWH (18:22). Not only does he offer an עולה at a location other than Jerusalem, he deliberately *re*-builds a YHWH altar, establishing continuity with (and thereby affirming) previous YHWH worship at Carmel (18:30, 32).

Elijah certainly does not go as far as Jeroboam in establishing a new ritual calendar and using images (1 Kgs 12:28–33).[8] In the context of 1 Kings 17–19, the storymakers approve of Elijah's actions, as YHWH validates his prophetic and priestly activities by consuming the sacrifice with fire from heaven (18:38). Moreover, Elijah's lament over the destruction of YHWH's altars throughout Israel (1 Kgs 19:10, 14) seems to express the original storymakers' acceptance of multiple cultic sites.

3.1 Traditional Justifications, Redaction-Critical Explanations

The potentially problematic nature of Elijah's actions at Mount Carmel has not been lost on biblical interpreters. Various explanations have been proposed to deal with Elijah's non-Deuteronomistic cultic activity. Interpreters who generally presume that the biblical texts must exhibit internal theological coherence have sought to justify Elijah's actions by harmonizing his activities with other biblical texts. Modern critical interpreters consider the problem to be evidence of a composite text, and debate the story's origin as well as when and why it came to

---

[7] For our purposes, it is more significant that the storymakers *believed* that high places were universally used for the worship of other deities (alongside or in place of YHWH), than whether specific high places were *in fact* used to worship deities other than YHWH.

[8] Sweeney suggests that the festival of Sukkot is the best fit for Elijah's sacrifice: "The absence of rain and other features of the sacrifice indicate that the offerings here are constructed as offerings required for the observance of Sukkot, which marks the end of the dry summer and the beginning of the rainy season in ancient (and modern) Israel"; Marvin A. Sweeney, "Prophets and Priests in the Deuteronomistic History: Elijah and Elisha," in *Israelite Prophecy and the Deuteronomistic History: Portrait, Reality, and the Formation of a History*, ed. Mignon R. Jacobs and Raymond F. Person Jr., AIL 14 (Atlanta: Society of Biblical Literature, 2013), 35–49 (38). But there is no evidence in the text that the offering occurs at Sukkot, which would have been simple to clarify.

be incorporated into the book of Kings (and a so-called Deuteronomistic History).

The "special circumstance" or "one-off" justification is that Elijah's action is a uniquely sanctioned event that demonstrates YHWH's superiority to Baʻal in an emergency situation. This explanation is offered to justify both Elijah's lack of Levitical pedigree and the non-Jerusalem sacrifice: "Rabbinic exegetes defended the building of the altar as a 'temporary regulation,' suspending the regulation of Deut 12 because of the emergency situation (see, e. g., *b. Yebam.* 90b; Qimḥi) ..."[9] The difficulty with the "one-off" explanation is that there is no such explanation or defense of Elijah given in the text. The storymakers could have provided something like the embarrassed explanation of Solomon's sacrifice at the Gibeon high place (1 Kgs 3:15)[10] – for example, "Now, Elijah used to sacrifice at the temple in Jerusalem, and henceforth only offered burnt offerings at the house of God that Solomon had built." But no such explanation is offered. Furthermore, this explanation fails to explain 1 Kings 18:30, 19:10, and 19:14, which imply that there had been Yahwistic altars at Carmel and other locations in Israel (and Judah) which had been torn down – the implication being that they should *not* have been torn down.

A second justification, which we might call the "Baʻal's home-field advantage" explanation, is that it was fitting to conduct the sacrifice at Mount Carmel in order to demonstrate YHWH's superiority over Baʻal (or to demonstrate Baʻal's non-existence), either because Mount Carmel was a prominent Baʻal cultic site, or because it was on the border between Phoenicia and Israel (thus representing the struggle with the cult introduced by Jezebel).[11] This explanation has some merit. Elsewhere in Kings, YHWH moves outside of his usual domain in order to demonstrate his superiority over other deities in locations that were supposed to be favorable for those other deities.[12] However, while providing an apt explanation of the irony that gives the narrative its meaning, this justification fails

---

[9] Mordechai Cogan, *1 Kings: A New Translation with Introduction and Commentary*, AB (New York: Doubleday, 2001), 442.

[10] See the contrast between 1 Kgs 3:3–4 and 2 Chr 1:3 in Giffone, "According to Which 'Law of Moses,'" 439–40, 443.

[11] "For Jezebel and her Phoenician family, Mount Carmel was no ordinary worship site but an important Baal sanctuary. This, of course, has a powerful influence on the way the prophets of Baal perceived Mount Carmel. Elijah had challenged them to demonstrate the power of Baal on precisely the piece of ground they presumed to have an advantage. Although an altar to the LORD had stood here in an earlier period, that altar had been destroyed. Thus while both the LORD and Baal had made a claim on this mountain, the ruined altar of the Israelite God made it clear who was king of this hill. It belonged to Baal. And the duel with Elijah was to occur on their home field." John A. Beck, "Geography as Irony: The Narrative-Geographical Shaping of Elijah's Duel with the Prophets of Baal (1 Kings 18)," *SJOT* 17.2 (2003): 298–99.

[12] In 1 Kings 20:13–30, YHWH (somewhat reluctantly) gives Ahab victory over the Arameans, because the Arameans had made the mistake of reasoning that YHWH as a mountain deity would not be able to give the Israelites victory on the plains, where their god had the advantage.

to explain a key detail. Beck rightly observes that Ba'al's defeat on his own sacred ground was greater than a defeat on neutral ground would have been.[13] For this reason, highlighting the previously-existing YHWH altar at Mount Carmel has the effect of diminishing YHWH's victory. Had the storymakers omitted the detail of the "altar that had been torn down," YHWH's glorious victory over Ba'al would actually be enhanced, as if YHWH had no previous connection to this location. In fact, there is no other biblical tradition of a YHWH altar at Mount Carmel,[14] so this detail would seem to be not only superfluous but troublesome.

Finally, it could be argued that the description, "the Tishbite, of the settlers of Gilead" (אליהו התשבי מתשבי גלעד, 1 Kgs 17:1[15]) at least leaves open the possibility that Elijah was a sojourning Levite – though not an Aaronide priest according to Deuteronomistic logic, since Aaron and his sons were allotted cities in Judah, Benjamin and Simeon (Josh 21:4–19). As is well known, the narrative contains numerous suggestive parallels to the lives of Moses and Aaron. But if the audience might have been troubled by a non-Levite officiating a sacrifice, Elijah's identity would have been relatively easy to clarify, or else the seemingly superfluous detail of Elijah's Manassite identity could have been omitted altogether.[16]

Each of these strategies for explaining Elijah's "illegal" activities was available to the storymakers of 1 Kings 17–19, who presumably could have achieved a more theologically consistent text without too much effort. Apparently, these details were not troublesome enough to prompt relatively easy editorial solutions. Other explanations for these phenomena must also be sought.

For readers who consider the theological coherence of the book of Kings to be a secondary concern or merely an open question, the solution to the "problem"

---

[13] "A defeat on this sacred ground was a more powerful defeat than one that would have occurred on more neutral ground. If Baal is unable to prove himself on this sacred ground, then where could his power be demonstrated?" Beck, "Geography as Irony," 299.

[14] Henry O. Thompson, "Carmel, Mount," *ABD* I.874–75.

[15] The LXX parallels the MT quite closely, the only plus being that Elijah was a "prophet": Ηλειού ὁ προφήτης ὁ Θεσβείτης ἐκ Θεσβῶν τῆς Γαλααδ.

[16] Regarding Elijah's identity as "a Tishbite, from the settlers of Gilead" – that is, not a Levite – this detail could perhaps have been omitted so as to leave open the possibility that Elijah was an Aaronide (or at least, a sojourning Levite). By comparison, the Chronicler "grafts" the Josephite prophet Samuel (1 Sam 1:1) into the line of Aaron, and the Kenizzite Caleb into the line of Judah in order to justify their specific roles in source narratives; presumably the storymakers of Kings could have done something similar for Elijah had they perceived the need to do so. See Gary A. Rendsburg, "The Internal Consistency and Historical Reliability of the Biblical Genealogies," *VT* 40 (1990): 197n25; Thomas Willi, "Late Persian Judaism and Its Conception of an Integral Israel According to Chronicles: Some Observations on Form and Function of the Genealogy of Judah in 1 Chronicles 2.3–4.23," in *Second Temple Studies 2: Temple Community in the Persian Period*, ed. Tamara C. Eskenazi and Kent H. Richards, JSOTSup 175 (Sheffield: Sheffield Academic, 1994), 159–60; Benjamin D. Giffone, *'Sit At My Right Hand': The Chronicler's Portrait of the Tribe of Benjamin in the Social Context of Yehud*, LHBOTS 628 (London: T&T Clark, 2016), 146–48.

is quite simple: the text is composite, with Elijah's sacrifice serving "as a marker of the pre-Deuteronomistic era, when multiple altars were the rule."[17]

There is nearly unanimous agreement that the Elijah–Elisha narratives in Kings were drawn from earlier Northern Israelite traditions, and incorporated after the fall of the Northern Kingdom – the debate is over precisely when and by whom. Due to the Northern provenance of the stories, the characters in the narratives are not consistently held to "Deuteronomistic" standards of behavior, not unlike the characters found in stories with Northern and Benjaminite origins in Judges and Samuel, in which prophets and "men of God" feature prominently and receive direct revelation (i.e., not guided by written "Law").[18] Elsewhere in the Former Prophets, it becomes obvious that neither Priestly nor Deuteronomistic cultic standards are strictly applied by the storymakers, with regard to what portions of sacrifices are eaten and also who conducts the sacrifice. Samuel, an Ephraimite (1 Sam 1:1), takes the priestly mantle from Eli, an Aaronide. Saul conducts an apparently legitimate sacrifice (1 Sam 11:15) and David's sons serve as "priests" (2 Sam 8:18).[19]

If the criterion of strict literary and theological consistency is set aside and the text is recognized as composite, it is plain that the basic aims of 1 Kings 17–19 as an atomized unit differ from the aims of the royal narratives in Kings – the Jeroboam narratives being one example. According to Elijah, who appears to express the central point of the 1 Kings 17–19 narrative (at least as it existed outside of the present book of Kings), the problem in Israel was not that they were sacrificing to YHWH at a plurality of sanctuaries, but rather that they were sacrificing to other deities ("How long will you waver between two opinions?" 18:24). Even the use of images does not appear to be a main concern of the text. The confrontation is not set in Bethel or Dan; no idols of Baʻal are mentioned as part of the ceremonies of his prophets, and no idols are torn down and ground to powder (*à la* Exod 32:20). This is in contrast to the polemic against the Bethel and Dan

---

[17] Cogan, *1 Kings*, 442.

[18] Noth noted the laxity of the pre-Jerusalem-temple cultic regime, and uses comparisons to Samuel and others as the Deuteronomist's "justification" for Elijah's sacrifice: "Dtr tacitly uses the presence of a 'man of God' or the like as a justification for sacrifices performed outside Jerusalem before the completion of the Jerusalem temple; this would apply to the sacrifice at the 'high place' of an unknown city in the presence of Samuel (1 Sam 9:12 ff.) and even to Elijah's sacrifice on Mount Carmel (1 Kgs 18:30 ff.). Dtr probably based this view upon 1 Sam 10:8 and 13:7b–14 – the secondary part of the old Saul tradition which, however, had formed a part of Dtr's source. Here it was a sin for Saul to perform a sacrifice without waiting for Samuel." Martin Noth, "The Central Theological Ideas," in *Reconsidering Israel and Judah: Recent Studies on the Deuteronomistic History*, ed. Gary N. Knoppers and J. Gordon McConville (Winona Lake, IN: Eisenbrauns, 2000), 27; reprinted from Martin Noth, *The Deuteronomistic History*, JSOTSup 15 (Sheffield: JSOT Press, 1981 [Eng. trans. of the 1957 German edition]), 95–96.

[19] Partially at odds with Noth, I have suggested that the pre-2 Sam 5–6 situation is different with respect to centralization, so that Elijah's cultic activities at Mount Carmel are a problem while Samuel's activities are not; see Giffone, "According to Which 'Law of Moses,'" 436–39.

sanctuaries (1 Kgs 12:25–14:18), where the location of YHWH worship and the use of images seem to be the main problems (see 12:28).

1 Kings 17–19 is therefore concerned about polytheism[20] – not with centralization, priestly identity, or use of images. 1 Kings 12–14, and a great deal of the rest of Kings, is concerned about centralization, priestly identity and idolatry, and only with polytheism secondarily at the end of the "slippery slope."

From this point, however, there is divergence of how to explain what McKenzie describes as "an intrusion into Dtr's framework."[21] McKenzie and others suggest that 1 Kings 17–19 is a post-Dtr insertion, in part because monotheism is presumed to be an exilic or post-exilic concept based on a certain model of the development of Israel's religion(s).[22] But whether 1 Kings 17–19 is pre- or post-

---

[20] "This narrative spoke clearly to the exilic community in Babylon, faced by a temptation to syncretism or apostasy. The point of the narrative is not just that Yahweh is the God of Israel, but that Yahweh is God, period. It might look for now as though the Babylonian god Marduk has beaten Yahweh in the arena of history, but the contest on Carmel is a reminder that this cannot be so. Marduk is a non-entity, just as Baal is. Yahweh does not lose in the contest of history. Yahweh's word makes history happen ... To Yahweh alone belongs the attribute 'God' (cf. 1 Cor. 8:5–6). What seems at first to be a battle between two competing gods turns out instead to be a contest between God and an empty delusion." Richard D. Nelson, *First and Second Kings*, IBC (Atlanta: John Knox, 1987), 120, 121.

[21] McKenzie, *The Trouble with Kings*, 87. "We have seen how 1 Kings 17–19 break unexpectedly into Dtr's report on Ahab so that they are better described as intruding into Dtr's framework rather than being integrated into it. Certainly Dtr had an aversion to both the Canaanite cults and the house of Ahab. However, in 1 Kings 11–16 Dtr traces the fall of the houses of Jeroboam and Baasha in fulfillment of prophetic oracles against them for the 'sin of Jeroboam,' i.e., the shrines he erected at Dan and Bethel. In 1 Kings 17–19 the concerns are different. Not only is Elijah more a miracle worker than a messenger (in contrast to Ahijah and Jehu ben Hanani) but there is no mention of the sin of Jeroboam. Elijah is now the focus, not the Northern royal house. Elijah's nemesis is not really Ahab but his alien wife, Jezebel. Dtr would no doubt agree with the perspective of 1 Kings 17–19, but the issues here are different than those Dtr has dealt with heretofore.

"The Elijah cycle in 1 Kings 17–19, then, was a late, post-Dtr insertion into Dtr's account of Ahab. Chapters 17–18 were added first and linked to Dtr's account of Naboth. Then, chapter 19 was added to prepare for the transition from Elijah to Elisha. This does not necessarily mean that the legends in the Elijah cycle are entirely of a late composition. Many of the late expressions noticed by Fohrer occur in redactional seams (cf. Dietrich 1972:122–23). The stories themselves may be much earlier, but they were edited and added to the DH in the exile or afterwards."

[22] This is one of the key arguments offered by Otto, "The Composition of the Elijah–Elisha Stories." Römer also writes, "The books of Kings contain prophetic stories that come close to anecdotes: the prophets appear as miracle-doers, healers, magicians and visionaries. Those stories often interrupt unexpectedly the Deuteronomistic reports and appear sometimes in the Greek version at different places; therefore one should consider them as post-Deuteronomistic additions ... The same observations apply to the Elijah and Elisha stories, with the possible exception of Elijah's confrontation with Ahab in 1 Kgs 21 and Elisha's implication in Jehu's revolt. The Elijah and Elisha cycles, as well as 1 Kgs 20 and 22*, were added to the books of Kings during the Persian period" (Römer, *So-called Deuteronomistic History*, 153–54). "According to Otto the Elijah and Elisha stories were composed about 750 in the Northern kingdom. This is quite possible for Elisha, [sic] the stories about Elijah do not reveal many pre-Deuteronomistic features: 1 Kgs 17–18 are close to the ideology of Deutero-Isaiah, and 1 Kgs 19 which criticize

Deuteronomistic, we still have a problem of two conceptions of centralization combined in the same work.

3.2 Evaluation

Traditional interpreters and redaction-critics have observed an important feature of the structure of Kings: 1 Kings 17–19 approvingly presents a non-Jerusalem, non-Levite-led sacrifice to YHWH, within the context of a larger work that elsewhere disapproves of such activities. While the "harmonizing" explanations have some merit, they are not able to encompass all the elements of the received text.

The most plausible explanation is that 1 Kings 17–19 is a tradition with its origins in a time and place where polytheism, syncretism, and chiseled altars are prohibited, but a plurality of YHWH cultic sites are accepted as legitimate. Elijah's sacrifice was therefore not originally considered illicit, and the history of YHWH worship at Mount Carmel as evidenced by the altar stones is a feature, not a bug.

But how then are we to understand the tension between this implicit belief and the perspective(s) of the final (Deuteronomistic?) storymakers? Those who maintain that a historiographical work must use "a consistent conception of history" assert that the additional stories must be "post-Dtr."[23] However, this theory would entail a post-Dtr editor introducing inconsistencies into a (hypothesized) theologically coherent text. Simply recognizing and assigning layers is not sufficient to explain the text we have, nor does it explain why the troublesome detail of Elijah's "illegal" sacrifice at Carmel was not so troublesome.

---

the ideology of the foregoing chapters must even be later" (Römer, *So-called Deuteronomistic History*, 154n109). Juha Pakkala also assigns 1 Kgs 18 to a later period based on this criterion; see *Intolerant Monolatry in the Deuteronomistic History*, PFES 76 (Helsinki: Finnish Exegetical Society; Göttingen: Vandenhoeck & Ruprecht, 1999), 161–62.

[23] "Like W. Thiel, I define the Deuteronomists as those editors who compiled the chronological framework and embedded traditional narratives into their work, using a specific language, style and theology. But since the Deuteronomists' intention was to present a coherent historical account of Israel – from Settlement to Exile in order to explain the past and to open a door to the future – I think it is necessary to presuppose a further criterion: the supposed Deuteronomistic approach has to match *the criterion of a consistent conception of history*. Therefore the texts will be examined by the criteria of language, style, theology and a consistent conception of history. Those texts which do not meet these criteria will be defined as post-Deuteronomistic additions – otherwise the clear model of the Deuteronomists would be incoherent" (Otto, "The Composition of the Elijah–Elisha Stories," 491, emphasis added). Yet contemporary interpreters must be cautious about imposing modern standards of consistency upon ancient works of history; see especially David M. Carr, *The Formation of the Hebrew Bible: A New Reconstruction* (New York: Oxford University Press, 2011), 117; Joshua A. Berman, *Inconsistency in the Torah: Ancient Literary Convention and the Limits of Source Criticism* (New York: Oxford University Press, 2017), passim.

4. Storymakers in Kings: Balancing Competing and Complementary Aims

It becomes apparent when we consider various expositions of Elijah's actions at Carmel offered by traditional and critical interpreters that the narrative of 1 Kings 17–19 cannot be considered coherent in every detail, nor is it entirely consistent with the theology of the rest of the book of Kings. In order to understand this phenomenon, we must recover the notion of authorial intent – in a form appropriate to ancient scribal culture – and recognize the complexity of human identities, intentions, and aims.

4.1 Storymakers, Authorizers, and the Promulgation of Biblical Texts

Most texts of the Hebrew Bible, including Kings, are composite works containing traditions that predate the final form of the text by several centuries. This basic notion is not controversial; however, scholars have not reached any sort of consensus on precisely how and why the texts were shaped into their present form.[24]

In a recent essay, I have tried to move beyond this mere observation, toward the normative statement that a basic presumption of some authorial and editorial intention[25] should guide our analysis:

> I presume that the final form of the text is the product of some conscious intention by an individual or a group of individuals who presented the text in [something close to] its present form to the community for retention, reverence, and reproduction. These persons who shaped the biblical texts are variously called redactors, editors, documentarians, tradents, or authors. Though they are not "authors" in the modern sense, they may perhaps be thought of as "authorizers" or promulgators of the texts, who confirm and propagate the texts' *authority* in the community.

When addressing narratives, I prefer the term "storymakers," which is neutral with respect to the various compositional theories but encompasses the notion of *intentionality*.[26] This is not to say that no compositional theory has any more merit than another. Rather, it is to acknowledge that 1) the text is composite; 2) in most cases we do not possess the pieces that preceded it, only the final form[27]; and 3) someone put the text together and propagated it as it currently stands.

---

[24] In addition to the ever-expanding body of literature on the Pentateuch and the Former Prophets, there is the problem of multiple "final forms" of these texts, including the Greek versions.

[25] Here I stand perhaps in partial disagreement with Karel van der Toorn, *Scribal Culture and the Making of the Hebrew Bible* (Cambridge, MA: Harvard University Press, 2007), who at certain points appears to imply that pre-Hellenistic Jewish scribal works do not exhibit coherence (5) but at other points suggests that scribal texts intentionally reflect the values and beliefs of communities (46–48).

[26] I have adopted this term from Gary E. Schnittjer, and I have not found it used by other scholars; see Schnittjer, "Individual versus Collective Retribution in the Chronicler's Ideology of Exile," *JBTS* 4.1 (2019): 113–32 [125]; and previously developed more comprehensively in Schnittjer, *The Torah Story: An Apprenticeship on the Pentateuch* (Grand Rapids: Zondervan, 2006).

[27] The book of Chronicles being a notable and instructive exception; see Giffone, "According to Which 'Law of Moses,'" 441 ff.

Any compositional theory which purports to make sense of the pieces must account for the intentionality of the whole.[28]

Moreover, we must think not merely in terms of a one-way process of presentation, but rather in terms of an interplay between the storymakers and their aims on the one hand, and community memory on the other:

> The narrative texts are neither ideologically neutral, "pure" historiography – nor are they strictly propagandistic fiction. Competing tendencies are reflected in these texts: on the one hand, the ideologies and rhetorical goals of the authors (including the survival of the community), and on the other hand, the parameters created by community memory and tradition. The scribes were not free to simply fabricate. Rather, I suggest that they shaped tradition gradually, "along the margin."[29]

Regardless of modern assessments of the degree of correspondence between the texts and actual flesh-and-blood events, the storymakers and their intended audiences appear to have *believed* that the events described actually happened.[30]

As the storymakers sought to propagate their ideologies within the constraints of existing tradition, community memory, and political and social realities, we perceive attempts to balance risks and benefits of including or excluding various stories or elements.[31] A single storymaker nearly always has more than one aim or audience in mind, and balances various concerns when deciding what to include or exclude from existing sources.[32]

---

[28] Benjamin D. Giffone, "'Israel's' Only Son? The Complexity of Benjaminite Identity between Judah and Joseph," *OTE* 32.3 (2019): 956–72 (961–62, emphasis original).

[29] Giffone, "'Israel's' Only Son," 962. See also Giffone, *'Sit at My Right Hand'*, 19–20 for further explication of this perspective.

[30] Regarding the book of Kings overall, the most extreme "minimalism" with regard to actual historical basis must be rejected. There are references to events and persons that correspond to external evidence; moreover, Kristin Weingart demonstrates by comparative and internal evidence that the chronographic data in Kings is likely drawn from a "Chronicle of the Kings of Israel … a continuously updated chronographic work, whose origins go back at least to the period of the Omrides and which served as a major source for the chronological arrangement and parts of the material included into the Book of Kings" ("Chronography in the Book of Kings," in this volume). A hypothesized chronographic book cannot be definitive evidence for historicity, but rather for the *perception* among ancient storymakers and audiences that the text re-presents historical events.

[31] I have discussed one such example in Giffone, "'Special Forces': A Stereotype of Benjaminite Soldiers in the Deuteronomistic History and Chronicles," *SJOT* 30.1 (2016): 16–29, following the suggestion of Gary N. Knoppers, *1 Chronicles 10–29*, AB 12A (New York: Doubleday, 2004), 530. Jonathan, Saul's son, is portrayed in the book of Samuel as an ideal Benjaminite: devoted to the "rightful" Judahite king, using his skill with "non-oppositional weapons" in support of David's claim to the throne (Giffone, "Special Forces," 25). Though the Chronicler, given his conciliatory message to Benjaminites (Giffone, *'Sit at My Right Hand'*, passim), would presumably have preferred to highlight Jonathan's early support for David, he evidently judged the risk to be too great: "Omitting all of the stories of David's relationships with Saul, Jonathan, and the members of Saul's house gives the writer a free hand to dissociate David from Saul" (Knoppers, *1 Chronicles 10–29*, 530; cf. Giffone, *'Sit at My Right Hand'*, 199–200).

[32] See, for example, the study of Woo Min Lee in this volume, identifying various possible au-

I suggest that the storymakers' decision to include 1 Kings 17–19 in its current form and narrative context – that is, with too many details that problematize a "coherentist" interpretation of Kings – represents an attempt to balance various aims: the complex representation of the identities of "Northern Israel" and "Benjamin" in the story of Judah and Greater Israel; bolstering the authority of Northern prophets (who in turn legitimize or delegitimize Northern rulers); supporting centralization of the cult in Jerusalem; and affirming intolerant monolatry (if not monotheism) as the proper way of worship.

4.2 Negotiating "Israel" and "Benjamin" within Judah's Bible

In a provocative 2012 study, *The Legacy of Israel in Judah's Bible*, Fleming examines the significance of the curious retention in the biblical texts of the identity "Israel" – which designates either a larger group encompassing "Judah," "Benjamin" and other identities; or, a smaller group identified with the Omride kingdom, the territory of the Ephraim hill country and north of it.[33] Inspired by Fleming's work, I have written more recently of Benjamin's complex legacy in DtrH and Chronicles[34] and in Genesis 35–50[35] as a border tribe between Israel and Judah:

> Given the apparent pro-Levi, pro-Judah agendas of the scribal communities that produced the biblical texts, the presence of Benjaminite and Northern Israelite material in the texts is remarkable in itself. Why did the communities that were called "Judah" – the Kingdom of Judah, and Yehud province under Babylonian and Persian rule – appropriate the identity and traditions of "Israel," while still maintaining identity of "Judah"?[36]

While the author of Kings is quite critical of Northern Israelite rulers, the attention given to the Northern people, prophets and rulers indicates the storymakers' belief that YHWH maintained a relationship (though strained) with Northern Israel and the descendants of the Northern tribes.[37] Numerous narratives found

---

diences for elements of 2 Kgs 19:30–31 ("The 'Remnant' in the Deuteronomistic Cultural Memory"). Lee utilizes the more common term "cultural memory"; I have here used "community memory" in a similar way, but perhaps more circumscribed in its scope.

[33] Daniel E. Fleming, *The Legacy of Israel in Judah's Bible: History, Politics, and the Reinscribing of Tradition* (New York: Cambridge University Press, 2012). Fleming and Lauren Monroe continue to explore the narrowest and widest definitions of the "Israel" designation in history and story, and I am grateful to them for sharing prepublication versions of their essays, now published as: Daniel E. Fleming, "The Bible's Little Israel: Terminological Clasts in a Compositional Matrix," *HeBAI* 10.2 (2021): 149–86; Lauren Monroe, "On the Origins and Development of Greater Israel," *HeBAI* 10.2 (2021): 187–227.

[34] Giffone, *'Sit at My Right Hand'*; Giffone, "Special Forces."

[35] Giffone, "'Israel's' Only Son."

[36] Giffone, "'Israel's' Only Son," 962.

[37] "Although Azariah recovers some territory for Judah, Israel shows even new vigour under Jeroboam II, with some rather extraordinary assistance: it is reported that Yahweh had resolved not to blot the name of Israel out, and so he saved them, ויושיעם, from their bitter plight through Jeroboam (2 Kgs 14.25–27). Marking the affiliation of the north to Yahweh in such 'unconditional' terms as these offers a counterpart to the 'unconditional' sanction for David, whose

in 1 Kings 12 to 2 Kings 16 show that YHWH still claimed an association with the Israelite people (1 Kgs 20:28), the Northern prophets and "men of God" (2 Kgs 2:3, 15), and the land itself (2 Kgs 5:17). This ongoing relationship offered Israel many opportunities to repent and avert national disaster, thus vindicating YHWH's ultimate decision to bring about the exile to Assyria. Moreover, even though Northern Israel is "rejected" by YHWH and exiled (2 Kgs 17:20), there are hints in Solomon's prayer of dedication (1 Kgs 8) – which many scholars consider to be exilic or post-exilic[38] – that the promise that YHWH would "hear and forgive" extends even to Northern individuals, and perhaps even Northern Israel as a whole.[39]

For a Babylonian- and Persian-era Judahite audience, this memory of YHWH's relationship with Northern Israel is more than simply a warning against disobedience. It was a record of the lengths to which YHWH went to maintain a relationship with his people, even through degrees and stages of "apostasy." The narrative of 1 Kings 17–19 supports this defense of YHWH's conduct with regard to Israel, and was therefore included by the storymakers despite its Deuteronomistically-problematic content.

4.3 Authority of Northern Prophets

A second important function of 1 Kings 17–19 that warranted its inclusion in Kings is that it bolsters the authority of the most significant Northern prophet, Elijah. Northern prophets and men of God, beginning with Ahijah the Shilonite (1 Kgs 11:29–30) and continuing through to Elisha, revoked or transferred legitimacy of Northern dynasties. Elijah pronounces the demise of the Omride dynasty because of Ahab's actions with respect to Naboth (1 Kgs 21:17–24).

It is apparent that 1 Kings 17–19 supports Elijah's authority by patterning his life and actions after Moses's. In addition to miraculous signs (1 Kgs 17), Elijah's sacrifice consumed by supernatural fire is reminiscent of the fire that consumed

---

dynasty now rules only Judah ... The presence of great prophets like Elisha and Elijah reinforces the sense of Israel as Yahweh's people, and their 'legitimate' religious heritage ... The memory of these prophets in the northern territory preserves a Yahwistic heritage for the north, in spite of Judah's exclusive hold on the temple during the time of the two monarchies"; James R. Linville, *Israel in the Book of Kings: The Past as a Project of Social Identity*, JSOTSup 272 (Sheffield: Sheffield Academic, 1998), 177–79.

[38] "The exilic redactors build upon the earlier text from the Josianic edition of Kings (v. 14–20*) and add, with a new introduction, a long prayer (vv. 22–51*) and a final blessing (vv. 54–56)." Romer, *So-Called Deuteronomistic History*, 119.

[39] Northern Israel experiences several of the punishments described in Solomon's prayer: "Rain Withheld" (1 Kgs 8:35–36; see 1 Kgs 17–18); "Famine Due to Blight, Insect or Siege" (1 Kgs 8:37–40; see 2 Kgs 6:24–7:20); and "Foreigner Prays to YHWH" (1 Kgs 8:41–43; see 2 Kgs 5:1–19). However, when those punishments are averted, it is not because the people turn toward Jerusalem and pray for forgiveness, but rather because YHWH intervenes in some other way, in another place – thereby demonstrating his continuing relationship with Northern Israel and his omnipresence.

Aaron's sacrifice when he was consecrated by Moses (Lev 9:24). The slaughter of the priests of Baʻal for promoting other gods (cf. Deut 13:1–5; 18:19–22) recalls Moses's mustering the Levites against those who had worshiped the golden calf (Exod 32:25–28). The parallels are clearest in Elijah's journey of forty days and nights to Horeb, where he encounters YHWH (1 Kgs 19:8, 11–18).

These parallels invite comparisons between Elijah, Elisha, and the ubiquitous "men of God" in 1 Kings 13 to 2 Kings 13, and the prophet-priests of pre-Jerusalem Israel who did not sacrifice according to Deuteronomistic requirements.[40] Particularly interesting is Samuel, a Josephite prophet (1 Sam 1:1) who serves as a judge and a priest (1 Sam 7:15–17).[41] Joshua, also a Josephite and miracle-working successor to Moses, presents Israel with a stark choice between serving YHWH and serving other gods (Josh 24), like Elijah does (1 Kgs 18:21).

Besides the significance of Elijah's authority for the narrative of Kings, the subordination of royal authority to prophetic authority is understood to be a feature of "Deuteronomism." The storymakers judged the prophets sufficiently important that stories comparing them to ancient heroes should be incorporated – despite the risks of including 1 Kings 17–19 and other "Deuteronomistically questionable" Northern material. Wilson writes:

Many of the stories focus on the miraculous deeds of the prophets and glorify both the prophets themselves and the God they represent. The writer of Kings has modified some of the stories in order to make them conform to Deuteronomic theology, but many non-Deuteronomic elements still remain.[42]

4.4 Balancing Centralization and Monolatry/Monotheism

Perhaps the most significant "balancing act" performed by the storymakers who incorporated 1 Kings 17–19 into Kings is the tightrope between Jerusalem centralization and monolatry/monotheism.

The received form of 1 Kings 17–19 clearly contains a strong polemic against Baʻal worship in Israel. It is an interesting question, however, whether the text represents *monotheism* (YHWH is the only deity and the gods of the nations are non-existent) or *monolatry* (YHWH is the only proper deity for Israel to worship, though other gods exist and it may be permissible for other nations to worship them). Pakkala, for example, considers 1 Kings 18:21–40 to belong to a post-Nomistic, monotheistic redaction of the book of Kings, corresponding to Deuteronomy 4:32–40 – as contrasted with the "intolerant monolatry" repre-

---

[40] See Noth, *Central Theological Ideas*, 95–96, as quoted above.
[41] See the evidence marshaled by Sweeney, "Prophets and Priests in the Deuteronomistic History," 35–36, 41, 48–49.
[42] Robert R. Wilson, "1 & 2 Kings," in *The Harper Collins Study Bible, Revised Edition*, ed. Harold W. Attridge (New York: HarperCollins, 2006), 508.

sented in Deuteronomy 4:19–20 and 29:25.[43] Though in certain verses Elijah appears to imply that Baʻal is in fact a non-entity (18:21, 24), the assignment of 1 Kings 18 to the category of "monotheism" is problematized by the statement that YHWH is "God *in Israel*" (כי־אתה אלהים בישׂראל) in 18:36b and the emphasis on YHWH's association with Israel (18:31). Such qualifications would seem to be unnecessary if YHWH were considered to be the only God that exists (and is therefore worthy of worship by all people).

Yet whether we align 1 Kings 18 with so-called "intolerant monolatry" passages or "monotheistic" passages in Deuteronomy, and even if such a development of Israelite/Judahite religion could be demonstrated, a strong monotheistic affirmation cannot in itself be grounds for viewing 1 Kings 17–19 as an "intrusion into Dtr's framework."[44] Surely the hypothesized monotheistic post-Deuteronomistic scribal elites would have believed in the primacy of Jerusalem. Given the existence of competing YHWH altars in the Babylonian and Persian periods, these Jerusalem scribal elites would surely have been cautious about narratives that could have provided legitimacy for other cultic sites.[45] These scribes would have needed to balance the strengths of the story (monotheism or monolatry) with its weakness (non-Jerusalem sacrifice), and were constrained from making certain types of changes in the narrative.

The key element of the narrative that makes the story palatable from a "Jerusalem-centralizing" perspective (whether Dtr or post-Dtr) is that the stones used for the altar are consumed by fire from YHWH. This precludes the possibility of the historic altar being rebuilt. By including the destruction of existing altar stones, which are troublesome for the "unique circumstance" justification for his actions (discussed previously), the storymakers imply that worship at Mount Carmel should not be repeated by future generations. Where the harmonizing "Baʻal's home turf" explanation fails to explain the reference to existing

---

[43] "Die Verehrung Jahves war das Zeichen dafür, dass man zu Israel gehörte, die Verehrung anderer Götter war wiederum ein Zeichen dafür, dass man kein Israelit war. Die Verehrung anderer Götter hätte die Identität, den Unterschied zwischen Israel und den anderen Völkern, gefährdet. Daher ist es verständlich, dass man die Existenz anderer Götter nicht abgestritten hat. Diese hatten eine wichtige Funktion in der neuen Theologie; sie waren die Götter anderer Völker. Israel hatte Jahve, und die anderen Völker hatten ihre Götter (Dtn 4,19–20; 29,25) … Obwohl der Unterschied zwischen den Nomisten und den späteren Autoren der Bücher Deuteronomium bis II Reg häufig eine schwierige Frage ist, unterscheiden sich einige Texte eindeutig in ihren Gotteskonzeptionen von den Nomisten. Redaktionskritisch gesehen gehören sie zu den spätesten Ergänzungen dieser Bücher. Die ausführlichsten und damit aufschlussreichsten für unser Thema sind Dtn 4,32–40; 7,7–11; II Sam 7,22–29; I Reg 8,54–66 und 18,21–40" (Pakkala, "Die Entwicklung der Gotteskonzeptionen," 242–43).

[44] McKenzie, *The Trouble with Kings*, 87.

[45] See, for example, the careful treatment of Benjaminite sites such as Gibeon and Bethel, in the book of Kings (Giffone, "According to Which 'Law of Moses,'" 440; 446–47; Giffone, '*Sit at My Right Hand*', 163–65). The Chronicler goes so far as to excise all named references to other cultic sites from his sources concerning Judah's history (Giffone, '*Sit at My Right Hand*', 206).

stones, this "extra" detail makes sense if the stones are consumed and Elijah's actions are not to be repeated in the storymakers' own day (the Persian period).

4. Conclusions and Ideas for Further Study

The rather cheeky title of this essay, "regathering too many stones," points to the difficulties for both traditional justifications and critical explanations of 1 Kings 17–19. The "regathering" of preexisting altar stones is itself a "superfluous stone" that creates problems for both approaches.[46] I have argued that the inconsistencies in the story are evidence of editorial attempts to integrate texts with different perspectives on cultic centralization – attempts which are constrained by practical concerns, desire to balance themes and perspectives, and community memory.

Lemaire correctly observes:

The two books of Kings therefore appear to be the culmination of literary activity spanning more than four centuries … At each of these literary stages these books were revised and updated: not only was recent history appended to the text, but previously recorded history was revised and systematically corrected when necessary.[47]

But as we have seen, there are several "corrections" that could have made 1 Kings 17–19 more coherent and consistent with the theology of the more clearly "Deuteronomistic" sections of Kings, that the storymakers did not make. Though there are numerous ways that the text of 1 Kings 17–19 could have been edited to integrate more coherently into a consistent framework (which, I would argue, is Deuteronomistic), theological inconsistencies still remain. I suggested that this compromise was acceptable to the Persian-era storymakers who "finalized" the text, because the consumption of the altar stones by fire prevents the text from being used to justify an altar at Mount Carmel.

Steven McKenzie writes: "The literary unevenness in so much of the DH [Deuteronomistic History] must be satisfactorily explained … In short, an acceptable reconstruction of the DH's formation must account both for its unity and its diversity – not an easy task!"[48] A more recent turn in efforts to reconstruct the formation of the DtrH and other texts is the application of "orality studies" to biblical criticism. Insights from studies of oral traditions have led some to ques-

---

[46] The original, even cheekier, title conceived of the redactional problem in Kings as layers of an onion – a "Carmelized" onion that induces tears when sliced.

[47] André Lemaire, "Toward a Redactional History of the Book of Kings," in *Reconsidering Israel and Judah: Recent Studies on the Deuteronomistic History*, ed. G. N. Knoppers and J. G. McConville, trans. Samuel W. Heldenbrand, SBTS 8 (Winona Lake, IN: Eisenbrauns, 2000), 459; translated from "Vers l'Histoire de la Rédaction des Livres des Rois," ZAW 98 (1986): 221–36.

[48] McKenzie, *Trouble with Kings*, 19.

tion the rigid application of the criterion of "literary unity" in discerning layers of editing or authorship.[49] While balance is needed in that debate,[50] it highlights the complexity and uncertainty at the heart of attempts to dissect the texts as we have received them, without (in most cases) much tangible evidence in the form of literary sources.[51]

In this study and in my earlier essay on cultic centralization in DtrH and Chronicles,[52] I have started mainly with synchronic analysis, and then moved cautiously (as I believe one must) to diachronic concerns. The starting point is the parameters and judgments that are explicit and implicit in the narratives: to what cultic standards are the characters held? Theological or literary inconsistencies in one text – Kings, or the DtrH broadly – may then be compared to those of other texts, especially the book of Chronicles where we find numerous narrative revisions that appear to be attempts to "solve" theological problems or "illicit" behavior in Samuel and Kings.

When diachronic models are permitted to inform synchronic analysis, we find that one of the main arguments in favor of post-Dtr integration of 1 Kings 17–19 is based on a developmental conception of Israelite religion that drives a wedge between "intolerant monolatry" and "monotheism," with the latter idea only developing in the Babylonian and Persian periods. This presupposed distinction needs to be challenged as arbitrary – and, moreover, unnecessary for understanding the texts of Kings and Deuteronomy. If, as I have shown, the "problems" of 1 Kings 17–19 for Deuteronomistic ideas of centralization and Levitical cultic leadership are not really that problematic (or rather, would have been *just as problematic* for post-Dtr scribes), then we might argue the other way from this

---

[49] For example, see Raymond F. Person Jr. and Robert Rezetko, eds., *Empirical Models Challenging Biblical Criticism*, AIL 25 (Atlanta: Society of Biblical Literature, 2016), especially Person's contribution to the volume, "The Problem of 'Literary Unity' from the Perspective of the Study of Oral Traditions," 217–37.

[50] Paul S. Evans has offered a helpful survey of "orality studies" in biblical scholarship and a welcome critique of some of its extremes: "Creating a New 'Great Divide': The Exoticization of Ancient Culture in Some Recent Applications of Orality Studies to the Bible," *JBL* 136.4 (2017): 749–64.

[51] See, for example, the measured critique of Benjamin Ziemer, "Radical Versus Conservative? How Scribes Conventionally Used Books While Writing Books," within this volume. Ziemer takes issue with the axioms of modern redaction criticism, particularly the *Wachstumsmodell*, which seems to be contradicted by extant evidence. Ziemer describes this excavation as an exercise in "tracing back their line of reasoning to the point where the method is no longer adapted to the text but the text to the method." Even though I am arguing for a kind of "conservatism" on the part of the storymakers, it is not the kind of rigid conservatism that only admits additions to a text (*Fortschreibung*) – a conservatism which Ziemer demonstrates cannot be proven. Rather, Ziemer rightly describes the task of the "master scribe": "The manifold metaphors for the growth model – growing forests, snowballs or archaeological tells – all suggest that the preservation of the original text in a new version is a natural thing. However, every writing process requires a conscious decision on the concrete text selection."

[52] Giffone, "According to Which 'Law of Moses.'"

text: 1 Kings 17–19 constitutes early evidence that *some* Northern Israelite prophets and laypeople at *some point* in Dtr's distant past believed that Israelites should only worship YHWH (monolatry), but that a variety of cultic sites were acceptable for such worship. This text was then integrated into Kings by a relatively light editorial hand, with potentially problematic elements left in the text.

In light of this conclusion that the presentation of a sacrifice by Elijah at Mount Carmel is not unbearably problematic in a Deuteronomistic framework, a thorough study of the presentation of Northern Israelite and Benjaminite cultic sites in the Hebrew Bible (particularly the Pentateuch and the Former Prophets) could provide an empirically-based understanding of how exactly the rhetoric of Jerusalem centralization functioned in the Babylonian and Persian eras. Why exactly did the authors and editors of the final forms of these texts ("books," and multi-scroll works) allow such varied accounts of sites Bethel, Shechem, and Mizpah – cultic sites in competition with Jerusalem – to stand in their works? If the presentation of Elijah's sacrifice at Mount Carmel is any guide, then nuanced examination of the narrative presentations of such sites is in order.

Bibliography

Beck, John A. "Geography as Irony: The Narrative-Geographical Shaping of Elijah's Duel with the Prophets of Baal (1 Kings 18)." *SJOT* 17.2 (2003): 291–302.

Berman, Joshua A. *Inconsistency in the Torah: Ancient Literary Convention and the Limits of Source Criticism*. New York: Oxford University Press, 2017.

Blanco Wißmann, Felipe. "'He Did What Was Right': Criteria of Judgment and Deuteronomism in the Books of Kings." Pages 241–59 in *Deuteronomy in the Pentateuch, the Hexateuch, and the Deuteronomistic History*. Edited by Konrad Schmid and Raymond F. Person Jr. FAT II 56. Tübingen: Mohr Siebeck, 2011.

Campbell, Antony F. *Of Prophets and Kings*. CBQMS 17. Washington: Catholic Biblical Association of America, 1986.

Carr, David M. *The Formation of the Hebrew Bible: A New Reconstruction*. New York: Oxford University Press, 2011.

Cogan, Mordechai. *1 Kings: A New Translation with Introduction and Commentary*. AB. New York: Doubleday, 2001.

Dozeman, Thomas B., ed. *Pentateuch, Hexateuch, or Enneateuch: Identifying Literary Works in Genesis through Kings*. AIL 8. Atlanta: Society of Biblical Literature, 2011.

Evans, Paul S. "Creating a New 'Great Divide': The Exoticization of Ancient Culture in Some Recent Applications of Orality Studies to the Bible." *JBL* 136.4 (2017): 749–64.

Fleming, Daniel E. "The Bible's Little Israel: Terminological Clasts in a Compositional Matrix." *HeBAI* 10.2 (2021): 149–86.

Fleming, Daniel E. *The Legacy of Israel in Judah's Bible: History, Politics, and the Reinscribing of Tradition*. New York: Cambridge University Press, 2012.

Freedman, D. N., ed. *Anchor Bible Dictionary*. 6 vols. New York: Doubleday, 1992.

Giffone, Benjamin D. "According to Which 'Law of Moses'? Cult Centralization in Samuel, Kings and Chronicles." *VT* 67.3 (2017): 432–47.

Giffone, Benjamin D. "'Israel's' Only Son? The Complexity of Benjaminite Identity Between Judah and Joseph." *OTE* 32.3 (2019): 956–72.

Giffone, Benjamin D. *'Sit At My Right Hand': The Chronicler's Portrait of the Tribe of Benjamin in the Social Context of Yehud*. LHBOTS 628. London: T&T Clark, 2016.

Giffone, Benjamin D. "'Special Forces': A Stereotype of Benjaminite Soldiers in the Deuteronomistic History and Chronicles." *SJOT* 30.1 (2016): 16–29.

Hutton, Jeremy M. *The Transjordanian Palimpsest: The Overwritten Texts of Personal Exile and Transformation in the Deuteronomistic History*. BZAW 396. Berlin: de Gruyter, 2009.

Knoppers, Gary N. *1 Chronicles 10–29*. AB 12A. New York: Doubleday, 2004.

Lee, Woo Min. "The 'Remnant' in the Deuteronomistic Cultural Memory: A Case Study on 2 Kings 19:30–31." Within this volume.

Lemaire, André. "Toward a Redactional History of the Book of Kings." Pages 446–61 in *Reconsidering Israel and Judah: Recent Studies on the Deuteronomistic History*. Edited by G. N. Knoppers and J. G. McConville. Translated by Samuel W. Heldenbrand. SBTS 8. Winona Lake, IN: Eisenbrauns, 2000; translated from "Vers l'Histoire de la Rédaction des Livres des Rois." *ZAW* 98 (1986): 221–36.

Linville, James R. *Israel in the Book of Kings: The Past as a Project of Social Identity*. JSOTSup 272. Sheffield: Sheffield Academic, 1998.

Lohfink, Norbert F. "Was There a Deuteronomistic Movement?" Pages 36–66 in *Those Elusive Deuteronomists: The Phenomenon of Pan-Deuteronomism*. Edited by Linda S. Schearing and Steven L. McKenzie. JSOTSup 268. Sheffield: Sheffield Academic, 1999.

McKenzie, Steven L. *The Trouble with Kings: The Composition of the Book of Kings in the Deuteronomistic History*. VTSup 42. Leiden: Brill, 1991.

Monroe, Lauren. "On the Origins and Development of Greater Israel." *HeBAI* 10.2 (2021): 187–227.

Müller, Reinhard, Juha Pakkala and Bas ter Haar Romeny. *Evidence of Editing: Growth and Change of Texts in the Hebrew Bible*. RBS 75. Atlanta: Society of Biblical Literature, 2014.

Na'aman, Nadav. "Prophetic Stories as Sources for the Histories of Jehoshaphat and the Omrides." *Bib* 78 (1997): 153–73.

Nelson, Richard D. *First and Second Kings*. IBC. Atlanta: John Knox, 1987.

Noth, Martin. "The Central Theological Ideas." Pages 20–30 in *Reconsidering Israel and Judah: Recent Studies on the Deuteronomistic History*. Edited by Gary N. Knoppers and J. Gordon McConville. Winona Lake, IN: Eisenbrauns, 2000; Reprinted from Martin Noth. *The Deuteronomistic History*. JSOTSup 15. Sheffield: JSOT Press, 1981 (Eng. trans. of the 1957 German edition).

Otto, Susanne. "The Composition of the Elijah–Elisha Stories and the Deuteronomistic History." *JSOT* 27.4 (2003): 487–508.

Pakkala, Juha. "Deuteronomy and 1–2 Kings in the Redaction of the Pentateuch and Former Prophets." Pages 133–62 in *Deuteronomy in the Pentateuch, the Hexateuch, and the Deuteronomistic History*. Edited by Konrad Schmid and Raymond F. Person Jr. FAT II 56. Tübingen: Mohr Siebeck, 2012.

Pakkala, Juha. "Die Entwicklung der Gotteskonzeptionen in den deuteronomistischen Redaktionen von polytheistischen zu monotheistischen Vorstellungen." Pages 239–48 in *Die deuteronomistischen Geschichtswerke: Redaktions- und religionsgeschichtliche Perspektiven zur "Deuteronomismus"-Diskussion in Tora und Vorderen Propheten*. Edited by Markus Witte, et al. BZAW 365. Berlin: de Gruyter, 2006.

Pakkala, Juha. *Intolerant Monolatry in the Deuteronomistic History*. PFES 76. Helsinki: Finnish Exegetical Society; Göttingen: Vandenhoeck & Ruprecht, 1999.

Person, Raymond F., Jr., and Robert Rezetko, eds. *Empirical Models Challenging Biblical Criticism*. AIL 25. Atlanta: Society of Biblical Literature, 2016.

Rendsburg, Gary A. "The Internal Consistency and Historical Reliability of the Biblical Genealogies." *VT* 40 (1990): 185–206.

Römer, Thomas. "The Case of the Book of Kings." Pages 187–201 in *Deuteronomy–Kings as Emerging Authoritative Books: A Conversation*. Edited by Diana V. Edelman. ANEM 6. Atlanta: Society of Biblical Literature, 2014.

Römer, Thomas. *The So-called Deuteronomistic History: A Sociological, Historical and Literary Introduction*. New York: T&T Clark, 2007.

Schnittjer, Gary E. "Individual versus Collective Retribution in the Chronicler's Ideology of Exile." *JBTS* 4.1 (2019): 113–32.

Schnittjer, Gary E. *The Torah Story: An Apprenticeship on the Pentateuch*. Grand Rapids: Zondervan, 2006.

Sweeney, Marvin A. "Prophets and Priests in the Deuteronomistic History: Elijah and Elisha." Pages 35–49 in *Israelite Prophecy and the Deuteronomistic History: Portrait, Reality, and the Formation of a History*. Edited by Mignon R. Jacobs and Raymond F. Person Jr. AIL 14. Atlanta: Society of Biblical Literature, 2013.

Toorn, Karel van der. *Scribal Culture and the Making of the Hebrew Bible*. Cambridge, MA: Harvard University Press, 2007.

Weingart, Kristin. "Chronography in the Book of Kings: An Inquiry into an Israelite Manifestation of an Ancient Near Eastern Genre." Within this volume.

Willi, Thomas. "Late Persian Judaism and Its Conception of an Integral Israel According to Chronicles: Some Observations on Form and Function of the Genealogy of Judah in 1 Chronicles 2.3–4.23." Pages 146–62 in *Second Temple Studies 2: Temple Community in the Persian Period*. Edited by Tamara C. Eskenazi and Kent H. Richards. JSOTSup 175. Sheffield: Sheffield Academic, 1994.

Wilson, Robert R. "1 & 2 Kings." Pages 474–559 in *The Harper Collins Study Bible*. Edited by Harold W. Attridge. Rev. ed. New York: HarperCollins, 2006.

Ziemer, Benjamin. "Radical Versus Conservative? How Scribes Conventionally Used Books While Writing Books." Within this volume.

The "Remnant" in the Deuteronomistic Cultural Memory: A Case Study on 2 Kings 19:30–31

Woo Min Lee

1. Introduction

In this article, I analyze 2 Kgs 19:30–31 with a focus on references to the "remnant" in terms of cultural memory collected and redacted by the Deuteronomistic scribes. The passage is a part of Isaiah's prophecy regarding Sennacherib's military campaign against Judah in 701 BCE. Specifically, it is included in YHWH's response to Hezekiah relayed through the prophet Isaiah. Regarding the usage of the term "remnant" and its implications, I argue that the passage reflects the pre-exilic scribal cultural memory in which eschatological perspective and Zion tradition were interwoven and integrated as a part of Isaiah's message to Hezekiah during Sennacherib's attack against Jerusalem.

As a part of the Deuteronomistic History, the passage of 2 Kgs 19:30–31 contains the term "remnant," which becomes a keyword in the prophecy of Isaiah (2 Kgs 19:14–34). One of the methodologies used to examine the past (or the remembered past) in biblical history is Jan Assmann's cultural memory theory.[1] Assmann's theory was derived from the collective memory philosophy developed by French sociologist Maurice Halbwachs.[2] In his work on collective memory, Halbwachs identified a social aspect to the memories of members of a society. Central to his collective memory concept is the fact that people's memories about the past are collected and reconstructed in the present. Subsequently, Assmann added individual memory to Halbwachs' social and collective memory in his cultural memory theory.[3]

Regarding the "remnant" in 2 Kgs 19:30–31, this article raises questions about scribal cultural memory related to the term, and its related historical context behind its usage. The "remnant" reflects an aspect of the scribes' cultural mem-

---

[1] Jan Assmann, "Collective Memory and Cultural Identity," trans. John Czaplicka, *NGC* 65 (1995): 125–33; Jan Assmann, *Religion and Cultural Memory: Ten Studies*, trans. Rodney Livingstone, CMP (Stanford, CA: Stanford University Press, 2006); Jan Assmann, *Cultural Memory and Early Civilization Writing, Remembrance, and Political Imagination* (Cambridge: Cambridge University Press, 2011).

[2] Maurice Halbwachs, *On Collective Memory*, trans. Lewis A. Coser (Chicago: University of Chicago Press, 1992).

[3] Assmann, *Religion and Cultural Memory*, 27.

ory in the context of the Deuteronomistic History. In particular, it is written in relation to certain places/spaces such as Judah, Jerusalem, and Mount Zion. Therefore, the analysis of the "remnant" in Isaiah's prophecy as described in 2 Kgs 19:30–31 should consider not only the literary context of the narrative of 2 Kgs but also the historical context of the scribes.

In search of possible answers to these questions, this article explores how cultural memory theories can be applied to 2 Kgs 19:30–31. It also analyzes the literary structure of 2 Kgs 18:13b to 2 Kgs 19:37 with a focus on 2 Kgs 19:30–31 in which the word, "remnant," was used with Judah, Jerusalem, and Mount Zion. Along with the literary analysis, this article explores eschatological features and Zion tradition implied in 2 Kgs 19:30–31. Finally, based on the literary analysis, the Deuteronomistic eschatology, and Zion tradition, this article suggests a possibility that the Deuteronomistic scribes' cultural memory implied in the passage of 2 Kgs 19:30–31 was developed since the pre-exilic period.

2. Deuteronomistic Cultural Memory

Maurice Halbwachs, who developed theories on collective memory, argued that the collective memory uses collective frameworks to reconstruct an image of the past in accord with the predominant thoughts of the society.[4] According to Halbwachs, collective memories are related to "a totality of thoughts common to a group" rather than contiguous in time.[5] Even though the group members' memories differ, they can be considered collective memories as long as the same group can call the memories to mind at the same time.[6] The frameworks for the collective memory exist in the specific social environment to which the members of the group belong.[7] In other words, collective memory is shared among people within a specific social context. Accordingly, collective memory would be affected by any contextual change.

Halbwachs described the religious collective memory as follows:

Although religious memory attempts to isolate itself from temporal society, it obeys the same laws as every collective memory: it does not preserve the past but reconstructs it with the aid of the material traces, rites, texts, and traditions left behind by that past, and with the aid moreover of recent psychological and social data, that is to say, with the present.[8]

Jan Assmann further developed the concept of the religious collective memory suggested by Halbwachs. Halbwachs' collective memory has been questioned

---

[4] Halbwachs, *On Collective Memory*, 40.
[5] Ibid., 52.
[6] Ibid., 52.
[7] Ibid., 53.
[8] Ibid., 119.

with regard to the social conditioning of memory. Assmann defined collective memory as "a collective concept for all knowledge that directs behavior and experience in the interactive framework of a society and one that obtains through generations in repeated societal practice and initiation."[9]

Assmann referred to memory conditioned by social and cultural contexts as "cultural memory,"[10] arguing that memory has not only a social basis but also a cultural basis.[11] He placed emphasis on the cultural effect on memories:

> We need a term to describe these processes and to relate them to historical changes in the technology of storage systems, in the sociology of the groups concerned, in the media, and in the structures of storage, tradition, and the circulation of cultural meaning – in short, to encompass all such functional concepts as tradition forming, past reference, and political identity or imagination. That term is cultural memory. It is "cultural" because it can only be realized institutionally and artificially, and it is "memory" because in relation to social communication it functions in exactly the same way as individual memory does in relation to consciousness.[12]

Based on Assmann's argument, cultural memory about the past is interrelated with the present social context in that they mutually affect each other. The cultural memory is consistently formed and conditioned by the present social and cultural context. It is even changed, modified, and updated according to changes in the present context. The memory then contributes to the formation of tradition, past reference, and identity of the present community. Those who are in the community share the memory to recognize the tradition and their past. A primary function or meaning of the memory culture is that it leads to future plans and hopes.[13] The present community will reproduce and (re-)interpret their past to project their hope for the future.

Assmann also delineated the relationship between cultural memory and identity. He explained that an important task of the collective memory developed by Halbwachs is to transmit a collective identity for those who belong to the society, by sharing memories.[14] Assmann suggested that one of the characteristics of cultural memory is "the concretion of identity."[15] He explained the relationship between cultural memory and identity:

> Cultural memory preserves the store of knowledge from which a group derives an awareness of its unity and peculiarity. The objective manifestations of cultural memory are defined through a kind of identificatory determination in a positive ('We are this') or in a negative ('that's our opposite') sense.[16]

---

[9] Assmann, "Collective Memory and Cultural Identity," 126.
[10] Assmann, *Religion and Cultural Memory*, 8; Assmann, *Cultural Memory*, 5.
[11] Assmann, *Religion and Cultural Memory*, 8.
[12] Assmann, *Cultural Memory*, 9.
[13] Ibid., 17.
[14] Assmann, *Religion and Cultural Memory*, 6–7.
[15] Assmann, "Collective Memory and Cultural Identity," 129–30.
[16] Ibid., 130.

Awareness of the unity and peculiarity of the group means that the members will have their own boundaries, which distinguish them from those who do not have any shared memory with them. This will be a collective identity for the members of the group. Collective memory or cultural memory as identity markers for a group would include reusable texts, images, and rituals specific to each society in each epoch.[17] These markers stabilize and convey that society's self-image.[18]

According to the collective or cultural memory theories by Halbwachs and Assmann, memory, identity, and society have a complementary relationship. First, the collective or cultural memory leads to the formation of shared identity, which contributes to the solidarity and maintenance of a society. As the members of a society in a certain epoch have shared memories among themselves, they have their own shared identity, which increases their solidarity and unity.

Meanwhile, the collective or cultural identity works as a boundary, which differentiates and distinguishes them from those who do not share the same cultural memories or identity. As a result, the society to which the members belong is maintained with solidarity. Along with the solidarity and maintenance of a society, the shared memories of the members of the society also develop and increase.

The solidarity and the maintenance of society become motivations for and outcomes of the collective memories and identity of those who belong to the society. The society is a place where the memories and identity are collected and shared by the members of the society and their own culture grows among them.

As Assmann implied, cultural memory and identity change as society changes. As the social and cultural contexts change throughout time, the members of the society have different experiences. As their experiences change, their shared memory also changes. Consequently, their shared identity would be adjusted to reflect the changed social context and shared memories.

Cultural memory has been recently introduced to the field of biblical studies.[19] In particular, Philip R. Davies suggested that the Bible as a whole can be considered a Judean cultural memory.[20] He argued that cultural memory is neither coherent nor monolithic.[21] Human memory inherently reflects discrete recollections in which personal and social identities are multilayered.[22] As a Judean cultural memory, the Bible is a fabric of warp-and-weft memories, woven over a long period of time. Since the biblical narrative is an agglomeration of

---

[17] Ibid., 132.
[18] Ibid.
[19] Philip R. Davies, *Memories of Ancient Israel: An Introduction to Biblical History, Ancient and Modern* (Louisville: Westminster John Knox, 2008), 111.
[20] Ibid.
[21] Ibid., 113.
[22] Ibid.

various scribal groups and traditions, it can also be considered as having been created out of "conflicting" and "collective" memories.

More specifically, Gaétane-Diane Forget suggested that the Deuteronomistic History should be considered as cultural memory.[23] Applying Halbwachs' collective memory theory to the biblical narrative, she proposed interrelatedness between the cultural memories of the past in the Bible and the identity of the biblical Israel: "Biblical Israel's identity was redefined and tweaked with each new crisis. Indeed, the exile was a most intriguing trigger as biblical Israel found itself without its markers of identity (no temple, no land), yet it found a way to renegotiate its identity and strengthen it."[24]

In particular, the Babylonian exile resulted in one of the identity crises for the Israelites.[25] Experiencing the fall of Jerusalem and the exile, the survivor group faced a huge challenge regarding their identity in the new sociocultural context. These challenges and their ensuing response are reflected in the Deuteronomistic History. Consequently, the Deuteronomistic History should be considered an example of the manipulation of memory, which created the identity for the exilic and the post-exilic community.[26] In addition, the new identity as "biblical Israel" in the Deuteronomistic History should be considered as a product of the scribes.[27]

Extending further from Forget's argument, I contend that the crisis caused by Sennacherib in 701 BCE became another important motivation for the formation of the cultural memory and the identity of the biblical Israel among the Deuteronomistic scribes. Even though the city of Jerusalem remained intact, the kingdom of Judah suffered from an extensive territorial loss and related damages during the Assyrian military campaign.

3. The Literary Context of 2 Kgs 19:30–31

The literary structure of 2 Kgs 18:13b–19:37 has long been an ongoing topic of discussion among scholars. Many believe that the account consists of two sources: A) 2 Kgs 18:13b–16 and B) 2 Kgs 18:17–19:37 (B1: 2 Kgs 18:17–19a, 36; B2: 2 Kgs 19:9b–35).[28] These two sources can be understood as two types of records or memories about the same past event. While source A provides a brief account of how Sennacherib subdued Hezekiah and received a tribute from the Judean king,

---

[23] Gaétane-Diane Forget, "Navigating 'Deuteronomistic History' as Cultural Memory," *R&T* 17.1–2 (2010): 1–12.
[24] Ibid., 4.
[25] Ibid., 7.
[26] Ibid., 8.
[27] Ibid., 10.
[28] Mordechai Cogan and Hayim Tadmor, *II Kings*, AB 11 (Garden City, N.Y: Doubleday, 1988), 240.

source B presents a long, prophetic narrative that describes how Sennacherib attacked Judah but withdrew from Jerusalem, leaving the city intact. Only source B notes that it was YHWH that thwarted Sennacherib's military campaign. More specifically, the angel of YHWH struck down the army of the Assyrian Empire, causing Sennacherib to withdraw from the siege against Jerusalem (2 Kgs 19:35–36). While source A describes the submission of Judah to Assyria without any sympathy for Hezekiah, source B highlights Hezekiah's consultation with Isaiah as well as YHWH's message to Hezekiah spoken through the prophet (2 Kgs 19:1–34). It appears likely that sources A and B came from different or even conflicting traditions or memories.

The passage of 2 Kgs 19:9b–35 is often referred to as "Hezekiah's prayer," but it actually consists of two parts: Hezekiah's prayer of supplication to YHWH and the divine answer to the king spoken through the prophet Isaiah. Meanwhile, 2 Chr 32:20 briefly describes Hezekiah and Isaiah praying to YHWH ("And the king Hezekiah and the prophet Isaiah, son of Amoz, prayed because of this and cried to the heaven"). "Hezekiah's prayer" as presented in the narrative of 2 Kgs 18:13b–19:37 describes the military conflict between the Assyrian Empire and the Kingdom of Judah in 701 BCE. In the military campaign, Sennacherib invaded Judah, and his Assyrian army prevailed (2 Kgs 18:13b). In this critical moment for Judah, Hezekiah prayed for the divine intervention from YHWH (2 Kgs 19:14–19). In response, Isaiah the prophet delivered the divine message to the king (2 Kgs 19:20–34), in which YHWH expressed disdain for Sennacherib and promised to protect the city of Jerusalem and the Davidic kingship. Finally, YHWH saved Hezekiah in Jerusalem, and the Assyrian king left the capital city of Judah intact (2 Kgs 19:35–36).

More specifically in 2 Kgs 19:20–34, Isaiah convinced the Judean king that divine help would come for an extraordinary restoration of Judah with an accusation and punishment against Sennacherib. In the prophecy, YHWH gives a sign of salvation to Hezekiah (2 Kgs 19:29–31). The sign, which is introduced in 2 Kgs 19:29, seemingly relates to the agricultural context of Judah at the time of the Assyrian military campaign. According to the message in the verse, the grain field of Judah would recover in three years. The agricultural metaphors used in reference to the sign are pertinent since the Assyrian army destroyed Judah's agricultural base during the military campaign.[29] The sign involves three years of agricultural recovery (2 Kgs 19:29).[30] According to the sign, for the first

---

[29] Cogan and Tadmor, 238; Marvin A. Sweeney, *I & II Kings: A Commentary*, OTL (Louisville: Westminster John Knox, 2007), 418.

[30] John Hayes and Stuart Irvine suggested two reasons for the three-year restoration: the Assyrian invasion from 701 BCE to 700 BCE and a sabbatical year from 700 BCE to 699 BCE (John H. Hayes and Stuart A. Irvine, *Isaiah, The Eighth-Century Prophet: His Times & His Preaching* [Nashville: Abingdon, 1987], 379–80). In the year of the Assyrian invasion, normal agricultural activity was not possible. In the following year, people should observe the sabbatical period. In the third year, people finally could resume their normal agricultural activity.

two years, the people of Judah would be able to eat without working the fields (2 Kgs 19:29a). In the first year after the Assyrian devastation, the people of Judah would eat whatever grows on its own.[31] In the second year, they would eat whatever grows afterwards. In the third year, however, the people would need to sow, reap, and plant vineyards to eat their fruit (2 Kgs 19:29b). In that year, the people would finally need to work to recover their agricultural base. Robert Cohn notes that the prophecy concerning the third year draws a picture of extraordinary fertility, which describes planting vineyards and eating their fruit in the same year.[32] Based upon Cohn's suggestion, this agricultural restoration in the third year implies a miraculous image which is related to the cultural memory about the restoration of Judah after Sennacherib's military campaign in 701 BCE.

The prophecy about the agricultural restoration is followed by a prophecy about the remnant. Brevard Childs argued that the theme of the agricultural restoration and the remnant resonates with Isaiah's son Shearjashub ("a remnant will return") in Isa 7:3 and continues with the sign of Immanuel ("God-with-us") in Isa 7:14.[33] The divine promise to David was confirmed again after Isaiah urged Ahaz to stand firm in faith (Isa 7:6–9).[34] Sweeney suggested that the agricultural metaphor is related to the regrowth of the remnant of Judah as described in Isa 11:1–16.[35] Furthermore, he pointed out that the statement described in 2 Kgs 19:31 about the remnant of Judah from Zion and the zeal of YHWH resonates with Isaianic language (cf. Isa 2:2–4; 4:2–6; 9:6).[36]

From the perspective that the passage of 2 Kgs 19:29–31 is about restoration by YHWH, it seems clear that the aftermath of the Assyrian military campaign against Judah would be significant. In that sense, the prophecy did not seem to predict what Hezekiah wanted to hear at the moment. The agricultural sign and the term, "remnant," meant that Judah would experience damage and loss in terms of its territory and people. Even though Jerusalem would remain intact, many cities of Judah were devastated by Sennacherib. It would take three years for Hezekiah and Judah to recover from the Assyrian invasion. In other words, the restoration of Judah would be a hopeful future but a time-consuming work for Hezekiah as well as Judah.

The prophecy about the restoration in 2 Kgs 19:29–31 reinforced YHWH's clear message about divine protection from the attack of Sennacherib against Hezekiah and Jerusalem, which is described in the following verses of 2 Kgs 19:32–34. In 2 Kgs 19:32, YHWH makes it clear that Sennacherib would not enter or cause any damage to the city. The prophecy also includes assurance that the

---

[31] Sweeney, *I & II Kings*, 418.
[32] Robert L. Cohn, *2 Kings* (Collegeville, MN: Liturgical Press, 2000), 138.
[33] Brevard S. Childs, *Isaiah*, OTL (Louisville: Westminster John Knox, 2001), 276.
[34] Ibid., 276.
[35] Sweeney, *I & II Kings*, 418.
[36] Ibid.

Assyrian king would return the same way that he came (2 Kgs 19:33). The last verse explains the reason for the divine protection: YHWH would defend the city for YHWH's own sake and for the sake of David, who was YHWH's servant (2 Kgs 19:34).

The divine protection is also closely related to Hezekiah himself. Christopher Seitz argued that Isaiah's prophecy about the remnant represented Hezekiah's obedience to YHWH, which is in sharp contrast with Ahaz.[37] Hezekiah is described as an ideal king of Judah in that YHWH's positive attitude toward Hezekiah is vividly expressed in 2 Kgs 19:31: "the zeal of YHWH will do this."[38]

YHWH's promise to Hezekiah through the prophet Isaiah was finally fulfilled (2 Kgs 19:35 [B2]–36 [B1]). On that night, the angel of YHWH attacked the Assyrian army (2 Kgs 19:35a); by the next morning, 185,000 were dead in the Assyrian military camp (2 Kgs 19:35b).[39] The scene is described from the perspective of the Jerusalemites ("they woke up in the morning and behold, all of the dead bodies!").[40] Cogan and Tadmor suggested that the image of the morning light after the dangerous night is associated with divine salvation (cf. Ps 90:4, 143:8; Exod 11:4, 12:29).[41] It was a painful morning for the Assyrian military camp, but it was a glorious morning for YHWH and the people of Jerusalem as well as for Hezekiah. Sennacherib left and went back to stay in Nineveh (2 Kgs 19:36).

Finally, 2 Kgs 19:37 describes the death of Sennacherib in his own land in the house of Nisroch. As he worshipped, Adrammelech and Sharezer killed him with a sword and then fled into the land of Ararat (2 Kgs 19:37a). Following Sennacherib's death, his son Esarhaddon became king (2 Kgs 19:37b). Sennacherib was assassinated in 681 BCE, leaving a twenty-year gap between his military campaign against Judah in 701 BCE and his murder. Assyrian and Babylonian documents show no direct connection between Sennnacherib's campaign and his assassination.[42] However, presenting his assassination in the concluding verse of 2 Kgs 19 seems to imply that his murder was related to his campaign against Judah. Therefore, Sennnacherib's assassination can be considered the fulfillment of another promise from YHWH to Hezekiah (2 Kgs 19:7).[43]

---

[37] Christopher R. Seitz, *Zion's Final Destiny: The Development of the Book of Isaiah: A Reassessment of Isaiah 36–39* (Minneapolis: Fortress, 1991), 89.

[38] Ibid.

[39] For more details, see Cogan and Tadmor, *II Kings*, 239; Lester L. Grabbe, "Of Mice and Dead Men: Herodotus 2.141 and Sennacherib's Campaign in 701 BCE," in *"Like a Bird in a Cage": The Invasion of Sennacherib in 701 BCE*, ed. Lester L. Grabbe, JSOTSup 363 (London: Sheffield Academic, 2003), 119–40.

[40] Cohn, *2 Kings*, 139.

[41] Cogan and Tadmor, *II Kings*, 239.

[42] Isaac Kalimi, *Reshaping of Ancient Israelite History in Chronicles* (Winona Lake, IN: Eisenbrauns, 2005), 33.

[43] Ibid.

4. Remnant, Eschatology, and Zion in 2 Kgs 19:30–31

Since the passage of 2 Kgs 19:30–31 is a part of the Deuteronomistic History, it is necessary to analyze how the terms "remnant," "the house of Judah," "Jerusalem," and "Mount Zion" are used together not only in the passage but also in the overall Deuteronomistic History. In a close analysis of the cultural memory, some specific words or expression would provide a clue for the explanation or clarification what is in or behind the memory. In the case of 2 Kgs 19:30–31, it would be important to understand the usage of the terms including "remnant," "the house of Judah," "Jerusalem," and "Mount Zion" throughout the Deuteronomistic History, as well as in the passage of 2 Kgs 19:30–31.

In 2 Kgs 19:30–31, Isaiah proclaimed through the message of YHWH that the surviving remnant of the house of Judah shall again take root downward and bear fruit upward (2 Kgs 19:30). A "remnant" shall go out or come out from Jerusalem and "those who escaped" from Mount Zion (2 Kgs 19:31). "The zeal of YHWH (of Hosts[44])" would do this (2 Kgs 19:31). This expression places emphasis on YHWH's support for the continued existence of the community.[45] With the ardent divine initiative, the future remnant would come forth.[46]

Both terms "remnant" (שאר/שארית) and "escaped remnant" (or, surviving remnant) (פליטה) are used twice in the passage of 2 Kgs 19:30–31.[47] In all cases, they are written in a feminine singular form.[48] The term שאר/שארית initially referred to those who survived the threat and destruction of communities in a negative sense, but later described those who survived with hope for a restored nation in a positive sense.[49] The word is used several times in the Deuteronomistic History (2 Sam 14:7; 2 Kgs 19:4, 21:14). In the book of 2 Samuel, the term refers to those who survived a blood vengeance in a family from Tekoa (2 Sam 14:7). The "remnant" in the books of Kings is applied to those who remained after the territorial loss of Israel and Judah.[50] In 2 Kgs 17:18, it is described that YHWH caused Israel to be conquered and removed by Assyria in 722 BCE and the tribe of Judah to remain alone.[51] Then, the "remnant" in 2 Kgs 19:4 clarifies the impending threat of Sennacherib upon Judah. The Assyrian army led by Sennacherib would advance against Judah and cause extensive damage. Regardless of the military threat, there would be survivors from the military campaign.

---

[44] Written in Hebrew MSS and Isa 37:32.
[45] Gerhard F. Hasel, *The Remnant: The History and Theology of the Remnant Idea from Genesis to Isaiah*, 2nd ed., AUMSR 5 (Berrien Springs, MI: Andrews University Press, 1974), 338.
[46] Ibid.
[47] יתר is basically synonymous with either of these terms, since it is used in parallelism with them elsewhere (Ezek 6:8, 14:22 [with פליטה]; Josh 11:22; Isa 4:3; Jer 34:7; 44:7 [with שאר]).
[48] Hasel, *The Remnant*, 336.
[49] R. E. Clements, "Šāʾar," *TDOT* 14:285.
[50] Ibid., 279.
[51] Ibid., 279.

Regarding the term פליטה, "escaped remnant" (or, "surviving remnant"), it refers to a remnant who is left over.[52] In particular, the term designates a remnant who has escaped from a war, a battle, or the like.[53] Hasel suggested that the word includes a positive notion of surviving a military action.[54] This escape can be related to salvation by YHWH.[55]

In the passage of 2 Kgs 19:30–31 (Isa 37:31–32), both of the "remnant" and the "escaped remnant" refer to remnants after Judah was weakened and lost its territory to Sennacherib of the Assyrian Empire.[56] Later, the "remnant" names those whom YHWH would cast out of YHWH's heritage along with Jerusalem and give into the hand of the enemies (2 Kgs 21:14).

The passage of 2 Kgs 19:30–31 does not explicitly mention any historical figure, such as Hezekiah or Sennacherib; it only describes the surviving remnant, or survivors. Continuing plant imagery in 2 Kgs 19:29, the remnant (or survivors) shall "take root downward," "bear fruit upward," and "go out." Seitz suggested the "remnant" in 2 Kgs 19:30–31 was interrelated to the reference in other passages in that the "remnant of the house of Judah" and "a remnant from Jerusalem" conform with Hezekiah's plea to Isaiah to pray "for the remnant that is left" (2 Kgs 19:4).[57] This supports the position that the distinctive poetic section is related to the narrative section through the repetition of the term "remnant."

As briefly written above, both the "remnant" and the "escaped remnant" are used in relation to specific origins or locations: the house of Judah, Jerusalem, and Mount Zion in 2 Kgs 19:30–31. In 2 Kgs 19:30, the remnant is described as being from the house of Judah (בית יהודה). While "the house of Judah" is written several times in the Deuteronomistic History and Isaiah (2 Sam 2:4, 7, 10, 11; 1 Kgs 12:21, 23; 2 Kgs 19:30; Isa 22:21, 37:31), it is used with "remnant" only in 2 Kgs 19:30/Isa 37:31.[58] Zobel pointed out that the expression "the house of Judah" originally referred to the monarchy of David at Hebron, but it later came to be used to contrast with the house of Israel.[59] The house of Israel had fallen to Assyria in 2 Kgs 17:1–23. After the fall, Israelites were exiled to Assyria, including in Halah; on the Habor, the river of Gozan; and in the cities of the Medes (2 Kgs 17:6). Furthermore, Assyria brought people from Babylon, Cuthah, Avva, Hamath, and Sepharvaim and placed them in the cities of Samaria (2 Kgs 17:24). In contrast to the devastated and fallen house of Israel, 2 Kings 19:30 explains

---

[52] Gerhard F. Hasel, "Pālaṭ," *TDOT* 11:560.
[53] Ibid.
[54] Ibid.
[55] Ibid. *yeter* can also have the same connotation.
[56] Clements, "Šāʾar," 279.
[57] Seitz, *Zion's Final Destiny*, 89.
[58] Nazek Khaled Matty, *Sennacherib's Campaign against Judah and Jerusalem in 701 B.C.: A Historical Reconstruction*, BZAW 487 (Berlin: de Gruyter, 2016), 170.
[59] Hans-Jürgen Zobel, "yehûdâ," *TWAT* 3:525.

that "the surviving remnant of the house of Judah" shall prosper like a plant with extraordinary fertility in security.[60]

According to 2 Kgs 19:31, a remnant shall go out from Jerusalem and a band of survivors from Mount Zion. In the verse, they are written in a parallel form with the verb phrase "go out" (*yṣ'*). Jerusalem was a pivotal place in the narrative about the military conflict between Hezekiah and Sennacherib. As the fortified cities of Judah were taken by the Assyrian army, Jerusalem was left alone (2 Kgs 18:13). Jerusalem was the place where the Assyrian king and Hezekiah confronted each other.

In apposition to Jerusalem, Mount Zion is mentioned as a place from where survivors shall go out in 2 Kgs 19:31, which is used only once in the Deuteronomistic History. Other than in 2 Kgs 19:31, Mount Zion can be found frequently in Psalms (Ps 48:2, 11; 74:2; 78:68; 125:1) and Isaiah (Isa 4:5; 8:18; 10:12; 18:7; 24:23; 29:8; 31:4; 37:32), as well as in Lamentations (Lam 5:18), Joel (Joel 2:32), Obadiah (Obad 17, 21), and Micah (Mic 4:7). Meanwhile, "Zion" is used three times in the Deuteronomistic History (2 Sam 5:7; 1 Kgs 8:1; 2 Kgs 19:21), referring to the city of David in the narrative (2 Sam 5:7; 1 Kgs 8:1) and in apposition to Jerusalem in Isaiah's prophecy to Hezekiah ("virgin daughter of Zion" and "daughter of Jerusalem") (2 Kgs 19:21). The parallel between Zion and Jerusalem in 2 Kgs 19:21 can be compared to the parallel between Jerusalem and Mount Zion in 2 Kgs 19:31.

Based upon the analysis of the term "remnant" in its relation to "the house of Judah," "Jerusalem," and "Mount Zion," it is possible that the passage of 2 Kgs 19:30–31 has an eschatological facet. Gerhard Von Rad suggested the presence of an "eschatological thread" in the book of Deuteronomy.[61] The promise of the land by YHWH was fulfilled in the past, but it still remained as a renewable promise in the future.[62] This renewable promise of land by YHWH and its eschatological aspect with a future hope suggested by Von Rad can be applied to 2 Kgs 19:30–31 in that the passage proclaims the restoration and even the prosperity of the house of Judah with the remnant from Jerusalem and Zion after the crisis caused by Sennacherib. The agricultural image in 2 Kgs 19:29 represents the vision of the prophet regarding YHWH's deliverance.[63] With the agricultural image, the prophecy continues to describe the remnant and the survivors in relation to the house of Judah, Jerusalem, and Mount Zion. Then, it is followed by another portion of prophecy (2 Kgs 19:32–34), in which YHWH would defend the city of Jerusalem from Sennacherib for the sake of YHWH and David. Paul

---

[60] Walter Brueggemann, *1 & 2 Kings* (Macon, GA: Smyth & Helwys, 2000), 509–10; Cohn, *2 Kings*, 138.

[61] Gerhard von Rad, *The Problem of the Hexateuch: And Other Essays*, trans. E. W. Trueman Decken (Edinburgh: Oliver & Boyd, 1966), 92–93.

[62] Ibid., 93.

[63] Brueggemann, *1 & 2 Kings*, 511–12.

Hanson argued that prophetic and apocalyptic statements have eschatological elements.[64] Due to the existence of the eschatological features in both phases in the prophetic tradition, he suggested terms such as "prophetic eschatology" and "apocalyptic eschatology."[65] He defined prophetic eschatology as "prophetic announcement to the nation of the divine plans for Israel and the world."[66] Meanwhile, apocalyptic eschatology is defined as "the disclosure to the elect of the cosmic vision of Yahweh's sovereignty."[67] The essential difference between prophetic and apocalyptic eschatology is in the realm of divine intervention.[68] While prophetic eschatology centers on divine activity in the politico-historical realm, apocalyptic eschatology encompasses divine activity in the cosmic realm.[69] Hanson emphasized that "the essential vision of restoration persists in both, the vision Yahweh's people restored as a holy community in a glorified Zion."[70] Considering these definitions and the categorization of the prophetic tradition suggested by Hanson, it is possible that the prophecy of Isaiah in 2 Kgs 19:30–31 contains prophetic eschatology with a future hope in YHWH. As noted earlier, the prophecy does not explicitly mention Hezekiah or Sennacherib, but it describes the divine intervention for salvation in the politico-historical realm of Judah at the time of the Assyrian military campaign against Hezekiah.

An eschatological aspect in 2 Kgs 19:30–31 can be found within the character of Hezekiah himself in the narrative of 2 Kgs 19:9b–35. Von Rad pointed out that 2 Kgs 25:27–30 represents the unresolved tension between judgment and hope in the books of Kings.[71] In the midst of such a tension, the narrative of Kings sets focus on the individual kings.[72] More specifically, the books of Kings assume that the righteousness of the kings in the eyes of YHWH had an impact on the whole kingdom.[73] Regarding the description of Hezekiah, a comparison between the books of Kings and Isaiah reveals the characterization of the king and its implication in the narrative of 2 Kgs 18–19. Provan asserted that Hezekiah has become a fully eschatological figure in the context of the book of Isaiah,[74] detached from any historical background.[75] According to Sweeney, the

---

[64] Paul D. Hanson, *The Dawn of Apocalyptic*, rev. ed. (Philadelphia: Fortress, 1983), 10.
[65] Ibid.
[66] Ibid., 11.
[67] Ibid.
[68] Ibid., 11–12.
[69] Ibid.
[70] Ibid., 12.
[71] Gerhard von Rad, *The Theology of Israel's Historical Traditions*, vol. 1 of *Old Testament Theology*, trans. D. M. G. Stalker, (Edinburgh: Oliver and Boyd, 1962), 334–47.
[72] Ibid., 344.
[73] Ibid., 344–45.
[74] Iain W. Provan, "The Messiah in the Books of Kings," in *The Lord's Anointed: Interpretation of Old Testament Messianic Texts*, ed. P. E. Satterthwaite, Richard S. Hess, and Gordon J. Wenham (Carlisle: Paternoster, 1995), 82–83.
[75] Ibid., 82.

description of Hezekiah in Isaiah was "a virtual whitewash of his character."[76] In terms of a diachronic order, it is possible that the narrative of Isaiah draws from Kings.[77] In the case of Hezekiah in Kings, both of his own ideal and weak (or even undesirable) dimensions are described. When Sennacherib advanced against him, he submitted and paid his tribute to Sennacherib (2 Kgs 18:13–16), which shows that Hezekiah had an undesirable aspect as king of Judah. Later, Hezekiah is described as depending upon YHWH's divine intervention during the Assyrian military campaign against Judah (2 Kgs 19:1–34). As a response to Hezekiah's desperate request, YHWH sent the angel of YHWH to strike down the Assyrian army in one night, after which Sennacherib returned home (2 Kgs 18:35–36).

A possible concern about the eschatological character of Hezekiah in the books of Kings is whether a distinction can be drawn between hope for the future that is this-worldly, national, and political, and hope for the future that is concerned with the final age itself: "eschatological."[78] It is difficult to determine if Hezekiah is described as a future-oriented ideal king in the present or even as a messianic king in mythological language.[79] At least, however, Hezekiah is described as having an eschatological aspect as an ideal king who depended upon YHWH in his time of crisis, while still having undesirable aspects including his tribute to Sennacherib (2 Kgs 18:13–16), in the narrative of Kings.

The eschatological aspects of 2 Kgs 19:30–31 and Hezekiah are reinforced by the Zion tradition reflected in the phrase, "Mount Zion" (2 Kgs 19:31). The origin of the tradition can be traced back to the pre-Davidic or pre-Israelite traditions.[80] Later, Mount Zion became often associated with the temple where

---

[76] Sweeney, *I & II Kings*, 411.

[77] There have been consistent debates about the diachronic relationship between Kings and Isaiah. R. E. Clements and Brevard Childs asserted that the "remnant" in 2 Kgs 19:30–31 seems to be interrelated to Shear-Jashub, Isaiah's son, ("a remnant will return") in Isa 7:3 and to the sign of Immanuel ("God-with-us") in Isa 7:14 (R. E. Clements, *Isaiah and the Deliverance of Jerusalem: A Study of the Interpretation of Prophecy in the Old Testament* [Sheffield: JSOT Press, 1980], 57; Childs, *Isaiah*, 276.). In particular, Clements proposed that the prophecy in 2 Kgs 19:29–31 is a secondary development of the theme of the remnant derived from the prophecy of Isaiah (Clements, *Isaiah and the Deliverance of Jerusalem*, 57; Brueggemann, *1 & 2 Kings*, 511). Accordingly, the overall theme would be the return of the remnant, even though it is not specified from where the remnant would return. Evans, however, argued that the connection between 2 Kgs 19 and Isa 7 is not clear (Paul S. Evans, *The Invasion of Sennacherib in the Book of Kings: A Source-Critical and Rhetorical Study of 2 Kings 18–19*, VTSup 125 [Leiden: Brill, 2009], 57). He suggests that the word "remnant" often calls up images of return from exile, which is not necessary (Ibid., 57–58). Richard Nelson suggested that exilic readers would have reinterpreted the "surviving remnant" in 2 Kgs 19:30 as themselves, even though it is related to the actual survivors from the Assyrian siege in the context of the passage (Richard D. Nelson, *First and Second Kings* [Louisville: Westminster John Knox, 1987], 241).

[78] Andrew Chester, *Future Hope and Present Reality*, WUNT 293 (Tübingen: Mohr Siebeck, 2012), 230.

[79] Ibid., 230.

[80] John H. Hayes, "The Tradition of Zion's Inviolability," *JBL* 82.4 (1963): 419–26.

YHWH dwelled.[81] The concept of a permanent place for the divine being belongs to the United Monarchy, but it was challenged during the period of the Hezekian-Josianic reforms.[82] During that period, the name of the divine was believed to reside in the sanctuary.[83] In a close relationship to Jerusalem, the Zion tradition was developed after the military campaign of Sennacherib against Hezekiah of Judah.[84] Clements suggested that the narrative was composed after the late 7th century, when the Assyrian control over Judah was declining.[85] According to 2 Kgs 18:17–19:37 (Isaiah 36–37), Jerusalem was not conquered during the military conflict with the divine protection of YHWH. Even though the Assyrian army of Sennacherib captured the fortified cities of Judah (2 Kings 18:13), the capital city of Judah was not captured. The belief in Zion's inviolability was formed after Jerusalem remained intact following Sennacherib's invasion.[86] The survival of Jerusalem and its Davidic monarchy in the midst of the Assyrian military campaign became evidence of the divine protection.[87] Although there have been consistent debates about the reason why the capital city of Judah was not destroyed, it is evident that the city was intact during the Assyrian military campaign against Judah. This occasion inspired the idea of the divine protection and the inviolability of Jerusalem. The interrelatedness between Jerusalem and Zion led to the advancement of the concept of the inviolability of Zion. Clements suggested that Israel's future was deeply related to the divine commitment to Mount Zion.[88]

Furthermore, Sweeney suggested that the passage of 2 Kgs 19:32–34 represents the Zion tradition.[89] The prophetic proclamation begins with לכן (2 Kgs 19:32), which is a typical introductory word for an announcement of divine judgment in a prophetic judgment speech.[90] It is followed by the messenger formula, "thus says YHWH to the king of Assyria," which represents the oracle by YHWH.[91] An arrow, a shield, and a siege-ramp from the Assyrian military camp signified the army's military tactics against Judah, especially, Lachish.[92] In relation to 2 Kgs 19:31, the oracle in 2 Kgs 19:32–34 repeats the theme of the Zion tradition,

---

[81] Moshe Weinfeld, *Deuteronomy and the Deuteronomic School* (Oxford: Clarendon, 1972), 196.

[82] Ibid., 197.

[83] Ibid.

[84] Clements, *Isaiah and the Deliverance of Jerusalem*, 72–89.

[85] R. E. Clements, "Zion as Symbol and Political Reality: A Central Isaianic Quest," in *Studies in the Book of Isaiah: Festschrift Willem A. M. Beuken*, ed. J. van Ruiten and M. Vervenne (Leuven: Leuven University Press; Peeters, 1997), 12.

[86] Clements, *Isaiah and the Deliverance of Jerusalem*, 85.

[87] Clements, "Zion as Symbol and Political Reality," 12.

[88] Ibid., 15.

[89] Sweeney, *I & II Kings*, 419.

[90] Ibid.

[91] Ibid.

[92] Ibid.

in which YHWH defends Jerusalem and the Davidic king.[93] The divine intervention and Sennacherib's return to Assyria described in the following verses of 2 Kgs 19:35–36 reinforce the Zion tradition.[94]

5. Second Kings 19:30–31 as Scribal Cultural Memory

As a part of the Deuteronomistic History, the passage of 2 Kgs 19:30–31 reflects the cultural memory of the scribes in that it was formed not only by a specific social context (a synchronic dimension) but also by concepts transmitted through generations which can be called traditions (a diachronic dimension).[95] In other words, the analysis of the cultural memory implied in 2 Kgs 19:30–31 needs to consider the date of writing and its related sociopolitical context(s). This is important in that it can help to elucidate any possible future hope or even eschatological element that can be found in the passage. In particular, the date of writing would clarify whom the Deuteronomists were referring to when mentioning the "remnant" in the passage.

Regarding the date of writing of 2 Kgs 19:30–31, however, it is difficult to determine exactly when it was written or redacted.[96] Campbell and O'Brien even suggested that the passage is too idiosyncratic to be easily characterized.[97] Related to the unspecified date of writing, there has been disagreement about the identity of the remnant in 2 Kgs 19:30–31. Related to the date of the writing of the phrase, "the surviving remnant of the house of Judah," Seitz suggested that it is difficult to relate the "remnant" in Isaiah's prophecy in Isa 37:30–32/2 Kgs 19:29–31 to a post-587 situation.[98] According to him, the phrase cannot be found in the vocabulary of the post-587 redaction.[99] He also pointed out that "house of Judah" is separated from the parallel of Jerusalem and Mount Zion in the prophecy.[100]

---

[93] Ibid.
[94] Ibid.
[95] Benjamin D. Giffone and Jin H. Han also explore the relationship between the transmission and the redaction of the Deuteronomistic History and cultural memory in their contributions to this volume. Giffone sets his focus on 1 Kgs 18 in terms of balancing between theological "risks and rewards" ("Regathering Too Many Stones? Scribal Constraints, Community Memory, and the 'Problem' of Elijah's Sacrifice for Deuteronomism in Kings"). Han deals with oneiromancy in Deut 13:2–6 in terms of the negotiation between its attraction and potential danger ("Did the Deuteronomist Detest Dreams?").
[96] Jutta Hausmann, *Israels Rest: Studien zum Selbstverständnis der nachexilischen Gemeinde*, BWANT 7 (Stuttgart: Kohlhammer, 1987), 132–33.
[97] Antony F. Campbell and Mark A. O'Brien, *Unfolding the Deuteronomistic History: Origins, Upgrades, Present Text* (Minneapolis: Fortress, 2000), 451.
[98] Seitz, *Zion's Final Destiny*, 90–91.
[99] Ibid., 90.
[100] Ibid., 91.

This separate use of "house of Judah" would reflect the historical reality that Sennacherib devastated Judah but not Jerusalem in 701 BCE.[101]

With the suggestions for a pre-exilic date of writing, a possibility of exilic and post-exilic work on the passage has also been suggested. The positive attitude towards the Davidic dynasty and Jerusalem as its core place is found in the Deuteronomistic History.[102] The Deuteronomists were interested in the Davidic monarchy and the cultic centralization of the Jerusalem temple.[103] Albertz proposed that they preserved their hope for the future in their writing, even after the exile.[104] The purpose of the Deuteronomistic History was to illustrate this hope with the restoration of the state cult of Jerusalem and the restoration of the Davidic monarchy.[105] The Deuteronomists intended to project a possibility for future restoration and return from their exile. Consequently, their memories and writing of their past related to the fall of Judah and the Babylonian exile would be modified and even changed in a positive aspect.

Cogan and Tadmor suggested that the passage of 2 Kgs 19:14–19 contains a postexilic element. According to them, Hezekiah's prayer conforms to the known form of petition.[106] In particular, the prayer includes "Deuteronomic echoes," such as "man's handicraft/mere wood and stone" (cf. Deut 4:28), "YHWH alone is God" (cf. Deut 4:35), "to destroy them" (cf. Deut 12:2), and "kingdoms of the earth" (cf. Deut 28:25, Jer 15:4; 24:9), which reveal its compositional origin.[107] In the prayer, the theme of creation appears in 2 Kgs 19:15b ("You [YHWH] made the heaven and the earth"). The cosmogonic concept, which was uncommon in the Deuteronomistic History, became an important element in the exilic and the postexilic liturgy.[108]

Regarding the passage of 2 Kgs 19:30–31, some other scholars suggested the exilic or post-exilic date of writing. Chester noted that the existence of eschatological messianic hope through kings, including Hezekiah in the books of Kings, can be considered a response to the disaster of 597/587 and beyond.[109] Furthermore, Hausmann argued that the accumulation of names from the house of Judah, Jerusalem, and Zion is to remove any doubt about Judah's positive future.[110] He suggested that it could be located in the exilic period or in the

---
[101] Ibid.
[102] Weinfeld, *Deuteronomy and the Deuteronomic School*, 169.
[103] Rainer Albertz, *Israel in Exile: The History and Literature of the Sixth Century B.C.E.*, trans. David Green, StBL 3 (Atlanta: Society of Biblical Literature, 2003), 281.
[104] Ibid., 281–82.
[105] Ibid., 302.
[106] Cogan and Tadmor, *II Kings*, 235.
[107] Ibid., 236.
[108] Weinfeld, *Deuteronomy and the Deuteronomic School*, 39; Cogan and Tadmor, *II Kings*, 236.
[109] Chester, *Future Hope and Present Reality*, 231.
[110] Hausmann, *Israels Rest*, 131–34.

post-exilic period.[111] Brueggemann also considered it possible that the use of "remnant" and "survivor" is related to the Isaiah tradition and also to an exilic or postexilic context.[112]

Among various perspectives and suggestions on this unresolved issue of the date of writing for 2 Kgs 19:30–31 as briefly written above, I assert the likelihood of the pre-exilic setting for the writing of the passage. As described in 2 Kgs 19:30, the surviving remnant of the house of Judah, which can be considered as a contrast to the house Israel, would settle down again to prosper. A primary reason for them to do so can be found in 2 Kgs 19:31; for a remnant shall go out from Jerusalem and a surviving remnant from Mount Zion. Without any implication or description about "return" of the remnant, which would be related to the exilic or the post-exilic historical situation, the verse describes that a remnant going out from Jerusalem and Mount Zion. In particular, the phrase, "Mount Zion," reflects the Zion tradition which was developed during the pre-exilic period not long after Sennacherib's campaign in 701 BCE.

6. Synopsis: 2 Kgs 19:30–31 as Pre-exilic Deuteronomistic Cultural Memory with an Eschatological Strand and the Zion Tradition

The passage of 2 Kgs 19:30–31 can be understood as pre-exilic scribal cultural memory about Sennacherib's military campaign against Judah. In other words, an earlier writing or redaction of the passage is possibly situated in the pre-exilic period after 701 BCE. In this socio-historical context, Isaiah's prophecy about the remnant in 2 Kgs 19:30–31 seems to represent those who survived the Assyrian military attack in 701 BCE. The aftermath of the Assyrian military campaign was devastating (2 Kgs 18:13; 19:29). In spite of the territorial and agricultural damage, the kingdom of Judah was able to preserve the Davidic kingship and Jerusalem until early 6th century BCE.

Based on the assumption of the pre-exilic setting for the 2 Kgs 19:30–31, it is possible to see how the Deuteronomists reflected upon their past, present, and future in their "collective" cultural memory with a hope in YHWH throughout their historical moments of crisis and turmoil. After Sennacherib's devastating military campaign in 701 BCE, the pre-exilic Deuteronomists developed the pre-existing Zion tradition about the inviolability of Jerusalem under YHWH's protection and the notion of the surviving remnant with an eschatological aspect. Therefore, the "remnant" in 2 Kgs 19:30–31 is both a historical and also an eschatological entity that reflects the pre-exilic Deuteronomists' cultural memory. Finally, their "collective" cultural memory gave a new identity to the group who

---

[111] Ibid., 132–33.
[112] Brueggemann, *1 & 2 Kings*, 511–12.

had survived Sennacherib's military campaign as the "remnant" from Jerusalem and Mount Zion with a future hope for the prosperity of the house of Judah.

Bibliography

Albertz, Rainer. *Israel in Exile: The History and Literature of the Sixth Century B.C.E.* Translated by David Green. StBL 3. Atlanta: Society of Biblical Literature, 2003.

Allen, Leslie C. *The Books of Joel, Obadiah, Jonah, and Micah*. Grand Rapids: Eerdmans, 2008.

Assmann, Jan. "Collective Memory and Cultural Identity." Translated by John Czaplicka. *NGC* 65 (1995): 125–33. https://doi.org/10.2307/488538.

Assmann, Jan. *Cultural Memory and Early Civilization Writing, Remembrance, and Political Imagination*. Cambridge: Cambridge University Press, 2011.

Assmann, Jan. *Religion and Cultural Memory: Ten Studies*. CMP. Stanford, CA: Stanford University Press, 2006.

Blenkinsopp, Joseph. *Isaiah 1–39: A New Translation with Introduction and Commentary*. 1st ed. New York: Doubleday, 2000.

Brueggemann, Walter. *1 & 2 Kings*. Macon, GA: Smyth & Helwys, 2000.

Campbell, Antony F., and Mark A. O'Brien. *Unfolding the Deuteronomistic History: Origins, Upgrades, Present Text*. Minneapolis: Fortress, 2000.

Chester, Andrew. *Future Hope and Present Reality*. WUNT 293. Tübingen: Mohr Siebeck, 2012.

Childs, Brevard S. *Isaiah*. 1st ed. OTL. Louisville: Westminster John Knox, 2001.

Clements, R. E. *Isaiah and the Deliverance of Jerusalem: A Study of the Interpretation of Prophecy in the Old Testament*. Sheffield: JSOT Press, 1980.

Clements, R. E. "Šāʾar." In *Theological Dictionary of the Old Testament*, edited by G. Johannes Botterweck, Helmer Ringgren, and Heinz-Josef Fabry, XIV:272–86. Grand Rapids, MI: William B. Eerdmans Publishing Co., 2004.

Clements, R. E. "Zion as Symbol and Political Reality: A Central Isaianic Quest." Pages 3–17 in *Studies in the Book of Isaiah: Festschrift Willem A. M. Beuken*. Edited by J. van Ruiten and M. Vervenne. Leuven: Leuven University Press; Peeters, 1997.

Cogan, Mordechai, and Hayim Tadmor. *II Kings*. 1st ed. AB 11. Garden City, NY: Doubleday, 1988.

Cohn, Robert L. *2 Kings*. Collegeville, MN: Liturgical Press, 2000.

Davies, Philip R. *Memories of Ancient Israel: An Introduction to Biblical History, Ancient and Modern*. Louisville: Westminster John Knox, 2008.

Evans, Paul S. *The Invasion of Sennacherib in the Book of Kings: A Source-Critical and Rhetorical Study of 2 Kings 18–19*. VTSup 125. Leiden: Brill, 2009.

Forget, Gaétane-Diane. "Navigating 'Deuteronomistic History' as Cultural Memory." *R&T* 17.1–2 (2010): 1–12. https://doi.org/10.1163/157430110X517889.

Fulton, Deirdre N. "The Exile and the Exilic Communities." Pages 230–35 in *Behind the Scenes of the Old Testament: Cultural, Social, and Historical Contexts*. Edited by Jonathan S. Greer, John W. Hilber, and John H. Walton. Grand Rapids: Baker Academic, 2018.

Grabbe, Lester L. "Of Mice and Dead Men: Herodotus 2.141 and Sennacherib's Campaign in 701 BCE." Pages 119–40 in *"Like a Bird in a Cage": The Invasion of Sennacherib in 701 BCE*. Edited by Lester L. Grabbe. JSOTSup 363. London: Sheffield Academic, 2003.

Greer, Jonathan S., John W. Hilber, and John H. Walton, eds. *Behind the Scenes of the Old Testament: Cultural, Social, and Historical Contexts*. Grand Rapids: Baker Academic, 2018.

Halbwachs, Maurice. *On Collective Memory*. Translated by Lewis A. Coser. Chicago: University of Chicago Press, 1992.

Hanson, Paul D. *The Dawn of Apocalyptic*. Rev. ed. Philadelphia: Fortress, 1983.

Hasel, Gerhard F. "Pālaṭ." In *Theological Dictionary of the Old Testament*, edited by G. Johannes Botterweck, Helmer Ringgren, and Heinz-Josef Fabry, XI:551–67. Grand Rapids, MI: William B. Eerdmans Publishing Co., 2001.

Hasel, Gerhard F. *The Remnant: The History and Theology of the Remnant Idea from Genesis to Isaiah*. 2nd ed. AUMSR 5. Berrien Springs, MI: Andrews University Press, 1974.

Hausmann, Jutta. *Israels Rest: Studien zum Selbstverständnis der nachexilischen Gemeinde*. BWANT 7. Stuttgart: Kohlhammer, 1987.

Hayes, John H. "The Tradition of Zion's Inviolability." *JBL* 82.4 (1963): 419–26.

Hayes, John H., and Stuart A. Irvine. *Isaiah, The Eighth-Century Prophet: His Times & His Preaching*. Nashville: Abingdon, 1987.

Kalimi, Isaac. *Reshaping of Ancient Israelite History in Chronicles*. Winona Lake, IN: Eisenbrauns, 2005.

Lambert, W. G. "A Document from a Community of Exiles in Babylonia." Pages 201–5 in *New Seals and Inscriptions, Hebrew, Idumean, and Cuneiform*. Edited by Meir Lubetski. Sheffield: Sheffield Phoenix, 2007.

Matty, Nazek Khaled. *Sennacherib's Campaign against Judah and Jerusalem in 701 B.C.: A Historical Reconstruction*. BZAW 487. Berlin: de Gruyter, 2016.

Nelson, Richard D. *First and Second Kings*. Louisville: Westminster John Knox, 1987.

Pearce, Laurie E. "'Judean': A Special Status in Neo-Babylonian and Achemenid Babylonia?" Pages 267–77 in *Judah and the Judeans in the Achaemenid Period: Negotiating Identity in an International Context*. Edited by Oded Lipschits, Gary N. Knoppers, and Manfred Oeming. Winona Lake, IN: Eisenbrauns, 2011.

Person, Raymond F., Jr. *Second Zechariah and the Deuteronomic School*. Sheffield: JSOT Press, 1993.

Provan, Iain W. "The Messiah in the Books of Kings." Pages 67–85 in *The Lord's Anointed: Interpretation of Old Testament Messianic Texts*. Edited by P. E. Satterthwaite, Richard S. Hess, and Gordon J. Wenham. Carlisle: Paternoster, 1995.

Seitz, Christopher R. *Zion's Final Destiny: The Development of the Book of Isaiah: A Reassessment of Isaiah 36–39*. Minneapolis: Fortress, 1991.

Sweeney, Marvin A. *I & II Kings: A Commentary*. 1st ed. OTL. Louisville: Westminster John Knox, 2007.

Van Seters, John. *In Search of History: Historiography in the Ancient World and the Origins of Biblical History*. New Haven: Yale University Press, 1983.

Von Rad, Gerhard. *Old Testament Theology*. Translated by D. M. G. Stalker. 2 vols. Edinburgh: Oliver & Boyd, 1962.

Von Rad, Gerhard. *The Problem of the Hexateuch: And Other Essays*. Translated by E. W. Trueman Decken. Edinburgh: Oliver & Boyd, 1966.

Weinfeld, Moshe. *Deuteronomy and the Deuteronomic School*. Oxford: Clarendon, 1972.

Nehemiah 5:1–13 as Innerbiblical Interpretation of Pentateuchal Slavery Laws*

Roger S. Nam

> "Debt is a social and
> ideological construct,
> not a simple economic fact."
> Noam Chomsky[1]

1. Introduction

For much of the twentieth century, biblical scholarship was singularly focused on reconstructions of texts. Nahum's Sarna's publication, "Psalm 89: A Study in Inner Biblical Exegesis" (1963) brought forth a new perspective in recognizing diachronic movements within biblical texts themselves.[2] As studies of intertextuality became widespread in other literary fields, these approaches were largely neglected in biblical studies, until the publication of Michael Fishbane's *Biblical Interpretation in Ancient Israel* and multiple studies by his students, particularly Benjamin Sommer, Bernard Levinson and William Schniedewind.[3]

---

* I am grateful to Johannes Unsok Ro in convening this group of scholars to continue the conversations on scribalism in relation to our collective understanding of the social world of ancient Israel. An earlier version of this paper was presented at a session in the joint session Intertextuality and the Hebrew Bible and Slavery, Resistance and Freedom. My thanks to Bernadette Brooten, Stacy Davis, Hyun Chul Paul Kim, and Shelley Long for facilitating this productive session.

[1] Noam Chomsky, "The People Always Pay," *The Guardian*, Jan 21, 1999, accessed Apr 26, 2022. http://www.theguardian.com/world/1999/jan/21/debtrelief.development3. Notably, this quote was made in the middle of the flourishing of Neo-classical economics and long before the debt crisis of 2008. Said crisis has caused the field of economics to pivot away from the free market advocacy of Ronald Reagan, Margaret Thatcher, and others; see Roger Nam, "Biblical Studies, COVID-19, and Our Response to Growing Inequality," *JBL* 139 (2020): 600–606.

[2] Nahum Sarna, "Psalm 89: A Study in Inner Biblical Exegesis," in *Biblical and Other Studies*, ed. A. Altmann (Cambridge, MA: Harvard University Press, 1963), 29–46.

[3] Michael Fishbane, *Biblical Interpretation in Ancient Israel* (Oxford: Clarendon, 1985); for representative examples, see Bernard Levinson, *Deuteronomy and the Hermeneutics of Legal Innovation* (Oxford: Oxford University Press, 1997); William Schniedewind, *Society and the Promise to David: The Reception History of 2 Samuel 7:1–17* (Oxford: Oxford University Press, 1999); Benjamin Sommer, *A Prophet Reads Scripture: Allusion in Isaiah 40–66* (Stanford, CA: Stanford University Press, 1998); the very terms of innerbiblical exegesis, early biblical interpre-

A parallel development took place in European scholarship, with Odil Steck's studies of the conjoining aspects of the different layers of Isaiah.[4] These foundational studies on intertextuality centered on specific lemma and techniques that signaled the adjustment and modification of another biblical text. But these approaches were not exclusive to textual studies. Rather, both Levinson and Schniedewind explicitly integrate their social settings into their studies of intertextuality. Pursuant to this volume, scribal activity does not occur within a vacuum, but within specific social settings that will impact all points throughout the "Making of the Hebrew Scriptures."

In this similar vein, I will look at the aspect of intertextuality, specifically the relationship of Neh 5:1–13 to pentateuchal passages. Rather than rely solely on traditional literary critical methods, I will use economic anthropology as a reading lens to think through Neh 5:1–13 as a form of scribal activity via interbiblical interpretation. Despite modern assumptions to the contrary, economic activity is not detached and merely transactional. Rather, economic activity is deeply embedded within social and cultural ideals. Consequently, in considering the intertextuality between Nehemiah 5 and related pentateuchal passages, I will contend that the shifting economic circumstances during the Persian period fundamentally influenced the textual development. These shifts redefined the economic language of terms like "loans, interests, credit, forgiveness, pledges" as they all relate to the phenomena of debt easement as portrayed in Neh 5. As other scholars have noted, pentateuchal texts informed these traditions. But, in addition, the shifting economic climate of Yehud also had a significant imprint on the passage, as it protests against the redistributive economy and calls for a return to a kinship-based economy based on reciprocity.

2. Prior Scholarship on the Intertextuality of Neh 5:1–13

Neh 5:1–13 occupies a pivotal shift in the overarching narrative of Ezra-Nehemiah. In the midst of the mandate for temple repair and reconstruction, Neh 5:1–13 interrupts the wall-building narrative of the surrounding chapters, and departs with the repetitive hear-formula ("And as Sanballat and Tobiah heard ..." Neh 4:1; 6:1). Surprisingly, Neh 5 essentially omits any mention of wall construction. In contrast, Neh 5 shares structure and content similarities with

---

tation, intertextuality, etc. are all nuanced with different assumptions. For a review, see William S. Schniedewind, "Innerbiblical Exegesis," *IVPBD* 6: 502–9.

[4] Odil Hannes Steck, *Studien zu Tritojesaja* (Berlin: de Gruyter, 1991); see also studies by R. Kratz, "Der Anfang des Zweiten Jesaja in Jes 40,1f. und das Jeremiabuch," *ZAW* 106 (1994): 243–61 and Konrad Schmid, *Buchgestalten des Jeremiabuches: Untersuchungen zur Redaktions und Rezeptionsgeschichte von Jer 30–33 im Kontext des Buches* (Neukirchen-Vluyn: Neukirchener Verlag, 1996).

Neh 13.[5] Neh 5 focuses on economic policies for the community in response to a crisis of famine. Considering that Ezra-Nehemiah is largely filled with hyperbolic claims of largess, Neh 5:1–13 presents a surprisingly candid admission of economic struggle due to oppressive royal taxation.[6] Although not directly faulted, the text refers to the Persian royal tax on Neh 5:4 as an indirect form of economic oppression that results in enslavement for the Judeans. The foundational source of the hardship is the royal tax, originating not in Judah, but in the Persian empire. It is this royal tax that leads to loans and then the repercussions of a broad default.[7] Nehemiah responds with a directive for the people, using kinship language and drawing from pentateuchal legislation regarding economic debts and manumission.

Scholars have long debated the specific connection between pentateuchal laws on economic ethics and Neh 5, though any consensus on the precise relationship has been elusive. Certain clusters of pentateuchal texts address issues like lending, manumission, interest rates and methods of debt easement. All of these measures appear in Neh 5:1–13. In addition, Ezra-Nehemiah display a proclivity, even an obsession towards the authority of written texts, particularly Torah. This sanctioning of Torah reaches a culmination in Neh 8, in which the reading of Torah occupies the central movement of a covenant renewal.[8] All of this naturally brings question on how some form of the Pentateuch served as a potential source material for Neh 5:1–13. Some scholars see very little direct correlation between Neh 5 and pentateuchal legal materials. Michael Fishbane suggests Neh 5:1–13 draws from a lengthy Mesopotamian royal scribal practice.[9] Multiple scholars identify structural similarities to Neo-Assyrian and Neo-Babylonian royal inscriptions with an autobiographical first-person perspective with social reform.[10] Several have noted the lack of shared lexicography in key economic words. For

---

[5] Jacob Wright, *Rebuilding Identity: The Nehemiah Memoir and its Earliest Readers* (Berlin: de Gruyter, 2004), 167–68.

[6] Examples of the largess include reference to generous donations to the temple by King Cyrus (Ezra 1:7–11) as well as the peoples' offerings (Ezra 2:68–69).

[7] The royal tax as a central source for the economic hardship is also implied in the appeal to imperial taxation in the adversaries' letter (Ezra 4:13) and the Persian response (Ezra 4:20).

[8] Although Neh 8 is widely considered as later in the literary growth of Ezra-Nehemiah (e.g. Williamson), this emphasis on written authority is broad and thorough throughout the book. For example, one can consider the opening reference to imperial written edict (Ezra 1:1), the centrality of written census for inclusion (Ezra 2, Neh 7, 11), the appeals to archival documents (Ezra 4:15) and the multiple references to that "which is written" (Ezra 3:2, 4; Neh 10:35, 37; 12:22).

[9] Fishbane, *Biblical Interpretation*, 130.

[10] Sean Burt, *The Courtier and the Governor: Transformations of Genre in the Nehemiah Memoir* (Göttingen: Vandenhoeck & Ruprecht, 2014); Josine Blok and Julia Krul, "Debt and Its Aftermath: The Near Eastern Background to Solon's *Seisachtheia*," *Hesperia* 86:4 (2017), 607–43.

example, Nehemiah avoids the terms of the Pentateuch of נשך and תרבית.¹¹ The avoidance of these terms is not related to linguistic chronology, as both terms appear in later texts (Ezek 18:8, 13, 17, 22) as well as post-biblical examples. Juha Pakkala suggests that the lack of direct pentateuchal references is problematic, particularly when compared to more direct quotation "As it is written," during the covenant ratification of Neh 8:13–18.¹² Ezra-Nehemiah deploys the expression "as it is written" in reference to pentateuchal texts in six instances, with four of those examples explicitly referring to Moses and/or the Torah (Heb. ככתוב; Ezra 3:2, 4; Neh 8:15; 10:35, 37; Aram. ככתב, Ezra 6:18). Yishai Kiel suggests that Ezra-Nehemiah displays a "semantic shift" in the understanding of Torah as a divinely revealed legal code in written form.¹³ If Neh 5 directly borrowed from the Pentateuch, the lack of deliberate appeal to this newly emerging concept of legal authority is puzzling.

Other scholars identify a more direct connection between Neh 5:1–13 and the Pentateuch. Although Neh 5:1–13 lacks an unmistakable lemma from different sources in the various pentateuchal slave laws, it makes clear allusions to multiple aspects of Torah regulation. Nearly every stipulation of Neh 5:1–13 has direct precedent in pentateuchal law: the taking of pledges (Exod 22:24; Deut 24:10–11), manumission (Exod 21:2–11; Deut 15:12–18), stipulation for female slaves (Exod 21:7–11), and strong kinship language (Deut 15:7–11). Joshua Berman argues that Neh 5 employs, what he calls a "legal blend" of pentateuchal material, not merely as a literary device but as a rhetorical strategy, aiming for sermonic effect on the audience.¹⁴ Specifically, he identifies sources in three related pentateuchal passages in the Holiness Code, the Covenant Code and the Deuteronomic Code. Neh 5:7–8 deliberately draws on kinship language of Lev 25:42, 46. Berman identifies four specific phrases in Exod 22:24–26 directly used in Neh 5:1–11: "crying out" (1); "loans of silver" (4); "I listened" (6), "returned" (11).¹⁵ He also sees direct phraseology in the language of "loan" from Deut 24:10 to Neh 5:7.

---

[11] Peter Altmann, *Economics in Persian Period Biblical Texts* (Tübingen: Mohr Siebeck, 2016), 252; Joshua Buch, "Neshekh and Tarbit: Usury from Bible to Modern Finance," *JBQ* 33 (2005): 13–22.

[12] Juha Pakkala, "The Quotations and References of the Pentateuchal Laws in Ezra-Nehemiah," in *Changes in Scripture: Rewriting and Interpreting Authoritative Traditions in the Second Temple Period*, ed. Hanne Von Weissenberg, Juha Pakkala, and Marko Martilla (Berlin: de Gruyter, 2011), 193–221.

[13] Yishai Keil, "Reinventing Mosiac Torah in Ezra-Nehemiah in Light of the Law (*dāta*) of Ahura Mazda and Zarathustra," *JBL* 136.2 (2017): 337. See also the essay by Lisbeth S. Fried and Edward J. Mills III in this volume, "Ezra the Scribe."

[14] Joshua Berman downplays the lack of similar terms in Nehemiah 5, rather citing that Nehemiah is inclined to use terms in distinct ways; see Joshua Berman, "The Legal Blend in Biblical Narrative (Joshua 20:1–9, Judges 6:25–31, 1 Samuel 15:2, 28:3–25; 2 Kings 4:1–7, Jeremiah 34:12–17; Nehemiah 5:1–12)," *JBL* 134.1 (2015): 105–25.

[15] Berman, "The Legal Blend," 109.

Some sort of literary influence is apparent, but the nature of the compositional relationship between Neh 5 and related pentateuchal sources is questionable.

Of course, this question of textual dependency necessarily depends on debated reconstructions of Torah and Ezra-Nehemiah. In the midst of these diachronic questions, recent academic debates such as the pre-exilic dating of P and the Persian authorization hypothesis associated with Peter Frei have further muddied the nature of the compositional links between Neh 5 and pentateuchal sources.[16] Within this discussion, the actual chronological setting of Neh 5 is under dispute. Some place the passage as a natural outgrowth of the events of wall-building, thus making Neh 5 a part of the Nehemiah Memoir and as early as the 5th century.[17] Other scholars see Neh 5, particularly verses 1–13 as too disjointed from the surrounding chronologies to date them as later additions to the building narratives. Jacob Wright provides one of the more cogent arguments for Neh 5:1–13 as a secondary insertion.[18] He recognizes the discontinuity of Neh 5 and its surroundings, as well as ties to Neh 13 as evidence of its place in an early Hellenistic setting. Whatever the setting, questions of compositional priority, or rather, who is revising whom, are much more complex. Early textual witnesses defy any clean linear progression, but rather reinforce the need for more sophisticated models of compositional history. In other words, the assumption of diachronic movement from Torah to Nehemiah is now in question.

To address this impasse, I propose that an investigation on the nature of the economic settings of Neh 5:1–13 can generate new insights on intertextual with related passages. In keeping with the perspective of this larger volume, scribal activity always occurs within distinct social contexts. Although the origins of the associated pentateuchal laws are unknown, Neh 5 definitely takes place under the aegis of a vast and tributary empire, whether later Persian or early Hellenistic. Consequently, Neh 5:1–13 must match the context of debt easement to this period. Analyzing the economic context of Neh 5:1–13 may enhance the understanding of the relationship with pentateuchal texts. Neh 5:1–13 deals with a specific set of economic problems: overwhelming taxation, differentiated social classes, and significantly the incursion of debt, leading to debt slavery. My hope is to examine economic categories in contexts of their own systems.

More broadly, this study also intends to demonstrate an intertextual study as much more than textual. Such an approach is not innovative, but more realis-

---

[16] Peter Frei, "Zentralgewalt und Localautonomie im Achämenidenreich" in *Reichsidee und Reichsorganisation im Perserreich*, ed. Peter Frei and Klaus Koch (Fribourg: Universitätsverlag, 1996), 8–131; cf. Peter Frei, "Persian Imperial Authorization: A Summary," in *Persia and Torah: The Theory of Imperial Authorization of the Pentateuch*, ed. James W. Watts (Atlanta: Society of Biblical Literature, 2001), 5–40.

[17] Hugh Williamson, *Ezra, Nehemiah* (Waco, TX: Word, 1985), 234–36.

[18] Wright, *Rebuilding Identity*, 165–71; Wright builds on earlier propositions by Loring Batten, *The Books of Ezra and Nehemiah: A Critical and Exegetical Commentary* (Edinburgh: T&T Clark, 1913), 237–40.

tically is a return to broader understandings of intertextuality during its nascent stage in social sciences. In Julia Kristeva's formulation, the "intertext" was the dialogical interplay of other textual traditions, but in doing so, necessitated commensurate weaving of theoretical approaches, whether literary, political, social, philosophical, or in this case, economic.[19] A broader intertextual understanding should challenge scholars to widen our concepts of ancient scribalism. All scribal communities in the ancient Near East were parts of intricate social systems with distinct and competing matrices of power and social authority. For this passage, I begin with the investigate on how the changing economic landscaped influenced the complex development of Neh 5:1–13.

3. The Economics Behind Neh 5:1–13

Economic anthropology has shown the social nature of economic transactions despite our tendencies to place economics in sterile terms of transactional descriptions.[20] The very words at the heart of the economic crisis: debt; interest, collateral, bondage all have symbolic value in the cultural world of ancient Israel. Economics is not merely transactional activity but rather deeply representative of social, cultural and political values within a society. Thus, economic policy necessarily has ethical components and social outcomes. It is unsurprising for Neh 5 to draw on legal tradition to articulate the moral underpinnings of fiscal policies within Yehud. Debt impacts more that the creditor and debtor, but has harsher repercussions across the wider community, particularly in the most vulnerable with sons and daughters, whose punishment is called "ravished."[21] This per-

---

[19] Julia Kristeva, *Desire in Language: A Semiotic Approach to Literature and Art* (New York: Columbia University Press, 1980); for a recent summative analysis, see Marianna Grohmann and Hyun Chul Paul Kim, introduction to *Second Wave Intertextuality and the Hebrew Bible*, ed. Marianna Grohmann and Hyun Chul Paul Kim (Atlanta: Society of Biblical Literature, 2019), 1–22.

[20] For a broad description of the theoretical foundations of economic anthropology, and its applicability to biblical studies, see Roger Nam, *Portrayals of Economic Exchange in the Book of Kings* (Leiden: Brill, 2012), 29–69; for a theoretical approach to extractive economies, see Roland Boer, *The Sacred Economy of Ancient Israel* (Louisville: Westminster John Knox, 2015), 9–52.

[21] Heb. נכבש, Neh 5:5. Early Jewish interpretation understood the intrinsic morality of interest-accruing debt, most famously with Hillel's innovation of the prosbul, which allowed for exceptions for lending with the expectation of manumission, e.g. Šeb. 10:3; other Jewish interpreters continued to interpret ethical injunctions concerning debt easement; for example, the Tosephta (Pe'ah 1:2) appears to support the prosbul, stating that "Good deeds yield principal and beats interest," though in contrast, "Sin creates capital but bears no interest" (Pe'ah 1:3). for a discussion of early Jewish interpretation on interest, though one that perhaps relies too heavily on modern economic assumptions, see Roman A. Ohrenstein and Barry Gordon, *Economic Analysis in Talmudic Literature: Rabbinic Thought in the Light of Modern Economics*, 3rd ed. (Leiden: Brill, 2009), 84–107; in Christian reception, the council of Nicea prohibited the

spective contrasts to modern notions of an individual economic activity. In socially-embedded economies, individualism gives way to broader communities. Because of the integration of ethical responsibility within economic settings, the intertextuality of this passage must be interpreted in light of the economic turmoil of the late Persian period. For earlier periods, Judah operated under an agrarian socially-embedded economy, based on kinships, whether real or fictive. With reliance on farming, droughts and pestilence and other forces of nature will inevitably lead to borrowing and lending. To a large degree, this is a natural part of the agrarian cycle to account for the capricious nature of farming in the southern Levant. Families will occasionally need to borrow, whether for seed or equipment, or to account for crop failures. For anthropologists, lending is not in itself an unethical transaction, as circulation of resources can bind communities together. Sympathetic relationships will undergird lending between kin.

Regardless of one's view on the precise chronological history of these biblical texts, it is undisputed that the economic systems of the Eastern Mediterranean from the fifth through third centuries BCE underwent seismic changes. Naturally, the textualization of Neh 5:1–13 would capture some of these changes. The prolific archaeological research of the last decade or so reveal a much more modest economic setting than the earlier monarchic periods, presumably due to a catastrophic event of the Babylonian exile.[22] The social displacements severely depopulated the region though the extent remains under contention. Alongside this depopulation, epigraphic evidence and sites like Ramat Rahel show a centralized redistributive economy, with extractive mechanisms.[23] Sealings appear in strategic locations, often attached to large storage jar handles with capacities

---

charging of interest on loans, threatening banishment from the church to violators. This would be a significant precedent that would last through many centuries of church history, reified by endorsements by powerful figures in church history, such as Aquinas and Calvin; Charles R. Geisst, *A History of Usury and Debt* (Philadelphia: University of Pennsylvania Press, 2013), 20–57.

[22] Recent years have seen an explosion in studies on the material culture of the Persian period. For major studies, see Avraham Faust, *Judah in the Neo-Babylonian Period: The Archaeology of Desolation* (Atlanta: Society of Biblical Literature, 2012); Oded Lipschits, *The Fall and Rise of Jerusalem: The History of Judah under Babylonian Rule* (Winona Lake, IN: Eisenbrauns, 2005); for summative works, see Ephraim Stern, *The Assyrian, Babylonian and Persian Periods (732–332 B.C.E.)*, vol. 2 of *Archaeology of the Land of the Bible* (New Haven: Yale University Press, 2001), 351–582; Charles David Isbell, "Persia and Yehud," in *The Old Testament in Archaeology and History*, ed. Jennie Ebeling et al. (Waco, TX: Baylor University Press, 2017), 529–56.

[23] Oded Lipschits et al., *What Are the Stones Whispering? Ramat Rahel: 3000 Years of Forgotten History* (Winona Lake, IN: Eisenbrauns, 2017); Oded Lipschits, Yuval Gadot, and Liora Freud, *Ramat Rahel III: Final Publications of Aharoni's Excavations*, MSSMNIA 35 (Winona Lake, IN: Eisenbrauns, 2016); Oded Lipschits, Manfred Oeming, and Yuval Gadot, *Ramat Rahel IV: The Renewed Excavations by the Tel Aviv-Heidelberg Expedition (2005–2010): Stratigraphy and Architecture*, MSSMNIA 39 (Winona Lake, IN: Eisenbrauns, 2020).

beyond households, and more fitting for in kind payment.[24] The innovation of the first coins appearing in Yehud at about 400 BCE signaled yet another level of change. Whatever the interpretation of this coinage, and there are a variety of interpretations from military payments to the emergence of a monetized economy, coinage necessitates some centralized power to sponsor the value of coinage.[25] The Persian empire, as the centralized power, selects Yehud to serve as a supporting agent within a wider extractive economy. This requires a disembedding of long-standing social relationships, particularly for agrarian economies at the subsistence level. The diasporic cycles of the Babylonian and Persian displacements naturally facilitated this social disembedding, as common to any forced migration. Ezra-Nehemiah outwardly endorses this shift to a centralized extractive economy. The opening verse names Cyrus as the continuation of the Davidic empire with the descriptor "The Lord stirred up the spirit of Cyrus" (Ezra 1:1).[26] The prologue further supports this endorsement with declaration of divine support to return the Judeans and sponsor the construction of the new temple. The prologue makes claims of a place for worship, but it is more of a place of revenue and fiscal control as Ezra 1:4 exhorts a collection of "silver and gold, with goods and with animals, besides freewill offerings for the house of God in Jerusalem" (Ezra 1:4).[27] Whatever the religious motivations, the opening prologue clearly directs a regular flow of goods, both in-kind and precious metals, to the reconstructed temple under the direction of Cyrus.

This collection of goods for the temple saturates much of Ezra-Nehemiah. But these temple donations, whether politically or socially coercive, are not the only means for centralization. Neh 5:4 introduces another kind of centralization in the מדת המלך, often translated as "king's tax" or "royal revenue." This particular phrase, only occurring here, signals the new mode of economic transaction in the

---

[24] Oded Lipschits and David Vanderhooft, *Yehud Stamp Impressions: A Corpus of Inscribed Stamp Impressions from the Persian and Hellenistic Periods in Judah* (Winona Lake, IN: Eisenbrauns,) 2011.

[25] Although coinage was not widespread in the late Persian Yehud, the limited examples display broad iconographic symbols such as an Athenian owl, falcon, dove, lily and Persian crown. All of these symbols are found broadly in Persian numismatic examples, suggesting that Yehud coinage was integrated deeply into the Persian Empire; for summary of evidence, see Charles Carter, *The Emergence of Yehud in the Persian Period: A Social and Demographic Study* (Sheffield: Sheffield Academic, 1999), 259–71. For the theory of coinage as military payments, see Peter Machinist, "The First Coins of Judah and Samaria: Numismatics and History in the Achaemenid and Early Hellenistic Periods," in *Achaemenid History VIII: Continuity and Change*, ed. Amelie Kuhrt and M. Cool Root (Leiden: Nederland Instituut voor Nabije Oosten, 1994), 365–80; for an exceedingly confident reconstruction of coinage as part of a growing monetary economy, see Morris Silver, *Prophets and Markets: The Political Economy of Ancient Israel* (Boston: Kluwer-Nijhoff), 1983.

[26] Although Ezra 1 and Neh 5 originate with distinct sources, the integration of these traditions deliberately framed the book in the context of Cyrus' mandate for return according to the Ezra 1:1–4 prologue.

[27] Cf. possible reference to Exod 11:2.

Persian empire. The מדת has an Akkadian cognate, *mandāttu*, and it is used for tribute that crosses political borders.²⁸ The מדת occurs twice in biblical Aramaic, without the genitival modifier "royal," both in Ezra-Nehemiah. In Ezra 4:20 in Aramaic as the adversaries disparagingly describe Jerusalem as one who will collect מדת from other nations. Ezra 6:8, presents an imperial promise that the rebuilding of the Jerusalem Temple will be supported from the tribute. Lisbeth Fried argues that this tribute is more like a rent, drawing from cognate usage in Aramaic (Elephantine) and Akkadian (Murashu) texts.²⁹ The implication of the מדת המלך is that the Persian king owned the land in Yehud, and thus the Judeans inhabitants owed regular rent in the form of a tribute. The concept of wealth flowing freely away from Yehud and towards the Persian Empire clashes with the socially-embedded economy of earlier times. The Judeans are paying rent on the very land that was granted to them according to divine promise. Wealth is no longer to be distributed according to kin relations and protected within the social lines. Instead, the issuance of the king's tax diminishes the community wealth in favor of the empire.

Neh 5:4 names this king's tax as culpable for the excessive financial burden. Unlike a reciprocally-based economy, the extractive economy moves goods away from Yehud and towards the Persians. This makes the financial ecology precarious and particularly vulnerable to external challenge such as a food shortage (Neh 5:3). Neh 5:7 complains of interest on these loans. The entire mode of extraction, from the complicit nobles and officials making the loans and the Persian government who instigated the royal tax, is all an oblique critique of the imperial economy. Nehemiah's solution alludes to legal materials.³⁰ This situation leads to a widespread debt slavery crisis. The king's tax is external to the Yehud community. Thus, an economy based on reciprocity and kinship is replaced by a socially-disembedded economy, as the victims of the debt slavery are treated as commodities. Neh 5:8 complains that their own kin are being sold. The

---

[28] Leo Oppenheim and Erica Reiner, "mandāttu," *CAD* 10:13–16.

[29] Fried draws on the *minda* paid as a toll for usage of the Nile in examples like *TAD* C3.7 as well as the usage of waterways in Nippur that the king leased out for usage in Murashu; Lisbeth S. Fried, *Ezra: A Commentary*, SPCC (Sheffield: Sheffield Phoenix, 2015), 214; also see cognates in Ugaritic *mnḥ*, G. del Olmo Lete and J. Sanmartín, "*mnḥ*," *DULAT* 562, and other Northwest Semitic texts *mndḥ₁*, Jacob Hoftijzer and Karen Jongling, "*mndḥ₁*," *DNWSI* 656.

[30] Exod 22:25; Lev 25:36–37; Deut 23:19. Significantly, there is no known legal prohibition against the charging of interest in the corpus of ANE law codes. Rather, Eshnunna and Hammurabi both limit interest to 20% on silver and 33% on grain, roughly in line with Old Babylonian loan documents. For some, the translation for נשׁה "interest" is in dispute with interpretations as "interest" but also some consideration for "pressing for repayment" or "pledge." The spelling of the final consonant he/aleph makes no suggestion on diachronic shift as earlier and later forms appear throughout the Hebrew Bible. Among English translations, most believe that Neh 5 is actually referring to the taking of interest. NJPS suggests that the people are guilty of forcibly demanding repayment. Others believe that the prohibition is against pledges. This would match other parts of the passage that explicitly refer to the pledge.

commodification of people in systems like debt slavery upend social cohesion with catastrophic results. Debt becomes a tool in such a disembedded economy. This view is recently popularized by David Graeber, but he is rehearsing earlier arguments by Karl Polanyi and Marcel Mauss.[31] Neh 5:5 concisely summarizes the crisis, "We are forcing our sons and daughters to be slaves." The category of debt slavery had generational consequences of abject poverty. Rich cuneiform evidence during this time demonstrates that slaves had a variety of economic circumstances, and that there are economic documents that show slaves owning land, houses and even other slaves. But despite the proclivity of scholars to pursue more sophisticated notions of slavery, we must pay attention to some of the Neo-Marxist interpreters, the most influential being Muhammed Dandamaev particularly his tome, *Slavery in Babylonia: From Nabopolassar to Alexander*: a massive 800 pages of translations and philological notes from Neo-Babylonian and Persian slave documents, and analysis.[32] Based on his study of the cuneiform evidence, Dandamaev challenged the broader spectrum of slavery to assert that slavery as a phenomenon was much more binary. Either you were owned, or you were not. Slaves were property. Dandamaev conceded that debt slavery was a way that one could hypothetically move from bondage to freedom, but Dandamaev insisted that there was very little indication that such transfer ever happened. In other words, once a person lost their very humanity, and were treated as a commodity, such a situation was rarely reversible. This type of devastating slavery constitutes the complaint of Neh 5:5.

4. Protesting the Extractive Economy

Innerbiblical interpretation of Neh 5:1–13 protests against these economic shifts. Whether drawing directly on written texts, or alluding to legal principals to later emerge, Neh 5:1–13 contextualizes these themes against the extractive economy. As mentioned above, Neh 5 and penteteuchal law both comment on interest, manumission, and slavery. The extent of adoption of these traditions is debatable, but there must be some connection to this known legal connection. Neh 5 integrates this tradition as an early biblical interpretation, specifically protesting against the Persian extractive economy.

---

[31] David Graeber, *Debt: The First 5,000 Years* (New York: Melville, 2011); Karl Polanyi, *The Great Transformation: The Political and Economic Origins of Our Time* (Boston: Beacon, 1944); Marcel Mauss, *The Gift: The Form and Reason for Exchange in Archaic Societies*, trans. W. D. Halls (London: Routledge), 1990.

[32] Muhammad A. Dandamaev, *Slavery in Babylonia: From Nabopolassar to Alexander the Great (626–331 BC)*, rev. ed., trans. V. A. Powell (DeKalb: Northern Illinois University Press, 1984).

The primary protest strategy of Neh 5 is the emphasis on kinship. As the extractive economy disembeds the social aspect of exchange by delivering goods to the distant imperial center, Neh 5:1–13 attempts to recapture the priority of kinship in economic distribution. Deut 15:7–11 utilizes kinship language of "brother/kin" four times (vv. 7 [2x], 9, 11). Deut 15 uses this kinship terminology to appeal to the notion of an inclusive community.[33] But in the content of repatriation, Neh 5:1–13 further amplifies the intentional community building aspect of debt reform through kinship language.

The commentators have noted the abundant kinship lexicography in Neh 5:1–13: "brother/kin" (vv. 1, 7, 8, 10); "Judean" (v. 1); "sons and daughters" (vv. 2, 5); "children" (v. 5); and "assembly" (v. 7). We also observe repeated usage of 1st common plural language in the 13 verses, for example "our fields, our vineyards, our houses" (v. 3); first common plural pronominal suffixes (21 times); independent first common plural pronouns (4 times); and verbal forms in first common plural finite verbal forms (5 times). The phonology of the first common plural forms reinforces the emphasis on the shared kinship. This highlight on kinship explicitly ties Neh 5 to pentateuchal sources, particularly with the language of Deuteronomy 15. Both passages exhort a broader support system for debt problems by appealing to a spirit of generosity via inclusion in a community. This community is defined by both ethnic boundaries (Deut 15:12; Neh 5:8) and past narrative of slavery (Deut 15:15; Neh 5:8). But this leaves the question on why Nehemiah never uses a limited number of key pentateuchal economic terms, such as "interest." Rather, the emphasis on community arises from a different motivation than simply reliance on earlier sources. I suggest that the emphasis on community implicitly draws on the Pentateuch, and explicitly promotes a re-embedding the economic transaction of lending back into a social relationship.[34] The redundant kinship language highlights the impact of debt bondage beyond the creditor-debtor to include families, particularly the vulnerable – sons and daughters – and also unborn progeny. Kinship language is also rhetorically effective in undoing the political position between creditor and debtor. This admonition to restore kinship is most pronounced in verse 5, "Now our flesh is the same as that of our kindred" (Neh 5:5). Such an exhortation fits with the deep emphasis on communal boundaries and strict identity throughout Ezra-Nehemiah, whether through census lists or rejection of the neighboring Samaritans. The emphasis on kin contrasts with the emerging imperial economy as a redistributive economy based on a pervasive taxation system.[35] This

---

[33] Sara Japhet suggests that this kinship language defines the "covenant community" (Sara Japhet, "The Relationship between the Legal Corpora in the Pentateuch in Light of Manumission Laws," in *Studies in Bible*, ed. Sara Japhet [Jerusalem: Magnes, 1986], 77).

[34] Wright (*Rebuilding Identity*, 180 ff.) also notes the abundance of kinship language.

[35] Biblical scholars have long suggested the temple as a central vehicle for a redistributive economy of Yehud, beginning with C. Torrey, "The Foundry of the Second Temple at Jerusalem,"

increasingly stratified taxation system clashed with traditional kinship economies.[36]

Neh 5 also protests against the economic structure in attacking specific societal groupings that emerge in the extractive economy. Most obviously, this comes in Neh 5:7 an invective against "nobles and officials" (Heb. חר, סגן). Throughout other portions of Ezra-Nehemiah, these terms refer to Judeans who have taken official authoritative positions to enforce the tribute.[37] In order to maximize the efficiency of the extractive economy, the central administration needs local support, in the form of authorized individuals, charged with collection. Significantly, the officials and nobles are not Persians, but Judeans. Neh 5:7 utilizes the labels of "nobles" and "officials," as a clear contrast to previously used kinship terms. Therefore, although Judean, the complicity of these nobles and officials excludes them from the Judean community. The accusation is followed by careful language that includes the nobles and officials as kin in pleading, "you are all taking interest from your *own* people."

JBL 55 (1936): 247–60, but more recently with the following: Joachim Schaper, "The Jerusalem Temple as an Instrument of the Achaemenid Fiscal Administration," *VT* 45 (1995): 528–39, Joachim Schaper, "The Temple Treasure Committee in the Times of Ezra-Nehemiah," *VT* 47 (1997): 200–206; Peter Altmann, "Tithes for Clergy and Taxes for the King: Separate or Combined Systems of Payments in Nehemiah?" *CBQ* 76 (2014): 215–29. Epigraphic evidence that suggests a strong taxation economy includes the distribution of Yehud seals (Oded Lipschits and David Vanderhooft, *The Yehud Stamp Impressions: A Corpus of Inscribed Impressions from the Persian and Hellenistic Periods in Judah* [Winona Lake, IN: Eisenbrauns, 2011]) as well as evidence for a wide taxation throughout the Persian Empire. For examples, see Matthew Stolper, *Entrepreneurs and Empires: The Murashu Archives, the Murashu Firm, and Persian Rule in Babylonia* (Leiden: Nederlands Instituut voor het Nabije Oosten, 1985); Kathleen Abraham, *Business and Politics under the Persian Empire: The Financial Dealings of Marduk-Nasir-Apil of the House of Egibi (521–487 BCE)* (Bethesda: CDL, 2004); Pierre Briant, ed., *Les archives des Fortifications de Persépolis dans le monde achemménide: Actes du colloque international sur les Archives de Persépolis, Collège de France, Paris, November 2006* (Paris: de Boccard, 2006); Laurie Pearce and Cornelia Wunsch, *Documents of Judean Exiles and West-Semites in Babylonia in the Collection of David Sofer* (Bethesda: CDL, 2014).

[36] Anthropological field studies have observed similar conflicts in later periods. The classic work by Marilyn Strathern, *No Money on Our Skins: Hagen Migrants in Port Moresby*, studies the rapid monetization of the post-colonial Pacific as it mixed with vestiges of a tribal brotherhood. As people engaged with international credit, namely as borrowers, inter-family loan requests continued. These requests were prefaced with the phrase "Hey brother" or "Hey sister." The recipient of such a request knew that the loan would be that of zero or negative interest. Strathern determined that elite-Fijians were able to get large interest free loans for school fees from relatives. But poor Indigenous Fijians could not. They were forced to take out sub-prime loans at super-prime rates. I take this recent example from Strathern as it illustrates the morality of debt. Traditional deals of kinship can effectively contend against detached extractive methods. The appeal to kinship in Nehemiah 5 is a deliberate plea for a return to socially embedded values in the Judean economic ethic. Marilyn Strathern, *No Money on Our Skins: Hagen Migrants in Port Moresby* (Canberra: Australian National University, 1975).

[37] Both terms appear in Neh 2:16; 4:8, 13; 7:5; חר appears in Neh 6:17; 13:17, 13; סגן appears in Ezra 9:2; Neh 5:17; 12:40; 13:11.

Similarly, the indictment of verse 5, "We are forcing our sons and our daughters to be slaves" presents tension against the covenantal promise. However one may opine on the historicity of Neh 5, debt slavery was a reality during this period.[38] To contest this, Neh 5 alludes to biblical law. The Holiness Code makes multiple references to provide generosity to the enslaved, particularly for kinspeople:

- "For they are my servants, whom I brought out of the land of Egypt; they shall not be sold as slaves are sold" (Lev 25:42).
- "But as for your fellow Israelites, no one shall rule over the other with harshness" (Lev 25:46).
- "You shall not lend them your silver at interest taken in advance or provide them food at a profit. I am the LORD your God, who brought you out of the land of Egypt, to give you the land of Canaan to be your God" (Lev 25:37–38).

By alluding to this tradition, Neh 5 emphatically presents the issue of debt slavery as contrary to the divine promise.[39] Instead of becoming natural heirs to generational possessions, the people are forced into slavery. Implicitly, this attacks the promise of freedom and exodus.

The solution also alludes to Torah. After thought and counsel, Nehemiah exhorts the people to "restore to them" all of the taken goods due to the debt problems. This aligns with general biblical law in both pentateuchal and Near Eastern sources.

- "Every seventh year you shall grant a remission of debts" (Deut 15:1).
- "If a member of your community, whether a Hebrew man or a Hebrew woman, is sold to you and works for you six years, in the seventh year you shall set that person free" (Deut 15:12).

Of course, the law of manumission is an established literary phenomenon that goes far beyond the biblical law to earliest known written law codes, as early as the Reform Texts of King Uru'inimgina of Lagash (24th c.). Similar laws are found in Old Babylonian (Code of Eshnunna, 18th c., Code of Hammurabi, 18th c.), Middle Assyrian Hittite, Middle Assyrian, Neo-Assyrian and Neo-Babylonian. Biblical Law inherits much of this tradition. Though unlike the ancient Near Eastern counterparts, this is not enforced politically, as it exceeds the authority

---

[38] The Wadi Daliyeh documents indicate slavery contracts among individuals with Yahwistic names during the fifth and fourth centuries BCE, most prominently displayed with Wadi Daliyeh 10: see Douglas Gropp, *Wadi Daliyeh II: The Samaria Papyri for Wadi Daliyeh*; Eileen Schuller et al., *Qumran Cave 4.XXVIII: Miscellanea, Part 2*, DJD XXVIII (Oxford: Oxford University Press, 2002), 36; and a more recent translation with commentary, Jan Dušek, *Les manuscrits araméens du Wadi Daliyeh et la Samarie vers 450–332 av. J.-C.* (Leiden: Brill, 2007), 240–47.

[39] The dissonance between actual enslavement and their status within community is paralleled in Ezra 9:7–8 and Neh 9:36–37; see Daniel Smith-Christopher, *A Biblical Theology of Exile* (Minneapolis: Fortress, 2002), 44.

of Nehemiah. Rather, it is enforced by the priests and through ritual (Neh 5:13).[40] It is grounded in authoritative traditions reflected in Torah. This emphasis on re-embedding the economy in social relations does more than change fiscal policy. In line with this emphasis on kinship, Neh 5:1–13 can be considered as a projection of identity for the post-exilic Judean community.

5. Conclusion

Scribal practice is a social activity. The textualization of Neh 5:1–13 occurred within specific social settings. Debt is indeed an ideological construct, and the form of the debt in this passage must be examined. Because of the similarities to different pentateuchal texts, intertextuality must carefully consider the degree of influence from different textual sources. But at the same time, the economic setting also impacted the appropriation of these sources. As the complexity of scribal practices continue to be revealed, our methods for studying these practices must reach commensurate sophistication. By doing so, we can more thoroughly contribute to the complex processes behind "Making Hebrew Scriptures."

Bibliography

Abraham, Kathleen. *Business and Politics under the Persian Empire: The Financial Dealings of Marduk-Nasir-Apil of the House of Egibi (521–487 BCE)*. Bethesda, MD: CDL, 2004.

Altmann, Peter. *Economics in Persian Period Biblical Texts*. FAT 109. Tübingen: Mohr Siebeck, 2016.

Altmann, Peter. "Tithes for Clergy and Taxes for the King: Separate or Combined Systems of Payments in Nehemiah?" *CBQ* 76 (2014): 215–29.

Batten, Loring. *The Books of Ezra and Nehemiah: A Critical and Exegetical Commentary*. Edinburgh: T&T Clark, 1913.

Berman, Joshua. "The Legal Blend in Biblical Narrative (Joshua 20:1–9, Judges 6:25–31, 1 Samuel 15:2, 28:3–25; 2 Kings 4:1–7, Jeremiah 34:12–17; Nehemiah 5:1–12)." *JBL* 134.1 (2015): 105–25.

Blok, Josine, and Julia Krul. "Debt and Its Aftermath: The Near Eastern Background to Solon's *Seisachtheia*." *Hesperia* 86.4 (2017): 607–43.

Boer, Roland. *The Sacred Economy of Ancient Israel*. Louisville: Westminster John Knox, 2015.

Briant, Pierre, ed. *Les archives des Fortifications de Persépolis dans le monde achemménide: Actes du colloque international sur les Archives de Persépolis, Collège de France, Paris, November 2006*. Paris: de Boccard, 2006.

---

[40] Tamara Eskenazi questions the legitimacy of this act, suggesting that it may be more akin to "extortion"; Tamara Eskenazi, *In an Age of Prose: A Literary Approach to Ezra-Nehemiah* (Atlanta: Scholars Press, 1988), 69.

Buch, Joshua. "Neshekh and Tarbit: Usury from Bible to Modern Finance." *JBQ* 33 (2005): 13–22.
Burt, Sean. *The Courtier and the Governor: Transformations of Genre in the Nehemiah Memoir*. Vandenhoeck & Ruprecht, 2014.
Carter, Charles. *The Emergence of Yehud in the Persian Period: A Social and Demographic Study*. Sheffield: Sheffield Academic, 1999.
Chomsky, Noam. "The People Always Pay." *The Guardian*. January 21, 1999. Accessed Apr 26, 2022. http://www.theguardian.com/world/1999/jan/21/debtrelief.development3.
Dandamaev, Muhammad A. *Slavery in Babylonia: From Nabopolassar to Alexander the Great (626–331 BC)*. Translated by V. A. Powell. Rev. ed. DeKalb, IL: Northern Illinois University Press, 1984.
Dušek, Jan. *Les manuscrits araméens du Wadi Daliyeh et la Samarie vers 450–332 av. J.-C.* Leiden: Brill, 2007.
Eskenazi, Tamara. *In an Age of Prose: A Literary Approach to Ezra-Nehemiah*. Atlanta: Scholars Press, 1988.
Faust, Avraham. *Judah in the Neo-Babylonian Period: The Archaeology of Desolation*. Atlanta: Society of Biblical Literature, 2012.
Fishbane, Michael. *Biblical Interpretation in Ancient Israel*. Oxford: Clarendon, 1985.
Frei, Peter. "Persian Imperial Authorization: A Summary." Pages 5–40 in *Persia and Torah: The Theory of Imperial Authorization of the Pentateuch*. Edited by James W. Watts. Atlanta: Society of Biblical Literature, 2001.
Frei, Peter. "Zentralgewalt und Localautonomie im Achämenidenreich." Pages 8–131 in *Reichsidee und Reichsorganisation im Perserreich*. Edited by Peter Frei and Klaus Koch. Fribourg: Universitätsverlag, 1996.
Fried, Lisbeth S. *Ezra: A Commentary*. SPCC. Sheffield: Sheffield Phoenix, 2015.
Fried, Lisbeth S., and Edward J. Mills III. "Ezra the Scribe." Within this volume.
Geisst, Charles R. *A History of Usury and Debt*. Philadelphia: University of Pennsylvania Press, 2013.
Graeber, David. *Debt: The First 5,000 Years*. New York: Melville, 2011.
Grohmann, Marianna, and Hyun Chul Paul Kim. Introduction to *Second Wave Intertextuality and the Hebrew Bible*. Edited by Marianna Grohmann and Hyun Chul Paul Kim. Atlanta: Society of Biblical Literature, 2019.
Gropp, Douglas M. *Wadi Daliyeh II: The Samaria Papyri for Wadi Daliyeh; Eileen Schuller et al., Qumran Cave 4.XXVIII: Miscellanea, Part 2*. DJD XXVIII. Oxford: Oxford University Press, 2002.
Hoftijzer, Jacob, and Karen Jongling. *Dictionary of the North-West Semitic Inscriptions*. 2 vols. Leiden: Brill, 1995.
Isbell, Charles David. "Persia and Yehud." Pages 529–56 in *The Old Testament in Archaeology and History*. Edited by Jennie Ebeling, J. Edward Wright, Mark Elliott, and Paul V. M. Flesher. Waco, TX: Baylor University Press, 2017.
Japhet, Sara. "The Relationship between the Legal Corpora in the Pentateuch in Light of Manumission Laws." Pages 63–89 in *Studies in Bible*. Edited by Sara Japhet. Jerusalem: Magnes, 1986.
Keil, Yishai. "Reinventing Mosiac Torah in Ezra-Nehemiah in Light of the Law (*dāta*) of Ahura Mazda and Zarathustra." *JBL* 136.2 (2017): 323–45.
Kratz, Reinhard. "Der Anfang des Zweiten Jesaja in Jes 40,1f. und das Jeremiabuch." *ZAW* 106 (1994): 243–61.

Kristeva, Julia. *Desire in Language: A Semiotic Approach to Literature and Art*. New York: Columbia University Press, 1980.

Levinson, Bernard. *Deuteronomy and the Hermeneutics of Legal Innovation*. Oxford: Oxford University Press, 1997.

Lipschits, Oded. *The Fall and Rise of Jerusalem: The History of Judah under Babylonian Rule*. Winona Lake, IN: Eisenbrauns, 2005.

Lipschits, Oded, and David Vanderhooft. *Yehud Stamp Impressions: A Corpus of Inscribed Stamp Impressions from the Persian and Hellenistic Periods in Judah*. Winona Lake, IN: Eisenbrauns, 2011.

Lipschits, Oded, Manfred Oeming, and Yuval Gadot. *Ramat Rahel IV: The Renewed Excavations by the Tel Aviv-Heidelberg Expedition (2005–2010): Stratigraphy and Architecture*. MSSMNIA 39. Winona Lake, IN: Eisenbrauns, 2020.

Lipschits, Oded, Yuval Gadot, and Liora Freud. *Ramat Rahel III: Final Publications of Aharoni's Excavations*. MSSMNIA 35. Winona Lake, IN: Eisenbrauns, 2016.

Lipschits, Oded, Yuval Gadot, B. Arubas, and Manfred Oeming. *What Are the Stones Whispering? 3000 Years on Forgotten History at Ramat Rahel*. Winona Lake, IN: Eisenbrauns, 2017.

Longman, Tremper, III, and Peter Enns. *InterVarsity Press Bible Dictionary*. 8 vols. Downers Grove, IL: InterVarsity Press, 2005.

Machinist, Peter. "The First Coins of Judah and Samaria: Numismatics and History in the Achaemenid and Early Hellenistic Periods." Pages 365–80 in *Achaemenid History VIII: Continuity and Change*. Edited by Amelie Kuhrt and M. Cool Root. Leiden: Nederland Instituut voor Nabije Oosten, 1994.

Mauss, Marcel. *The Gift: The Form and Reason for Exchange in Archaic Societies*. Translated by W. D. Halls. London: Routledge, 1990.

Nam, Roger. "Biblical Studies, COVID-19, and Our Response to Growing Inequality." *JBL* 139 (2020): 600–606.

Nam, Roger. *Portrayals of Economic Exchange in the Book of Kings*. Leiden: Brill, 2012.

Ohrenstein, Roman A., and Barry Gordon. *Economic Analysis in Talmudic Literature: Rabbinic Thought in the Light of Modern Economics*. 3rd ed. Leiden: Brill, 2009.

Olmo Lete, G. del, and J. Sanmartín. *A Dictionary of the Ugaritic Language in the Alphabetic Tradition*. 2nd rev. ed. Leiden: Brill, 2004.

Oppenheim, A. Leo, Erica Reiner, and Martha T. Roth, eds. *The Assyrian Dictionary of the Oriental Institute of the University of Chicago*. 26 vols. Chicago: Oriental Institute of the University of Chicago, 1956–2010.

Pakkala, Juha. "The Quotations and References of the Pentateuchal Laws in Ezra-Nehemiah." Pages 193–221 in *Changes in Scripture: Rewriting and Interpreting Authoritative Traditions in the Second Temple Period*. Edited by Hanne Von Weissenberg, Juha Pakkala, and Marko Martilla. Berlin: de Gruyter, 2011.

Pearce, Laurie, and Cornelia Wunsch. *Documents of Judean Exiles and West-Semites in Babylonia in the Collection of David Sofer*. Bethesda, MD: CDL, 2014.

Polanyi, Karl. *The Great Transformation: The Political and Economic Origins of our Time*. Boston: Beacon, 1944.

Sarna, Nahum. "Psalm 89: A Study in Inner Biblical Exegesis." Pages 29–46 in *Biblical and Other Studies*. Edited by A. Altmann. Cambridge, MA: Harvard University Press, 1963.

Schaper, Joachim. "The Jerusalem Temple as an Instrument of the Achaemenid Fiscal Administration." *VT* 45 (1995): 528–39.

Schaper, Joachim. "The Temple Treasure Committee in the Times of Ezra-Nehemiah." *VT* 47 (1997): 200–206.

Schmid, Konrad. *Buchgestalten des Jeremiabuches: Untersuchungen zur Redaktions und Rezeptionsgeschichte von Jer 30–33 im Kontext des Buches.* Neukirchen-Vluyn: Neukirchener Verlag, 1996.

Schniedewind, William S. *Society and the Promise to David: The Reception History of 2 Samuel 7:1–17.* Oxford: Oxford University Press, 1999.

Silver, Morris. *Prophets and Markets: The Political Economy of Ancient Israel.* Boston: Kluwer-Nijhoff Publishing, 1983.

Smith-Christopher, Daniel. *A Biblical Theology of Exile.* Minneapolis: Fortress, 2002.

Sommer, Benjamin. *A Prophet Reads Scripture: Allusion in Isaiah 40–66.* Stanford, CA: Stanford University Press, 1998.

Steck, Odil Hannes. *Studien zu Tritojesaja.* Berlin: de Gruyter, 1991.

Stern, Ephraim. *The Assyrian, Babylonian and Persian Periods (732–332 B.C.E.).* Vol. 2 of *Archaeology of the Land of the Bible.* New Haven: Yale University Press, 2001.

Stolper, Matthew. *Entrepreneurs and Empires: The Murashu Archives, the Murashu Firm, and Persian Rule in Babylonia.* Leiden: Nederlands Instituut voor het Nabije Oosten, 1985.

Strathern, Marilyn. *No Money on Our Skins: Hagen Migrants in Port Moresby.* Canberra: Australian National University, 1975.

Torrey, C. C. "The Foundry of the Second Temple at Jerusalem." *JBL* 55 (1936): 247–60.

Williamson, Hugh. *Ezra, Nehemiah.* Waco, TX: Word, 1985.

Wright, Jacob. *Rebuilding Identity: The Nehemiah Memoir and its Earliest Readers.* Berlin: de Gruyter, 2004.

Chronography in the Book of Kings: An Inquiry into an Israelite Manifestation of an Ancient Near Eastern Genre

Kristin Weingart

Chronography is inseparably linked to writing. Assembling king lists, keeping day books, putting together chronicles – all these are genuinely scribal endeavors, done in writing, and – unlike other genres – usually not intended for oral presentation. Chronographic documents can serve very practical aims: Annals may support a ruling king by presenting his reign as a chain of successes and great deeds. King lists can provide dynastic legitimation by setting a king into a continuous line of illustrious predecessors. Records of the Nile floods or lists of market prices may serve economic needs. But beyond day-to-day necessities, chronography is also connected to the intellectual enterprise of ordering the world by setting a multitude of events into an established order, of structuring history along temporal lines – all in all an enterprise deeply rooted in and associated with the intellectual exploration of the (historical) world.

Chronography, therefore, is a widespread literary genre attested all over the Ancient Near East. Chronographic documents display some local unique features but also share comparable practices and pragmatics.[1] It is hardly a surprise that the Old Testament literature which is in many ways part of the greater stream of ANE literary production has its share in the chronographic realm – the Book of Kings being the most prominent example. The book not only contains a plethora of chronological data, but also applies a distinctive chronological framework in presenting the parallel histories of the kingdoms of Israel and Judah.[2] This paper

---

[1] For collections and discussions of ANE chronographic works and documents see e.g. Albert Kirk Grayson, *Assyrian and Babylonian Chronicles*, TCS 5 (Locust Valley, NY: Augustin, 1975); Donald B. Redford, *Pharaonic King Lists, Annals and Day Books: A Contribution to the Study of the Egyptian Sense of History* (Missisauga: Benben, 1986); Jean-Jacques Glassner, *Mesopotamian Chronicles*, WAW (Leiden: Brill, 2005); for an overview on compositions comparable to the Book of Kings see Kristin Weingart, *Gezählte Geschichte: Systematik, Quellen und Entwicklung der synchronistischen Chronologie in den Königebüchern*, FAT 142 (Tübingen: Mohr Siebeck, 2020), 85–121.

[2] The ordering principle has long been recognized, so for instance by Samuel R. Driver, *An Introduction to the Literature of the Old Testament*, ITL (Edinburgh: T&T Clark, 1891), 179: "In the arrangement of the reigns of the two series of kings a definite principle is followed by the compiler. When the narrative of a reign (in either series) has once been begun, it is continued to its close …; when it is ended, the reign or reigns of the other series, which have synchronized

seeks to investigate its chronographic base, i. e., the synchronistic chronology, as an outcome of scribal work by addressing three points:

(1) How was the chronological framework compiled?

(2) Which were its sources? Here, the discussion will focus on the material regarding the Northern Kingdom and on one chronographic document still discernable as a source text.

(3) The results shall then be discussed with regard to their implications: What does the inquiry tell us about scribal culture in Israel?

1. The Synchronistic Chronology in the Book of Kings – Systematics and Compilation

Most of the chronological data within the Book of Kings is to be found within the so-called regnal frame, i. e. the formulaic introduction and conclusion given for most kings that establishes the overall ordering principle of the book and at the same time provides the history recounted with a continuous structure and interpretation.[3] For the nineteen kings of the Northern Kingdom of Israel, the regnal frame records data for their length of reign and for seventeen kings there also is a synchronistic date for their accession.[4] Of the likewise nineteen kings of the Kingdom of Judah starting with Rehoboam, only eleven have a synchronistic accession year date, the seven kings after Hezekiah could obviously no longer be synchronized to any Israelite king. For all of them the length of reign is re-

---

with it, are dealt with; the reign overlapping it at the end having been completed, the compiler resumes his narrative of the first series with the reign next following, and so on."

[3] The latter, i.e., an interpretation of history is mainly done by means of the judgement formulae. So, it is not surprising that research on the introductory formulae of the regnal frame was predominantly focused on these (see e.g. Helga Weippert, "Die 'deuteronomistischen' Beurteilungen der Könige von Israel und Juda und das Problem der Redaktion der Königsbücher," *Bib* 53 [1972]: 301–39; Baruch Halpern and David S. Vanderhooft, "The Editions of Kings in the 7th–6th Centuries B.C.E.," *HUCA* 62 [1991]: 179–244; Benjamin D. Thomas, *Hezekiah and the Compositional History of the Book of Kings*, FAT II 63 [Tübingen: Mohr Siebeck, 2014], 124–77; Felipe Blanco Wißmann, *"Er tat das Rechte ...": Beurteilungskriterien und Deuteronomismus in 1 Kön 12 – 2 Kön 25*, ATANT 93 [Zürich: TVZ, 2008]; or Sang-Won Lee, "Die Königsbeurteilungen und die Literargeschichte des Deuteronomistischen Geschichtswerks: Anmerkungen zu einer kontroversen Diskussion," *VT* 68 [2018]: 581–605, to name just a very few recent contributions). Compared to the intensive debates on the judgment formulae, the role of the numerical data as a component of the Deuteronomistic regnal frame was hardly ever discussed. This might be due to the fact that the numbers themselves were widely seen as older source material taken up by the author of Kings – or the Deuteronomist – and integrated into his work. So already Martin Noth, *Überlieferungsgeschichtliche Studien: Die sammelnden und bearbeitenden Geschichtswerke im Alten Testament*, 2nd ed. (Darmstadt: WBG, 1957), 74.

[4] For Jeroboam I and Jehu, there is no date of accession; for the last king of Israel Hoshea, 2 Kgs 15:30 and 17:1 name two different dates.

corded, and for most of them also the age at accession.[5] An investigation of the synchronistic chronology therefore has to address two issues: (1) the numerical data and its compilation, and (2) the textual presentation of the data within the regnal frame.

1.1 The Compilation of the Chronological Data

As is well known, the chronological data within the Book of Kings has prompted a never-ending history of research, and the attempts to extract a chronology of Israel's monarchic period, consistent in itself and compatible with the external data, fill a considerable number of shelf meters.[6] The main obstacles have been frequently pointed out: inconsistencies within the chronological data, e.g. conflicting synchronisms or regnal year totals for Israel and Judah; variant numerical data in the ancient versions; uncertainties regarding the calendar in ancient Israel, e.g. the date of the New Year; uncertainties regarding the counting methods for regnal years (postdating or antedating); the occurrence and handling of coregencies, and the frequent incompatibility with external data, i.e. Assyrian or Babylonian sources which also date specific events related to the history of Israel and Judah.[7] Within the scholarly debates, the main focus has been on the establishment of a reliable historical timetable, but the inner systematics of the numerical data in the Book of Kings were only marginally addressed.

Looking at the numerical data within the regnal frame, a number of peculiarities catch the eye which allow one to draw some preliminary conclusions regarding their character:

a) The numerical data of the regnal frame are in all likelihood no writing-desk fiction,[8] but rather the result of a processing of existing data. Unlike the symbolic number of 40 years given for the reigns David or Solomon (2 Sam 5:4; 1 Kgs 2:11; 11:42), the plethora of different and seemingly insignificant numbers

---

[5] Rehoboam, like Jeroboam I, lacks an accession date. For queen Athaliah no regnal frame is provided and therefore no chronological data.

[6] The critical discussion was started by Julius Wellhausen, "Die Zeitrechnung des Buches der Könige seit der Theilung des Reiches," *JDT* 20 (1875): 607–40, the latest monographs are Antti Laato, *Guide to Biblical Chronology* (Sheffield: Sheffield Phoenix, 2015); Christine M. Tetley, *The Reconstructed Chronology of the Divided Kingdom* (Winona Lake, IN: Eisenbrauns, 2005); David Miano, *Shadow on the Steps: Time Measurement in Ancient Israel*, RBS (Leiden: Brill, 2011), as well as Weingart, *Gezählte Geschichte*. For a more detailed overview on the history and trends of the scholarly debates, see ibid., 2–16.

[7] See already Joachim Begrich, *Die Chronologie der Könige von Israel und Juda und die Quellen des Rahmens der Königsbücher* (Tübingen: Mohr Siebeck, 1929), 55–101, or the critical discussion of a number of ways to cope with these difficulties in Laato, *Guide*, 13–24.

[8] So already Ernst Krey, "Zur Zeitrechnung des Buchs der Könige," *ZWT* 20 (1877): 404–8, who saw the chronology as a result of "arbitrary playfulness" (407), or James R. Linville, *Israel in the Book of Kings: The Past as a Project of Social Identity*, JSOTSup 272 (Sheffield: Sheffield Academic, 1998), arguing that the whole Book of Kings presents a fictitious historical image aimed at creating an Israelite collective identity in the Persian Period.

in terms of numerical symbolism or ideology point to recorded rather than invented figures. Even more significant: the frequent inconsistencies regarding the numbers themselves as well as their calculation[9] also speak against a made-up system. On the other hand, certain portions of the data do display an inner consistency, so that one cannot easily dismiss the whole material as chaotic or as resulting from corruption during the processes of textual transmission. Furthermore, the textual witnesses rather indicate a tendency to harmonize and to resolve contradictions.[10]

b) One of the portions of overall consistency is the data for the Israelite Kings. With very few exceptions, regnal year totals and synchronistic accession year dates match each other perfectly. Moreover, the data indicate a consistent use of antedating – as far as the method of reckoning is discernable – up to the time of Menachem.[11] For the later kings, Pekahiah, Pekah, and Hoshea, postdating is applied.[12]

c) The data for the Judahite kings does not display a comparable degree of consistency and the numbers are consequently more puzzling. One issue is whether post- or antedating is applied to calculate the regnal years of a king. There are only very few instances which allow to relate a regnal year total to the subtraction of the synchronistic dates (Abijam, Jehoram, and Jotham). These cases seem to indicate antedating; but all of them are problematic either because of contradictory data (Abijam) or recorded irregularities (Jehoram, Jotham; for Jehoram see below). Moreover, the case of Ahaziah clearly implies postdating, because a regnal year total of one year is logically impossible in antedating.[13] The

---

[9] Not only does the sum of the regnal year totals of the Judahite kings differ from that of the Israelite kings, also the method of counting regnal years, i.e., postdating or antedating, varies (for these methods see n11 below).

[10] For harmonization procedures discernable in the textual witnesses as well as a discussion of their methodology see Kristin Weingart, "Harmonizing Biblical Chronology: On Procedures, Pitfalls, and Ramifications," in *Methodik im Diskurs: Harmonisierungen*, ed. Raik Heckl & Thomas Wagner, BThSt (Göttingen: Vandenhoeck & Ruprecht, 2023), forthcoming.

[11] The case of Nadab in 1 Kgs 15:25, 33 can serve as an example for antedating. His reign starts in the second year of Asa, his successor Baasha ascends to the throne in the third year of Asa. The total given for his regnal years is two. This implies that the year of his accession, though shared with Jeroboam I, is counted as a full regnal year. As usual in cases of antedating a subtraction of the synchronisms is one year short in comparison to the listed regnal years.

For a case of the alternative counting method, i.e., postdating, see Pekah in 2 Kgs 15:27: His reign parallels the 50th, 51st, and 52nd year of Azariah. Therefore, he ascends to the throne during the 50th year of Azariah, which is treated as his accession year and not yet counted as a regnal year. The 51st and 52nd year of Azariah are attributed to him as regnal years, the sum of which adds up to two. In the case of postdating, the subtraction of the synchronisms equals the regnal years given.

[12] The difficult cases are Omri (1 Kgs 16:23), Menahem (2 Kgs 15:17), and Hoshea (2 Kgs 15:30; 17:1); for a discussion of these see Weingart, *Gezählte Geschichte*, 33–36, 69–71.

[13] Regnal years were always counted from the New Year. If the New Year fell into the reign of a king, even if the actual time span of his reign might have covered only a few months, he was

overall interplay of synchronistic dates and regnal year totals, therefore, rather points to postdating. In addition, the dating formula in the book of Jeremiah mentioning a בראשית ממלכת or בראשית מלכות of several kings seems to refer to an accession year and thus indicates that postdating was in use in Judah at least in the later monarchic period.[14]

If the chronological data are no random collection of incoherent information, how were they put together? Older research was preoccupied with the alternative that either the regnal year totals or the synchronistic accession dates were secondary and calculated on the basis of the other set of numbers.[15] Eventually, the many unsuccessful attempts to retrace the calculation have clearly demonstrated that the basic assumption is wrong: one can neither calculate the synchronisms out of the regnal year totals, nor vice-versa.

But there is a certain logic to the material. The synchronistic chronology in the Book of Kings is best explained as a compilation on the basis of two sets of numbers: (1) a collection of regnal year totals and synchronistic accession year dates for the kings of Israel, and (2) a collection of regnal year totals for the kings of Judah. The synchronistic dates for the accessions of the Judahite kings were secondarily calculated by combining Judahite regnal year totals and Israelite accession dates. The result is a series of consecutive combinations, i.e., synchronistic interlacings of the two sets of numbers, coherent in themselves but limited in range.

The issue has been treated in a more comprehensive way elsewhere,[16] but one important observation underlying the proposal shall be named and exemplified: only in the Judahite material, there are occasional deviations from the stereotype regnal frame which aim at combining otherwise irreconcilable numerical data. A good case to illustrate the matter is the chronological treatment of the period around Jehu's assumption of power concerning the Judahite kings Jehoshaphat, Jehoram, and Ahaziahu.

---

attributed two regnal years. If the New Year lay outside his regnal period, he was attributed no full regnal year; see the explanations in Begrich, *Chronologie*, 90–93, or Edwin R. Thiele, *The Mysterious Numbers of the Hebrew Kings: A Reconstruction of the Chronology of the Kingdoms of Israel and Judah*, 2nd ed. (Exeter: Paternoster, 1965), 16–22.

[14] Jer 26:1; 27:1; 28:1; 49:34; see already Begrich, *Chronologie*, 93.

[15] See e.g. Wellhausen, "Zeitrechnung," 608; Gustiav Löv, "Das synchronistische System der Königsbücher," *ZWT* 43 (1900): 161–79, for the regnal year totals as basis of the compilation or e.g. Julius Lewy, *Die Chronologie der Könige von Israel und Juda* (Gießen: Töpelmann, 1927), 9; Martin Thilo, *Die Chronologie des Alten Testamentes dargestellt und beurteilt unter besonderer Berücksichtigung der masoretischen Richter- und Königszahlen: Mit vier großen graphischen Tafeln* (Barmen: Hugo Klein's Verlag, 1917), preferring the synchronisms. Both sides have to change great portions of the data and/or assume a large degree of textual corruption in order to retrace the assumed calculations.

[16] See Weingart, *Gezählte Geschichte*, 23–55.

Israel		Regnal Year Total	Synchronism
Ahab	1 Kgs 16:29	22	38th Asa
Ahaziah	1 Kgs 22:52	2	17th Jehoshaphat
Joram	2 Kgs 3:1	12	18th Jehoshaphat
Jehu	2 Kgs 10:35 f.	28	

The Israelite data place the accession of the Israelite Ahaziah in the 17th year of Jehoshaphat and that of his successor Joram in the 18th year of Jehoshaphat. The takeover of Jehu is not dated but, according to 2 Kgs 9, has to coincide with the deaths of Joram of Israel and Ahaziahu of Judah.

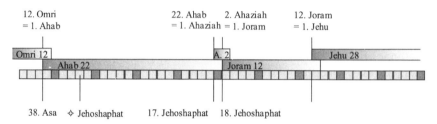

Fig. 1: Data for the Kings of Israel Omri to Jehu.

The Judahite regnal year totals for the period amount to 25 years for Jehoshaphat, 8 years for Jehoram and 1 year for Ahaziahu.

Judah		Regnal Year Total	Synchronism
Asa	1 Kgs 15:9 f.	41	20th Jeroboam
Jehoshaphat	1 Kgs 22:41 f.	25	4th Ahab
Jehoram	2 Kgs 8:16 f.	8	5th Joram
Ahaziahu	2 Kgs 8:25 f.	1	12th Joram
Jehoash	2 Kgs 12:1 f.	40	7th Jehu

As Joram of Israel and Ahaziahu of Judah supposedly died in the same year, their successors should take reign at the same time. But it becomes immediately apparent, that the Israelite and Judahite data do not fit. The beginning of Jehu's and Athaliah's reign does not coincide.

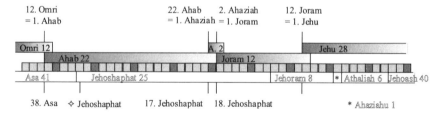

Fig. 2: Data for the Kings of Israel Omri to Jehu and Judahite Regnal Year Totals.

The solution to the problem is found in 2 Kgs 8:16, a deviation from the usual formula of the regnal frame indicating a coregency of Jehoshaphat and Jehoram:[17]

8:16 וּבִשְׁנַת חָמֵשׁ לְיוֹרָם בֶּן־אַחְאָב מֶלֶךְ יִשְׂרָאֵל וִיהוֹשָׁפָט מֶלֶךְ יְהוּדָה מָלַךְ יְהוֹרָם בֶּן־יְהוֹשָׁפָט מֶלֶךְ יְהוּדָה׃

With an overlap of four years in the reign of these two kings the remaining synchronisms nicely fall into place.[18]

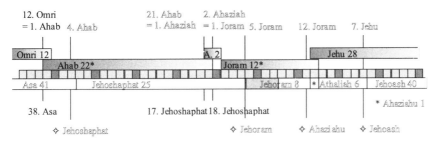

Fig. 3: Compilation Jehoshaphat to Jehoash.

For the beginning of Jehoram's coregency no accession year is included, but this corresponds to all the other cases of overlapping reigns within the chronology of the Judahite kings (Azariah, Jotham). One important word of caution is in order: the reconstruction does not imply that the mentioned coregency is an historical fact; it is just the way the compiler tried to make sense of the data at his disposal.

Comparable notes either within the context of the regnal frame or in the narrative material appear also in 2 Kgs 14:17 and 14:22. Here as well, they help to combine Judahite regnal year totals and accession dates of Israelite kings which would be otherwise irreconcilable. Besides the comprehensible combination

---

[17] Many commentators see ויהושפט מלך יהודה as a gloss secondarily inserted into the text and disturbing the usual sequence of the introductory formula (see e. g., Otto Thenius, *Die Bücher der Könige*, 2nd ed., KEH [Leipzig: Hirzel, 1873], 312; Wellhausen, "Zeitrechnung," 616; James Shenkel, *Chronology and Recensional Development in the Greek Text of Kings*, HSM [Cambridge, MA: Harvard University Press, 1968], 73; Volkmar Fritz, *Das zweite Buch der Könige*, ZBK [Zürich: TVZ, 1998], 43). The words are also missing in some textual witnesses ($\mathfrak{G}^{Nmin}$, Syh, $\mathfrak{S}$, $\mathfrak{U}^{Mss}$) prompting the apparatus of the BHS to suggest their deletion. 8:16 obviously deviates from the usual regnal frame, but this characterizes the phrase rather as a *lectio difficilior probabilior*: a secondary adjustment to the regular formula, i. e., a deletion of the clause, is much more plausible than a later addition (Jürgen Werlitz, *Die Bücher der Könige*, NSKAT [Stuttgart: Kath. Bibelwerk, 2002], 234; cf. Burke O. Long, *2 Kings*, FOTL [Grand Rapids: Eerdmans, 1991], 108). Besides, it is hard to explain what information the assumed gloss ויהושפט מלך יהודה should have conveyed. That Jehoshaphat was a king of Judah is implied by the filiation in 16b. Indicating a coregency, the phrase has a recognizable function within the introductory formula, and one does not have to assume a gloss or interpolation.

[18] The new compilation results in the problem that Ahab's regnal year total of 22 years no longer fits, but the concern of the compiler was more on the data of the Judahite kings. Conflicting Israelite regnal year totals were usually not adapted.

of these two sets of numbers, these "corrective notes" hint most clearly at the method of compilation.

1.2 The Presentation of the Chronological Data

The observation that the scribe(s) compiling the synchronistic chronology worked with these two sets of numbers, i.e., a collection of regnal year totals for the kings of Judah and a collection of regnal year totals and synchronistic accession dates for the kings of Israel, points to another question leading back to the texts: what were the documents providing these numbers?[19]

One might expect that they were taken out of two chronographic works, which might have also influenced the way the data is presented within the Book of Kings. But a closer look at the regnal frame shows not two, but three different patterns of introductory formulae (see appendix):[20]

Pattern A is characteristic for the kings of Judah. It contains specific details (age at accession, information on the king's mother) and is rigid in the sequence of the elements. Syntactically it is construed out of two verbal clauses, both with מלך. In the formulae of the last kings of Judah beginning with Manasseh, the elements 1–3 are missing, but all the other parts are extant and identical in sequence and phraseology.

Pattern B is used for five kings of Israel: Nadab (1 Kgs 15:25), Ahab (1 Kgs 16:29), Ahaziah (1 Kgs 22:52), Joram (2 Kgs 3:1) and Shallum (2 Kgs 15:13). It starts with the name of the king and his territory before the synchronistic date. Syntactically, it consists of two verbal clauses ו... מלך ... וימלך. The sequence of the elements is slightly more variable than in pattern A.

Pattern C begins like pattern A with a synchronism and continues with the elements known from pattern B. Here we have only one clause with מלך in the second position. The introductory formulae of the remaining kings of Israel follow this pattern.

---

[19] Scholarly wisdom has it – and rightly so – that the data within the regnal frame goes back to king lists recording chronological data for successive kings in Israel and Judah or perhaps to chronicles of a king's reign; so already Noth, *Überlieferungsgeschichtliche Studien*, 72–76; Shoshana Bin-Nun, "Formulas from Royal Records of Israel and of Judah," *VT* 18 (1968): 414–32, or – more recently – Nadav Na'aman, "Sources and Composition in the Book of Kings: The Introductory and Final Verses of the Kings of Judah and Israel," (Hebr.), in *Shai Le-Sara Japhet: Studies in the Bible, Its Exegesis and Its Language*, ed. Moshe Bar-Asher et al. (Jerusalem: Bialik, 2007), 97–118; Nadav Na'aman, "The Sources Available to the Book of Kings," in *Recenti tendenze nella ricostruzione della storia antica d'Israele* (Rome: Accademia Nazionale dei Lincei, 2005), 105–20; and Jonathan M. Robker, *The Jehu Revolution: A Royal Tradition of the Northern Kingdom and its Ramifications*, BZAW 435 (Berlin: de Gruyter, 2012), who reconstructs an Israelite source recounting the history of the Northern Kingdom from Jeroboam I up to Jeroboam II.

[20] These patterns have long been recognized; the following considerations build and expand upon the systematic treatment in Bin-Nun, "Formulas," cf. also Weingart, *Gezählte Geschichte*, 121–39.

Do these patterns lead back to the sources used by the scribe(s) compiling the regnal frame? Pattern A, used for the Judahite kings, and pattern C, used for most Israelite kings, bear the greatest resemblance. Pattern C matches exactly the first clause of pattern A, which is only supplemented by the residency and regnal year total. On the other hand, pattern A and pattern B differ considerably, in regard to their contents, the sequence of elements and the syntactical structure. So, for any source-critical considerations patterns A and B seem to be the best point of departure.

Pattern B is easily conceivable as the basic grid of a king list or if supplemented by some additional content on the various kings' reigns as a chronicle,[21] which recorded:

- the name of the king,
- his territory,
- a synchronistic accession date,
- his residence,
- a regnal year total, and
- (if applicable) notes on wars and building measures.[22]

Because this pattern is only used for Israelite kings, it could lead back to an Israelite document which was utilized by the compiler of the regnal frame.

Pattern A, used for the Judahite kings, is attested with and without a synchronism in the beginning. In its form without the synchronistic accession date and the elements 2–3, as used for the Judahite kings after Hezekiah, it does not resemble a sufficient introductory section for a king list or chronicle. Starting with the age at accession, a proper introduction of the king – naming his function and patronym – is missing. Yet, it is unlikely that the synchronistic accession dates were already included in the source. The main reason was already named by Shoshana Bin-Nun in her groundbreaking study on the introductory formulae:[23] In any king list or chronicle, it would be highly unusual that the name of a neighboring – or any other king – was mentioned before the king the entry is dealing with.[24] This is confirmed by all ANE chronicles, annals and king lists

---

[21] For an inquiry into the basic structure of various chronicles, annals, and king lists, see Thomas, *Hezekiah*, 46–61; Weingart, *Gezählte Geschichte*, 85–115.

[22] Unlike the burial notes for the Judahite kings, the closing formulae of the Israelite kings do not contain any new information. The burial place, if mentioned, always matches the residence. Therefore, the burial notes are probably modelled after the Judahite examples present in pattern A.

[23] Bin-Nun, "Formulas," also reiterates another argument originally going back to Wellhausen, "Zeitrechnung," 611 f., and repeated ever since (see again Robker, *Jehu Revolution*, 74 f.): the phrasing of pattern C – and to a lesser degree also of pattern A – is considered awkward or even logically impossible, because מלך is used both in an inchoative and a durative sense. The semantics of מלך do allow both possibilities and if the formulation was indeed impossible, one may wonder why any later redactor should have created it.

[24] Bin-Nun, "Formulas," 426.

known so far.[25] In addition, the introduction of the new king is not missing at all, if the closing formula of the regnal frame is brought into the picture. Each new king is introduced in the succession formula וימלך ... בנו תחתיו. Taken together with the synchronistic accession date in the beginning and read continuously one would even end up with a double and thus redundant introduction.

Therefore, a probable chronographic *Vorlage* might have contained:

- a succession note introducing the king,
- his age at accession,
- his regnal year total,
- his residence,
- particulars regarding the king's mother,
- (possibly) notes on wars, building measures etc., and
- a burial note.

However, recognizing the synchronistic dates in pattern A as secondary does not imply that this applies for synchronistic accession dates universally. Pattern B shows that synchronistic dates could well be included in an introductory – or for that matter – king list formula which gives no occasion for literary critical operations.

Pattern C constitutes the most concise form of the introductory formulae. It is identical to the first clause of pattern A and contains the elements of pattern B. With the synchronism up front, it probably does not resemble any king list and rather is a creation of the compiler of the regnal frame who by supplementing a Judahite source with synchronistic dates created pattern A, which then served as a model for integrating data on the kings of Israel that were originally taken from a source text still discernable behind pattern B. The result of the combination was pattern C.

The analysis of the three patterns of introductory formulae therefore leads back to two sources,[26] king lists or chronicles – each with a distinctive content and structure – and provides indications for their redactional reworking in the development of the third pattern. This conclusion corroborates the results of the

---

[25] Cf. already William F. Albright, "The Chronology of the Divided Monarchy of Israel," *BASOR* 100 (1945): 16–22, 19; Thomas, *Hezekiah*, 75. In Neo-Assyrian Eponym Chronicles the name of the eponymous official may precede the name of the king whose accession is reported. Also, the Neo-Babylonian Chronicles do not provide any counterexample. The accession dates for some Assyrian and Elamite kings are included following the name and regnal year of the Babylonian king, but these accessions are treated as events happening during the ruling period of the respective Babylonian king whose reign is the object of presentation.

[26] Although a discussion of the so-called source citations within the closing formulae of the regnal frame lies outside the scope of this paper (see Weingart, *Gezählte Geschichte*, 175–83), it should be noted that they refer to two sources for the account of the history of the parallel kingdoms as well: a chronicle of the kings of Israel (ספר דברי הימים למלכי ישראל) and a chronicle of the kings of Judah (ספר דברי הימים למלכי יהודה).

earlier discussion of the numerical data, which led to the proposition of two sets of numbers – a combination of regnal year totals and synchronistic accession dates for the kings of Israel and a collection of regnal year totals for the kings of Judah. The scribes working out the regnal frame did so in utilizing (at least) two chronographic sources: on the one hand, an Israelite source containing regnal year totals and synchronistic accession year dates as well as most of the other data found in pattern B; and on the other hand, a Judahite source containing regnal year totals and other data on the successive Judahite kings.

2. The Chronicle of the Kings of Israel

So far, our considerations concerned the skeleton of the synchronistic chronology, i.e., the regnal frame, and led to a distinction between material compiled and composed by the scribe(s) putting together the synchronistic chronology, thus establishing the basic framework of Kings, and material taken over from the sources they used. If the analysis is correct, it suggests that the scribes responsible for the regnal frame could already take recourse to existing chronographic documents which provided the greater part of the numerical data as well as two out of the three patterns for its presentation. One of the two chronographic documents was concerned with the kings of the Northern Kingdom of Israel, one with the kings of the Kingdom of Judah.

The following considerations will focus on the material concerning the Kingdom of Israel and propose a reconstruction of the chronographic source pertaining to it. Unlike its Judahite counterpart, it is easier to grasp in its structure and contents.[27] The source contained numerical data on the kings' dates of accession and lengths of reign and organized these in a sequence that stands behind pattern B of the regnal frame. Although any reconstruction of this chronographic source has to remain speculative, a few attempts to further characterize it can be dared:

2.1 Content

It is self-evident that the genuinely Deuteronomistic materials as well as the post-Deuteronomistic additions do not originate from the older chronographic doc-

---

[27] Compared to the material on the Northern Kingdom within the Book of Kings, the material on Judah is much more extensive and diverse. It also lacks a comparable structural uniformity (for that see below). It stands to reason that the scribes assembling the synchronistic history of the two kingdoms had at their disposal a wider range of material and traditions on Judah. As a result, it is even harder to identify and differentiate between specific sources; for a discussion of conceivable options see Weingart, *Gezählte Geschichte*, 163–69.

ument.[28] Thus, the range of possible source material is noticeably reduced; it comprises the two larger narrative blocks on the division of the kingdom (1 Kgs *11:26–14:20) and the Jehu revolt (2 Kgs 9:1–10:27) as well as a whole series of shorter notes.

The short notes can be assigned to three subject areas: (1) They concern irregular seizures of power, especially *coups d'état* and the associated murders of incumbent rulers and the replacement of dynasties. These can be extremely concise factual notes (1 Kgs 15:27 f.; 16:9 f.; 2 Kgs 15:10, 14, 25, 30a) or, in the case of Omri, a slightly more detailed account (1 Kgs 16:15–19). The six short coup notes have a recognizably parallel structure. The basic pattern is best discernable in 2 Kgs 15:30a. The other notes almost always have the same elements (...קשר הכה...המית...מלך...תחת) in an analogous sequence, at times supplemented by brief additional information on the location and circumstances of the coup. The case of Omri, who is initially appointed as a counter-king to Zimri and must then assert himself against the counter-king Tibni, is more complicated and more freely narrated, but the basic pattern returns explicitly in 16:16. (2) A further group of notes are reports on military campaigns and the resulting territorial gains or losses, or tribute obligations (2 Kgs 13:24–25a; 14:25a; 15:19–20, 29; 17:3–6). (3) For Omri, construction measures are mentioned (1 Kgs 16:24).

The information conveyed in these short notes is highly individual and specific.[29] Although there are no external sources for the coups that could be used

---

[28] The Elijah and Elisha narratives (1 Kgs 17–19; 2 Kgs 1:1–17 and 2 Kgs 2:1–25; 4:1–8:15; 13:14–25) are post-deuteronomistic additions (for the integration of the Elijah-narratives into the Deuteronomistic Book of Kings, see Erhard Blum, "Der Prophet und das Verderben Israels: Eine ganzheitlich historisch-kritische Lektüre von 1 Regum xvii–xix," in *Textgestalt und Komposition: Exegetische Beiträge zu Tora und Vordere Propheten*, ed. Wolfgang Oswald, FAT 69 [Tübingen: Mohr Siebeck, 2010], with further references; for the Elisha-stories see e.g. Hermann-Josef Stipp, "Ahabs Buße und die Komposition des Deuteronomistischen Geschichtswerks," *Bib* 76 [1995]: 471–97; Susanne Otto, "The Composition of the Elijah-Elisha Stories and the Deuteronomistic History," *JSOT* 27 [2003]: 487–508; or Ruth Sauerwein, *Elischa: Eine Redaktions- und religionsgeschichtliche Studie*, BZAW 465 [Berlin: de Gruyter, 2014], 111); on 1 Kgs 18 also see the contribution by Benjamin D. Giffone in the present volume ("Regathering Too Many Stones"). The same applies to the stories of the man of God from Judah in Bethel (1 Kgs 13, cf. Frank Ueberschaer, *Vom Gründungsmythos zur Untergangssymphonie: Eine text- und literar-geschichtliche Untersuchung zu 1 Kön 11–14*, BZAW 481 [Berlin: de Gruyter, 2015], 220 f., 239 f. with further references) and of Nabot's vineyard (1 Kgs 21, cf. Erhard Blum, "Die Nabotüberlieferungen und die Kompositionsgeschichte der Vorderen Propheten," in *Textgestalt und Komposition: Exegetische Beiträge zu Tora und Vordere Propheten*, ed. Wolfgang Oswald, FAT 69 [Tübingen: Mohr Siebeck, 2010], 355–74) as well as to the reports of wars with Aram (1 Kgs 20, 22) and Moab (2 Kgs 3:4–27), which are linked to Ahab and Joram in the present context (see Stipp, "Ahabs Buße," 489–93). Of Deuteronomistic origin are the judgment formulae within the regnal frame, the dynastic oracles and their fulfillment notes (1 Kgs 14:7–16; 15:29 f.; 16:1–4, 11–13; 21:20–22, 24) as well as the promise for the Jehu dynasty (2 Kgs 10:30) and its fulfillment notes regarding Joahas (2 Kgs 13:4–7), Jerobeam II (2 Kgs 13:25b–27) and Zechariah (2 Kgs 15:12).

[29] So also, Lester L. Grabbe, "Mighty Oaks from (Genetically Manipulated?) Acorns Grow:

to verify or falsify them, analogies such as the news of coups in Elam (ABC[30] 1, ii 32–35; iii 13–15), the assassination of Sennacherib by his sons (ABC 1, iii 34f., cf. 2 Kgs 19:37), or irregular seizures of power in Tyros[31] or Assyria[32] show that such details are part of a broader repertoire of chronographic works and are highly likely to preserve historical facts. It would be hard to explain why information on the exact location of a coup (1 Kgs 15:27; 16:9; 2 Kgs 15:14, 25), the suicide of Zimri (1 Kgs 16:18), the military successes of Jeroboam II (2 Kgs 14:25) or the tribute payment of Menachem (2 Kgs 15:19 f.) should have been invented without any basis in reality. With the exception of the territorial expansions by Jeroboam II (2 Kgs 14:25), the information on armed conflicts is supported by Assyrian or Aramean sources.[33]

Moreover, the structural uniformity especially in the notes on the coups is striking. One could argue that it points to the work of the author of the Book of Kings who shows a clear interest in recurring phraseology, e.g., in the judgment formulae. On the other hand, it is revealing that deviations, where they occur, coincide with peculiarities of the narrative account within the Book of Kings: as seen above, the description of Omri's assumption of power deviates from the usual pattern of the coup notes.[34] The longer account of the Jehu revolt in 2 Kgs 9f. differs from the short factual notes on the other coups in its broader narrative

---

The Chronicle of the Kings of Judah as a Source of the Deuteronomistic History," in *Reflection and Refraction: Studies in Biblical Historiography in Honour of A. Graeme Auld*, ed. Robert Rezetko, Timothy H. Lim and W. Brian Aucker, VTSup 113 (Leiden: Brill, 2007), 155–73, 157, who however wants to trace the information back to a Judahite chronicle.

[30] Grayson, *Chronicles*.

[31] The King List from Tyre which is cited by Josephus mentions a number of these incidents, cf. e.g., Josephus, *Contra Apionem* 1.122–24.

[32] Seizures of power are a recurrent topic also in the Assyrian King List, cf. in the so-called Khorsabad-List B: i 39–47; ii 4, 6–11, 45–46; iii 1, 21–22; iv 1–4 (see Glassner, *Mesopotamian Chronicles*, 136–45).

[33] Although there is no direct Aramean evidence for the events mentioned in 2 Kgs 13:24, the Tel Dan Inscription confirms the lengthy conflict between the Northern Kingdom and Aram. For 2 Kgs 15:19–20 see e.g., Hayim Tadmor, *The Inscriptions of Tiglath-pileser III, King of Assyria: Critical Edition, with Introduction, Translations and Commentary*, Fontes ad res Judaicas spectantes (Jerusalem: Israel Acad. of Sciences and Humanities, 1994), Ann. 13*: 10, or Ann. 27: 2; for 15:29 see ibid., Ann. 18: 2'–7'; Ann. 24: 1'–11'. The exact reconstruction of the conquest of Samaria (2 Kgs 17:3–6) is subject of an ongoing debate, see e.g., the contributions in Shuichi Hasegawa, Christoph Levin, and Karen Radner, *The Last Days of the Kingdom of Israel*, BZAW 511 (Berlin: de Gruyter, 2019).

[34] The differences to the usual structure are obvious: Omri's inauguration is reported immediately after the introductory formula for Zimri and not following the judgment formula. As a result, the judgment formula for Zimri lacks the usual introduction עשה הרע/הטוב בעיני יהוה and follows the note on Zimri's death. A burial and succession note for Zimri are missing. An account of Omri's conflict with Tibni is placed between the source citation for Zimri and the chronological information on Omri. All in all, the rule of two kings and an account of Omri's irregular way to the throne are combined into one episode. The trajectory clearly lies on Omri. The rule of Zimri as well as the conflict with Tibni are presented as a mere prelude to Omri's rule.

design, its theological concern, and its noticeable disinterest in chronological matters.[35] Its origins lie elsewhere,[36] and its combination with the material taken from the chronographic source may have been the reason for the absence of the usual closing formula for Joram and the opening formula for Jehu.

A distinct profile of the chronographic source document emerges. It is best described as a Chronicle of the Kings of Israel, which contained information on the individual kings concerning the date of their accessions and their lengths of reign, their area of rule and residence, as well as – if relevant – concise intelligence about coups, military campaigns, and construction measures.[37]

2.2 Genre

The Chronicle's form and design is first and foremost structured by a rigid chronological framework. The latter consists of synchronistic accession dates for the individual kings and data on their respective lengths of reign, occasionally supplemented by additional synchronistic dates (1 Kgs 15:28; 16:10).[38] The formal structure is best preserved in pattern B of the introductory formulae. Within this structure, the Chronicle is narrative in its basic layout and differs in this respect from pure lists. The individual entries are drawn up as short narrative paragraphs; the predominant verbal form is *wayyiqtol*, which is characteristic of Hebrew prose. Asyndesis – if it appears – marks a new theme (2 Kgs 14:25; 15:19, 29; 17:3) and occasionally the beginning of a new ruling period (cf. 1 Kgs 22:52; 2 Kgs 15:13), thus also following Hebrew narrative conventions.

In terms of design and content, the Chronicle corresponds to the thematic orientation of numerous chronographic works from the wider ANE context:[39]

---

[35] The same holds true for the account of the division of the kingdom in 1 Kgs *11:26–14:20, which – although being part of the older northern Israelite material integrated into Kings – has its own style and pragmatics (see Kristin Weingart, "Jeroboam and Benjamin: Pragmatics and Date of 1 Kgs 11:26–40 and 12:1–20," in *Saul, Benjamin, and the Emergence of Monarchy in Israel: Biblical and Archaeological Perspectives*, ed. Joachim J. Krause, Omer Sergi, and Kristin Weingart, AIL 40 [Atlanta: Society of Biblical Literature, 2020], 133–59).

[36] For the recent debates see e.g., Susanne Otto, *Jehu, Elia und Elisa*, BWANT 152 (Stuttgart: Kohlhammer, 2001); Robker, *Jehu Revolution*; or Shuichi Hasegawa, *Aram and Israel During the Jehuite Dynasty*, BZAW 434 (Berlin: de Gruyter, 2012); cf. also Weingart, *Gezählte Geschichte*, 146–49.

[37] While the current discussion focusses on the character of one of the sources used for the Book of Kings, the source's integration into another chronographic document, namely the Book of Kings, can also serve as an example for the pluriformity of methods scribes utilized in order to form new ones out of existing texts, for the phenomenon see the contribution by Benjamin Ziemer in this volume ("Radical Versus Conservative").

[38] Cf. already Noth, *Überlieferungsgeschichtliche Studien*, 74 f., who proposed that the data and information were extracted out of court annals. Also, Na'aman, "Sources available," 111, reckons with an Israelite chronicle as source of information; he assumes, however, that the chronological data were copied from a separate king list.

[39] This assessment and the following considerations concern chronographic works dealing

(1) ANE chronographic royal chronicles and king lists may vary in the kind of numerical information they provide,[40] but there are certain focuses. They usually record the length of reign of a king (and sometimes additionally the length of reign of a dynasty[41]). In contrast, the accession dates of individual kings are only occasionally provided, so for instance in the Neo-Babylonian Chronicles or the Neo-Assyrian Eponym Chronicles. Sometimes there are also numerical data on biographical matters like the lifetime[42] or the year of death.[43] With its specific set of numerical data, the Chronicle of the Kings of Israel reminds of the Neo-Assyrian Eponym Chronicles, although they use the eponym canon as an external chronology in order to record the accession years and does not refer to the regnal years of another line of rulers. Like in the Chronicle of the Kings of Israel any new king's accession to the throne is dated and opens a new section.[44]

(2) With regard to the dating formula itself, the Chronicle has a close parallel in the Neo-Babylonian Chronicle; their respective dating formulas both follow the same sequence:[45] synchronistic date, name of the king, territory, seems to match the dating formulas in the Book of Kings.[46] It should be noted, however, that in the Neo-Babylonian Chronicle the dating formula is applied for dating the accessions of the neighboring Assyrian or Elamite kings, not the Babylonian kings themselves, whose reign is described and whose regnal years provide the chronological structure of the composition. Therefore, a comparable dating formula is used, yet integrated into a differing structure.[47]

(3) Although synchronizing the accession of the Israelite kings with an external (here Judahite) chronology, the Chronicle is not a synchronistic work interlacing two parallel lines of rulers like the Synchronistic King List[48] or the Synchronistic History.[49] Instead, the Chronicle of the Kings of Israel concen-

---

with the sequence of rulers and dynasties; there are of course also numerous chronographic works with a completely different (cultic, administrative, economic etc.) orientation.

[40] See the overview in Weingart, *Gezählte Geschichte*, Anhang III.

[41] So e.g., the Turin King List, the Sumerian King List, the King List from Larsa, the Babylonian King Lists A, B, and C, or the Dynastic Chronicle. Occasionally also the number of kings within a dynasty is included.

[42] So e.g., in the Turin King List or the King List from Tyre.

[43] The date of Nabupolassar's death is recorded in the Neo-Babylonian Chronicle (Grayson, *Chronicles* 5, r 10).

[44] In some textual witnesses of the Eponym Chronicle, the individual reigns are graphically divided by horizontal lines, see Alan Millard, *The Eponyms of the Assyrian Empire 910–612 BC*, SAAS 2 (Helsinki: The Neo-Assyrian Text Corpus Project, 1994), 12–13.

[45] So e.g., Grayson, *Chronicles* 1, i 9: "The fifth year of Nabopolassar: Humban-nikaš ascended to the throne in Elam" (cf. ibid., 1, i 38; ii 32; iii 6, 13, 19, 28).

[46] In fact, the closest parallels are patterns A and C, and not pattern B which goes back to the Chronicle of the Kings of Israel.

[47] This speaks against a direct literal dependency of the regnal frame from the Neo-Babylonian Chronicles as proposed by Blanco Wißmann, *Beurteilungskriterien*, 213–23.

[48] Albert Kirk Grayson, "Königslisten und Chroniken: B. Akkadisch," *RlA* 6:86–135, 116–21.

[49] Grayson, *Chronicles* 21.

trates solely on one line of kings, namely that of Israel. Judahite kings are only mentioned insofar as it is necessary for dating the accessions of the Israelite kings. The Judahite kings themselves or even their complete line are not the object of the presentation.[50]

(4) In its contents, the Chronicle of the Kings of Israel picks up the predominant topics found in those ANE chronicles and king lists, which are not limited to mere chronological information.[51] They usually record successions – regular as well as irregular ones. Accordingly, the Sumerian King List mentions special cases in the dynastic succession,[52] so does the Assyrian King List[53], the King List from Tyre,[54] or the Neo-Assyrian Eponym Chronicle.[55] The great deeds of specific kings and their military pursuits are of course an important and very frequent topic, as well as construction projects (temples, irrigation systems, fortifications etc.).[56]

All in all, the Chronicle of the Kings of Israel displays clear similarities in content and structure to other examples of the chronographic genre. It is best understood as regional or individual manifestation of the widely-attested genre (locally and temporally) of ANE chronography. None of its elements is unique in itself, but the present combination and sequence is nevertheless specific.

2.3 Date

Dating Old Testament texts remains a notoriously difficult task; dating their supposed sources or precursors leads to an even shakier ground. Usually, a number of different indicators can be used to situate a text within the literary history of ancient Israel or the Ancient Near East: linguistic features of the texts, provided they can be located within linguistic-historical developments, stratigraphic

---

[50] Accordingly, the names Rehoboam, Abijam, or Jehoram do not appear in the material taken over from the Chronicle.

[51] Examples of pure chronographic lists which only contain the kings' names and regnal year totals are the Turin King List, the King Lists from Ur-Isin or Larsa or the Babylonian King Lists A, B, C or the Synchronistic King List.

[52] Dietz-Otto Edzard, "Königslisten und Chroniken: A. Sumerisch," RlA, 6:77–86, 77–84; cf. Glassner, *Mesopotamian Chronicles 1*: G v 31–33; vi 39–40.

[53] Grayson, "Königslisten," 101–15; Glassner, *Mesopotamian Chronicles 5*: B i 39–47; ii 4, 6–11, 45–46; iii 1, 21–22, 27–29, 34–36; iv 1–4.

[54] See e.g., Josephus, *Contra Apionem* 1.122–23.

[55] The revolt that led to the ascension of Tiglat-Pileser is recorded in B1[74–80] (see Millard, *Eponyms*).

[56] The King List from Lagaš being a persiflage of the genre perfectly illustrates the literary conventions associated with these chronographic compositions (Edzard, "Königslisten," 84–85, Glassner, *Mesopotamian Chronicles* 6). It records the sequence of kings and their (mostly legendarily long) lengths of reign; in addition, it records great deeds of the kings, predominantly construction measures. It does not mention military campaigns, but the theme is well attested in numerous other king lists and chronicles.

relations to other texts datable with a higher degree of certainty, or links to specific events or discourses related to a certain period within the history of Israel.[57]

In the case of a reconstructed text, one has to be doubly cautious when relying on certain linguistic peculiarities. Is it feasible that these did not only survive the processes of later textual transmission, but also the text's primary integration into its new literary context? In the case of the Chronicle of the Kings of Israel, the relevant texts are limited to the five occurrences of pattern B (1 Kgs 15:25; 16:29; 22:52; 2 Kgs 3:1; 15:13) the short notes on *coups d'état* (1 Kgs 15:27 f.; 16:9 f., 15–19; 2 Kgs 15:10, 14, 25, 30a), military campaigns and building measures (1 Kgs 16:24; 2 Kgs 13:24–25a; 14:25a; 15:19–20, 29; 17:3–6), none of which show any datable linguistic peculiarities.

Reading the Chronicle against the background of ANE chronography has illustrated how deeply this Israelite manifestation of the genre is rooted within the wider ANE genre. Specific intertextual relations that would help to date the text are not detectable. With regard to the literary stratigraphy of the Old Testament itself, the incorporation of the Chronicle into the regnal frame provides a *terminus ad quem*. The compilation of the regnal frame is usually and with good reason associated with the work of one or successive Deuteronomistic editor(s) working in the exilic or late monarchic period. In addition, it stands to reason that the Chronicle included material on the last kings of the Northern Kingdom (cf. the introduction of Shallum following pattern B or the coup notes on Pekah in 2 Kgs 15:25 or Hoshea in 15:30). So, it might have covered the fate of the Northern Kingdom up to its very last king. Taken together, this points to its completion in the late monarchic period.

It would be misleading, however, to identify the last event mentioned with a *terminus a quo* for the composition as a whole. Here, one needs to take into account one of the specifics of the chronographic genre: king lists and chronicles tend to be continuously kept, i.e., they were updated and supplemented over a longer period of time.[58] There are clear indications that this also applies to the Chronicle of the Kings of Israel:

---

[57] For the categories see Erhard Blum, "The Linguistic Dating of Biblical Text: An Approach with Methodological Limitations," in *The Formation of the Pentateuch: Bridging the Academic Cultures of Europe, Israel, and North America*, ed. Jan Christian Gertz et al., FAT 111 (Tübingen: Mohr Siebeck, 2016), 303–28.

[58] The process is well known from later Roman or medieval annalistics, but also sufficiently attested in the ANE. Very few examples may suffice: for the Sumerian King List, the extant textual witnesses testify subsequent additions (see e.g., Piotr Steinkeller, "An Ur III Manuscript of the Sumerian King List," in *Literatur, Politik und Recht in Mesopotamien: FS Claus Wilcke*, ed. Walther Sallaberger, OBC 14 [Wiesbaden: Harassowitz, 2003], 267–92, 284–86), the numerous royal inscriptions of Salmanassar III illustrate how older texts were reused and extended in later compositions (cf. Shigeo Yamada, *The Construction of the Assyrian Empire: A Historical Study of the Inscriptions of Shalmaneser III (859–824 B.C.E.): Relating to His Campaigns to the West*, CHANE 3 [Leiden: Brill, 2000]), in the series of the Neobabylonian Chronicles (ABC, cf.

- As already noted, notes on the circumstances of *coups d'état*, military events, tribute payments etc. contain very specific details that are not easily explained as later constructions: why should anyone invent a tax levied by Menachem, the drunkenness of Ela or the suicide of Zimri? It stands to reason that the intelligence reflects historical circumstances that were recorded shortly after the events in question.[59] The same applies to the chronological data which are almost completely devoid of any round or symbolic numbers and therefore also speak against a "writing-desk construction" accomplished at a certain later date.
- The occasionally possible cross-references to external sources suggest a fundamental historical plausibility of the data. Menachem's tribute or the territorial losses of Pekah are confirmed by Assyrian sources.[60]
- The change from antedating to postdating in counting the regnal years also points to a continuously kept chronicle. Such shifts in the method of reckoning are conceivable in a continuously updated chronographic document but not in a retrospect construction.

If the Chronicle is to be understood as a continuously updated chronographic document, when was it begun? For the emergence of a synchronistic dating practice, much points to the era of the Omrides. The period was characterized by close family and political ties between the ruling houses of the Northern and Southern kingdom. Athaliah, a Northern Israelite princess,[61] was the wife of the Judahite king Jehoram and the mother of his successor Ahaziahu. Athaliah's marriage into the Jerusalemite royal house most likely had a political dimension and was aimed at securing and strengthening the Omridic influence on Judah. The close relations between the ruling houses, from the military alliance against Aram to Ahaziahu's sick call to Joram (2 Kgs 8:29), fit well into the picture. Accordingly, Shoshanna Bin-Nun proposed that the earliest synchronisms in the Israelite records stem "from the time of the alliance between the House of Ahab and that of Jehoshaphat".[62] In addition, at the time of the Omrides distinct administrative structures become visible for the first time in Israel[63] and the North-

---

Grayson, *Chronicles*) which from earlier to later chronicles shows a tendency to become more and more extensive in its individual entries, a gradual development is recognizable.

[59] Cf. the cautious assessment of Robker, *Jehu Revolution*, 286: "The various political revolts in the early days of Israel are also possible, i.e., at least no evidence can be found to contradict them." Even if one assumes – like Robker – that the dynastic stability of the Nimshides shall be painted positively against the quickly changing dynasties in other periods, there would be no need to invent and/or narrate such specific details.

[60] See above n33.

[61] 2 Kgs 8:18 and 8:26 contradict each other in describing Athaliah as daughter of Omri or of Ahab.

[62] Bin-Nun, "Formulas," 426.

[63] See Israel Finkelstein, *The Forgotten Kingdom: The Archaeology and History of Northern Israel*, ANEM 5 (Atlanta: Society of Biblical Literature, 2013), 113–15, or Christian Frevel, *Geschichte Israels*, ST (Stuttgart: Kohlhammer, 2016), 94–95.

ern Kingdom of Israel appears as a political agent on the international stage (and here immediately as a significant actor in the conflicts of the Central Palestinian states with Assur). The development of administrative infrastructure may have contributed to a growing interest in chronological matters. The examples of Tyre or Moab illustrate that one does not have to travel far away from Israel at this time in order to encounter both king lists and chronicles as well as an interest in chronology.[64]

The information attributed to the Chronicle does lead even further back to Jeroboam I (regnal years) or his successor Nadab (regnal years and synchronistic accession date). The first detailed information on a coup is already available for the transition from Nadab to Baasha. Did the chronographic recording of events begin even earlier, or do we have to reckon with memories retrospectively put into writing? That can hardly be decided anymore. The circumstances of the first coup described in 1 Kgs 15:27 f. refer to conflicts with the Philistines and an army camp in Gibbeton as the site of Nadab's murder. Due to the lack of additional sources, they can neither be ascertained nor refuted. Moreover, a decisive clue regarding oral or written tradition would also not necessarily follow. The accessions from Nadab to Ahab are all synchronized with the lengthy reign of the Judahite Asa, so, if the lengths of reign of the kings were known, their accession dates could have been easily calculated. Irrespective of whether the data on the first kings are based on early entries in a royal chronicle or were put in writing later, they are – as noted above – hardly conceivable as a pure invention without any historical reference.

3. The "Chronicle of the Kings of Israel" and Scribal Culture in Israel

Chronography is a written genre. Its contents, the plethora of numbers, names, and details, are hardly imaginable as an oral tradition. It has its primary function in administrative contexts (e.g. dating treaties and records) and its legitimatory pragmatics (e.g. indicating dynastic continuity, listing great deeds of a successful ruler). Both aspects point to royal courts[65] which are generally considered

---

[64] For the King List from Tyre, see above n31 and also the assessment of Wolfgang Zwickel, "Die Tyrische Königsliste und die Annalenangaben des Alten Testaments," in *Text – Textgeschichte – Textwirkung: FS S. Kreuzer*, ed. Thomas Wagner et al., AOAT 419 (Münster: Ugarit-Verlag, 2014), 83–92, that the list proves the existence of trustworthy records which go back to the 10th century. Also, the Mesha Stele from Moab (Herbert Donner and Wolfgang Röllig, *Kanaanäische und aramäische Inschriften. Mit einem Beitrag von O. Rössler, I. Texte*, 5th ed., [Wiesbaden: Harassowitz, 2002], No. 181) has a regnal year total for Mesha's predecessor (line 2).

[65] Accordingly, it was almost taken for granted in older research and is still occasionally assumed today, that the chronological data within the royal framework were copied out of "official court annals," the existence of which at the respective residences was not called into question

one of the primary institutional contexts for the development and maintenance of writing and scribal culture. Therefore, it is hardly surprising that the extant chronographic documents from Mesopotamia also include a number of scribal exercises.[66]

The identification of a Chronicle of the Kings of Israel as a continuously updated chronographic work, whose origins go back at least to the period of the Omrides and which served as a major source for the chronological arrangement and parts of the material included into the Book of Kings, in a certain regard goes against a current trend in recent scholarly debates. In many current reconstructions dealing with the development of a scribal culture in Israel it is considered an established fact that the beginnings of a scribal culture in Israel can only be dated into the 8th century.[67] Therefore, seeking substantial texts or literary compositions from earlier periods is no longer an option; chronographic documents whose beginnings go back to the early 9th or even 10th century would be out of the question.

Two main arguments stand behind the focus on the 8th or early 7th century: an archaeological one concerning the epigraphic evidence, and a socio-cultural one concerning the infrastructure necessary for the development of a scribal culture. The first one starts from the observation that the chronological distribution of the extant Hebrew inscriptions shows a significant accumulation in the 8th century, while only very few and isolated finds can be attributed to the earlier periods.[68] The second argument links the existence of professional scribes to the processes of state formation and the emergence of administrative structures; where territorial expansion, socio-economic differentiation, and political development require the development of an administrative infrastructure, there one also finds

---

(see e.g., Noth, *Überlieferungsgeschichtliche Studien*, 72–76, or more recently Ernst A. Knauf, *1 Könige 1–14*, HThKAT [Freiburg: Herder, 2016], 89). The Chronicle of the Kings of Israel, proposed here, does not readily fit the category "annals," as documents structured on a yearly basis. It is rather structured by a sequence of kings, whose respective reigns mark time periods or epochs.

[66] The Babylonian King Lists B and C are usually understood as exercise texts, see Grayson, "Königslisten," 96–97, 100.

[67] Israel Finkelstein, a strong proponent of this view, sees in Israel "no evidence for compilation of complex texts before the early 8th century" ("History, Historicity and Historiography in Ancient Israel," in *Story and History: The Kings of Israel and Judah in Context*, ed. Johannes Unsok Ro, FAT II 105 [Tübingen: Mohr Siebeck, 2019], 15–30, 21); John Van Seters argues that "not until the late 8th century was Judah sufficiently advanced as a state that it could produce any written records" (*The Biblical Saga of King David* [Winona Lake, IN: Eisenbrauns, 2009], 60), cf. also Finkelstein, *Forgotten Kingdom*, 35, or Israel Finkelstein and Benjamin Sass, "The West Semitic Alphabetic Inscriptions, Late Bronze II to Iron IIa: Archaeological Context, Distribution and Chronology," *HeBAI* 2 (2013): 149–220, 190–99.

[68] For an overview see e.g., Hermann M. Niemann, "Kein Ende des Büchermachens in Israel und Juda (Koh 12,12): Wann begann es?" *BK* 53 (1998): 127–34, 129.

a scribal culture.[69] According to the current interpretation of the archaeological findings, this point was not reached in Israel before the very end of the 9th century and in Judah not before the 8th century. Therefore, a scribal culture and the production of substantial literature cannot be expected before this period.

The number of extant inscriptions, as well as the fact that growing administative necessities resulted in the development of a scribal culture, and a corresponding schooling and training system for scribes, can hardly be disputed. It is questionable, however, whether both observations indeed exclude the possibility of literary production in earlier times and thus also the existence and maintenance of chronographic records. Two recent studies by Matthieu Richelle and Erhard Blum raise justified doubts in this regard.[70] Both point to the methodological difficulties of directly relating the quantity of finds and the use of writing to each other. The difficulties concern the dating of the individual inscriptions, the question of the literary genres involved,[71] but above all the inevitable contingency of the findings.[72] The assumption that one can only reckon with writing and scribes in those historical periods for which epigraphic evidence is attested cannot be upheld, if other periods in the history of Israel, such as the Persian period, are considered as well. The one-to-one relation between administrative structures and literary production is called into question by a series of extensive literary compositions from earlier periods. Blum points to royal inscriptions stemming from the 9th century (Mesha Stele, Tel-Dan Inscription) and to further examples of a developed scribal culture which originating from the 8th century but turning up not at the big rural centers but in the periphery, like the Gezer Calender, the ostracon of Khirbet Qeiyafa, or the wall inscriptions from Deir 'Alla and Kuntillet 'Ajrud. Richelle stresses the fact that the creation of lit-

---

[69] David W. Jamieson-Drake, *Scribes and Schools in Monarchic Judah: A Socio-Archaeological Approach*, JSOTSup 109 (Sheffield: Almond Press, 1991), proved to be very influential in his estimation.

[70] Matthieu Richelle, "Elusive Scrolls: Could any Hebrew Literature have been Written prior to the Eighth Century BCE?" *VT* 66 (2016): 556–94; Erhard Blum, "Institutionelle und kulturelle Voraussetzungen der israelitischen Traditionsliteratur," in *Konstruktion, Transmission und Transformation von Tradition(en) im Alten Israel*, ed. Ruth Ebach and Martin Leuenberger, FAT 127 (Tübingen: Mohr Siebeck, 2019), 3–44.

[71] The known ostraca and short inscriptions from the 8th century are predominantly economic or legal documents and letters, but no literary texts (see Blum, "Voraussetzungen," 4–10).

[72] The problem of the varying durability of writing materials is discussed by Richelle, "Elusive Scrolls," 564–67, the contingency of the finds by ibid., 570–71, as well as Blum, "Voraussetzungen," 25–26 (see also Alan Millard, "Only Fragments of the Past: The Role of Accident in Our Knowledge of the Ancient Near East," in *Writing and Ancient Near Eastern Society: Papers in Honour of Alan R. Millard*, ed. Piotr Bienkowski et al., LHBOTS 429 [New York: T&T Clark, 2005], 301–19). The example of the Persian Period remains striking: although usually seen as the formative period within the literary history of the Old Testament, the number of epigraphic finds from this period is surprisingly small (cf. William M. Schniedewind, *How the Bible Became a Book: The Textualization of Ancient Israel* [Cambridge: Cambridge University Press, 2004], 170–72).

erary works does not require an extensive scribal community and educational institutions, but only a limited number of scribes.[73]

Given these reflections, assuming of the existence of chronographic literature in Israel already in the first half of the 9th century is not only feasible but adds another point to the observations of Blum and Richelle. Isolated but nevertheless noteworthy hints like the familiarity of Israelite scribes with Hieratic numerals, pointing to long-lasting transregional writing traditions,[74] or the indicators for the existence of chronographic compositions in Tyre or Byblos[75] further support the assumption that chronological and historical data were collected in Israel since the early 9th century. The Chronicle of the Kings of Israel, which is still discernable as one of the sources of the Book of Kings, offers an additional testimony. Keeping a chronicle does not require widespread literacy, but the existence of a few professional scribes whose training included practical exercises in and on relevant genres as well as an intellectual education accomplished not least by means of internalizing older texts and traditions – basically what David Carr calls "the oral-written educational-enculturational model".[76] This would also explain why this Israelite chronographic document integrates itself so smoothly into the wider field of Ancient Near Eastern chronography.

---

[73] Richelle, "Elusive Scrolls," 588–89, points to the fact that the Book of Samuel mentions only two scribes at the court of David: Seraiah (2 Sam 8:17) and Sheva (2 Sam 20:25). Zwickel, "Königsliste," 84, had already referred to these texts (and 1 Kgs 4:3) as indicators of a rather early occurrence of professional scribes in Judah.

[74] See Stefan Wimmer, *Palästinisches Hieratisch: Die Zahl- und Sonderzeichen in der althebräischen Schrift*, ÄAT 75 (Wiesbaden: Harrassowitz, 2008), 279: "Das Szenario, wonach die mindestens im südlichen Kanaan offenbar gut etablierte, hieratische Schreibtradition der pharaonischen Administration in der Zeit des Neuen Reiches, bzw. der Spätbronzezeit, zum Phänomen der in Juda und Israel üblichen Notierung von Zahl- und Sonderzeichen mit beigetragen hat, bleibt wahrscheinlich."

[75] The Egyptian Story of Wenamun, a 10th century composition, mentions chronographic records in Byblos (Bernd U. Schipper, *Die Erzählung des Wenamun: Ein Literaturwerk im Spannungsfeld von Politik, Geschichte und Religion*, OBO 209 [Fribourg: Academic Press; Göttingen: Vandenhoeck & Ruprecht, 2005], 192–93, 333).

[76] David M. Carr, *Writing on the Tablet of the Heart: Origins of Scripture and Literature* (Oxford: Oxford University Press, 2005), 292.

Appendix: Three Patterns of Introductory Formulae in the Regnal Frame

Pattern A

1	Synchronism	בשנת ... (שנה) ל... (בן ...) (מלך ישראל) מלך
2	Name of the King	... (בן ...)
3	Territory	ביהודה / על יהודה / מלך יהודה
4	Age at accession	בן ... שנה היה / ... במלכו
5	Regnal year total	שנים / שנה ... מלך
6	Residence	בירושלם
7	Mother of the king	ושם אמו ... בת ... / מ... / Ø

Pattern B

1	Name	... בן ... מלך
2	Territory	על ישראל
3	Synchronism	בשנת ... (שנה) ל... מלך יהודה וימלך
4	Residence	בשמרון
5	Regnal year total	... שנה

Pattern C

1	Synchronism	בשנת ... (שנה) ל... (בן ...) מלך יהודה מלך
2	Name of the King	... (בן ...)
3	Territory	על (כל) ישראל / מלך ישראל
4	Residence	בתרצה / בשמרון
5	Regnal year total	שנים / שנה ...

Bibliography

Albright, William F. "The Chronology of the Divided Monarchy of Israel." *BASOR* 100 (1945): 16–22.
Begrich, Joachim. *Die Chronologie der Könige von Israel und Juda und die Quellen des Rahmens der Königsbücher.* Tübingen: Mohr Siebeck, 1929.
Bin-Nun, Shoshana. "Formulas from Royal Records of Israel and of Judah." *VT* 18 (1968): 414–32.
Blanco Wißmann, Felipe. *"Er tat das Rechte ...": Beurteilungskriterien und Deuteronomismus in 1 Kön 12–2 Kön 25.* ATANT 93. Zürich: TVZ, 2008.
Blum, Erhard. "Der Prophet und das Verderben Israels: Eine ganzheitlich historisch-kritische Lektüre von 1 Regum xvii-xix." Pages 339–53 in *Textgestalt und Komposition: Exegetische Beiträge zu Tora und Vordere Propheten.* Edited by Wolfgang Oswald. FAT 69. Tübingen: Mohr Siebeck, 2010.
Blum, Erhard. "Die Nabotüberlieferungen und die Kompositionsgeschichte der Vorderen Propheten." Pages 355–74 in *Textgestalt und Komposition: Exegetische Beiträge zu Tora und Vordere Propheten.* Edited by Wolfgang Oswald. FAT 69. Tübingen: Mohr Siebeck, 2010.
Blum, Erhard. "Institutionelle und kulturelle Voraussetzungen der israelitischen Traditionsliteratur." Pages 3–44 in *Konstruktion, Transmission und Transformation von Tradition(en) im Alten Israel.* Edited by Ruth Ebach and Martin Leuenberger. FAT 127. Tübingen: Mohr Siebeck, 2019.
Blum, Erhard. "The Linguistic Dating of Biblical Text – an Approach with Methodological Limitations." Pages 303–28 in *The Formation of the Pentateuch: Bridging the Academic Cultures of Europe, Israel, and North America.* Edited by Jan Christian Gertz, et al. FAT 111. Tübingen: Mohr Siebeck, 2016.
Carr, David M. *Writing on the Tablet of the Heart: Origins of Scripture and Literature.* Oxford: Oxford University Press, 2005.
Donner, Herbert, and Wolfgang Röllig. *Kanaanäische und aramäische Inschriften: Mit einem Beitrag von O. Rössler: I. Texte.* 5th ed. Wiesbaden: Harassowitz, 2002.
Driver, Samuel R. *An Introduction to the Literature of the Old Testament.* ITL. Edinburgh: T&T Clark, 1891.
Ebeling, Erich, et al., eds. *Reallexikon der Assyriologie.* Berlin: de Gruyter, 1928–2018.
Finkelstein, Israel. "History, Historicity and Historiography in Ancient Israel." Pages 15–30 in *Story and History: The Kings of Israel and Judah in Context.* Edited by Johannes Unsok Ro. FAT II 105. Tübingen: Mohr Siebeck, 2019.
Finkelstein, Israel. *The Forgotten Kingdom: The Archaeology and History of Northern Israel.* ANEM 5. Atlanta: Society of Biblical Literature, 2013.
Finkelstein, Israel, and Benjamin Sass. "The West Semitic Alphabetic Inscriptions, Late Bronze II to Iron IIa: Archaeological Context, Distribution and Chronology." *HeBAI* 2 (2013): 149–220.
Frevel, Christian. *Geschichte Israels.* ST. Stuttgart: Kohlhammer, 2016.
Fritz, Volkmar. *Das zweite Buch der Könige.* ZBK. Zürich: TVZ, 1998.
Glassner, Jean-Jacques. *Mesopotamian Chronicles.* WAW. Leiden: Brill, 2005.
Grabbe, Lester L. "Mighty Oaks from (Genetically Manipulated?) Acorns Grow: The Chronicle of the Kings of Judah as a Source of the Deuteronomistic History." Pages 155–73 in *Reflection and Refraction: Studies in Biblical Historiography in Honour of*

A. Graeme Auld. Edited by Robert Rezetko, Timothy H. Lim, and W. Brian Aucker. VTSup 113. Leiden: Brill, 2007.

Grayson, Albert Kirk. *Assyrian and Babylonian Chronicles*. TCS. Locust Valley, NY: Augustin, 1975.

Halpern, Baruch, and David S. Vanderhooft. "The Editions of Kings in the 7th–6th Centuries B.C.E." *HUCA* 62 (1991): 179–244.

Hasegawa, Shuichi. *Aram and Israel During the Jehuite Dynasty*. BZAW 434. Berlin: de Gruyter, 2012.

Hasegawa, Shuichi, Christoph Levin, and Karen Radner. *The Last Days of the Kingdom of Israel*. BZAW 511. Berlin: de Gruyter, 2019.

Jamieson-Drake, David W. *Scribes and Schools in Monarchic Judah: A Socio-Archaeological Approach*. JSOTSup 109. Sheffield: Almond Press, 1991.

Knauf, Ernst A. *1 Könige 1–14*. HThKAT. Freiburg: Herder, 2016.

Krey, Ernst. "Zur Zeitrechnung des Buchs der Könige." *ZWT* 20 (1877): 404–8.

Laato, Antti. *Guide to Biblical Chronology*. Sheffield: Sheffield Phoenix, 2015.

Lee, Sang-Won. "Die Königsbeurteilungen und die Literargeschichte des Deuteronomistischen Geschichtswerks: Anmerkungen zu einer kontroversen Diskussion." *VT* 68 (2018): 581–605.

Lewy, Julius. *Die Chronologie der Könige von Israel und Juda*. Gießen: Töpelmann, 1927.

Linville, James R. *Israel in the Book of Kings: The Past as a Project of Social Identity*. JSOTSup 272. Sheffield: Sheffield Academic, 1998.

Long, Burke O. *2 Kings*. FOTL. Grand Rapids: Eerdmans, 1991.

Löv, Gustav. "Das synchronistische System der Königsbücher." *ZWT* 43 (1900): 161–79.

Miano, David. *Shadow on the Steps: Time Measurement in Ancient Israel*. RBS 64. Leiden: Brill, 2011.

Millard, Alan. "Only Fragments of the Past: The Role of Accident in Our Knowledge of the Ancient Near East." Pages 301–19 in *Writing and Ancient Near Eastern Society: Papers in Honour of Alan R. Millard*. Edited by Piotr Bienkowski, et al. LHBOTS 429. New York: T&T Clark, 2005.

Millard, Alan. *The Eponyms of the Assyrian Empire 910–612 BC*. SAAS 2. Helsinki: The Neo-Assyrian Text Corpus Project, 1994.

Na'aman, Nadav. "Sources and Composition in the Book of Kings: The Introductory and Final Verses of the Kings of Judah and Israel." (Hebr.) Pages 97–118 in *Shai Le-Sara Japhet: Studies in the Bible, Its Exegesis and Its Language*. Edited by Moshe Bar-Asher, Nili Vazana, Emanuel Tov, and Dalit Rom-Shiloni. Jerusalem: Bialik, 2007.

Na'aman, Nadav. "The Sources Available to the Book of Kings." Pages 105–20 in *Recenti tendenze nella ricostruzione della storia antica d'Israele*. Rome: Accademia Nazionale dei Lincei, 2005.

Niemann, Hermann M. "Kein Ende des Büchermachens in Israel und Juda (Koh 12,12): Wann begann es?" *BK* 53 (1998): 127–34.

Noth, Martin. *Überlieferungsgeschichtliche Studien: Die sammelnden und bearbeitenden Geschichtswerke im Alten Testament*. 2nd ed. Darmstadt: Wissenschaftliche Buchgesellschaft, 1957.

Otto, Susanne. *Jehu, Elia und Elisa*. BWANT 152. Stuttgart: Kohlhammer, 2001.

Otto, Susanne. "The Composition of the Elijah-Elisha Stories and the Deuteronomistic History." *JSOT* 27 (2003): 487–508.

Redford, Donald B. *Pharaonic King Lists, Annals and Day Books: A Contribution to the Study of the Egyptian Sense of History*. Missisauga: Benben, 1986.

Richelle, Matthieu. "Elusive Scrolls: Could any Hebrew Literature have been Written prior to the Eighth Century BCE?" *VT* 66 (2016): 556–94.

Robker, Jonathan M. *The Jehu Revolution: A Royal Tradition of the Northern Kingdom and its Ramifications.* BZAW. Berlin: de Gruyter, 2012.

Sauerwein, Ruth. *Elischa: Eine Redaktions- und religionsgeschichtliche Studie.* BZAW 465. Berlin: de Gruyter, 2014.

Schipper, Bernd U. *Die Erzählung des Wenamun: Ein Literaturwerk im Spannungsfeld von Politik, Geschichte und Religion.* OBO 209. Fribourg: Academic Press; Göttingen: Vandenhoeck & Ruprecht, 2005.

Schniedewind, William M. *How the Bible Became a Book: The Textualization of Ancient Israel.* Cambridge: Cambridge University Press, 2004.

Shenkel, James. *Chronology and Recensional Development in the Greek Text of Kings.* HSM. Cambridge, MA: Harvard University Press, 1968.

Steinkeller, Piotr. "An Ur III Manuscript of the Sumerian King List." Pages 267–92 in *Literatur, Politik und Recht in Mesopotamien: FS Claus Wilcke.* Edited by Walther Sallaberger, et al. OBC 14. Wiesbaden: Harassowitz, 2003.

Stipp, Hermann-Josef. "Ahabs Buße und die Komposition des Deuteronomistischen Geschichtswerks." *Bib* 76 (1995): 471–97.

Tadmor, Hayim. *The Inscriptions of Tiglath-pileser III, King of Assyria: Critical Edition, with Introduction, Translations and Commentary.* Fontes ad res Judaicas spectantes. Jerusalem: Israel Acad. of Sciences and Humanities, 1994.

Tetley, Christine M. *The Reconstructed Chronology of the Divided Kingdom.* Winona Lake, IN: Eisenbrauns, 2005.

Thenius, Otto. *Die Bücher der Könige.* KEH. 2nd ed. Leipzig: Hirzel, 1873.

Thiele, Edwin R. *The Mysterious Numbers of the Hebrew Kings: A Reconstruction of the Chronology of the Kingdoms of Israel and Judah.* 2nd ed. Exeter: Paternoster, 1965.

Thilo, Martin. *Die Chronologie des Alten Testamentes dargestellt und beurteilt unter besonderer Berücksichtigung der masoretischen Richter- und Königszahlen: Mit vier großen graphischen Tafeln.* Barmen: Hugo Klein's Verlag, 1917.

Thomas, Benjamin D. *Hezekiah and the Compositional History of the Book of Kings.* FAT II 63. Tübingen: Mohr Siebeck, 2014.

Ueberschaer, Frank. *Vom Gründungsmythos zur Untergangssymphonie: Eine text- und literargeschichtliche Untersuchung zu 1 Kön 11–14.* BZAW 481. Berlin: de Gruyter, 2015.

Van Seters, John. *The Biblical Saga of King David.* Winona Lake, IN: Eisenbrauns, 2009.

Weingart, Kristin. *Gezählte Geschichte: Systematik, Quellen und Entwicklung der synchronistischen Chronologie in den Königebüchern.* FAT 142. Tübingen: Mohr Siebeck, 2020.

Weingart, Kristin. "Harmonizing Biblical Chronology: On Procedures, Pitfalls, and Ramifications." In *Methodik im Diskurs: Harmonisierungen.* Edited by Raik Heckl & Thomas Wagner. BThSt. Göttingen: Vandenhoeck & Ruprecht, 2023 (forthcoming).

Weingart, Kristin. "Jeroboam and Benjamin: Pragmatics and Date of 1 Kgs 11:26–40 and 12:1–20." Pages 133–59 in *Saul, Benjamin, and the Emergence of Monarchy in Israel: Biblical and Archaeological Perspectives.* Edited by Joachim J. Krause, Omer Sergi, and Kristin Weingart. AIL 40. Atlanta: Society of Biblical Literature, 2020.

Weippert, Helga. "Die 'deuteronomistischen' Beurteilungen der Könige von Israel und Juda und das Problem der Redaktion der Königsbücher." *Bib* 53 (1972): 301–39.

Wellhausen, Julius. "Die Zeitrechnung des Buches der Könige seit der Theilung des Reiches." *JDT* 20 (1875): 607–40.

Werlitz, Jürgen. *Die Bücher der Könige.* NSKAT. Stuttgart: Kath. Bibelwerk, 2002.

Wimmer, Stefan. *Palästinisches Hieratisch: Die Zahl- und Sonderzeichen in der althebräischen Schrift*. ÄAT 75. Wiesbaden: Harrassowitz, 2008.

Yamada, Shigeo. *The Construction of the Assyrian Empire: A Historical Study of the Inscriptions of Shalmanesar III (859–824 B.C.E.) Relating to His Campaigns to the West*. CHANE 3. Leiden: Brill, 2000.

Zwickel, Wolfgang. "Die Tyrische Königsliste und die Annalenangaben des Alten Testaments." Pages 83–92 in *Text – Textgeschichte – Textwirkung: FS S. Kreuzer*. Edited by Thomas Wagner, et al. AOAT 419. Münster: Ugarit-Verlag, 2014.

Radical Versus Conservative?
How Scribes Conventionally Used Books While Writing Books

Benjamin Ziemer

1. The Cultural Background of a Central European Protestant Old Testament Scholar

We owe the whole Hebrew Bible as a written document to scribes – in their functions as copyists as well as authors, and editors.[1] Who were they, and how did they work? Concerning the explicit references to named scribes, Ezra is described as having "the law" (דת) in his hands (Ezra 7:14), and later reading it publicly from a "book" (Neh 8),[2] whereas Baruch is described as writing books following oral instruction by another person, Jeremiah.[3] However, in most cases the scribes' names are unknown. Regardless of whether alleged authors of texts are mentioned in superscriptions like those of psalms, proverb collections and prophetic books, most Hebrew scriptures have a prehistory that includes other books.

The purpose of this paper is to ask how the anonymous scribes handled their written sources. Certainly, sometimes the scribes introduced new material and new ideas into given contexts known from other, older books. The question is: did such radical innovation require the composition of a new literary work or a new edition which usually coincides with making selective use of its sources,

---

[1] See Karel van der Toorn, *Scribal Culture and the Making of the Hebrew Bible* (Cambridge, MA: Harvard University Press, 2007), 109, for these "aspects of the scribal profession."

[2] For a new view on Ezra's mission see the contribution of Lisbeth S. Fried and Edward Mills III, "Ezra the Scribe," in this volume. However, their reconstruction of an "authentic letter" in Ezra 7 is a prime example for the circularity of the usual growth model. If an author or editor had access to authentic Achaemenid letters he or she could easily use their formulae to fabricate a letter like that in Ezra 7 with a mix of more or less authentic-sounding elements. The theoretical possibility to cut out a smaller, more authentic sounding letter out of the present text says nothing about the historicity of this "reconstruction." To be clear: if any editor deliberately changed the message of an authentic letter to an authentic person, this should be named forgery – whereas the use of formulae to fabricate such letter illustrating a legendary tradition can be regarded as legitimate stylistic device. Both seem possible, but if the editor forged an authentic letter it is (beyond the circular axioms of the growth model described in the following) not plausible why he or she should have refrained cautiously from omissions or reformulations.

[3] For Baruch's role in the versions of the book of Jeremiah and the book of Baruch, see Johanna Erzberger's contribution in this volume, "Israel's Salvation and the Survival of Baruch the Scribe."

rearranging or reformulating them? Or was such expansion convenient in the frame of a conservative approach preserving the older text in its entirety? The Hebrew scriptures give little information on the scribes' behaviour apart from the fact they are suspected to lie (Jer 8:8). Therefore we have to examine those cases in which written books can be compared with their sources. Both the parallels between different biblical books and the differences between extant versions of one book show how scribes dealt with their real *Vorlagen*.

Because this volume is a collection of contributions from different cultural backgrounds I would like to say a few words on where my specific interest in the scribal behaviour comes from first. My background is in European Protestant Old Testament research. Its own scribal culture has been described by Stephen A. Kaufman nearly 40 years ago:

> In spite of a welcome tendency in recent years toward holistic treatments of biblical texts, complex reconstructions of the redaction history of Pentateuchal and other biblical material continue to stream from the pens of Bible scholars, especially in Europe. It is not unusual for savants to claim the ability to accurately reconstruct three, four, five or more stages in the development of a given text, all this using methodologies never subjected to empirical verification.[4]

Since then, the situation has not meaningfully changed. Especially in Germany, where scholars have to write two books – dissertation and habilitation – before gaining professorship, the precise dissection of biblical texts into layers in a specified historical sequence is a welcomed template for dissertations to be accepted within the closed circle of "savants", to use Kaufman's terminology.

The *Central European*, especially German background may be responsible for the romantic ideal to go back to the roots and to find the "oldest document of the human race."[5] For the Prophetic books, the "original words" of the prophets were sought. Among the poetry, the most archaic-sounding compositions found the greatest interest.

The *Protestant* perspective is characterised by the principle of *sola scriptura*, the high estimation of scripture against tradition. Its ideal is a self-interpretation of the scripture, "*sacra scriptura sui ipsius interpres*," claimed by Christoph Levin not only as an exegetical rule but as an adequate description of the formation process of the Hebrew Bible.[6] Joshua Berman recently used this Protestant theo-

---

[4] Stephen A. Kaufman, "The Temple Scroll and Higher Criticism," *HUCA* 53 (1982): 30.

[5] Compare the title of Johann Gottfried Herder's "Älteste Urkunde des Menschengeschlechts" (Riga: Hartknoch, 1774–76).

[6] Christoph Levin, *Das Alte Testament*, 4th ed. (München: Beck, 2010), 26: "Man kann die Art des Wachstums 'Schneeballsystem' nennen: Einmal ins Rollen gebracht, gewinnt der Schneeball mit jeder Umdrehung eine neue Schicht. Das Alte Testament ist auf diese Weise zu großen Teilen seine eigene Auslegung, 'sacra scriptura sui ipsius interpres'. Es gibt fast keine Texteinheit, die nicht aus mehreren literarischen Schichten besteht."

logical background to explain the widespread bias against empirical evidence from the Ancient Near East.[7]

Protestant theologians are, as *Christian* theologians, familiar with the four Gospels, and with the idea of Gospel harmonies, at least for the stories of the birth, the passion and the resurrection of Jesus. Such harmony would allow, to a limited extent, immediate reconstruction of different parallel sources. This has been the most important empirical model for the Pentateuch, not only for German Protestant scholars like Otto Eißfeldt but also for other scholars with Christian background like Jean Astruc or George F. Moore.[8]

Over the last decades, in my cultural environment the questions concerning the scribes of the biblical books have changed: while former generations of German Old Testament scholars, like Julius Wellhausen or Bernhard Duhm, looked down on the "late Jewish" scribes with arrogance, this attitude has changed after World War II. "Schriftgelehrter" (literally "scholar of scripture"), the term Martin Luther used to translate סֹפֵר in the Old and γραμματεύς in the New Testament, as well as the abstract noun "Schriftgelehrsamkeit" have been used as slander among Old Testament scholars of the first half of the twentieth century, as an antithesis (cf. 2 Cor 3:6) to people gifted with spirit, like the prophets or Jesus. Nowadays, the same words have turned into compliments.[9] The romantic desire to unravel the "original" has been replaced by a positive interest in the younger "layers" of the books, which can be attributed to those "scholars of scripture". However, the optimism of being able to pursue text archaeology has increased. And turning away the romanticisation of the individual heroes of the prophetic era has led to throwing out the baby with the bathwater: the scribes to whom we owe the Hebrew scriptures are not thought of as individuals anymore.

This background has led me to ask about these scribes and their work. The theory of growing texts seems to be well in accordance with the conception of the autonomy of texts.[10] But even autonomously "growing" texts would need scribes to write them down consciously. Those "editors editing the work of editors, with no original authors at all"[11] would still be human beings. Before dealing with the question of whether "growth" or "evolution" are adequate terms to describe the

---

[7] Joshua Berman, "Empirical Models of Textual Growth: A Challenge for the Historical-Critical Tradition," *JHS* 16/12 (2016): 1–25, doi:10.5508/jhs.2016.v16.a12.

[8] See Benjamin Ziemer, *Kritik des Wachstumsmodells: Die Grenzen alttestamentlicher Redaktionsgeschichte im Lichte empirischer Evidenz*, VTSup 182 (Leiden: Brill, 2020), 98–99.

[9] E.g., Konrad Schmid, *Schriftgelehrte Traditionsliteratur: Fallstudien zur innerbiblischen Schriftauslegung im Alten Testament*, FAT 77 (Tübingen: Mohr Siebeck, 2011).

[10] See Erhard Blum's critique of this concept in "Notwendigkeit und Grenzen historischer Exegese: Plädoyer für eine alttestamentliche 'Exegetik'," in *Grundfragen der historischen Exegese: Methodologische, philologische und hermeneutische Beiträge zum Alten Testament*, ed. Kristin Weingart and Wolfgang Oswald (Tübingen: Mohr Siebeck, 2015), 17–22.

[11] John Van Seters, *The Edited Bible: The Curious History of the "Editor" in Biblical Criticism* (Winona Lake, IN: Eisenbrauns, 2006), 395.

prehistory of the Hebrew scriptures, I would like to label some basic assumptions of redaction criticism and their consequences for how the implicit editors would have looked at their *Vorlagen*.

2. The Axioms of the "Growth Model" and its Implicit Editors

The presumed axioms of a redaction criticism which is able to reconstruct a text's or a book's prehistory in several stages have been described variously elsewhere.[12] I name this set of axioms the "growth model" ("Wachstumsmodell") since it claims to adequately reconstruct the prehistory of the Hebrew Bible as *growth*, be it as continuous "Fortschreibung" by elements of text added here or there by multiple hands, or as a multi-stage series of thoroughly-edited book versions each supplemented by a number of characteristic additions. A reconstruction of such "growth" is theoretically possible only if two axioms are presupposed.

Firstly, the *principle of addition* ("additives Prinzip"):[13] the editor-scribes confined themselves to additions and refrained from omissions, reformulations or rearrangements. Obviously, no former version can be fully reconstructed from a later version if this principle is violated. To take an example: The MT and LXX versions of Jeremiah differ in the superscription and the arrangement. One version, titled "The Word of God which came to Jeremiah", has the Oracles Against the Nations (OAN) in the centre of the book (LXX); the other is titled "The Words of Jeremiah" (MT) and has the OAN in a different order at the end of the book, just before the concluding chapter. One of the titles and one of the arrangements has to be closer to the original. But, irrespective of the direction of dependance, one would not be able to reconstruct the former state of the book out of the later one without external evidence. So, even if a modern redaction critic would be right in subtracting a pericope like Jer 33:14–26 (MT), which indeed is not present in the LXX, she could not be sure about the content, the arrangement and the wording of the *Vorlage* if we take the differences of the known versions as standard.

Secondly, the *principle of difference* ("Differenzprinzip") is presupposed: the added elements are distinguishable from the surrounding text, whether in style or content. This means that the editors left traces. As with the first principle,

---

[12] Cf., among others, Blum, "Notwendigkeit," 5–6; Juha Pakkala, *God's Word Omitted: Omissions in the Transmission of the Hebrew Bible*, FRLANT 251 (Göttingen: Vandenhoeck & Ruprecht, 2013), 16–25.

[13] This is essentially the same as the "rule of preservation" or the "principle of preservation" named by Pakkala, *Omitted*, 15, 289 (and more often). Blum describes as implicit condition for the "literarkritische Methodik" "dass die Texte während ihrer gesamten Überlieferungsgeschichte ausschließlich additiv erweitert wurden" (Blum, "Notwendigkeit," 6).

no former version can be reconstructed correctly out of a later version if this principle is violated. To take an example: the Samaritan Pentateuch in its account of the Plagues of Egypt – in this case faithfully rendering the so called Pre-Samaritan Pentateuch attested by manuscripts such as 4QpaleoExod^m – reports YHWH's announcements of each plague twice: firstly as YHWH's instruction to Moses what he shall say before Pharaoh in his name; and secondly as execution of this instruction – how Moses repeated these words before Pharaoh. In contrast, the MT and the LXX contain only one of the speeches – either YHWH's instruction (e. g., Exod 9:1–5) or Moses' execution (e. g., Exod 10:3–7). Even if a literary critic would suspect this annoying repetition to be an editor's mark, she would not be able to reconstruct which part of the repetition is added by the editor: YHWH's instruction, or its quotation by Moses. However, the redaction critic probably would not even be interested in it because the reconstructed *Vorlage* would not show any difference in content.

A third axiom is usually presupposed to explain the absence of external evidence for an assumed growth process: The *single-copy axiom* (Singularitätsprinzip) means that only one exemplar of a book existed at a given time which was irreversibly superseded by the next, then revised exemplar.[14] If this principle is violated and several versions of one book survive we could compare them and determine whether the other axioms are valid. Denying the possibility of parallel transmission enables scholars to ignore the existing external evidence.

Assuming these axioms of the growth model were valid in the making of the Hebrew scriptures, the editor-scribes would have been somehow schizophrenic. These scribes ideally would retain all old text present in the respective *Vorlage*, omit nothing, reformulate nothing and rearrange nothing. Thereby they would honour the tradition. But, at the same time, they would have added new material, including new tendencies and theological conceptions. Since they would not have declared their additions unmistakably as a commentary, they would implicitly claim the same dignity for their own additions and the elements of text taken over from their respected *Vorlage*.

But why would any person add something to an older, existing, honoured book? The sole reason seems to be that the book would have been looked at as insufficient in a certain respect, either outdated, unintelligible, or incomplete. Something was thought to be missing, so the old book was regarded as deficient. For a classical or canonical work, this could be a commentator's task. He answers open questions, actualises the work by his explanations, or even changes the argument by sophisticated exegesis. But the commentator would not change the work itself, and would not mix his commentary with the text. In the latter case his commentary would lose its function – it could easily be revealed as forgery. Finally, the imagined "redactor" of the growth model, while introducing

---

[14] Cf. van der Toorn, *Scribal Culture*, 147.

new elements not declared as such, would have replaced his *Vorlage* by another, new version. We need the single-copy axiom to spare him from being accused as a forger.

However, he honoured his *Vorlagen* by allegedly leaving them unchanged. This would imply that the interpolation of new elements has once been regarded as a less fundamental change than omission, reformulation or rearrangement. Was expansion, even by new elements, regarded as an allowed improvement of a classical text whereas other changes were regarded as sacrilege?[15]

If this was the case it should be visible in the frame of so called empirical models and empirical examples for biblical criticism as well. The question is: how did real scribes, according to the external evidence, look at their *Vorlagen*? Did they make a difference between the certain modes of change?

3. Typologies and Their Limits

Scribes served different functions. The main distinction is made between authors or editors on the one hand and copyists on the other.[16] However, to avoid modern misunderstandings of the terms "redactor" or "author" and to acknowledge the fact that the Hebrew term סֹפֵר, "scribe", does not differentiate between these aspects, I prefer the term "master scribe" coined by Sara J. Milstein. The "master scribes" are defined by Milstein as those scribes who "had both the ability and the authority to introduce changes into a tradition, to bring like material together, even on occasion to produce 'new' works," to be discerned from scribes who were "mere copyists."[17] There have been several attempts to classify those anonymous master scribes of the Hebrew scriptures and the changes made by them.

3.1 Uwe Becker

I take Uwe Becker's textbook[18] on Old Testament exegesis as an example of how scribal changes are classified in frequently-used German-language scholarly literature. Becker, in his description of the method of redaction criticism, describes the following range of characteristics of editorial processes ("redaktionelle Bearbeitungsvorgänge"): "They range from simple and unique explanations (glosses) to extensive and comprehensive editorial layers."[19] The claimed com-

---

[15] Cf. Levin, *Das Alte Testament*, 24–25.

[16] Van der Toorn, *Scribal Culture*, 126, emphasises this distinction.

[17] Sara J. Milstein, *Tracking the Master Scribe: Revision through Introduction in Biblical and Mesopotamian Literature* (New York: Oxford University Press, 2016), 210.

[18] Uwe Becker, *Exegese des Alten Testaments: Ein Methoden- und Arbeitsbuch*, 2nd ed. (Tübingen: Mohr Siebeck, 2008).

[19] "Sie reichen von einfachen und einmaligen Erläuterungen (Glossen) bis zu umfangreichen und übergreifenden Redaktionsschichten." Becker, *Exegese*, 89.

plexity is nothing more than a differentiation between several types of additions, named "Zufügung" ("addition") or "Ergänzung" ("supplementation"), be it in the frame of "Bearbeitung" (editing), "Komposition" (composition), "Kompilation" (compilation), "Fortschreibung" or "relecture".[20] Redactional activity, according to Becker, solely consisted in additions.[21] A description of the changes made by scribes in the course of centuries would therefore result in an adequate reconstruction of the literary history of a given book – as linear growth.

3.2 Stephen A. Kaufman, "The Temple Scroll and Higher Criticism"

However, Becker's description is widely ignorant for processes to be observed within the so called empirical models for literary criticism. Stephen Kaufman, in contrast, offered a typology of changes made in one of the most important examples of "redaction" coming to light in the 20th century, comparing the Temple Scroll with the Pentateuch.

He discerns six "major compositional patterns" the composer of the Temple Scroll used:

(1) Original composition; (2) Paraphrastic conflation; (3) Fine conflation; (4) Gross conflation; (5) Modified Torah quotation; (6) Extended Torah quotation.[22]

Line by line he assigns the composition of the Temple Scroll to these patterns. Notably, three of the six patterns (2, 3 and 4) describe how several sources were mixed together without copying one of them in full length. This is an important contribution to evaluate source criticism, whereas actual tendencies in redaction criticism in Central Europe favour a linear model with a chain of supplementing editors. In this respect, three patterns remain: "Original composition" (1) of a certain passage,[23] "modified quotation" (5) and "extended quotation" (6). According to Kaufman, there would be certainly hope to distinguish between "original composition" and "extended quotation" even without knowing the sources. However, it would still not be possible to reconstruct the wording of a *Vorlage*. His conclusion is:

In sum, the various compositional patterns used in the Temple Scroll, especially the extremely complex patterns of paraphrastic conflation, fine conflation and modified torah quotation must be assumed to have been used in the formation of the biblical text as well. But the very complexity and variety of those patterns makes higher criticism a dubious endeavor.[24]

---

[20] Becker, *Exegese*, 89–92.
[21] For characteristic examples in German redaction criticism, see Ziemer, *Kritik*, 86–98.
[22] Kaufman, *Temple Scroll*, 34.
[23] That means additions formulated by the master scribe, the equivalent in German redaction critical language would be "redaktionelle Eigenformulierungen" (e.g., Reinhard G. Kratz, "Redaktionsgeschichte/Redaktionskritik I. Altes Testament," *TRE* 28: 369).
[24] Kaufman, *Temple Scroll*, 42.

3.3 Juha Pakkala, "God's Word Omitted"

Juha Pakkala, in his important monograph "God's Word Omitted," seeks to combine the conventional assumptions on literary growth with the empirically-proven processes which include rewriting, reordering and omitting elements of the used *Vorlagen*. He has given an overview of the "different types of editors" that "can be identified" from his point of view, which I quote here:

> When we investigate the prehistory of texts that are not documented, the chain of editors may consist of any of the following:
> 1) Author editor, who collected the composition rather freely (sources of the Pentateuch, for example the Yahwist).
> 2) Copyist editor, who mainly made small changes perhaps interpretative expansions, clarifications and glosses, for his main task was to copy the text.
> 3) A conservative editor who updated the text to correspond to the changed environment and circumstances. Working within an ideological paradigm, he made only expansions (e.g., the SP in relation to the MT or the MT of Jeremiah in relation to the LXX version).
> 4) A radical editor who was working during a paradigm shift or was otherwise part of such a shift. He could have made comprehensive changes to the texts such as omitting and rewriting parts of the older text (e.g., First Esdras and Chronicles).
> 5) A rewriter-editor who mainly created a new composition but who followed the source to a great extent (e.g., Chronicles in relation to 1–2 Kings, the Temple Scroll in relation to the Pentateuch or Jubilees in relation to Genesis–Exodus).
> 6) A censor editor who mainly purged the older text of conceptions that had become offensive and unacceptable (evidence for such activity can be found especially in 1 Samuel and 1–2 Kings).
> 7) An editor who used a section of another literary work for part of his own text. This could be a quotation or allusion, for example.[25]

This list gives an idea of the manifold possibilities of master scribes – whereby categories 1–6 presuppose that only one main source has been used at a time, and only category 7 considers the possibility that a scribe may have drawn from several sources. The source compilation, i.e. the assumed procedure of the Pentateuchal editor, which in terms of research history stood at the beginning of literary-critical research and is part of Becker's as well as of Kaufman's typology, does not occur here at all. Neither a shortening edition is mentioned, nor a collection of small, unrelated units. Moreover, the formulation of categories 2) and 3), both of which correspond to the growth paradigm, is strongly influenced by wishful thinking: The small changes made by a "copyist editor" (2), who primarily liked to copy the text, usually include the whole arsenal of changes that must be reckoned with in the history of text always and everywhere. These would not only be the "small interpretative additions, clarifications and glosses" Pakkala names, which could be subsumed under "deliberate additions for a better understanding of the text". The "small changes" of a "copyist editor" generally include corrections that are not extensions: A supposedly incorrect or erroneous text passage may have been corrected by various orthographic, morphological or syn-

---

[25] Pakkala, *Omitted*, 379.

tactic changes, but also by omitting or replacing individual words or phrases. Not to mention that the more copyists are assumed the more unintentional changes must be taken into account including omissions due to *parablepsis*.

The two examples mentioned under category 3) – the Samaritan Pentateuch and Jeremiah-MT – may be called "conservative." However, they differ from their *Vorlagen* not only by additions. And the additions are not limited to "updating", but consist to a large extent (in case of Jer MT) or almost completely (in case of the SP) of harmonising and homogenising supplementation of texts that were already contained elsewhere in the *Vorlage*. So, Pakkala's claim "We have seen that there are editors whose toolbox only contained expansions"[26] is not substantiated by empirical evidence. On the contrary, his distinction between expansion as a "conservative" tool versus "omissions, rewritings and relocations" as "more radical methods"[27] is problematic. An addition not declared as such[28] requires a master scribe who has the "ability and the authority to introduce changes into a tradition."[29] So, the question remains: were there any master scribes who confined themselves to additions and abstained from making any other emendations?

3.4 Changes on the Text's Surface: Additions, Omissions, Reformulations and Reorderings

The three cited catalogues of editorial activities show how difficult it is to find generally valid categories for editors and editorial processes. The most important category according to Kaufman ("conflation") is missing from Pakkala's catalogue, while the most important category according to Pakkala ("made only expansions") is not found in Kaufman's. However, both Kaufman and Pakkala acknowledge the importance of the empirical evidence and address (like others) the gap between the conventional redaction criticism and the empirical examples. Kaufman's conclusions are pessimistic, whereas Pakkala remains optimistic that "Much of the transmission of the Hebrew scriptures accords with the conventional assumption that the editors only made expansions and preserved the older text." "It is fair to assume that this type of conservative transmission

---

[26] Pakkala, *Omitted*, 379.
[27] Pakkala, *Omitted*, l.c. and more often.
[28] This is to be differentiated from additions made clearly visible for each learned reader. The Habakkuk Pesher adds explanations to Habakkuk's prophecy claiming to reveal its original message – while making a clear distinction between the cited verses and the commentary by the keyword "pesher." The vocal signs, accents and Masoretic notes in a Masoretic Codex are useful additions compared to a Torah scroll and claim to express the text more exactly than the scroll – but they do not deny their later origin. Every reader can distinguish between the letters of the written text (Ketiv) and the other signs, added subsequently by the Masoretes.
[29] Milstein, *Tracking*, 210. Cf. van der Toorn, *Scribal Culture*, 126.

forms the main bulk of the overall development of most texts of the Hebrew scriptures."[30]

But how does Pakkala come to his conclusion? He tends to distribute complex editorial processes among several successively active persons whose work may have spanned many generations – "the chain of editors."[31] If the differences between Chronicles and Samuel, or between the two extant editions of the book of Jeremiah are distributed along such "chain of editors," it is easy to attribute the omissions and text changes to the one, "radical" editor, and everything else to the other editors who would only have added. This sounds like arbitrary circularity, but it is common practice in many cases where text comparison is possible. In reconstructions of the literary history of Deuteronomy, for example, it is usually assumed that a first, quite free, "rewriting" of the Covenant Code would have been followed by a series of editors, who would then, almost exclusively, have added.[32] But this mixes the external evidence of the differences to be seen between the Covenant Code and Deuteronomy with the conventional assumptions about textual growth.

Kaufman, on the other hand, does not presume such "chain of editors." He compares the text of the Temple Scroll with that of the Pentateuch, often concluding that for a text passage of the Temple Scroll not only a single passage of the original text but several thematically related passages in the Pentateuch served as *Vorlagen*. This is similar to the procedure of the Pentateuchal editor assumed in the documentary hypothesis – with the decisive difference that the author of the Temple Scroll must have formulated much larger parts himself and often greatly modified the adopted parts. However, Kaufman did not find any evidence in the Temple Scroll that a section of its source had been expanded but otherwise remained unchanged in its wording. The rule for Pakkala and many redaction critics was not even found as an exception by Kaufman.

As distinct as the cited catalogues are, a more general classification of editorial techniques could gain general acknowledgement: if two given textual witnesses do not offer exactly the same text, but show such great similarities that they must be connected with each other in terms of their literary prehistory, then all differences can be formally divided into four types.

On the one hand, there can be quantitative differences. Depending on which text is considered to be closer to the original, they can be described as *additions* or *omissions* compared to the *Vorlage*.

And on the other hand, there can also be qualitative differences, if the wording or the text sequence differs. These must be described, regardless of the assumed order of origin, as modifying *reformulations* or *rearrangements* of the text

---

[30] Pakkala, *Omitted*, 384.
[31] Pakkala, *Omitted*, 379.
[32] Cf. Pakkala, *Omitted*, 361, with n12.

of the *Vorlage*. These modes of changes – additions, omissions, reformulations and rearrangements – are often listed.[33] It is Molly Zahn who, in her analysis of the Reworked Pentateuch manuscripts, made a further distinction which is very important for the evaluation of an editor's "toolbox": Concerning quantitative differences it is useful to differentiate between additions of new material ("what we most readily think of as 'addition'") and additions "from elsewhere", be it from the main source itself (as a duplication) or from other "scriptural" texts.[34]

In empirical examples where extant texts are compared, pluses in one book or version usually coincide with pluses in the other book or version and with differences in wording and sequence, so that very often quantitative (addition of new material, duplication of material from elsewhere, omission) and qualitative changes (reformulations, reordering) are found side-by-side.

3.5 Were There Any Editors Confining Themselves to Additions and, If So, Was This the Rule?

In almost all Old Testament publications focused on redaction criticism, an edition that only adds to the *Vorlage* and preserves it in its entirety is the rule.[35] The underlying growth model is easy to apply and, thanks to its circular reasoning, can lead to subjectively convincing results – the reconstructed, thoroughly comprehensible preliminary texts grow step by step under the guidance of the redaction critic eventually turning into the final text, which is often confusingly complex – but attested in the Biblia Hebraica.

A realistic editorial history, on the other hand, has a hard time: if one describes what remains of Samuel in Chronicles,[36] or how the text of 1QIsa[a] differs from the MT and the protomasoretic Qumran texts, it is not possible to "present" hitherto unknown works or versions.

However, the lack of empirical foundation of the growth model is not some aesthetic problem of Old Testament science, since literary and redaction analysis lead, in a much clearer way than most other exegetical methods, to factual as-

---

[33] See Pakkala, *Omitted*, 379, for a fourfold enumeration ("expansions," "omissions, rewritings and relocations"). Some authors subsume reformulations and rearrangements under a broader category of changes. Cf. Molly M. Zahn, *Rethinking Rewritten Scripture: Composition and Exegesis in the 4QReworked Pentateuch Manuscripts*, STDJ 95 (Leiden: Brill, 2011), 17–19 ("additions," "omissions," "alterations"), Kratz, "Redaktionsgeschichte/Redaktionskritik," *TRE* 28:369 ("Änderungen, Auslassungen und Zufügungen").

[34] Zahn, *Rethinking*, 17–18.

[35] Cf. Pakkala, *Omitted*, 38: "If one looks at the conclusions of literary- and redaction-critical approaches, the reconstructed literary layers follow this principle [i.e., the principle of preservation] so that it is very difficult to find reconstructions of the literary development of any text of the Hebrew scriptures where one literary layer is only partially preserved. The main exception to this rule is the oldest literary layer, or the 'original' source, which, as seen above, is often assumed to have been used selectively and thus preserved only fragmentarily."

[36] Cf. Berman, "Empirical Models," 21–22; Ziemer, *Kritik*, 248–52.

sertions that are historically either true or false.[37] Describing the structure or the topic of a certain passage in the context of a synchronic text analysis does not logically exclude that the structure or topic of the same passage can be described in a different way. A document can be read differently, and readers' responses in new contexts may change what is perceived as structure or topic of the text. Thus in the book of Ezekiel, depending on the perspective of reading, both the Babylonian Golah and the worldwide Diaspora can be addressed, both the prophecy of doom and the prophecy of salvation can be seen as essential, and both the vision reports and the oracles against the nations can be perceived as structurally significant.

If, on the other hand, the existence of a Golah-oriented version of the book of Ezekiel is postulated, adding within Ezek 43 exactly the 22 words of Ezek 43,6a.7a MT, or if the formulation of Jer 30:1–3 MT is traced back to an editor in the late 4th century who would have introduced the "new covenant" into the book of Jeremiah, or if an exact distribution of the wording of Exod 12 MT over seven different diachronically differentiated layers is presented as the result of scientific work,[38] then such "results" are necessarily either historically right or wrong. Either the books postulated existed in this form, or they did not exist. In the positive case, one could build on such hypotheses, in the negative case not. Since there are no textual witnesses to Exodus, Jeremiah or Ezekiel from pre-Hellenistic times, a direct verification or falsification of such hypotheses is not possible. When dealing with such "research results" it should matter how probable it is that scribes regularly followed the axioms of the growth model. In order to test this, the existing empirical examples of "editing" must be taken into account.

The question therefore is twofold: were there any editors at all whose "toolbox" consisted solely of updating expansions? And do the observations possible in concrete text comparison allow the conclusion that such a merely expanding edition could have been the rule?

It would be an easy task to enumerate cases where scribes did *not* follow these axioms whether they clearly abbreviated their sources[39] or that they made eclectic use of formulations or traditions of older sources.[40] However, in view of my cultural background where the "internal evidence" usually is seen as sufficient to prove redaction-critical hypotheses, I made another decision in testing the axioms of the growth model: I started with a catalogue given by Reinhard G. Kratz in the relevant TRE article on redaction criticism. Kratz

---

[37] Cf. the statements on the growth of the texts of the Hebrew Bible quoted in Ziemer, *Kritik*, 22–23, n48.

[38] See the studies discussed in Ziemer, *Kritik*, 86–98.

[39] E.g., comparing 1 Chr 1 with Gen 1–36, or the subsequent editions of the royal annals of Assyria (cf. Hans Jürgen Tertel, *Text and Transmission: An Empirical Model for the Literary Development of Old Testament Narratives*, BZAW 221 (Berlin: de Gruyter 1994).

[40] E.g., comparing motives of the Psalms with Ugaritic epics, or Prov 22:17–23:11 with the Instruction of Amenemope.

enumerates a list of examples which allow "to evaluate the relationship between the original text and the edited work in the versions received."[41] I took all these empirical examples of "redaction history", listed by a leading German Protestant redaction critic, to question if they can substantiate the axioms of the growth model: The Gilgamesh epic, the Book of the Dead, Chronicles against Samuel/Kings, MT versus LXX in Jeremiah, Daniel and Esther, 1 Esdras against Chronicles and Ezra–Nehemiah, Jubilees, the Genesis Apocryphon and the LAB against Genesis, compositions discovered in Qumran like 4Q174, 4Q175, 11QPs[a], 11QTemple, the different versions of the Community Rule, the Damascus Document and the War Scroll, the Enoch literature, the Synoptic Gospels and Gospel harmonies.[42] For all these (and three other oft-cited) empirical examples I analysed how far the principle of addition (or preservation) and the principle of difference are suitable descriptions of what happened in their redaction history. In the interest of brevity I refer the reader to the detailed cases presented elsewhere,[43] and here present a summary of my conclusions.

4. Examining the Empirical Examples for "Redaction"

4.1 The Task of the Master Scribe: Not to Develop But to Select What to Write

The examination of this comprehensive list of empirical examples[44] has led to a sobering conclusion. Not in a single case the original text was preserved completely in the new book or version. Pakkala's "conservative editor" whose toolbox consisted solely of additions was not found among the examples enumerated by Kratz.

The manifold metaphors for the growth model – growing forests, snowballs or archaeological tells – all suggest that the preservation of the original text in a new version is a natural thing. However, every writing process requires a conscious decision on the concrete text selection.

Anyone who begins to write on a clay tablet, papyrus or leather scroll must begin by selecting what he or she wishes to write. This is true for a copyist as well as for an editor or an author. A *copy* for a temple or state archive, intended to preserve tradition, has to reproduce the content of the *Vorlage* as accurately and completely as possible. In case of a copy for private or liturgical purposes, other criteria may have played a role. An excerpt manuscript like 4Q41 (4QDeut[n]) or a collection of testimonia like 4Q175 was less expensive than a manuscript of the

---

[41] Kratz, "Redaktionsgeschichte/Redaktionskritik," *TRE* 28:367 ("eine Reihe von Beispielen, bei denen das Verhältnis von Textvorlage und Redaktion an den jeweils erhaltenen Fassungen abgelesen werden kann").
[42] Ibid.
[43] See for this Ziemer, *Kritik*, 131–694.
[44] See for this Ziemer, *Kritik*, 131–694.

complete Deuteronomy. A Deuteronomy manuscript was cheaper than a copy of the complete Pentateuch. Additions of new material played only a marginal role, if any, in the context of copies. This is shown by the Qumran manuscripts of the books nowadays known as "biblical"[45] as well as in their later textual history,[46] which in this respect does not differ from the textual history of other ancient literary texts.[47]

This principle of conscious selection also applied to "editors" and "authors," i.e., master scribes. A master scribe can be distinguished from a copyist as follows: the book he aimed to write did not yet exist in this form. In cases in which it is certain that written *Vorlagen* existed (i.e., in all the examples named here), the master scribe therefore found his *Vorlage(n)* in need of improvement in one respect or another – otherwise the scribe (or the person who gave instruction to write this new version or new work) could have been satisfied with a copy. Although it is theoretically possible that he adopted the wording of his *Vorlage(n)* in its entirety he was more likely to select elements of the *Vorlage(n)* that he wished to reproduce, to revise them more or less systematically if necessary,[48] and to add what he considered to be missing. As far as the latter is concerned, a review of all the empirical examples of "redaction" mentioned by Kratz suggests that an edition which updates the text through additions and the complete preservation of the original text are mutually exclusive opposites.[49]

Of course the fact that each writing process is necessarily preceded by a conscious selection has serious consequences for the possibility to reconstruct any *Vorlage*: The optimal result is not the reconstruction of the actual *Vorlage*, but the correct identification of the chunks the author/editor has selected from his respective *Vorlage*.[50] However, those parts of the text would still have the possibly "late" form the editor has given them.

---

[45] See Ziemer, *Kritik*, 545, 684–89 for 1QIsa[a] and ibid., 691n54 for 1QIsa[b]. For the generally greater inclination of scribes to accidentally omit information, see also ibid., 61n54.

[46] See, exemplarily, ibid., 352–65 on the inner Greek textual history of Jeremiah; ibid., 64–70, 689 on Codex L, and 426–34 on the Esth-AT tradition in ms. 93 (Rahlfs).

[47] See Ziemer, *Kritik*, 189–92, on the Ptolemaic manuscripts of the Book of the Dead as well as studies on details of the textual history of SB Gilgamesh (ibid., 141–51), Jeremiah (ibid., 289–94, 339–52, 355–65), Jubilees (ibid., 463–65), the Damascus Document (ibid., 564–69) or the Enoch literature.

[48] As a rule, editors show an effort for consistency, but are not able to achieve it; cf. Emanuel Tov, "Some Reflections on Consistency in the Activity of Scribes and Translators in Textual Criticism," in *Textual Criticism of the Hebrew Bible, Qumran, Septuagint: Collected Essays Vol. 3*, VTSup 167 (Leiden: Brill, 2015), 36.

[49] If updated (Chronicles, Jubilees, Temple Scroll), the *Vorlage* is not fully preserved; if the *Vorlage* is (nearly) fully preserved (Samaritan Pentateuch), nothing new is added.

[50] Cf. David M. Carr, *The Formation of the Hebrew Bible: A New Reconstruction* (New York: Oxford University Press, 2011), who speaks of the "tendency of ancient scribes to draw selectively on the ancient traditions they appropriated (even as they might expand on the particular chunks selected)" (112).

To look at an empirical example does not mean to know beyond doubt how the differences arose. For all examples examined, the scholarly discussion already produced hypotheses that "stages of growth" or "layers" can be observed. In most cases this has to do with the fact that the growth model has been taken for granted. Therefore in my book I have refrained from mentioning such theses or tracing back their line of reasoning to the point where the method is no longer adapted to the text but the text to the method.[51] Likewise, at least for the biblical books, there is always the opposite hypothesis, that they are original creations without the use of written *Vorlagen* – a thesis often advocated by religious fundamentalists. Again, in my study I have refrained from analysing the structure of argument or giving an overview of such theses.

Both extremes offer a general key to the understanding of biblical literature, excluding one thing wherever possible: That the people to whom we ultimately owe the creation of the biblical books have consciously chosen their respective written *Vorlagen* and have consciously transformed their text. In order to be able to counter both possible extremes, my aim was to discern the transmission situation for each individual example as immediately as possible and, if necessary, to examine several theoretically possible interpretations with regard to their consequences for the growth model. On the one hand, I found that in all the "examples of editing" mentioned by Kratz, the respective "new whole" was actually created with the help of written *Vorlagen* and thus did not appear from nowhere. On the other hand, however, none of these editorial processes correspond to the axioms of the growth model.

Of course, there are also studies for each of these cases abstaining from such dogmatic presuppositions and therefore achieving more realistic interpretations of the textual findings; fortunately, this is the rule. But often studies dealing with the transmitted evidence are influenced by the growth model,[52] attempting to understand what is observed as an exception confirming the rule.[53]

According to my survey, the alleged "rule" that the Hebrew scriptures had grown in stages or layers never applied as such. Books obviously do not grow like a tree with its growth rings, not like a snowball and not like an archaeological tell. A new book or the new version of a book does not physically evolve from a *Vorlage*, but always requires a new production through a concrete writing process. Books are written by people who consciously choose what to adopt and what to leave out from the used *Vorlagen*. They were neither forced to fully integrate their *Vorlagen* nor to reformulate everything anew.

---

[51] I made an exception for Chronicles, where the interpretation as "growth" stands in particularly blatant contradiction to the textual reality, see Ziemer, *Kritik*, 252–66.

[52] See my critique of Hermann Joseph Stipp's approach concerning Jeremiah (Ziemer, *Kritik*, 334–39).

[53] So Pakkala, *Omitted*, 384.

Not a single empirical example of the "phenomenon of editing" cited by Kratz[54] corresponds to the axioms of the growth model, and in no case would it be possible to reconstruct the older version simply by analysing the younger version. This applies to all theoretically conceivable directions of dependence.

In most cases, additions are accompanied by omissions and extensive text alterations. Even when one tries to explain the quantitative differences by the auxiliary construction of a common *Vorlage* in which the pluses of both textual witnesses were missing, the qualitative text changes and the rearrangements remain unexplained. In this respect, the phenomena of "editing" in the field of "biblical" literature do not differ from the "extra-biblical" examples.[55]

4.2 The Empirical Examples to Learn What "Redaction" Was

Regrettably, there will be no alternative standard model to be used in future reconstructions of the prehistory of biblical texts. Since the axioms of the growth model did not apply, Kaufman was right in claiming that a reconstruction of lost sources "in other than their broadest outlines is a consummately fruitless endeavor."[56] And beyond this, it is to be expected that the various books were created differently. It is highly unlikely that collections of psalms came into being in the same way narratives, law codes or prophetic books did. That is why I will review the series of examples named by Kratz and others as models to learn about how "redaction" functioned and say a few words about their respective model character.

Probably the most frequently cited Ancient Near Eastern model for the phenomenon of editing is the Gilgamesh Epic.[57] Its "Standard Babylonian" version (SB), attested by numerous copies especially from Nineveh, relates to its *Vorlagen* in a manner similar to the relationships of Chronicles or the Book of Jubilees to their respective *Vorlagen*. The main *Vorlage* (Old Babylonian Gilgamesh) is copied almost word-for-word for large portions, and at the same time carefully updated linguistically. Simultaneously, entire passages are left out. Other sources (e.g. the Akkadian Atrahasis epic in SB XI and the Sumerian poem "Gilgamesh, Enkidu, and the Netherworld" in SB XII) are used as well, and this integration of different sources certainly left its mark.[58] The new frame in SB I:1–28 and XI:322–28 with the older beginning in SB I:29 cited is a good example for "revision through introduction."[59] However, recognising and cutting

---

[54] Kratz, "Redaktionsgeschichte/Redaktionskritik," 28:367 ("Phänomen der Redaktion").

[55] Cf. Molly M. Zahn, "Innerbiblical Exegesis: The View from beyond the Bible," in *The Formation of the Pentateuch: Bridging the Academic Cultures of Europe, Israel, and North America*, ed. Jan C. Gertz et al., FAT 111 (Tübingen: Mohr Siebeck, 2016).

[56] Kaufman, *Temple Scroll*, 29.

[57] Cf. Ziemer, *Kritik*, 136–69.

[58] Cf. Carr, *Formation*, 40–48.

[59] Milstein, *Tracking*.

off this frame does not unearth an older, once existing version of the epic. Such a procedure would result in an incomplete SB Gilgamesh including the chunks of both OB Gilgamesh and other sources *Sîn-lēqi-uninni* selected to build on, in the linguistic form he gave them. The formation of the Pentateuch and of other books (e.g., Joshua, Judges, Samuel, Kings[60] or Ezra–Nehemiah) that seem to contain a continuous story while using several sometimes-contradictory *Vorlagen* should be imagined in a similar way. According to the analogy of SB XI and XII, it seems possible to evaluate where and how sources were used in these books. However, based on the analogy of the Gilgamesh Epic, there is little certainty about the concrete scope, the exact wording and the literary character of these direct sources without external evidence, and almost nothing about the literary history of these sources. A continuous "Fortschreibung" by a "chain of editors" cannot be observed in the history of the Gilgamesh material.[61] This should not surprise since, according to Van der Toorn, "The notion of an ongoing *Fortschreibung* is simply not consistent with Ancient Near East scribal practice."[62]

Whereas not a single complete copy of the Gilgamesh Epic has survived, the Egyptian Book of the Dead (BD)[63] and related text corpora like the Pyramid Texts and the Coffin Texts are preserved in numerous complete and reliably dated textual witnesses. The history of the tradition of the BD is therefore an inexhaustible and incomparable source of what was possible and customary in the textual and literary history of religious works which were anonymously handed down but highly valued in antiquity. Therefore, the study of these works promises a considerable gain for Hebrew Bible research.[64] There were different phases to this history of tradition: In the New Kingdom there was great freedom in the selection of individual sayings, the prehistory of which can often be traced back to *Vorlagen* from the Second Intermediate Period or the Middle Kingdom. In the Third Intermediate Period a far-reaching break in tradition occurred. The subsequent Saite "editing" of the BD was essentially giving a fixed order to a compilation of sayings which, as individual sayings, already belonged to the corpus of the BD in the New Kingdom. This editing offers perhaps the best analogy for the collection of classical Hebrew literature that must have happened in the exilic or early post-exilic period. Later copies of the BD are either more-or-less-complete copies of their respective *Vorlagen*, or shorter copies that are limited to a selection and sometimes combine BD spells with sayings from other text corpora. The situation is thus strikingly similar to the psalm manuscripts in

---

[60] For Kings, cf. the contribution of Benjamin D. Giffone in this volume, "Regathering Too Many Stones."
[61] For the Middle Babylonian and Assyrian evidence see Ziemer, *Kritik*, 155–58: None of these exemplars show an intermediate stage.
[62] Cf. van der Toorn, *Scribal Culture*, 149.
[63] Cf. Ziemer, *Kritik*, 170–220.
[64] Cf. ibid., 209–20.

Qumran. Adding something new was a rare exception in the more than 2000-year history of the BD – comprehensible when "millionfold proven" spells were available for selection.[65] Longer and shorter versions of the same spells were transmitted over centuries side by side; in many cases the shorter versions are proven as secondary by the empirical evidence. There was no "literary growth" in case of this by far best-witnessed empirical example for multi-stage redaction in the ancient world.

Among the books of the Hebrew Bible, there is only one that can be empirically compared with its Hebrew counterparts and should therefore occupy a prominent place in every textbook dealing with redaction history: Chronicles.[66] Comparing Chronicles with Samuel and Kings shows that there is no chance to reconstruct the real sources out of the work using them.[67] Such comparison can show exemplarily that addition, omission, rearrangement and exchange of text elements usually complement each other as editorial techniques and serve a single purpose. An editor who likes to rework an old topic should try to make the written *Vorlagen* he used serve his purpose. He would choose what fits his plan, he would leave unchanged what he can make his own, and he would look for an appropriate place for what he likes to supplement. He is neither forced to copy his *Vorlage* or even parts of it word-for-word, nor to reformulate everything anew. He cannot eliminate the sources he used for his work out of the cultural memory – and would therefore hardly strive to do so. He knows, in contrast, that his work has to compete with the *Vorlagen* and will therefore seek not to contradict them unless he believes to have good reasons to do so. To describe the edition of Chronicles, in view of the fact that editors who delt with their sources in a similar way – the authors of Jubilees, Pseudo-Philo, Temple Scroll or SB Gilgamesh – it is not necessary to assume additional hypothetical "preliminary" or "intermediate stages." On the contrary: the relationship of Chronicles to its sources can serve as an aid to understanding the editors of other books whose sources are no longer extant, like the Pentateuch.[68]

Besides Chronicles, the comparison of Jer LXX (short text) and Jer MT (long text)[69] should be given a prominent place in every Old Testament introduction. In this case the quantitative differences are distributed so unevenly that one version of the text is contained almost completely in the other version. Another much-discussed example of such a situation is the Community Rule with the fragmentary versions found in Cave 4 in Qumran (including the short texts 4QS^b, 4QS^d and 4QS^e) compared to 1QS (long text). The proven existence of

---

[65] Book of the Dead, chapters 18, 19, 20, 31, 72, 89, 100, 101, 125, 134, 144, 148, 155, and 157. Cf. Ziemer, *Kritik*, 211.
[66] Cf. Ziemer, *Kritik*, 221–72.
[67] See Berman, "Empirical Models," 21–22; Ziemer, *Kritik*, 248–52.
[68] Cf. Ziemer, *Kritik*, 270–72.
[69] Cf. ibid., 273–383.

short and long texts does not mean, however, that the short text inevitably is the older version and the *Vorlage* of the long text. Often the priority of the long text is established beyond doubt, especially in case of extreme quantitative differences like those between the Pentateuch and the Qumran phylacteries. Be this as it may, in the case of Jeremiah as well as in the case of the Community Rule, the oldest known manuscripts of the long version are older than those of the short version: 4QJer^a (cognates of MT) is older than 4QJer^{b,d} (cognate of the Hebrew *Vorlage* of the LXX), and 1QS is older than 4QS^{b,d,e}. This can mean two things: Either the long text is also the older version – then we get no example of an expanded, but of a shortened version. Or the short texts have been transmitted alongside the long text for decades and centuries, perhaps with the presumption that they offer a more original version of the text – in which case we get an example of an expanding edition, but its result would not have been generally accepted, contrary to the single-copy axiom. The text-historical fact of the parallel transmission of different versions of Jeremiah and the Community Rule in Qumran proves in any case that short versions could prevail against long versions. This seems to have been the case even or especially when the short texts had hardly any independent textual components compared to the long texts. This is easy to explain psychologically: A rewriting that shortens its *Vorlage* but does not add anything new is conservative: It does not contain anything that is not in its *Vorlage*. If one has the choice between two versions, but does not know which one is older or even "original," the least wrong thing to do is to prefer the short text. Therefore, the absence of any such shorter edition of, e.g., Isaiah in Qumran is an indication that probably no short version of this book existed in post-exilic times, regardless of whether it would have been a more original or a secondarily shortened version. Be that as it may: Most pluses of Jer MT are duplications of material present in Jer LXX as well. Even if Jer MT is understood as a secondary expanded edition compared to a shorter version of Jeremiah as testified by Jer LXX (which indeed seems most likely), this does not give an example of the growth model, but rather the pattern of a homogenising edition, which hides its traces making a reconstruction of the *Vorlage* impossible.

As far as the relationship between LXX and MT is concerned, Jeremiah with its one-sided distribution of quantitative differences is a rare exception, comparable only with the book of Job where it is generally admitted that the LXX version is the result of conscious shortening. Normally books which have the highest number of pluses in the LXX are among the books with the highest number of minuses as well and vice versa. This is true for Esther, Daniel, Exodus, Joshua, 1 Samuel and 1 Kings if using the Tov/Polak synopsis of the MT and LXX.[70] The

---

[70] Cf. ibid., 275–81.

Books of Daniel[71] and Esther,[72] known for the deuterocanonical "additions" in the Greek versions, show that an expanding edition is usually accompanied by great freedom with regard to the *Vorlage*. The direction of dependence is more clear-cut here than in the case of Jeremiah. Moreover, two Greek versions are available for each book and can be included in the discussion. The value as an empirical model for the prehistory of the Hebrew-Aramaic books in the MT version is, however, limited by the fact that here, as in the case of 1 Esd (a shortening "edition"),[73] and in contrast to e.g. Jer LXX, the Greek versions are in all probability not simply translations of their Hebrew-Aramaic *Vorlagen*, but rather recompositions with heterogeneous pieces composed in the course of translation. The Qumran Daniel fragments allow to say that only the book edition exemplified by the MT was in use there. Minor similarities of the Qumran fragments with Dan LXX and Dan θ' (Theodotion) against MT suggest that the Hebrew-Aramaic *Vorlagen* of the Greek translations also belonged to this book edition. Dan LXX, Est LXX and 1 Esd equally show that additions do not happen without simultaneous omissions and/or rewriting. However, an optimistic aspect is that a diachronic text hypothesis, which is based on genres when hypothesising the amount of *Vorlagen* (cf. the hymns in Dan 3 LXX or the prayers in Est C LXX), is safer than a layered reconstruction, which hopes to come closer to an actual *Vorlage* by *Tendenz*-critical subtraction of individual verses or parts of verses. This is because Dan LXX, Est LXX and 1 Esd are each new compositions including new, clearly defined text passages, while the sections taken from the *Vorlage* are either not expanded at all (Dan 1–2; 7–12 LXX, 1 Esd) or only in the course of general rewriting with simultaneous omissions (Est LXX; Dan 4; 5–6 LXX). 1 Esd allows the comparison with five other ancient reports covering the end of the Kingdom of Judah: Kings, Jer LXX, Jer MT, Chronicles, and Josephus' Antiquities. This comparison shows that in the field of biblical historiography eclectic procedures rather than updating expansions are the rule rather than the exception.[74]

The classical examples of rewriting – Jubilees, Genesis Apocryphon and LAB[75] – obviously cannot be examples of "literary growth."[76] It is important to note that this rewriting took place at a time when the Torah had long since been literarily completed and was available in several very similar versions – the Qumran manuscripts attest to the existence of different text types, of which Proto-MT, Pre-SP and the Hebrew *Vorlagen* of LXX for the individual books are

---

[71] Cf. ibid., 384–422.
[72] Cf. ibid., 423–45.
[73] Cf. ibid., 446–60.
[74] Cf. ibid., 450–60.
[75] Cf. ibid., 461–82.
[76] As far as the Genesis Apocryphon is concerned, I had to revise some of the hypotheses put forward in my own dissertation.

best described by their later descendants, which have been handed down independently by Jews, Samaritans and Christians. The texts did not gradually gain authority.[77] In fact, different approaches to a literary work coexisted. For some Pentateuchal traditions, Sidnie White Crawford described even a gradually increasing freedom in dealing with the *Vorlage*.[78] These new works or new editions can serve, along with Chronicles, as evidence of how new books could be made from old narrative traditions, and are further aids to understanding the creation of books whose immediate sources have not been handed down.

With the "selective text compilations"[79] it is even clearer that they do not prove "growth." 4Q175 (4QTestimonia)[80] is recognisable as a collection of quotations – the incoherence between the individual quotations certainly indicates that the individual sections are taken from different contexts, and suggests that they originally belonged to different works. However, no one would think of using a subtraction method to cut complete sources out of 4Q175, since these are not independent units but extracted parts of much larger works (Exodus, Numbers, Deuteronomy, Joshua Apocryphon). The situation is different with 4Q174 ("4QFlorilegium" or 4QMidrEsh[a]):[81] Here, too, the sources are reproduced only in extracts, but they are clearly identified by certain formulae and separated from the commentary and other quotations used. The example of 4QMidrEsch makes it clear that the biblical books, even if some commenting elements seem to exist here and there, are not commentaries. I have already mentioned the Temple Scroll.[82] Kaufman made it clear nearly 40 years ago that its editing questions the prevailing growth model. This scroll is still one of the most important empirical models, especially for the development of the Pentateuch, in particular for the editing of legal texts.[83]

11QPs[a] is also named by Kratz among the "selective text compilations." Starting from there, I compared the existing Psalter versions.[84] The Psalter is, along with Genesis, Deuteronomy and Isaiah, one of the most popular books in Qumran; but unlike those, the arrangement and selection of the individual pieces varies greatly. Some of the psalm scrolls found in Qumran differ from the Psalter as known from the canonical versions (MT, LXX), in the same way various unusual Ptolemaic copies of the BD differ from the Saite recension represented by the equally Ptolemaic Turin Papyrus: Each of these is a different selection from a text

---

[77] So among others Pakkala, *Omitted*, 354–55.
[78] Sidnie White Crawford, *Rewriting Scripture in Second Temple Times* (Grand Rapids: Eerdmans, 2008), 149.
[79] Cf. Kratz, "Redaktionsgeschichte/Redaktionskritik," *TRE* 28:368 ("selektive Textzusammenstellungen"), Ziemer, *Kritik*, 483–547.
[80] Cf. Ziemer, *Kritik*, 484–91.
[81] Cf. ibid., 491–96.
[82] Cf. ibid., 517–29.
[83] Cf. ibid., 525–29.
[84] Cf. ibid., 496–517.

corpus. On the other hand, at least in Hellenistic times, an order existed for the Psalter as well as for the BD, which on the long run was established as the standard. Given the great variety in selection and arrangement between 11QPs[a] and other "Qumran psalters" in comparison to the MT and the LXX, the individual psalms only differ slightly between the various versions, with no particular tendency in terms of content. This might also be a model for the development of other books which, like the Psalter, appear as collections of independent pieces, such as Proverbs or the Book of the Twelve, and perhaps also for Edition I of the Book of Jeremiah. In all of these books, the individual pieces are identified and separated from each other within the text by headings. This makes it possible to assume that different pieces in the collection were written at different times. In analogy to 11QPs[a], however, one should not expect a successive "growth" of the individual pieces, but instead a partial linguistic update and homogenisation, which can obscure the dating of the sources. It is impossible to reconstruct the exact appearance and size of earlier collections, because regrouping or omitting individual pieces leaves no clear traces.

The extent to which the various editions and versions of the Community Rule, the Damascus Document and the War Scroll[85] can provide helpful analogies for the process of handing down biblical books is an open question. As far as the genres are concerned, these works stand at the transition between literary texts and "texts of a more technical nature," whose transmission was governed by different customs in antiquity.[86] In terms of research history, the versions of the Community Rule have attracted particular interest. It is an example of how strongly the interpretation of the findings of the tradition is determined by the respective presuppositions. Those who are accustomed to the growth model will be more willing to reconstruct two or three preliminary stages that have not been handed down than to accept a shortening tendency. On the other hand, those who also reckon with the possibility of shortening editions can explain the findings more easily. In any case, the versions handed down in parallel prove that short texts were transmitted alongside long texts, so that a reconstruction of a short text which is not represented by any textual witness is always a weak hypothesis.

The findings in the Enoch literature[87] are similar in their complexity to those of the Book of the Dead and the Gilgamesh Epic, to which there are also thematic connections (journeys to the beyond; celestial bodies). In this case, "redaction history" is ultimately a history of *reduction*, as can be seen, e.g., in the diminution of the path of the moon through the Qumran manuscripts, the Ethiopic, the

---

[85] Cf. ibid., 548–77.
[86] Cf. Leighton D. Reynolds and Nigel G. Wilson, *Scribes and Scholars: A Guide to the Transmission of Greek and Latin Literature*, 3rd ed. (Oxford: Clarendon, 1991), 234–37.
[87] Cf. Ziemer, *Kritik*, 577–88.

Slavonic and the Hebrew book of Enoch.[88] It is a prime example of the fact that the Hebrew Bible itself is nothing else than a conscious selection from the Hebrew and Aramaic Israelite literature of the Second Temple period.

The Gospels[89] have always played a role as an analogy for the Christian research of the literary history of Old Testament books. The Gospels of Matthew and Luke are two of the best-known examples of the fact that the authors of books later recognised as canonical also used written sources. However, even a brief glance at a New Testament synopsis shows that, as is the rule with new writings, there are additions next to omissions, rearrangements and reformulations.

In early Christianity, the unease with this situation led to the program of a gospel harmony,[90] be it as an independent work or in the form of canon tables added to the manuscripts. Gospel harmonies stood at the beginning of German-language Bible-related literature. They have been among the oldest literary works both for the Old Low German (Heliand)[91] and the Old High German (Tatian translation).[92] While the literary principle of the gospel harmony – creating a new whole from several sources, if possible without adding one's own – has long been regarded as the best (and only) model for the documentary hypothesis of the Pentateuch,[93] another analogy between the ancient concept of a gospel harmony and the modern growth model has not yet been seen: Both are universal tools to resolve contradiction in the Holy Scriptures but in a complementary way. The idea of the gospel harmony is to restore the whole true story behind the gospels, presuming that the four evangelists never erred and did not add anything of their own but only told a part of this true story. The possibility of uniting every bit of information contained in each of the four Gospels in one harmony has been seen as proof for the extraordinary trustworthiness of the Evangelists, although it would be possible to create a harmony out of forged testimonials as well. The idea of the growth model is, on the contrary, to restore the true literary history behind the Hebrew scriptures presuming that the editors never left out anything their predecessors had written. The possibility of "reconstructing" a literary history with completely preserved layers is seen as proof for the extraordinary trustworthiness of the biblical redactors, who only made expansions, although it would be possible to postulate such "layers of growth"

---

[88] Compare 4Q209 (4QEnoch[b]) with 1 En. 73–74, 2 En. 16 and 3 En. 17:5. See Ziemer, *Kritik*, 585–88.

[89] Cf. Ziemer, *Kritik*, 589–603.

[90] Cf. ibid., 604–9.

[91] See MS München, Bayrische Staatsbibliothek, Cgm 25, accessed Apr 26, 2022: https://daten.digitale-sammlungen.de/bsb00026305/image_5. Cf. Ziemer, *Kritik*, 708.

[92] See MS St. Gallen, Stiftsbibliothek, Cod. Sang. 56, accessed Apr 26, 2022: https://www.e-codices.ch/en/csg/0056/25/0/Sequence-262 (Latin and Old High German). Cf. Ziemer, *Kritik*, 708.

[93] Since Astruc's *Conjectures*, cf. Ziemer, *Kritik*, 98.

for every modern text as well.[94] It remains to be noted that a gospel harmony, because nothing new is added compared to its *Vorlagen*, cannot serve as an example for the growth model.

Thus, among the twenty empirical examples mentioned by Kratz, there was not a single case in which "*Vorlage* and redaction had formed a new whole together"[95] in such a way that the "well-founded distinction between *Vorlage* and redaction" (Kratz' definition of redaction criticism) could be "made on one and the same text."[96] Thus, the assertion that the conventional redaction-critical methodology is appropriate to the particular way in which the biblical texts are handed down is clearly refuted.

Beyond Kratz' catalogue, I reviewed three other cases: The juxtaposition of different legal texts in the Pentateuch on the basis of a series of Passover texts cited by Reinhard Müller, Juha Pakkala and Bas ter Haar Romeny as empirical examples of editing,[97] and the only two cases of independent Hebrew textual witnesses to biblical books preserved in their entirety: the Samaritan Pentateuch (SP), compared to the Masoretic Text (MT),[98] can be called an expanded edition. However, the additions do not consist of new material but duplicate information already contained in the earlier version. And the quantitatively relevant special readings of 1QIsa^a compared to Isa MT and Isa LXX,[99] interpreted by Eugene Ulrich as evidence of continued textual growth, proved to be unintentional omissions or attempts to correct them again.

The resulting picture may be considered representative for those cases of rewriting that are usually cited as examples of "editing." In these cases, the following applies: addition of new text never happens alone, but only in combination with other processes, such as homogenisation, rearrangement and/or omission of elements of the original text. Common to all of the examined rewritings is the fact that the responsible master scribes worked selectively – with respect to the concrete text volume and/or the text arrangement or the selected text version as well as with respect to the formulae, formulations and other linguistic means ever used.

The study does not claim to be representative of the ancient scribal culture as a whole. Everyday texts, such as administrative lists or chronicles, may well "grow" just like an archive, but their production is not a model for literary texts. The vast majority of documents with literary content, on the other hand, were copies that did not intend to change the content of their respective originals, even if they de-

---

[94] Cf. Ziemer, *Kritik*, 75.
[95] Kratz, "Redaktionsgeschichte/Redaktionskritik," *TRE* 28:370 ("Vorlage und Redaktion bilden gemeinsam ein neues Ganzes").
[96] Kratz, "Redaktionsgeschichte/Redaktionskritik," *TRE* 28:368 ("die begründete Unterscheidung von Text und Redaktion" … "an ein und demselben Text vorgenommen").
[97] Cf. Ziemer, *Kritik*, 610–36.
[98] Cf. ibid., 637–68.
[99] Cf. ibid., 669–94.

viate from their *Vorlage* here and there, often unintentionally. This applies to the manuscripts in the library of Assurbanipal as well as to those in the Qumran "library." In terms of statistics, probably shortened versions, abstracts or excerpts of known works would range in second place. Collections or anthologies are relatively common too, i.e., compilations of various works or excerpts thereof, as well as commentaries. Only then newly composed works would rank. Even rarer are revisions of existing works with regard to content, whereby one would have to differentiate between conscious forgeries, tacitly updating and text-critically motivated new editions.

Once a work exists in different versions, such as Jeremiah, or once a story is present in different works, like the story of David in Samuel and Chronicles, a copyist has usually copied only one particular *Vorlage* – Sam *or* Chr, Edition I *or* Edition II of Jeremiah – whether complete or abridged. Regarding the Gilgamesh Epic, often only one tablet was copied, regarding the Pentateuch, often only one book was copied. If one takes the completely preserved Qumran texts as the starting point for a statistic, then excerpts and eclectic compilations such as 4QDeut^n, 4QTest and some of the phylacteries were dominant – not only because small documents simply have a greater chance of being completely preserved but also since there are many fragmentary excerpt manuscripts as well.[100]

The more examples one consults, the clearer the picture emerges: Adding new material to old books is an exception. If books have been newly written, the use of several sources is the rule: The Chronicler used, next to Samuel and Kings, at least Gen, Deut, Josh, Jer and Ps; the author of Jubilees used, next to Genesis, at least Ex, Lev and Deut as well as parts of the Enoch literature – similar procedures can be assumed for the "editor" of the Book of Kings, the "editor" of the first edition of Jeremiah and the "editor" of the Pentateuch. If books were revised they were homogenised (Jer MT, SP). If books were translated, they could have been shortened simultaneously (Job LXX, Exod LXX, Vulgate),[101] newly arranged according to chronological criteria (Book of the Twelve, Daniel and 1 Esd in the LXX)[102] or theologically revised (Esth-LXX).[103] The easiest thing for the translator was, however, to follow the particular original text faithfully, of course irrespective of whether this *Vorlage* later turned out to be a Jewish "standard text" (e.g., Num LXX, 2 Esd), or not (Jer LXX, 1 Sam LXX).

---

[100] For these see ibid., 483n2.

[101] For the Vulgate see ibid., 524–25.

[102] The Greek Book of the Twelve has the three oldest prophets (Hosea, Amos, Micah) first. Daniel LXX has chapters 5–6 after chapter 8 getting the order Nebuchadnezzar–Belshazzar–Darius; 1 Esd has rearranged Ezra 2–4 getting the order Darius–Xerxes in 1 Esd 5.

[103] God and the Jewish religion are mentioned explicitly several times throughout the book (Esth 2:20; 4:8; D:8, 6:1, 13 LXX; and more often), see Ziemer, *Kritik*, 438–41.

5. Conclusion

In conclusion, the following rule of thumb emerges: The authors of new compositions, revisions, and translations who were most inclined to add new material, never reproduced their *Vorlagen* unchanged and in their entirety. No one should be surprised by this. Introducing new elements into an old text is a radical change, even more radical than producing a shortened version. Conservative copyists would not dare to do so.[104] Even conservative editors – editors in the literal sense of the word – were reluctant to introduce new material into their work. This is true for the scrupulous compilers of gospel harmonies as well as for the editors of the Samaritan Pentateuch or the Saite recension of the Book of the Dead. In contrast, combining new, updated formulations with classical texts is not a conservative approach but a sign of freedom in relation to the *Vorlage*. Scribes who inserted new elements into their texts were not the slaves of a preservation principle but true masters of the tradition. These master scribes, while copying large strings of their sources, simultaneously added, omitted, substituted and rearranged elements of the text. If anything can be named as the main tool used consciously while using sources, it is the selection of the sources and of the strings to be copied. However, small-scale additions, omissions, homogenising reformulations and linguistic updates may occur unconsciously as well. If such differences come to light in text comparison it is not always clear if they were consciously made by an editor or unconsciously by a copyist. For a copyist whose duty was the "faithful reproduction of the text as received",[105] such changes could have been seen as a sign of untrustworthiness. For a master scribe they could be a mark of quality. Thorough new editions have been a rare event in literary history, therefore, a "chain of editors" is most unlikely. The empirical evidence shows that such editions usually included additions, omissions, reformulations and rearrangements at once. We owe the Hebrew Bible to master scribes who felt enabled to perform such radical innovations. However, fortunately there do not seem to have been many radical revisions for a given book. Most scribes, as shown by the Qumran scrolls of the prophets which barely revealed any previously unknown elements,[106] acted rather conservatively, hesitating to perform large scale interpolations, omissions or other alterations – as copyists. Thanks to a chain of more-or-less-trustworthy copyists, we are able to study the Hebrew scriptures today.

---

[104] Cf. van der Toorn, *Scribal Culture*, 126.
[105] Ibid.
[106] Cf. Ziemer, *Kritik*, 381n263, for the Jeremiah manuscripts, and ibid., 692, for Isaiah.

Bibliography

Becker, Uwe. *Exegese des Alten Testaments. Ein Methoden- und Arbeitsbuch*. 2nd ed. Tübingen: Mohr Siebeck, 2008.

Berman, Joshua. "Empirical Models of Textual Growth: A Challenge for the Historical-Critical Tradition." *JHebS* 16.12 (2016): 1–25. DOI:10.5508/jhs.2016.v16.a12.

Blum, Erhard. "Notwendigkeit und Grenzen historischer Exegese: Plädoyer für eine alttestamentliche 'Exegetik'." Pages 1–29 in *Grundfragen der historischen Exegese: Methodologische, philologische und hermeneutische Beiträge zum Alten Testament*. Edited by Kristin Weingart and Wolfgang Oswald. FAT 95. Tübingen: Mohr Siebeck, 2015.

Carr, David M. *The Formation of the Hebrew Bible. A New Reconstruction*. New York: Oxford University Press, 2011.

Erzberger, Johanna. "Israel's Salvation and the Survival of Baruch the Scribe." Within this volume.

Fried, Lisbeth S., and Edward J. Mills III. "Ezra the Scribe." Within this volume.

Giffone, Benjamin D. "Regathering Too Many Stones? Scribal Constraints, Community Memory, and the 'Problem' of Elijah's Sacrifice for Deuteronomism in Kings." Within this volume.

Kaufman, Stephen A. "The Temple Scroll and Higher Criticism." *HUCA* 53 (1982): 29–42.

Kratz, Reinhard G. "Redaktionsgeschichte/Redaktionskritik I. Altes Testament." *TRE* 28 (1997): 367–78.

Levin, Christoph. *Das Alte Testament*. 4th ed. München: Beck, 2010.

Milstein, Sara J. *Tracking the Master Scribe: Revision through Introduction in Biblical and Mesopotamian Literature*. New York: Oxford University Press, 2016.

Müller, Reinhard, Juha Pakkala, and Bas ter Haar Romeny. *Evidence of Editing: Growth and Change of Texts in the Hebrew Bible*. RBS 75. Atlanta: Society of Biblical Literature, 2014.

Pakkala, Juha. *God's Word Omitted: Omissions in the Transmission of the Hebrew Bible*. FRLANT 251. Göttingen: Vandenhoeck & Ruprecht, 2013.

Reynolds, Leighton D., and Nigel G. Wilson. *Scribes and Scholars: A Guide to the Transmission of Greek and Latin Literature*. 3rd ed. Oxford: Clarendon, 1991.

Tertel, Hans Jürgen. *Text and Transmission: An Empirical Model for the Literary Development of Old Testament Narratives*. BZAW 221. Berlin: de Gruyter, 1994.

Toorn, Karel van der. *Scribal Culture and the Making of the Hebrew Bible*. Cambridge, MA: Harvard University Press, 2007.

Tov, Emanuel. "Some Reflections on Consistency in the Activity of Scribes and Translators in Textual Criticism." Pages 36–44 in *Textual Criticism of the Hebrew Bible, Qumran, Septuagint. Collected Essays Vol. 3*. VTSup 167. Leiden: Brill, 2015.

Van Seters, John. *The Edited Bible: The Curious History of the "Editor" in Biblical Criticism*. Winona Lake, IN: Eisenbrauns, 2006.

White Crawford, Sidnie. *Rewriting Scripture in Second Temple Times*. Grand Rapids: Eerdmans, 2008.

Zahn, Molly M. "Innerbiblical Exegesis: The View from beyond the Bible." Pages 107–20 in *The Formation of the Pentateuch: Bridging the Academic Cultures of Europe, Israel, and North America*. Edited by Jan C. Gertz, et al. FAT 111. Tübingen: Mohr Siebeck, 2016.

Zahn, Molly M. *Rethinking Rewritten Scripture. Composition and Exegesis in the 4QReworked Pentateuch Manuscripts*. STDJ 95. Leiden: Brill, 2011.

Ziemer, Benjamin. *Kritik des Wachstumsmodells: Die Grenzen alttestamentlicher Redaktionsgeschichte im Lichte empirischer Evidenz*. VTSup 182. Leiden: Brill, 2020.

List of Contributors

Peter Altmann, Senior Researcher in Old Testament, University of Zurich

Daniel Bodi, Professor of History of Religions of Antiquity, Sorbonne University

Johanna Erzberger, Laurentius Klein Chair for Ecumenical and Biblical Theology, Jerusalem School of Theology/Research Associate, Faculty of Theology, University of Pretoria

Lisbeth S. Fried, Visiting Scholar, Department of Middle Eastern Studies, University of Michigan

Benjamin D. Giffone, Associate Professor of Biblical Studies, LCC International University/Research Associate, Faculty of Theology, Stellenbosch University

Jin H. Han, Professor of Biblical Studies, New York Theological Seminary

Benjamin Kilchör, Professor of Old Testament, Staatsunabhängige Theologische Hochschule Basel

JiSeong James Kwon, Professor, Nehemiah Christian Institute

Woo Min Lee, Adjunct Professor, McCormick Theological Seminary

Edward J. Mills III, Adjunct Professor of Hebrew and Christian Traditions, Tusculum University

Roger S. Nam, Professor of Hebrew Bible, Emory University

Sungwoo Park, Professor, Department of Political Science & International Studies, Seoul National University

Johannes Unsok Ro, Professor of Biblical Studies, International Christian University

William R. Stewart, Honorary Scholar in Theology, Alphacrucis College

Kristin Weingart, Professor of Old Testament, Ludwig-Maximilians-Universität München

Benjamin Ziemer, Professor of Old Testament, Martin-Luther-Universität Halle-Wittenberg

Index of Biblial and Ancient Sources

1. Old Testament

Exodus
18:20   181–82
24:1   129
24:9   129
24:12   166, 178–79
24:14   129
29:38–42   168–69

Numbers
28   186
28:3–8   168–69

Deuteronomy
12:1–17:7   193–94
13   197, 205–6, 208–9
13:1   194
13:2–6   27, 193–96
13:7–10   196
17:10–11   181–82
17:18–19   166, 172
18   194–95
27–31   166

Joshua
1   170–72, 166, 186
8   166
23   166
24:26   166

Judges
2:11–19   198
7–9   198
7   197–200

Samuel–Kings
1 Sam 22–1 Kgs 2   113

1 Samuel
3   197–98, 200–2
28   197–98, 201–3

2 Samuel
7   101
13–21   117
22–24   114
24   101

1 Kings
1–2   114
2:3   170–72, 175
3   197–98, 203–5
5:3   116
8:23   175
8:25   174
14:25   175
15:9–24   176
17–19   213–231

2 Kings
10:31   166
18:4   182–83
18:13b–19:37   236, 239–242, 244
19:14   23
19:30–31   235–252
22–23   166
22   160, 184
23:1–3   184–185
23:1   160
23:28   185
24–25   155, 162
25:8   159

1 Chronicles
10:13   203
16:40   168–70, 183, 185–86
18–20   101, 115–16
19:1–5   101, 115
21–29   113–17
22–29   100
22:12–13   170–72, 175, 186

Index of Biblical and Ancient Sources

23:27–28	173	9	161
28:3	101	12:41	4

2 Chronicles | | *Esther* | |
1	205	3:13	29
2:11–18	101, 116	8:10	29
6:14	175	9:20	29
6:16	174, 186	9:26	29
8–9	101, 115	9:29	29
12:1–5	174–76, 186	9:30	29
14–15	173, 176		
17:3	186	*Isaiah*	
17:6	186	1:19–20	52
17:7–9	177–80, 182	8:18	27
19:5–11	177, 180–82, 186	37:14	23
20:30	173		
23:18	173	*Jeremiah*	
30:1	29	1	50
30:6	29	8:8	302
30:16	173	13:1–11	51
31:3–4	182–83, 185–86	19:1–13	41, 44–53, 55–57
34:14–15	184–85	19:1	160
35:1–19	184–85	25	158
36:26–27	184–85	25:1–13(14)	157
		32	155
Ezra		36	155, 157–58, 160–61, 163
2:36	4		
3:2	4	36:2	128
4:8	29	39	159, 162
4:11	29	43 LXX	155
5:6	29	45	155–163
6:9	4	52	159, 162
7–10	139–151		
7:14	301	*Ezekiel*	
7:26	179	4:3	27
		5:10, 12	51, 53
Nehemiah		12:6	27
2:7	29	43:11	128
2:8	29	45:17	183, 186
2:9	29		
3:22	4	*Daniel*	
5:1–13	256–68	2	146–47
5:12	4	6	147–48
6:5	29	7	148–49
6:17	29	9:2	161
6:19	29		
7:64	4	*Amos*	
8	139, 145, 150, 301	8	5

Index of Biblical and Ancient Sources 333

2. Apocrypha

1 Maccabees
3:48   151

3. Dead Sea Scrolls

4Q389 1.7	160	4Q174	321
11QPs[a]	321–22	4QSam[a]	3
4Q175	321	4QpaleoExod[m]	305

4. Ancient Jewish Authors

Josephus
*Ant.*10.179   159

Ben Sira   145

5. Ancient Near Eastern Texts

Tell Fekheryeh statue	15, 16	Mari Letters	
Darius's Behistun Inscription	142	A.730	25
		ARM 1 3:1	23
Baba Meṣi'a 6:3	29	ARM 4 68:17–22	23
Codex Hammurabi		ARM(T) 10 78:9–10	24
Epilogue of CH (CH xli52)	25	ARMT 10 4:1–13	
		= ARM 26/1 207 [A.996]	25–26
Ostracon	85	ARM 10 4	27
Cuneiform texts		ARM 10 6	27
A.6458	20	ARM 10 9	27
CT 16 8:280/281	20–1	ARM 26/1 196 [A.3719]:1–10	28
CT 39	22	ARM 26/1	39
K.2764	24	ARM 26/1.206	
Šumma ālu		= WAW 41, no. 16	41–59
Tablet 11 Omen 26'	22	ARM 26/1.207:4	42
Tablet 11 Omen 35'	22	ARM 26/1.212.2'	42
Tablet 20 Omen 35	21	ARM 26/1.237.5	42
Tablet 95	22	FM 14:iii 35	4
Neo-Assyrian		Egyptian	
SAA 9	40	*The Dialogue of a Man and His Ba (Soul)*	
SAAS 7	40		69, 86, 88
SAA 2.6:547–50	53		

The Tale of the Eloquent Peasant	69–70, 86–9, 91	Mesopotamian (Sumerian–Babylonian)	
		Sumerian Man and His God	74–5, 86–9, 91
The Dialogue of Ipuur and the Lord of All	70–2, 86, 88	Babylonian Man and His God	75–6
		Ludlul bēl nēmeqi	76–9, 86–91
The Words of Neferti	72, 86	The Babylonian Theodicy	79–80, 86, 88–90
The Instruction of Ankhsheshonq	73, 88	A Pessimistic Dialogue between Master and Servant	81, 87–88
The Instruction of Papyrus Insinger	74, 90		
Book of the Dead	313, 317, 321–22, 326	Aramaic	
		Sayings of Ahiqar (Ahiqar Proverbs)	91
Saite Recension	317, 321, 326	Ugaritic	
		The Epic of Keret (Kirtu Epic)	83–4, 87–9

6. Classical Authors

Herodotus		Plato	
Histories		*Menexenus*	99–120
8.98	29		
		Thucydides	
		History	100, 104, 106, 115, 118

Index of Modern Authors

Achenbach, Reinhard 132
Albertz, Rainer 91, 250
Albright, William F. 18
Altmann, Peter 7, *163*
Assmann, Aleida 207
Assmann, Jan 89, 207–8, 235–38
Astruc, Jean 303

Bakhtin, Mikhail 125
Barthes, Roland 36
Barton, John 6, 38–40, 58–59
Beck, John A. *218*, 219
Becker, Uwe 306, 308
Ben Zvi, Ehud 3
Ben-Dov, Jonathan 37
Berman, Joshua A. 258, 302
Bin-Nun, Shoshana 281, 290
Blum, Erhard 293–94, *304*
Bodi, Daniel 5–6, 55
Bogaert, Pierre-Maurice 161
Bottéro, Jean 81
Braulik, Georg 133, 135
Brettler, Marc Zvi 57
Brueggemann, Walter 251
Buss, Martin J. 144

Campbell, Antony F. 249
Carr, David M. 3–4, 127, 132, 134
Charpin, Dominique 40
Cheney, Michael 88
Chester, Andrew 250
Childs, Brevard S. 24
Clements, R. E. 248
Cogan, Mordechai 18, 242, 250
Cohn Robert L. 241
Collins, John J. 166, 179
Crawford, Sidnie White 321
Crowell, Bradley L. 85

Dahood, Mitchell Joseph 82
Dandamayev, Muhammad A. 264

Davies, Philip R. 2, 59, 238
Day, John 84
Dossin, George 26
Dozeman, Thomas B.
Driver, Samuel R. *273*
Duhm, Bernhard *157*, 303
Durand, Jean-Marie 18, 24, 27, 39–40, 43, 46, 54

Eissfeldt, Otto 303
Erzberger, Johanna 7
Eskenazi, Tamara Cohn 150, *268*

Falkenstein, Adam 23
Feinberg, Charles L. 82
Finet, André 27
Finkelstain, Israel *292*
Finsterbusch, Karin 128
Fischer, Georg 134
Fishbane, Michael 255, 257
Fitzpatrick-McKinley, Anne 166
Fleming, Daniel E. 225
Forget, Gaétane-Diane 239
Freedman, Sally M. 22
Frei, Peter 259
Fried, Lisbeth S. 7, 263

Gibson, John C. L. 83
Giffone, Benjamin D. 8, *249*
Gordon, Robert P. 47
Graeber, David 264
Graupner, Axel *157*
Gray, John 76, 86
Guichard, Michaël 54

Halbwachs, Maurice 235–39
Hallo, William W. 23, 44
Han, Jin H. 8, *249*
Hanson, Paul D. 246
Harvey, Paul B. Jr. 165, 182
Hasel, Gerhard F. 244

Hausmann, Jutta 250
Huffmon, Herbert B. 40–41, 52

Jacobsen, Thorkild 90
Japhet, Sara *175*, 176–77, 183, *265*
Jiang, Shuai 165, 167–68, 170, 173

Kaufman, Stephen A. 15, 302, 307–10, 316
Keil, Yishai 258
Kilchör, Benjamin 7
Klein, Jacob 75–76
Knoppers, Gary N. 165, 180, 182
Köbert, Raimund 17
Kramer, Samuel N. 75
Kratz, Reinhard G. 312–16, 321, 324
Krey, Ernst *275*
Kristeva, Julia 260
Kwon, JiSeong J. 6

Landesberger, Benno 15, 18–19, 21
Lee, Woo Min 8
LeFebvre, Michael 166, 181
Lemaire, André 229
Levin, Christoph 3, 302
Levinson, Bernard 255–56
Lohfink, Norbert F. 134
Loraux, Nicole 102

Magdalene, F. Rachel 86
Malamat, Abraham 47, 54
Mankowski, Paul V. 15, 17
Margalit, Baruch 83
Markl, Dominik 132–33
Maskow, Lars 165, 173–74, 185
Mauss, Marcel 264
McKenzie, Steven L. 221, 229
Mills, Edward J, III 7
Milstein, Sara J. 9, 306
Moor, Johannes C. de 82
Moore, George F. 303
Müller, Reinhard 324

Na'aman, Nadav *286*
Nam, Roger 8
Naveh, Joseph 29
Nelson, Richard D. 47

Niditch, Susan 91, 199
Nihan, Christophe 132
Nissinen, Martti 37, 40–41, 52
Noegel, Scott B. 49
Nora, Pierre 209
Noth, Martin 215, *220*, *286*

O'Brien, Mark 249
O'Connor, Daniel 84
Oppenheim, A. Leo 16, 18, 27

Pakkala, Juha 227, 258, 313, 308–10, *311*, 324
Park, Sungwoo 6
Parkinson, Richard B. 69, 89
Parpola, Simo 40
Pearce, Laurie E. 16
Person, Raymond F. Jr 3–4
Pfeiffer, Robert H. 84–85
Polanyi, Karl 264
Polzin, Robert 125–26
Provan, Iain W. 246

Richelle, Matthieu 293–94
Ro, Johannes Unsok 6
Roberts, J. J. M. 52
Romeny, Bas ter Haar 324
Römer, Thomas 2

Sanders, Seth L. 134–35
Sarna, Nahum 255
Sasson, Jack M. 26–27
Sasson, Victor 85
Saussure, Ferdinand de 3
Schaper, Joachim 36, 38
Schmid, Konrad 86
Schneider, Thomas 74
Schniedewind, William M. 135, 255–56
Schopenhauer, Arthur 197
Schorch, Stefan 37
Seitz, Christopher R. 242, 244, 249
Sherwood, Yvonne M. 48
Soden, Wolfram von 17–18
Sommer, Benjamin 255
Sonnet, Jean-Pierre 126–27, 129, 132–33, 135
Speiser, Ephraim A. 81
Sperling, David 18

Steck, Odil Hannes 256
Stewart, William R. 6
Strathern, Marilyn *266*
Sweeney, Marvin A. 241, 246, 248

Tadmor, Hayim 16, 242, 250
Thiel, Winfried *157*
Thomas, Samuel I., 59
Thureau-Dangin, François 18
Tigay, Jeffrey H. 59
Twelftree, Graham H. 45

Ulrich, Eugene 324
Ungnad, Arthur 18, 23

Van der Toorn, Karel 88, *223*, 317
Van Seters, John *292*
Venema, Geert J. 128

Von Rad, Gerhard 245–46
Vroom, Jonathan 166

Weinfeld, Moshe 86
Weingart, Kristin 8, *224*
Wellhausen, Julius 35, 39, 58–59, 303
Wilcke, Claus 18, 26–27
Willi, Thomas 174
Wilson, Robert R. 227
Witte, Markus 177
Wright, David P. 51
Wright, Jacob L. 259

Zadok, Ran 16
Zahn, Molly M. 311
Ziemer, Benjamin 9, *230*
Zimmern, Heinrich 17
Zobel, Hans-Jürgen 244

Index of Subjects

1 Esdras, book of 313, 320, 325

Addressee(s) 24, 126, 129–33, *132*, 135, 139, 156, 160–61, *see also* Audience
Audience 56, 69, 89, 117, 125–35, 160, 176, 178, 195, 219, 224, 226, 258, *see also* Addressee(s)
Author's purpose 90–92, 99–101, 103, 107, 113, 118, 120, 145–46, 162–63, 193–96, 200–8, 214, 216–31, 239, 280, 285, 288, 318, *see also* Rhetorical strategy

Baruch, book of 155–163

Canonization 2, 323
Chronicles, book of 3, 99–120, 165–187, 318, 321, 325
Collective identity 100–3, 106–9, 112–14, 116, 118–20, 207–10, 225, 236–39
Community memory, *see* Cultural memory
Community Rule 313, 318–19, 322
Compositional process, *see* Text production
Cultural identity, *see* Collective identity
Cultural memory 3–5, 87, 101–2, 106–7, 120, 193, 198, 206–10, 214, 224, 229, 235
– Deuteronomistic 207, 235–239, 243, 249, 251

Daniel, book of 320
Dead Sea scrolls 3, 314, 317–22, 325–26
Deuteronomism 215–16, 227
Deuteronomist(s) (dtr) 8, *53,* 125, 193–98, 200–2, 205–7, 215–16, *220–21*, 235–36, 239, 251, 289
Deuteronomistic History (DtrH) 4, 8, 101, 113–14, 116, 118, 193, 197–98, 205–10, 213–15, 218, 225, 229–30, 236, 239, 243–44, 250
Deuteronomy 4, 125–136, 310

Divine letter 20–23, 27, 30, 46
Diviner 37, 42, *43*, *45*, 56–57, 77–78, 146, 193–96, *201*, 206–9
Documentary hypothesis 310, 323

Ecclesiastes 92
Enoch, book of 322–23, 325
Esther, book of 320
Ezekiel, book of 36, 183, 312
Ezra–Nehemiah 150, 256–59, 262–63, 265–66

Form criticism 86–87, 92

Genesis Apocryphon 320
Gilgamesh Epic 316–17, 322, 325
Gospels 303, 323, *see also* Matthew, Luke
Growth model 9, *230, 301*, 304–6, 311–24

Historicity 45, 57, *224, 301*
Historiography 105, 107, 113, *193*, 195, 206, 221, 224, 273–74, 285, 320

Intertextuality 255–56, 259–61, 264–68, 301

Jeremiah, book of 7, 155, 157, 160–62, 208–9, 312, 319–20, 322, 325
– Masoretic 160, 304, 309, 318–19
– Septuagint 160, 304, 318–19
Job, book of 6, 67–92, 321
Jubilees, book of 320, 325

Kings, book of 8, 113, 167–68, 185, 213–231, 273–295, 325

Langue 3, 4
Law, divine 7, 18, 165, 167–68, 176, 179, 181–82, 186, *see also* Torah, divine
Law, written 92, 141, 148–50, 166, 267
Layer(s), literary *157, 216*, 302–3, 306, *311*

Index of Subjects

Letter, ANE terms for
- egēru 15, 30
- egirrû 6, 16–21, 24–25, 28, 30
- egirtu 6, 15–17, 19–21, 24, 28–30
- 'iggĕrâ 17, 29
- inim.gar 19–23, 30

Luke, book of 323

Making, *see* Text production
Mantic arts 37–38, 41, 59
Mari Letters 24, 30
Matthew, book of 323
Morpheme 142
Morphology 308–9

Nevi'im 36–39, 50, 57

Omen 21–22, 26–27, 42, 49, 52, *see also* Sign texts
Oral communication 125–129, 133
Oral culture 1–2, 5, 209, 213, 229, 291, 294
Orality, primary vs secondary 128–29, 133, 135, 144

Parole 3, 4
Paronomasia 48–51, 59, see also Pun(s)
Pentateuch 7, 8, 58, *102*, *130*, 131, 165–87, 231, 256–60, 265–68, 307–11, 314, 317, 319, 321, 323–26
Phenomenology 37, 39–40, 43–44, 57–58
Prophet as author 5, 43–44, 58–59, 125
Proverbs, book of 92
Psalms, book of 321–22
Pun(s) 38, 41, 48–52, 59, see also Paronomasia

Redaction criticism 9, 213, 230, 304–12, 324, *see also* Growth model
Rhetorical strategy 78, 86–89, 92, 99, 134, 194, 198, 201, 203, 205–206, *218*, 227, 229, 258, 273, 307, *see also* Author's purpose, Text production
- dialogue 67–92, 99–100, 102, 119
- prose-tale 67–80, 83–88, 90, *91*, 92
- sufferer's motif 6, 67, 74–80, 87–88

Samaritan Pentateuch 305, 309, 324, 326
Samuel
- Masoretic 3
- Septuagint 3
Samuel–Kings 3, 113, 165, 167, 183, 186
Scribal culture 1, 3–5, 37, 58, *67–68*, 86, 213, 215, 223–25, 228, 235, 239, 256, 259–60, 268, 291–94, 302, 306, 318, 323–24, 326
Scribal practice 5, 39, 59, 86–87, 92, 198, 214–15, 222, 228, 231, 235, 239, 250, 256, 268, 294, 301, *301*, 303, 305, 307–8, 312–13, 316, 318, 324–26 *see also* Author's purpose, Rhetorical strategy, Scribalism
Scribalism 100, 102, 118–20, 260
Scribe
- role of a *67–68*, 139, 145, 149–51, 155–57, 160, 301, 304, 306, 308–9, 312, 314–15, *see also* Scribal practice, Scribal culture
- post-deuteronomistic 222, 228, 230
- various ANE terms for 16–17, 140, 149
Scripturalization 2, 166, 168, 175, *see also* Textualization, Torahization
Sign texts 6, 27, 38, 41–57, 194–95, 240–41, *see also* Omen
Standard Babylonian Omen series 21
Šumma ālu 21-2

Temple Scroll 307, 310, 318, 321
Text production 5, 92, 207–8, 213, 216, 220, 223–24, 251, 256, 273–74, 279, 281–83, 286, 289–92, 302–26, *see also* Rhetorical strategy
- regnal frame 274–91, 295
Textualization 58, 125, 135, *150*, 155, 261, 268, 277, *see also* Scripturalization
Torah
- as icon 150–51
- cultic application of 7, 168–69
- divine 7, *92,* 166–70, 179, 184, 186, 258
- judicial application of 92, 181, 186
- oral 126–28, 130–33, 135, 175
- written 125–35, 165–87
Torahization 175, *see also* Scripturalization

Forschungen zum Alten Testament

Edited by
Corinna Körting (Hamburg) · Konrad Schmid (Zürich)
Mark S. Smith (Princeton) · Andrew Teeter (Harvard)

FAT I publishes works that give important momentum to Old Testament research all over the world. There are no religious or denominational preferences, and the series has no limits defined by certain positions. The sole determining factor for the acceptance of a manuscript is its high level of scholarship. Monographs, including habilitations, essay collections by established scholars and conference volumes on key subjects from the fields of theology and religious history define the profile of the series.

FAT II makes a point of publishing outstanding works of scholars at the beginning of their career and welcomes explorative research. As in *FAT I*, there are no religious or denominational preferences, and the series has no limits defined by certain positions. In addition to dissertations and monographs by recent doctorates and established scholars, *FAT II* publishes conference volumes on subjects from the fields of theology and religious history with an interdisciplinary focus.

FAT I:
ISSN: 0940-4155
Suggested citation: FAT I
All published volumes at
www.mohrsiebeck.com/fat1

FAT II:
ISSN: 1611-4914
Suggested citation: FAT II
All published volumes at
www.mohrsiebeck.com/fat2

Mohr Siebeck
www.mohrsiebeck.com